Winston S. Churchill

VOLUME I

Youth

1874–1900

Second Lieutenant Winston S. Churchill
4th Hussars, 1895

RANDOLPH S. CHURCHILL

Winston S. Churchill

VOLUME I · Youth · 1874 - 1900

ILLUSTRATED WITH PHOTOGRAPHS
AND MAPS

HOUGHTON MIFFLIN COMPANY BOSTON
The Riverside Press Cambridge
1966

First Printing R

Copyright © 1966 C & T Publications Limited
Library of Congress Catalog Card Number: 66–12065
Printed in the United States of America

Theme of Volume I

How an under-esteemed boy of genius
of noble character and daring spirit
seized and created a hundred opportunities
to rise in the world
and add glory
by his own merit and audacity
to a name already famous

Theme of the Work

He shall be his own biographer
                    —*Lockhart*

Acknowledgements

THE AUTHOR WISHES first to acknowledge his indebtedness to Her Majesty the Queen, who graciously gave permission for him to have access to the Royal Archives and to use other documents which are her copyright. For guidance in the selection of this material the author is grateful to Mr Robert Mackworth-Young, Librarian at Windsor Castle.

The author's main source is the papers in the Chartwell Trust established by Sir Winston Churchill in 1946, which he directed in 1960 should be placed at the author's disposal. The author records his thanks to the Trustees of the Chartwell settlement, Baroness Spencer-Churchill, Sir Leslie Rowan, Mr Jock Colville and Mr Anthony Moir, who have been most helpful in causing the papers to be sorted and arranged at the Public Record Office under the supervision of Mr Lionel Bell.

Acknowledgements are also due to those who have kindly allowed the author access to their Archives: Mr Ian B. Hamilton, Sir Shane Leslie, the Duke of Marlborough (Blenheim Papers), Mrs Edward Phillips, the Earl of Rosebery, the Marquess of Salisbury and Viscount Wimborne; the Trustees of Sir Aylmer Haldane; Birmingham University Library (Joseph Chamberlain), the Trustees of the British Museum (Balfour Papers), New York City Public Library (Cockran Papers), and the Director of Government Archives, Pretoria.

Copyright permission has also been kindly provided by the Trustees of the late Maurice Baring, the Marquis de Breteuil, Rear-Admiral Sir Anthony Buzzard, Mrs Norah Brown (Goodacre), Mr

Peregrine S. Churchill, Miss K. M. Clegg, Brother Norwood Coaker, CR, Mr Angus Davidson, the Earl of Derby, Mr Henry Drummond-Wolff, Dr A. R. B. Haldane, Mr Charles James and Mrs F. L. Klin, Sir Frederic Johnstone, Dr C. F. Keuzenkamp, Mrs Janet Leeper and Mrs George Shield (Hamilton), Mrs Anita Leslie, Sir Shane Leslie, Pamela, Countess of Lytton, the Duke of Marlborough, Mrs Terence Maxwell (Joseph Chamberlain), Mr Iain Murray (Aylesford), Sir Frederick Rawlinson, Lady Rayleigh (Blood), Viscount Runciman, Lady Tweedmouth, A. P. Watt & Sons, Lord Wigram (Colonel Neville Chamberlain), the Earl of Wilton and Mr Leonard Woolf. And also by the following publishers: A. S. Barnes & Company, *Lord Randolph Churchill* by Robert Rhodes James (published in England by Weidenfeld and Nicolson); Blackwood, *How We Escaped from Pretoria* and *A Soldier's Saga* by Aylmer Haldane; Century Publishing Company, *Reminiscences* by Lady Randolph Churchill (published in England by Edward Arnold); Charles Scribner's Sons, *The World Crisis, A Roving Commission (My Early Life), Amid These Storms (Thoughts and Adventures)* — all published in England by Odhams Press — and *Marlborough* (published in England by George G. Harrap); Gale and Polden, *History of the Fourth Hussars* by David Scott Daniell; Hogarth Press, *The Development of English Biography* by Harold Nicolson; Hodder and Stoughton, *An Ambassador of Peace* by Lord D'Abernon; Methuen and Co, *The Relief of Ladysmith* by J. B. Atkins; John Murray, *Parliamentary Reminiscences and Reflections* by Lord George Hamilton; Odhams Press, *The River War, Savrola,* and *Lord Randolph Churchill* — all by Winston S. Churchill. Also *Encounter* and *The Star,* Johannesburg.

The events recorded in these pages happened many years ago, and in some cases it has not been possible to trace the holders of copyright. Will any copyright holders who have been omitted please accept the author's apologies?

For reminiscences the author is indebted to Mr Humphrey Bingham, Baroness Spencer-Churchill, the late Mrs John Churchill, Mr A. M. Davey of the University of South Africa, Brigadier Jack Gannon, Mr Lewis C. B. Howard, Dr C. F. Keuzenkamp, Mrs Anita Leslie, Sir Shane Leslie, Pamela, Countess of Lytton, Dr Jan Ploeger, and the late Mrs Muriel Warde.

To the following the author expresses his thanks for reading the proofs and for tendering valuable advice: Hon Sir George Bellew, Mr R. A. Bevan, Mr Anthony Montague Browne, Mr Lyonel Capstickdale, Baroness Spencer-Churchill, Mr Peregrine S. Churchill, Mr Winston S. Churchill, Mr Jock Colville, Colonel F. S. Corke, Mr Robert Rhodes James of All Souls, Sir Shane Leslie, Mr Robert Mackworth-Young, Hon Mrs Christopher Soames, Mr Robert Taylor of Nuffield College, Oxford, and Mr Ivan Yates.

Finally the author desires to express his indebtedness to the following who have assisted in sorting, assembling and studying the material: Mr Michael Wolff, who has from the beginning directed the research; Mr Andrew Kerr and Mr Martin Mauthner, who have been chiefly concerned with work on this volume; Mr Martin Gilbert of Merton College, Oxford, and Mr George Thayer, who have been more concerned with work on later volumes; and Mr Michael Molian. Also to his secretarial staff: Miss Eileen Harryman, archivist, and Miss Barbara Twigg, personal secretary; Mrs Trevor Adams; Mrs Margaret Bentley, Miss Lynette Parker, Miss Alice Golding, Mrs Bettye Verran and Mrs Richard von Goetz. And to Mrs Robert Bevan, who assembled the illustrations and advised on their selection.

Contents

Illustrations

xvii

Bungalow at Bangalore

The Regimental Polo Team

Attached to 21st Lancers

Near Omdurman 2 September 1898: Two Messages

The Armoured Train (*The Star, Johannesburg: Barnett Collection*)

Captain Aylmer Haldane and Lieutenant Le Mesurier (*Blackwood*)

Pamela Plowden, 1892

Winston Churchill, 1900

"Winston" (*Vanity Fair*)

Member for Oldham

MAPS

BY JOAN EMERSON

§

Preface

BROUGHT UP TO ADMIRE his grandfather, and daily growing throughout his youth and manhood in his love and veneration for his father the author has long aspired to write a filial and objective biography. This is evidenced by two telegrams that passed in 1932 between the author, who had not yet come of age, and his father, who was lecturing in America.

RSC to WSC
(Stour Papers)
TELEGRAM

[27 February 1932]   72 Glebe Place
                                                            Chelsea

Have been offered 450 pounds advance on substantial royalties for biography of you have you any objection to my accepting if I do it will naturally be unauthorised unofficial and undocumented my aim would be present political history last thirty years in light unorthodox fashion believe could produce amusing work without embarrassing you mummie looking very well all counting days to your return love
                                                                      R

WSC to RSC
(Stour Papers)
TELEGRAM

27 February 1932   Indianapolis

Strongly deprecate premature attempt hope some day you will make thousands instead of hundreds out of my archives most improvident

xxi

anticipate now stop lecture pilgrimage drawing wearily final stage much love show mamma

FATHER

This sensible advice was naturally heeded, resulting in advantages to the family even more abundant than Mr Churchill had predicted.

In planning what will be a colossal work, I have been guided very much by the lectures which that master of biography, Sir Harold Nicolson, gave in 1927 and which were first published in 1928 in the Hogarth Lectures on Literature. In *The Development of English Biography*, Sir Harold points out that Izaak Walton revived the "admirable practice of introducing original letters into the text." He later says of Mason, who wrote the *Life and Letters* of Gray: "He is said to have first conceived of this method on reading Middleton's *Cicero;* but he expanded it, and allowed the letters to tell their own story, introducing them only with short explanatory captions, or explaining them by sensible and vivid notes. 'In a word,' as he says, 'Mr Gray will become his own biographer.' " Sir Harold also observes in the same series of lectures:

> For the *Life of Johnson* is a work of art, not merely in its actual excellence of outline, but in the careful adjustment of internal spaces. We have thus the absence of comment, or rather the very skilful interspacing of comment — the way in which Boswell first provides the evidence, and then, at a later period, confirms by comment the conclusion which the reader had already reached.

I have also been influenced by what Lockhart, the son-in-law and biographer of Sir Walter Scott, wrote:

> I have endeavoured to lay before the reader those parts of Sir Walter's character to which we have access, as they were indicated in his sayings and doings through the long series of his years — making use, whenever it was possible, of his own letters and diaries rather than of any other materials — but refrained from obtruding almost anything of comment. It was my wish to let the character develop itself.

I have also been fortified in my conception of my task by what Lockhart wrote to Scott's friend William Laidlaw, ". . . that his sole object was to do Scott justice 'or rather to let him do himself justice, by so contriving it that he shall be, as far as possible, from first to last, his own biographer . . .' " thus echoing what Mason had written.

Churchill himself in prefacing his Life of his father wrote:

> For a thing so commonly attempted, political biography is difficult. The style and ideas of the writer must throughout be subordinated to the necessity of embracing in the text those documentary proofs upon which the story depends. Letters, memoranda, and extracts from speeches, which inevitably and rightly interrupt the sequence of his narrative, must be pieced together upon some consistent and harmonious plan. It is not by the soft touches of a picture, but in hard mosaic or tessellated pavement, that a man's life and fortunes must be presented in all their reality and romance. I have thought it my duty, so far as possible, to assemble once and for all the whole body of historical evidence required for the understanding of Lord Randolph Churchill's career. Scarcely anything of material consequence has been omitted, and such omissions as have been necessary are made for others' sakes and not his own. Scarcely any statement of importance lacks documentary proof. There is nothing more to tell. Wherever practicable I have endeavoured to employ his own words in the narration; and the public is now in a position to pronounce a complete, if not a final, judgement.

And even earlier, writing to his mother:

WSC to Lady Randolph
EXTRACT

31 March [1898]   Camp Peshawar

. . . As to the Biographer — who may investigate another human wretch's life — I would say as Oliver Cromwell did to Sir Peter Lely — "Paint me as I am" and thereupon was painted wart and all. . . .

With the wealth of material which has been entrusted to the author about a man who was in his own lifetime widely saluted as a patriot, a hero and a genius, it would scarcely be possible to write a dull book. Nonetheless the epic of his life, the innumerable activities in which he was involved, the vast number of personalities with whom he was brought into conflict or contact or with whom he transacted business, have presented the author with problems and decisions often of a tortuous complexity. What to put in? What to leave out? What to relegate to appendixes? These have not been easy questions to answer. After much thought and consultation the author decided upon the following method:

To assemble the body of relevant original and unpublished documents and letters in one or two independent appendix volumes as companions to each volume of the main work; to compile these first, and to use them as the raw material from which each volume of the main work was to be written. The general reader may rest assured that each volume of the main work will contain all that is most interesting and exciting in the life of Sir Winston Churchill, while the student and historian who wish to have access to the full documentation will find it readily available in the Companion Volume or Volumes to the main work, as each Companion comes from the press.

Every effort has been made in this volume and will be made in succeeding volumes of the main work to spare the reader the distraction of otiose footnotes which might have disfigured the pages: to avoid what Mr John Betjeman has called the "rash of foot and note disease." Whenever it has been possible without interrupting the flow of the narrative, references have been incorporated in the text. When no references are given it should in general be assumed that the information comes from Sir Winston's papers in the Chartwell Trust which have been carefully sorted and catalogued by the Public Record Office and which will eventually be available to students of the period. Spelling has for the most part been corrected and brought up to date except where it has been thought desirable to retain the "period flavour" of the original. In the case of the subject of the biography, however, his original spelling and punctuation is preserved until he comes to manhood at the age of twenty, on the death of his father, after which obvious slips are corrected. Addresses and dates have been standardized. Where square brackets are used in letters or quotations it should be understood that they contain interpolations by the author; round brackets, where they occur, are those of the original writer.

Those characters who have short biographies at the beginning of the volume will be found to have their names set in small capitals in the index. Those who do not warrant such biographies will, wherever possible, have the necessary details of rank and identification in the index. In addition, fuller details of the subordinate characters may be found in the Companion Volumes.

RANDOLPH S. CHURCHILL

Stour
East Bergholt
Suffolk
April 1966

Short Biographies
of the Principal Characters

BALFOUR Arthur James (1848–1930); eldest son of James Mait-
land Balfour and Lady Blanche Cecil, second daughter of 2nd Marquess of Salisbury. Succeeded his uncle, 3rd Marquess of Salisbury,
as Prime Minister 1902–5 and leader of the Tory Party 1902–11.
Conservative MP for Hertford 1874–85, for Manchester East 1885–
1906, for City of London 1906–22. For a time a member with Lord
Randolph Churchill of the Fourth Party. President of Local Government Board 1885–6; Secretary for Scotland 1886–7; Chief Secretary
for Ireland 1887–91; Leader of the House and First Lord of the
Treasury 1891–2, 1895–1905. Succeeded WSC as First Lord of the
Admiralty 1915; Foreign Secretary 1916–19; Lord President of the
Council 1919–22, 1925–9. Earl 1922.

BARING Hugo (1876–1949); sixth son of 1st Baron Revelstoke.
Lieutenant 4th Hussars, in India with WSC. Served in Boer War
(severely wounded), and in First World War (wounded). Married
1905 Evelyn Harriet, widow of 2nd Baron Magheramorne, second
daughter of 8th Earl of Shaftesbury.

BARNES Reginald Walter Ralph (1871–1946); son of Prebendary
R. H. Barnes of Stoke Canon, near Exeter. He and WSC were fellow-
subalterns in the 4th Hussars and they went to Cuba in 1895. Major-
General and KCB 1919.

BEACONSFIELD 1st Earl of — see DISRAELI.

BLANDFORD Albertha Frances Anne (Bertha), Marchioness of (1847–1932); sixth daughter of 1st Duke of Abercorn and Louisa Jane, daughter of 6th Duke of Bedford. She had seven brothers, and was one of seven sisters, all of whom married into the peerage. She married in 1869 George Charles, Marquess of Blandford (qv below) eldest son of 7th Duke of Marlborough (qv). This marriage was dissolved in 1883; the decree nisi was awarded five months before her husband succeeded to the dukedom, but was not made absolute until four months after. However, she preferred to retain the style of Marchioness of Blandford, though by 1896 she was one of five ladies then living who were or had been entitled to the style of Duchess of Marlborough. The others were Jane, widow of 6th Duke; Fanny, widow of 7th Duke; Lily, widow of 8th Duke; and Consuelo, wife of 9th Duke.

BLANDFORD George Charles, Marquess of (1844–92); eldest son of 7th Duke of Marlborough (qv) whom he succeeded 1883 and brother of Lord Randolph Churchill (qv). Married (1) 1869, Albertha (qv above), daughter of 1st Duke of Abercorn; (2) 1888 at the Tabernacle Baptist Church, New York, Lilian Warren (Duchess Lily), widow of Louis Hammersley and daughter of Cicero Price, Commodore US Navy. Succeeded as 8th Duke in 1883.

BLOOD Bindon (1842–1940); son of W. B. Blood, of County Clare, and a descendant of the celebrated Colonel Thomas Blood, who attempted to steal the Crown Jewels from the Tower of London in 1671. As Major-General commanding Malakand Field Force 1897 he afforded WSC opportunities for active service. KCB 1896, GCB 1909. Retired as General 1907.

BRABAZON John Palmer (1843–1922); son of Major H. Brabazon of County Mayo and Eleanor Ambrosia, daughter of Sir W. H. Palmer, 3rd Bart. Served in Grenadier Guards and 10th Hussars; appointed to command 4th Hussars 1893. Later commanded 2nd Cavalry Brigade in South Africa. Major-General and KCB 1911.

BRETEUIL Henri Charles Joseph le Tonnelie, Marquis de (1848–1916); son of Alexandre Charles Joseph de Breteuil and Charlotte

Fould, daughter of Napoleon III's finance minister, Achille Fould. Served with distinction in Franco-Prussian War. Member of Chamber of Deputies 1877–92, sat as a conservative and monarchist, and was noted as an authoritative speaker on finance matters and foreign affairs. Close friend of Lord and Lady Randolph's.

CASSEL Ernest Joseph (1852–1921); born at Cologne, youngest son of Jacob Cassel, a small banker. In 1869 came to England, where he amassed a vast fortune: he became an intimate friend of the Prince of Wales, later King Edward VII, and of Lord Randolph Churchill. Knighted 1899.

CHAMBERLAIN Joseph (1836–1914); eldest son of Joseph Chamberlain, a boot and shoe manufacturer, and Caroline, daughter of Harry Harben, a provision merchant. Made a substantial fortune as screw manufacturer in Birmingham; three times Mayor of Birmingham 1873–5, MP 1876–1914. President of the Board of Trade under Gladstone 1880–5, and President of Local Government Board 1886, when he left the Liberal party on the issue of Home Rule and allied himself with Tories as Liberal Unionist. Secretary of State for Colonies 1895–1903, when he left the Tory government to campaign for imperial preference. Three times married; one son (Austen) became Chancellor of the Exchequer and Foreign Secretary, the other (Neville) Chancellor of the Exchequer and Prime Minister.

CHURCHILL John Strange Spencer- ("Jack") (1880–1947); younger brother of WSC. Born in Dublin 4 February 1880; educated at Harrow; served in the South African War where he was wounded and mentioned in despatches, and in First World War at Gallipoli. By profession a stockbroker. He married in 1908 Lady Gwendeline Bertie (1885–1941), daughter of 7th Earl of Abingdon.

CHURCHILL Lady Randolph Spencer- ("Jennie") (1854–1921); mother of WSC and Jack Churchill. She was born on 10 January 1854 in Brooklyn, New York, second daughter of Leonard Jerome (qv), and married (1) Lord Randolph Churchill (qv below); (2) on 28 July 1900 Captain George Cornwallis-West, whom she divorced 1913; (3) 1919 Montagu Porch.

CHURCHILL Lord Randolph Henry Spencer- (1849–95); father of WSC and Jack Churchill (qv). Born in London 13 February 1849, third but second surviving son of 7th Duke of Marlborough. Educated Eton and Merton College, Oxford. He married 15 April 1874 Jennie Jerome. MP for Woodstock 1874–85, and for South Paddington 1885–95. Secretary of State for India 1885–6; Chancellor of the Exchequer and Leader of the House of Commons July–December 1886. He died in London 24 January 1895.

COCKRAN William Bourke (1854–1923); American lawyer and politician. Born in County Sligo, he went to America in 1871. Democratic Member of Congress for New York 1891–5, 1904–9, 1920–3.

CROMER Evelyn Baring, 1st Earl of (1841–1917); sixth son of Henry Baring MP, a member of the family of merchant bankers, and Cecilia, daughter of Admiral William Windham. British Agent and Consul-General in Egypt 1883–1907. Baron 1892, Viscount 1899, Earl 1901.

CURZON George Nathaniel (1859–1925); eldest son of Reverend Alfred Curzon, 4th Baron Scarsdale, and Blanche, daughter of Joseph Senhouse of Netherhall. Viceroy of India 1899–1905. Earlier, Tory MP for Southport 1886–98; Under-Secretary of State for India 1891–2; Under-Secretary of State for Foreign Affairs 1895–8. Later Lord Privy Seal 1915–16; Lord President of the Council 1916–19; Foreign Secretary 1919–24. Married (1) 1895 Mary, daughter of Levi Leiter of Washington, D.C., who died in 1906; (2) 1917 Grace, daughter of J. Monroe Hinds of the United States and widow of Alfred Duggan of Buenos Aires. Created Baron Curzon of Kedleston (Irish Peerage) 1898; Earl Curzon of Kedleston, Viscount Scarsdale and Baron Ravensdale 1911; Marquess Curzon and KG 1921.

DISRAELI Benjamin (1804–81); son of Isaac D'Israeli, author and literary critic. Twice Prime Minister, 1868, 1874–80; Tory MP for Buckinghamshire 1847–76. Wrote more than a dozen novels, the last, *Endymion,* published in 1880. Created Earl of Beaconsfield 1876; KG 1878.

ELGIN Victor Alexander, 9th Earl of and 13th Earl of Kincardine (1849–1917); eldest son of 8th Earl, Viceroy of India 1862–3, and of Lady Mary Louisa, eldest surviving daughter of 1st Earl of Durham. He himself was Viceroy of India 1894–8 while WSC was serving there, and later Secretary of State for the Colonies when WSC became Under-Secretary in 1905. His grandfather, 7th Earl, salvaged in 1801 the marble frieze of the Parthenon (now known as the "Elgin Marbles") later acquired by the British Museum where it can still be seen to great advantage.

EVEREST Elizabeth Ann (1833–95); born in Kent. Children's nurse, first with Rev Thompson Phillips of Carlisle, then with Lord Randolph Churchill 1875–93. Nicknamed by Winston and Jack "Woom" or "Woomany".

FINCASTLE Alexander Edward, Viscount (1871–1962); eldest son of 7th Earl of Dunmore. Major 16th Lancers; served with Sudan Field Force 1896; ADC to Viceroy of India 1895–7; served with Malakand Field Force and ADC to Sir Bindon Blood 1897 (VC, despatches three times). Published *A Frontier Campaign* 1898. In Boer War he raised and commanded Fincastle's Horse (despatches); and in World War I (DSO, despatches four times) was wounded twice. Succeeded as 8th Earl of Dunmore 1907.

FREWEN Clara (1850–1935); eldest daughter of Leonard Jerome (qv). She married Moreton Frewen (qv); they had two sons, and a daughter, Clare, who married Wilfred Sheridan, a descendant of Richard Brinsley Sheridan, eighteenth-century playwright and politician. Clare Sheridan achieved fame as a sculptress and as a traveller in North Africa.

FREWEN Moreton (1853–1924); son of Thomas Frewen MP, of Northiam, Sussex, and Helen Louisa, daughter of Frederick Homan of County Kildare. Married 1881 Clara (qv above), eldest daughter of Leonard Jerome. A knowledgeable if unlucky student of economic affairs, he was the author of a number of works on bi-metallism. MP for North-East Cork, 1910–11.

GLADSTONE William Ewart (1809–98); fourth son of Sir John Gladstone, 1st Bart, and Anne, daughter of Andrew Robertson, Provost of Dingwall. Three times Chancellor of the Exchequer and four times Prime Minister 1868–74, 1880–5, 1886, 1892–4. Liberal MP for Newark, Oxford University, South Lancashire, Greenwich (1868–80) and Midlothian (1880–95). Author of numerous works on religious and philosophical topics.

GUEST — see WIMBORNE.

HALDANE (James) Aylmer Lowthorpe (1862–1950); eldest son of Daniel Rutherford Haldane and Charlotte, daughter of James Lowthorpe of Welton Hall, Yorks. Joined Gordon Highlanders 1882; served in India and South Africa with WSC. He was in command of the Chieveley armoured train when he and WSC were captured and imprisoned in Pretoria. KCB 1918; retired as General 1925.

HAMILTON Ian Standish Monteith (1853–1947); born in Corfu, the son of Col Christian Hamilton and Corinna, daughter of 3rd Viscount Gort; he married 1887 Jean, daughter of Sir John Muir, 1st Bart, and Lady Muir. Commanded 3rd Brigade, Tirah Campaign, 1897–8. Served in South Africa, 1899–1901, where he took part in the defence of Ladysmith, and later commanded one of the mobile columns described by WSC in *Ian Hamilton's March*. At the battle of Majuba Hill 1881 received a wound in his wrist which afflicted his left arm for the rest of his life. Commanded Mediterranean Expeditionary Force 1915, which attempted to capture the Gallipoli Peninsula. KCB 1900; General 1905.

JAMES Henry (1828–1911); lawyer and politician, befriended Lord and Lady Randolph and later WSC. Liberal MP for Taunton 1869–85, for Bury 1885–6. Twice Attorney-General under Gladstone 1873–4, 1880–5. With Chamberlain and Hartington left Liberal party and became Liberal Unionist (MP for Bury 1886–95). Chancellor of Duchy of Lancaster 1895–1902. Knighted 1873; created Baron James of Hereford 1895.

JEROME Clara (1825–95); wife of Leonard Jerome (qv below) whom she married in 1849 and mother of Clara (Frewen), Jennie (Spencer-Churchill) and Leonie (Leslie) qv. Youngest daughter of Ambrose

Hall, a member of New York State Assembly, and Clarissa daughter of David Willcox whose father and grandfather had been blacksmiths in Dartmouth, Massachusetts. Lived for many years in Paris with her three daughters. After they were married she settled in England and died at Tunbridge Wells.

JEROME Leonard Walter (1817–91); husband of Clara Jerome (qv), fifth son of Isaac Jerome of Pompey, New York, and Aurora, daughter of Reuben Murray of Connecticut. First a lawyer and small-town newspaper proprietor, he came to New York in 1855 and became a successful stockbroker and financier, and for a period principal proprietor of the *New York Times*. American Consul in Trieste 1851–2. A keen yachtsman, founder of the American Jockey Club and a patron of the opera.

JEUNE Mary Susan Elizabeth, Lady (1845–1931); daughter of Keith Stewart Mackenzie of Seaforth and Hannah, eldest daughter of James Hope-Vere of Craigie Hall. Married (1) 1871 John, second son of 2nd Baron Stanley of Alderley (d. 1878); and (2) 1881 Sir Francis Jeune 1st Bart, later 1st and last Baron St Helier, President of the Probate Divorce and Admiralty Division of the High Court. Celebrated London hostess who befriended WSC.

KINSKY Count Charles (1858–1919); son of Ferdinand, seventh Prince Kinsky, and Marie, Princess Liechtenstein. Friend and admirer of Lady Randolph. Served in Austro-Hungarian diplomatic service, first in London and later at Brussels and Paris. A great sportsman and rider to hounds, he rode his own horse Zoedone to victory in the Grand National of 1883. Married 17 January 1895 Elisabeth, Countess Wolff Metternich, and succeeded as Prince 1904.

KITCHENER Horatio Herbert (1850–1916); second son of Lieutenant-Colonel Henry Horatio Kitchener of Cossington, Leicestershire and his first wife Anne Frances, daughter of the Rev John Chevallier, vicar of Aspall, Suffolk, who kept a lunatic asylum there and became a noted agriculturist. Commissioned in the Royal Engineers, he was Sirdar of the Egyptian Army 1892–9, planning and executing the campaign that ended in the Battle of Omdurman 1898 and led to the reconquest of the Sudan. Chief of Staff to Lord Roberts (qv) in South Africa, 1899–1900; Commander-in-Chief 1900–2; Commander-in-Chief India 1902–9; British Agent and Consul-General, Egypt 1911–14; Secretary of State for War 1914–15. Drowned in HMS *Hampshire* on way to Russia. KCMG 1894, KCB 1896, Baron 1898, Viscount and OM 1902, Earl (Kitchener of Khartoum) 1914, KG 1915.

KNOLLYS Francis (1837–1924); second son of General Sir William Knollys, and Elizabeth, sister of Sir Edward St Aubyn 1st Bart. Private Secretary to the Prince of Wales from 1870, continued to serve in that capacity on the Prince's accession as Edward VII in 1901, and to King George V until 1913. KCMG 1886. Baron 1902 and Viscount 1911.

LANSDOWNE Henry Charles Keith, 5th Marquess of (1845–1927); elder son of Henry, 4th Marquess of Lansdowne and Emily Jane Mercer, Baroness Nairne in her own right. Under-Secretary for War 1872–4; Under-Secretary for India 1880; Governor-General of Canada 1883–8: Viceroy of India 1888–94; Secretary of State for War 1895–1900; Foreign Secretary 1900–5. Married 1869 Maud Evelyn Hamilton, daughter of 1st Duke of Abercorn and sister of Albertha, Marchioness of Blandford (qv).

LESLIE Leonie Blanche (1859–1943); youngest daughter of Leonard and Clara Jerome (qqv), favourite aunt of WSC. Educated in France, she married 1884 John, only son of Sir John Leslie, 1st Bart, of Glaslough, County Monaghan. Their son, John Randolph Shane (born 1885), was a godson of Lord Randolph.

MARJORIBANKS Edward (1849–1909); eldest son of Dudley, 1st Baron Tweedmouth, whom he succeeded 1894. Married 1873 Lady Fanny Spencer-Churchill, third daughter of 7th Duke of Marlborough. Liberal MP for Berwick 1880–94, Chief Whip 1892–4; Lord Privy Seal and Chancellor of Duchy of Lancaster 1894–5, First Lord of the Admiralty 1905–8, Lord President of the Council 1908. His son Dudley (1874–1935) was at Harrow with Winston, joined Royal Horse Guards 1895; married 1901 Muriel, eldest daughter of W. St John Brodrick, at that time Secretary of State for War.

MARLBOROUGH Charles, 9th Duke — see SUNDERLAND.

MARLBOROUGH Frances Anne Emily ("Fanny"), Duchess of (1822–99); first daughter of Charles, 3rd Marquess of Londonderry, by his second wife, Frances, daughter and heiress of Sir Henry Vane-Tempest, Bart. She married John Winston, Marquess of Blandford (later 7th Duke of Marlborough, qv below), in 1843, and had five sons and six daughters. Only two of the sons (Lord Blandford, the eldest, and Lord Randolph, the third) survived their early childhood.

MARLBOROUGH John Winston, 7th Duke of (1822–83); eldest son of George, 6th Duke of Marlborough and Jane, eldest daughter of 8th Earl of Galloway. Father of Lord Randolph Churchill and grandfather of WSC. Tory MP for Woodstock 1840–5 and 1847–57, when he succeeded to the dukedom. Lord President of the Council 1867–8; Viceroy of Ireland 1876–80. Married 1843 Frances Anne, daughter of 3rd Marquess of Londonderry (qv above).

MILBANKE John Peniston (1872–1915); eldest surviving son of Sir Peniston Milbanke, 9th Bart, whom he succeeded in 1899. Came to Harrow (The Head Master's House) 1886, left December 1889, but remained close friend of Winston. Joined 10th Hussars through Militia 1892; won Victoria Cross during Boer War. Killed in action commanding Sherwood Rangers at Hill 70, Gallipoli. His younger brother Mark was at The Head Master's 1888–92; an artist, his early sketches were published in *The Harrovian;* later he exhibited at the Royal Academy.

MILNER Alfred (1854–1925); son of Dr Charles Milner of London and Mary, daughter of Major General Ready, Governor of the Isle of Man. A brilliant administrator, he was Under-Secretary for Finance in Egypt at the age of thirty-five; and Chairman Board of Inland Revenue at thirty-eight. High Commissioner for South Africa 1879–1905. Member of War Cabinet without Portfolio 1916–18, Secretary of State for War 1918–19, Secretary of State for Colonies 1919–21. KCB 1895, Baron 1901, Viscount 1902.

MINSSEN Bernard Jules (1861–1924); modern languages master at Harrow 1891–1921. Winston stayed with him and his parents at his home in Versailles, 1891–2.

MORIARTY Louis Martin (1855–1930); Army Class master at Harrow, where he also taught Classics and French, and was a house-master, 1889–1917.

PLOWDEN Pamela Frances Audrey (born 1874); daughter of Sir Trevor John Chichele Chichele-Plowden and Millicent Frances, daughter of General Sir C. J. Foster. As a young girl accompanied her father to Hyderabad, where he was the Resident. Married 1902 Victor, 2nd Earl of Lytton.

ROBERTS Frederick Sleigh (1832–1914); born at Cawnpore, son of General Sir Abraham Roberts and Isabella, widow of Major Hamilton Maxwell. Won VC in Indian Mutiny 1858 (his son won a posthumous VC in South Africa). Exponent of the "forward policy" on the Indian frontier, led the march from Kabul to Kandahar which resulted in the pacification of Afghanistan 1880. Lord Randolph Churchill, as Secretary of State for India, was instrumental in his appointment as Commander-in-Chief, India 1885–93. Field Marshal and C-in-C Ireland 1895–9. Commander-in-Chief, South Africa 1899–1900. KCB 1879, GCB 1880 and Bart 1881, Baron Roberts of Kandahar 1892, Earl Roberts of Kandahar and Pretoria, and KG 1901.

ROOSE Robson (1848–1905); third son of Francis Finley Roose. An eminent and well-connected physician who practised in London and Brighton and attended Lord Randolph Churchill and his family.

ROSEBERY Archibald Philip, 5th Earl of (1847–1929); son of Lord Dalmeny (d. 1851) and Catherine, daughter of 4th Earl Stanhope. Succeeded his grandfather 1868. Friend of Lord Randolph at Oxford and later of WSC. Secretary of State for Foreign Affairs 1886 and 1892–4; Leader of Liberal Party, Prime Minister 1894–5. Racehorse owner: won the Derby 1894, 1895, and 1905. Married 1878 Hannah, only child and heir of the Austrian Baron Meyer Amschel de Rothschild, who died 1890.

SALISBURY Robert Arthur Talbot, 3rd Marquess of (1830–1903); three times Prime Minister 1885–6, 1886–92, 1895–1902. Second son of 2nd Marquess of Salisbury and of Frances Mary, only daughter of Bamber Gascoyne MP. Conservative MP for Stamford 1853–68; Secretary of State for India 1866–7 (resigned in protest against Disraeli's reform bill). Succeeded his father 1868. Secretary of State for India 1874–8, Foreign Secretary 1878–80, 1885–6, 1887–92 and 1895–1900.

SOMERVELL Robert (1851–1933); English master at Harrow 1887–1911, and Winston's first form master. He also taught History and Classics. He was Bursar of the School 1888–1919 and Housemaster 1904–11.

SUNDERLAND Charles Richard John, Earl of ("Sunny") (1871–1934); courtesy title of eldest son of Marquess of Blandford (qv) whom he succeeded 1892 as 9th Duke of Marlborough. Became close friend of his cousin WSC. Served with Queen's Own Oxfordshire Hussars, staff captain with Imperial Yeomanry in South Africa. Paymaster-General of the Forces 1899–1902, Under-Secretary of State for the Colonies 1903–5; Joint Parliamentary Secretary to the Board of Agriculture and Fisheries 1917–18. Married (1) 1895 Consuelo, daughter of Commodore William Vanderbilt of New York (marriage dissolved 1921), (2) 1921 Gladys, daughter of Edward Parke Deacon of Boston.

WALES Albert Edward, Prince of (1841–1910); eldest son of Queen Victoria, whom he succeeded as King Edward VII 22 January 1901. Married 1863 Princess Alexandra (1844–1925), daughter of King Christian IX of Denmark.

WELLDON James Edward Cowell (1854–1937); son of Rev Edward Welldon, sometime Master at Tonbridge School. Educated Eton and King's College, Cambridge. Headmaster of Harrow, at the age of thirty-one 1885–98; WSC was in his house. Chaplain in Ordinary to the Queen 1892–8. Bishop of Calcutta and Metropolitan of India 1898–1902; Canon of Westminster 1902–6; Dean of Manchester 1906–18; Dean of Durham 1918–33.

WILSON Lady Sarah Isabella Augusta (1864–1929); eleventh and youngest child of 7th Duke of Marlborough. Married 1891 Gordon Chesney Wilson (1865–1914), Royal Horse Guards, eldest son of Sir Samuel Wilson MP, and was besieged with him in Mafeking.

WILTON Laura Caroline, Countess of (1842–1916); youngest daughter of William Russell, Accountant-General of the Court of Chancery, who was a great-grandson of 4th Duke of Bedford. Married (1) 1862 Seymour John Grey Egerton (1839–98), younger son of Thomas 2nd Earl of Wilton, who succeeded 1885 his elder brother Arthur as 4th Earl. She married (2) 1899 Sir Frederick John William Johnstone (1841–1913), 8th Bart. Befriended Winston when he was at Harrow, and called herself his "Deputy Mother."

WIMBORNE Cornelia Henrietta Maria, Lady (1847–1927); eldest daughter of 7th Duke of Marlborough, aunt of WSC. Married 1868 Sir Ivor Bertie Guest, 2nd Bart, who was created 1880 1st Baron Wimborne. When young, WSC frequently stayed at their house near Bournemouth with his first cousin Ivor (1873–1939) who succeeded as 2nd Baron 1914 and was created Viscount 1918.

WOLFF Henry Drummond (1830–1908); born in Malta: only child of Rev Joseph Wolff and Lady Georgiana, daughter of Horatio (Walpole), 2nd Earl of Oxford. Married 1852 Adeline, daughter of Walter Sholto-Douglas. Conservative MP Christchurch, Hants 1874–8, MP for Portsmouth 1880–5. With Lord Randolph Churchill, John Gorst and Arthur Balfour, formed the Fourth Party. Founder, with Lord Randolph, of the Primrose League. Ambassador at Madrid 1892–1900. GCMG 1878, PC 1885, GCB 1889.

WOOD (Henry) Evelyn (1838–1919); son of Rev Sir John Page Wood, 2nd Bart, rector of St Peter's Cornhill, London, and Caroline, daughter of Admiral Sampson Michell. Midshipman 1852. Served in Crimean War, in trenches before Sebastopol. Transferred to Army 1855; served Indian Mutiny 1857; VC 1859. Adjutant-General 1897–1901. KCB 1879, GCMG 1882, GCB 1891. Field Marshal 1903. His sister, Katherine, was married first to Captain W. H. O'Shea and, after being divorced, to Charles Stewart Parnell.

Winston S. Churchill

VOLUME I

Youth

1874–1900

I

Birth

WINSTON LEONARD SPENCER-CHURCHILL was born at Blenheim Palace in Oxfordshire on 30 November 1874. His father was Lord Randolph Churchill, second surviving son of the 7th Duke of Marlborough and Frances, a daughter of the 3rd Marquess of Londonderry. Winston's mother, Jennie Jerome, was the second of the four daughters, three of whom were still living, of Mr and Mrs Leonard Jerome of New York City. It had been intended that the child should be born at the young couple's new London house, 48 Charles Street, Mayfair; but the birth was two months premature — hence Lady Randolph Churchill's Blenheim confinement. Lady Randolph's mother was in Paris at the time with her eldest daughter Clara; Lord Randolph hastened to send her the news:

Lord Randolph to Mrs Leonard Jerome

Monday 30 [November 1874]   Blenheim Palace
12.30 p.m.   Woodstock

Dear Mrs Jerome,
    I have just time to write a line, to send by the London Dr to tell you that all has up to now thank God gone off very well with my darling Jennie. She had a fall on Tuesday walking with the shooters, & a rather imprudent & rough drive in a pony carriage brought on the pains on Saturday night. We tried to stop them, but it was no use. They went on all Sunday. Of course the Oxford physician cld not come. We telegraphed for the London man Dr Hope but he did not arrive till this morning. The country Dr is however a clever man,

& the baby was safely born at 1.30 this morning after about 8 hrs labour. She suffered a good deal poor darling, but was vy plucky & had no chloroform. The boy is wonderfully pretty so everybody says dark eyes and hair & vy healthy considering its prematureness. My mother & Clementine have been everything to Jennie, & she cld not be more comfortable. We have just got a most excellent nurse & wet nurse coming down this afternoon, & please God all will go vy well with both. I telegraphed to Mr Jerome; I thought he wld like to hear. I am sure you will be delighted at this good news and dear Clara also I will write again tonight. Love to Clara.

Yrs affty
RANDOLPH S. C.

I hope the baby things will come with all speed. We have to borrow some from the Woodstock Solicitor's wife.

Lord Randolph's mother Duchess Fanny, as she was known to her family, also wrote:

Duchess of Marlborough to Mrs Leonard Jerome

30 November [1874]   Blenheim

My dear Mrs Jerome,
     Randolph's Telegram [*which has not survived*] will already have informed you of dear Jennie's safe confinement & of the Birth of her Boy. I am most thankful to confirm the good news & to assure you of her satisfactory Progress. So far indeed she could not be doing better. She was in some degree of Pain Saturday night & all Sunday & towards evg of that day we began to see that all the remedies for warding off the Event were useless. Abt 6 of P.M. the Pains began in earnest.
     We failed in getting an *accoucheur* from Oxford so she only had the Woodstock Doctor; we telegraphed to London but of course on Sunday ev there were no trains.
     Dr Hope only arrived at 9 of this Morg to find dear Jennie comfortably settled in bed & the baby washed and dressed! She could not have been more skillfully treated though had he been here than she was by our little local doctor. She had a somewhat tedious but perfectly safe & satisfactory Time. She is very thankful to have it over & indeed nothing could be more prosperous.
     We had neither cradle nor baby linen nor any thing ready but

fortunately *every* thing went well & all difficulties were overcome. Lady Camden, Lady Blandford & I were with her by turns & I really think she could not have had more care. She has had an anxious Time and dear Randolph and I are much thankful it is over. I will be sure to see you receive a Bulletin every day.

We expect today a 1st Rate Nurse. Best love to Clara & Believe me,

Yrs sincerely

F. MARLBOROUGH

Lady Camden (Clementine) was the daughter of the 6th Duke of Marlborough by his second wife, so that she was an aunt of Lord Randolph's, though only a year older. She had married in 1866 the future 3rd Marquess Camden and had borne him four children, but was widowed in 1872. She became one of the godparents of the newly arrived baby. Lady Blandford, Albertha, was the sixth daughter of the 1st Duke of Abercorn, at that time Viceroy of Ireland. She had been married for five years to the eldest son and heir of the 7th Duke of Marlborough, the Marquess of Blandford, who was soon to be involved in a serious public scandal; she had already had a son and two daughters.

The London doctor who was supposed to have attended the confinement of Lady Randolph was Mr William Hope, who at the age of thirty-seven had already become one of the leading obstetricians of the day. His inability to travel to Blenheim on a Sunday gave an unexpected opportunity to the local physician Dr Frederic Taylor. He had established himself in Woodstock not only as the principal doctor in the district but also as something of a local worthy, for he sat on the Bench and acted as Coroner for Woodstock until he left to practice in London in 1887. Lord Randolph expressed himself appreciative of his "skilful management of and careful attention to her Ladyship during her confinement," and Dr Taylor received a fee of twenty-five guineas for his professional services. The greatest initial embarrassment at the unexpected and premature arrival was the lack of baby clothes. Of course all the preparations were being made in Charles Street, though a lot of the baby clothes had not yet been purchased — Mrs Jerome and Lady Randolph's elder sister Clara had promised to buy some of them in Paris. After a week Lord Randolph wrote to Mrs Jerome: "The *layette* has given great

satisfaction but the little shawls with *capuchons* have not arrived.
Jennie says they are much wanted, also the pillow cases have not
come." Fortunately, Mrs Thomas Brown, the wife of the local
solicitor, had been more provident than Lady Randolph. She was
expecting her first child towards the end of January and it was the
baby things prepared for this arrival that were borrowed by Lord
Randolph to deal with the emergency caused by the premature birth
of his son.

Lord Randolph and his mother continued to send daily bulletins
to Mrs Jerome in Paris. In three consecutive letters Lord Randolph
somewhat querulously complained that he had had no reply to his
telegram to his father-in-law. "I telegraphed to Mr Jerome yesterday," he wrote on December 1, "and did expect he would have
answered but he has not yet." And on December 2: "I wonder Mr
Jerome has not answered my telegram"; and when there had been
no reply by December 4, Lord Randolph complained: "I think Mr
Jerome might have answered my telegram I sent him. It is so
unsatisfactory when people don't appreciate one's news."

Lord and Lady Randolph asked Mr Jerome to be godfather to
their child, but there is no record whether he was or not. However,
the fact that Winston was given the extra name of Leonard certainly
lends credibility to the supposition.

*

Thirty years later the child whose premature arrival had caused
such a commotion at Blenheim and in Woodstock gave this description of his birthplace and its history when writing his father's Life:

> The cumulative labours of Vanbrugh and "Capability" Brown have
> succeeded at Blenheim in setting an Italian palace in an English park
> without apparent incongruity. The combination of these different
> ideas, each singly attractive, produces a remarkable effect. The palace
> is severe in its symmetry and completeness. Nothing has been added
> to the original plan; nothing has been taken away. The approaches
> are formal; the wings are balanced; four equal towers maintain its
> corners; and the fantastic ornaments of one side are elaborately
> matched on the other. Natural simplicity and even confusion are, on

the contrary, the characteristic of the park and gardens. Instead of that arrangement of gravel paths, of geometrical flower beds, and of yews disciplined with grotesque exactness which the character of the house would seem to suggest, there spreads a rich and varied landscape. Green lawns and shining water, banks of laurel and fern, groves of oak and cedar, fountains and islands, are conjoined in artful disarray to offer on every side a promise of rest and shade. And yet there is no violent contrast, no abrupt dividing-line between the wildness and freshness of the garden and the pomp of the architecture.

The whole region is as rich in history as in charm; for the antiquity of Woodstock is not measured by a thousand years, and Blenheim is heir to all the memories of Woodstock. Here Kings — Saxon, Norman and Plantagenet — have held their Courts. Ethelred the Unready, Alfred the Great, Queen Eleanor, the Black Prince loom in vague majesty out of the past. Woodstock was notable before the Norman conquest. It was already a borough when the Domesday Book was being compiled. The park was walled to keep the foreign wild beasts of Henry I. Fair Rosamond's Well still bubbles by the lake. From the gatehouse of the old manor the imprisoned Princess Elizabeth watched the years of Mary's persecution. In the tumults of the Civil Wars Woodstock House was held for King Charles by an intrepid officer through a long and bitter siege and ravaged by the victorious Roundheads at its close. And beyond the most distant of these events, in the dim backward of time, the Roman generals administering the districts east and west of Akeman Street had built their winter villas in this pleasant, temperate retreat; so that Woodstock and its neighbourhood were venerable and famous long before John Churchill, in the early years of the eighteenth century, superimposed upon it the glory of his victories over the French.

Whether ancestry or environment play the greater part in influencing the character and destiny of human beings has long been disputed and is still an open question. The degree of influence must vary from case to case. It is diverting to speculate why such care is devoted to the breeding of dogs and horses while the human race prefers to reproduce itself in a largely indiscriminate and haphazard fashion. More than fifty years later, when Winston was writing his magnificent history of John, Duke of Marlborough, he set down a careful account of the origins of the Churchill family:

Besides attending to his son's education Winston [John's father] in
his studious leisure bethought himself often of his pedigree and his
arms. His researches into genealogy have produced as good an account of the origin of the Churchills as is likely to be required. He
traced his "Lyon Rampant, Argent upon a Sable coat," to Otho de
Leon, Castelan of Gisor, "whome we call our common ancestor."
The said Otho had two sons, Richard and Wandrill, Lord of Cour-
celle, "whose youngest son came into England with William the
Conqueror." After recounting conscientiously several generations,
Winston rested with confidence upon "John . . . Lord of Currichill,
or as 'tis in divers records Chirechile, since called Churchill in Som-
ersetshire," whose son, Sir Bartholomew de Churchill, "a man of
great note in the tyme of King Steven, . . . defended the castle of
Bristow against the Empress Maud and was slaine afterward in that
warr." In the time of King Edward I, after the Barons' War, the
lordship of Churchill was seized by the Crown and given to some
favourite, whose posterity continued in possession till "nere about
Henry VIII, his tyme." After passing through the hands of a family
of the name of Jennings . . . it was sold eventually in 1652 to a Sir
John Churchill, sometime Master of the Rolls, "and had come to my
son in right of his wife, had it not been so unfortunately alianated by
her said father."

All this was very fine, but when, descending these chains, we come
to John, "ancestor of the present Churchills of Munston, and Roger,
who by the daughter of Peverell, relict of Nicholas Meggs, had issue
Mathew, father of Jaspar, my grandfather," we enter a rather shady
phase. Edward Harly rudely asserts "that John Churchill's great
grandfather was a blacksmith who worked in the family of the
Meggs," and certainly, as his great-great-great-grandfather married a
Mrs Meggs, this seems very suspicious and even disquieting. In any
case, there are strong grounds for believing that John's grandfather
solidly improved the fortunes of this branch of the Churchill family.
He was a practising lawyer, a deputy registrar of Chancery as well as
member of the Middle Temple, and lawyers were a prosperous class
at this date. Not only did he make a marriage himself into an aristo-
cratic family, the Winstones, but he seems to have arranged a step
for his eldest son. For all the genealogical table produced by Winston, the Drakes were a more renowned and substantial family than
the Churchills, of whom there were numerous branches of various
conditions, some quite lowly, in Dorset alone; whereas John Drake's

family descended eight in line from father to son, and all called John, through the Bernard Drakes, who were already in good repute at the Court of Queen Elizabeth, and passed on the properties at Musbury which had been in their hands from the fifteenth century. Bernard Drake had been a man of so robust quality that he had physically assaulted his relation, the renowned Sir Francis Drake, for daring to display upon his coat of arms a wyvern which he deemed poached from him. Hearing this, Queen Elizabeth conferred upon Sir Francis a wyvern dangling head downward from the yards of a ship, and asked Sir Bernard what he thought of that! He replied with some temerity, "Madam, though you could give him a *finer* yet you could not give him an *ancienter* coat than mine." So the marriage arranged for Winston with Lady Drake's daughter Elizabeth was socially satisfactory, and was . . . a veritable salvation during the Civil Wars.

Another streak of blood, strange and wanton, mingled in the child John's nature. His grandmother, Lady Drake, was herself the daughter of John, Lord Boteler, who had married the sister of George Villiers, Duke of Buckingham, the favourite of James I and Charles I. Some students have amused themselves in tracing all the men — some of the greatest and wickedest in our history — who have descended from George Villiers, father of Buckingham. They are said to have repeatedly produced across the centuries, the favourites, male and female, of kings and queens; and Chatham, and Pitt, as well as Marlborough, bear the distinction of this taint or genius.

When at length, at the end of her life, Sarah, Duchess of Marlborough, read — tardily, for it had been kept from her — Lediard's history of the Duke, she made the following extremely up-to-date comment upon this part of the subject: "This History takes a great deal of Pains to make the Duke of Marlborough's Extraction very ancient. That may be true for aught I know; But it is no matter whether it be true or not in my opinion. For I value nobody for another's merit."

Be this as it may, students of heredity have dilated upon this family tree. Galton [in his *Hereditary Genius*], cites it as one of the chief examples on which his thesis stands. Winston himself has been accounted one of the most notable and potent of sires. Had he lived the full span, he would have witnessed within the space of twelve months his son gaining the battle of Ramillies and his daughter's son [the Duke of Berwick and Alba] of Almanza; and would have

found himself acknowledged as the progenitor of the two greatest
captains of the age at the head of the opposing armies of Britain and
of France and Spain. Moreover, his third surviving son, Charles,
became a soldier of well-tried distinction, and his naval son virtually
managed the Admiralty during the years of war. The military strain
flowed strong and clear from the captain of the Civil Wars, student
of heraldry and history, and champion of the Divine Right. It was
his blood, not his pen, that carried his message.

An older strain and one equally potent in Winston's blood was
that of the Spencers. The Spencers are first heard of in the latter part
of the fifteenth century. They were then Warwickshire shepherds
whose flocks were to prove the foundation of the family fortune. By
1504 John Spencer had risen sufficiently in the world to obtain a
grant of arms. He owned large estates at Wormleighton in Warwickshire, and later at Althorp in Northamptonshire. He was knighted
by Henry VIII and Winston was descended from him in direct male
descent through fifteen generations. This Sir John Spencer, who died
in 1522, had a grandson, another Sir John Spencer, who built a
substantial Elizabethan dwelling. The present (7th) Earl Spencer,
who by his careful organization and study of the papers in the Muni-
ment Room at Althorp has done so much to make known the earlier
history of the family, some years ago put on record for the benefit
of the author his account of an ancestor of his who died in 1586, two
years before the Spanish Armada:

He increased his wealth by sheepfarming, but, although his flocks
multiplied, tradition asserts that neither he nor his successors were
ever able to possess as many as 20,000 sheep. Though often their
flocks reached a total of 19,999, yet some fate, such as disease or
accident, always befell them before their number amounted to 20,000.
His riches seem to have been very great, for as well as leaving his
paternal property to his eldest son and successor he settled an estate
on each of his four younger sons.

It was to each of three daughters of this Sir John Spencer, Elizabeth, Alice and Ann, that Edmund Spenser dedicated a poem, and
also, in *Colin Clouts come home againe* he wrote:

Nor less praiseworthy are the sisters three,
The honor of the noble familie
Of which I meanest boast myself to be.

On the strength of this Edward Gibbon wrote in his autobiography, *Memoirs of my Life and Writings:* "The nobility of the Spencers has been illustrated and enriched by the trophies of Marlborough; but I exhort them to consider the Fairy Queen as the most precious jewel of their coronet." Alas, there is no apparent connection between the poet Spenser's family, who at the end of the thirteenth century held a freehold at Worsthorne, near Burnley, Lancashire, and Sir John Spencer's family, which traces its descent from the Despensers, notably Hugh, a prominent favourite at the courts of Edward I and II between 1287 and 1326.

In 1603 the Spencer of the day, fourth in direct descent from the first Sir John Spencer, was made a baron, and it was his grandson, the 3rd Lord Spencer, who married Lady Dorothy Sidney at Penshurst in 1639. She was the celebrated "Sacharissa" of Waller's poems. The 3rd Lord Spencer was created Earl of Sunderland in 1643 by Charles I. Within a few months he was to die, with his great friend Lord Falkland, at the Battle of Newbury. Of him Clarendon wrote: "A lord of a great fortune, tender years . . . and an early judgement; who, having no command in the army, attended upon the King's person under the obligation of honour; and putting himself that day into the King's troop a volunteer, before they came to charge was taken away by a cannon bullet."

"Sacharissa" was the chatelaine of Althorp during her son's minority of nineteen years. Her son, the 4th Lord Spencer and 2nd Earl of Sunderland, succeeded to Althorp in 1662 when he came of age. "Sacharissa" Sidney had taken great pains to ensure that her son was a staunch Protestant, and while at Oxford he early gave proof of his attachment to the Reformed Church by joining William Penn, founder of the State of Pennsylvania, in a demonstration in Tom Quad in Christ Church against the wearing of surplices, which had recently been enjoined upon the authorities by King Charles II. Penn and some others were rusticated, and Sunderland left the University in sympathy with his friends. In 1665 he married Lady

Anne Digby, daughter of the 2nd Earl of Bristol, and grand-daughter of the 4th Earl of Bedford. She was a striking beauty and also heiress to the great estates of her brother, the 3rd Earl of Bristol, who died in 1698.

While Cromwell ruled in England, Sunderland had travelled widely in Europe. After the restoration of Charles II he was appointed Ambassador first at Madrid at the age of thirty-one and then at Paris. He thus had the opportunity, which he embraced, of becoming a discerning patron of the arts. He acquired that splendid collection of pictures to which every succeeding generation of the family has had the good sense to add works by the leading artists of their day. He was a powerful minister who filled numerous offices under Charles II, James II, and even William III. These various appointments under three different sovereigns could not have been achieved by a man who did not have a marked flexibility of character and principle.

He was succeeded in 1702 by his second and only surviving son Charles, who as Lord Spencer had three years before in 1699 married Lady Anne Churchill as his second wife. His first wife was Lady Arabella Cavendish, daughter and co-heiress of the Duke of Newcastle, who had died in 1698. The Cavendish dukedom of Newcastle antedated the Devonshire creation by 29 years. It was extinguished by the death of the second Duke in 1691. Three years later it was recreated for the benefit of John Holles, Earl of Clare, who had married Margaret Cavendish, daughter of the second Duke of Newcastle. Lady Anne was the third and much loved daughter of John, Earl of Marlborough who was raised to a Dukedom shortly after Queen Anne's accession to the throne in 1702. Of this match Winston, in his *Marlborough,* was to write:

[Lord Spencer] had none of the insinuating charm and genial courtesy of his incomprehensible father. He was an ultra-Whig of the straitest and most unbending type. He did not trouble to conceal his republican opinions. He was so conscious of the rights of his order and of Parliament against the Crown that he had little sympathy left for the commonalty. According to his philosophy, citizens of the worst republic were free, while subjects of the best king were slaves. He was a keen book-lover, and the Sunderland Library remained for many generations his monument. The Whig Party took a lively interest in the development of his mind. It was thought that experience would mellow his orthodox severity, and they already saluted him as the future champion of the cause for which "Hampden had died in the field and Sidney on the scaffold."

Sarah, that sturdy Whig, may have shared these hopes; but Marlborough's temperamental Toryism was repulsed by the harshness alike of Lord Spencer's doctrine and disposition. Anne was his favourite daughter, and by every account was a brilliant and fascinating creature. Intimate and subtle as were his relations with Sunderland in State affairs, important as were the reciprocal services which might be rendered, magnificent as was the inheritance, he was disinclined to mingle that wayward blood with his own, or to countenance a marriage which might not bring his daughter happiness. He was therefore very hard to persuade. However, he gradually yielded to Sarah's persuasions, and, being at length convinced of Lord Spencer's sincerity, he finally consented. Once again [*as she had done the year before for the marriage of Marlborough's eldest daughter, Henrietta, to Francis Godolphin*] Princess Anne, who was the girl's godmother, matched the family dowry with a gift of £5000. Sunderland, who seems to have longed for the marriage, wrote in a remarkable letter (to Mrs Boscawen [young Godolphin's aunt] on 31 December 1698):

> If I see him so settled I shall desire nothing more in this world but to die in peace if it please God. I must add this that if he can be thus happy he will be governed in everything public and private by my Lord Marlborough. I have particularly talked to him of that and he is sensible how advantageous it will be to him to be so. I need not I am sure desire that all this may be a secret to everybody but Lady Marlborough.

These expectations were not fulfilled, and Spencer's personality and conduct were to become after his father's death a cause of serious political embarrassment. It is, however, by this marriage that the Marlborough blood, titles, and estates have descended to posterity, for his [Marlborough's] only surviving son, Lord Churchill, Master of the Horse, in the Duke of Gloucester's household, had almost as short a span to live as the little Prince he served.

Charles Spencer, 3rd Earl of Sunderland, was to play a great role in politics during the lifetime of his father-in-law. After a career of lively political intrigue, during which he held many offices, he

was First Lord of the Treasury from 1718 to 1721. It was the third
son of this marriage who in 1733, at the age of twenty-six, inherited
Blenheim and the Marlborough dukedom from his aunt, Henrietta,
Countess of Godolphin and, by Special Remainder, Duchess of
Marlborough. This boy, another Charles, had meanwhile become
5th Earl of Sunderland and had succeeded to Althorp in 1729 on the
death of his elder brother.

Under a family compact made many years before, Charles vacated
Althorp to his brother Jack, eighteen months younger, when he
inherited the dukedom and Blenheim. Their grandmother Sarah,
the old Duchess, disapproved of them both because of their extravagance, but Jack was her favourite and to him she left most of the
family property, pictures and treasures which were not entailed with
Blenheim. Thus it is that the finest family pictures and plate are
today at Althorp and not at Blenheim. In the same way, the immensely valuable estates at Wimbledon and St Albans, together with
several millions of cash, were alienated from the senior branch of the
family. She further alienated from the Marlborough dukedom such
trophies as the sword of Ramillies and Marlborough's campaign maps
to another daughter who was married to the Duke of Montagu,
whose heiress, Elizabeth, married the 3rd Duke of Buccleuch. These
treasures now repose at Boughton in Northamptonshire.

What had now become the cadet branch of the Spencer family
proved capable from their firm base at Althorp of producing politicians and statesmen of high capacity. Jack Spencer sat in the House
of Commons. His son became 1st Earl Spencer in 1765. The 2nd
Earl Spencer was First Lord of the Admiralty in the days of Nelson,
and his son, the 3rd Earl, was a powerful Whig politician and one
of the men who carried the Reform Bill in 1832. He was succeeded,
as 4th Earl, by his brother Frederick, a Rear-Admiral who fought at
Navarino and was later Lord Chamberlain and Lord Steward of the
Household. His son, John Poyntz, 5th Earl, who was famous for his
red beard, was Viceroy of Ireland and later First Lord of the
Admiralty under Gladstone. The 6th Earl Spencer sat in the House
of Commons for twenty years before he succeeded to his title and was
Lord Chamberlain of the Household to King Edward VII and King
George V.

By contrast, the holders of the Dukedom who succeeded Marlborough were somewhat undistinguished for several generations. Charles, 3rd Duke of Marlborough and 5th Earl of Sunderland, it is true, had an honourable career in the Army, commanded a brigade of foot guards at the Battle of Dettingen, the last battle at which a King of England, George II, was personally in command, and became Lord Privy Seal and Master General of the Ordnance. His son George succeeded as 4th Duke at the age of twenty, and remained the occupier of Blenheim for fifty-eight years until his death in 1817. It was he who employed Capability Brown in the 1760s and commissioned Reynolds and Romney to paint portraits of his family. Indeed, many of the pictures that made the Blenheim collection one of the most renowned in Europe were acquired by him or by younger members of his family. This was the most splendid time the Palace knew: when George III visited Blenheim in 1786 he was prompted to remark: "We have nothing to equal this."

Spencer remained the family name of the Dukes of Marlborough until 1817 when by Royal Licence the 5th Duke, shortly after he succeeded to the dukedom, changed it to Spencer-Churchill. He was authorized to "take and use the name of Churchill, in addition to and after that of Spencer . . . in order to perpetuate in his Family a Surname to which his illustrious ancestor the said John the first Duke of Marlborough &c by a long series of transcendant & heroic Achievements added such imperishable Lustre. . . ." The arms were quartered, the first and fourth quarters for Churchill, the second and third for Spencer, and were surmounted by two crests, a lion for Churchill, and a griffin's head for the Spencer family. In more recent times the Churchills have tended to drop the Spencer from their surname.

The 5th and 6th Dukes lived up to their age's reputation for profligacy and were noted for nothing so much as for their extravagance, which ruined the family. Gronow, the celebrated writer of reminiscences of the early nineteenth century, relates an astonishing story of how the 6th Duke, before he had succeeded and when he was still Marquess of Blandford, produced, while travelling in his coach, fifty £1,000 notes which he said he had borrowed. "You see, Gronow," he explained, "how the immense fortune of my family will be frittered away; but I can't help it; I must live. My father inherited £500,000 in ready money and £70,000 a year in land; and in all probability when it comes to my turn to live at Blenheim I shall have nothing left but the annuity of £5,000 a year on the Post Office." After he became Duke "he lived in one remote corner of his magnificent Palace, a melancholy instance of extravagance."

His son, John Winston, was left vastly impoverished by the folly of his predecessors. He devoted himself to politics, sat in the House of Commons for some fifteen years as Member for Woodstock and, after his succession as 7th Duke, became Lord President of the Council and a member of Lord Derby's third cabinet and of Disraeli's first cabinet for nearly two years. The great family talent, however, which had lain largely fallow during all these years and which had only burgeoned in the cadet Spencer branch, was not to erupt until Lord Randolph Churchill, younger son of the 7th Duke, entered Parliament in 1874.

When Winston was born his father was twenty-five. Lord Randolph had been the Conservative Member for the family seat of Woodstock for nine months but he had so far done little more in the House of Commons than make his maiden speech. His speech did not excite great interest but prompted an amiable letter from the Prime Minister to Lord Randolph's mother which has been published in Winston's *Lord Randolph Churchill*. But Disraeli also wrote the same day what was perhaps a more objective letter to the Queen:

Benjamin Disraeli to Queen Victoria

(*Royal Archives*)

EXTRACT

22 May 1874   2 Whitehall Gardens
                                                                        S.W.

. . . Tonight, there was an amusing debate respecting making Oxford a military centre. Mr Hall, the new Conservative member for Oxford city, made a maiden speech, of considerable power and promise — a fine voice, a natural manner, and much improvisation. While he was sitting down, amid many cheers, Lord Randolph Churchill rose and though sitting on the same side of the House upheld the cause of the University against the city, and answered Mr Hall.

Lord Randolph said many imprudent things, which is not very important in the maiden speech of a young member and a young man, but the House was surprised, and then captivated, by his energy, and his natural flow, and his impressive manners. With self control and study he might mount. It was a speech of great promise. . . .

*

Winston's mother, Lady Randolph, was twenty at the time of his birth. She was a woman of exceptional beauty in an age of famous beauties. They glittered around the circle of the Prince of Wales and they continued to glimmer after his accession to the throne as King Edward VII in 1901.

Lady Randolph's father, Leonard Jerome, was a financier of great drive and ability who in 1855 had settled in New York, where he joined the stock exchange and became a partner in a brokerage business with William R. Travers. He won and lost several large fortunes in the course of a daring and brilliant career. He was active in politics, serving for about eighteen months as American Consul in Trieste; and for a period he was the principal proprietor of the *New York Times*. But his name is best remembered as a founder of the American Jockey Club and a patron of the American turf. He built the race track in the Bronx, New York City, which was named Jerome Park after him. He was also a generous benefactor of the arts, particularly of opera, and an ocean-racing yachtsman. He was the fifth of seven sons of Isaac Jerome, whose great-grandfather Timothy had, along with other Huguenot families, sailed from the Isle of Wight to America in 1710. Leonard's mother, Aurora Murray, was of Scots extraction, her great-grandfather Jonathan Murray having come to Connecticut in the early 1680s.

Leonard Jerome married in 1849 Clarissa Hall, whose elder sister Catherine had married, five years before, Leonard's younger brother Lawrence. Clarissa, known after marriage as Clara, was a noted beauty in her day: a woman of good but expensive tastes, she spent most of her time in Europe, chiefly in Paris, after she had accompanied her husband to Trieste in 1852–3. She was the daughter of Ambrose Hall, a member of the New York State Assembly, whose family were settled in Connecticut before 1650. Her mother, Clarissa

Willcox, was the grand-daughter of Eleazur Smith, of Dartmouth, Massachusetts, and Meribah (no maiden name recorded), who is believed to have been an Iroquois Indian. At least two of Leonard's forebears fought against the British in the American War of Independence: one great-grandfather, Samuel Jerome, served as a sergeant in the Berkshire County Militia; another great-grandfather, Major Libbeus Ball of the 4th Massachusetts Regiment, was with Washington at Valley Forge and fought in the Mohawk Valley. Leonard Jerome's maternal grandfather, Reuben Murray, served as Lieutenant in Connecticut and New York regiments, while Clara's grandfather, Ambrose Hall, was a Captain in the Berkshire County Militia at Bennington.

Leonard Jerome's marriage to Clarissa Hall was to produce four daughters: Clara, born 1850, Jennie (1854), Camille (1855), who died at the age of seven, and Leonie (1859). Like many beautiful women, Jennie sought at this time of her life to disguise her age. We find her writing to Lord Randolph on 8 January 1883: "How sweet of you to send me a present. Just in time for my birthday tomorrow — *29* my dear! but I shall not acknowledge it to the world, 26 is quite enough." It is rare for people as young as Jennie was to camouflage their age; but she was approaching thirty, then thought to be as deadly as the age of forty today. This letter plainly indicates that she was born on 9 January 1854. Further evidence of the date is that her christening mug is engraved *Jennie Jerome 1854*. Subsequently, when she was in need of money and was writing her Reminiscences in 1908, she was obviously short of material: for while admitting that she was born in Brooklyn, she recounted in a lively, indeed exuberant style, the impressions that Trieste had made upon her: described an exciting journey back across the Mont Cenis Pass in deep snow: and stated that until the age of six she spoke only Italian.

Leonard Jerome served in Trieste from April 1852 until November 1853. Jennie was not born until after the Jeromes' return to America. If we are to believe Lady Randolph's Reminiscences, it would mean that she was born at least as early as 1851 and that she was three years older than she candidly reported to Lord Randolph at a time when she was pretending to be three years younger than her true date of birth. There is an easy explanation for this discrepancy. In 1908 Lady Randolph was fifty-four. Perhaps her age did not then matter so much; but she needed material for the Reminiscences and it is reasonable to suppose that all the tales she had heard in the nursery from her older sister and from her parents were so indelibly etched on her memory for her to believe that she had experienced them herself. As to the preference for the Italian tongue until the age of six, it is very possible that the Jeromes brought back an Italian governess from Trieste and that Jennie was born into a nursery where Italian was the principal language.

Lord Randolph had first met his future wife at a reception and dance at Cowes in August 1873. The original invitation to Mrs Jerome and her daughters is preserved:

To meet
Their Royal Highnesses the Prince and Princess of Wales
and
*Their Imperial Russian Highnesses the
Grand Duke Cesarewitch and Grand Duchess Cesarevna
Captain Carpenter and the officers of H.M.S. 'Ariadne'*
request the honour of the Company of
MRS & MISSES JEROME
On board, on Thursday, August 12th, from 3.30 to 7.30 pm
DANCING
Boats will be in attendance at the R.Y.C. Landing Place.
R.S.V.P.

Afterwards Jennie wrote on her invitation card between the lines, immediately below *To meet,* one word — Randolph.

It seems on both sides to have been love at first sight — both were hot-blooded and impetuous. Lord Randolph in particular sought to brush aside all suggestions of delay either by his father, the Duke, or by his brother Blandford, or by Mr Jerome. Mr Jerome was at first overjoyed at the news his daughter Jennie and his wife had sent to New York. He wrote:

Leonard Jerome to Jennie Jerome

EXTRACT

11 September [1873]   Union Club

. . . I must say I have been very happy all day. I have thought of nothing else. I telegraphed your mother immediately that I was "delighted" and that I would arrange £2000 per year for you which she says in her letter will do. I cannot imagine any engagement that would please me more. I am as confident that all you say of him is true as though I knew him. Young, ambitious, uncorrupted. And best of all you think and I believe he loves you. He must. You are no heiress and it must have taken heaps of love to overcome an Englishman's prejudice against "those horrid Americans." I like it in every way. He is English. . . .

This last was of prime importance to Mr Jerome. Earlier he had written to Jennie: "You know my views. I have great confidence in you and still greater in your mother and any one you would accept and your mother approves I could not object to Provided always he is not a Frenchman or any other of those Continental cusses."

The Duke, on the other hand, had his reservations: "My father and mother," Lord Randolph wrote to Mrs Jerome, "have been very much taken by surprise & find it difficult to convince themselves of the reality & probable permanence of our feelings for each other."

The Duke had written to Lord Randolph on August 24: "You have indeed taken me by surprise & to use a Cowes speech you have brought up all standing; I am afraid this kind of marineering is full of changes."

A week later the Duke revealed that Lord Randolph's impetuosity was not the only cause of his doubts.

Duke of Marlborough to Lord Randolph

(Blenheim Papers)

31 August [1873]   Guisachan

My dearest Randolph,
    It is not likely that at present you can look at anything but from your own point of view but persons from the outside cannot but be struck with the unwisdom of your proceedings, and the uncontrolled state of your feelings, which completely paralyses your judgement; never was there such an illustration of the adage *"love is blind"* for you seem blind to all consequences in order that you may pursue your passion; blind to the relative consequences as regards your family & blind to trouble you are heaping on Mamma and me by the

anxieties this act of yours has produced. I do but write the expression of my constant thoughts when I say this, that you must not think me unkind for telling it to you.

Now as regards your letter I can't say that what you have told me is reassuring. I shall know more before long but from what you told me & what I have heard this Mr J. seems to be a sporting, and I should think vulgar kind of man. I hear he drives about 6 and 8 horses in N.Y. (one may take this as a kind of indication of what the man is). I hear he and his two brothers are stock brokers, one of them bears a *bad* character in commercial judgement in *this* country, but which of them it is, I do not know, but it is evident he is of the class of speculators; he has been bankrupt once; and may be so again: and when we come to think of N.Y. speculators & their deeds look at Fiske and *hoc genus omne.*

Everything that you say about the mother and daughters is perfectly compatible with all that I am apprehensive of about the father & his belongings. And however great the attractions of the former they can be no set off against a connection shd it so appear wh no man in his senses could think respectable. I can say no more at present till I have seen you, & get some further replies to enquiries I have set on foot. I am deeply sorry that your feelings are so much engaged; and only for your own sake wish most heartily that you had checked the current before it became so overpowering.

May God bless and keep you straight is my earnest prayer.

Ever your affectionate father
MARLBOROUGH

Lord Randolph's determination to marry Jennie somewhat mollified the Duke but he continued to be obstinate. Lord Randolph reported to Mrs Jerome on 30 September 1873 "that taking into consideration the suddenness & rapidity of the attachment formed he [the Duke] said he wld give his consent if we were of the same mind in a year hence." Lord Randolph succeeded in bearing down his father who agreed that the marriage might take place as soon as the General Election, due to be held soon, was over and Lord Randolph had been elected for the family borough of Woodstock. The election took place on February 3, and Lord Randolph defeated the Liberal candidate George Brodrick, polling 569 votes against 404.

Further complications were soon to arise about the marriage

settlement. Lord Randolph was receiving £1000 a year as a result of
a settlement made by the Duke shortly before the election. Mr
Jerome, as we have seen, was very willing to settle £2000 a year on
his daughter: this income was to be derived from a settlement of
£40,000 consisting of a house in New York on the corner of Madison
Avenue and 25th Street. The Duke's solicitors at first suggested that
the settlement should be raised to £50,000 on the grounds that "it
was not usual to give trustees power to make investments which
yield 5%." British solicitors and trustees at that time thought that
all trustee settlements must be confined to gilt-edged securities which
produced between 2½ and 3 per cent per annum. A more serious
objection to Mr Jerome's plans was now raised. Mr Jerome intended
that the £2000 be paid to his daughter: the Duke of Marlborough
would have none of this. "Such a settlement," wrote the Duke's
solicitor, Frederick L. Capon, to Lord Randolph on February 25,
"as far as Lord Randolph is personally concerned cannot be considered as any settlement at all, for . . . Miss Jerome is made quite
independent [of Lord Randolph Churchill] in a pecuniary point of
view, which in my experience is most unusual, & I think I might add
in such a case as the present without precedent — and His Grace
desires it to be distinctly understood that in accepting Mr Jerome's
proposal you have done so in direct opposition to his [the Duke's]
views & wishes and solely upon your own responsibility."

As a compromise it was suggested that Lady Randolph should be
given "pin money," first £300, then £500, then £600, and that the
residue of the £2000 should be paid to Lord Randolph. In the end
Mr Jerome agreed that half the allowance of £2000 a year should be
paid to his daughter and half to Lord Randolph. "My daughter
although not a *Russian* Princess is an American and ranks precisely
the same and you have doubtless seen that the Russian settlement
recently published claimed *everything* for the bride." Mr Jerome
was referring to the settlement on the Grand Duchess Marie Alex-
androvna, only daughter of Tsar Alexander II, who married on
23 January 1874 Queen Victoria's second son, the Duke of Edinburgh. She was given a marriage portion of 2 million roubles
(£250,000), and the marriage treaty stipulated that the capital was
to be considered as her property, and the income from the 5 per cent
interest was to be "for her separate and exclusive use and enjoyment."

Even then the matter was not finally resolved. Mr Jerome had wanted to leave the disposal of the capital sum of £50,000 to be entirely at the discretion of Lady Randolph should she die before Lord Randolph. Now this was changed, so that the apportionment of the £50,000 was to be decided, in the event of there being children, between Lord Randolph and Lady Randolph, or, if no apportionment was made, for the sum to be divided equally between the children. If there were no children and Lady Randolph died before Lord Randolph, half the £50,000 was to be paid to Lord Randolph and the other £25,000 to Lady Randolph's family. The following letter from Mr Leonard Jerome expresses his view on the final position:

Leonard Jerome to Duke of Marlborough

(Blenheim Papers)

9 April [1874]   Paris

Dear Duke,

Your very kind letter of the 7th reached me this morning. I learned on my arrival on Wednesday that you and the Duchess had paid a visit to Paris and I am extremely gratified to know that the impression you formed of my daughter was so favourable. The assurances you give me of the kindly manner in which she will be received into your family afford me much pleasure. I have every confidence in Randolph and while I would entrust my daughter to his sole care alone in the world still I can but feel reassured of her happiness when I am told that in entering your family she will be met at once with "new and affectionate friends and relatives."

I am very sorry you are not able to come over to the wedding. We had all hoped to have had the pleasure of seeing both yourself & the Duchess. Under the circumstances however, we must of course excuse you — and we do this the more readily as we know the occasion has your best wishes & the young people your blessing.

In regard to the settlement — as it has finally, I am happy to say, been definitely arranged — little more need be said. In explanation of my own action in respect to it I beg to assure you that I have been governed purely by what I conceived to be in the best interests of *both* parties. It is quite wrong to suppose I entertain any distrust of Randolph. On the contrary I firmly believe there is no young man in the world safer, still I can but think your English custom of making the wife so utterly dependent upon the husband most unwise.

In the settlement as is finally arranged I have ignored American custom & waived all my American prejudices. I have conceded to your views & English custom in every point save one. That is simply a — somewhat unusual allowance of pin money to the wife. Possibly the principle may be wrong but you may be very certain my action upon it in this instance by no means arises from any distrust of Randolph.

With kind regards, Believe me dear Duke, Yours most sincerely

LEONARD JEROME

On 14 April 1874 Lord Randolph was able to report to his mother: "Things are all going now as merrily as a marriage bell. I expect the settlements over tonight and they will be signed tomorrow." And the Duke wrote from London on the same day:

Duke of Marlborough to Lord Randolph
(Blenheim Papers)

EXTRACT

14 April [1874]   London

My dearest Randolph,

I must send you a few lines to reach you tomorrow, one of the most important days of your life & which I sincerely pray will be blessed to you & be the commencement of a united existence of happiness for you & for your wife. She is one whom you have chosen with less than usual deliberation but you adhered to your love with unwavering constancy & I *cannot* doubt the truth & force of your affection: & now I hope that as time goes on, your two natures will prove to have been brought, *not* accidentally, together: may you both be 'lovely & pleasant in your lives' is my earnest prayer. I am very glad that harmony is again restored, & that no cloud obscures the day of sunshine but what has happened will show that the sweetest path is not without its thorns & I must say ought not to be without its lesson to you. . . .

On April 15 Lord Randolph and Jennie Jerome were married at the British Embassy in Paris by the Reverend Dr Edward Forbes in the presence of Mr and Mrs Jerome, the Marquess of Blandford (Lord Randolph's elder brother) and Mr Francis Knollys, private secretary to the Prince of Wales.

2

Ireland

LORD AND LADY RANDOLPH and their newly born son, Winston, spent the Christmas of 1874 with the Marlboroughs at Blenheim and two days later on December 27 the baby was baptised in the chapel of Blenheim by the Duke's chaplain, the Reverend Henry William Yule. On their return from their honeymoon Lord and Lady Randolph had lived for three months in Curzon Street until their short lease had expired at the end of July 1874. Early in the New Year they moved into the house they had rented in Charles Street. Shortly after their return to London, Mrs Everest, who will play a striking role in these pages, was engaged as Winston's nanny. Lord and Lady Randolph gave themselves up to the delights of the London season and Lord Randolph does not seem to have been particularly attentive to his parliamentary duties. Indeed, in the course of the year, he only made two speeches, the first defending John, Duke of Marlborough, against the sneers of some Irish members: and the second defending the family borough of Woodstock which he had the honour of representing in the House of Commons. The Prince of Wales attended the second of these two speeches and sat in the traditional place of the heir to the Throne, behind the clock above the Speaker's chair.

Winston was later to give some account in his Life of Lord Randolph of the style in which his father and mother lived in Charles Street:

> . . . they continued their gay life on a somewhat more generous scale than their income warranted. Fortified by an excellent French

cook, they entertained with discrimination. The Prince of Wales, who had from the beginning shown them much kindness, dined sometimes with them. Lord Randolph's college friend, Lord Rosebery, was a frequent visitor. . . . But in the year 1876 an event happened which altered, darkened, and strengthened his [Lord Randolph's] whole life and character. Engaging in his brother's quarrels with fierce and reckless partisanship, Lord Randolph incurred the deep displeasure of a great personage. The fashionable world no longer smiled. Powerful enemies were anxious to humiliate him. His own sensitiveness and pride magnified every coldness into an affront. London became odious to him. The breach was not repaired for more than eight years, and in the interval a nature originally genial and gay contracted a stern and bitter quality, a harsh contempt for what is called "Society," and an abiding antagonism to rank and authority. If this misfortune produced in Lord Randolph characteristics which afterwards hindered or injured his public works, it was also his spur. Without it he might have wasted a dozen years in the frivolous and expensive pursuits of the silly world of fashion; without it he would probably never have developed popular sympathies or the courage to champion democratic causes. . . .

At the time when Winston wrote his father's Life thirty years later he probably did not know the full details of the event which caused Lord Randolph's temporary exile in Ireland. Moreover, so far as he knew the facts, they could hardly at that time be presented to the public. The "great personage" had now become, at the time of writing, King Edward VII. Many accounts have appeared of Lord Randolph's quarrel with the Prince of Wales but none of them has been complete. Here it is proposed to put down all the details that are known, for it is important that the causes which led Winston and his parents to spend three years in Dublin are understood.

On 11 October 1875 the Prince of Wales left England on a tour of India. Among those who accompanied the Prince were the Earl of Aylesford and his brother-in-law Colonel Owen Williams of the "Blues." Aylesford had, as Lord Guernsey, married Edith Williams in January 1871, just ten days before he succeeded to the earldom. Although he was only twenty-six when he went to India, he had already acquired a reputation which earned him the nickname of Sporting Joe. He owed this not only to his activities on the turf, where he was known for his perseverance rather than for any success, but also to the fact that he was a man of violent disposition and extravagant tastes with a fondness for pugilism, cock-fighting, and the pleasures of the notorious Cremorne Gardens.

The Prince of Wales, Lord and Lady Randolph, Lord Randolph's elder brother Blandford and the Aylesfords had all been part of the same social group. For many months before the events that must now be described, Blandford had become very susceptible to the charms of Lady Aylesford. While the Royal party was away in India Blandford moved his horses to stables near Packington, the Aylesford seat in Warwickshire, and took up his residence in a nearby inn. Early in 1876 Lady Aylesford volunteered news of her infidelity to Lord Aylesford who was still in India. On receipt of this letter Aylesford at once telegraphed to his mother to send for his two children from Packington Hall and to keep them until his return to England: "a great misfortune has happened." Word was sent to his brother-in-law Owen Williams, who had just left the Royal party on his way home to be with his wife Fanny, who was seriously ill. Aylesford's mother complied with her son's directions and the young Lady Aylesford then wrote the following poignant letter which came to light in a subsequent legitimacy case in the House of Lords:

Lady Aylesford to Dowager Countess of Aylesford
(Copy: Minutes of Evidence, House of Lords, 1 July 1885)

Friday night [?25 February 1876]   [Packington Hall]

Dear Lady Aylesford,

By the time this letter reaches you I shall have left my home for ever. Guernsey knows of this, which will account for his telegram to you. I do not attempt to say a word in self defence, but you can imagine I must have suffered much before I could have taken such a step; *how* much it would be impossible to tell you, but it is the only reparation I can make to Guernsey, and he will now have the opportunity of getting rid of one who he has long ceased to care for. You do not know, you never can know, how hard I have tried to win his love, and without success, and I cannot live uncared for. I do not ask you to think kindly of me; I know you could not do it, but for God's sake be kind to the children, and do not teach them to hate their wretched mother, let them think I am dead, it will be the best. I heard from Minna [Aylesford's sister Lady Anne Murray] the other day, but never answered her letter; she will know why.

You have always been most kind to me, and it is the last word I shall ever say to you; do not be offended if I thank you for all your kindness and tell you how very wretched it makes me feel to think that I should have brought such sorrow and disgrace upon you all. Oh! Lady Aylesford, if it is possible, try and forgive me, as you hope for forgiveness. I know that Guernsey does not care for me, therefore, I do not think he will feel my loss, and perhaps may be glad to be free; but what it costs me to leave my children I cannot tell you, and I cannot bear to think; that they will be cared for I know, as you will be a mother to them, but my God I shall *never* see them again, it is like being dead and yet alive. I could not give orders about the children; they, therefore, know nothing, so please give the necessary orders yourself. I have left the diamonds with James, and as regards the things belonging to me, I have written to him to send them, and they will be forwarded to me. I wrote to Madge [sister of Lady Aylesford, and wife of Sir Richard Williams-Bulkeley] to come to me today. I have told her all as I have told you; she has just returned to town, and I am left alone completely broken-hearted. I bring this letter to town myself. I would have seen you, but feel that perhaps you would rather not see me. God bless you, dear Lady Aylesford, and for the last time farewell, and try not to think too hardly of

EDITH

A week or so later one of the Duke of Marlborough's sons-in-law, Edward Marjoribanks (later Lord Tweedmouth), wrote to the Duke, who was in his yacht off Greece:

Edward Marjoribanks to Duke of Marlborough
(Blenheim Papers)

1 March 1876   134 Piccadilly

My dear Duke,

   I write in fulfillment of my promise in the telegram I sent to Zante to explain to you the circumstances which led to it.

   I hope you will forgive what may seem presumption on my part when I said that I think that any steps that you may take to influence Blandford to give up Lady Aylesford would be for the present at any rate entirely thrown away.

   The only thing we can hope for at present is to postpone his final departure for as long as possible. Any suggestion of the possibility of parting them only serves to increase his obstinate determination. The one argument that seems to move him is the wretched position that Lady Aylesford will be placed in if she goes off with him, more particularly should anything happen to him.

When I first became aware for certain that Blandford intended to go away with Lady Aylesford the position was as follows.

Lady Aylesford had written to Aylesford informing him that she had been untrue to him and asking Aylesford to telegraph whether they were to leave at once or to wait till he arrived in England, at the same time saying that should he still wish it she was ready to live as his wife before the world but no more. Blandford at the same time wrote Col Williams telling him of his intentions, expressing his readiness to meet Aylesford & promising that if a meeting was Aylesford's wish he would not go away with Lady Aylesford till after it had taken place. . . .

. . . On Friday Feb 25 Sir R. Bulkeley and Mr Hwfa Williams and other members of the family consulted at Linners Hotel. Mr H. Williams expressed his intention of calling Blandford out and also stated that should Blandford refuse to meet him he would shoot him down sooner than see him go off with his sister.

Randolph went into Linners during the evening of Friday 25 Febr and said to Sir R. Bulkeley and Mr H. Williams and Lord Hartington (who had been called in by them for advice) that Blandford would meet no one but Aylesford and that he (Randolph) would take measures to prevent a breach of the peace.

On Saturday morning Feb 26 Randolph received a letter from Lord Hartington strongly urging him to induce Blandford if possible to postpone his departure till Col Williams' return.

Randolph and I at once went to Blandford and persuaded him after much difficulty to consent to allow matters to remain absolutely *in statu quo* until Col Williams' return. He also pledged himself not to have any interview with Lady Aylesford during that period.

Mr Hwfa Williams still seeming bent on serious mischief Randolph thought it advisable to take steps to prevent the possibility of anything occurring and accordingly had detectives placed to watch Blandford and Mr H. Williams. These detectives were withdrawn on Monday 28th, Randolph having received an assurance from Mr Williams that he would hold his hand till his brother's return.

On Sunday morning Feb 27 Randolph & I were with Blandford all morning and after much argument he expressed himself willing to concede to proposals of the following nature viz that Aylesford

should consent to be merely separated from his wife and not
divorced.

That an establishment and position should be provided for her.

That she should be allowed to retain her children.

That these objects being attained he (Blandford) would absent
himself from England for a year. This is the position until Col
Williams' return.

It is proposed that Lady Aylesford shall go down for the present to
Aylesford with the Dowager Lady Aylesford who has been very kind
and seems to impute some at any rate of the blame to her son. I think
it may be considered that she will either do this or go down to Wales
tomorrow.

Whatever happens Blandford seems now inclined to take no decisive steps till Aylesford obtains a divorce.

Every pressure has been put upon the Prince to induce Aylesford
to reconsider his determination and we now hear that Aylesford is
to proceed home at once. I hope you will think that I have put the
whole case sufficiently intelligibly before you. I don't think anything
is very generally known as yet only the following people are aware of
everything: The Duchess of Manchester, the Princess of Wales, the
Charles [Innes-] Kers and Bulkeley, Hartington and Lord Alington
and Lansdowne. Cornelia and Ivor [Guest] know nothing and Rosamond and Clemmie don't even know of Blandford's interview with
Bertha. I showed the main portion of the letter to Lansdowne and
he thinks that it adequately represents the state of affairs.

I think there is just a hope that it will eventually be arranged but
I cannot speak sanguinely about it. Randolph is doing and has done
all he can to influence Blandford but he is very difficult to move.

Believe me my dear Duke very affectionately yours

E. MARJORIBANKS

As will soon be seen, Marjoribanks was a trifle naïve in thinking
that a secret that was "only" known to eight people was likely to
remain a secret for long. At this stage Lord Randolph intervened
in a dramatic and perhaps inexcusable way. He believed that a
divorce would not only cause grave scandal but also that it would
not be in the best interests of Blandford and his wife and four children. Furthermore he had reason to believe that the Prince of Wales
himself had shown attentions to Lady Aylesford and he felt that his

brother Blandford was being made a scapegoat. Moreover Aylesford
had spread the Prince's strictures on Blandford all over London.
Accordingly he took upon himself to call on the Princess of Wales.
He was accompanied by a young newly created peer, Lord Alington.
They pointed out to the Princess that it would be undesirable for
divorce proceedings to be instituted and they asked her to tell the
Prince to stop Aylesford continuing with his divorce plans. At the
same time, Lord Randolph let it be widely known that he had in his
possession certain letters which the Prince of Wales had written to
Lady Aylesford; and Sir Charles Dilke recollected that he said: "I
have the Crown of England in my pocket." Thus he was espousing
in ardent fashion the cause of his brother — not always to the satisfaction of Blandford himself who was still intent on divorce and
re-marriage.

The Queen was furious: "What a dreadful disgraceful business,"
she wrote to the Prince of Wales, "and how unpardonable of Lord
Alington to draw dear Alex into it! Her dear name should never
have been mixed up with such people. Poor Lord Aylesford should
not have left her. I *knew* last summer that this was going on. Those
Williamses are a bad family." The whole affair was now getting so
out of hand that it was essential to call in the aid of the Prime
Minister, Disraeli. Where Hartington and Lansdowne, great Lords
of the Whig and Tory parties had failed, it was hoped that the subtle
Jew would succeed. He did. To Disraeli the Queen caused her Lady
of the Bedchamber, the Marchioness of Ely, to write: "The Queen
says you are so kind — so full of tact and judgement, Her Majesty
feels you will manage this perfectly."

Meanwhile Edward Marjoribanks again reported to the Duke of
Marlborough:

Edward Marjoribanks to Duke of Marlborough

(Blenheim Papers)

EXTRACT

22 March [1876]   134 Piccadilly

. . . I have not written before this because really I have nothing
to tell you. Owen Williams returned and will do all he can to

prevent Aylesford applying for divorce. He says very truly that Aylesford is already so unsavoury that it will not do for him to appear in the Divorce Court. In any case I think it is very unlikely that Aylesford will apply for anything more than a separation. Great pressure can be applied to prevent him doing more than this.

Aylesford will not come to England at all so O. W. says. I do not know for what reason but I expect his money affairs will not allow of his doing so. I know he had not at the time of going to India paid one penny of his succession duty. There is not now the least question of a duel but if there were steps have already been taken to make it impossible.

Lady Aylesford is now at Eastbourne with her sister Mrs Seaton Montgomery. I am sorry to say the whole affair is now known to everybody, even details are pretty accurately known. I attribute this to the Williams family who chose it to be known at Kimbolton and Crichel. Blandford is wildly infatuated. I feel the only chance of a favourable issue is that he is prevented from actually going away with her or marrying her. Time will possibly work a change in his feelings towards her. I fear it is not likely.

I think you ought to know that Randolph has been most active in doing all he can to influence Blandford and his arguments have great force with him. In fact it is mainly if not entirely due to Randolph that Blandford has not yet taken any entirely irrevocable step. . . .

The Prince of Wales, who was still in India, had of course now been fully informed. He was incensed. He wrote a furious letter from India to one of his courtiers, Lord Hardwicke, Master of the Buck Hounds. Lord Randolph replied: "I can only understand His Royal Highness' letter to you as a demand for an apology or a meeting. If I have acted indiscreetly or have been guilty of the slightest disrespect to Her Royal Highness the Princess of Wales by approaching her on so painful a subject I must unreservedly offer their Royal Highnesses the Prince of Wales and Princess of Wales my most humble and sincere apologies. This is the only apology which circumstances warrant my offering. With regard to a meeting no-one knows better than his Royal Highness the Prince of Wales that a meeting between himself and Lord Randolph Churchill is definitely out of the question. Please convey this to his Royal Highness."

The threat of a duel between the Prince of Wales and Lord Randolph caused the highest personages in the land to meet in secret confabulation. In due course the Prime Minister, the Lord Chancellor, Lord Cairns, and Lord Hartington, the arbiter of all social questions at the time, drafted a formal apology which Lord Randolph, some months later, reluctantly signed, but with an ungracious addendum which was to make it unacceptable to the Prince.

In the meantime the Prince of Wales had left India, though he did not hasten his return to England, spending a few agreeable weeks on the Continent while matters were sorted out. On his arrival in London he made it quite clear that not only would he not meet the Randolph Churchills at any house in London but that he would himself not go to any house where they were received. One staunch friend alone resisted the cut. When the Prince of Wales reproached Mr John Delacour, a Yorkshire country gentleman, for seeing too much of "the Randolph Churchills," Delacour replied: "Sir, I allow no man to choose my friends." For a young and socially ambitious bride like Lady Randolph it was indeed a sombre edict of the Prince's. Nor was life for the young Member for Woodstock any more palatable. It was under these circumstances that Disraeli offered to the Duke of Marlborough the post of Viceroy of Ireland which the Duke had already refused several times in preceding years. The purpose of this project was that Lord Randolph should be the Duke's private secretary. Lord Randolph's mother, the Duchess of Marlborough, who adored her younger son, recalled later in a memoir of her son which is preserved in the Wimborne Papers: "Lord Beaconsfield said to me, 'My dear Lady, there's but one way: make your husband take the Lord Lieutenancy of Ireland and take Lord Randolph with him. It will put an end to it all.' " But there were objections to this: if Lord Randolph were paid it might mean that he would have to give up his seat in the House of Commons. Eventually it was decided that Lord Randolph should act as unpaid private secretary. In view of the animosity of Court and Society, which Lord and Lady Randolph had only temporarily escaped by taking a summer trip to America, it seemed best to leave the country as gracefully as possible.

The Duke, though he refused to see his son or his family humiliated at the hands of the Court, was reluctant to leave Blenheim and involve himself in the discomforts and the expenses that the Viceroyalty in Dublin would involve. Though he appreciated Lord Beaconsfield's good intentions (Disraeli was elevated to an earldom in the midst of these transactions) the Duke protested vehemently against not being made a member of the Cabinet (he had been included in 1867–8) if he took up the appointment in Dublin. Worse still, he felt slighted that the Chief Secretary for Ireland, Sir Michael Hicks-Beach, was to be included in the Cabinet while he was excluded. Lord Beaconsfield showed himself to be a skilful negotiator, and the Duke after a show of resistance saw that it was in the best interests of himself and of his family that he should go to Ireland. "He always did," as Winston was later to remark, "whatever Lord Beaconsfield told him to do." And many years later the Duchess had to concede: "The Viceroyalty was a great success and Lord Beaconsfield used to congratulate me on his foresight."

Blandford was eventually divorced by his wife in 1883. Aylesford emigrated to America in 1882 and bought 27,000 acres at Big Springs, Texas, where he was "exceedingly popular" with the cowboys, and where he died of dropsy and hardening of the liver, shortly before his thirty-sixth birthday in 1885. Lady Aylesford, who was five years older than Aylesford, survived him by twelve years. She and Blandford lived together for some time and she gave birth to a son Bertrand in Paris in 1881. But though he was free to do so, Blandford never married her: instead, he married in 1888 the American widow of Mr Louis Hammersley. Lady Aylesford however was not quite forgotten: on her death in 1897 a wreath was sent to her funeral by the Prince and Princess of Wales.

To clear the way for the Duke of Marlborough's entry into Dublin, it was necessary to dispense with the services of the incumbent viceroy, the Duke of Abercorn. This again involved some embarrassment since Bertha, the aggrieved wife of Blandford, was herself the daughter of the Duke of Abercorn. So the change-over between the two Dukes was very much a family affair and Lord Beaconsfield handled it with his usual address.

The Marlboroughs travelled to Dublin early in January 1877 to take up the Duke's new appointment. Their arrival was signalized

by *The Times* with less than that newspaper's usual high standard
of sub-editing:

> Few noblemen have come into the Irish capital to assume the high
> and responsible office of Viceroy in more auspicious circumstances.
> He finds the country peaceful and prosperous.
> Their Graces the Duke and Duchess of Marlborough left London
> yesterday morning in a special saloon carriage attached to the Irish
> Limited Mail. They were accompanied by Lord and Lady Randolph
> Spencer Churchill, Sir Ivor and Lady Cornelia Guest, Lady Rosa-
> mond Spencer Churchill, Lady Georgiana and Lady Sarah, and Lord
> Winston Spencer Churchill, their children.

Master Winston Spencer-Churchill was the only child then born
to Lord and Lady Randolph, and he had no right to the courtesy title
bestowed on him by *The Times*. And, of course, Lady Cornelia,
Lady Rosamond, Lady Georgiana and Lady Sarah were not his sisters
but his aunts. The reader may find this a convenient moment to
consult the genealogical tree.

The peace and prosperity in Ireland to which *The Times* had
alluded were to be short-lived. Already the movement for Home
Rule, led by Isaac Butt, was gaining ground; but though 59 Home
Rulers had been elected to Westminster in the election of 1874,
they made little progress by Parliamentary methods and the young
member for County Meath, Charles Stewart Parnell, returned at a
by-election in 1875, was soon to assert himself as the leader of a more
militant faction among the Irish. At this time too, the first cargoes
of cheap wheat were coming across the Atlantic to Europe. Within
two years the unprotected agricultural industry of Britain suffered
its worst depression since the 1840s: in England, with most of its
population in urban areas, the cheap food at least favoured the
majority; in Ireland, largely a farming community, this was aggra-
vated by the failure of the potato crop 1877–9, which led to ruin and
famine and opened the way to agrarian revolt and the terrorism that
accompanied it.

Among the numerous retinue which accompanied the Viceroy to
Dublin was Winston's nanny, Mrs Everest, who until her death in

1895, when Winston was twenty, was destined to be the principal confidante of his joys, his troubles, and his hopes. It was not until after the death of Mrs Everest and of Lord Randolph that there opened that period of warm-hearted eager companionship between mother and son which was to prove so valuable to both. Many touching examples survive of the devotion of this faithful servant to her young charge and of his life-long gratitude to her.

Mrs Everest was not only the friend and companion of his youth, schooldays and early manhood; she remained warmly cherished in his memory throughout his life. Four years after her death we find Winston writing in his only novel *Savrola* — an under-regarded work:

> Savrola's thoughts were interrupted by the entrance of the old woman with a tray. He was tired, but the decencies of life had to be observed; he rose, and passed into the inner room to change his clothes and make his toilet. When he returned, the table was laid; the soup he had asked for had been expanded by the care of his housekeeper into a more elaborate meal. She waited on him, plying him the while with questions and watching his appetite with anxious pleasure. She had nursed him from his birth up with a devotion and care which knew no break. It is a strange thing, the love of these women. Perhaps it is the only disinterested affection in the world. The mother loves her child; that is maternal nature. The youth loves his sweetheart; that too may be explained. The dog loves his master; he feeds him; a man loves his friend; he has stood by him perhaps at doubtful moments. In all these are reasons; but the love of a foster-mother for her charge appears absolutely irrational. It is one of the few proofs, not to be explained even by the association of ideas, that the nature of mankind is superior to mere utilitarianism, and that his destinies are high.

Winston's mother from the earliest days exercised an exceptional fascination for him. She died in 1921 at the age of sixty-seven. Nine years after her death, in *My Early Life,* Winston evoked his own childhood memories of those days in Ireland:

> My picture of her in Ireland is in a riding habit, fitting like a skin and often beautifully spotted with mud. She and my father hunted continually on their large horses; and sometimes there were great

scares because one or the other did not come back for many hours after they were expected.

My mother always seemed to me a fairy princess: a radiant being possessed of limitless riches and power. She shone for me like the Evening Star. I loved her dearly — but at a distance.

Lord D'Abernon, the celebrated Edgar Vincent, international banker in Turkey, Ambassador in Berlin, and an arbiter of fashion, in his memoirs etched this portrait of Lady Randolph as she was during these Irish days:

I have the clearest recollection of seeing her for the first time. It was at the Viceregal Lodge at Dublin. The Viceroy was on the dais at the farther end of the room surrounded by a brilliant staff, but eyes were not turned on him or on his consort, but on a dark, lithe figure, standing somewhat apart and appearing to be of another texture to those around her, radiant, translucent, intense. A diamond star in her hair, her favourite ornament — its lustre dimmed by the flashing glory of her eyes. More of the panther than of the woman in her look, but with a cultivated intelligence unknown to the jungle. Her courage not less great than that of her husband — fit mother for descendants of the great Duke. With all these attributes of brilliancy, such kindliness and high spirits that she was universally popular. Her desire to please, her delight in life, and the genuine wish that all should share her joyous faith in it, made her the centre of a devoted circle.

Winston, quoting this passage in *My Early Life,* added that these were words for which he was grateful. The three years in Ireland were, in the nature of things, unproductive of much correspondence that concerns Winston. Occasionally when Lord Randolph is attending the House of Commons in London, some letters to him from Lady Randolph survive, but they only afford fugitive glimpses of the young boy.

. . . Winston is flourishing tho' rather X the last 2 days more teeth I think. Everest has been bothering me about some clothes for him saying that it was quite a disgrace how few things he has & how shabby at that. . . .

. . . Winston has just been with me — such a darling he is — "I can't have my Mama go — & if she does I will run after the train & jump in" he said to me. I have told Everest to take him out for a drive tomorrow if it is fine — as it is better the stables shd have a little work. . . .

. . . I bought Winston an elephant this afternoon which he has been asking me for some time, & I was on the point of saying to the shop-woman "An ephelant" I just stopped myself in time. . . .

. . . Winston is flourishing and has learnt a new song "We will all go hunting today etc". . . .

In *My Early Life* Winston was subsequently to recall, though not with perfect accuracy, what he then remembered about his childhood days in Dublin: the Little Lodge, about a stone's throw from the Viceregal, where he lived; the riflemen in Phoenix Park; the burning down of the Theatre Royal; the unveiling by his grand-father the Viceroy of the Gough statue: "A great black crowd, scarlet soldiers on horseback, strings pulling away a brown shiny sheet, the old Duke, the formidable grandpapa, talking loudly to the crowd. I recall even a phrase he used: 'And with a withering volley he shattered the enemy's line.' " His recollection at the age of fifty-five was surprisingly good, but not exact: the contemporary report of the unveiling records the Duke as saying: "With a crashing volley the enemy was fiercely beaten back." Moreover, these events did not occur when he was scarcely four, as Winston supposed, but in February 1880, when he was more than five, and a week or two before the family left Dublin.

Winston was very young at the time of the sojourn in Ireland; but indirectly, through their influence on Lord Randolph, the years in Ireland proved important. Fox-hunting all over Ireland with his young wife Lord Randolph obtained a keen insight into the country and its inhabitants. As secretary of his mother's Famine Fund campaign he gained invaluable knowledge of the life of the poor. His work as private secretary to his father brought him in further contact with all the many extremes of political thought and the ruddy pool of rebellion. He visited London quite frequently and attended the House of Commons, though he did not make many speeches. In September 1877, however, he excited the annoyance of the Tory party and embarrassed his father by making a speech in his constituency at Woodstock, at the dinner of the local agricultural and horticultural Show, in which he berated the Government for their policy in Ireland: "I have no hesitation in saying that it is inattention to Irish legislation that has produced obstruction [in the House of Commons]. There are great and crying Irish questions which the Government have not attended to, do not seem to be inclined to attend to and perhaps do not intend to attend to." Lord Randolph's father, the Duke, wrote to Sir Michael Hicks-Beach, the Chief Secretary: "The only excuse I can find for Randolph is that he must either be mad or have been singularly affected with local champagne or claret."

Except for such interludes this was the period which afforded scope for repose and meditation and it was certainly in this period that Lord Randolph's powers first came to fruition. All this early training, all this new-found knowledge in Ireland was to prove invaluable to him when he became the protagonist in the fight against Mr Gladstone's Home Rule Bill. His understanding of Irish politics enabled him in 1886 to assure Parnell that he would not be a member of any Government which renewed the Irish Coercion Bill. On this Parnell volunteered that in that case the Tory party would receive the Irish vote in England. In 1886 Gladstone was able to secure the Irish vote for the Liberals because of his support for Home Rule, but the Tories swept the country because of the adhesion of the English electorate to an anti-Home Rule platform. This too was the period in which he brooded much upon the injustices, as he thought them, that society had meted out to himself and his wife; and he acquired the fierce and sometimes bitter driving force which, in the next decade, was to carry him within a hair's breadth of the summit of power.

3

Ascot

EARLY IN 1880 Lord and Lady Randolph together with Winston and his brother Jack, who had been born in Dublin on February 4, re- turned to England to face the General Election which took place in April. Lord Randolph successfully held the family seat, Woodstock, by 60 votes, though his majority was reduced by 105. In the country as a whole Lord Beaconsfield's Government went down to defeat and so the Duke of Marlborough's term as Viceroy came to an end. Mr Gladstone and the Liberals returned to Parliament 106 stronger than the Tories and with an overall majority against Tories and Irish combined of 46. Mr Gladstone seemed supreme. The political situa- tion in the Parliament of 1880 was later to be vividly described by Winston in his *Lord Randolph Churchill*.

. . . The position of the Conservative Party, upon the other hand, was weak and miserable in the extreme. The sympathies and the intellect of the nation were estranged. Lord Beaconsfield, the only man who could touch the imagination of the people, was withdrawn from the popular assembly. Many of the Tory strongholds — family boroughs and the like — were threatened by approaching Redistribu- tion. The Front Opposition Bench, cumbered with the ancient and dreary wreckage of the late Administration, was utterly unequal to the Government in eloquence or authority. The attendance of Con- servative members, as in all dispirited Oppositions, was slack and fitful. Outmatched in debate, outnumbered in division, the party was pervaded by a profound feeling of gloom. They had nothing to give to their followers, nothing to promise to the people; no Garters for Dukes, no peerages for wealth, no baronetcies or knighthoods or trinkets for stalwarts. Although the new spirit created by Disraeli — *Imperium* abroad, *Libertas* at home — still lived in the Tory party, it had been profoundly discouraged by the results of the election; and many of those who swayed Conservative counsels could think of no plan of action except an obstinate but apathetic resistance to change. . . .

What political prophet or philosopher, surveying the triumphant Liberal array, would have predicted that this Parliament, from which so much was hoped, would be indeed the most disastrous and even fatal period in their party history? Or who could have foreseen that these dejected Conservatives in scarcely five years, with the growing assent of an immense electorate, would advance to the enjoyment of twenty years of power? It needed a penetrating eye to discover the method, and a bold heart first to stem and finally to turn the tide. Who would have thought of breaking up the solid phalanx of Liberalism by driving in a wedge between the Radicals and the Whigs; or dreamt of using the Irish to overthrow the great apostle of reconciliation between peoples; and who without the audacity of genius would have dared to force the Conservative party to base the foundations of their authority with confidence upon the very masses they dreaded and to teach those masses to venerate and guard the institutions they had formerly despised? . . .

This was the political background against which Winston was to live the four sensitive years of his life between the ages of five and nine. On their return to London Lord and Lady Randolph moved into a new house at 29 St James's Place, next to that of Sir Stafford Northcote, Lord Randolph's nominal leader in the House of Commons. A few months later Northcote was to write in his diary:

I asked him [Beaconsfield] whether Randolph Churchill was forgiven yet in high quarters. He said he was all right so far as the Queen was concerned, but that the Prince of Wales had not yet made it up with him; which Lord B thought very unfair, as he and Hartington had been called in as umpires and had decided that Randolph should make an apology (which was drawn up by Cairns) under the full

impression that the matter was to end there, but the Prince having
got the apology, still kept up the grievance, but nothing, said the
Chief, will help Randolph into favour again so much as success in
Parliament. The Prince is always taken by success.

Though after their return from Ireland the general cut by London
society was progressively relaxed it was to be another three years
before Lord and Lady Randolph were to be reconciled with the
Prince of Wales; but eventually Beaconsfield's prophecy was to be
fulfilled.

Even before Lord and Lady Randolph accompanied the Marlboroughs to Dublin the Queen had sought to exercise a mollifying
influence on the Prince of Wales. On Christmas Day 1876 she had
caused her private secretary, General Ponsonby, to write to the
Prince's private secretary, Mr Francis Knollys, saying that she could
not altogether exclude Lord Randolph from Court festivities. No
occasion, however, festive or otherwise, seems to have arisen for any
attendance at Court until 25 February 1883 when the Dowager
Duchess of Roxburghe, Lady of the Bedchamber (and mother-in-law
of one of Duchess Fanny's daughters), wrote from Windsor to
Duchess Fanny and suggested that Lady Randolph would be welcome
at one of the Queen's Drawing Rooms and that Lord Randolph
should attend one of the Levées. It is not known whether Lord Randolph complied with the suggestion but it is known that Lady Randolph attended a Drawing Room on March 14 of that year.

Another year was to pass before the reconciliation was complete.
Lord Randolph and the Prince both met at a dinner given by Sir
Henry James MP (later Lord James of Hereford). The object was
evidently achieved since Knollys wrote to Sir Henry a few days later
saying he was glad to hear the dinner had been a success and that he
had heard, evidently from the Prince, that "R. Churchill's manner
was *just* what it ought to have been."

St James's Place was to be Winston's home for the next two years;
then after Lord and Lady Randolph had again visited the United
States, the family moved to 2 Connaught Place. But it is from
Blenheim that we have Winston's first known letter to his mother.

Winston to Lady Randolph
[Postmark 4 January 1882]   [Blenheim]

My dear Mamma
I hope you are quite
well I thank you
very very much
for the beautiful
presents those

Soldiers and
Flags and Castle
they are so nice
it was so kind
of you and dear
Papa I send

you my love
and a great
many kisses
Your loving
Winston

*

The long remorseless process by which Mr Gladstone's Government was to be worn down and destroyed was already in train. It
began over what seemed to be a trifling affair, that of Charles Brad-

laugh, who had been elected as a radical member for Northampton in 1880, and, being a proclaimed atheist, had declined to take the Oath; instead he had expressed a desire to affirm. This led to the formation of the Fourth Party — Lord Randolph Churchill, Sir Henry Drummond Wolff, Mr John Gorst, with Mr Arthur Balfour, Lord Salisbury's nephew, in loose attendance. With Balfour's access to Hatfield, Gorst's knowledge of the party machinery, Wolff's instinct for Parliamentary procedure, and Lord Randolph's skill and panache in debate, the Fourth Party quickly became master of a confused situation and undermined Sir Stafford Northcote's position as effective leader of the Tory opposition in the House of Commons. Five times in all Parliament voted that Bradlaugh should not take his seat; five times the electors at Northampton returned him as their member. It was in a sense a repetition of what had happened in the case of John Wilkes in the years 1763 to 1774; the electorate in the end prevailed. The sequence of events which arose weakened the self-confidence of the Liberal administration and threatened the authority of Mr Gladstone himself. Lord Randolph and his friends were unremitting in exploiting the situation which progressively developed to the disadvantage of Mr Gladstone's government.

Early in 1882 the Bradlaugh affair took a new turn. Winston was later in his Life of Lord Randolph to describe it in this fashion:

. . . On February 21 there was another Bradlaugh scene. The member for Northampton, advancing suddenly to the table, produced a book, said to be a Testament, from his pocket, and duly swore himself upon it, to the consternation of the members. Lord Randolph was the first to recover from the surprise which this act of audacity created. He declared that Mr Bradlaugh, by the outrage of taking in defiance of the House an oath of a meaningless character upon a book alleged to be a Testament — "it might have been the *Fruits of Philosophy*" [*a pamphlet advocating birth control published in 1878 by Bradlaugh and Mrs Annie Besant*] — had vacated his seat and should be treated "as if he were dead." In moving for a new writ he implored the House to act promptly and vindicate its authority. Mr Gladstone, however, persuaded both sides to put off the decision till the next day. On the 22nd therefore a debate on privilege ensued. Sir Stafford Northcote merely moved to exclude Mr Bradlaugh from the precincts of the House, thus modifying Lord Randolph's motion for a new writ. Lord Randolph protested against such "milk and water" policy and urged the immediate punishment of the offender. After a long discussion, in which the temper of all parties was inflamed by Mr Bradlaugh's repeated interruptions, Sir Stafford substituted for his simple motion of exclusion a proposal to expel Mr Bradlaugh from the House; and this being carried the seat for Northampton was thereby vacated.

Lord Randolph seems to have gained much credit in Tory circles for the promptness and energy with which he had acted. . . .

A few days after Lord Randolph's successful intervention, which humiliated his own leader Sir Stafford Northcote as much as it embarrassed Mr Gladstone, Lord Randolph was taken ill with a serious inflammation of the mucous membrane.

Winston to Lord Randolph

20 March [1882]   Blenheim

My dear Papa,
I hope you are getting better. I am enjoying myself very much. I find a lot of primroses every day. I bought a basket to put them in. I saw three little Indian children on Saturday, who came to see the house. Best love to you and dear Mamma.

I am, Yr loving son
WINSTON

*

Winston's school days were the only unhappy part of his life. His pugnacious and rebellious nature never adapted itself to discipline. The neglect and lack of interest in him shown by his parents were remarkable, even judged by the standards of late Victorian and Edwardian days. His letters to his mother from his various schools abound in pathetic requests for letters and for visits, if not from her, from Mrs Everest and his brother Jack. Lord Randolph was a busy politician with his whole interest absorbed in politics; Lady Randolph was caught up in the whirl of fashionable society and seems to have taken very little interest in her son until he began to make his name resound through the world. It will later be seen how neglectful she was in writing to him when he was for three years a subaltern in India and when his father and Mrs Everest were dead. His brother Jack, more than five years younger, could not be a satisfactory correspondent and Winston was to feel exceptionally lonely and abandoned.

Yet his love for his mother never abated. Hesketh Pearson recalls that Bernard Shaw said of his mother: "Her almost complete neglect of me had the advantage that I could idolize her to the utmost pitch of my imagination and had no sordid disillusioning contacts with her. It was a privilege to be taken for a walk or a visit with her, or an excursion."

These comparable circumstances may suggest a similar explanation of Winston's extravagant adoration of his own neglectful mother.

Winston was later to write the story of his schooldays and as it is impossible to improve upon his own account, considerable extracts from *My Early life* follow:

The School my parents had selected for my education was one of the most fashionable and expensive in the country. It modelled itself upon Eton and aimed at being preparatory for that Public School above all others. It was supposed to be the very last thing in schools. Only ten boys in a class; electric light (then a wonder); a swimming pond; spacious football and cricket grounds; two or three school treats, or "expeditions" as they were called, every term; the masters all M.A.'s in gowns and mortar-boards; a chapel of its own; no hampers allowed; everything provided by the authorities. It was a dark November afternoon when we arrived at this establishment. . . .

I was taken into a Form Room and told to sit at a desk. All the other boys were out of doors, and I was alone with the Form Master. He produced a thin greeny-brown, covered book filled with words in different types of print.

"You have never done any Latin before, have you?" he said.

"No, sir."

"This is a Latin grammar." He opened it at a well-thumbed page. "You must learn this," he said, pointing to a number of words in a frame of lines. "I will come back in half an hour and see what you know."

Behold me then on a gloomy evening, with an aching heart, seated in front of the First Declension.

Mensa	a table
Mensa	o table
Mensam	a table
Mensae	of a table
Mensae	to or for a table
Mensa	by, with or from a table

What on earth did it mean? Where was the sense in it? It seemed absolute rigmarole to me. However, there was one thing I could always do: I could learn by heart. And I thereupon proceeded, as far as my private sorrows would allow, to memorize the acrostic-looking task which had been set me.

In due course the Master returned.

"Have you learnt it?" he asked.

"I think I can *say* it, sir," I replied; and I gabbled it off.

He seemed so satisfied with this that I was emboldened to ask a question.

"What does it mean, sir?"

"It means what it says. Mensa, a table. Mensa is a noun of the First Declension. There are five declensions. You have learnt the first singular of the First Declension."

"But," I repeated, "What does it mean?"

"Mensa means a table," he answered.

"Then why does mensa also mean o table," I enquired, "and what does o table mean?"

"Mensa, o table, is the vocative case," he replied.

"But why o table?" I persisted in genuine curiosity.

"O table, — you would use that in addressing a table, in invoking a table." And then seeing he was not carrying me with him, "You would use it in speaking to a table."

"But I never do," I blurted out in honest amazement.

"If you are impertinent, you will be punished, and punished, let me tell you, very severely," was his conclusive rejoinder.

Such was my first introduction to the classics from which, I have been told, many of our cleverest men have derived so much solace and profit. . . .

How I hated this school, and what a life of anxiety I lived there for more than two years. I made very little progress at my lessons, and none at all at games. I counted the days and the hours to the end of every term, when I should return home from this hateful servitude and range my soldiers in line of battle on the nursery floor. The greatest pleasure I had in those days was reading. When I was nine and a half my father gave me *Treasure Island,* and I remember the delight with which I devoured it. My teachers saw me at once backward and precocious, reading books beyond my years and yet at the bottom of the Form. They were offended. They had large sources of compulsion at their disposal, but I was stubborn. Where my reason, imagination or interest were not engaged, I would not or I could not learn. . . .

The school which Winston later discreetly camouflaged as St James's was St George's, at Ascot, and the headmaster was the Rev H. W. Sneyd-Kynnersley. Winston entered the school on 3 November 1882, five weeks after the beginning of term and some four weeks before his eighth birthday.

Such of Winston's letters as have survived do not seem to confirm the recollections which he subsequently recorded in middle age: but children seldom complain to their parents about their schools, except possibly on the grounds of the bad food. Young children tend — and probably more so in Winston's day — to assume that parents will be on the side of authority.

Winston to Lady Randolph

[? 3 December 1882]   Ascot

My dear Mamma,
    I hope you are quite well. I am very happy at school.
    You will be very glad to hear I spent a very happy birthday. I must now thank you for your loveley present you sent me. Do not forget to come down on the 9th Decer.

With love and kisses I remain your loveing son
WINSTON
kisses

Winston to Lord Randolph

[3 December 1882]   Ascot

My dear Papa,
    I am very happy at chool. You will be very plesed to hear I spent a very happy birthday. Mrs Kynersley gave me a little bracket. I am going to send a Gazette wich I wish you to read.

With love and kisses, I remain your loving son
WINSTON

Lady Randolph to Lord Randolph [in Monte Carlo]

EXTRACT

26 December 1882   2 Connaught Place
W.

. . . I send you the enclosed [? Report] which is all Kynnersley has
sent me as regards Winston. He also sends the bill £55 for next term
— to be paid in advance. I must own I think it is rather a strong
order to have to pay £52 for one month. As to Winston's improvement I am sorry to say I see none. Perhaps there has not been time
enough. He can read very well, but that is all, and the first two days
he came home he was terribly slangy and loud. Altogether I am
disappointed. But Everest was told down there that next term they
meant to be more strict with him. He teases the baby more than ever
— when I get well I shall take him in hand. It appears that he is
afraid of me. I am going to make him write to your mother today. . . .

Schoolmasters who preside over fashionable establishments tend
to mitigate the severity of their reports to influential parents lest
these should encourage the parents to believe that it is a bad school
and take the children away. Even bearing this in mind Winston's
reports throughout his schooldays were almost uniformly bad and
seldom redeemed by the insight of a master who saw his point and
detected his possibilities.

At the end of his first term at St George's his report read:

Division Master's Classical Report

Place in 4th Division of 11 boys for ½ term: 11th
Grammar: Has made a start
Diligence: He will do well, but must treat his work in general more
         seriously next Term

Set Master's Report

Place in 3rd Set of 14 boys: 14th
Mathematics: Very elementary
French: Knows a few sentences, but knowledge of Grammar is very
         slight

Scripture: f

History ⎫
Geography ⎭ Fair

Writing and Spelling: Writing good but so slow — spelling weak

General Conduct: Very truthful, but a regular "pickle" in many
ways at present — has not fallen into school
ways yet — but this could hardly be expected.

Total place for Term   11th

Times late   4

At the same time Lord Randolph's colleague Sir Henry Drummond Wolff was writing that he had seen Jack at Connaught Place and had asked him if he was good, to which Jack had replied: "Yes, but brother is teaching me to be naughty."

The following summer Winston was reported as being late nineteen times in the second half-term. His classical composition was described as "very feeble," his translation as "good," his grammar as "improving." Of mathematics the report stated "Could do better than he does"; of French "Fair"; of diligence "Does not quite understand the meaning of hard work — must make up his mind to do so next term." Geography was "Very fair"; "Writing good but so terribly slow — spelling about as bad as it well could be." But History was described as "Very good."

During the summer holidays Winston was taken to Blenheim by his mother but was then left alone with Jack and his cousin Sunny who was just three years older. Lord Randolph was at this time touring the Continent with his brother Blandford, now 8th Duke of Marlborough, following the death of their father the 7th Duke on July 5. Lady Blandford had obtained a divorce from him in February on the grounds of his adultery with Lady Aylesford.

Lord Randolph to Lady Randolph

EXTRACT

9 September [1883]   Schweitzerhof
Lucerne

. . . I hope you had a nice time at Blenheim & that Winston was good. I think it is rather rash of you letting him be at Blenheim

without you. I don't know who will look after him & Sunny & keep
them in order. . . .

Winston to Lady Randolph

15 September 1883   [Blenheim]

My dear Mamma,
   I hope you are quite well. I went out fishing today & caught my
first fish by my self. Jack & I are quite well. With love & kisses.

> I am your loving
> WINSTON

   In the autumn term of 1883 Winston's report on diligence said
"Began term well but latterly has been *very* naughty! — on the whole
he has made progress"; French was "Not very good"; Geography
"Weak"; Drawing "Very elementary"; General Conduct "On the
whole he has improved though at times he is still troublesome."
Times late — 6. But History "Good."

Winston to Lord Randolph

9 December 1883   Ascot

My dear Papa,
   I hope you are quite well. We had gymnastic trials yesterday. I
got 39 marks out of 90. I beat some of the boys in two classes above
me. The play room is getting ready for concert we are learning to
sing for it. It is about 75 feet long & 20 broad and lighted by 920 cp
[candlepower] lamps it will show a very bright light wont it.

> With love and kisses I remain yours affet
> WINSTON

X one big kiss   and a lot of little ones.

   His half-term report for the first term of 1884, by which time he
was nine, shows some improvement. Under mathematics we are
told "Shows decided signs of being very good"; French "Fair — does
not learn the grammar with sufficient care"; Scripture "Good" — this
was largely due to the good grounding he received from Mrs Everest;
History and Geography "Very erratic — sometimes exceedingly
good"; Writing and Spelling "Both very much improved"; Drawing

"Fair"; General Conduct "Much better"; headmaster's remarks "He is, I hope, *beginning* to realize that school means work and discipline. He is rather greedy at meals."

At St George's the food is believed to have been above average. Since, however, the food at English private and public schools alike is competitively bad and most boys who attend them have to supplement their ill-cooked prison rations in one fashion or another, licit or illicit, one might have thought that Mr Sneyd-Kynnersley would have appreciated the fact that one at least of his pupils enjoyed a good appetite. Not at all: Winston was written off as "greedy."

In the second half of this term the reports for Composition Translation, Grammar, Mathematics and French all read "Improved"; while Writing and Spelling are described as "Both very much improved"; Music as "Promising," a promise not fulfilled in later life; and Drawing as "Fair, considering" — considering what we are not told. But the headmaster seems to have taken a different view from that of his assistant masters. Under Diligence he reported "Conduct has been exceedingly bad." He is not to "be trusted to do any one thing." Mr Kynnersley, however, covered himself with Lord and Lady Randolph by adding: "He has however notwithstanding made decided progress." Winston was late twenty times in this half term on which one master commented "Very disgraceful" and the headmaster reported "Very bad." And under General Conduct the headmaster reported "Very bad — is a constant trouble to everybody and is always in some scrape or other. He cannot be trusted to behave himself anywhere" — and again, however, lest his parents should remove him "He has very good abilities."

In the summer term of 1884 things seem to have gone slightly better. Diligence — "Better on the whole but still far from satisfactory"; only late twice — "Great improvement"; History and Geography "V. good"; Spelling "Improved"; Writing "Full of corrections and untidy"; General Conduct "Better — but still troublesome." Under Diligence for the second half of this term we are told "Fair on the whole, occasionally gives a great deal of trouble." Headmaster's Remarks: "He has no ambition" wrote that percipient man. Mr Roy Jenkins in his Life of Sir Charles Dilke records that after a walk at Mentmore with Lord Rosebery one Sunday afternoon in May 1880, Dilke noted that he "came to the conclusion that Rosebery was the most ambitious man I had ever met." Many years later Dilke wrote in the margin alongside this opinion: "I have since known Winston Churchill."

Maurice Baring, who arrived at St George's shortly after Winston, has left, recorded in his book *The Puppet Show of Memory,* published in 1922, the following impression which Winston had made upon the school:

> Dreadful legends were told about Winston Churchill, who had been taken away from the school. His naughtiness appeared to have surpassed anything. He had been flogged for taking sugar from the pantry, and so far from being penitent, he had taken the Headmaster's sacred straw hat from where it hung over the door and kicked it to pieces. His sojourn at this school had been one long feud with authority. The boys did not seem to sympathise with him. Their point of view was conventional and priggish.

The fact that Winston had not complained overmuch to his parents about this school, but complained about it bitterly later in *My Early Life,* might have inclined one to believe that in his fifties he was exaggerating the degrading conditions in which he found himself as a boy of eight. It is only necessary to read the Life of Roger Fry by Virginia Woolf to realize that this is a false assumption. Mrs Woolf quotes a number of letters which Fry wrote to his parents from the same school at the time. Fry describes how disagreeable it was as head boy to have the painful duty imposed on him of holding the other boys while they were being birched; but he does not make very much of it in his letters to his parents.

Fry went to St George's five or six terms before Winston. Many years later he put down an account of what life was like there. He makes no reference to the fact that Winston was there after him; and though he lived long enough to have read *My Early Life,* the account of which Mrs Woolf made use was probably compiled before he could have read it.

Roger Fry records amongst other things:

> . . . Mr Sneyd-Kynnersley had aristocratic connections, his double name was made even more impressive by an elaborate coat of arms with two crests, one the Sneyd the other the Kynnersley, which ap-

peared in all sorts of places about the house and was stamped in gold on the bindings of the prizes. He was a tall thin loose-limbed man with an aquiline nose and angular features. He was something of a dandy. The white tie and the black cloth were all that marked him as a clergyman — he eschewed the clerical collar and coat. But his great pride and glory was a pair of floating Red Dundreary whiskers which waved on each side of his flaccid cheeks like bat's wings. How much satisfaction they afforded him was evident from the way in which during lessons he constantly fondled them distractedly. He was as high church as was consistent with being very much the gentleman, almost a man of the world. But he spoke of respect for his cloth with unction and felt deeply the superiority which his priesthood conferred on him. He was decidedly vain. . . .

He was however genuinely fond of boys and enjoyed their company. He was always organising expeditions — during a cold winter he took the upper form boys for long afternoons skating on the Basingstoke canal — in summer we went to Eton and always we were *treated* very lavishly with high teas and strawberries and cream. The school was I think a very expensive one but everything was done in good style and the food was a good deal better than what I was accustomed to at home. . . .

Mr Sneyd-Kynnersley explained to us with solemn gusto the first morning that we were all gathered together before him he reserved to himself the right to a good sound flogging with the birch rod. . . .

But as I was from the fiᵣst and all through either first or second in the school I was bound *ex officio* to assist at the executions and hold down the culprit. The ritual was very precise and solemn — every Monday morning the whole school assembled in Hall and every boy's report was read aloud.

After reading a bad report from a form master Mr Sneyd-Kynnersley would stop and after a moment's awful silence say "Harrison minor you will come up to my study afterwards." And so afterwards the culprits were led up by the two top boys. In the middle of the room was a large box draped in black cloth and in austere tones the culprit was told to take down his trousers and kneel before the block over which I and the other head boy held him down. The swishing was given with the master's full strength and it took only two or three strokes for drops of blood to form everywhere and it continued for 15 or 20 strokes when the wretched boy's bottom was a mass of blood. Generally of course the boys endured it with fortitude but sometimes there were scenes of screaming, howling and struggling which made me almost sick with disgust. Nor did the horrors even stop there. There was a wild red-haired Irish boy, himself rather a cruel brute, who whether deliberately or as a result of the pain or whether he had diarrhoea, let fly. The irate clergyman instead of stopping at once went on with increased fury until the whole ceiling and walls of his study were spattered with filth. I suppose he was afterwards somewhat ashamed of this for he did not call in the servants to clean up but spent hours doing it himself with the assistance of a boy who was his special favourite.

I think this fact alone shows that he had an intense sadistic pleasure in these floggings and that these feelings were even excited by the wretched victim's performance or else he would certainly have put it off till a more suitable occasion. . . .

You will no doubt long ago have come to the conclusion that Mr Sneyd-Kynnersley was at least an unconscious Sodomite but on looking back I feel fairly convinced that he was not and that his undoubted fondness for boys was due to his own arrested development. He was certainly very vain and his very meagre intellectual culture left him I suspect always with a feeling of slight humiliation among grown-up people. I attribute to that the care with which he got rid of any master of intelligence and supplied his place with imbeciles.

It was natural therefore that he felt happiest among boys where he could more than hold his own and whose sense of humour was of his own elementary brand. . . .

Boswell records that Dr Johnson said "A schoolmaster is a man among boys, and a boy among men." Winston was to be withdrawn after less than two years at the school. Mr Sneyd-Kynnersley did not long survive Winston's departure: he died of heart failure in November 1886 at the early age of thirty-eight.

*

The first two terms of 1884, Winston's last year at St. George's, were a time of hectic and successful political activity on the part of Lord Randolph. Early in the New Year he made what is still today considered his most famous speech, the "chips" speech at Blackpool.

After observing that Mr Gladstone was "the greatest living master of the art of political advertisement," and that "Holloway, Colman and Horniman are nothing compared with him," Lord Randolph went on to advert to Mr Gladstone's autumn holiday, for which purpose "a large transatlantic steamer is specially engaged, the Poet Laureate [Tennyson] adorns the suite and receives a peerage as his reward, and the incidents of the voyage are luncheon with the Emperor of Russia and tea with the Queen of Denmark."

Lord Randolph went on to describe how a deputation of working men from the "immaculate borough of Chester" had been received at Hawarden Castle; how they were not received in the house, the study, the drawing room or even in the dining room, for that would have been "out of harmony with the advertisement 'boom' ": but had instead been conducted through the ornamental grounds into the wide spreading park "strewn with the wreckage and the ruins of the Prime Minister's sport. All around them, we may suppose, lay the rotting trunks of once umbrageous trees; all around them, tossed by the winds, were boughs and bark and withered shoots. They came suddenly on the Prime Minister and Master Herbert, in scanty attire and profuse perspiration, engaged in the destruction of a gigantic oak, just giving its last dying groan. They are permitted to gaze and to worship and adore, and, having conducted themselves with exemplary propriety, are each of them presented with a few chips as a memorial of that memorable scene."

In his peroration Lord Randolph exploited the theme of chips which, he said, was all that Mr Gladstone had given to those who had sought him in 1880 — "Chips to the faithful allies in Afghanistan, chips to the trusting native races of South Africa, chips to the Egyptian fellah, chips to the British farmer, chips to the manufacturer and the artisan, chips to the agricultural labourer, chips to the House of Commons itself. To all who leaned upon Mr Gladstone, who trusted him, and who hoped for something from him — chips, nothing but chips — hard, dry, unnourishing, indigestible chips. . . ."

A Redistribution Bill was at this time going through Parliament. Under one of its provisions rotten and family boroughs like Woodstock were to be abolished. A few days after the "chips" speech Lord Randolph announced that at the next General Election he would fight the Central Division of Birmingham, a city at that time represented in Parliament by three Liberal members, Joseph Chamberlain, John Bright and Philip Henry Muntz. The announcement that Lord Randolph was to carry the fight for Tory democracy into the very citadel of radicalism and that he was going to challenge John Bright and through him the mighty Joe himself on his home ground galvanized the Tory Party throughout the country. Lord Randolph overnight became the established hero and darling of Tory working men throughout the land and his name was on every political lip. The Birmingham candidature even became a matter of discussion in the academic and sadistic groves of St George's.

Winston to Lady Randolph

16 March [?1884]   Ascot

My dear Mama,

I hope you are quite well. Mrs Kynnersley went to Birmingham this week. And she heard that they were betting two to one that Papa would get in for Birmingham. We all went too a sand pit the other day and played a very exciting game. As the sides are about 24 feet high, and a great struggle, those who got out first kept a fierce strugle with the rest.

With love & kisses
I remain your affet
WINSTON

During the first six months of this year, Lord Randolph was also concerned in a lively fight for control of the National Union of Conservative Associations. This was the organization whose local branches, as today, did all the donkey work in the constituencies and got the vote out at election times. Then as now, however, all real political authority was concentrated in London at the Conservative Central Office. It was this latter body, known at the time as the Central Committee, which raised the money and, subject to the Party leader, exercised control over policy. Lord Randolph wished to increase his power inside the Party and to impose his own policies upon it. To this end he waged a double campaign — (1) to obtain the Chairmanship of the National Union and (2) to increase the powers of that body at the expense of the Central Committee. His second objective naturally aided his first. These tactics were exceedingly distasteful to the mandarins of the Party in London; they had installed on the National Union their tame protégés (notably Lord Percy, son and heir of the Duke of Northumberland) who saw to it that the body they controlled confined itself to loyal resolutions supporting what had been decided in London.

Lord Randolph triumphantly carried the day, gained a majority on the Council, and was elected its Chairman. The Central Committee in London was abolished and, though real power still remained in the Party leadership (at this time divided between Salisbury and Northcote, respectively leaders of the House of Lords and House of Commons), Lord Randolph obtained for the National Union what at least appeared on paper to be considerable new powers in shaping Party policy and management. He also obtained official recognition for the Primrose League; this was a new organization which he and his friends had set on foot in memory of Lord Beaconsfield and to procure for the Party a vast body of voluntary canvassers, because the 1883 Corrupt Practices Act was to make illegal the employment of paid canvassers at election time. These were substantial gains. To the surprise and dismay of many of his supporters Lord Randolph did not press his fight against the leadership, but having attained recognition of his new position acted, at any rate temporarily, with an unwonted sense of responsibility. No documentary proof exists, but it seems likely that it was at this time that Lord Randolph came to some arrangement with Lord Salisbury as to the terms on which he would be prepared to join the next Conservative Government, which was to take office in the following years.

4

Brighton

THE EXACT CAUSES which led Lord and Lady Randolph to take
Winston away from St George's at the end of the summer term of
1884, and to send him in the middle of the following term to what
was to prove for Winston a more agreeable school at Brighton, are
not known. It is believed that Mrs Everest saw the wounds of his
birchings and told his mother about it. In any case, Jack was sent to
a different preparatory school at Elstree, and the Frewen and Leslie
cousins went to Ludgrove and Speldhurst Lodge, Tunbridge Wells.
In *My Early Life* Winston merely records that he had fallen into a
low state of health at St George's and after a serious illness was transferred to Brighton. Apart from the sea air, Brighton had the advantage that the family doctor, the celebrated Robson Roose, had at that
time his main practice there. The school was at 29 & 30 Brunswick
Road, Hove, and there Winston came under the jurisdiction of two
elderly spinsters, the Misses Thomson. Winston was much happier
there. As he later wrote:

> This was a smaller school than the one I had left. It was also
> cheaper and less pretentious. But there was an element of kind-
> ness and of sympathy which I had found conspicuously lacking
> in my first experiences. At this school I was allowed to learn
> things which interested me: French, History, lots of Poetry by
> heart, and above all Riding and Swimming. The impression of
> those years makes a pleasant picture in my mind, in strong con-
> trast to my earlier schoolday memories.

Indeed his earliest letters to his mother say that he is happy, ask for more stamps, confess to extravagance in the purchase of a stamp album and ask for more money.

That winter Lord Randolph undertook a trip to India. Though again there is no documentary evidence, it seems likely that he did so partly to recover from a recent illness but, more importantly, because Lord Salisbury had indicated to him that if he should form a government after the next election Lord Randolph would be Secretary of State for India. In April 1952 the author had occasion to give a lecture on Lord Randolph to the City of London Conservative Association. When this was to be printed by the Conservative Political Centre as one of a series on Conservative leaders the author asked his father for his views upon it:

WSC to RSC

(Stour Papers)

6 April 1953   10 Downing Street

Dearest Randolph,

Many thanks for sending me this, I have added a few notes and queries.

The practical cause of Lord Randolph's rise, apart from the House of Commons, was his mastery of the National Union of Conservative Associations, which had great power, in those days. On this Lord Salisbury came to terms. The fact that my Father went on a four months' visit to India in 1884/5 was no doubt a proof of the office Lord Salisbury had led him to expect.

Your loving Father
WINSTON S. CHURCHILL

Lord Randolph's visit to India caused a stir in the family.

Mrs Leonard Jerome to Lady Randolph

EXTRACT

22 December 1884   New York Hotel

Dear darling Jennie,

I write you a few words to wish you & ys, a happy New Year. I seldom write to you my dear child I don't know why unless it is, I hear all about you so often, that I almost imagine that I hear from you. We read about Randolph's departure in the newspapers. His friends wishing him bon voyage, & a safe return, it must have been quite an ovation. Dear Randolph, I think he well deserved it, & I hope he will come back well, & strong to enjoy life for many long years. He has made himself such a good name so early in life, he ought to reap a rich harvest later. I suppose the dear children are both with you for the holidays. Clara writes me that Winston has grown to be such a nice, charming boy. I am so pleased. Will you give him my best love, and my little Jack. I hope he is the same darling boy as ever. I am dying to see them again. What a delightful surprise it must have been for Jack [Leslie] & Leonie, to be with you at Connaught Place instead of going to Clarges Street, I can't get over it, such a nice house, & such a lot of jolly little people living together. I do hope you will all keep well & try to be *good* & enjoy yourselves. . . .

During the Christmas holidays at Connaught Place Winston wrote to his father:

Winston to Lord Randolph

1 January 1885   2 Connaught Place

My dear Papa,

I hope you are quite well. Jack had such a beautiful box of soldiers sent him from Lady de Clifford. I have been out to tea to Aunt Bertha's this evening and enjoyed myself very much indeed. We had a Christmas tree and party here this year, which went off very well. My Stamp Book is gradually getting filled. I am very glad to hear you arrived safely. Will you write and tell me all about your voyage, was it rough at all? I wrote to you once when the ship stopped at Gibraltar. How nice for sailing all over the sea. Jack is quite well & so am I.

I hope you had a happy Christmas, and a glad New Year (Jackey is quite well). Chloe [his dog] is very fat indeed, I give her a run every day to take her fat down.

With love and kisses I remain, yours affect
WINNY

Lady Randolph to Lord Randolph

EXTRACT

2 January 1885   2 Connaught Place

. . . Winston brought me down the enclosed, which he wrote last night — the handwriting is moderate — but the spelling is not

bad. They both went to tea with Sunny [Sunderland] yesterday —
they all met in the Park and Bertha wrote & asked if they might
come — so I let them. . . .

During the Spring term of 1885 Winston began to prosper. A
number of unimportant letters to his mother treat of such subjects as
visits to the doctor, his goldfish, his riding and his stamp collection:

Winston to Lady Randolph

28 January [1885]   Brighton

My dear Mamma,

I hope you are quite well. I ride three times a week. I have
one hour on Tuesday, an hour and a half on Wednesday, and an
hour on Friday. Do you think Papa will stay long in India?
Have you heard from him lately? Is Jacky quite well and happy?
does he cry at all now? I am quite well and, very happy. How is
old Chloe, has she been shaved yet? I make my pony canter when
I go out riding. I will send you a list of the work we have. A
master here is going to give a lecture on Chemistry, is it not wonderful to think that water is made of two gases namely hydrogd-
gen and nitrodgen I like it, only it seems so funny that two
gases should make water. With love and kisses.

I remain, Your loving son
WINSTON

He had not then met Professor Lindemann (see Volume IV), who
would have told him it was oxygen, not nitrogen, that together with
hydrogen constitute water.

Lady Randolph to Lord Randolph

EXTRACT

30 January [1885]   London

. . . The children are flourishing & I hear a much better account of
Winston. Miss Thompson says he is working so much harder this
term. . . .

Winston to Lord Randolph

Friday
[14] February 1885   Brighton

My dear Papa,

   I hope you are enjoying yourself in India. Mamma came to see me
on the 12th February. Is it not bad about poor Col Burnaby? I hear
you have been out shooting at Calcutta and shot some animals.
When are you coming home again. I hope it will not be long. I am
at school now and am getting on pretty well. Will you write and
tell me about India what it's like. It must be very nice and warm
out there now, while we are so cold in England. Will you go out
on a tiger hunt while you are there? Are the Indians very funny?
I hope you are quite well, and will keep so till you come home again.
I hope Mr Thomas [Lord Randolph's private secretary] is quite
well. Try and get me a few stamps for my stamp album, Papa. Are
there many ants in India if so, you will have a nice time, what with
ants and mosquitos. Every body wants to get your signature will
you send me a few to give away? I am longing to see you so much.
   I think you will be glad to know I am well and happy. We had a
play here on the 12th Feb and a grand party. We went on dancing
till ten o'clock and I enjoyed myself very much indeed it was so
nice. I am learning dancing now and like it very much indeed.
I am afraid it will boor you very much to read my scribble so I will
not write much more. I went out riding this morning and cantered.
Now I must say good-bye.

                              With love and kisses I remain,
                                        Your loving son
                                     WINSTON CHURCHILL

   Colonel Frederick Gustavus Burnaby (1842–85), Royal Horse
Guards, was a worthy of the Victorian era. He was killed on January
17, "sword in hand, while resisting the desperate charge of the Arabs
at the battle of Abu Klea." His enterprises included a ride through
Asia Minor to Persia, service as a War correspondent for *The Times,*
and a solo balloon flight from Dover to Normandy. In 1880 he had
stood unsuccessfully as a Conservative candidate for Birmingham,
and early in 1884 he had arranged to contest one of the Birmingham
seats again, this time with Lord Randolph as a candidate in another.

Leonard Jerome in New York was following Lord Randolph's rising career with interest and sympathy:

Leonard Jerome to Lady Randolph

EXTRACT

26 February 1885   Union Club
                                        First Avenue & 21st St

. . . I read the English news with the greatest possible interest. I see *Saturday Review, The Mail* (*Times*) *Pall Mall Budget, Vanity Fair, Truth, World* & various periodicals. I read them all thoroughly so that I think very little of any thing said by or about Randolph escapes me. I have watched with wonder Randolph's rise in the political world. Over & over he has been smashed "pulverised" so (?) ruthlessly squelched that he was considered done for ever. And yet a little after, up he comes smiling as though he had never been hit at all. I confess I am amazed, so young! so reckless inexperienced & impulsive! That he should have fought his way up through the fiery elements without as the trotters say a "skip or a break" is indeed wonderful. I hope he will come home soon & that he will find himself in accord with Lord Salisbury touching Egyptian affairs. After what has happened & the blood and treasure still to be spent there the English ought to stay. . . .

Two letters at this time show some advance in Winston's style of writing:

Winston to Lord Randolph

5 April 1885   Brighton

My darling Papa,

I hope you are quite well. The weather continues very fine though there has been a little rain lately. I have been out riding with a gentleman who thinks that Gladstone is a brute and thinks that "the one with the curly moustache ought to be Premier." The driver of the Electric Railway said "that Lord R. Churchill would be Prime Minister." Cricket has become the foremost thought now. Every body wants your Autograph but I can only say I will try, and I should like you to sign your name in full at the end of your letter.

I only want a scribble as I know that you are very busy indeed. With love and kisses.

I remain your loving son
WINSTON

Winston to Lady Randolph

30 May 1885   Brighton

My dear Mamma,

I hope you are quite well. The parade is perfectly crammed. I received a "Pictorial world" this morning and I guessed from which quarter of the globe it came from. The first Cricket Match came of on Wednesday, we were beaten as the weather did not permit us to practice sufficiently. But there has been a change for the better lately in the weather and we have been able to practise regularly for the match on Saturday. I am learning to swim and getting on capitally. Do write to me and tell me if Chloe is better as I should be very sorry if she were to die. Thank Everest for her letter and give her my best love. Will you tell me if Jack is well? Do you miss me much? I go out riding very often now. Will you send me the paper with Victor Hugo's funeral in it.

I am getting on with my French and Latin but am rather backward with Greek, but I suppose I must know it to get into Winchester so I will try and work it up.

Do you mind me having a riding suit as I am getting on very well. I am quite well and very happy. I am learning a piece of Poetry called Edinburgh after Flodden. There are no new boys this term except a very little one. The matches are comming in very quick succession.

With love and kisses, I remain
Your loving son
WINSTON

No doubt the educational standards at Brighton were not as high as those at St George's, and Winston was able to earn more favourable reports at his new school than had ever been vouchsafed by Mr Sneyd-Kynnersley. It is, moreover, legitimate to infer that he was much happier and responded to the more kindly treatment he was receiving. But though in his second and third terms he was respectively 29th out of 29 and 30th out of 30 for conduct, in his third term he was also 1st in Classics and his report said: "Very marked progress made during the term. If he continues to improve in steadiness and application, as during this term, he will do very well indeed."

For part of the summer holidays Winston was sent to Cromer on the east coast:

Winston to Lady Randolph

2 September 1885   Chesterfield Lodge

My dear Mama,

I have recd your letter this morning. The weather is very fine. But, I am not enjoying myself very much. The governess is very unkind, so strict and stiff, I can't enjoy myself at all. I am counting the days till Saturday. Then I shall be able to tell you all my troubles. I shall have ten whole days with you. I like the stamps very much indeed. My temper is not of the most amiable, but I think it is due to the liver as I have had a billious attack which thoroughly upset me, my temperature was 100 once instead of 98 & $\frac{2}{5}$ which is normal.

                              With love and kisses I remain your loving son
                                                           W. CHURCHILL

                                   *

Into the eighteen months from June 1885 to December 1886 was crowded the final crescendo, drama and tragedy of Lord Randolph's unique political career. Gladstone's Government, whose members were increasingly divided among themselves, almost courted defeat. It was not in the immediate interests of the Tories to bring the Government down. The Reform Bill of 1884 had given votes to two million more householders. The Queen would not have granted a dissolution to either party until the new electoral registers were ready, so that if the Tories were to defeat the Liberals in the House and Lord Salisbury were to be asked to form a Government he would be unable to go to the country to secure a majority until the late autumn of 1885. Nevertheless, five years of bitter opposition had built into the Tories an instinctive reflex action to grab at any opportunity of pulling down the Government. The occasion came on 8 June 1885 when on an unimportant amendment to the Budget concerning beer and spirit duties the Government was defeated by 12 votes and resigned forthwith.

Opinion was much divided among the Tory leaders as to whether Salisbury should agree to form a Government. The Queen was put in the embarrassing position of having to ask Gladstone whether, if Salisbury refused, he would carry on with his existing Cabinet. Mr Gladstone said that he would not. Lord Randolph did not help Salisbury much in his difficulties — he had never held office: he was not a Privy Councillor: he was only thirty-six: but some time before he had let Salisbury know that he could not join a Government in which Sir Stafford Northcote was the Leader of the House of Commons.

The Queen herself was shocked by Lord Randolph's obduracy and telegraphed to Salisbury: "With due consideration to Lord R. Churchill, do not think he should be allowed to dictate entirely his own terms, especially as he has never held office before." Lord Salisbury sought to see Lord Randolph before going to Balmoral to see the Queen, but Lord Randolph, despite all the pressure that was brought to bear on him, declined to do so and rested on his position. Lord Randolph won. Sir Stafford Northcote went to the House of Lords as the Earl of Iddesleigh, Sir Michael Hicks-Beach who had supported Lord Randolph in this crisis became Leader of the House of Commons, and Lord Randolph was sworn of the Privy Council and became Secretary of State for India and a member of the Cabinet in what was known as the Caretaker Government since it was only intended to hold office until the General Election could take place.

Salisbury must by now have begun to realize that Lord Randolph was going to be a difficult colleague; but he knew, and the Tory Party knew, that the following general election could not be won without the magic of Lord Randolph's eloquence, particularly now that two million electors had been newly enfranchised. Lord Randolph further emphasized his growing authority by ensuring that his political lieutenants did not go unrewarded. Sir Henry Drummond Wolff was sworn of the Privy Council and entrusted with an important mission to the Porte in Constantinople, while Mr Gorst entered the Government as Solicitor General. Mr Balfour needed no recommendation from Lord Randolph; he was Lord Salisbury's nephew, and he became President of the Local Government Board, but without as yet a seat in the Cabinet.

*

This is no place to speak of Lord Randolph's short but successful tenure of the India Office during which Burma was annexed to the Crown. Salisbury dissolved at the earliest possible moment and the election was held in November.

Lord Randolph was fighting against John Bright for the Central Division of Birmingham and thereby challenging the great Joe and his party manager Schnadhorst on their own ground.

Winston to Lord Randolph

28 November 1885   Brighton

Dearest Papa,

I hope most sincerely that you will get in for Birmingham, though when you receive this the Election will be over. There is another whole holiday to-morrow. There is a boy here whose Pater is going to put up for Winchester he is a Conservative, his name is Col Tottenham. If he gets in for Winchester and you get in for Birmingham I Believe we are going to have a supper.

With much love I remain, Ever your loving son
WINSTON CHURCHILL

Lord Randolph, who had been largely responsible for the Tory successes in the boroughs, had fought a valiant but unsuccessful fight in Birmingham against Bright but he was defeated by 4,989 to 4,216, a margin of 773. He had, however, availed himself of the offer of an admirer who had stood down in South Paddington in Lord Randolph's favour so that on the following day he was elected to the new Parliament, being returned by 1,706 votes.

The Liberals were sure that with the mighty prestige of Gladstone and two million new voters they would be triumphantly returned. In fact their majority compared with five years before fell by twenty. The figures were: Liberals 335, Tories 249, Irish Nationalists 86. It was clear that whoever undertook the Government of the United

Kingdom would be dependent on the Irish vote. For the time being Lord Salisbury carried on but only a few weeks after the election, on December 15, Herbert Gladstone, the G.O.M.'s son and private secretary, flew the "Hawarden kite" when he disclosed that his father had espoused Home Rule for Ireland. Mr Gladstone's denials were delphic. But Lord Salisbury's administration was eventually defeated at the end of January 1886 on an amendment concerning agricultural labourers in England. Lord Salisbury resigned: Gladstone formed his third Cabinet at the beginning of February and it quickly became apparent that he was going to introduce a measure of Home Rule which would involve a separate Parliament for Ireland. In embracing Home Rule he split the Liberal leadership from top to bottom. Though the rank and file of the Liberal Party remained faithful to Mr Gladstone, such party chieftains as Lord Hartington, Joseph Chamberlain and Mr Henry James broke with him and entered into a confederacy with the Tories.

Lord Randolph instantly perceived that Gladstone had played into the hands of the Tory Party. There was at this time no question of partitioning Ireland; and the project was that Ulster should come under a Dublin Parliament. Lord Randolph wrote to his great Irish friend, Lord Justice Fitzgibbon, on 16 February 1886: "I decided some time ago that if the G.O.M. went for Home Rule, the Orange card would be the one to play. Please God it may turn out the ace of trumps and not the two."

Lord Randolph travelled to Belfast, where on February 22 in the Ulster Hall he made the famous speech which for its effect upon the audience was, according to his son and biographer, "one of the most memorable triumphs of his life."

If it should turn out that the Parliament of the United Kingdom was so recreant from all its high duties, and that the British nation was so apostate to traditions of honour and courage, as to hand over the Loyalists of Ireland to the domination of an Assembly in Dublin which must be to them a foreign and an alien assembly, if it should be within the design of Providence to place upon you and your fellow Loyalists so heavy a trial, then, gentlemen, I do not hesitate to tell you most truly that in that dark hour there will not be wanting to you those of position and influence in England who would be willing to cast in their lot with you and who, whatever the result, will share your fortunes and your fate. There will not be wanting those who at the exact moment, when the time is fully come — if that time should come — will address you in words which are perhaps expressed by one of our greatest poets:

> "The combat deepens; on, ye brave,
> Who rush to glory or the grave.
> Wave, Ulster — all thy banners wave,
> And charge with all thy chivalry."

The poet was Thomas Campbell, writing of the battle of Hohenlinden. Lord Randolph omitted to tell his audience that he had taken the liberty of substituting Ulster for Munich. A few weeks later, in a letter to a Liberal Unionist, Lord Randolph wrote:

If political parties and political leaders, not only Parliamentary but local, should be so utterly lost to every feeling and dictate of honour and courage as to hand over coldly, and for the sake of purchasing a short and illusory Parliamentary tranquillity, the lives and liberties of the Loyalists of Ireland to their hereditary and most bitter foes, make no doubt on this point — Ulster will not be a consenting party: Ulster at the proper moment will resort to the supreme arbitrament of force; *Ulster will fight, Ulster will be right.*

This famous slogan became the watchword of Ulster; it pithily explains why Ulster is still part of the United Kingdom of Great Britain and Northern Ireland.

*

Despite the bracing climate of Brighton and the more kindly treatment he received there, in March 1886, when he was eleven, Winston suffered an attack of pneumonia which nearly carried him away. This dangerous illness in his childhood is of exceptional interest in the light of the series of pneumonic attacks from which he was to suffer during and after the Second World War. In those early days there was no "M & B" which was later to cure him so promptly. There was, however, Dr Robson Roose, the trusted family physician, whose presence there was one of the reasons, as we have seen, why Lord and Lady Randolph had sent their son to this Brighton school. Lord and Lady Randolph hastened to their son's bedside. Dr Robson Roose's bulletins and letters speak for themselves and show that the young Winston was at this time closer to death than at any time during his daring and adventurous life.

Dr Robson Roose to Lord Randolph

Sunday 10.15 p.m.   29 & 30 Brunswick Road
[14 March 1886]   Brighton

Memo: W. Churchill
Temp: 104·3 right lung generally involved — left lung of course feeling its extra work but, as yet, free from disease. Respirations more frequent. Pulse increased.

N.B. This report may appear grave yet it merely indicates the approach of the crisis which, please God, will result in an improved condition should the left lung remain free.

I am in the next room and shall watch the patient during the night — for I am anxious.

ROBSON ROOSE

Dr Robson Roose to Lord Randolph

6 a.m.
[15 March 1886]   [Brighton]

Dear Lord Randolph Churchill,
The high temp: indicating exhaustion I used stimulants, by the mouth and rectum, with the result that at 2.15 a.m. the temp: had fallen to 101, and now to 100, thank God! I shall give up my London work and stay by the boy today.

R. R.

Dr Robson Roose to Lord Randolph

1 p.m.
[15 March 1886]   Brighton

Dear Lord Randolph Churchill,
We are still fighting the battle for your boy. His temperature is 103 now but he is taking his nourishment *better* and there is no increase of lung mischief. As long as I can fight the temp and keep

it under 105 I shall not feel anxious, and by Wednesday the fever ought to have subsided and the crisis be past. Nourishment, stimulants and close watching will save your boy. I am sanguine of this. I shall remain here until 3.30 when I will walk to the Orleans [Club] and leave a report but I shall not leave the house for more than an hour.

Yours faithfully and gratefully
ROBSON ROOSE

Pardon this shaky writing. I am a little tired. R. R.

Dr Robson Roose to Lord Randolph

11 p.m.
15 March 1886   Brighton

Dear Lord Randolph Churchill,

   Your boy, in my opinion, on his perilous path is holding his own well, right well! The temp is 103·5 at which I am satisfied, as I had anticipated 104! There can *now* be no cause for anxiety for some hours (12 at least) so *please* have a good night, as we are armed at all points!

Ys faithfully
ROBSON ROOSE

Dr Robson Roose to Lord Randolph

16 March 1886   Brighton

Dear Lord Randolph Churchill,

   We have had a very anxious night but have managed to hold our own the temp now is 101, the left lung still uninvolved, the pulse shews still good power and the delirium I hope may soon cease and natural sleep occur, when one might hope he would awake free from the disease — on the other hand we have to realise that we may have another 24 hours of this critical condition, to be combatted with all our vigilant energy. I have telegraphed that I remain here today.

Ys gratefully
ROBSON ROOSE

I have given you a statement of fact, your boy is making a wonderful fight and I do feel please God he will recover.

Dr Robson Roose to Lord Randolph

Wed 7 a.m.
[17 March 1886]   Brighton

Dear Lord Randolph Churchill,
   I have a very good report to make. *Winston has had 6 hours quiet sleep.* Delirium has now ceased. Temp: 99, P. 92, respiration 28. He sends you and her ladyship his love.
   I will call in on my road to the station, and I meet Rutter in consultation at 8.45 so that I will bring his report too. I shall not return tonight as now the case will I hope not relapse and nourishment the *avoidance* of *chill, rest* and quiet are the essential factors. I will however come down tomorrow night or Friday as the lung will I hope begin to be clearing up and must be carefully examined. I leave the case in Rutter's hands in whom I have every confidence.
                                        Yours faithfully
                                        ROBSON ROOSE

Dr Robson Roose to Lady Randolph

Wed   The Station
[17 March 1886]   [Brighton]

Dear Lady Randolph Churchill,
   Forgive my troubling you with these lines to impress upon you the absolute necessity of quiet and sleep for Winston and that Mrs Everest should not be allowed in the sick room today — even the excitement of pleasure at seeing her might do harm! and I am so fearful of relapse knowing that we are not quite out of the wood yet.
                                        Ys faithfully and obliged
                                        ROBSON ROOSE

In London also the anxiety — and relief — were marked. Lady Randolph received a typewritten letter from her brother-in-law:

Moreton Frewen to Lady Randolph

17 March 1886   18 Chapel Street
                                           Park Lane

My dear Jennie,
   It is such a relief to us all to hear that you regard the crisis as past; I am *so* glad you dear thing. Poor dear Winny, & I hope it will

leave no troublesome after effects, but even if it leaves him delicate
for a long time to come you will make the more of him after being
given back to you from the very threshold of the unknown.

Everyone has been so anxious about it; the Prince stopped the
whole line at the levée to ask after him, & seemed so glad to hear (on
Monday) that he was a little better.

Bless you both; When do you come back.

Yours ever

M

Duchess of Marlborough to Lady Randolph

17 March 1886   46 Grosvenor Square

Dearest Jennie,

I do indeed congratulate you & pray that now all will go on well.
You must have had a most anxious Time.

Such hours make one years older & one feels how one's Happiness
in this world hangs on a thread. I hope dear you will come to town
& have a little Change. [? I move] for the Day. I saw dear R and
thought him pretty well and he dines here tomorrow.

The Accts [? of Cannes] are much the same, no worse.

The weather is beastly, no real Change. I am sure you will insist
on grand cure and *quiet* after such an illness. I hope Everest will be
sensible and not gushing so as to excite him. This certainly is not
wise.

God bless you. I am so thankful for God's Goodness for preserving
your dear Child.

Yours most affectionately

F. M.

In haste — dining out.

Eight months later Winston was able to write:

Winston to Lady Randolph

EXTRACT

23 November 1886   Brighton

. . . We had Gymnastic Examination on Monday, I find that in addition to having gained back my strength, I have gained more than I
possessed before, I will give you an Illustration Last Christmas term

I beat Bertie Roose by 1 Mark, Last term he beat me by 10 marks. This term I beat him by 3 marks getting top of the school by a majority of 1 mark, I got 60 out of 64.

I am in good health. It is superfluous to add that I am happy. . . .

*

Gladstone's Government survived for four months in a precarious equipoise. Then, in June, on the Home Rule Bill, it was brought down by a majority of 30. Gladstone resigned. The Queen sent for Salisbury who asked for an immediate dissolution. A General Election took place in July, the Tories and Liberal Unionists being returned with a clear majority over all other parties of 118. The figures were:

Conservatives	316
Liberal Unionists	78
Liberals	191
Irish Nationalists	85

It had been Lord Randolph's victory. He had pioneered it, engineered it and executed it. His exceptional services to the Party had to be recognised. He was indispensable to it. He was appointed Chancellor of the Exchequer and Sir Michael Hicks-Beach, twelve years his senior, when offered the leadership of the House of Commons again, persuaded both Lord Salisbury and Lord Randolph that it would be absurd for him to have the job. Many years later Sir Michael Hicks-Beach put his views on this matter in writing:

> I felt that Lord Randolph Churchill was superior in eloquence, ability and influence to myself; that the position of Leader in name, but not in fact, would be intolerable; and that it was better for the party and the country that the Leader in fact should be Leader also in name. Lord Salisbury very strongly pressed me to remain, saying that character was of most importance, and quoting Lord Althorp as an instance; but I insisted.
>
> I had great difficulty in persuading Lord Randolph to agree. I spent more than half an hour with him in the Committee Room of the Carlton before I could persuade him, and I was much struck by

the hesitation he showed on account of what he said was his youth and inexperience in taking the position. He insisted on my going to Ireland, pointing out that I could only honorably give up the Leadership by taking what was at the moment the most difficult position in the Government.

Lord Randolph accepted Sir Michael's advice and became Leader of the House of Commons as well as Chancellor of the Exchequer. Sir Michael accepted Lord Randolph's advice and became Chief Secretary for Ireland.

Lord Randolph proved a highly successful Leader of the House. He was diligent in his attendance and by his ready grace and wit much facilitated the progress of Government business. He also showed a high degree of punctilio in his nightly reports to the Queen on the progress of business in the House of Commons. At the end of the first session of the new Parliament the Queen, who had no reason to love him, began to mellow. She wrote to Lord Randolph on September 22: "Now that the session is just over, the Queen wishes to write and thank Lord Randolph Churchill for his regular and full and interesting reports of the debates in the House of Commons, which must have been most trying. Lord Randolph has shown much skill and judgement in his leadership during the exceptional session of Parliament."

*

While these stirring affairs were afoot Winston was still at Brighton. His letters show that he had followed his father's political fortunes with interest. Lord Randolph improved his own majority at South Paddington from 1,706 to 1,807.

Winston to Lady Randolph

[? 6 July 1886]   Brighton

My darling Mummy,

I hope you are well. Has Everest gone for her holiday yet? I should like you to come and see me very much. I am very glad Papa got in for South Paddington by so great a majority. I think that was a victory. I hope the Conservatives will get in, do you think they will?

Give my love to Jack and Everest.
>   With love and kisses I remain, Your loving son
>   WINSTON S. CHURCHILL

For a while Winston's interest in politics was mingled with a passionate desire to learn to play the 'cello. Winston was never to become musical and it is useless to speculate whether he might have been encouraged if this whim, passing as it was, had been indulged.

Winston to Lady Randolph

13 July [1886]   Brighton

My dear Mama,

I am sorry I have not written to you before. Has Everest gone for her holiday yet? I want to know if I may learn the Violincello or if not The Violin instead of the Piano, I feel that I shall never get on much in learning to Play the piano, but I want to learn the violincello very much indeed and as several of the other boys are going to learn I should like to very much, so I hope you will give sanction I would be delighted. I hope you are quite well. I had a very nice ride this morning. The weather kept fine till Monday when it rained from dawn of day till evening without intermission. Do you think the Conservatives will get in without any of the Unionist Liberals. I am very sorry to say that I am bankrupt and a little cash would be welcome.

>   With much love I remain, Your loving son
>   WINSTON

Winston to Lady Randolph

27 July [1886]   Brighton

My dear Mamma,

I received Papa's letter this morning, it was so kind of him to write to me when he was so busy. Do you think he will be Secretary of State for India, or that he will have a new post. Our Examinations have begun already, and we go home on the fourth of August. Has Everest come back from Ventnor yet? If she has, will you ask her to write to me. The weather has been very wet, but to-day it was fine. Have you made any plans for the holidays I should like to go to Jersey very much. We had a lecture on Science and Astronomy

by Mr Woodman. Give my best love to Jack and Everest and tell
Jack that I shall soon be home and then we will have some fine
barricades.

   Are you quite well I received the P.O.O. which you sent me and
am very thankful for it. You have not said anything about the
Violincello, in your letter. One of our boys passed into Clifton
Colledge.

With best love, I remain, Your loving son
WINSTON S. CHURCHILL

   By the Autumn of 1886 Lord Randolph was beginning to prepare
his Budget and his instinct for economy in public expenditure seems
to have been communicated to his son. "The parade is being greatly
enlarged. I think it is a great waste of money 19000£ it cost,"
Winston wrote to his mother on 28 September 1886 from Brighton.

   Lady Randolph, as has been seen, was wont to complain about
Winston being "slangy." The following rather stilted letter may well
have been written in reply to such a complaint:

Winston to Lady Randolph

5 October 1886   Brighton

My dear Mamma,

   I have much joy in writing "Ye Sealed Epistle" unto thee. I will
begin by informing you the state of the weather after that, I will
touch on various other equally important facts. I received your letter
and intend to correspond in the best language which my small vocabulary can muster. The weather is fearfully hot. We went to the
Swimming Baths to-day, I nearly swam the length which is about
60 feet. We are going to Play a Football Match tomorrow. Last
night we had a certain Mr Beaumont to give a lecture on Shakespeare's play of Julius Caesar. He was an old man, but read
magnificently.

   I am in very good health and am getting on pretty well. Love
to all.

I remain, Your loving son
WINSTON S. CHURCHILL

   On October 3, Lord Randolph, without consulting the Prime
Minister, made a fateful speech at Dartford before 14,000 people.
He demanded closer links with Germany and Austria in countering

Russian influence in the Balkans, a proposal quite out of tune with the Government's policy of friendship towards France and hostility towards the Turks. As for home affairs, he ran counter to party opinion in demanding procedural reforms in Parliament (including the closure by simple' majority), increased expenditure on local government, improvements for agricultural labourers, and reductions in Government expenditure. The Dartford Programme, as it came to be called, created a sensation. Lord Randolph left on a short continental holiday "secretly and silently" immediately afterwards but returned in time to repeat his manifesto to the National Union of Conservative Associations at Bradford on October 30.

Winston to Lord Randolph

19 October 1886　　　　　　　　　　　　　　　　　Brighton

My darling Papa,

I received your kind letter, and the Autographs and stamps. I heard about the fire at Connaught Place, It is very unfortunate, Is it not? We have had a tremendous gale here, several seats on the parade were smashed, and some twenty feet of wall destroyed.

We are learning Paradise Lost for Elocution, it is very nice. I am getting on very well indeed in my work. We are going to be Photographed tomorrow. I will try and send you a copy. I am very well indeed and trust you are the same.

I am trying for the Classical Prize and hope I shall get it. I am also getting on well in my swimming. The weather is gradually settling down. I hope you will [be] as successful in your speech at Bradford as you were at Dartford, and regularly "cut the ground from under the feet of the Liberals." I trust that you will have a pleasant crossing. I too find how quickly time flies, especially the holidays. I cannot give you any more information, for the simple reason that there is no more to tell you.

With much love, I remain, Your loving son
WINSTON S. CHURCHILL

The winter term was filled with concerts and plays — "They are going to act the Finale of the First Scene of the Mikado, and various other things," Winston told his mother on 24 October 1886; "the highest ticket price is 5/– and Miss Kate says That if you would come and play, she would double the prices at once and make it

10/– instead of 5/–. It would give me tremendous pleasure, do come please."

"When you come to see me," Winston wrote on November 2, "bring Jack and Everest with you. I am getting on splendidly, and am very happy. What are you going to allow me to have for Christmas? I propose that we have a Christmas party, and tree, and have about 18 of my juvenile friends. We will have another Conjuror etc etc. We are going to have a play at the end of this term and I hope you will come and see it."

On December 7 Winston wrote: "I am working hard at the Play, which is getting on admirably. There is to be a Rehearsal this evening. Mind and Come down to distribute the prizes. You had better spend the Saturday night and Sunday in Brighton."

But as was to be the case for many years to come, Lady Randolph had other ideas about spending her evenings.

Winston to Lady Randolph

14 December [1886]   Brighton

My darling Mama,

I hope you will not think my demand unreasonable or exorbitant, but nevertheless I shall make it all the same. Now you know that you cannot be watching a juvenile Amateur Play in the borough of Brighton, and at the same time be conducting a dinner party at,

2 Connaught Place
London.

If you go up to town in time for the dinner party you will not be able to see the Plays, but simply distribute the prizes and go.

Now you know I was always your darling and you can't find it in your heart to give me a denial, "I want you to put off the dinner party and take rooms in Brighton and go back on Monday morning . . ." and perhaps take me with you, No II is more moderate, "not bring Jack if inconvenient, but come alone and go back by about the 10.30 p.m. train, bring Jack if you can." I am quite well and hope you are the same. You know that mice are not caught without cheese: —

Programme is as near as I can guess as follows:

English Play
French Play

Latin & Greek
Recitations
Supper
Dancing

commencing 4.30 p.m. ending 12 p.m.
This petition I hope you will grant.

Love to all, I remain, Your loving son
WINSTON S. CHURCHILL

Lord Randolph, too, was not always as considerate as he might have been:

Winston to Lord Randolph

10 November [1886]   Brighton

My dear Papa,

I hope you are quite well. The weather is very wet today. You never came to see me on Sunday when you were in Brighton. We went to the Museum on Saturday. I was very much interested in the Curiosities, there were several Mummies, also some curious fish. And there were some curious Instruments of Torture used about two centuries ago in the Holy Spanish Inquisition, which one of the masters kindly explained to us.

I require another half dozen autographs if you please. Give my love to Mamma and tell her I will write to her soon

With much love, I remain,Your loving son
WINSTON S. CHURCHILL

Lord Randolph's resignation is chronicled in detail in the reminiscences of those who watched it. On December 20, accompanied by Lord George Hamilton, the First Lord of the Admiralty, he went to Windsor to dine and sleep. There he wrote a letter to Lord Salisbury in which he told the Prime Minister that in view of the fact that neither Lord George Hamilton nor W. H. Smith at the War Office were prepared to decrease their estimates for the coming year "I cannot continue to be responsible for the finances." Lord George Hamilton records in his Memoirs that he told Lord Randolph: "You cannot send a letter like that to Salisbury. Won't you consult somebody?"

"No I won't consult anybody."

"Have you spoken to your mother the Duchess?"

"No."

After dinner Lord Randolph had an audience of the Queen but said nothing to her. Later Winston was to write in his Life of Lord Randolph about the events of the following morning, December 21: "Both Ministers left Windsor and returned to London. Lord Randolph bought, as was his custom, a number of newspapers, but found that neither he nor Hamilton had any change. The train was about to start, and the bookstall keeper, who knew both his customers by sight, cried: 'Never mind, my lord — when you come back next time will do.' Lord Randolph looked sideways at his companion and said, with a quaint smile, 'He little knows I shall never come back.' "

Sir Henry Drummond Wolff, who had returned from a mission to Egypt, now takes up the story:

On Tuesday [December 22] Lord Randolph Churchill received no answer from Lord Salisbury; neither did one arrive on Wednesday morning. On that day, however, Lord Randolph lunched at the Carlton with Mr W. H. Smith who said that he had received a communication from Lord Salisbury and plainly showed that it was considered that Lord Randoph's resignation had been accepted.

The same evening Lord Randolph dined with me at the Carlton and in the middle of dinner received a letter from Lord Salisbury. This he at once showed me, and it seemed to cut out all chance of negotiation and to accept the resignation in the most positive manner.

On this, Lord Randolph wrote a letter to Lord Salisbury, which he sent down to Hatfield by Special Messenger, and it arrived there late — there being a ball going on.

Lady Randolph was waiting at home at 2 Connaught Place to be picked up by Sir Henry and Lord Randolph with whom she was to go to the Strand Theatre to see a performance of *The School for Scandal* in which Edward Compton was taking the lead:

Although [wrote Lady Randolph] the recipient of many confidences, so little did I realise the grave step Randolph was contemplating, that I was at that moment occupied with the details of a reception we were going to give at the Foreign Office, which was to be lent to us for the occasion. Already the cards had been printed. The night before his resignation we went to the play with Sir Henry Wolff. Questioning Randolph as to the list of guests for the party, I remember being puzzled at his saying: "Oh! I shouldn't worry about it if I were you; it probably will never take place." I could get no explanation of his meaning, and shortly after the first act he left us ostensibly to go to the club, but in reality to go to *The Times* office and give them the letter he had written at Windsor Castle three nights before.

Mr Robert Rhodes James writes in his Life of Lord Randolph:

Various accounts have been given of the interview between Churchill and Buckle [the highly regarded Editor of *The Times*]. It is at least certain that he showed Buckle copies of the letters and that when Buckle saw the last one he said, "You can't send that." "It has gone," replied Lord Randolph. According to one account Churchill then asked Buckle to support him in his leading article and that when he refused, Churchill protested that "there is not another paper in England what would not show some gratitude for such a piece of news." Buckle replied by saying that "you cannot bribe *The Times*." The full truth of what was said at this interview will in all probability never be known, but when Churchill left Buckle had his full permission to publish the news of his resignation.

Meanwhile Lord Salisbury was host at the ball at Hatfield attended by, among others, the Duchess of Teck and her daughter, the future Queen Mary, and the Duchess of Marlborough, Lord Randolph's mother. Mr Rhodes James records that "Lord Salisbury was talking to the Duchess of Teck in the middle of the ball at Hatfield shortly before half-past one in the morning of the 23rd when a red dispatch box was brought to him; excusing himself, he opened it, read the one letter that it contained, and then resumed the conversation with unbroken composure. The ball continued until the early hours; Salisbury told no one of the nature of the single letter in the dispatch box; he did not communicate with the Queen; he did not warn the editor of *The Times;* he simply went to bed. He was woken early by Lady Salisbury, who reminded him that they must get up to see the Duchess of Marlborough off, as she was catching an early train. 'Send for *The Times* first,' was the sleepy response. 'Randolph resigned in the middle of the night, and if I know my man, it will be in *The Times* this morning.' It was. The Duchess of Marlborough to her intense indignation, was allowed to leave Hatfield without seeing either her host or hostess."

At Connaught Place the scene that morning was recorded by Lady Randolph:

> When I came down to breakfast, the fatal paper in my hand, I found him calm and smiling. "Quite a surprise for you," he said. He went into no explanation, and I felt too utterly crushed and miserable to ask for any, or even to remonstrate. Mr Moore [his private secretary], who was devoted to Randolph, rushed in, pale and anxious, and with a faltering voice said to me, "He has thrown himself from the top of the ladder, and will never reach it again!" Alas! he proved too true a prophet.

It is agreeable to the historian that so many different accounts are in substantial harmony. That is not what usually happens. Lord Randolph's resignation proved fatal to his career and cast a gloom over the homes of his mother, his wife and his children. He nearly destroyed Lord Salisbury, who took eleven days to find a new Chancellor, but in the event Lord Randolph destroyed himself. Asked some years later why he did not bring Lord Randolph back, Lord Salisbury said, "Have you ever heard of a man having a carbuncle on his neck wanting it to return?"

It has been thought right to tell the story of Lord Randolph's resignation at such length since it was against this background that Winston was to grow up between the ages of twelve and twenty when his father died. The small family at Connaught Place long nourished the hope that Lord Salisbury would relent and that Lord Randolph's political fortunes could be restored. Perhaps if Lord Randolph's health had not soon collapsed this might have happened; it was not to be.

Nearly five years later he was to write to his wife from Johannesburg: "So Arthur Balfour is really leader — and Tory Democracy, the genuine article, at an end. Well, I have had quite enough of it all. I have waited with great patience for the tide to turn, but it has not turned, and will not now turn in time. In truth; I am now altogether *déconsidéré*." A little more than three years later Lord Randolph was dead.

*

Winston was to spend another four terms at Brighton. Football, amateur theatricals, cricket, and Queen Victoria's Golden Jubilee were the dominating themes of his letters in the first half of the year.

Winston to Lady Randolph

25 January 1887   Brighton

My dear Mamma,
    I am in good health and hope you are the same. I am also getting on very well in Conduct. My marks are as follows: — 10, 9, 7, 7, 10 not bad for me.
    Little Kim [Lord Kimbolton] seems to like school very much indeed, and gets on very well indeed.
    I am in the first eleven in football. Give my love to all.
With much love, I remain, Your loving son
WINSTON S. CHURCHILL

On 22 January 1887 Lord and Lady Randolph attended the first performance of the new Gilbert and Sullivan opera *Ruddy-Gore,* later euphemized as *Ruddigore.*

Winston to Lady Randolph

1 February 1887   Brighton

My dear Mamma,
    If you are as well as I am, you will do no harm. I should like to see Ruddy-Gore acted, you must take me to see it when I come home, however there is plenty of time to look forward to it. Do not forget to get the set of chess for me. I should like the board to be red and white and not black and white. In our singing classes, we are now learning an Operetta entitled "The merry men of Sherwood forest," I am Robin Hood and Bertie Roose [the doctor's son] is

Meg Marian and the remaining characters are Little John, Much the Miller's son, Friar Tuck and Will Scarlett.

Give my love to all.
I remain, Your loving son
WINSTON S. CHURCHILL

Winston to Lady Randolph

3 May 1887   Brighton

My dearest Mama,

I hope you are quite well; I, at present, am blessed with that inestimable treasure, i.e. "Good Health," which I trust will not be withdrawn from me, for a long time.

I recieved your letter this morning. I am quickly settling down, though I have not got into full swing quite yet. The weather, though showery, is fine and rather hot. We had a game of Cricket this afternoon, I hit a twoer, as the expression goes, my first runs this year.

I hope to improve this year in Cricket as well as in my studies.

As we were out this morning on the Parade, we saw a wreck which had been run down by a steamer, about 3 miles out at sea & was being towed in by tugs bit by bit.

Now I must close this scrawl with the usual amount of love.

Give my love to Everest and thank Jack for his letter tell him I will write Friday.

I remain, Your loving son
WINNY

This interest in cricket was not confined to his own performances:

Winston to Lady Randolph

31 May 1887   Brighton

Dear Mamma,

I hope that you have not been looking for a letter, from me, long. I try and think of sensible sentences for my letter, but they are very hard to think of. There is a Grand Match in Cricket at the County ground between Gloucestershire and Sussex; W. G. Grace who is playing for Gloucester made 53 runs, his side was 230 and 3 more wickets to go down yesterday afternoon, but as it is a three-days-match the result is uncertain, as yet. I am, at present quite well, and hope I shall continue so for a long time.

The weather is very fine & hot. We are going to play our first match of the season tomorrow afternoon. Give my best love to all. With love to yourself.

I remain Your loving son
WINNY

P.S. Remember the "Jubilee"

Cricket was not an interest that survived his school-days.

Though his father was by this time in the wilderness, Winston's interest in politics was not diminished: "About a dozen boys have joined the Primrose League since yesterday. I am among the number & intend to join the one down here, and also the one which you have in London. Would you send me a nice badge as well as a paper of Diploma, for I want to belong to yours most tremendously," he wrote to his mother on 24 May 1887.

That summer was taken up with Queen Victoria's Golden Jubilee and Winston was much looking forward to participating in the celebrations in London on June 21. When one of the Miss Thomsons sought to deny him this pleasure, Winston used all his powers of pleading to reverse her verdict:

Winston to Lady Randolph

[Postmark 11 June 1887]   [Brighton]

My dear Mamma,

Miss Thomson doesn't want me to go home for the Jubilee and because she says that I shall have no place in Westminster Abbey and so it is not worth going. Also that you will be very busy and unable to be with me much.

Now you know that this is not the case. I want to see Buffalo Bill & the Play as you promised me. I shall be very disappointed, disappointed is not the word I shall be miserable, after you have promised me, and all, I shall never trust your promises again. But I know that Mummy loves her Winny much too much for that.

Write to Miss Thomson and say that you have promised me and

you want to have me home. Jack entreats you daily I know to let me come and there are 7 weeks after the Jubilee before I come home. Don't disappoint me. If you write to Miss Thomson she will not resist you, I could come home on Saturday to stay till Wednesday. I have got a lot of things, pleasant and unpleasant to tell you. Remember for my sake. I am quite well but in a torment about coming home it would upset me entirely if you were to stop me.

Love & kisses, I remain, Yours as ever, Loving son
WINNY

(Remember)

Winston to Lady Randolph

Sunday [? 12 June 1887]   [Brighton]

My dear Mamma,

I hope you are as well as I am. I am writing this letter to back up my last. I hope you will not disappoint me. I can think of nothing else but Jubilee. Uncertainty is at all times perplexing write to me by return post please!!! I love you so much dear Mummy and I know you love me too much to disappoint me. Do write to tell me what you intend to do. I must come home, I feel I must. Write to Miss Thomson a letter after this principle so: — My dear

> Could you allow Winston to come up to London on Saturday the 18th for the Jubilee. I should like him to see the procession very much, and I also promised him that he should come up for the Jubilee.
>
> I remain, Yours
> JSC

I think that the above will hit its mark, anyhow you can try. I know you will be successful.

I am looking forward to seeing Buffalow Bill, yourself, Jack, Everest, and home.

I would sooner come home for the Jubilee and have no amusement at all than stay down here and have tremendous fun.

The weather is fine.

Please, as you love me, do as I have begged you.

Love to all I remain as ever, Your loving son
WINNY

For Heavens sake Remember!!!

Winston to Lady Randolph

[June 1887]   [Brighton]

Dear Mamma,

    I am nearly mad with suspense. Miss Thomson says that she will let me go if you write to ask for me. For my sake write before it is too late. Write to Miss Thomson by return post please!!!

                          I remain Your loving son
                                  WINNY

Winston's unremitting pertinacity seems to have prevailed.

His letters at this time give more detailed accounts of his work, a fact not perhaps unconnected with threats of a tutor in the holidays.

Winston to Lady Randolph

24 June 1887   Brighton

My dear Mamma,

    I arrived hear alright yesterday, and took a cab to the school, at which I arrived at 7.15. I am settling down alright now, though rather dull at first. The weather is beautifully fine. We went to the baths to day they were fine.

I hope you will soon forget my bad behaviour while at home, and not to make it alter any pleasure in my summer Holidays. I telegraphed to Everest as soon as I arrived at the station. All serene.

Kim came back to day, another boy will come back tomorrow, so I was not the latest back.

I am getting on capitally in Euclid. I and another boy are top of the school in it we have got up to the XXX Proposition. Will you send me a book to read I have got nothing at all to read now. I should like "She" or "Jess" very much indeed — I am quite well.

Please be quick and send me the autographs 6 of yours & 6 of Papa's.

With much love, I remain as ever, Your loving son
WINNY

Winston to Lady Randolph

28 June 1887   Brighton

My dear Mamma,

I am getting on capitally in everything especially Euclid which I like tremendously now, also in Greek & Latin.

We went to the baths this morning, I am getting on in swimming very well, I jumped off the top spring board. Weather beautiful, not too hot, & not to warm. We break up on the 28th of July. I want to collect Butterflies in the Holidays so much, I enjoy it immensely.

I should so much like to have "Jess" by Haggard I want something to read very much, Will you send it to me soon.

My Money will last a long time yet, I think. Please write soon to me, I rather want a letter.

Please send me the autographs 6 of yours & 6 of Papa's.

Love to All, I remain As Ever,
Your loving son
WINNY

The "long time" proved to be six days.

Winston to Lady Randolph

5 July 1887   Brighton

My dear Mamma,

I received your letter this morning, it gave me a good deal of pleasure. The weather on Monday was so intensely hot that we kept our whites on all day for coolness. But to-day the oppressive heat was relieved in the morning by a refreshing shower which cooled the whole day, and gave a beautiful freshness to all things.

Tomorrow we are going to Bramber for our annual treat, we start about 10 a.m. and return at about 8 p.m. I will tell you all about it next letter. I am looking forward to the book, autographs, & holidays. The latter commence on the 28th of this month. We were unable to go to the Baths today, owing to the repainting of the same. I have now got a piece of good news for you, viz. I am told by Mr Best that I am getting on much better in my Greek. Now Greek is my weak point & I cannot get into Winchester without it, so I am very glad I have made a start. We have got up to the end of the Passive voice of the verb λυω. I believe I am beginning to like Greek now. In Euclid, too, we have got up to the XXXIV Proposition.

It was Miss Kate's Birthday on Monday & it is for that we have our treat, we *do* enjoy ourselves. I am getting on allright in the character of "Robin Hood" we have learnt to the end of it.

Do you think there will be a chance of my going to Paris in the Holidays or somewhere on the continent. I should like 5/- as I am absolutely bankrupt.

Give my best love to all at home.

I hope you will be, when this reaches you as well as I am when it leaves me.

With much love, I remain As ever, your loving son
WINNY

Winston to Lady Randolph

[? 8 July 1887]   [Brighton]

Dear Mamma,

I am in want of 5/- because Miss Kates Birthday Present has taken 5/- out of my Exchequer. I want "Jess" or "She" soon. Autographs for goodness sake. My darling I hope you don't intend to make my Holidays miserable by having a Tutor.

Love & Kisses
I remain, Your loving son
WINNY

Winston to Lady Randolph

[July 1887]   [Brighton]

My dear Mamma,

I am told that "Mr Pest" is going to be my tutor in the Holidays.
Now as he is a Master here and I like him pretty well I shall not
mind him at all, on one condition viz. "Not to do any work" I give
up all other conditions except this one I never have done work in
my holidays and I will not begin now. I will be very good if this
is not forced upon me and I am not bothered about it. When I am
doing nothing I don't mind working a little, but to feel that I am
forced to do it is against my principles. Without this I might have
very happy holidays.

Hoping you will grant this.

I remain, Your loving son
WINNY

Winston to Lady Randolph

[? 14 July 1887]   Brighton

My dear darling Mummy,

I received your letter yesterday evening & I was very pleased to get
the Autographs + 5/- but I did not enjoy the letter quite so much,
nevertheless I deserved it, I know. I promise you I will be a very
good boy indeed in the Holidays. Only *do* let me off the work because I am working hard this term & I shall find quite enough to do
in the Holidays.

I am never at a loss for anything to do while I am in the country
for I shall be occupied with 'Butterflying' all day (I was last year).
Do let me try it for a week & then if it becomes a burden let me off
it. (I ask this as a favour).

For even if it is only 1 hour a day I shall feel that I have got to be
back at a certain time and it would hang like a dark shadow over
my pleasure.

Do you think you could possibly come down to see me Saturday.
It is 3 weeks to day since I came back & I want to see you very, very
much.

Do come if you can, I have got so many things to talk to you
about, more than would fill a quire of Paper.

> You may have thought me unaffectionate
> but I always was, & always will be, Your loving son
> WINNY

During the summer of 1887 Lord Randolph sought the advice of his sister Fanny's husband — Edward Marjoribanks — as to a suitable public school for Winston. Marjoribanks had put his own son, only a few months older than Winston, down for Harrow and he now wrote on behalf of Lord Randolph to the young newly arrived Headmaster, the Reverend J. E. C. Welldon. The latter replied on September 24 that it would be a pleasure for him to find room for Lord Randolph's son "somewhere." "It is difficult to speak positively about vacancies; and my own house is terribly full. But with Lord Randolph's leave I will make an arrangement by which his son may go temporarily into a Small House and may then pass from it into my own house, or, at the worst, into some other Large House."

Winston was told of these arrangements and wrote to his mother on September 25: "I am very glad that I am going to Dr Wildon's house. It is very kind of him indeed." It appears that until quite late in the day Winston was intended for Winchester. His cousin Sunny had already been there for three years; but it is possible that a family quarrel about the sale of the Blenheim pictures was a contributory factor. The quarrel had arisen between Lord Randolph and his brother after the latter had succeeded to the Dukedom. The 7th Duke of Marlborough, out of dire necessity — he was no spendthrift — had himself started the break-up of the family treasures. First in 1875, he had sold the Marlborough Gems for £10,000; then in 1882–3 the Sunderland Library for nearly £60,000; and in 1883 the Blenheim enamels for more than £73,000. But Blandford, after he had succeeded, felt constrained to sell — against the wishes of the rest of the family — some of Blenheim's finest pictures. Of eleven sold, nine went abroad and two, Raphael's Madonna degli Ansidei and Van Dyck's equestrian portrait of Charles I, were bought for the nation for £70,000 and £17,500 respectively. They may now be seen in the National Gallery.

The new Duke did not spend it all on personal extravagance: he installed an early telephone and electric light, and spent a good deal

of money improving the Blenheim estates. In 1888 he married Mrs
Lilian Warren Hammersley of New York, who brought with her a
considerable fortune, he installed with his new wife's money in place
of the pictures which had been sold at one end of the long Library
a Willis organ on which are inscribed words written by the Duke
which showed that he was far from illiterate:

> In memory of happy days
> and as a tribute to
> this glorious home
> we leave thy voice to
> speak within these walls
> in years to come, when
> ours are still.
> 1891

Lord Randolph agreed that Winston should go to Harrow and
Mr Welldon replied on October 4: "I shall look forward with much
pleasure to his coming, & I hope I may be useful to him, when he is
here. You may rely upon my placing him in a House where his
health will be carefully watched, if I cannot find room for him
immediately in my own."

Winston to Lord Randolph

8 October 1887   Brighton

Dearest Father,

I am very glad to hear that I am going to Harrow & not to Winchester. I think I shall pass the Entrance Examination, which is not
so hard as Winchester. I shall know by the time I go there the 1st
2nd and part of the 3rd books of Euclid. In arithmetic we are doing
"Square Root" and have quite mastered Decimal fractions & Rule of
three. Greek, however is my weakest subject as I have yet to learn
the Verbs in μ which are very hard. Will you send me some of your
autographs. We are, at the end of the term going to act Molière's
"*Médecin Malgré lui*." I take the part of "Martine."

We are getting up a Greek play too, in which, there are only 2
characters one of whom is myself. The Play is called "The Knights"

by "Aristophanes." Of course we are only doing one extract but I think it will prove very amusing to all. I wish you would come to the distribution of prizes at the end of this term, but I suppose it is impossible. The weather, today is moderately fine, but we have had some severe storms. I went to see Grandmamma a fortnight ago, & she read me your speech on the Distribution of Prizes for the school of Art, it was just the sort of speech for school boys. You had great luck in Salmon fishing, I wish I had been with you I should have liked to have seen you catch them. Did you go to Harrow or Eton? I should like to know.

Please do not forget the autographs.

With Love & Kisses I remain, Your loving son
WINSTON S. CHURCHILL

It seems strange that a boy of nearly thirteen who was about to go to Harrow should not have known that his father had been to Eton. The implication is a remoteness between father and son and an excessive parental disposition to decide things above a child's head without any reference to the child. An agreeable contrast is afforded by Winston's treatment of his own son more than thirty years later; when he gave his son the choice of Eton or Harrow, the latter inspected both institutions, and opted for Eton.

The Churchills had been an Etonian family for six generations in direct descent from the 3rd Duke of Marlborough who went there about 1722, down to Lord Randolph who went there in 1862. It appears that the decision to send Winston to Harrow rather than to Eton was based upon the severe attack of pneumonia which Winston had suffered at Brighton, and the idea that Harrow-on-the-Hill would be more bracing and less injurious to his lungs than Eton surrounded by the fogs and mists of the Thames Valley. Quaintly enough, in the course of a long life, though frequently assailed by pneumonia, Winston never suffered from lack of lung power, either on the political platform or in the House of Commons.

Even stranger is the fluke that seventy-four years later his grand-daughter, Arabella Spencer Churchill, the author's daughter, played the same role, Martine, in *Médecin malgré lui* at her school, Lady-mede, near Princes Risborough.

In December Winston began to make plans for Christmas.

Winston to Lady Randolph

[? 13 December 1887]   [Brighton]

Dearest Mother,

I have not written to you lately but I will try to write now.

I am very hard at work what with Play and Examinations. You said you would not mind a "scribble" if I wrote to you 1 decent letter a week.

When Papa came down he asked Miss Thomson to let us have a half-holiday and she let us have one.

We will not have a Christmas tree this year, But I think a good 3 guinea Conjuror and a Tea and amusements and games after tea would answer better. You see the Conjuror for 3 guineas gives "ventriloquisim" and an hours good conjuring which always causes some amusement. I will get a lot of addresses this time. We might have

> Vince
> Finch
> Beauville
> Horne
> Roper
> Wroughton
> Rusle
> and a lot of others

I must now say good bye

> With love and kisses
> I remain, Your loving son
> WINSTON S. CHURCHILL

But then, almost before Winston could have known of it, Lord and Lady Randolph were to depart on a seven week visit to Russia.

Winston to Lady Randolph

14 December 1887   Brighton

Dearest Mother,

Miss Thomson told me your plans before your letter arrived. I am very disappointed at hearing that I must spend my holidays without you. But I am trying to make the "Best of a bad job." We shall not be Able to have a party of course. Try and get Mr Best to stay with me and Jack in the holidays. Jack will not want a governess if Mr Best comes. I shall see you on Saturday and I have no doubt you will try your best to make me happy.

I remain, Your loving son
WINSTON

He spent Christmas with Jack, looked after by Mrs Everest, at Connaught Place.

Winston to Lady Randolph

26 December 1887   [2 Connaught Place
London W.]

Dearest Mother,

I did not know your address or how to send it (the letter). I have got two prizes one for English Subjects & one for Scripture.

I must tell you about Christmas Day.

Auntie Clara was too ill to come so Auntie Leonie & Uncle Jack were our only visitors. We drank the Queens health Your health & Papa's. Then Everest's and Auntie Clara and Uncle Moreton. In the Evening I went to Stratford Place and played games till 6.30.

I get on all right with Mademoiselle. Auntie Leonie & Auntie Clara both gave me 10/- which I was to spend on a theatre. Auntie Leonie also gave me 20/- from Papa so I am well up in "[?Jam]."

Grandmama wrote to me from Blenheim and wanted me to go to Blenheim but I told Auntie Leonie and she is arranging it. I don't want to go at all.

I am so glad you arrived safely.

Bertie Roose came to luncheon to day. My darling Mummy I do wish you were at home it would be so nice. But you must come and see me when you come back. In fact you might have me back from school for a day or two. Please thank my dear Papa for the 20/-

Excuse my writing but I will write very often now I know what to do.

With much love I remain, Your loving son
WINSTON S. CHURCHILL

It is very dull without you. But after all we are very happy. Jack sends His love to you & Papa and is going to write.

It seems quite clear from this letter that his Grandmother's invitation to Blenheim did not attract Winston and that it was he who persuaded his Aunt Leonie to turn it down. The old Duchess reacted strongly:

Duchess of Marlborough to Lord Randolph

(Blenheim Papers)

EXTRACT

26 December [1887]   Blenheim

. . . I hope you & Jennie will not be angry with me, I have asked Winston to come to stay *a week* with me. I would be responsible for him. He wrote me such a nice little letter & I *never* see him. B [Blandford] was very pleased & I will take great care of him. I expect him tomorrow & send to Oxford for him. . . .

. . . Just got a Tel from Leonie that Winston is not to be allowed to come & see me! I feel much aggrieved & shall trouble no more about my Gd Children. I should have thought I was as able to take care of him as Leonie & Clara. . . .

Winston was soon to go to Blenheim anyway. On New Year's Day disquieting news reached Lord and Lady Randolph in St Petersburg.

Lord Randolph to Duchess of Marlborough

EXTRACT

2 January [1888]   Hotel de France
                                                                    St Petersburg

Dearest Mama,

We were troubled yesterday by receiving a telegram from Roose saying that Everest had got bad diphtheria and that he had moved the two boys into his own house. This was a very disquieting message for New Years day. We got another message last night to say that the boys were perfectly well and that Everest was doing well. We have telegraphed to Clara to take the boys into her house for a time, which I hope she may be able to do. . . .

Winston to Lady Randolph

[? 30 December 1887]   45 Hill Street
                                                    Berkeley Square

Dearest Mother,

I suppose you have heard about Everest's illness. I & Jack at present (Sat 30) are staying at Dr Roose's. It is very hard to bear — we feel so destitute. Dr Gordon says that Everest has 2 patches down her throat but that is more Quinzy than Diphtheria.

Darling I hope you will come down to see me when you come home and bring Everest.

I feel very dull — worse than school. I must now end. Thank you for your letter.

                                        Good bye my dear
                                        I remain, Your loving son
                                        WINSTON S. CHURCHILL

The old Duchess quickly took away the two boys to Blenheim.

Duchess of Marlborough to Lord Randolph

(Blenheim Papers)

EXTRACT

3 January [1888]   Blenheim

. . . I fear you will have been bothered about this misfortune of Everest having diphtheria but she appears to be recovering & the 2 children are here safe & well with their nice gov. Such a contrast to Bertha's X scowling gov. They will go to 46 [Grosvenor Square] on Monday when all leave this place & I can keep them there till you return. Poor Leonie was much perplexed abt them & glad to telegraph to me in her difficulty so that I am appeased as regards Winston not to have been allowed to come here. . . .

Duchess of Marlborough to Lord Randolph

(Blenheim Papers)

EXTRACT

8 January 1888   Blenheim

. . . The boys are very well. The gov is a nice sensible person & seems to be quite happy about them. They leave here & go to Grovr Sq tomorrow so you might write (or Jennie might in your

name) a line to B for having had them here. It has done them
good & I keep Winston in good order as I know you like it. He is a
clever Boy & really not naughty but he wants a firm hand. Jack
required *no* keeping in order. They will stay at 46 till you return. . . .

Winston to Lady Randolph

12 January 1887 [1888]   46 Grosvenor Square

Dearest Mother,

Grandmamma has kindly allowed us to sleep here until you come
back. I do long to kiss you my darling Mummy. I got your kind
letter yesterday. How I wish I was with you, in the land of the
"Pink, green & blue roofs."

We have been staying at Blenheim lately — it was very nice.
Everest is much better — thanks to Dr Roose. My holidays have
chopped about a good deal but as I expect an exeat in the term I
do not wish to complain. It might have been so much worse if Woomany had died. You will let me come up for a week to see you &
Woomany I am sure.

I am going to a Play called "Pinafore" tonight (Thursday) with
Olive Leslie [*Sir John Leslie's 15-year-old daughter who married in
1894 Walter Murray Guthrie*].

Tomorrow I am to go to Dr Godson's Party. Sat Sir G. Womwell
[*the Sir George Wombwell who rode in the Charge of the Light
Brigade at Balaclava*], is going to take me to Drury Lane so I am
making up for other inconveniences. Auntie Leonie & Auntie Clara
gave me together a beautiful theatre which is a source of unparal-
leled amusement.

I must perform before you when you come back. Have you heard
that Uncle Jack [Leslie] has resigned the army? Having told you all
the news.

I remain, With Love & Kisses, Your loving son

WINSTON S. CHURCHILL

P.S. Give my best love to Papa.

Duchess of Marlborough to Lord Randolph
(Blenheim Papers)
EXTRACT

15 January [1888]   46 Grosvenor Square

. . . I hope you neither of you worry about the Children. They are
here all right & I will look after them. But do not mind if you hear

I am strict & discourage going out & keep Winston in order. I only do as if they were my own. I do not like Winston going out except Leonie & Clara take him & are responsible. I gave them the room downstairs to sit in & do not let them rampage. I make Sped a sort of *usher* or tutor to look after them at breakfast & the Gov is very nice & sensible & she now comes at 10 & goes away at 7 o'clock. I have got little Francis Curzon as their house is painting & I expect Kelso [later 8th Duke of Roxburghe] on his way back to school so that I consider this is the real Churchill home! I only tell you this that Jennie & you should not worry. Sir George Wombwell took both boys to the pantomime last night, it was very good-natured of him, & I expect it is to pander to you. . . .

Duchess of Marlborough to Lord Randolph
(Blenheim Papers)
EXTRACT

19 January [1888]   46 Grosvenor Square

. . . I am glad to report well of the Children. I fear Winston thinks me very strict, but I really think he goes out too much & I do object to late parties for him. He is so excitable. But he goes back to school on Monday. Meantime he is affectionate & not naughty & Jack is not a bit of trouble. I feel unhappy about your house. Roose has been making investigations there. I certainly do not advise anything being done till you can consider the matter & you can always use this house if you choose. . . .

Duchess of Marlborough to Lord Randolph
(Blenheim Papers)
EXTRACT

23 January [1888]   46 Grosvenor Square

. . . Winston is going back to school today. Entre nous I do not feel very sorry for he certainly is a handful. Not that he does anything seriously naughty except to use bad language which is bad for Jack. I am sure Harrow will do wonders for him for I fancy he was too clever & too much the Boss at that Brighton School. He seems quite well & strong & very happy — Jack is a good little boy & not a bit of trouble. . . .

Winston's last term at Brighton was devoted to preparations for the Harrow Entrance Examination — in between joining in the "Theatre Rage." "Please," Winston wrote to his mother on 14 February 1888, "ask Everest to send down all the things and Scenes connected with the Play 'Aladdin' & the stage as soon as the 5 trap doors are made. Also please send me a bottle of Sperm oil for the 8 footlights. I am very ambitious to beat the others. Ask Auntie Leonie to be quick with Britannia & Fairies."

"I shall have a hard job to beat the others," Winston wrote a week later, "but if I get all the requisites I think I can make a pretty good attempt. Everest says that 'Sperm oil' is rather expensive but I think you can manage to stand me a bottle, also a small bottle of 'Spirits of Camphor' as that is the best thing to burn in the footlights."

Winston to Lady Randolph

28 February 1888 [Brighton]

My dear Mother,

I am working hard for Harrow. I hear Miss Thomson is going to take me up for my Exam. I sincerely hope I shall pass well. I am not very good at Latin Verse but it is of very little importance. Prose being the chief thing in which I am rapidly improving. I am going through the first book of Euclid again & although I have not done more than 27 Propositions I can safely say that I should not make *many* mistakes in them. We are doing L.C.M.'s [Lowest Common Multiples] in Algebra & Simple Interest in Arithmetic.

You will be pleased to hear that we are learning the Geography of the U.S. When I come home you must question me. Many days will not elapse I hope before I receive a Postal Order.

With love & Kisses I remain, Your loving son
W. CHURCHILL

Winston to Lord Randolph

6 March 1888 Brighton

Dearest Father,

I am working hard for my Examination which is a very Elementary one, so there is all the more reason to be careful & not to miss in the easy things. We are getting through the 2nd Book of Virgil's Aeneid all-right, I like that better than anything else. I have done

the 1st 30 Propositions in Euclid & I should not be very afraid of missing in them. In Greek we have finished the Verbs in "$\mu\iota$" & are now
revising the Elementary work. In Arithmetic we have finished Simple & Compound Interest — Rule of Three — Double Rule of three
& are now simply working up the Fractions, Vulgars & Decimals.

In Algebra we are doing L.C.M.'s. In English History the Saxon
Period. In Ancient History the 2nd Persian Invasion & in Geog-
raphy the Continents of North & South America. I hope I shall pass
— I think I shall —

Will you come down & see me after the Exam & I will tell you all
about it.

I will take your advice about doing the most paying questions
first & then the others.

Please come down & see me afterwards. Give my love to Mamma.

Miss Thomson has got the Dictionaries but I have not seen them
yet.

Write to me & let me know if you will come down or not.

Hoping you are well, I remain, Your loving son
WINSTON S. CHURCHILL

When the day of the examination came, Winston's tentative
optimism was sorely tested and began to evaporate. Looking back
on the event forty-two years later, he wrote in *My Early Life:*

. . . I should have liked to be asked to say what I knew. They
always tried to ask what I did not know. When I would have willingly displayed my knowledge, they sought to expose my ignorance.
This sort of treatment had only one result: I did not do well in
examinations.

This was especially true of my Entrance Examination to Harrow.
The Headmaster, Mr Welldon, however, took a broad-minded view
of my Latin Prose: he showed discernment in judging my general
ability. This was the more remarkable, because I was found unable
to answer a single question in the Latin paper. I wrote my name
at the top of the page. I wrote down the number of the question
"I." After much reflection I put a bracket round it thus "(I)." But
thereafter I could not think of anything connected with it that was
either relevant or true. Incidentally there arrived from nowhere in
particular a blot and several smudges. I gazed for two whole hours
at this sad spectacle: and then merciful ushers collected up my piece
of foolscap with all the others and carried it up to the Headmaster's

table. It was from these slender indications of scholarship that Mr Welldon drew the conclusion that I was worthy to pass into Harrow. . . .

Winston's contemporary letters to his father and mother make it plain that his examination papers cannot have been quite so inadequate as he later persuaded himself and his readers to believe. Just as his greatest friend of later days, F. E. Smith, was wont to exaggerate the poverty of his youth, Winston was inclined to exaggerate his own early ignorance. Both no doubt subconsciously felt in later years that their brilliant successes would be enhanced, set against a sombre background of poverty and stupidity.

Winston to Lady Randolph

16 March 1888   Brighton

Dearest Mother,

I have passed, but it was far harder than I expected. I had 12 or 13 lines of very, very, hard Latin Translation & also Greek Translation. No Grammar in which I had hoped to score no French — no History no Geography the only things were Latin & Greek Trans Latin Prose — 1 or 2 questions in Algebra & Euclid. And a very easy Arithmetic paper in which I scored I think. However I am through, which is the great thing.

I was afraid that I had not passed after the Examination it was so much harder than I expected in every way. We had luncheon with the Head Master Mr Weldon, who is very nice. One of the boys fainted in the morning as he was dressing.

The roads were in a horrible condition mud & water & in some places the road was covered with water which reached up to the carriage step and extended for over 200 yrd.

Well, I saw Papa as he may have told you and he told me that I was coming home on the 6th of April. I was not excited before the Examination but felt very (uncomfortable in every way & sick) afterwards. I am very tired now but that does not matter now I know that I have passed. I am longing to go to Harrow it is such a nice place — beautiful view — beautiful situation — good swimming bath — a good Gymnasium — & a Carpentering shop & many other attractions.

You will often be able to come & see me in the summer it is so near to London you can drive from Victoria in an hour & 15 minutes or so. They say that the subscriptions in the summer term amount to 30/– or more & that every boy is supposed to have 2/– a week pocket money.

Mr Weldon's sisters are very nice. I like them very much we talked to them after the Exam.

If my writing is bad you must excuse it as I am telling you a good deal of news.

"My funds are in rather a *low condition the Exchequer would bear replenishing.*"

I am very tired so I must conclude.

With love & kisses
I remain, Your loving son
WINSTON S. CHURCHILL

P.S. Please show this letter to Everest as I am to tired to write anymore tonight.

WINSTON

Miss Charlotte Thomson's letter of excuse confirms Winston's own account:

Miss Charlotte Thomson to Lord Randolph

(Blenheim Papers)

16 March [1888]   29 & 30 Brunswick Road
                                                               Brighton

My Lord,

I hear from Mr Welldon today that Winston passed the examination yesterday.

My worst fears were realised with regard to the effect the nervous excitement would produce on his work: and he has only scraped through.

He was terribly upset after his morning's work and assured me over and over again that he had never translated Latin into English so of course he could not do the piece of prose set on the paper.

As I knew that he had for more than a year been translating Virgil and for much longer Caesar, I was rather surprised by the assertion but of course I did not contradict him.

I am glad to find Winston today much more composed, and I think he will soon recover from the excitement.

He had a severe attack of sickness after we left Harrow and we only reached Victoria in time for the 7.5 train.

If Mr Welldon would allow him to try again on the 18th April, I believe that Winston would do himself more justice; but I think the permission would be difficult to obtain.

Believe me, very truly yours
CHARLOTTE THOMSON

5

Harrow

WINSTON ENTERED HARROW on 17 April 1888, and three days
later he was giving his first impressions to his mother:

Winston to Lady Randolph

[Postmark 20 April 1888]   [Harrow]

My dear Mamma,
    I am writing according to promise. I like everything immensly.
I bought a "frouster" the cheapest I could find it was only 3/6 a sort
of deck chair canvass bottom. It is perfectly true that I shall have
to have 30/- for subscriptions. Boys generally bring back hampers.
I shall not have to find my breakfast. They only do that in large
houses. At tea a boy had a chicken and jam and those sort of things.
If you will send me a

> 1 Chicken
> 3 pots jam
> 1 plum cake

I think that will be all. I am afraid I shall want more money.
    I want to learn Gymnastis *and carpentering. You make what you
like with the assistance of the car.* [The italicized passage is crossed
through in the original.] Gymnastics is all I want.
    Dudley [Marjoribanks] is here and Luke White, Sterling [Stirling]
2 boys from Brighton.
    I will write tomorrow evening to say what form I'm in. It is going
to be read out in the speech room tomorrow.
                            With love & kisses I remain, Your loving son
                                            WINSTON S. CHURCHILL

Before he went to Harrow, Winston had expressed a desire to go into Crookshank's House, because he knew some boys there. But the Headmaster himself, the Reverend J. E. C. Welldon, had consented to take Winston into his own House, although he was not able to promise immediate entry. So Winston was sent to "wait" in one of the Small Houses which was run by Mr H. O. D. Davidson. It was not until a year had passed, in April 1889, that there was room for Winston in the Headmaster's.

Davidson, who was Winston's "tutor" for most of his time at Harrow even after he had moved into the Headmaster's House, was an Old Harrovian, a keen player of games, a kindly but conventional schoolmaster. Mr Welldon was a different type. An Etonian, a great classical scholar, and a fine preacher of sermons, he had been appointed Headmaster of Harrow in 1885, at the age of thirty-one. Winston has described how Mr Welldon had looked in a helpful manner on his entrance examination. Throughout his school career Welldon showed infinite patience, and took considerable pains with Winston; ever afterwards the two retained an admiration for each other.

Winston's next letter from Harrow gives further details of his financial and academic positions:

Winston to Lady Randolph

[? 21 April 1888]   [Harrow]

My dear Mamma,

Please send me some more money. This evening I had to give 10/- to the Cricket subscription. Which doesn't leave me much.

Most boys, at least those I have questioned, about 5 in number say they usually bring back £3 and write for more. I shall be asked for more subscriptions tomorrow or perhaps tonight amounting to 10/- more. So I do not know what to do. Please send me the money as soon as possible you promised me I should not be different to others.

I have some more pleasing intelligence to come. Though I am in the 3rd 4th just above Harry Sterling I have gained in Arith a place in the 1st div of the 4th very high indeed.

The master said my Entrance paper in arith was *the best*.

With love & kisses I remain Your loving son
WINSTON

He had been placed in the bottom form of the School, the third division of the Fourth Form, under the supervision of Mr Robert Somervell. Few of his early companions in his first form were to distinguish themselves greatly in after life: though the father of one of them, Archibald John Campbell Colquhoun, was for some years owner of Chartwell, near Westerham in Kent, destined to become Winston's home for the last forty years of his life. As the new boys were placed in alphabetical order, young Spencer-Churchill found only two below him, so that he "gained no more advantage from the alphabet than from the wider sphere of letters." When these two disappeared "through illness or some other cause," he found himself at the bottom of the school. Visitors to the school, anxious to catch a glimpse of the great Lord Randolph's son as he filed past the master at Bill, the Harrow roll-call, were frequently heard to remark: "Why, he's the last of all." Winston himself objected strenuously to appearing under the letter S. "I am called, and written Spencer Churchill here and sorted under the S's," he complained to his father in a postscript to a mid-term letter. "I never write myself Spencer Churchill, but always Winston S. Churchill. Is it your wish that I should be so called? It is too late to alter it this term but next term I may assume my proper name." Since it was Lord Randolph who ten years before had remarked "how often we find mediocrity dowered with a double-barrelled name" it might have been supposed that Lord Randolph would have been in sympathy with his son's wishes. But neither the next term, nor in any subsequent term did either Winston or his brother Jack succeed in dropping the Spencer, and they continued to be listed under S in the school register.

It did not take Winston long to discover a way of rising above his lowly position. "I am learning 1000 lines of Macaulay for a prize," he wrote to his father on June 3. "I know 600 at present." And he added, with disarming candour: "Any one who likes to take the trouble to learn them can get one, as there is no limit to the prizes." Among the lines he chose to learn were Horatius from *The Lays of Ancient Rome,* and his capacious and retentive memory permitted him all his life to recite with gusto and relish the lines he learned when he was thirteen. The stirring patriotism these verses evoked abided with him for ever and were the mainspring of his political conduct. The Harrow School Songs also stirred his youthful patriotism. In 1940 the author accompanied his father to the first of those annual singings of the School Songs at Harrow which Churchill was to attend throughout the war and for some years thereafter. Driving back he said with lively emotion: "Listening to those boys singing all those well-remembered songs I could see myself fifty years before singing with them those tales of great deeds and of great men and wondering with intensity how I could ever do something glorious for my country."

Winston certainly took trouble, and persevered even when he found shortly before the day of recitation that it was 1200, and not 1000 lines he had to learn. His efforts were rewarded with a success which, he later recalled, was thought incongruous for one "stagnated" in the lowest form. To the end of his career at Harrow his name in the school register carried after it the distinction of an italic *p* commemorating the fact that he had gained a prize in the Speech Room. The collection of this prize, on the evening before the end of term, 30 July 1888, clearly put a strain on the administrative resources of the Churchill household, as the following letter to his mother shows:

Winston to Lady Randolph

[29 July 1888]   [Harrow]

Dearest Mamma,

I have got a plan which I sincerely hope will meet with your approval. I am going up to get my prize in speech-Room on Monday night at about 6 o'clock — Now I want my best trousers & jacket & waistcoat, because I cannot go up untidily.

Could you let Everest come down bring my clothes + 10/- for "journey money" & she could help me pack up and take my big portmanteau home so I should not have the anxiety about it on Tuesday morning. I am sure I shall lose it amongst 500 others' portmanteaus.

Do let Everest come, because my ideas of packing are very limited. I know you will do this as it is the only way in which I can get my "journey money" & trousers. It only cost 1/6 for Everest to come 2nd Class return — do let her come. I should have written before — I did only I forgot to post the letter & so it would now be impossible for anything to be sent to-day being Sunday.

You will get this 1st Post tomorrow morning — if you will let

Everest come please telegraph by what train *she will arrive* at once or I shall not know what to do. I think I am 3rd in Terms order & so I shall probably get my remove. I shall be able to bring my Essay back with me on Tuesday and 1 copy & 1 prize.

Good Bye my dearest Mummy I remain Your loving son

WINSTON S. CHURCHILL

P.S. Don't forget to telegraph *at once* Monday is a whole holiday anytime after dinner will do for Everest to come.

The term had not been however without its difficulties for the new boy. His housemaster had written earlier in the term:

H. O. D. Davidson to Lady Randolph

12 July 1888   Harrow

Dear Lady Randolph Churchill,

After a good deal of hesitation and discussion with his form-master, I have decided to allow Winston to have his exeat: but I must own that he has not deserved it. I do not think, nor does Mr Somervell, that he is in any way *wilfully* troublesome: but his forget-fulness, carelessness, unpunctuality, and irregularity in every way, have really been so serious, that I write to ask you, when he is at home to speak very gravely to him on the subject.

When a boy first comes to a public school, one always expects a certain amount of helplessness, owing to being left to himself so much more in regard to preparation of work &c. But a week or two is generally enough for a boy to get used to the ways of the place. Winston, I am sorry to say, has, if anything got worse as the term passed. Constantly late for school, losing his books, and papers, and various other things into which I need not enter — he is so regular in his irregularity, that I really don't know what to do: and some-times think he cannot help it. But if he is unable to conquer this slovenliness, (for I think all the complaints I have to make of him can be grouped under this head, though it takes various forms); he will never make a success of a public school. I hope you will take the opportunity to impress upon him very strongly the necessity of putting a check on himself in these matters, and trying to be more businesslike. As far as ability goes he ought to be at the top of his form, whereas he is at the bottom. Yet I do not think he is idle: only his energy is fitful, and when he gets to his work it is generally

too late for him to do it well. I thought it wd do him good to spend
a day with you, and have therefore let him go: but unless he mends
his ways, he will really have to be heavily punished and I cannot
help thinking he does not deserve any special treat during the exeat!
I have written very plainly to you, as I do think it very serious that
he should have acquired such phenomenal slovenliness. At his age,
very great improvement is possible if he seriously gives his mind
to conquering his tendencies: but I am sure that unless a very determined effort is made it will grow upon him. He is a remarkable
boy in many ways, and it would be a thousand pities if such good
abilities were made useless by habitual negligence.

I ought not to close without telling you that I am very much
pleased with some history work he has done for me.

I am afraid this is a very long letter, but my excuse must be my
interest in the boy.

Believe me yours sincerely
H. O. D. DAVIDSON

Winston's other great interest at Harrow was the School Rifle
Corps. A few days after he had arrived at Harrow, on 3 May 1888,
the school magazine, *The Harrovian,* carried an indignant letter
from a correspondent Miles Harroviensis, complaining about the
state of the Rifle Corps. He said that the Harrow Rifle Corps ought
to have at least 200 members "whereas we have scarcely over 100, the
majority of whom are inefficient." The correspondent went on to
consider the reason for this "lack of energy and interest" in the Corps.
"It is due mainly to the fellows who belong to it themselves. The
majority of them join merely for the pleasure of going to Wimbledon, and think it monstrous if they are obliged to attend twenty
drills in the Summer term. The consequence is that whenever the
Corps makes its appearance the drilling is bad, the marching is
slovenly, and it becomes the laughing stock of the rest of the School.
This is why it is so difficult to get smart and influential fellows to
join."

Winston, at this time, was neither smart nor influential, but he
joined the Corps straightaway and derived great pleasure from it.
On May 12 he took part in his first Field Day which took the form of
a battle with Haileybury at Rickmansworth. *The Harrovian* re-

ported: "The action began about three o'clock. The manœuvres were simple. The Haileybury Corps, regardless of life, advanced gallantly over a large open space, and would, without doubt, have been annihilated, if it had not been for an unfortunate mistake made by the right flank of Harrow, who mistook a flag supposed to represent a company of 100 for a detachment of four men. They were obliged to retire in ignominious haste." Winston found the battle very exciting. He drew a sketch map of the positions (see next page) in his letter to his mother on May 14. "As I had not got a uniform I only carried cartridges. I carried 100 rounds to give away in the thick of the fight consequently my business enabled me to get a good view of the field. It was most exciting you could see through the smoke the enemy getting nearer & nearer. We were beaten & forced to retire."

Meanwhile the holidays, particularly the summer holidays, presented a problem. Winston and Jack were usually packed off to the seaside with Mrs Everest. Part of the summer holidays of 1888 were spent at Ventnor in the Isle of Wight where Mrs Everest's brother-in-law, Mr Balaam, was a senior warder at Parkhurst Prison:

Winston to Lady Randolph

Thursday [Postmark 2 August 1888]   [2 Verona Cottages
                                               Ventnor I.O.W.]

Dearest Mother,

We are enjoying ourselves very much indeed — I went in the sea this morning — and for a long walk over the downs this afternoon. We are staying at Woomany's sister's House & are very comfortable: Address

                    2 Verona Cottages
                    Ventnor I.W.

Jackey is very happy & said as he got into bed to-night "Well I think this *has* been a successful day." I enjoyed myself tremendously, we (that is I & Jack) eat about a ton a day.

It was raining in the morning, but it came over so warm & fine that we have had a jolly walk.

We had a good "go" at some raspberries and gooseberries which we picked ourselves & eat.

The plan of battle was (as best as I could make out) side thus

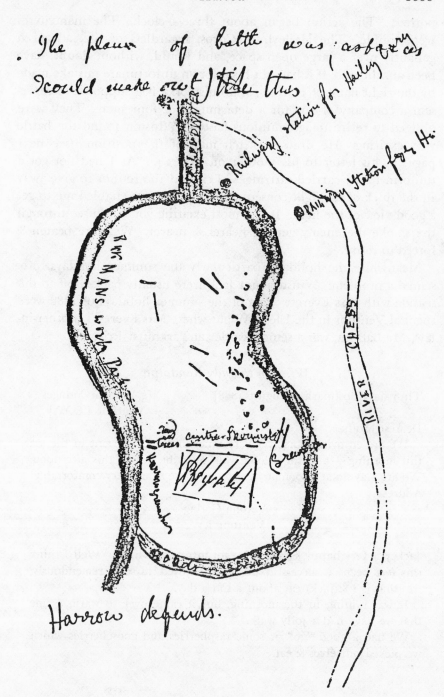

Harrow defends.

Everything is very Jolly & nice
Hoping you are quite well

I remain Your loving son
WINSTON S. CHURCHILL

At the end of the Summer term, Winston had been third, as he had forecast on July 23, in the final order of his form: but he did not get his remove. The two boys above him were promoted, so that Winston began his second term at the top of his own class. Considering the fact that he was much the youngest in his form, this was no bad achievement. He had additionally won the prize for recitation and a "copy," or prize (but not given in Speech Room), for his work in History. The following term, animated by his success, he entered for the Shakespeare prize. The boys had to "learn and work up the notes in Merchant of Venice, Henry VIII and Midsummer Night's Dream." Winston came fourth out of twenty-five boys for the Lower School prize — and some of those he beat were much older than himself, and several forms above him. Winston expressed himself well satisfied with obtaining 100 marks, the boy who won the prize getting 127.

Winston's interests were now broadening:

Winston to Lady Randolph

7 November 1888   [Harrow]

Dearest Mamma,

I am going to write you a proper epistle, hoping you will forgive my former negligence. On Saturday we had a lecture on the

"Phonograph"

By "Col Gouraud." It was very amusing he astonished all sober-minded People by singing into the Phonograph

"John Brown Body lies — Mouldy in the grave
And is soul goes marching on
Glory, glory, glory Halleluja"

And the Phonograph spoke it back in a voice that was clearly audible in the "Speech Room"

He shewed us it in private on Monday. We went in 3 or 4 at a time.

His boys are at Harrow.

He fought at Gettysburg.
His wife was at school with you.
Papa gave him letter of introduction to India.
He told me to ask Papa if he remembered the "tall Yankee."
I want to be allowed to join the Harrow work shop for they then supply you wood and I want to make some scenery for the nursery if we have any Party. 3 or 4 scenes cost about ½ a sovereign and the man who is in charge thoroughly understands scenery making.

With love & kisses I remain
WINSTON S. CHURCHILL

P.S. Will you write to say whether I may join as I have no imploy-ment for odd half hours. W. C.

Winston wrote little about his work at this time but those letters that do deal with work seem imbued with characteristic optimism.

Winston to Lady Randolph

[Postmark 11 December 1888]   [Harrow]

My darling Mummy,
My "Remove" I think is pretty certain. I have got a "Copy" for History like last term & hope to get another one for Arithmetic. I am all right and working very hard. I am going to write to Papa tomorrow and try and persuade him to come down for "Cock House Match" I am working up my Bible for the Examination tomorrow morning.
I hope to come out "top." I have come out "top" in my other Roman History Paper.
I expect to come out first in

Roman Hist	
English Hist	1st
Repetition	
French	

and to come out among the 1st 6 in

Greek Construe
Latin Construe
Anglice Reddenda
Construe
Latin Grammar
Euclid

I feel in "working trim" & expect many rises in my position.

With love My darling Mummy I remain Your loving son

WINSTON S. CHURCHILL

At Christmas the boys spent the holidays with their parents at 2 Connaught Place. Lord Randolph wrote to his mother, who, since the marriage of her son the 8th Duke (Blandford) a few months earlier, had become known as Frances, Duchess of Marlborough.

Lord Randolph to Frances, Duchess of Marlborough

(Wimborne Papers)

EXTRACT

30 December 1888　　　　　　　　　　2 Connaught Place

. . . Of course the boys have made themselves ill with their Christmassing, & yesterday both were in bed with Roose and Gordon hopping in & out of the house. Jack is better this morning but Winston has a sore throat & some fever. I hope it is nothing but biliousness & indigestion. . . .

Winston's illness was obviously a little more than biliousness and indigestion, but this did not seem to have prevented Lord and Lady Randolph from going away:

Winston to Lady Randolph

EXTRACT

Wednesday 2 January 1889　　　　　　[? 2 Connaught Place]

My darling Mamma,

I have just recd your nice letter, it was quite disennuye-ing.

My throat is still painful & swelled — I get very hot in the night — & have very little appetite to speak of. I am not allowed to go to the Circus by Doctor Gordon. But he says there is no reason why Jacky may not go.

I asked Dr Gordon to ask Bertie Roose to come & sit with me.

How slow the time goes — I am horribly bored — & slightly irritable — no wonder as my liver is still bad — Medecin 6 times a day is a horrible nuisance. I am looking forward to your return with "feelings, better imagined than described."

It is awful "rot" spending ones holidays in bed or one room. . . .

Once again the boys were sent to Ventnor for a short visit of recuperation and Winston returned to Harrow towards the end of January 1889 to find that he was still in Mr Davidson's Small House but that he had at last got his remove one division higher to the second (instead of the third) division of the Fourth Form. This merited a telegram to Mrs Everest. He later furnished a full account to his mother:

Winston to Lady Randolph

[? 3 February 1889]   [Harrow]

My darling Mummy,

How long is it since I have written to you? I am ashamed to say! But I will try and write a nice letter to you now.

To begin with I told you how I got my remove. I am getting on very well in that form & the master says I have much improved since the Summer Term.

I came out 2nd in Holiday Task getting 71 marks.

I am very happy & am getting on very well indeed in my house as I am on very good terms with the boys. One night we had a "Sale by Auction" & I did not sell any of the things which I had brought from home but only a few things I had bought down here. What I sold were probably worth 2/- but I made 5/9 off it. One Boy got 13/6. But then he sold a Racket & an Electric Battery.

I am very interested in my work & am getting on in a way which quite satisfies me, that *if* I only keep it up I shall get my remove again & that would be "awfully decent" because then I might get another and change on to the Modern side.

Saturday is Jack's Birthday. Everest is going to see him. Tomorrow we are going for a Paper Chase, & hope to have great fun. I & another boy are hares & all the rest of the house are hounds. The weather is fair & cold & snowy & dry & then warm and bright and sunny & dull about 3 times a day.

I am keeping my Room in much better order than in any preceding term. By the way I have been steadily advancing in Arithmetic ever since I went to Miss Thomsons & now, you will be pleased to hear, I have begun "Stocks." It (is not) or rather (they) are not at all easy they require a good "Stock" of knowledge but still they are very interesting.

One of them reads like this

"When Cash Price is £300 & Quotation £90 find the nominal value of stock of consuls."

It is rather a "swot."

I hope you (& the bonnets) are well & enjoying your "spree on the Continong." I wrote an order for a "Squash Racket" to-day and have had several good games.

We (the rifle Corps) are going to have a sham fight with Haileybury in the football field this term. If you are in London you must try & come down to it.

Forgive me, my Mummy, for not writing.

Hoping you will be as lenient as you can.

> I remain As ever your loving son
> WINSTON S. CHURCHILL

During this term Winston was taken ill and he was away from the schoolroom for some time. His letters to his mother from the sick-room at Harrow consisted mainly of pleas to allow "Woomany" — Mrs Everest — to come down to see him. By the end of the term, however, he was well enough to take part in another great sham fight with the Rifle Corps — this time at Aldershot. "It was great fun," he wrote to his father on March 27. "The noise was tremendous. There were 4 Batteries of Guns on the Field & a Maxim, & several Nordenfeldts. We were defeated because we were inferior in numbers & not from any want of courage. I have bought a Book on Drill as I intend going in for the Corporal Examinations next term. I went down to the Range on Tuesday & fired away 20 rounds."

At the same time Winston asked his father to remind Mr Welldon of his promise to take him into the Headmaster's House. This Lord Randolph did, and Welldon replied on 2 April 1889 that he would take Winston into his House the following term, explaining:

> If I have left him so long as I have in a Small House, the reason is only that in Davidson's opinion, and, I may add, in my own it seemed to be best for him, as he was very much of a child, when he first came, to be under more personal care, than can well be given to a boy who is one of a large number. However, as it happens, I told Davidson a fortnight ago that I should like to take him into my

own House next Term. He has some great gifts and is, I think, making progress in his work.

Mr Welldon also took the opportunity of dropping a hint to Lord Randolph that it might "perhaps not be disagreeable" to him and to Lady Randolph to come some time in the summer and take "at least the opportunity of seeing what Winston's school life is like." It looks as if it was to be another six months, and altogether eighteen months after Winston had first gone to Harrow, before Lord Randolph first went down to see the school.

Winston's first letter from the Head Master's was received by Lady Randolph at the beginning of the Summer term:

Winston to Lady Randolph

[Postmark 2 May 1889]   [The Head Master's
                                          Harrow School]

My dear Mamma,

I arrived safe & am now comfortably lodged in Welldon's new house No 4. I have got into a 2 Room, that is a Room with only 2 boys in it. I am one, & as the other does not come back yet I have it all to myself. I have bought a Mantle-Board and a big fan. It is an awfully nice room, it has two windows and is much bigger than Davidsons Rooms. Will you tell Woom that I want

1. a pair of Blue Rugs
2. The Vases she gave me
3. My table cloth
4. My Draw-cover
5. and all my fans

Will you buy me a nice Rocking Chair as there is lots of Room for one.

I also want my curtains.

Good bye my dear Mummy
Am getting on very well and Remaining your loving son
WINSTON S. CHURCHILL

Winston supplemented Mr Welldon's broad hints with entreaties of his own, begging his father to come to Harrow for Speech Day.

Winston to Lord Randolph

[? 2 July 1889]   [Harrow]

My dear Papa,
    I am writing to tell you all about Speech-day. If you take the 11.7
from Baker Street you will get to Harrow at 11.37. I shall meet you
at the station with a fly, if I can get one.
    The "Speeches" begin at 12. But dont let the name hinder your
coming. Speeches simply mean the Greek-English-French-German
plays & the distribution of Prizes by Mr Welldon who makes a short
speech to each of the prizemen.
    I don't think that you will be asked to make a speech. In fact I
should think it will be very improbable. I do hope both you &
Mamma will come as last Speech day nobody came to see me & it
was vy dull.
    You have never been to see me & so everything will be new to you.
Ducker is reserved specially for the visitor to look at. You will see
the Vaughan Library — the Gymnasium — the Racquet Courts —
My room — & other places. Am going to school this morning, so I
must say "Good Bye" & Love & Kisses
                                        Remain Your loving son
                                        WINSTON S. CHURCHILL
P.S. I shall be awfully disappointed if you don't come.

"Do try to get Papa to come," he wrote to his mother. "He has
never been." But Lord Randolph did not go.
    Winston compensated himself for these disappointments with a
new toy:

Winston to Lord Randolph

[15 May 1889]   [Harrow]

My dear Papa,
    I am writing to thank you for the money to buy the Bicycle — It
is so kind of you. I should have written long ago only I wanted to
wait until I could write and say that I could ride it. I can now, on
Saturday I rode 8 miles with it, it is a beautiful little machine. 2 days
ago I had written the letter, but that evening the money came so
I am writing a different letter. I would also have written yesterday
but I was part of a Guard of Honour *all* the afternoon, for the
Princess Louise.

I am very well I like Welldon's awfully.

Good Bye dear Papa once more thanking you

I remain Your loving son

WINSTON S. CHURCHILL

P.S. Do come & see me soon

Evidently he did not learn to ride the bicycle as well as he had thought, for on June 20 Mr Welldon had to write to Lady Randolph to inform her that Winston had fallen off his bicycle, and though he was not seriously hurt, he would have to remain in the sick-room for a week or so to get over "slight concussion." That term Lord Randolph expressed his desire that Winston should go into the Army. No doubt he had been much impressed by the obvious enthusiasm with which Winston was describing his outings with the Rifle Corps. Winston, however, later recorded in *My Early Life* an episode that may have earlier influenced his father in coming to this decision:

. . . This orientation was entirely due to my collection of soldiers. I had ultimately nearly fifteen hundred. They were all of one size, all British, and organised as an infantry division with a cavalry brigade. My brother Jack commanded the hostile army. But by a Treaty for the Limitation of Armaments he was only allowed to have coloured troops; and they were not allowed to have artillery. Very important! I could muster myself only eighteen field-guns — besides fortress pieces. But all the other services were complete — except one. It is what every army is always short of — transport. My father's old friend, Sir Henry Drummond Wolff, admiring my array, noticed this deficiency and provided a fund from which it was to some extent supplied.

The day came when my father himself paid a formal visit of inspection. All the troops were arranged in the correct formation of attack. He spent twenty minutes studying the scene — which was really impressive — with a keen eye and captivating smile. At the end he asked me if I would like to go into the Army. I thought it would be splendid to command an Army, so I said "Yes" at once: and immediately I was taken at my word. For years I thought my father with his experience and flair had discerned in me the qualities of military genius. But I was told later that he had only come to the conclusion that I was not clever enough to go to the Bar. However that may be, the toy soldiers turned the current of my life. Henceforward all my education was directed to passing into Sandhurst, and afterwards to the technical details of the profession of arms. Anything else I had to pick up for myself. . . .

Accordingly Winston joined the Army Class in September 1889. Until 1888, apart from a handful of bright fifth-formers who anyway usually went to Woolwich and not Sandhurst, it was the rule rather than the exception for candidates for the Army examination to spend six months or more at a London crammer's after they had left Harrow. It was to discourage this premature loss from the school of boys of sixteen and seventeen that Mr Welldon, as part of his far-reaching reforms in the curriculum of the school, had reconstituted the Army Class. Although boys still nominally belonged to the regular forms, they were taken away from the main stream of ordinary school instruction and given special lessons in those subjects which were dear to the hearts of the Civil Service Commissioners who were responsible for selecting entrants to Sandhurst, as to all branches of the Government Service. Not only did this involve extra lessons in the evenings and on half-holidays, but it also meant that it was difficult for an Army Class boy to rise high enough in his ordinary form to obtain a Remove at the end of the term. This was apt to prove frustrating to the boys and irksome to their parents. In Winston's case, it meant that he never in fact got out of the Lower School throughout his four and a half years at Harrow; though after three years he was no longer compelled to fag. Mr Wellsford and Mr L. M. Moriarty, the Army Class tutors, did not consider Winston good enough in Mathematics to pass into Woolwich, the Military Academy for cadets seeking commissions in the Royal Artillery or the Royal Engineers. It was thought best that he should try to pass into Sandhurst which catered primarily for the Infantry and Cavalry.

That term, Winston continued to do well at shooting and he began to learn to fence, as he himself said, with an eye to its being useful when he got into the Army. That term too, Lord Randolph paid his first recorded visit to Harrow. But from an academic point of view it seems to have been a bleak period for Winston. Quite early on he was put on "reports" — that is to say he had to obtain weekly reports on his work and show them to his tutor or to the Headmaster. "Please do try and come on Thursday," he wrote to his mother at the end of October, "as I want you to jaw Welldon about keeping me on reports for such a long time." It seems that Lady Randolph for once did as she was asked: but it was of no avail.

Winston to Lady Randolph

[Postmark 11 November 1889]   [Harrow]

My dear Mamma,

   You know that you spoke to Welldon, when you came down last, about taking me off reports. Well he said that he would do so of course the moment I got a good report. I am on still.

> My reports have been as follows
> Quite satisfactory   1 week
> No Complaint
> _____
> Satisfactory   another week
> Satisfactory
> _____
> Quite satisfactory ⎫
> Quite satisfactory ⎬ this morning

   It is a most shameful thing that he should keep me on like this.

   Well you know that you promised to help me when I wrote & told you; so that's what I am doing now. I am awfully cross because now I am not able to come home for an absit [overnight leave] on Thursday which I very much wanted to do.

   I hope you don't imagine that I am happy here. It's all very well for monitors & Cricket Captains but its quite a different thing for fourth form boys. Of course what I should like best would be to leave this *hell of a* [subsequently crossed out] place but I cannot expect that at present. But what I want you to do is to come down and speak to Welldon on Tuesday. Please don't be afraid of him because he always promises fair & acts in a very different way. You must stick up for me because if you don't nobody else will. Its no good writing to him, so Please come down yourself. Now you know Mamma that you told me to rely on you & tell you everything so I am taking your advice.

Good Bye my own Mummy, Hoping to see you on Tuesday,
I remain, Your loving son
WINSTON S. CHURCHILL

Throughout this black year, however, he remained under the supervision of Mr Somervell, and that was considerable compensation.

We were considered such dunces [he recalls in *My Early Life*], that we could only learn English. Mr Somervell — a most delightful man, to whom my debt is great — was charged with the duty of teaching the stupidest boys the most disregarded thing — namely, to write mere English. He knew how to do it. He taught it as no one else has ever taught it. Not only did we learn English parsing thoroughly, but we also practised continually English analysis. Mr Somervell had a system of his own. He took a fairly long sentence and broke it up into its components by means of black, red, blue and green inks. Subject, verb, object: Relative Clauses, Conditional Clauses, Conjunctive and Disjunctive Clauses! Each had its colour and its bracket. It was a kind of drill. We did it almost daily. As I remained in the Third Fourth (β) three times as long as anyone else, I had three times as much of it. I learned it thoroughly. Thus I got into my bones the essential structure of the ordinary British sentence — which is a noble thing. And when in after years my schoolfellows who had won prizes and distinction for writing such beautiful Latin poetry and pithy Greek epigrams had to come down again to common English, to earn their living or make their way, I did not feel myself at any disadvantage. Naturally I am biassed in favour of boys learning English. I would make them all learn English: and then I would let the clever ones learn Latin as an honour, and Greek as a treat. But the only thing I would whip them for is not knowing English. I would whip them hard for that. . . .

During the Christmas holidays Winston had measles — passing the disease on, incidentally, to Lady Randolph's friend Count Kinsky. The illness had this advantage in Winston's eyes, that he did not have to do his holiday task, so he was full of enthusiasm when he returned to Harrow at the beginning of the Spring term in January 1890; the more so as he obtained his Remove into the first division of the Fourth Form.

Winston to Lady Randolph
EXTRACT

[? January 1890]   [Harrow]

Darling Mummy,

I am getting on capitally in my new form & I think I shall come
out much higher than I did in the one below it. I am going up for
my "preliminary Exam" for "Sandhurst" in June. Mr Welldon is
back, immensely pleased to find I have got my remove.

I am very anxious to learn drawing. Papa said he thought singing
was a waste of time, so I left the singing class & commenced drawing. But Mr Davidson said that it was one thing to "take drawing
lessons" & another to "Learn Drawing" I get now an hour & a half a
week & if I had another hour with the army class boys who learn
Drawing in the Evening I am sure I should get on, as you know I
like it. Drawing count 1200 marks in the further [examination] &
every mark is useful.

Also I want to go on fencing & as you will perceive am vy anxious
to have my Bicycle cleaned. . . .

Winston was supposed to take the Preliminary Examination for
Sandhurst in the summer of 1890, but at the last moment Mr Welldon decided that he was not yet ready for it, his geometrical drawing
being considered his greatest weakness. Lady Randolph replied to
this news:

Lady Randolph to Winston

Thursday 12 June 1890   2 Connaught Place

Dearest Winston,

I am sending this by Everest, who is going to see how you are
getting on. I would go down to you — but I have so many things
to arrange about the Ascot party next week that I can't manage it.
I have much to say to you, I'm afraid not of a pleasant nature. You
know darling how I hate to find fault with you, but I can't help
myself this time. . . . In the first place your Father is very angry
with you for not acknowledging the gift of the 5£ for a whole week,
and then writing an offhand careless letter.

Your report which I enclose is as you see a *very* bad one. You
work in such a fitful inharmonious way, that you are bound to come

out last — look at your place in the form! Yr Father & I are both more disappointed than we can say, that you are not able to go up for yr preliminary Exam: I daresay you have 1000 excuses for not doing so — but there the fact remains! If only you had a better place in your form, & were a little more methodical I would *try* & find an excuse for you. Dearest Winston you make me very unhappy — I had built up such hopes about you & felt so proud of you — & now all is gone. My only consolation is that your conduct is good, & that you are an affectionate son — but your work is an insult to your intelligence. If you would only trace out a plan of action for yourself & carry it out & be *determined* to do so — I am sure you could accomplish anything you wished. It is that thoughtlessness of yours which is your greatest enemy. Your Father threatens to send you with a tutor off somewhere for the holidays — I can assure you it will take a great deal to pacify him, & I do not know how it is to be done. I must say I think you repay this kindness to you very badly. There is Jack on the other hand — who comes out at the head of his class every week — notwithstanding his bad eye.

I will say no more now — but Winston you are old enough to see how serious this is to you — & how the next year or two & the use you make of them, will affect your whole life — stop and think it out for yourself & take a good pull before it is too late. You know dearest boy that I will always help you all I can.

Your loving but distressed
MOTHER

Winston replied manfully:

Winston to Lady Randolph

[Postmark 19 June 1890]   [Harrow]

My darling Mummy,

I have not written till now because I can write a much longer letter. I will not try to excuse myself for not working hard, because I know that what with one thing and another I have been rather lazy. Consequently when the month ended the crash came I got a bad report & got put on reports etc etc. That is more than 3 weeks ago, and in the coming month I am *bound* to get a good report as I have had to take daily reports to Mr Davidson twice a week and they have been very good on the whole. . . . My own Mummy I can

tell you your letter cut me up very much. Still there is plenty of
time to the end of term and I will do my *very best* in what remains.
I want to go in for my Preliminary & I will explain the whole thing
to you.

If in your examination you succeed in passing any 3 of the 8 subjects you need only compete in those you failed in. Now I knew that
if I worked at

1 Geography
2 French
3 & English Dictation & Composition

I should pass in all these.
3. I knew that work however hard at Mathematics I could not pass
in that. All other boys going in were taught these things & I was
not, so they said it was useless.

> Goodbye my own
> With love I remain Your own
> WINSTON S. CHURCHILL

Earlier he had written to his father a full and frank account of
how he saw matters:

Winston to Lord Randolph

EXTRACT

[? 1 June 1890]   [Harrow]

. . . Millbank [Jack Milbanke] came down here yesterday. He is at
Wellington Barracks drilling as he is in the militia. I wish I could
go into the army through the Militia. Much more amusing — much
easier & instead of being unacquainted with drill I shall have passed
the full standard required in the Army. Any way here, I shall never
get through my further. 1 Percent of those boys who go up pass
their further from Harrow. The Army Class loses me my remove,
takes me away from all the interesting work of my form & altogether
spoils my term. Still I am sure I can pass my preliminary from here
but more than that is not in the bounds of possibility.

9/10 of the boys in the Army Class will go to a Crammer before
their Exam. They all dislike the Army Class because it makes them
come out low in their forms. Of course Mr Welldon will tell you
that a Public School etc but he cannot deny that a boy who gives

2 hours a day to Army Class work has not so good a chance as a boy who gives 6 hours.

Harrow is all right for a Preliminary Examination but 6 months & James or any other crammer is more to a chap than 2 years at Harrow. I should like to go in through the militia because then you begin much earlier which is a distinct point. It is a well known thing that a fellow who goes through the militia is always much more use than a Sandhurst Cadet. Be that as it may I have to pass my further if I go to Sandhurst and then pass out.

While I only have to pass out of the Militia. Another difference is that on one side one gets practical instruction & on the other theoretical.

Harrow is a charming place but Harrow & the Army Class don't agree. . . .

Actually Winston was luckier than he, or even his teachers, realised. When he was at last allowed to take the Preliminary Examination for Sandhurst in November 1890 he was still only just above the Fourth Form, in Modern Third Shell. It was just in time. This was the last Preliminary Examination at which Latin was an optional subject: the new regulations made it one of the obligatory subjects — in place of English Essay. It is interesting to speculate on what might have happened if Winston had failed to pass his Preliminary Examination before the new rules took effect. Certainly at the time only Winston himself was at all sanguine as to the outcome:

Winston to Lady Randolph

[? November 1890]   [Harrow]

My darling Mama,

I hear that you are greatly incensed against me! I am very sorry — But I am very hard at work & I am afraid some enemy hath sown tares in your mind. I told you I thought I should not pass my preliminary on account of my being put under a master whom I hated & who returned that hate. Well I complained to Mr W. & he has arranged all things beautifully. I am taught now by masters who take the greatest interest in me & who say that I have been working very well. Now I have got over 3 weeks & I may easily do it. I am working very hard & if I am not slanged too much I stand a very fair chance & I have much the best chance of knowing. I said I should pass if I had a fair chance & I have got one now so I'll have a pretty good try at it. Arithmetic & Algebra are the dangerous subjects. I am sure of English

Nearly sure of Geography

Euclid &

French

Can work up Geometrical drawing.

Besides if you want to give me a chance please let me know the extent of the evil of which I am accused.

As for the rest — that can be seen to later. I am thinking only of my preliminary. If you will take my word of honour to the effect that I am working my very best, well & good, if not — I cannot do anything more than try.

Goodbye my darling Mummy with love from

WINNY

Lady Randolph to Lord Randolph

EXTRACT

Sunday 23 [November 1890]   2 Connaught Place

. . . I went to Harrow on Thursday & had an interview with Welldon — who told me he thought Winston was working as hard as he possibly cld & that he would pass his preliminary exam. It appears that Winston was working under a master he hated — & that one day the master accused him of a lie — whereupon Winston grandly said that his word had never been doubted before & that he wld go straight to Welldon — which he did. Welldon quite approved, took him away from the master, & now he is with one he likes & works very well with — I thought him looking pale, but he was very nice & full of good resolutions which I trust will last. . . .

When it came to the examination, Winston had an astonishing piece of good fortune:

Winston to Lady Randolph

[Postmark 10 December 1890]   [Harrow]

Darling Mama,

Of course I cannot judge whether or not I have passed in this day's exam. But I can tell you that I am very contented with the result.

Last night I thought I would try & see if I could learn up the right map. Therefore I threw all the maps (their names on little scraps on Paper) into my hat & drew out one with my eyes shut. New Zealand was the one and New Zealand was the very first question in the Paper. I consider that this is luck. To draw the right map out of 25 different scraps of paper. Of course I had learnt all about New Zealand. I think I can say I have passed

English

Geography

& I should [not] be at all surprised if I passed in Geometrical Drawing.

I have had a very successful day.

Of course this is only my opinion still I am very pleased.

The subjects for the essay were

   i. Rowing versus Riding

  ii. Advertisements Their use & abuse

 iii. The American Civil War

I did the last.

Show this to Everest as she is awfully keen.

A Remittance would not be altogether misplaced.

Tomorrow { Algebra & arithmetic / Euclid / French

Wish me luck

I remain Your loving son

WINSTON S. CHURCHILL

Winston passed in all subjects. Of the twenty-nine candidates from Harrow, only twelve succeeded in doing that, and of these Winston was from much the lowest form. Two fifth-formers and his cousin Dudley Marjoribanks were among the six who passed in four out of five subjects; four boys passed in only three subjects; and six failed altogether. "I have received very many congratulations from scores of boys and many masters," Winston told his mother. "Dudley has not spoken to me. Vive la joie!! He has not passed and is furious." And Lady Randolph hastened to send a glowing, indeed an overglowing, account to her husband, who was on his way home from a visit to Egypt. For, as we have seen, twelve boys passed from Harrow, not four as she avers:

Lady Randolph to Lord Randolph

EXTRACT

Monday 26 [January 1891]   2 Connaught Place

. . . I am sure you will be delighted to hear that Winston has passed his P.E. [Preliminary Examination] in *everything* — one of the only 4 boys of Harrow who got in. Dudley Marjoribanks hasn't passed, and he is 18 months older and in a much higher form. Winston writes that he is in the special Sandhurst class working with the boys of the 6th and 5th forms. I hope he won't break down, for I am sure it is hard work, and unfortunately he has got to go through a sort of treatment for his throat, which will be a great bore and tedious. I will tell you all about it when we meet — it is too long to write about. I think you might make him a present of a gun as a reward. He is pining for one, and ought to have a little encouragement. Mr Welldon is very pleased — I enclose his letter. . . .

The year 1890, which had promised to be dispiriting and ended triumphantly, brought new interests to Winston in a number of other fields. That summer Lord and Lady Randolph took Banstead, a small property at Newmarket. Lord Randolph, though he had bought his first horse at Newmarket while he was still Chancellor in October 1886, had only started taking an interest in racing after his resignation. He was in partnership with Lord Dunraven, who, as Under-Secretary of State for the Colonies, was the only other Minister to resign at the same time as Lord Randolph. Some horses were entered in Lord Randolph's name, others in Lord Dunraven's. The horses were trained by R. Sherwood at St Gatien House, Newmarket. In his first season as an owner, 1887, Lord Randolph only had one winner in his colours of pink, chocolate sleeves and cap (these colours were later adopted by his son Winston) and that a nominal prize of £100. But in September 1887 he bought the cheapest of Mr James Snarry's five yearlings which were up for sale at Doncaster; she was a black filly by Trappist out of Festive which Lord Randolph named L'Abbesse de Jouarre. This name was the choice of Lady Randolph who had been reading the French novel of that title by Renan. In her first season the Abbess, nicknamed by the racing public the "Abscess on the Jaw," won three Weight-for-Age races with a total value of £935, but in the following year she won the Oaks (£2600) at odds of 20 to 1. Lord Randolph was not at Epsom to see his filly win this classic race. Nor, even more annoying, did he back it, Sherwood the trainer having advised both Lord Dunraven and Lord Randolph that the Abbess, having lost a number of races, had no chance on her recent form.

This was not, however, to be her last victory, though it was her only one in that year, 1889. In the following year she won no fewer than four races, including the valuable Manchester Cup (£2202), again at 20 to 1, a race in which Lord Randolph insisted on entering the Abbess against the advice of her trainer. It was after this race that Lord Randolph sent Winston £5 which, to his great annoyance, as communicated in the letter on page 124, the latter failed to acknowledge promptly. In 1891 the Abbess won only one race but again a valuable one, the Hardwicke Stakes (£2412). That was the end of her racing career, in which she had won more than £10,000 in stake money for Lord Randolph and his racing partner. This is very little by modern standards in England and America but in those days it was substantial. She was sold for 7000 guineas and Lord Dunraven gave the following account of her in her retirement in November 1893: "I never saw a more lovely picture than the Abbess and her foal. The old mare looked simply perfection for a brood mare and the filly, though small which is natural, is the image of her mother and I do not think those joints are going to be much detriment to her." The Abbess died at Welbeck and Lady Randolph recalls "with great satisfaction" that she saw a grandson of hers, Land League, win the Cambridgeshire in 1907. Between 1889 and 1893 either Lord Randolph or Lord Dunraven were always among the leading winning owners on the turf. Lord Randolph was elected a member of the Jockey Club in 1890 and during these years racing and family racing friends like Colonel North and Colonel Montagu, the trainer Sherwood and his younger son Bob, provided Winston and Jack with lively company.

Naturally, both Winston and Jack were enormously excited that they had a country house to go to having spent so many holidays in London or at the sea-side in boarding houses. Mrs Everest realized how much her two young charges welcomed the change:

Mrs Everest to Lady Randolph
(Blenheim Papers)

1 January 1891   Banstead

My Lady,

We arrived here safely at 3 o'clock yesterday & I am very sorry but I quite forgot to send you a telegram until we had got some way on the road here. I hope you got Master Winston's letter he wrote last evening. They are both so happy & delighted & in towering spirits. Mr Winston walked from Cheveley up to the house yesterday & said he left all his bad throat in the train he feels nothing of it. They danced all evening & were out before breakfast this morning & have been out with the keeper the whole morning, killed 5 rabbits & frightened 50. They have just had luncheon & gone off again. They do not need pressing to go out here. On the contrary now I have the trouble to get them to come in to their meals. But they are so happy & well today. The house is very comfortable & warm. The weather changed in the night & it has been thawing today — otherwise the pond is beautiful for skating. They were looking forward to it, but if the thaw continues they will be able to ride. I should like to keep Master Jack here untill Mr Winston returns from Canford. Mr W could come up with Walter the boy. It is so much better for them than London. I am desired to enclose drawings of last night with their best love & kisses.

Your ladyship's obednt servant
E. A. EVEREST

At Banstead Winston built the Den. It was quite a large hut constructed, with the aid of a few of the men who worked on the estate, of mud and planks, and carpeted with straw inside. With his brother Jack, his cousins Shane Leslie and Hugh Frewen and the gardener's son and other children on the estate, Winston built intricate fortifications around it. The author is indebted to Sir Shane Leslie for some accounts of these activities. There was a moat and a drawbridge. The entrance to the Den was guarded by a large home-made elastic catapult which propelled green apples with great force at any target which hazarded into the vicinity, notably a cow which was occasionally hit. Winston now graduated from drilling his toy soldiers in Connaught Square to drilling his brother, his cousins and his other "volunteers" in the field outside the Den and it was at the end of the drilling that he marched his troops across the drawbridge into the Den, raised the drawbridge and defended the citadel against all comers with the aid of his powerful catapult. Before Winston returned to Banstead for the summer holidays in 1891, Jack, who had gone on before, sent the following report:

Jack to Winston

EXTRACT

Sunday ? [26 July 1891]   Banstead

. . . The Den is dirty inside but has withstood the weather well Nothing is spoilt except the bag's ropes are broken and there is something rong with the lever. I dont know quite what it is, but I will find out, I will try and get the Den clean by the time you come It is very hard to aproach for huge thistles & stinging nettles are all around about, and the ditch is empty of water. I shall not make much noise for there are a lot of Rabbits in the gras there which has grown very high and we will have a feast. . . .

Winston and Jack also kept chickens at Banstead. Mrs Everest wrote from Banstead: "I go to look at your chickens they look thriving there are 2 Bantam chickens & 3 or 4 others. Bell has got 2 of your Hens sitting on some Turkey's Eggs. The guinea pig died & 2 of the little Rabbits & Herbert told me he has sold all the eggs for 1/6d so I am afraid your farming will not pay the labourer's wages." And again: "I often go to see your chickens the old Cock is a noisy old fellow he wakes me up all hours of the night crowing. I think your hens must lay plenty of eggs for they are constantly cackling. Herbert seems to keep them well supplied with corn but they never seem to have much water." To his father Winston reported proudly on May 27: "My hens have had one brood of four chickens and laid eighty eggs."

At school at this time, Winston suffered a good deal from toothache and had to make numerous visits to a succession of dentists some of whom were thought inadequate in their duties. He also suffered a strain which was evidently some form of incipient hernia and for which he consulted an eminent specialist in hernia surgery, Sir William MacCormac. Nearly sixty years later he had to undergo an operation for this complaint which involved an eight-inch scar across the belly. This he triumphantly survived.

Winston was a mischievous boy and one of many devices. With four companions he broke up a disused factory in Harrow. What is engaging, or artful, about him is that he immediately reported his malpractice to his parents — perhaps out of a sense of honesty, or perhaps because he thought they would hear about it anyway.

Winston to Lady Randolph

EXTRACT

[? 17 May 1891]   [Harrow]

. . . I am well & all right, but have just been in the deuce of a row for breaking some windows at a factory. There were 5 of us & only 2 of us were discovered. I was found, with my usual luck, to be one of these 2. I've no doubt Mr Welldon has informed you of the result. . . .

Winston to Lord Randolph

(Blenheim Papers)

EXTRACT

Wednesday   [Harrow]
27 May [1891]

. . . There was rather a row about some broken windows not long ago. I, young Millbank [Mark Milbanke] and three others went out for a walk a week ago and discovered the ruins of a large factory, into which we climbed. Everything was in ruin and decay but some windows yet remained unbroken; we facilitated the progress of time with regard to these, with the result that the watchman complained to Welldon, who having made enquiries and discoveries, "swished" us. However this is not a serious row, and Welldon never even mentioned it to Mama yesterday. . . .

Lord Randolph was in fact far away. In April 1891 he had sailed for a lengthy visit to South Africa in search of health and with expectation of making some money for his wife and children. He was oblivious of the fact, but his family had by now begun to accept that he would never recover his health or restore his political fortunes.

During Lord Randolph's absence in South Africa a benefactress entered into Winston's life. She was Lady Wilton, a close friend of both Lord and Lady Randolph Churchill. It may be surmised that she comprehended the difficulties which Winston's parents had in coping with one whom they regarded as an awkward boy amid their social and political pre-occupations and circumscribed as they were by increasingly limited means — the result of their joint extravagances.

Lady Wilton, who was a daughter of William Russell, nephew of the 5th and 6th Dukes of Bedford, married in 1862 the youngest son of the 2nd Earl of Wilton, who somewhat unexpectedly succeeded as 4th Earl in 1885. He was a rich landowner principally around Manchester. She took Winston under her wing; she was a keen fisherwoman and often asked Winston to stay at her house, The Hatch, near Windsor, on her summer visits to England. She also seems to have tempted him to come and stay with her at her villa Le Nid in the south of France. This project does not seem to have been realized.

Like most boys and indeed most grown-ups Winston was usually short of money. He seems to have been exceptionally extravagant. His parents were somewhat capricious, but on the whole generous; and Winston had at least one regular source of revenue which was unknown to his parents. A typical ending to a letter from Lady Wilton is:

. . . Enclosed £2 with best love & a kiss

from yr Deputy Mother
LAURA WILTON

Lady Wilton's great friend was Sir Frederick Johnstone, the 8th Baronet, who like his father and grandfather before him had sat in Parliament for Weymouth. He subsequently married Lady Wilton in 1899 after her husband had died. Sir Frederick was a considerable race-horse owner, and in 1891 had a half-share in the three-year-old Common, which won the 2000 Guineas and the Derby, and went on

to win the St Leger in September of that year. Sir Frederick also had
a nephew at Harrow, but in a different house from Winston's.

Sir Frederick Johnstone to Winston

Sunday 14 June 1891   9 Arlington Street
                                                      Piccadilly S.W.

Dear Winston,
   I am afraid I was rather indiscreet, but I suppose that does not
matter when I enclose your £5. I hope you will come down to the
Hatch this summer.

                                                      Yrs very truly
                                                      F. JOHNSTONE
I have got a nephew at Druries you must be nice to him.

There is some mystery here. A likely explanation of Sir Frederick's
indiscretion is that he offered Winston this generous tip in front of
Lady Randolph and was reproved by her for doing so. Anxious to
make a friend for his nephew he forwarded it later.
   While Lord Randolph was away in South Africa, Lady Randolph
was increasingly caught up in the world of fashion and society, and
was more and more surrounded by a competitive band of handsome
young admirers, of whom the famous Count Kinsky was the most
prominent.
   Winston seems to have resigned himself to seeing little of his
mother; but naturally not wishing to feel "left out of it" on those
occasions, like Speech Day, when most boys are visited by their
parents, he appealed to her to make other arrangements.

Winston to Lady Randolph

[? June 1891]   [Harrow]

Dear Mamma,
   I wish you would try & get someone to come down here on Speech
Day. I suppose grand mamma Duchess could not come.
   Try and get Auntie Clara to come if no inconvenience to her. Do
get someone as I shall be awfully "out of it" if no one comes. Next
Thursday is Speech Day.
   Please try and arrange something darling Mummy. I hope to be

able to spend Lord's at Banstead with you. Jack will probably be
well enough by then.

Good Bye Mamma with Love & Kisses
I remain Your loving son
WINSTON S. CHURCHILL

Jack had had mumps, and Winston showed a touching concern
for him, which went so far as copying out for Jack's benefit one of
Lord Randolph's quite lengthy letters from South Africa — all this,
it should be remarked, at a time when the disparity in their ages was
probably most marked, for Winston was already sixteen and Jack
only eleven.

Winston to Lady Randolph

[? June 1891]   [Harrow]
Darling Mummy,
    It was a pity you could not come to see me on Sat. I did not expect
you & so was not disappointed. Mr. Searle says there is every chance
of my being allowed to come to your concert, however we can talk
it over at "Lords."
    I have copied out Papa's letter and sent it to Jack.

Good Bye my darling Mummy.
With love & Kisses
I remain, Your loving son
WINSTON S. CHURCHILL

While Winston was at Brighton and at Harrow there were numer-
our references in their correspondence to Lady Randolph's "Concerts." She was a gifted amateur pianist, good enough to be in demand for charity concerts — and not merely on account of her social
position.

Twice, in rapid succession, Winston made references to "Lord's."
The annual cricket match between Eton and Harrow, played early in
July at Lord's cricket ground in London, was the occasion for a mid-
term holiday. All boys at Harrow were allowed to go to Lord's for
the cricket, and nearly all made the most of their opportunity and
spent the rest of the holiday at home. Shortly before the "Lord's"
holiday Winston learned that he might be deprived of this treat.

Winston to Lady Randolph

[3 July 1891]   [Harrow]

My darling Mummy,

Please do all you possibly can for me. Think how unhappy I should be being left at Harrow when 90 out of every hundred boys are enjoying themselves. You promised me I should come. It is no special exeat but a regular holiday given in the Summer Term to every boy whose conduct has been such as to merit it. I was terribly frightened when I got your letter this morning. The Possibility of my not being able to come being to my mind entirely out of the question. Could you not ask Grandmamma Marlborough to let me stay with her (at least.)

I managed all right about Speech day (having taken the precaution of writing & of telegraphing). Mummy darling if you knew or had known how much I was looking forward to my "Lords" I am sure you would have endeavoured to avoid that Engagement, or make some provision for my holiday.

It will be a poor time indeed for me if I have to go to Lords, Friday & Saturday as a Harrow boy & answer my name every 2 hours & not leave the ground etc (as 100 other unfortunates usually have to do).

My darling Mummy I am sure you have not been very much troubled about me this term. I have asked for no visits & I forfeited the pleasure of seeing you on Speech Day therefore I do hope you will endeavour not to disappoint me utterly with regard to July 11th & 12th.

Please do come down in any case on Tuesday [July 7].

I have many things to talk to you about which take so much longer to write than to tell. How is poor little Jack? I have written several times & sent several newspapers & books for him to read but I have recd. no answer; so I conclude he is not well enough to write. I have had Mumps so there is no danger for me.

Where is everybody?

No one has written to me to tell me any news for a long time. Where is Everest. Do try my Darling Mummy to please your

                                                    Loving son
                                            WINSTON S. CHURCHILL

Lady Randolph to Winston

Sunday [5 July 1891]   Banstead

Oh! dear oh! dear what an ado!! You silly old boy I did not mean
that you would have to remain at Harrow only that I cld not have
you here, as I am *really* obliged to go to Stowe on Saturday. But I
shall see you on Friday & can arrange something for you. I shall
be at Aunt Clara's. Perhaps she can put you up too. I will write &
let you know. I believe Jack is all right — so Everest writes — but
he has not written to me tho' I sent him some fruit. I had a long
letter from Papa in Johannesburg — in very good spirits & health.
He sent his best love to you both — I suppose you write to him?
The mail leaves Friday night.

Goodbye my darling. Write to Aldford Street [her sister Clara's
house] where I go tomorrow.

Your loving

MOTHER

Mrs Everest to Winston

EXTRACT

Monday 11 a.m. [6 July 1891]   2 Verona Cottages
                                                        Ventnor

. . . Well my dearest the reason Mamma cannot have you home is
the house is to be full of visitors for the race week which commences
on the Tuesday tomorrow week. But I don't see why you could not
go from Friday till Monday because you could go by yourself & I
talked to Jackie about it & he said he did not care about going
much & should not feel at all disappointed if I don't go. Mr Sander-
son [headmaster of Jack's school at Elstree] asked him if he would
like to go to Lords he has got a Break to go. He is such a contented
little Lamb. But I should think you could go quite well but if you
do go alone [to Banstead] please be careful & get into the right
train & change at Cambridge. You see you would return to Harrow
the day before the visitors go to Banstead and then perhaps Aunt
Clara or some one would see you off to Harrow. Let me know the
decision dear soon as you know it yourself. . . .

Lady Randolph to Winston

Monday [6 July 1891]   18 Aldford Street

Dearest Winston,

It is all right Grandmamma Marlborough will put you up & Jack up Friday night & I suppose you go back Saturday evening? Write & tell me. I am trying to arrange for a coach — for Lords' —

You must come here the first thing — & mind you make yrself *very* smart —

Yr loving mother
JSC

It seems that Winston prevailed.

Lady Randolph to Lord Randolph
(Blenheim Papers)

EXTRACT

11 July [1891]   18 Aldford Street

. . . Winston is here and is sleeping at your mother's as there is no room here. We spent the day at Lords yesterday — very hot and tiring and Harrow is getting much the best of it. Jack is too infectious with the remains of mumps to be allowed up. They both have good reports, but Welldon says W should have special help for the French this summer. I am going to try and find a little governess (ugly) who wants a holiday. Just to talk and read with him . . . As you may imagine the whole town is in a ferment about the German Emperor and Empress . . . The Emperor begins his day at eight in the Park riding with half a doz ADCs in uniform and he changes his clothes about five times a day. Margot Tennant [*who three years later was to marry Mr H. H. Asquith*] sallied forth yesterday on a prancing steed determined to make his acquaintance and she did. . . .

Winston to Lord Randolph
(Blenheim Papers)

[11 July 1891]   [50 Grosvenor Square]

Dear Papa,

I am so sorry you have not recd my letters. I have written three times. I am up for the Lords exeat Harrow as usual are winning easily. I am staying with Grandmama at Grosvenor Square.

Last night I dined with Millbank [Jack Milbanke] and afterwards went on to the Naval Exhibition. I suppose Mama has told you about the Eclipse Stakes. Surefoot, Gouverneur, Common.

I am going to try and see the fireworks tonight at the Crystal Palace. They will be wonderful as the Emperor will be there. Poor Jack cannot come up for his exeat on account of infection, but is consoled by Mama's having purchased a beautiful pony for him. I have got a good report so says Mama.

Do send me some stamps in your next letter.

Hoping you will have luck health and pleasure.

I remain ever your loving son
WINSTON S. CHURCHILL

Winston to Jack

[? 11 July 1891]   [Harrow]

My darling Jack,

I sit down to write you an account of the exeat from beginning to end. But first let me tell you how sorry I was you could not come.

Having eluded the Masters I escaped with the sanction of the authorities to London which I reached on Friday at 11 o'clock. I went, as Mamma had told me to Aldford Street, where I found Mamma & Count Kinsky Breakfasting. (I have been staying you know with Grandmamma at 50.) I then went on to see Grandmamma & after that I went to Lords. I lunched with Grandmamma. In the Afternoon I went again to Lords. Came back & Dined with Milbanke at the Isthmian Club. After dinner we went on to the "Naval Exhibition." Most beautiful models & guns of every description. Got home at 11.45.

Sat.

Breakfasted with Mamma at 18 Aldford Street. Arranged with Count Kinsky that he should take me to the Crystal Palace, where the German Emperor was going. (he Drove me in his phaeton.)

The programme of what we saw (everything of course was awfully well done on account of the Emperor) is as follows.

Wild Beasts. (wonderful never seen any thing like them.)

Fire Brigade Drill before the Emperor.

This was perfectly splendid. There were nearly 2000 firemen & 100

Engines. They all marched past the Emperor to the music of a band of infantry.

Then the Engines trotted past & finally all the lot Galloped past as hard as they could go. Then we went & had dinner.

The head man said he could not possibly give us a table but Count K. spoke German to him & it had a wonderful effect. Very tolerable dinner. Lots of Champagne which pleased your loving brother very much.

Then ensued a most exciting incident.

"Row with Kaffir."

We went to see Panorama but it was closed so we went to the Switch Back Railway. On the way however we came across a new thing called the "Aerial Car" which rushed across a wire Rope nearly 300 yards in length & awfully high. We waited about 10 minutes for our turn & then the thing went wrong, & the Gun summoning people to the fireworks went off, so Count K & I clambered over the rails in anger & wished to go. However a half bred sort of Kaffer who was in charge attempted to stop Count K. caught him

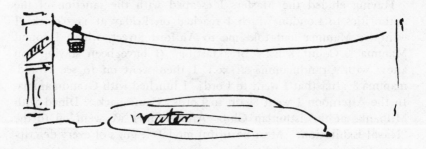

by the coat tail. The Count whom you know is immensely strong grew furious and caught hold of the blackguards hand, crushing the fingers in his grasp; the Mulatto dropped the coat & took to swearing telling Count K. that He should think himself "d—d lucky" that he did not pitch him over the bannisters. "By ——" said Count Kinsky "I should like to see you touch me." "You go and learn manners" retorted the cad. "But not from you" said Count K.

Then the audience & the other people made the scoundrel be quiet & we went on our way angry but triumphant.

The Fireworks were wonderful & I wished you had been there to see them.

They began with a perfect volley, rockets etc.

Then there were two great set pieces of Cornflowers & Roses (the Emperors Favourit Flowers) which after ward changed to the heads of the Emperor & Empress. Then there was the Battle of the Nile.

The ships actually moved & the cannonading was terriffic. Finally L'Orient blew up. Then a great mixture when everything was let off in all directions.

Then we went & got our coat & had each an American drink & then we went to our carriage. Count K. drives beautifully & we passed with our fast pair of horses everything on the road.

I must describe the Emperor's uniform. A helmet of bright Brass surmounted by a white eagle nearly 6 inches high.

A polished steel cuirass & a perfectly white uniform with high boots.

Of course you know Harrow won by 5 wickets. I could not "smash an Eton hat" as I had to leave the ground early to go to the Crystal Palace.

I hear your pony is a regular beauty & the fastest on Newmarket heath, but I don't believe he will beat the "Gemelet."

I saw "Touty" [de Forest] at the Match. Kim [Kimbolton] I saw looking dirty disreputable & ill.

The "City Clerk" is at Staines.

I shall soon see you so will now say good bye.

Ever your loving brother
WINSTON S. CHURCHILL

Winston to Lord Randolph

(Blenheim Papers)

EXTRACT

22 July 1891

. . . I spent the "Lords Exeat" with Grandmamma in London. I had tremendous fun. On the Saturday I got Count Kinsky to take me [to the] Crystal Palace, whither the German Emperor was going. There was a grand review of all the Country Fire Brigades before H.I.M. About 3000 Firemen & 100 Engines, a fine sight. We had splendid seats & saw without any crush or struggle. The Emperor's uniform is worthy of description. A bright brass helmet coming right down the

nape of his neck surmounted by a magnificent white eagle nearly
6 inches high. Black tin cuirass and white uniform.

Then of course there was a most splendid show of Fireworks. The
German Emperor has made a great impression I believe, though
there are those who denounce him as a prig.

Of course Harrow won the match, by 7 wickets. I am going to
camp out at the end of the term for 5 or 6 days at Aldershot. I shall
think of you, who will probably be doing the same thing, some distance away. . . .

His earlier account giving Harrow's margin of victory as 5 wickets
was wrong, doubtless because he had left the match before the end
and had relied on gossip.

Lord Randolph had been away for nearly three months on his
tour of southern Africa. He has left a record of his travels in *Men,
Mines and Animals in South Africa*. About this time Winston received the following letter:

Lord Randolph to Winston

27 June 1891   Johannesburg

Dearest Winston,

You cannot think how pleased I was to get your interesting & well
written letter & to learn that you were getting on well. I understand
that Mr Welldon thinks you will be able to pass your examination
into the army when the time comes. I hope it may be so, as it will
be a tremendous pull for you ultimately. I have been having a most
agreeable travel in this very remarkable country. I expect that when
you are my age you will see S Africa to be the most populous &
wealthy of all our colonies. I suppose Mama has read you my letters
& that you have seen my letters in the *Daily Graphic,* for I cannot tell you more than I have already written. You would have enjoyed an expedition I made last week for shooting purposes. A regular gipsy life, sleeping on a mattress in a bell tent, dressing and
washing in the open air & eating round a camp fire. The sport was
vy fair & wild & there was much variety of game to shoot. Here I
have been examining gold mines & investing money in what I hope
will be fortunate undertakings for I expect you & Jack will be a
couple of expensive articles to keep as you grow older.

Tomorrow we start for our journey up country staying a few days at Pretoria on the way. My waggons have been slowly treking up through Bechuanaland with Captain Giles, Rayner & the others since the middle of May & ought to be now at Fort Juli in Matabele Land where I hope to join them in about 10 or 12 days. I expect that we shall be vy comfortable & jolly when we get to the waggons. I have not had any roughing it or discomfort yet, as we have always been put up by friends and have avoided the Hotels which are most dirty & uncomfortable. We have a six or seven days journey before us from Pretoria to Juli. We travel in a "spider" a sort of light framed waggonette with eight mules, and so about 50 miles in the day.

The accommodation on the road for the night is said to be vy indifferent. I suppose this will just reach you as you are going home for the holidays. I hope you will have a good time at Banstead & that you and Jack will amuse yourself well. Give him my vy best love & tell him how glad I am to hear of his good place in the school. Perhaps he will write to me before long. Goodbye take care of yourself, don't give Mama any trouble.

Ever yr most affte father
RANDOLPH S. CHURCHILL

I am doubtful about being able to bring home a tame antelope. The Bechuanaland stamps I think I can obtain: I have a pointer called Charlie & a shooting pony called Charlie both excellent animals. When we travel we always have our guns ready to secure any game which may show itself.

*

The term after Winston had passed his Preliminary Examination to Sandhurst was comparatively tranquil as far as the demands made upon him by his masters were concerned, but in the Summer Term, immediately after the Lord's exeat, Mr Welldon raised the question of Winston going abroad during the summer holidays in order to perfect his languages.

Reverend J. E. C. Weldon to Lady Randolph

13 July 1891   Harrow

Dear Lady Randolph Churchill,
    You will, I am sure, forgive my making a suggestion about Winston. Mr Moriarty, the master who takes charge of my Army boys,

is very anxious that he should spend his holidays or a good part of his holidays in France, so as to enhance his getting more marks in French when his examination comes on. It will probably be suggested that he should spend some future holidays in Germany.

I do not know if the idea of sending him to France will fall in with your own plans, and of course, if he goes there, it will be necessary that he should go with a steady purpose of work; but I may say that I have again and again found it convenient to send many boys abroad for the holidays, and I could easily recommend a family in which he might live, if you could spare him.

I broke this painful subject to him in conversation some days ago and I do not doubt it involves some self sacrifice, but Lord Randolph has so strongly argued the importance of letting him enter the Army straight from Harrow that it seems only right to point out a means of increasing his prospect of success.

Believe me, Sincerely yours
J. E. C. WELLDON

Winston reacted forcibly and unequivocally.

Winston to Lady Randolph

[? 14 July 1891]   [Harrow]

My darling Mummy,

Mr Welldon told me last night that he had written to you about my going to spend "at least 4 weeks" in France. His ideal of course is a "family" one of his own "specials." I told Papa when he came down that I ought (in Mr W's opinion) to go, but he said "utter nonsense, if you like I'll get a German scullery maid for Banstead." I'm sure you would not like me to be away the greater part of the holidays with some horrid French Family. It would be perfectly —— well unpleasant. Besides practically there is no hurry. I have very nearly 3 years at the outside limit.

Furthermore Dudley is not going & he has 9 months less time than I. How can you expect me to work all the term & then go to a filthy den all the holidays.

How frightfully dull it would be. I shouldn't see Jack nor you, nor Everest at all. Of course it is (as says Welldon) entirely in your hands. But I am sure you will not send me to any such abominable drudgery with your free consent.

Even if the worst comes to the worst you could send me to some of your friends & not to the "respectable creatures." A governess would

I am sure answer all the immediate colloquial requirements. As
Papa absolutely veto'ed the idea & as I beg you to let me have a bit
of fun.

I remain, Your loving son
WINSTON S. CHURCHILL

P.S. Really I feel less keen about the Army every day. I think the
church would suit me much better. Am well, safe, & happy. About
Fire works ask Count K.

Winston's suggestion of going into the Church does not appear to
have been seriously considered in one way or the other though he
was later briefly to refer in *My Early Life* to this fugitive idea. Discussing what might have happened if he had not passed his Army
examination, he wrote: "I might have gone into the Church and
preached orthodox sermons in a spirit of audacious contradiction to
the age."

Some ingenious writer might well come to indite a thesis on the
supposition that Winston Churchill had taken Holy Orders and had
pursued a career in the Church of England: of how he had later
crossed the aisle and joined the Church of Rome and had become a
cardinal; and of how in his old age he had reconciled himself to the
Church of England. The theme could concern the reunification of
Christian Churches around the year 1937 after the summoning of an
oecumenical conference, and the avoidance of the Second World
War; with his own acceptance in 1940 of the Papal Tiara and his
installation as the first English Pope since Adrian IV, 1154–9. This
might have been celebrated by the retrocession of the Papal States to
the Vatican by that magnanimous and pacific statesman Signor
Mussolini; and by the consequent political unification of Europe
under the double leadership of Britain and the Church of Rome.
Such fantasies, however, must be left to some more imaginative pen.

"I hope she will turn a deaf ear," wrote Winston to his father in
telling him of Mr Welldon's request. Lady Randolph went to see
Mr Welldon and succeeded in persuading him to compromise at any
rate for the summer holidays. "He thinks," Lady Randolph reported
to her husband on July 24, "that a good governess will do as well —
and I think so too if I can find the right kind — but if I can't I shall
have to send him away. Welldon gave me an excellent account of
him and said his next report would be very good and he was most

anxious to meet your views and get him to Sandhurst next year —
'a triumph for me and for the boy'. . . ."

A few days later Lady Randolph had changed her mind. She wrote
to Lord Randolph on July 29: "I am trying to arrange now to get a
French tutor over from Cambridge 3 or 4 times a week and the other
days Winston can prepare lessons. He is quite alive to the necessity
of working — he has improved very much in looks and is quite
sensible now."

It was towards the end of August that Lady Randolph succeeded in
finding "a rather nice young man from Cambridge." There is no
record as to whether or not the three weeks of intermittent tutorials
benefited Winston. But on his return to Harrow towards the end
of September Dr Welldon showed that he was not entirely happy.

Reverend J. E. C. Welldon to Lady Randolph
(Blenheim Papers)

21 September 1891   Harrow

Dear Lady Randolph Churchill,

Thank you very much for your letter about Winston. I will not
be hard upon him. I am anxious for him to make as much progress
as possible this year. The only condition on which he can pass into
Sandhurst is that he should work hard. Will you let me arrange
for his Christmas holiday after carefully discussing with my army
masters what is best for him? They will probably send him to Germany. I should, of course, not wish to take any step that you might
disapprove, but I promised Lord Randolph that I would spare no
effort to get him into the army.

With kind regards, Sincerely yours
J. E. C. Welldon

Lady Randolph sent this letter on to Lord Randolph who was
making preparations for his return home at the end of the year.

Lady Randolph to Lord Randolph
(Blenheim Papers)

EXTRACT

25 September [1891]   2 Connaught Place

Dearest R,

At last I have seen the boys safely off. Winston conveniently
worked himself into a bilious attack and had to stay on a couple

of days. On the whole he had been a very good boy — but honestly
he is getting a bit too old for a woman to manage. After all he will
be 17 in 2 months and he really requires to be with a man. I send
you Welldon's letter. You will have time to answer me before I decide anything. Of course it will be hard upon him not spending his
holidays at home — but after all I shan't know what to do with
him, and it will be impossible for him to pass his exam if he does
not get a smattering of German. Young Millbank spent the last
week at Banstead — but he is rather dull and stupid. Winston
will be all right the moment he gets into Sandhurst. He is just at
the "ugly" stage — slouchy and tiresome. I managed to get a very
nice little man from Cambridge — very clever spoke 12 languages.
He might be made use of later to travel with him. It will be all the
better for Jack to be without him — the difference in their ages is
beginning to tell and poor Jack is quite worn out rushing about
after Winston. . . .

Unless Winston's looks greatly fluctuated it would seem that Lady
Randolph was somewhat capricious in her judgment for only two
months before she had written that he had improved very much in
looks. Early in October Lady Randolph went down to Harrow to see
Winston. "I am delighted to give you a very good account of Winston," she wrote to Lord Randolph. "Mr Welldon told me that since
his return he has worked very hard — and that he thinks he is
certain to pass in June. I thought Winston looking very well he was
full of enquiries as regards you."

In that winter term of 1891, just before his seventeenth birthday,
Winston was instructed for his confirmation in the Church of
England.

Lady Randolph to Lord Randolph

EXTRACT

6 November 1891

. . . Winston is going in for his Confirmation. Perhaps it will steady
him — Welldon wrote that Winston wished to become a candidate
— I am afraid only because it will get him off other work! . . .

We have seen how the term before he had, perhaps somewhat un-
thinkingly and prematurely, contemplated taking Holy Orders. We

have no evidence as to how seriously he viewed the important event of confirmation. Certainly from manhood onward he was not a regular communicant; he was apt to say that what with the daily chapel prayers — twice on Sundays — imposed on him in his youth, he had built up a solid reserve of church attendance in his religious bank and that this, augmented through the years by attendances at christenings, marriages, funerals and memorial services, had amply fortified his bank balance. He would often quote with approbation Disraeli's comment that "all sensible men are of the same religion" and Disraeli's reply when pressed by his interlocutor as to the nature of that religion: "Sensible men never say." Winston's first cousin, Sir Shane Leslie, who was ten years younger than he, recalls how after he had become a Roman Catholic in 1908 he had a long talk with Winston "about religion of the church kind." He recalled that Winston had said that he "had been confirmed but Communion he had received once and never again."

It is of interest that Sir Shane remembers the phrase "religion of the church kind." For though Winston was not religious in the literal sense of the word, namely "being bound," like most serious-minded people, he frequently speculated on the mysteries of the universe — why we were here, what we were supposed to be doing and where we were going. Frequently the author heard him say that he thought the reason we were here was to find out why; but that when we did find out, the world would come to an end, as we would have achieved our objective.

*

Winston's half-term report did not live up to the expectations aroused by Dr Welldon's favourable opinion at the beginning of the term.

Reverend J. E. C. Welldon to Lady Randolph

24 November 1891   Harrow

Dear Lady Randolph,

You will, I hope, forgive me troubling you with one more letter about Winston. It seems to me essential that he should make the best use of his coming holidays. He has worked better this term

than before but he is fitful, and he will need all the marks that he
can get. If you will let me, I should like to send him to a M.
Elmering whose address is

9 Rue de la Ferme
Rouen.

M. Elmering has had Harrow boys under his care before and has
taught them well. Of course I must count upon his being willing
to go and upon his working steadily when he is there; for I cannot
exercise the same control over him in the holidays as in the term
time, and it will be in his power to defeat the project made for his
good, unless he is sensible. But I ought to say plainly that his chance
of passing his examination for Sandhurst depends upon himself, and,
sorry as I am to spoil the pleasure of his holidays, I cannot doubt
that I am advising you in his true interest.

His cousin, Dudley Marjoribanks, is going off at the beginning of
the holidays, to a family in Baden.

If arrangements are made for Winston's going to Rouen, they
ought to be made as soon as possible.

Believe me, Sincerely yours
J. E. C. WELLDON

"Welldon makes all the arrangements. I shall have to let him go,"
Lady Randolph told Lord Randolph. Winston himself seemed by
now conditioned to the idea of having to go abroad: "But let me beg
you," he wrote to his mother, "No Family! No Family! Ugh!"
There then began a long struggle over the next three weeks in which
Winston showed himself a tenacious but unsuccessful fighter. " I beg
and Pray that you will not send me to a vile, nasty, fusty, beastly
French 'Family.' " He was allowed to go to London for the wedding
of his Aunt Sarah to Captain Gordon Chesney Wilson, but he had to
return to Harrow almost immediately. "It was very 'bad luck'
having to go just as the fun was commencing," he wrote to his mother
on November 22. "It is still worse having to look forward to such a
time as you and Welldon seem to be planning out for me next
Christmas." It appears that at least Winston, through Lady Randolph had persuaded Dr Welldon to drop the Rouen "family," for it
was arranged that Winston should stay at the Versailles home of one
of the French masters at Harrow, M. Minssen. But then arose the

JOHN CHURCHILL, 1ST DUKE
OF MARLBOROUGH, AND SARAH,
DUCHESS OF MARLBOROUGH

Formerly attributed to Kneller,
but probably School of Lely

The north front

BLENHEIM, ABOUT 1880

The west and south fronts

JOHN WINSTON, 7TH DUKE
OF MARLBOROUGH

FRANCES, DUCHESS
OF MARLBOROUGH

LEONARD JEROME
AND CLARA HALL JEROME

LORD AND LADY RANDOLPH, 1874

"B"

Vanity Fair Cartoon
18 June 1881

THE MARQUIS
OF BLANDFORD

"The eldest son of the Duke of Marlborough was born clever. This accident of birth occurred to him thirty-seven years ago, and he has not yet recovered from it. He went into the 'Blues,' where he was remarked for the audacity of his notions and the brilliancy of his declamation, and where he made among his fellow officers many friends, some of whom adhered to him with courage and fidelity. At five-and-twenty he married the charming daughter of the Duke of Abercorn, and soon afterwards undertook with her a voyage to India, to inform himself of the rule of that country by the middle classes. Being at that time the most intimate and independent friend of the Prince of Wales, his Eastern stories had a great share in inducing the Prince to undertake his patriotic visit to India. At this time however Lord Blandford desisted from all attempts to be courtier, and retired to the purity of domestic life and the study of advanced and other philosophers. Gifted by Nature with an unobtrusive modesty, he has devoted his period of study less to original thought by his own active brain than to the acquisition of the opinions of others. The result has been to make him for the present the consort and ally of the apostles of Change. The unobtrusive dignity of his dress is a source of general envy. He has long endured his brother and patronized his father with great patience. He is neither proud nor bigoted. He is bright, vivacious, and witty, and a very ready and facile talker out of a copious vocabulary. He is a man of brilliant parts and acute intelligence, ready to receive audacious ideas and to adopt solemn paradoxes. But he will one day be a man of property and Duke of Marlborough."

LADY RANDOLPH IN IRELAND
About 1877

WINSTON AND HIS MOTHER, 1876
The first known photograph

"A Younger Son"
Vanity Fair Cartoon by Spy, 10 July 1880

" . . . He is so bold and so independent as to have once taken sides in a quarrel with the Prince of Wales otherwise than for the Prince; and withal he is so clever, that, by making bold and independent speeches in the House of Commons, he has won for himself the interest as well as the attention of that middle-aged assembly, for which he is well-informed enough to entertain the smallest amount of respect consistent with its privileges. He is a staunch Conservative as becomes his birth, yet he is neither proud nor narrow-minded, and he is so bright and cheerful a companion, and so brilliant and witty a speaker, that he is justly looked upon as one of the hopes of his Party. Withal he is a staunch friend and a faithful brother."

Mrs Everest

LADY RANDOLPH WITH JACK AND WINSTON, ABOUT 1881

2 CONNAUGHT PLACE, THE DRAWING ROOM

MRS JEROME AND HER DAUGHTERS: (FROM LEFT) LEONIE LESLIE
CLARA FREWEN, JENNIE SPENCER CHURCHILL

LORD RANDOLPH IN HIS PRIME

LETTER FROM BRIGHTON
Supervised — 17 May 1887

LETTER FROM BRIGHTON
Unsupervised — postmarked
20 May 1887

JUBILEE AT BRIGHTON
29 and 30 Brunswick Road,
June 1887

THE SCHOOLBOYS
ABOUT 1887
Winston with Bertie
Roose (left) and Jack
(standing)

LADY RANDOLPH, 1889

question — when should Winston go? Dr Welldon wanted him to lose no time in getting to France after term had ended. This meant spending Christmas away from home.

Winston to Lady Randolph

[? 6 December 1891]   [Harrow]

My darling Mama,

I had written a long letter to you but on second thoughts I decided not to send it. I hear Papa will be nearly a fortnight later coming back. Mr Welldon is in consequence very keen on my going to Paris straight from here. Darling Mummy, I shall think it will be very unkind and unnatural of you if you allow him to do me out of my Christmas. Out of all this school not 5 boys are going away at all and I believe Dudley is the only one who goes before Christmas. Please dont *you* put pressure on me. Welldon got very angry last night when I told him I couldn't give up coming home. He said "very well then you must give up the Army." That is all nonsense. But Mummy don't be unkind and make me unhappy. I have firmly made up my mind not to go abroad till after the 27th. If you in spite of my entreaties force me to go I will do as little as I can and the holidays will be one continual battle. I am sure Papa would not turn me away from home at Christmas or indeed at any time. If you do all you possibly can to make things nice for me I will go after the 27th and return so as to have 4 days with Papa.

Please don't be unkind
Ever your loving son
Winston S. Churchill

Lady Randolph to Winston

Tuesday [? 8 December 1891]   London

Dearest Winston,

I was beginning to wonder why you had not written. My dear boy, I feel for you in every way & can quite understand your anxiety & desire to be at home for Xmas, but quite apart from other considerations, the tone of your letter is not calculated to make one over lenient. When one wants something in this world, it is not by delivering ultimatums that one is likely to get it. You are old enough not to play the fool, & for the sake of a few days pleasure, give up the chance of getting through yr exam: a thing which may affect yr whole life. You know how anxious Papa is that you shld go to Sandhurst this summer — I have received a letter from him this morning, dated 7th Nov in which he says "Please tell Mr Welldon that I gladly agree to any arrangement which he may be kind enough to make for Winston's studies during the Xmas holidays." He also says "I have such a nice letter from Winston please thank him for it & give him my best love." Of course if you don't "intend" going abroad till after the 27th & have "firmly" made up yr mind to return here for the inside of a week, I suppose that wld give you about a fortnight at Versailles. If possible I will come & see you on Thursday. Meanwhile I will think it over. You can be quite certain my darling that I will decide for what is best, but I tell you frankly that *I* am going to decide not *you*. If you have to go, I shall see if it is possible to make it up to you in another way. I *count* on you helping me & not making a useless fuss. I will let you know what train I come by Thursday — until then bless you & work so that Papa may see a good report.

Yr loving
MOTHER

Winston to Lady Randolph

[? 9 December 1891]   [Harrow]

My darling Mamma,

I received your letter this morning. I hope that you will come down tomorrow as it is so much easier to explain things. You ought not however to be so sarcastic to me since it is I not you who have to make the sacrifice. You say that "You tell me frankly" very well Mamma I only told you frankly my intentions. Not intending or wishing to overcome you *sine vi aut fraude.*

I merely stated *frankly* that I would throw every obstacle in the way of my going abroad before the 27th.

You say it is for you to decide. I am required to give up my holidays — not you, I am forced to go to people who bore me excessively — not you. You were asked to give up a short part of the year to take me abroad — you promised — refused & I did not press the point.

I am very much surprised and pained to think that both you & Papa should treat me so, as a machine. I should like to know if Papa was asked to "give up his holidays" when he was at Eton.

It also seems to me that in your letters there is an inaccuracy. You state that 5 weeks − 5 days − 4 days = 14 days. This is a mistake. 5 weeks − 5 days − 4 days = 26 days.

You blame me for being frank to you. You say that "if I want to gain my point, other methods than those dictated by honour and honesty should be used."

Please do come down on Thursday, if possible for lunch because if you come by the 3.30 & leave by the 4.37 it does not give very much time.

Please do have a little regard for my happiness. There are other and higher things in this world than learning, more powerful agents than the Civil Service Commissioners.

With Love & kisses I remain
Ever your loving son
WINSTON S. CHURCHILL

Lady Randolph went down to Harrow to pacify Winston but then a new difficulty arose. To go to France on Monday, December 21, Winston would have to leave Harrow before the end of term. When would Mr Welldon allow him to come home?

Winston to Lady Randolph

[? 13 December 1891]   [Harrow]

My darling Mummy,

I am afraid by your not answering my letter that you are angry with me. I hope this is not so. If you want me to go to France next holidays very much I suppose I shall have to go, but I can't help feeling very unhappy about it.

You will see that beggar won't let me out of his clutches much.

Do please write to Mr Welldon and ask that I may be allowed to come home on the Friday night. It would mean a great deal to me. The difference of 1 night in 3 days holidays is most noticeable.

I am awfully low about it. First feeling I won't go & then that I must.

Woomany told me that you were trying to make arrangements with Baron H. [Hirsch] for me. I expect this little French brute will spoil it all.

—— Welldon; he is the cause of all my misfortunes but for him I should be looking forward to as nice a holidays, & as merry a Christmas as I have ever had.

Goodbye my darling Mummy, With much love & many kisses
I remain, Ever your loving son
WINSTON S. CHURCHILL

Lady Randolph to Winston

Tuesday [? 15 December 1891]   2 Connaught Place

Dearest Winston,

I have only read one page of yr letter and I send it back to you —
as its style does not please me. I confess after our conversation the
other day I did not expect you to go back on yr word, & try & make
everything as disagreeable for yrself & everyone else as possible. My
dear you won't gain anything by taking this line. Everything that
I can do for you to make things as smooth & palatable as possible
I will do — more I cannot promise. I don't think I can write to
Mr Welldon again — but you can ask him to let you come Friday —
& say that I shld be very glad if he wld let you.

Yr loving
MOTHER
Write to me a nice letter!

Winston to Lady Randolph

[? 16 December 1891]   [Harrow]

*[At the top of this letter Winston wrote: "P.S. I send the other
letter back that you may peruse it." He then crossed it out.]*

My darling Mummy,

Never would I have believed that you would have been so unkind.
I am utterly miserable. That you should refuse to read my letter is
most painful to me. There was nothing in it to give you grounds
for rejecting it. I am glad however that I waited 3 hours before
answering or I would have sent you something that would have
startled you. I can't tell you how wretched you have made me feel
— instead of doing everything to make me happy you go and cut
the ground away from under my feet like that. Oh my Mummy!

I made up my mind I would write no letter to you of any length
in future as in my letters length I can perceive a [reason] for your
not reading it. I expect you were too busy with your parties and
arrangements for Christmas. I comfort myself by this. As to the

style — it was rather good. A letter of mine to the Harrovian has recently been accepted & pronounced good.

IMPORTANT

READ THIS

I have got to tell you that the Frenchman wants to know what time he can come & see you on Friday. Please let me know by return of post, or tell Everest to if you feel very "spiteful."

Darling Mummy — I am so unhappy but if you don't read this letter it will be the last you'll have the trouble to send back. I think you might keep your promise to me & write to W. [Welldon] Likely he'd let me go isn't it? (on my own recommendation).

If you don't — I refuse to go to Paris till Tuesday though you will probably be so unkind that I shall be glad to get away.

I am more unhappy than I can possibly say. Your unkindness has relieved me however from all feelings of duty. I too can forget. Darling Mamma if you want me to do anything for you, especially so great a sacrifice don't be so cruel to

Your loving son
WINNY

Winston to Lady Randolph

[? 17 December 1891]   [Harrow]

My darling Mummy,

Please don't be so unkind. Do answer my letter and let me know about the Frenchman. I am very unhappy. I think you might keep your promise about Friday.

Do be kind to your Loving son
WINSTON S. CHURCHILL

Winston to Lady Randolph

[? 18 December 1891]   [Harrow]

My darling Mummy,

Welldon whom I have just seen says "I am going to let you go home for the Sunday and that's all." He says one thing to you, but quite another to me. If he doesn't let me come home till Sat. I do hope you will let me have 2 or 3 more days. Darling Mummy, do attend to my letter. I am so wretched. Even now I weep. Please my darling Mummy be kind to your loving son. Don't let my silly letters make you angry. Let me at least think that you love me. — Darling Mummy I despair. I am so wretched. I don't know what to do. Don't be angry I am so miserable.

Please don't expect me to go on Monday if he doesn't let me come till then. Oh how I wish I had not believed him. How I have been tricked. I don't know what to do. Do please write something kind to me. I am very sorry if I have "riled" you before I did only want to explain things from my point of view.

> Good Bye my darling Mummy.
> With best love I remain, Ever your loving son
> WINSTON

Lady Wilton, evidently unaware of the full details of the fierce family dispute that was raging, intervened at this time with a well-meant but unhelpful letter:

Lady Wilton to Winston

[? 18 December 1891] *In pencil*   Le Nid

My dear Winston,

Very many thanks for yours. So you are coming to France to study the "lingo." Well — I think you might study it here! under my maternal wing! What do you say? Its lovely nice weather here & I'm very fit just at present. Do you remember my Cockatoo? He is better-looking than ever & so nice. I take him about on my hand — only he tries to destroy all the furniture!

How is Jack? & when do you expect your Father? When next you write to your Mama, do give her my love. & with much to yourself

> Ever your very affecte Deputy Mother
> LAURA WILTON

For a boy of just seventeen Winston had fought a staunch rear-guard action, but he was beaten. Authority, personified by his mother and the headmaster, prevailed:

Reverend J. E. C. Welldon to Lady Randolph

[Friday] 18 December 1891   [Harrow]

Dear Lady Randolph,

I am afraid Winston cannot leave School until tomorrow, but he shall come to you early then. Mr Minssen, who has received an in-vitation from Winston, is anxious to see you and would like to call upon you tomorrow at 12, if that were a convenient time for you. He would prefer tomorrow to Monday as he may wish to have some conversation with me after seeing you.

I have had two conversations with Mr Minssen and I shall talk to Winston once more to-day.

The arrangement seems eminently satisfactory. I am confident that Mr Minssen will be kind, careful and considerate but much depends upon Winston himself. Mr Minssen will do everything for him, if he is docile and industrious; but he will not let him waste his time and, if he is idle, he must be sent home.

It is, I think, essential that he should not accept invitations to any family where he will speak English, I want him to make as much progress as possible in French conversation.

He tells me Baron Hirsch's sons, with whom he hopes to ride speak English fluently; but if that were so, it would be a loss to him to be much with them. Mr Minssen will probably ask you not to let him accept more than three invitations a week, and it is clearly bad for him to be out alone at night. Mr Minssen will, if you wish, supply him with such pocket money as is necessary. It is, I fear, somewhat of an intrusion for me to enter into these details; but my excuse is that I have set my heart upon his passing into Sandhurst and he has no time to lose.

I fully believe he will go in a sensible and right spirit.

Sincerely yours
J. E. C. WELLDON

P.S. Just as I finished writing this letter, Winston came in to say you had asked to see Mr Minssen to-day.

Lady Randolph to Lord Randolph
(Blenheim Papers)

EXTRACT

[? 18 December 1891]   2 Connaught Place

. . . Winston comes home tomorrow and on Monday goes to Ver-sailles. He starts with the French Master of Harrow with whose parents he is to stay. Mr Welldon has arranged all.

I can't tell you what trouble I have had with Winston this last fortnight he has bombarded me with letters, cursing his fate and everyone. Of course it is a great disappointment to him not being home for Xmas but he makes as much fuss as tho' he were going to Australia for 2 years. Welldon insisted on his going at once, otherwise he wd not have time enough there to derive any benefit from it.

I have just seen Mr Minssen the tutor in whose family he is going and I think I have arranged everything satisfactorily. . . .

Throughout those tempestuous weeks Mrs Everest, as always, tried to be a calming, comforting influence. "If you have to go to France without coming home I will send or bring your big tweed coat & some Fine Flannel Shirts for you to sleep in those you wore at Banstead."

Considering the protracted battle Winston accepted his capitulation in reasonable spirit:

Winston to Lady Randolph

Tuesday evening after post   18 Rue de Provence
[22 December 1891]   [Versailles]

My darling Mummy,

I was too tired to write last night. We travelled 2nd classe but notwithstanding a horrible smell of Brandy & beer on the boat, I was not sick. Au contraire I slept all the time.

We arrived at Dieppe où nous partook of de bon Cafe au lait. Le chemin de fer etait très incommode. Pour quatres heures I waited having nothing to do. Nous arrivames au gare St Lazare. J'ai déclaré my boite des cigarettes. But they did not charge me anything nor did they open mon mal.

We reached Versailles at 9 o'clock. I telegraphed to Everest immediately. "Arrived safe. Good passage." Apres le dejeuner we went for a walk. We saw soldiers, nothing but soldiers — De Seine de l'artillerie, des cuirassiers et de chasseurs a pieds. There are 6,000 hommes dans la garrison, and on Sat week there is to be a great review. 10,000 men march past. C'est une nation bien militaire. We then went into the "Grand Trianon" I saw that there was much to see. The skating is perfect. I want you to buy me a pair of skates. I do not like parting with 15 fr and a bad pair are useless.

*

Fatigue, the passage, The strange food, The cold, home sickness, the thoughts of what was behind & what was before nearly caused me to write a letter which would have been painful to you. Now I am better & I think that I will wait here my month though not one day more. Today we went to the "Bon Marché" in Paris. We spent 3 hours there. I bought a present for you, a blotting pad which I hope will give you as much pleasure to receive & it has me to buy; and for Jack I purchased something too, Also a "Sachée" for Everest.

The food is very queer, But there is plenty, & on the whole it is good. There is wine & beer to drink. I have a room to myself but it is awfully cold. However with rugs overcoats, dressing gowns etc I managed to sleep.

Tomorrow I am going to ride, in my boots.

I have already made great progress in French. I begin to think in it, in the manner in which the first part of my letter is written. M. Minssen says I know far more than he thought I did. These people are very kind. Of course I would give much to return, if you wish it I will come tomorrow — but considering all things I am prepared to stay my month.

I don't know how to get to see Baron Hirsch I am afraid you have not written. I would like very much to go and see them.

If you cannot get skates made to fit me — send me a line to the effect that you wish me to have them and are willing.

Goodbye my darling Mummy
Read this to Jack
With love I remain Your loving son
WINSTON

Winston to Lady Randolph

"Christmas Eve" [1891]   [Versailles]

Darling Mummy,

Thanks awfully for your telegram. I appreciate it muchly. We went for a long ride of 3 hours on the "chevaux de louage" [hired hacks] they were all right but M.M. rides very well & very hard at full gallop on the 'ard'igh road. Les chevaux ne sont pas mal. Ils sont veritablement rosses. Mme Monsieur M's mere ne dit rien que "Son progres est marveilleux." "N'est ce pas extraordinaire" etc etc.

Write to Baron Hirsch. Do! I have not heard a word from all those "friends" you spoke about.

With much love & kisses
I remain your loving son
WINSTON

Mrs Everest to Winston

EXTRACT

Saturday 11 a.m. [26 December 1891]   2 Connaught Place

My darling Winny,

I recd 2 letters from you this morning & it is such a relief to hear you are comfortable. Lucky for you that you have not been here we have not seen day light since last Monday 5 days utter darkness & no electric light scarcity of gas could not make any so I have lived in this room with a candle till I am half blind. This morning there is a change for the better. Your suit of clothes have come from Nicoll's, shall be sent on Monday. No Booking Office open today Boxing Day. I see it is just like Jacks.

Your letters shall be forwarded to Mamma today if she does not come home we don't know yet whether she is coming today or Monday. Jackie says in a letter to me he is getting on with his skating. The Gardener stands on the Bank with a cape for him. I see Baron Hersch is in Paris: Soon as you get your new clothes you must go & call on them. Winny dear do try & keep the new suit expressly for visiting, the Brown one will do for every day wear please do this to please me. I hope you will not take cold my darling take care not to get wet or damp.

I hear Papa started on the 24th so he will be here in 16 days. I expect he & Mamma will be coming to Paris to see you.

We had a very happy Xmas here. Edney [the butler] made himself very agreeable. We had an excellent Xmas dinner & supper & after supper they all sang songs & then we went into the kitchen & they put aside the table & danced for dear life no music Edney whistled & I played the comb with a piece of paper & comb like we used to do in our good old nursery days & they all thoroughly enjoyed themselves in a quiet way. Edney made a long toast or speech after dinner & we drank to the health & happiness of Mamma & Papa, Mr Winston & Mr Jack which of course I heartily joined in you may be sure. I have had 22 Xmas cards sent me. There were 2 letters came for you this morning so I took the envelopes off to enclose them in this because I should have had to pay 5d. instead of 2½ otherwise. Pray forgive me for so doing. One only had a card in it, from one of your school fellows I think. No writing on it only on the envelope & looked like a Boy's writing.

I hope you will try & feel happy. You will be seeing people you know then you will feel more reconciled. Charlie Balaam [her nephew] has been summoned up to be examined by the Bank authorities next Friday so I expect he will get in.

Thank you so much dearest for getting me a present it has not yet arrived. It is very kind of you but you know my Lamb I would rather you did not spend your money on me. Have you given Monsieur Minnsen the 5£ to keep for you that will have to last you I expect so be careful don't make it fly too fast. You don't know what you may want. I will write again — soon as I receive your present. Cheer up old Boy enjoy yourself try & feel contented you have very much to be thankful for if you only consider & fancy how nice it will be to be able to parlez vous francais. . . .

Winston to Lady Randolph

[? 27 December 1891]   [Versailles]

My darling Mummy,

I received your letter on Christmas Day. I spent a quiet Christmas. The mother is an English woman so we had the orthodox thing Turkey and plumpudding. Also a little fun on Christmas Eve.

Last night I went to the theatre to see Michel Strogoff, and did not return till 1 o'clock. I am very tired to day in consequence. I also went for a long ride yesterday with M.M. for 3 hours. The horses are very good considering. I have one somewhat like Gem, only capable of being galloped on the hard high road. He has a hogged mane, & lots of pluck, & eats biscuit.

Not a word from Baron Hirsch — Not a line from M. de Breteuil — Not a sound from Mr Trafford. I don't know any of their addresses so what can I do?

I would awfully like to have gone to-day to B.H. but . . . . . Please try and do something. A week will have gone when you receive this.

Monday 3 weeks I come home — at least my month is up. I will remind you of the promise you made me at Harrow of an extra week [at home] if I gave up my Christmas. A promise is a promise & as I have fulfilled my part I rely on you my darling mummy to do the rest. I know you won't chuck me like that.

I am longing to return. I think if all is well I shall be home on Monday 3 weeks. I count the hours. I won't travel 2nd again by Jove. They are too funny here. Last night we arrived (I & M) at 10 o'clock & we had nearly a mile to go through wet & mud. I had on my shoes. There were plenty of cabs — we needs must walk. That sort of thing is absurd.

I am going to have a look at the palace this afternoon so I must end.

Goodbye my darling Mummy
Hoping to see you in 3 weeks 21 hours, I remain your loving
WINSTON S. CHURCHILL

Winston to Lady Randolph

Tuesday [29 December 1891] 11 o'clock   [Versailles]

My dear Mamma,

It seems to me that with you "out of sight and out of mind" indeed. Not a line from anybody. You promised to write 3 times a week — I have recd 1 letter. There seems to be something wrong in the Postal arrangements between France & England as between Africa & London.

It is not at all kind of you, and, my darling Mummy, I am very unhappy about it. This is the 3rd letter I have written to you. I have also sent 2 to Jack & 3 to Everest. I wish you would try my mummy to fulfill your promise. Baron Hirsch may be in Jericho for all I know.

Please do something for
Your loving son
WINSTON S. CHURCHILL

The same day Mrs Everest wrote to express her delight at the sachet, which she had just received. As always she was solicitous about Winston's health. "If you feel sick or feverish or stomach out of order get a bottle of Eno fruit salt & take a tea spoon full in water. I should buy plenty of fruit & eat if I were you keep you *regular you know dear.*"

On 1 January 1892 the Marquis de Breteuil sent Winston a charming invitation asking him to propose himself any day for luncheon. Baron Hirsch also responded to Lady Randolph's instructions:

Winston to Jack

[? January 1892]   [Versailles]

Darling Jack,
    Just recd your letter. Many thanks. Keep the £1. J'ai assez.
When I return we will have much fun & great games with the army.
I have seen here such beautiful soldiers. At the "Bon Marche" I saw
a sho[?] of soldiers. Among many other French and Russian there
was a box of artillery men with 3 black cannons. They were in all
positions for loading & firing. Ramming home etc. Only 7 francs
= 5/-. I will, if you like to send me the money in about a week buy a
few battalions of Russians for you. 2 francs the dozen. And artillery
men, who have "fascines" for myself I think I will buy a box of
cannon also. The Russians are like this [sketch].
    So glad you like the present. Write to me. I wish I could meet
Papa. Lucky boy you are! Why didn't you burn that letter?
                              Good Bye, Much love
                                          WINNY
N.B. Invitations have come. Baron Hirsch Friday last Mr Trafford
Sat yesterday. Baron Hirsch Tomorrow M. de Breteuil Tuesday.
WSC

Winston to Lady Randolph

Friday [? 8 January 1892]   [Versailles]

Darling Mummy,
    Thank you very much for your telegram, I will go with much
pleasure Sunday. Have you recd my present? Is it arranged that I
return Monday week? Please give Papa my best love & tell him I am
so sorry not to be able to welcome him myself. If you are not too
busy, you might send me a line. I have recd my new suit. It fits
very well.
                    Good bye my darling Mummy,
            With much love, I remain, Your loving son
                                          WINSTON S.

Jack to Winston

Saturday 8 [9] January 1892   Canford Manor
                                              Wimborne
Dear Winney,
    Papa arrived yesterday morning looking very well [picture] but

with a horrid beard so raged [ragged]. He was expected to arrive on Thursday night and we started in the evening from Dorset. We had 9 miles to drive to the Sation and we missed the train by 6 minits. We had to wait 2 hours for the next train and then we had to wait ¾ of an hour at Salisbury. In the morning Mamma was fast asleep when she was woken up by Pace [her lady's maid] who said that the tender would start to meet the Scot in 15 minutes. The Glob [Globe] said Lady R. Churchill nimbly ran across the dock.

I remain Your loving brother
JACK S. CHURCHILL

Papa gave me Spanish notes for 2½
Thomas brought stamps.

Lady Randolph to Winston

Sunday 10 [January 1892]   Canford Manor
                                                              Wimborne
Dearest Winston,

Yr letter received today was very short — you do not tell me anything either of yr visit to Mr de Breteuil or to the Hirschs. What have you been doing? I am afraid that Mr Minssen was rather vexed at my letting you go out so often — I trust it does not make you neglect yr work. Write & tell me all about yrself & whether Mr Minssen is still pleased with you. Papa arrived on Friday. Jack & I went to meet him — Jack has written to you I know & has probably told you all we did. We return to London tomorrow. Papa is very well & in great spirits but his beard is a "terror." I think I shall have to bribe [him] to shave it off. Dearest boy don't be so lazy & neglectful about writing — you only seem to do so when you want something — & then you are very prolific with yr pen! I don't know when yr time is up. You must find out. I will write again shortly.

Best love Yr
MOTHER

Winston to Lord Randolph

[? 12 January 1892]   [Versailles]

My dear Papa,

Much Love and many kisses! I am so glad to hear from Mamma that you have come back safe and well. I was very sorry not to be able to go & meet you with everybody else. I have missed every thing this year. Christmas, New Years Day etc.

I went to see M. de Breteuil yesterday. I saw the M. "Tonton" he told me to tell you so. Afterwards Baron Hirsch took me to see the Morgue. There were only three.

Mamma says you are to come to Paris in 10 days. My month is up on Monday or ought to be for M. Minsen says a calendar month & I maintain a Lunar month was meant. The chief inducement Mamma held out to me to go to France was the promise of an extra week. Please do see what you can arrange for me. I have seen nothing of you or Jack or any body. I have only been home 2 days. If you would like me to wait here till you come to Paris and you would give me an extra week I would be delighted to do so. But I want to see Jack a little.

> Hoping to see you soon
> I remain Your loving son
> WINSTON S. CHURCHILL

Winston to Lady Randolph

[? 13 January 1892]   [Versailles]

My darling Mummy,

Il faut que je vous explique quelque choses. You addressed your letter to me a Paris. Result sent back and again forwarded by Edney. I had not recd. a letter from you for a fortnight when it arrived.

I have had lots of invitations. Last Monday I went to M. de B. and B. Hirsch after. He took me to the morgue. I was much interested. Only 3 Macabres — not a good bag. It is freezing hard and I am going skating this afternoon. I make much progress and Minnsen and I get on capitally.

I want either to come home Monday and see Jack and go on to France with you and Papa or — to wait here for Papa. I don't mind much which only you might easily bring Jack here too; But I am of course counting, my Mummy, on you to fulfil your promise which was more than anything the reason of my coming here willingly.

I must remind you it was a regular promise. I am willing and happy to leave all in your hands only I do hope . . .

I have written to Papa. Please write to me by return of post.

Winston S. Churchill,
   18 Rue de Provence,
      Versailles,
         France.

> With love and kisses I remain, Your loving son
> WINNY

Lord Randolph to Winston

15 January 1892   2 Connaught Place

Dearest Winston,

I was very glad to get your letter this morning. I think I will not try and get you an extra week because really every moment is of value to you now before you go up for your examination in June. The loss of a week now may mean your not passing, which I am sure you will admit would be very discreditable & disadvantageous. After you have got into the army you will have many weeks for amusement and idleness should your inclinations go in that direction, but now I do pray you my dear boy to make the most of every hour of your time so as to render your passing a certainty.

I remember when I was going up at Oxford for "final schools" I took something of an extra week & consequently altogether neglected what was called "special subjects." The result was that I just missed the First Class degree and only took a Second, & I have often thought since what a fool I was to lose the chance of a First for a few hours or days amusement. If you return Monday as I understand you will, we shall have a few days together before you return to Harrow, and after that the Easter holidays will soon be upon us, tho I must say I hope you will work like a little dray horse right up to the summer examination, only about four months off.

Your mother and I have just come back from Penn, Lord & Lady Howe's place where there was to have been a party for the Prince of Wales. Of course he could not come on account of the illness of the Duke of Clarence, & the party was broken up by the death of the poor Duke one of the saddest events I have ever known. Our party was naturally gloomy & dull. I shall stay on in London now & not go to Paris till Saturday week at the earliest. I think you must have had a novel & not unpleasant experience staying at Versailles. Hoping to see you back all safe Monday

Believe me ever Your most affte father
RANDOLPH S. C.

There was nothing Lady Randolph could do. "Papa showed me his letter to you," she wrote to Winston on the same day. "He won't hear of yr asking for an extra week. I am very sorry — but if you come home Monday you will have nearly a fortnight at home."

On his return to Harrow, Winston reported to Lord Randolph:

Winston to Lord Randolph

(*Blenheim Papers*)

Sunday 31 January [1892]   Harrow

My dear Papa,
   You will be glad to hear I have got my Remove. I was not very
pleased as I had hoped for a double. However Mr Welldon says if I
work well for a fortnight he will give me a Special Remove. I am
working hard at my fencing as I hope, with luck, to be champion.
Mr W. congratulated me on having enjoyed my holidays. I am in
Monsieur Minssen's French Prose division. I find that I have greatly
improved in French. There is of course no news, except that the
authorities try to avert the influenza by quinine pills and by prayers.
   Hoping you will come down and see me soon, I remain

                                             Your ever loving son
                                             WINSTON S. CHURCHILL

   Winston was small but pugnacious and the art of fencing came
easily to him. He had spent a good deal of time in the gymnasium.
His first authenticated published work, a letter to *The Harrovian*
written over the pseudonym of Junius Junior, complained of lack of
encouragement to boys to take a greater interest in the gymnasium's
activities, and was published in December 1891. He did indeed become fencing champion of the school in March 1892. He wrote to
Lady Randolph in the South of France:

Winston to Lady Randolph

[? 24 March 1892]   [Harrow]

Darling Mummy,
   I have won the Fencing. A very fine cup. I was far and away first.
Absolutely untouched in the finals. I have written to Papa. The
oranges were luscious.
   My eyes are alright, though I have to wear glasses when doing fine
work.
   I will write again tomorrow but it is awfully late.

                                             Ever your loving son
                                             WINNY

Lord Randolph to Winston

25 March 1892   2 Connaught Place

Dearest Winston,

I congratulate you on your success. I only hope fencing will not too much divert your attention from the army class. I enclose you £2 with which you will be able to make a present to yr fencing master. Jack came up the other day looking vy well & fit. Your mother writes that they are having lovely weather out at the Riviera. She does not yet speak of coming home.

Ever yr most affte father
RANDOLPH S. C.

Lady Randolph was in Monte Carlo. This was only the second time in his life that Winston had won anything on his own and Lord Randolph responded. Winston replied asking his father to come and see him at the Public School Championships at Aldershot and also, incidentally, asking for more money.

Lord Randolph to Winston

29 March 1892   2 Connaught Place

Dearest Winston,

I send you a P.O. £1, but you are really too extravagant. Do you mean to say you spent the £2 I sent you on the present to yr fencing master. If you were a millionaire you could not be more extravagant. I fear I cannot possibly get to Aldershot on the 7th it is Sandown races which I must go to. I think you have got through about £10 this term. This cannot last, & if you are not more careful should you get into the army six months of it will see you in the Bankruptcy Court. Do think this over & moderate your ways & ideas.

Ever yr most affte father
RANDOLPH S. C.

Winston to Lord Randolph
(Blenheim Papers)

[? 30 March 1892]   [Harrow]

Dear Papa,

Thank you so much for the £1. I must confess that I only spent £1 on a present for Sergt Queese, the other I employed in paying off some small sums I owed to various people. You don't know how easily one's money goes here. I have to get my own teas and generally my own breakfasts — say 2/- a day then comes another shilling on fruit, and "food." Total three shillings per diem = 18/- a week + 2/- for Sat night biscuits etc. — This comes up to £1 a week. There have been 11 weeks as yet!!!

The competition is not on the 7th but on Friday the 8th. If this should by any chance be more convenient to you — please write. If not don't trouble, as I know how busy you are.

Mr Welldon tells me that I must write and "stir you up" to come down and deliver a "jaw" on S. Africa. I can't tell you how much it would be appreciated by the Boys. Lord Wolseley's lecture on the Red River expedition would be quite eclipsed. Therefore let me beg you to come as soon as you can.

I remain ever your loving son
WINSTON S. CHURCHILL

At Aldershot Winston again won, beating Johnson of Bradfield and Ticehurst of Tonbridge to become the Public Schools Fencing Champion. It was only the second time that a Harrovian had won this championship and Winston was the only Harrovian champion at Aldershot that year. His cousin Dudley Marjoribanks was beaten in the final of the heavy-weight boxing championships and the gymnastics team, of which Leo Amery was the Captain, came fourth. Winston's success, according to *The Harrovian,* arose from the fact that he did not fight in the orthodox way, and "was chiefly due to his quick and dashing attack which quite took his opponents by surprise." Later *The Harrovian* commented again: "Churchill must be congratulated on his success over all his opponents in the fencing line, many of whom must have been much taller and more formidable than himself."

This was Winston's only individual sporting achievement at Harrow but during the Summer term he was one of the three swimmers who represented Welldon's in the final of the House swimming races and, by taking second and third places, beat Bushell's.

Winston's letters to *The Harrovian* — another one from Junius Junior was published in March — seemed to have borne fruit, for at the Assault at Arms in the gymnasium in December "the programme

contained a great deal more school work than it did last year. . . .
Long before the half-hour, the gymnasium was packed, nearly all the
school being present besides a large number of visitors." The fencing
event in which Winston was the star "passed off well."

The Summer term of 1892 was devoted to working for the Entrance Examination to Sandhurst — the "Further" as distinct from
the Preliminary Examination which Winston had passed in the
winter of 1890. The Examination took place in July and in the
middle of August Winston learned the result. He had failed. Out of
693 candidates he was 390th scoring 5100 marks; the minimum, at
this Examination, for entrance into the Cavalry was 6457 and into
the Infantry 6654. Winston's marks were as follows:

	Mathematics	Latin	French	English History
Maximum	2000	2000	2000	2000
WSC	568	601	1218	987

	Chemistry	English Comp	Drawing: Freehand	Geometrical
Maximum	2000	500	500	1000
WSC	829	305	196	495

It may be noted that his marks in English History were comparatively good. Out of 415 candidates who took the subject Winston
was 18th.

Mr Louis Moriarty the Army Class tutor, to whom, Winston later
acknowledged, he owed a great deal, sought to comfort him:

Louis Moriarty to Winston

EXTRACT

23 August 1892   [Harrow]

. . . I think your marks & place very creditable for your first try,
and I think you will remember that I had estimated the marks at less.
If you work earnestly & sensibly & above all keep it up through the
term I think you will pass all right this winter. But remember that
it is by no means a certainty, 1500 marks are a good deal to make in
about 3 months. (The Exam is on 20th Nov I think) Lang who was

only about 100 places out last December, & who since then had been working all day at Wren's, has failed I see. I think he would have been more likely to pass from here, as I am sure they over-crammed him. I am glad you are going to cram up your Euclid — there are marks to be made in that and I feel sure that your history might be more accurate, but I wish you were reading a few French novels (with a dictionary, & notebook for new words.) One can learn a lot of French like that, without apparent effort. . . .

Mr Welldon, however, was less pleased:

Reverend J. E. C. Welldon to Winston

10 September 1892   [Harrow]

My dear Churchill,

Thank you for sending me your marks, which have just reached me. I shall have something to say to you about them when we meet. But I feel it to be essential that in coming back to school you should come resolved to work not by fits & starts but with regular persistent industry.

The grammatical foundation of your languages is so uncertain that you lose marks which other boys gain. You have therefore ground to make up as well as new ground to cover.

If I did not think you would be sensible I should wire your father to take you away from Harrow now and send you to a "coach." But all depends on yourself.

Sincerely yours
J. E. C. WELLDON

And Lord Randolph was also displeased:

Lord Randolph to Frances, Duchess of Marlborough

EXTRACT

[? September 1892]   Banstead

. . . I don't think Winston did particularly well in the army examination. He was 300 places off the successful candidates 1500 marks less than the lowest successful & 700 marks less than Dudley M. However he has had two-vy kind and encouraging letters from his army class tutor & his mathematical master. His next try is on Nov 24th. If he fails again I shall think about putting him in business. I could get him something very good either through Natty [Rothschild] or Horace [Farquharson] or Cassel. . . .

At this time Lord and Lady Randolph with their family and servants moved to 50 Grosvenor Square and doubled up with Duchess Fanny. Both families were feeling the pinch. Lord Randolph had left 2 Connaught Place during the summer of 1892 and he gave up Banstead in October.

In September Winston returned to Harrow for what was to be his last term. Older boys at Harrow were, like the boys at Eton, allowed to have their own room but those who had brothers there could share a room with them.

Winston to Lady Randolph

[? September 1892]   [Harrow]

Dear Mamma,

We have now quite settled down. The room is very beautiful. We purchased in London sufficiency of ornaments to make it look simply magnificent.

Papa has written to Jack & says that you are better for the change. I rejoice.

I got my remove & when you come down to Harrow you will see yours truly in "Tails." Jack is getting on capitally though I think he finds he has plenty of work to do & that it is rather hard.

One of our hampers was spoiled "in transitu" owing to the careless manner in which it was packed.

There is of course no more news except that we both send our love & I remain

Your loving son
WINSTON S. CHURCHILL

P.S. I hope you can read this & if so I hope that you will not read it out for the amusement of those staying at Invermark. wsc

Lady Randolph was on her annual autumn round of the houses of her friends and relations in Scotland; but when she returned to London early in October she became gravely ill:

Lord Randolph to Winston

25 October 1892   50 Grosvenor Square

Dearest Winston & Jack,

Your dear mother was extremely ill yesterday & we were rather alarmed. But thank God today there is an improvement & the doctors are vy hopeful. I only got up to town this evening. I will keep you informed as to how yr dear mother progresses.

You will have heard of the vy sad death of your poor Uncle Roxburgh who taken vy ill last Monday had to undergo an operation Saturday to which he succumbed. You did not know him much but I was vy much attached to him & my poor sister Annie is quite heartbroken. Troubles accumulate just now. I pray you try & concentrate your thoughts on your work. Your mother would be in such good spirits if she thought you were going to do real well in yr examination. Kiss Jack for me.

Ever your affte father
RANDOLPH S. C.

In fact Lady Randolph had been very unwell for at least two weeks before Lord Randolph wrote this letter. It seems that she was suffering from a form of peritonitis for which at that time surgery was not recommended — the first well-known case for removal of the appendix was ten years later when King Edward VII was the patient. Lord Randolph was all this time in Scotland but an alarming letter from Dr Roose had brought him home to London in the third week of October.

These alarms came just as Winston was finishing his preparation for his second attempt at the Entrance Examination which took place late in November at the time of his eighteenth birthday. Mr. Welldon took the trouble to write a kindly letter to Lord Randolph:

Reverend J. E. C. Welldon to Lord Randolph

28 November 1892   Harrow

Dear Lord Randolph,

Winston is anxious that I should write to you about his prospect of success in the Examination which begins tomorrow. I do so gladly. His work this term has been excellent. He understands now the need of taking trouble, and the way to take it, and, whatever happens to him, I shall consider that in the last twelve months he has learnt a lesson of life-long value.

The two disadvantages under which he lies are that he was not well grounded, when he came here; hence he is still not safe against bad mistakes; and that he partially wasted the beginning of his public schooldays.

Still, when this is said, I am of the opinion that he is now well up to the level of passing into Sandhurst according to the standard which has been usual in past years. We are aware however that the level tends to rise and that, owing to the change which is being made in the age of admission, it is likely to be very high this time. At the next examination it will be normal again.

On the whole so far as I can judge from my own observation and the reports of his masters, I should say he has a very fair chance of passing now and is certain to pass in the summer if not now.

In giving this opinion I do not forget the perils of exercising the prophetic art; but it is due to him to say that of late he has done all that could be asked of him.

I hope Lady Randolph is recovering her health.

Believe me sincerely yours
J. E. C. Welldon

The legend, partly fostered by himself, that Winston was a preternaturally stupid little boy has doubtless encouraged habits of indolence in many generations of other schoolboys, and has no doubt often afforded some solace to their parents. We have seen enough of his work to denounce this legend as false. He was not stupid; indeed he early showed originality of mind. He was obstinate, rebellious and mischievous. No one could make him do or learn anything against his will. Unthinking schoolmasters found it easier to write him off as stupid than to scrutinize and adapt their own methods. Yet despite his ostensible failure at school, these unhappy years were far from wasted. His parents kept him at a distance and this, combined with his mutinous outlook at school, early compelled him to stand on his own feet and to make his way in the world by his own exertions and by his own methods. He had to fight every inch of his road through life; nothing came easily to him, not even oratory and writing, in which he was later to excel. To achieve success he had to develop that intense power of concentration which, as it grew, was to serve him and his fellow countrymen so well. In later life he was fond of quoting Napoleon's phrase: *L'art de fixer les objets longtemps sans être fatigué.* This priceless gift was perhaps intuitive to Napoleon — but it had to be remorselessly mastered by Winston. Nonetheless history may decide that he ultimately exercised this mental power as abundantly as did Napoleon.

6

Sandhurst

ON ABOUT 20 JANUARY 1893, Winston heard that he had failed in his "Further" Examination for Sandhurst for the second time. On this occasion he came 203rd out of 664 candidates with 6106 marks, compared with 5100 at his previous attempt.

	Mathematics	Latin	French	English History
Maximum	2000	2000	2000	2000
WSC	1063	425	1004	1273

	Chemistry	English Comp	Drawing: Freehand	Geometrical
Maximum	2000	500	500	1000
WSC	1229	264	247	601

Winston had declared himself shortly after taking the examination, "awfully depressed now that the examination is over." But he had added in a letter to his mother: "I did the Chemistry practical quite correctly and shall get good marks." For once Winston was right in his confident view about Chemistry. Out of 2000 marks he was awarded 1229. This was 400 more than he had obtained on the previous occasion. Of the 134 candidates who took this subject (and only 15 of them were successful) Winston was 8th. On the other hand he did less well in Latin, French and English Composition. Still, even if he had retained his previous marks in these subjects he would have failed in obtaining a cavalry cadetship by five marks. As Welldon had predicted, the standard this time was much more severe than before.

When it was clear that Winston had failed, but before the full details of the result were known, Lord Randolph had written to Welldon asking for advice as to what to do with Winston. Welldon replied:

Reverend J. E. C. Welldon to Lord Randolph

(*Blenheim Papers*)

EXTRACT

20 January 1893   Harrow

. . . I wish that, before answering [your questions], I could have seen Winston's marks in the recent examination. It will be a disappointment to me if it does not prove that he has so far improved his position in respect of his marks as to make it clear that he would have been successful, had the standard remained what it was a year or eighteen months ago, and that his chance of succeeding if he competes again will be excellent. Unless I am wrong, the total number of marks required for admission has in the last two examinations risen by as many as six hundred. It will clearly fall again — though nobody can say how much — at the next examination. On the other hand it is necessary to take into account the possibility of his not being well or not having reasonable good fortune in his papers.

If there were an opportunity then of getting him at once into a cavalry regiment, I should upon the whole be disposed to take advantage of it. The most successful "crammer" for the Sandhurst Examination is, I believe, Capt James. . . .

And to Winston Welldon wrote:

Reverend J. E. C. Welldon to Winston

23 January 1893   Harrow

My dear Churchill,

I am very much obliged to you for sending me the telegram. It seems to me to bear out what I have ventured to say to your father and yourself, *viz* that you would have passed or would have been on the borderline of passing, if the standard of marks had remained what it was two years ago, and that, if you make the same progress in the next six months as you made in the last your passing is assured. That is in my opinion not an unsatisfactory result; only, if you are going up again, do let me beg you to begin work at once and to carry it on with the greatest energy and regularity. I wish I had got you here.

Sincerely Yours
J. E. C. WELLDON

But Winston had left Harrow, and it was decided that he should go to Captain James's establishment.

Captain W. H. James to Lord Randolph

28 January 1893   5 Lexham Gardens

London W.

My Lord,
I shall be very happy to receive your son and should be pleased to see you at 12.30 on Monday next.

Yours faithfully
WALTER H. JAMES

Before these arrangements could be implemented, however, Winston first had to recover from an accident in which he came near to killing himself in a reckless escapade on January 10, at his aunt Cornelia's place, Canford, at Branksome Dene, near Bournemouth. Winston later provided a full account in *My Early Life:*

My Aunt, Lady Wimborne, had lent us her comfortable estate at Bournemouth for the winter. Forty or fifty acres of pine forest descended by sandy undulations terminating in cliffs to the smooth beach of the English Channel. It was a small, wild place and through the middle there fell to the sea level a deep cleft called a "chine." Across this "chine" a rustic bridge nearly 50 yards long had been thrown. I was just 18 and on my holidays. My younger brother aged 12, and a cousin aged 14, proposed to chase me. After I had been hunted for twenty minutes and was rather short of breath, I decided to cross the bridge. Arrived at its centre I saw to my consternation that the pursuers had divided their forces. One stood at each end of the bridge; capture seemed certain. But in a flash there came across me a great project. The chine which the bridge spanned

was full of young fir trees. Their slender tops reached to the level
of the footway. "Would it not," I asked myself, "be possible to leap
on to one of them and slip down the pole-like stem, breaking off each
tier of branches as one descended until the fall was broken?" I
looked at it. I computed it. I meditated. Meanwhile I climbed over
the balustrade. My young pursuers stood wonderstruck at either end
of the bridge. To plunge or not to plunge, that was the question!
In a second I had plunged, throwing out my arms to embrace the
summit of the fir tree. The argument was correct; the data were
absolutely wrong. It was three days before I regained consciousness
and more than three months before I crawled from my bed. The
measured fall was 29 feet on to hard ground. But no doubt the
branches helped. My mother, summoned by the alarming message
of the children, "He jumped over the bridge and he won't speak
to us," hurried down with energetic aid and inopportune brandy.
It was an axiom with my parents that in serious accident or illness
the highest medical aid should be invoked, regardless of cost. Eminent specialists stood about my bed. Later on when I could understand again, I was shocked and also flattered to hear of the enormous
fees they had been paid. My father travelled over at full express
from Dublin where he had been spending his Christmas at one of
old Lord [Justice] Fitzgibbon's once-celebrated parties. He brought
the greatest of London's surgeons with him. I had among other
injuries a ruptured kidney. It is to the surgeon's art and to my own
pronounced will-to-live that the reader is indebted for this story. But
for a year I looked at life round a corner. They made a joke about
it in those days at the Carlton Club, "I hear Randolph's son met
with a serious accident," "Yes?" "Playing a game of 'Follow my
Leader' " — "Well, Randolph is not likely to come to grief in that
way!"

In this account Winston, as will emerge, had somewhat exaggerated the length of his convalescence. In fact he was able to go back
to work in less than two months. One feels too, from this account, that
his decision to jump from the bridge may have been influenced by
Macaulay's lines of brave Horatius, which he had memorized at Harrow nearly five years before.

Lord Randolph's racing partner, Lord Dunraven, wrote from Ireland: "I do hope the boy is getting on all right. I suppose boys will

be boys, but I see no necessity for them believing themselves to be birds or monkeys and acting as such. . . ."

Winston's arrival at James's was thus delayed for some time. On February 8, Dr John Rose, a Harley Street specialist who had been called in, wrote to Dr Robson Roose advising that "Young Mr Churchill should not return to hard study any more than he should take vigorous exercise." This no doubt suited Winston. He was convalescing at Brighton, where he stayed with his aunt, Duchess Lily, whose husband, Blandford, the 8th Duke, had died in November. Blandford's death made Winston next-in-line to the Dukedom after his cousin Sunny and Lord Randolph. He remained in this perilous situation for four years until 1897 when Consuelo, the wife of Sunny, the 9th Duke, gave birth to a son who is now 10th Duke of Marlborough. It is amusing to speculate as to what would have happened to Winston's political career had his cousin Sunny died within those four years. Of course at that time Lord Salisbury was Prime Minister and it was not thought in any way unnatural for a peer to hold that office. But would Winston have espoused a political career in the House of Lords?

Winston did not arrive at James's until the end of February. Immediately he seems to have come into conflict with authority:

Captain W. H. James to Lord Randolph

(Blenheim Papers)

7 March 1893   5 Lexham Gardens

Dear Lord Randolph,

I have issued orders for your son to be kept at work and that in future he is to do the full hours. I had to speak to him the other day about his casual manner. I think the boy means well but he is distinctly inclined to be inattentive and to think too much of his abilities. These are certainly good and if he do as he ought he should pass very well in the summer, but he has been rather too much inclined up to the present to teach his instructors instead of endeavouring to learn from them, and this is not the frame of mind conducive to success. I may give as an instance that he suggested to me that his knowledge of history was such that he did not want any more teaching in it! I think you will agree with me that this is problematical. I have no doubt that between the two of us we can manage him well enough and I am glad to have received your letter of today.

I am sorry that I cannot see him personally as I am confined to my room with a bad cold on my chest but he will be spoken to and I shall let you know how he gets on.

The boy has very many good points in him but what he wants is very firm handling.

Yours very truly
WALTER H. JAMES

My Early Life recorded the methods used at this "crammer's" establishment:

It was said that no one who was not a congenital idiot could avoid passing thence into the Army. The Firm had made a scientific study of the mentality of the Civil Service Commissioners. They knew with almost Papal infallibility the sort of questions which that sort of person would be bound on the average to ask on any of the selected subjects. They specialised on these questions and on the answering of them. They fired a large number of efficient shot-guns into the brown of the covey, and they claimed a high and steady average of birds. Captain James — if he had known it — was really the ingenious forerunner of the inventors of the artillery barrages of the Great War. He fired from carefully selected positions upon the areas which he knew must be tenanted by large bodies of enemy troops. He had only to fire a given number of shells per acre per hour to get his bag. He did not need to see the enemy soldiers. Drill was all he had to teach his gunners. Thus year by year for at least two decades he held the Blue Ribbon among the Crammers. He was like one of those people who have a sure system for breaking the Bank of Monte Carlo, with the important difference that in a great majority of cases his system produced success. Even the very hardest cases could be handled. No absolute guarantee was given, but there would always be far more than a sporting chance.

For the Easter holidays Winston again went to stay with Duchess Lily at Brighton. "I am glad to have Winston with me," she wrote to Lord Randolph on April 5, "for I have grown really fond of the boy. He has lots of good in him and only needs sometimes to be corrected, which he always takes so smartly and well." But on resuming at James's there were more complaints:

Captain W. H. James to Lord Randolph

(*Blenheim Papers*)

29 April 1893   5 Lexham Gardens
Private

Dear Lord Randolph,
   I am sure you will feel that I am only impelled by kind motives in writing to you about your son. I have no definite complaint to make about him but I do not think that his work is going on very satisfactorily. All the tutors complain that while he has good abilities he does not apply himself with sufficient earnestness to his reading. He can and will succeed if he will but give up everything to the examination before him but I doubt his passing if he do not do this. Of course I feel that at a time like the present it is difficult for him not to take an interest in current political topics, but if this be done to an extent which takes his mind away from his studies, the result is bad for the latter. I have spoken to him on the question and I hope you will give him a little paternal advice and point out, what I have done, the absolute necessity of single-minded devotion to the immediate object before him, and the extreme desirability of thoroughness and detail [*sic*] attention to all he attempts.

Yours very truly
WALTER H. JAMES

Winston has described in *My Early Life* how, on 21 April 1893, he was squeezed into the Distinguished Strangers' Gallery to hear Mr Gladstone wind up the second reading of the Home Rule Bill. Out of affection for his father and out of interest, the lively young man was already beginning to be noticed in a small circle. The recently elected member for Dublin University, Edward Carson, with whom he was to be associated politically for the next forty years, invited him to dine at the House of Commons and afterwards to listen to the debate.

   "I have had a letter from Mr Carson," he wrote to his father on May 30, "inviting me to dine with him at the House on Friday evening. I have accepted as I have very little work on Saturday. If you would rather I would not go, please send me a line." But Mr Carson had to write postponing the visit: he had forgotten it was a Friday and that the House adjourned early.

Towards the end of June Winston sat for the Sandhurst Entrance Examination for the third time.

Captain W. H. James to Lord Randolph

(Blenheim Papers)

19 June 1893   5 Lexham Gardens

Dear Lord Randolph,

Without saying that your son is a certainty I think he ought to pass this time. He is working well and I think doing his best to get on but, as you know, he is at times inclined to take the bit in his teeth and go his own course.

I believe, however, I have convinced him that he has got to do what you wish him to do, and I have lately had no cause to complain of him.

It would not do to let him know what I think of his chance of success as with his peculiar disposition this might lead him to slacken off again.

I tell him that if he worked till he go up he ought to have a fair chance and though I think this is a minimum estimation still I feel it would not be advisable to say more to him.

Yours very truly
WALTER H. JAMES

On this occasion he was successful — but only just. He came 95th out of 389, four places and 18 marks too low to gain an infantry cadetship, but enough for a cavalry cadetship.

	Mathematics	Latin	French	English History
Maximum	2000	2000	2000	2000
WSC	1236	362	1233	1278

	Chemistry	English Comp	Freehand	Geometrical
Maximum	2000	500	500	1000
WSC	825	312	338	725

An indication of the fact that though Winston had to be crammed, he was always reading on his own outside the subjects to which the

Examiners attached particular importance is apparent in his marks for English History. Of the 104 successful candidates 53 took this subject, and Winston's 1278 out of 2000 was by far the highest. This achievement seems finally to nail the myth that he was a stupid or a lazy boy. When his interest was excited he could excel. By contrast his Latin marks show a different story. Of those who succeeded only five scored fewer marks than Winston.

Winston received the news of his success just as he was about to leave England for a walking tour in Switzerland with his brother and a tutor, Mr J. D. G. Little, a young master from Eton. Winston telegraphed to his father, to Duchess Lily and to Welldon. "I was so pleased to get your wire today and to know you had 'got in'!!!" wrote Duchess Lily on August 3. "Never mind about the Infantry: you will *love* the Cavalry, and when Papa comes back we will get the charger." Welldon wrote:

Reverend J. E. C. Welldon to Winston

4 August 1893   Harrow

My dear Churchill,

Your telegram being sent from Dover Pier makes me think you must have been on the point of leaving England.

But, even if it is long before you get this letter, I cannot help saying how much I rejoice in your success, and how keenly I feel that you have deserved it.

You have I hope learnt now what hard work is, and it will be a lesson of enduring value to you.

Sincerely yrs
J. E. C. WELLDON

Fortified by what he regarded as a scholastic triumph Winston wrote a somewhat insouciant letter to his father.

Winston to Lord Randolph

(Blenheim Papers)

6 August [1893]   Schweizerhof Hotel
Lucerne

Dear Papa,

I was so glad to be able to send you good news on Thursday. I did not expect that the list would be published so soon & was starting off in the train, when Little congratulated me on getting in. I looked in the paper & found this to be true. Several boys I know very well have got in too.

At Dover I sent off a lot of telegrams, and on the boat I received one from Grandmamma telling me I had passed.

We had a very rough crossing & poor Jack was very sick. At Calais we secured an empty first class carriage & travelled very comfortably to Amiens where 5 horrid people got in & stayed with us all night — till we got to Bale. Very uncomfortable it was — 8 people in one carriage.

We changed carriages at Bale & came on here in a coupe.

This is a splendid hotel — lifts, electric light, & fireworks (every Saturday). Tomorrow we are going away to Andermatt where our address will be . . . . Hotel Bellevue Andermatt. We leave here on the 9th. Lucerne is a lovely place. There are excellent swimming baths, & good food, & magnificent scenery. Yesterday we went up Pilatus, which was very interesting, & came down by the mountain Railway to Alpnack & so home by steamer. I had a telegram from Duchess Lily saying that she was going to look out for a good horse for me when I return . . . Also a letter.

*

I like Mr Little very much. He is unfortunately very lame, but is getting better slowly.

Miss Welldon is here with her husband a Harrow master named Stephen. She was married 3 days ago & this is the honeymoon. I talk lots of French to the waiters etc. Altogether we are enjoying ourselves immensely & I should be very sorry to come back if I were not going to Sandhurst.

Hoping that you are quite well & that the waters suit you

I remain your ever loving son
WINSTON S. C.

P.S. If you have time to write to us write to Hotel des Couronnes, Brigue.

This letter drew upon him one of the most formidable rebukes of Lord Randolph that survive; a short holograph extract is first reproduced:

Lord Randolph to Winston

9 August 1893　　　　　　　　　　　　　　　　　　Kissingen

My dear Winston,

I am rather surprised at your tone of exultation over your inclusion in the Sandhurst list. There are two ways of winning an examination, one creditable the other the reverse. You have unfortunately chosen the latter method, and appear to be much pleased with your success.

The first extremely discreditable feature of your performance was missing the infantry, for in that failure is demonstrated beyond refutation your slovenly happy-go-lucky harum scarum style of work for which you have always been distinguished at your different schools. Never have I received a really good report of your conduct in your work from any master or tutor you had from time to time to do with. Always behind-hand, never advancing in your class, incessant complaints of total wants of application, and this character which was constant in yr reports has shown the natural results clearly in your last army examination.

With all the advantages you had, with all the abilities which you foolishly think yourself to possess & which some of your relations claim for you, with all the efforts that have been made to make your life easy & agreeable & your work neither oppressive or distasteful, this is the grand result that you come up among the 2nd rate & 3rd rate class who are only good for commissions in a cavalry regiment.

The second discreditable fact in the result of your examination is that you have not perceptibly increased as far as my memory serves me the marks you made in the examination, & perhaps even you have decreased them, in spite of there being less competition in the last than in the former examination. You frequently told me you were sure to obtain 7000 marks. Alas! your estimate of your capacity was, measured arithmetically, some seven hundred marks deficient. You say in your letter there were many candidates who succeeded whom you knew; I must remind you that you had very few below you some seven or eight. You may find some consolation in the fact that you have failed to get into the "60th Rifles" one of the finest regiments in the army. There is also another satisfaction for you that by accomplishing the prodigious effort of getting into the Cavalry, you imposed on me an extra charge of some £200 a year. Not that I shall allow you to remain in the Cavalry. As soon as possible I shall arrange your exchange into an infantry regiment of the line.

Now it is a good thing to put this business vy plainly before you. Do not think I am going to take the trouble of writing to you long letters after every folly & failure you commit & undergo. I shall not write again on these matters & you need not trouble to write any answer to this part of my letter, because I no longer attach the slightest weight to anything you may say about your own acquirements & exploits. Make this position indelibly impressed on your mind, that if your conduct and action at Sandhurst is similar to what it has been in the other establishments in which it has sought vainly to impart to you some education. Then that my responsibility for you is over.

I shall leave you to depend on yourself giving you merely such assistance as may be necessary to permit of a respectable life. Because I am certain that if you cannot prevent yourself from leading the idle useless unprofitable life you have had during your schooldays & later months, you will become a mere social wastrel one of the hundreds of the public school failures, and you will degenerate into a shabby unhappy & futile existence. If that is so you will have to bear all the blame for such misfortunes yourself. Your own conscience will enable you to recall and enumerate all the efforts that have been made to give you the best of chances which you were entitled to by your position & how you have practically neglected them all.

I hope you will be the better for your trip. You must apply to
Capt James for advice as to your Sandhurst equipment. Your
mother sends her love.

Your affte father
RANDOLPH S. C.

That Lord Randolph's annoyance was genuine and was not merely
put on as a spur to Winston's future endeavours was shown by the
following:

Lord Randolph to Frances, Duchess of Marlborough

EXTRACT

5 [August] 1893   Hotel Victoria
                                             Kissingen

... I cannot think highly of Winston's [result]. He missed the last
place in the infantry by about 18 marks which shows great slovenliness of work in the actual examination. He only made about 200
hundred marks more than last time, I think not so many even as 200.
He has gone & got himself into the cavalry who are always 2nd rate
performers in the examination and which will cost me £200 a year
more than the infantry wld have cost. I have told you often & you
never would believe me that he has little [claim] to cleverness, to
knowledge or any capacity for settled work. He has great talent for
show off exaggeration & make believe. In all his three examinations
he has made to me statements of his performance which have never
been borne out by results. Nothing has been spared on him; the best
coaches every kind of amusement & kindness especially from you &
more than any boy of his position is entitled to. The whole result of
this has been either at Harrow or at Eton to prove his total worth-
lessness as a scholar or a conscientious worker. He need not expect
much from me. He will go up to Sandhurst when for the first time
in his life he will be kept in order & we shall see whether he can
stand military discipline. If he can he may rub along respectably.
I shall try & get Brabazon who has a regiment of Hussars to take
him & after 2 or 3 years shall exchange him with the infantry. Now
this is all truth & it is better to look facts in the face. When he is
at Sandhurst I wont have any running backwards & forwards to
London. He shall be kept to his work so that he may acquire the
elementary principles of a military education.

I will not conceal from you it is a great disappointment to me. I never had much confidence, James's 2 or 3 revelations as to his manner of working & his attitude to the tutors stopped all confidence. But I did hope seeing the chances he had he would show a considerable improvement on his last examination but one. There was much less competition in his last and the result was much worse & much more discreditable in a relative sense for Winston. Now dearest Mama goodbye; the above is only meant for you alone & need not be communicated to any of the family. After all he has got into the army & that is a result which none of his cousins have been able to do, but still that is a vy wretched & pitiable consolation.

Ever yr affte son
RANDOLPH S. C.

Lord Randolph had less than eighteen months to live. His performances alike in private and public were already causing deep concern to his friends and family. He was in the grip of the progressive mental paralysis from which he was to die. Allowance must therefore be made for the mental aberrations in the above letter, which lead him to a jumbled expression as to Winston's marks and also to the extraordinary delusion that Winston had been at Eton as well as at Harrow. The shadows were closing very quickly around him. On his return to England in the autumn he embarked on another programme of political speeches up and down the country. But it was a pathetic tour: his son recalled how "the crowds who were drawn by the old glamour of his name departed sorrowful and shuddering at the spectacle of a dying man, and those who loved him were consumed with embarrassment and grief."

Winston's mother also wrote:

Lady Randolph to Winston
EXTRACT

Monday 7 August [1893]   Kissingen

Dearest Winston,

We have just received your letters & are very pleased to think you are enjoying yrselves — I am glad of course that you have got into Sandhurst but Papa is not very pleased at yr getting in by the skin of yr teeth & missing the Infantry by 18 marks. He is not as pleased over yr exploits as you seem to be! . . .

Winston replied to his father's rebuke :

Winston to Lord Randolph

EXTRACT

14 August 1893   Continental Hotel
                                                   Milan

Dear Papa,

I received your letter this morning. It had been forwarded here from Brigue. I am very sorry indeed that you are displeased with me. As however you tell me not to refer to the part of your letter about the Examination I will not do so, but will try to modify your opinion of me by my work & conduct at Sandhurst during the time I shall be there. My extremely low place in passing *in* will have *no* effect whatever on my chance there. . . .

All the necessary equipment & outfit are supplied at Sandhurst at a charge of £30. I have nothing to do but to be there on the 1st Sept.

Thank you very much for writing to me. I am very sorry indeed that I have done so badly.

                                       Ever your loving son
                                       WINSTON S. CHURCHILL

P.S. Excuse smudge &c as pens & blotting paper are awfully bad.

                                                                WSC

Mr Little, in a letter to Lord Randolph, gives some idea of the effect of Lord Randolph's letter on Winston:

J. D. G. Little to Lord Randolph
(*Blenheim Papers*)

EXTRACT

19 August [1893]   Hotel de Zermatt
                                                   Zermatt

. . . Your letter to Winston arrived while we were at Milan. I had not of course received your letter to myself. When he showed me your letter, we had a long talk and he told me a good deal about his views of men and things. He was a good deal depressed; I pointed out to him that in going to Sandhurst he began, what was practically a new page in his Life; and that such opportunities were a completely new start, occurred at most but once or twice in a lifetime, and ought therefore to be made the most of. Whatever he did at Sandhurst would have a permanent effect on his career in the army, and he ought therefore to make a sustained effort for the next year and a half to do his best, and pass out high. I think he intends to try hard. . . .

Mr Little had been recommended to Lord Randolph by his old Merton contemporary (and opponent at Woodstock) George Brodrick, from whom he received the highest recommendation — "He is a thorough gentleman and anything but a Don." Both Mr Little and Winston sent detailed accounts of their holiday to Lord and Lady Randolph who were at Kissingen for the cure. Winston did not, however, tell either his tutor or his father of the narrow escape he had from drowning while on the lake near Lausanne. It is related in *My Early Life*. He rowed out with another boy a mile from the shore; they took off their clothes and went swimming. Suddenly a breeze sprung up and it was only with the utmost difficulty that Winston managed to regain the boat and row back for his companion. He had seen Death, he recalled later, "as near as I believe I have ever seen him. He was swimming in the water, whispering from time to time in the rising wind . . ."

As usual Lord Randolph was not very sanguine about the progress being made by Winston and his tutor:

Lord Randolph to Frances, Duchess of Marlborough

EXTRACT

20 August 1893   Kissingen

. . . We have heard from the boys from Brienz & they were going on to Zermatt & Chamonix. I do not at all approve of their having gone down into Italy & to such a dirty unhealthy town at this time of year as Milan. Besides that tearing about & not remaining for some days in one place is very expensive & I doubt if they have much money left. I have written to Little to let me know how the funds are & if the money is all gone I shall tell them they had better return to England. I expect Winston has overpowered Little & taken the entire command of all the travelling arrangements. . . .

In fact Mr Little still had plenty of money in hand, having spent £27 on the return fare from London to Lucerne and £81 on the first three weeks of the tour, leaving him with £92 of the £200 that Lord Randolph had given him for the six weeks' tour. Mr Little's own remuneration amounted to £25 for the six weeks which he considered "very adequate." Winston left Mr Little and Jack in Geneva and set out for London on August 28. He told Lord Randolph before his return:

Winston to Lord Randolph

EXTRACT

23 August 1893   Hotel des Couronnes
                                                                   Brigue

. . . I should start from Geneva for London — via Basle and Paris on Monday night. We have to be back at Sandhurst by 8 o'clock on Friday. This I learn from some "gentleman cadets" I met on a walking tour.

The only clothes I want are a dark blue serge or cloth morning suit. I have only got smart clothes for London and shooting suits. What I want is a light suit to wear for travelling or in the country. If you think this unnecessary I could manage by having a pair of trousers to match one of my *knee breeches suits.* If I don't hear to the contrary I will order the former. This will save you writing about it unless you object.

Otherwise I think that I have everything except the uniform — which they will supply to me. I am looking forward to going there very much more especially as it gives me an altogether fresh start on a course which is certainly "paved with good resolutions". . . .

On his arrival in London he found that because a number of other aspirants had failed to take up their cadetships to Sandhurst that year, he had after all been given the opportunity of going into the Infantry:

Winston to Lord Randolph
(*Blenheim Papers*)

30 August 1893   50 Grosvenor Square

Dear Papa,

I am writing to you to explain my telegram of this morning. As to the Infantry Cadetship: on arriving in London last night I called at Grosvenor Square for letters and found, among others, this enclosure from the Military Secretary. I have no doubt that you will be pleased to find that I have got an Infantry cadetship and shall be able, after all, to enter the 60th. [*The enclosure has not survived*].

As regards the money I had when I left Geneva about 140 fr (£5.10.0.) This, the expenses of the journey — viz diner — dejeuner — porters — cabs — registration of luggage — hotel in Paris etc etc reduced to £2.13.6d. which sum I have by me at the present time.

There are sure to be some things I shall *have* to pay at once on joining. Others that I ought to pay — for instance, Clubs and subscriptions — as soon as I can. Then there are the expenses of today and tomorrow in London and of the ticket and cab to Sandhurst on Friday. There are also such expenses as furnishing my room etc. If I have a room with two other boys I shall be expected to do my share. If I get a room to myself it will want some sort of decoration. I enclose a circular which I have received which will show you that this *furnishing* is not uncommon.

I hope you will not be angry with me for writing to you on this subject. I should so much like to have an annual allowance — payable quarterly. Out of it I would get my clothes, pay for my amusements — railway journeys — and sundries (cigarettes etc): in fact everything. I would then know how much I was going to have and what I had to do with it. You would also know what I was given. Whereas at present (the last 6 months particularly) you have given me money when I wanted it — (more or less). (I am afraid I don't make my meaning very clear).

As to the amount, you know, much better than I do, what I ought to have. Sandhurst, is, very much, on the same footing as the "Varsity," except of course for the military discipline — and I should think the expenses would be about the same.

You see in 18 months I shall be in the army — and I should like very much to have a trial beforehand.

Please do not be displeased with me for writing to you on this point. I am afraid I have been very extravagant in the past and have frittered a great deal of money away. But I have had no responsibilities to bear. I should very much like a trial on the allowance system during the next 18 months.

You will see on the enclosure that you will be expected to pay £150 per annum to the College. Harrow used to cost £80 a term or £250 a year (clothes and pocket money extra). There will be no extras at Sandhurst at all. If you decide to give me an allowance I will promise to keep account of what I spend and send them to you regularly.

I have written a very long letter and have taken up a lot of your time. Hoping you will send me some money for my immediate needs (I don't know what to do if you don't) & you will not be angry with me for what I have written,

I remain ever your loving son
WINSTON S. CHURCHILL

Address after Friday
Royal Military College Sandhurst

Winston had also written to his mother to enlist her help:

Winston to Lady Randolph

30 August 1893   50 Grosvenor Square

Dear Mamma,

I got your letter this morning. You did not say anything about the absorbing topic — money. I have written a long & respectful letter to Papa to ask him to give me an allowance. Please try & persuade him. It would be much better & cheaper than the present arrangements which are

"Spend as much as I can get"
"Get as much as I can"

I have been very anxiously awaiting a letter from Papa. But I have had none since the one he wrote me on my examination 3 weeks ago. I hope he will be pleased to hear that I have got into the infantry after all.

I had a very tiring journey from Geneva. I stayed 5 hours in Paris — hoping to see the Eiffel Tower but 'twas shut. I went to the Hotel de Louvre & had bath & breakfast. (I wanted both after 18 hours in train). Then I walked about till it was time to go & so came safely here.

I do not know what I shall do unless I get some money before the 1st proximo. I would have written & asked for some only I expected by every post a letter from Papa. Good-Bye dear Mamma — I will write to you from Sandhurst on Sunday.

I remain, Your Ever loving son
WINSTON S. C.

Lord Randolph agreed:

Lord Randolph to Frances, Duchess of Marlborough

EXTRACT

3 September 1893   Staubinger Hof
Gastein

. . . I am very glad that Winston has got an infantry cadetship. It will save me £200 a year. I shall see the Duke of Cambridge when I get back & remind him about the 60th Rifles. I enclose you a letter I received from Winston. I wrote telling him that I thought he was somewhat precipitate in his ideas about an allowance & that his figures were too summary. I told him I would give him £10 a month out of which he would have to pay for small articles of clothing, & for other small necessaries but that I will continue to pay his tailor & haberdasher while he was at Sandhurst. I also demurred to paying for furniture for his rooms till [I] was better informed as to what was necessary. I also told him to send me a list of the subscriptions which he considered he had to pay. I think that £10 is ample of the present. I wrote very kindly to him & did not lecture. I don't agree with you about the Duchess Lily being a useful friend to him. I think her very silly & gushing and I should be horrified if he got money from her. . . .

To Lord Randolph Winston gave the first detailed account of his life at Sandhurst. He wrote on his first Sunday:

Winston to Lord Randolph

(Blenheim Papers)

3 September [1893]   Royal Military College
Sandhurst
Camberley

Dear Papa,

I am very glad to be able to write to you on this extremely smart paper. [*It bears the Royal Arms surrounded by standards surmounted by the Crown with the motto* Vires Acquirit Eundo. *The whole device is gold, red and blue.*]

On Friday I left London by the 12.20 and got down here in time for lunch. Since then I have had little or nothing to do. Yesterday there was a drill at 10 o'clock for an hour and today there has been a parade and Church.

The first 3 days are devoted chiefly to being measured for the Uniform and finding one's way about — the latter no easy task in so huge a building. Tomorrow (Monday) however, work begins in earnest. At 6.30 Revelly sounds and you have to be dressed by 7 o'clock.

I am very contented and like the place very much — though it is freely said that it "combines the evils of the life of a private school-boy with those of a private soldier." The room I have with 2 others is very large and divided into cubicles like stalls in a stable [diagram]. I had first choice and so have the best of the 3.

Of course it is very uncomfortable. No carpet or curtains — No ornamentation or adornments of any kind — No hot water and very little cold (as far as I can make out) but the motto of the college is *"Nec aspera terrent."*

The Discipline is extremely strict — Far stricter than Harrow. Hardly any *law* is given to juniors on joining. No excuse is ever taken — not even with a plea of "didn't know" after the first few hours: and of course no such thing as unpunctuality or untidiness is tolerated. Still there is something very exhilarating in the military manner in which everything works; and I think that I shall like my life here during the next 18 months very much.

I am in E. Company the "crack" Company of the battalion, and next term I shall have a room to myself. In addition to your own room — each cadet can go and sit in the Company *ante-room* — which is furnished very comfortably as a smoking room and where are *all* the daily and weekly papers. Besides this there are 2 billiard rooms to each Company and a capital Library and reading room with chess and card tables.

The Food here is not very good but you can add to it by ordering extras e.g. jam — coffee — wine — fruit etc. Smoking is allowed everywhere and cigarettes are handed round after dinner — I should say "mess."

This is the great meal of the day and counts as a parade. As our mess uniforms are not finished we have to wear the ordinary dress-clothes and in these we assemble in the ante room. Then the Company butler solemnly announces dinner and you walk down a quarter of a mile of stone passage till you reach the dining hall. The dinner is very grand — and the names of the dishes are written in

French on the menu. There is nothing else French about them. After dinner there is no work and billiards and whist finish the day.

"My Servant" sounds very nice — but this part of College machinery is rather out of gear and requires frequent oiling. He will however black boots — pipe clay belt and clean rifle — clear away slops and on occasion (when he has been tipped) do odd jobs for you.

Altogether, I like the life. I am interested in the drill and in the military education I shall receive; and now that the army *is* to be my trade I feel as keen as I did before I went in for any of the Examinations. At any rate I am sure that I shall be mentally, morally, and physically better for my course here. Hoping you will write to me and send me some money for myself.

I remain ever your loving son
WINSTON S. CHURCHILL

And the following day he resumed:

. . . The work is very heavy for the first 6 weeks & there are many extra parades for juniors.

Of course for the present I have very little time. Reveille is at 6.30. 1st study at 7. Breakfast 8 — parade at 9.10. Study from 10.20 to 1.50. 2 o'clock luncheon — 3 o'clock afternoon parade (¾ hour); 5 o'clock to 6 Gymnastics. 8 o'clock Mess. So you see there is hardly any time for writing or idling. The only five subjects they teach here are

    1 Fortification (with geometrical drawing)
    2 Tactics
    3 Topography
    4 Military law
    5   "   administration

I like the work — but the physical exertion of one day is so severe that at the end of one day I feel regularly fatigued. . . .

My position in the College is that of a junior. That is to say one who has passed the last exam. In four months I shall become an "intermediate" and my last term here a "senior." Everyone is technically equal except the corporals and under-officers — but it is more usual for juniors to associate mainly with cadets of their own standing. I am sure I shall get on here with the boys — as I know a

good many and have of course been with many at James's. Do you
know he passed 20 this time. Thank you very much for your very
generous allowance. . . .

The Royal Military College was founded in 1802 and ten years
later it was established on its present site near the village of Sandhurst, some thirty miles from London on the main Portsmouth road.
About 120 young men were accepted for cadetships every half year,
and when Winston was there the course consisted of three terms
spread over 16 months. The college was divided into six companies
each under the command of an officer-instructor. Winston's, E
Company, was commanded by Major Oswald James Henry Ball of the
Welsh Regiment. The commandant, or Governor as he was then
known, had arrived at Sandhurst at the same time as Winston. He
was Major-General Cecil James East. Unlike Major Ball, who had
the misfortune of never having seen active service, General East had
been present at the siege of Sevastopol and had taken part in the
fighting in the Indian mutiny in which he was severely wounded.
The cadets themselves received promotion while they were at the
college, each company having a quota of under-officers, senior
corporals and corporals. They wore a uniform of blue serge, and for
full dress, one of scarlet and gold. A number of changes were made
at Sandhurst around the time Winston was there. Musketry became
a compulsory subject — one in which Winston was to persevere after
he had obtained his commission; polo, on the other hand, was soon
to be abolished on the grounds of expense. The Visitors who reported on the college in 1893 complained of "great laxity in collecting
the mess bills of the college"; the consequent reforms more than once
led Winston into financial embarrassment.

*

We have seen in Lord Randolph's letter of August 5 to Duchess
Fanny how he was determined that Winston should go to London
as little as possible. This question of Winston's leave soon became
pressing: it was immediately evident that Lord Randolph's earlier
view was not a passing whim.

Winston to Lord Randolph

(*Blenheim Papers*)

10 September [1893]   [53 Seymour Street]

Dear Papa,

I have received the £10 alright; thank you very much for that. My Company Officer Major Ball says he prefers that instead of a list of relations etc parents should send a signature to say "Please place no restrictions on my son's leave."

He is an awfully good sort — though fearfully strict on parade — and says he like to feel he can trust his Company.

I have now been ten days at Sandhurst and like it more than ever. Major Ball told me he would give me leave for yesterday and today as he always gives one leave without waiting for the home list or permission so I am staying with Grandmama Jerome. Tonight I go back to RMC.

The work is very interesting and extremely practical. Shot and shell of all kinds — bridges, guns, field and siege, mapping, keeping regimental savings bank accounts — inspecting meat etc form the "study" work. Then there are all the parades and drills.

It is not a bit of good turning up for parade or study *punctually*. You are bound to be *in your place* when the bugle sounds. So far I have been ten minutes too early for everything. Public opinion of the College is tremendously against unpunctuality.

I want your leave to ride, also, as there are excellent horses in the village. Please send me the two signatures as I want to ride very much.

There does not seem to be much fury against the House of Lords for throwing out the HR [Home Rule] Bill [*having been carried in the Commons on September 1 after 82 nights of discussion*].

Thanking you very much for your letter

I remain ever your loving son
WINSTON S. CHURCHILL

Lord Randolph to Frances, Duchess of Marlborough

EXTRACT

15 September 1893   Gastein

. . . I send you a letter from Winston. I have demurred to "unrestricted leave," and have told him he can come to town when his mother is there. I have declined paying for horses. I do not see what an infantry cadet wants with a horse. Winston's letters are generally full of requests for unnecessary things and articles. . . .

Frances, Duchess of Marlborough to Lord Randolph

(Blenheim Papers)

EXTRACT

20 September [1893]   Guisachan

. . . I quite agree with you about Winston's letter which I keep for you. It is the nature of all Boys of his age especially sharp ones to be rather scratching to get all they can in order to compare favourably with their fellows & I think you are right to turn a deaf ear & to make your favours in proportion to his merits. Still I prefer his open requests & there is one advantage he is very frank and open in his pertinacity. I think the *no restriction* permission is most objectionable & the request for a Horse unnecessary. You give him such a liberal Allowance that it would seem he could easily hire one occasionally. But the great thing is for him to feel he is not the son of a rich man and also that he is at Sandhurst not for amusement but to distinguish himself. I know how easy it is to preach and yet how difficult to guide a Boy! I begin to think a *strict* training is the best. . . .

Winston to Lady Randolph

17 September [1893]   [Sandhurst]

My dear Mamma,

Your letter arrived last night, and made me feel rather unhappy. I am awfully sorry that Papa does not approve of my letters. I take a great deal of pains over them & often re-write entire pages. If I write a descriptive account of my life here, I receive a hint from you that my style is too sententious & stilted. If on the other hand I write a plain and excessively simple letter — it is put down as slovenly. I never can do anything right.

Thank you very much for your letter. I am afraid that you have reason to be cross with me for not writing to *you*. I will not give you cause again. Do come back as soon as you can as I am longing to see you.

I find that you do not have to obtain permission from home to ride — but only to play polo — so the Infantry cadet will be allowed to ride for amusement until next term when *all* the boys are taught together. As to leave — it is very hard that Papa cannot grant me the same liberty that other boys in my position are granted. It is only a case of trusting *me*. As my company officer said he "liked to know the boys whom their parents could trust" — and therefore recommended me to get the permission I asked for. However it is no use my trying to explain to Papa, & I suppose I shall go on being treated as "that boy" till I am 50 years old.

It is a great pleasure to me to write to you unreservedly instead of having to pick & choose my words and information. So far I have been extremely *good*. Neither late nor lazy, & have had always 5 minutes to wait before each parade or study. Yesterday I went out riding with a charming Eton boy (he is 19½) whose acquaintance I have made. We got to Aldershot & were having a stiff gallop when his saddle slipped round & he fell on his head. Of course he was stunned & has now got concussion of the brain. I revived him as well as I could — with brandy & water & then had to hire a cab to drive all the way back to Sandhurst. I took him to see a doctor on the road who said he had had a marvellous escape of breaking his neck. The whole thing was a great responsibility & rather expensive.

When I got to the college they treated it most coolly: were not the least disturbed or put out. He was taken to the casualty ward & attended by a gorgeously clothed surgeon. Today he is quite sensible & I have had a long talk with him.

Well I have told you all about my life. I am cursed with so feeble a body, that I can hardly support the fatigues of the day; but I suppose I shall get stronger during my stay here.

The drill is progressing and my shoulders are greatly improved.

Goodbye dear darling Mummy.

Ever so much love & more kisses from your ever loving son

WINSTON S. CHURCHILL

P.S. You see I have tried to spoil my handwriting for your sake. Is it any better?

Winston's administration of brandy and water would seem to imply that he did not until some time later consider its administration to concussed people as "inopportune" — the phrase which he much later applied in *My Early Life* to his mother's first aid in the chine at Bournemouth.

As to being "cursed with so feeble a body" Winston, though he was soon to become more robust, seems at this period to have had physique and stamina that were a little below standard. According to the Sandhurst measurements his height was 5 feet 6½ inches: a report submitted by the authorities in September 1893 showed that his chest measurement was 31 inches with an expansion of 2½ inches. This was thought inadequate, and he and a number of other cadets who were also listed were held to be unfit for commissions unless they could increase their chest measurement and expansion powers before they left Sandhurst. In these circumstances it seems exceptionally unreasonable for Lord Randolph to have grudged his son a horse.

In *My Early Life* Winston has put on paper his considered views on horses:

> Horses were the greatest of my pleasures at Sandhurst. I and the group in which I moved spent all our money on hiring horses from the very excellent local livery stables. We ran up bills on the strength of our future commissions. We organised point-to-points and even a steeple-chase in the park of a friendly grandee, and bucketed gaily about the country-side. And here I say to parents, and especially wealthy parents, "Don't give your son money. As far as you can afford it, give him horses." No one ever came to grief — except honourable grief — through riding horses. No hour of life is lost that is spent in the saddle. Young men have often been ruined through owning horses, or through backing horses, but never through riding them; unless of course they break their necks, which, taken at a gallop, is a very good death to die.

Winston's earlier anxieties about money and about the prompt payment of his allowance unfortunately recurred:

Winston to Lady Randolph

EXTRACT

20 September 1893   Sandhurst

. . . I am looking forward to see you — but shall have to continue looking for some time yet. I want you to explain to Papa that on the 6th of October I have to pay the Canteen bill & extra messing account: probably over £4. They only give 24 hours notice & anyone not producing the money — is posted on a blackboard. Of course it will come out of my £10 per month. Only I want you to remind Papa — so that he should not send it late — as a day would make all the difference. I hope in future months to have a balance — but the expense of coming here — of carpet & chairs etc have swallowed that. I have however sufficient to keep me going till the 3rd or 4th of October. . . .

Unfortunately at this time Lord and Lady Randolph were themselves particularly sharply beset by money problems:

Lord Randolph to Lady Randolph

EXTRACT

6 October 1893

. . . Dearest I am vy sorry but I have no money at the present moment & balance overdrawn at bank. I am selling Deep Levels [*South African mining shares in which he had invested £10,000 in 1891.*] but it is vy difficult to get 46 for them now, & I must not sell more than £500. I will try & send you £105 to Paris to Hotel Scribe. . . .

However, Lord Randolph seems to have been impressed by Winston's progress and to have realized that the £10 per month allowance was inadequate.

Winston to Lady Randolph

EXTRACT

21 October 1893   Tring Park

. . . Papa was very pleased to see me and talked to me for quite a long time about his speeches & my prospects. He seemed very interested in the RMC intelligence [*news of Sandhurst*] & gave me a cheque for £6 to pay my mess bill with. . . .

Lord Randolph to Frances, Duchess of Marlborough

EXTRACT

24 October 1893

. . . I took Winston to Tring on Saturday. He had to leave at 4.30 afternoon to get back to Sandhurst. He has much smartened up. He holds himself quite upright and he has got steadier. The people at Tring took a great deal of notice of him but [he] was very quiet & nice-mannered. Sandhurst has done wonders for him. Up to now he has had no bad mark for conduct & I trust that it will continue to the end of the term. I paid his mess bill for him £6 so that his next allowance might not be *"empieté"* [encroached] upon. I think he deserved it. . . .

Though his mind by this time was clouded Lord Randolph seemed to show more understanding of Winston's latent interests and ambitions. In *My Early Life* the son was to give a sympathetic account of his father's treatment of him at this time:

Once I became a gentleman cadet I acquired a new status in my father's eyes. I was entitled when on leave to go about with him, if it was not inconvenient. He was always amused by acrobats, jugglers, and performing animals; and it was with him that I first visited the Empire Theatre. He took me also to important political parties at Lord Rothschild's house at Tring, where most of the leaders and a selection of the rising men of the Conservative Party were often assembled. He began to take me also to stay with his racing friends; and here we had a different company and new topics of conversation which proved equally entertaining. In fact to me he seemed to own the key to everything or almost everything worth having. But if ever I began to show the slightest idea of comradeship, he was immediately offended; and when once I suggested that I might help his private secretary to write some of his letters, he froze me into stone. I know now that this would have been only a passing phase. Had he lived another four or five years, he could not have done without me. But there were no four or five years! Just as friendly relations were ripening into an Entente, and an alliance or at least a military agreement seemed to my mind not beyond the bounds of reasonable endeavour, he vanished for ever.

At this time the financial embarrassments with which Lord and Lady Randolph were much afflicted combined with difficulties inseparable from "doubling up" with relations, even in Grosvenor Square with Duchess Fanny, who herself was not very well off, resulted in what one must be inclined to regard as the rather shabby treatment of Mrs Everest. This provoked an honourable and intrepid reaction from Winston. It should, however, in justice to Duchess Fanny and Lord and Lady Randolph, be pointed out that Winston cannot have known of the financial difficulties which explained, if they do not excuse, what seems on the face of it to have been a particularly thoughtless action:

Winston to Lady Randolph

EXTRACT

29 October [1893]   [Sandhurst]

My dear Mamma,

I have felt very uncomfortable since I got here about Everest. I fear that at the time you told me — I was so occupied with Jack & Harrow that I did not think about it seriously. Now however — I have a very uneasy conscience on the subject. It is quite easy, dear Mamma, for you to say that it is not my business or for you to refuse to read what I have got to say — but nevertheless I feel I ought in common decency to write to you at length on the subject.

In the first place if I allowed Everest to be cut adrift without protest in the manner which is proposed I should be extremely ungrateful — besides I should be very sorry not to have her at Grosvenor Square — because she is in my mind associated — more than anything else with *home*.

She is an old woman — who has been your devoted servant for nearly 20 years — she is more fond of Jack and I than of any other people in the world & to be packed off in the way the Duchess suggests would possibly, if not probably break her down altogether.

Look too at the manner in which it would be done. She is sent away — nominally for a holiday as there is no room at Grosvenor Square for her. Then her board wages are refused her — quite an unusual thing. Finally she is to be given her congé by letter — without having properly made up her mind where to go or what to do.

At her age she is invited to find a new place & practically begin

over again. Of course I am extremely fond of Everest & it [is] perhaps from this reason that I think such proceedings cruel & rather
mean.

I know you have no choice in the matter & that the Duchess has
every right to discharge a servant for whom she has "no further
use." But I do think that you ought *to arrange that she remains at
Grosvenor Square — until I go* back to Sandhurst & Jack to school.

In the meantime she will have ample time to make up her mind
where to go — to find a place & resign herself to a change.

Then when a *good* place *has been* secured for her she could leave
and be given a pension — which would be sufficient to keep her from
want — & which should continue during her life.

This is what I should call a fair and generous method of treating
her. It is in your power to explain to the Duchess that she *cannot* be
sent away until she has got a good place.

She has for 3 months been boarding herself out of her own money
and I have no doubt is not at all well off. Dearest Mamma — I
know you are angry with me for writing — I am very sorry but I
cannot bear to think of Everest not coming back much less being
got rid of in such a manner. If you can arrange with the Duchess &
persuade her to let Everest stay till after Christmas — I should feel
extremely relieved. If you can't, I will write and explain things to
Papa, who will I am sure forgive me troubling him. . . .

*

Leave was to continue to be a source of dispute with Lord
Randolph:

Lord Randolph to Winston

EXTRACT

10 February 1894   Le Nid

. . . If you get through this time well, the rest will follow more
easily. Mind if you do well at Sandhurst & get good reports good
positions in the classes & even the good conduct medal you would go
to your regiment so much higher in credit & more thought of. So if
you feel at times like giving way or falling off "Don't." Pull your-

self together & keep yourself well abreast & even ahead of those you are competing with. I rather advise you not to come up to London too often. Your mother & I can run down. It does not seem such an awful journey. Lastly take care of your health. Keep down the smoking, keep down the drink & go to bed as early as you can. . . .

Even when his reports showed him doing well, Lord Randolph still maintained restrictions:

Lord Randolph to Winston

13 April 1894   50 Grosvenor Square

My dear Winston,

I have to thank you for two letters. The Bradford meeting in St George's Hall was very fine & crowded in every corner. Mr Balfour made a very fine speech and received an enthusiastic greeting.

Now I turn to another subject on which I must write seriously. You have written two letters, one to your grandmother, one to me, announcing your intention of coming up to town on Saturday. Now to this I particularly object. You have been just one day over a week at Sandhurst & you get restless & want to get away. Now this is your critical time at Sandhurst and you have got to work much harder than in the former term. If you are always running up to town every week on some pretext or other & your mind is distracted from your work besides being an unnecessary expenditure of money. Now I am not [going to] have you this term come to London more than once a month, and I give you credit for not coming to London without my knowledge. Now it is no use your telling me there is nothing to do on Sunday, because you can do work on Sunday instead of loitering about as I expect you do & getting through no work. I remind [you] that your holidays you rode in Knightsbridge riding school & that practice placed you ahead of the other cadets.

The same result will arrive if you devote on Sunday at least 3 hours of real study. You will have that advantage of extra knowledge over those cadets who take their leave for Saturday & Sunday, or who do nothing all day. You not only gain Sunday but you gain some two hours extra on Saturday. Now all this may seem to you very hard & you may be vexed and say that "all work & no play makes Jack a dull boy." But it is no use complaining about what I

tell you to do, for if you act as I advise you, you will excel at Sandhurst and the sacrifice of your taking your leave so frequently will be
amply rewarded, and I shall be ten times more pleased with you than
if you resumed your habits of coming to London many times in the
term.

You are 20 & in November 21 [*he was a year out in his calcula-
tions*] & you must remember always that you are a military cadet
and not a Harrow schoolboy. Now is the time to work & work hard;
when you are in the regiment your work may be slightly relaxed,
by the performance of regimental duties. But even then if you desire to be thought smart & well trained & well informed about all
the details of your profession you should still carefully keep up all
your Sandhurst acquirements. Why do I write all this. Because
when you go into the army I wish you to make your one aim the
ambition of rising in that profession by showing to your officers
superior military knowledge skill & instinct.

This is all written in perfect kindness to you. If I did not care
about you I should not trouble to write long letters to you. I shall
always take a great interest in you & do all I can for you if I am
certain you are wrapped up in your profession. You need not answer
this letter. I only want you to think over it and agree with it.

Lord Randolph's attitude made Winston "rather unhappy."

In his second term at Sandhurst Winston was involved in a misadventure which shed much light on the characters of both Winston
and his father: he lost his watch. It was a good gold watch which he
had been given by his father. One day it was broken and taken to
Messrs Dent's, who early in March 1894 informed Winston that the
watch required a new balance staff, minute wheel, pinion, second
hand and glass, re-adjustment, compensation, a repaired case and
cleaning. The cost would be £3, and a watch was being forwarded on
loan by registered post. As ill luck would have it Lord Randolph,
six weeks later, went into Mr Dent's to see about his own watch.

Lord Randolph to Winston

21 April 1894   50 Grosvenor Square

Dear Winston,

I have received your letter of yesterday's date & am glad to learn that you are getting on well in your work. But I heard something about you yesterday which annoyed & vexed me very much. I was at Mr Dent's about my watch, and he told me of the shameful way in which you had misused the very valuable watch which I gave you. He told me that you had sent it to him some time ago, having with the utmost carelessness dropped it on a stone pavement & broken it badly. The repairs of it cost £3 17s. which you will have to pay Mr Dent. He then told me he had again received the watch the other day and that you told him it had been dropped in the water. He told me that the whole of the works were horribly rusty & that every bit of the watch had had to be taken to pieces. I would not believe you could be such a young stupid. It is clear you are not to be trusted with a valuable watch & when I get it from Mr Dent I shall not give it back to you. You had better buy one of those cheap watches for £2 as those are the only ones which if you smash are not very costly to replace. Jack has had the watch I gave him longer than you have had yours; the only expenses I have paid on his watch was 10/s for cleaning before he went back to Harrow. But in all qualities of steadiness taking care of his things & never doing stupid things Jack is vastly your superior.

Your vy much worried parent
RANDOLPH S. CHURCHILL

Once again Lord Randolph did not confine his angry words to Winston. He wrote to Lady Randolph in Paris:

. . . I have written a letter to Winston he wont forget . . . I assure [you] the old Mr Dent was quite concerned at one of best class of watches being treated in such a manner. . . . I wound up by telling him that in all qualities of steadiness taking care of thing[s] and of not doing stupid things Jack was vastly his superior. You see I was really very angry for I cannot understand anybody not taking the greatest care of a good watch, but also because he had never told me a word about it. However as I said he wont forget my letter for some time & it will be a long time before I give him anything worth having. I wanted you to know this as he may tell you a vy different story. . . .

Winston replied to his father:

Winston to Lord Randolph

(Blenheim Papers)

22 April [1894]   Sandhurst

My dear Father,

I have been very unfortunate about the watch — which I kept safely the whole time I was at James's during our tour in Switzerland — and all last term. But about 6 weeks ago I broke it and within a fortnight of its being mended it is broken again. So really I have had it for over a year without an accident and then come 2 in a fortnight. Yet I have been no less careful of it during that fortnight than during the preceding year.

The first accident was not my fault at all. I had a leather case made for the watch — during the daytime to protect it and I was putting it into it when it was knocked out of my hand by a boy running past.

This time I am more to blame. I placed the watch (last Sunday) in my breast pocket — not having with uniform a waistcoat to put it in — and while walking along the Wish Stream I stooped down to pick up a stick and it fell out of my pocket into the only deep place for miles.

The stream was only about 5 inches deep — but the watch fell into a pool nearly 6 feet deep.

I at once took off my clothes and I dived for it but the bottom was so uneven and the water so cold that I could not stay in longer than 10 minutes and had to give it up.

The next day I had the pool dredged — but without result. On Tuesday therefore I obtained permission from the Governor to do anything I could provided I paid for having it all put straight again.

I then borrowed 23 men from the Infantry Detachment — dug a new course for the stream — obtained the fire engine and pumped the pool dry and so recovered the watch. I tell you all this to show you that I appreciated fully the value of the watch and that I did not treat the accident in a casual way. The labour of the men cost me over £3.

I would rather you had not known about it. I would have paid for its mending and said nothing. But since you know about it — I feel I ought to tell you how it happened in order to show you that I really valued the watch and did my best to make sure of it.

I quite realise that I have failed to do so and I am very very sorry that it should have happened. But it is not the case with all my things. Everything else you have ever given me is in as good repair as when you gave it first.

Please don't judge me entirely on the strength of the watch. I am very very sorry about it.

I am sorry to have written you such a long and stupid letter, but I do hope you will take it in some measure as an explanation.

> With best love
> I remain ever your loving son
> WINSTON S. CHURCHILL

Thus early did Winston reveal his resourcefulness, his ability to organize and his talent for command. Lady Randolph at once wrote to soothe Winston:

Lady Randolph to Winston

Sunday [22 April 1894]   Hotel Scribe

Dearest Winston,

I am *so* sorry you have got into trouble over yr watch — Papa wrote to me all about it. I must own you are awfully careless & of course Papa is angry after giving you such a valuable thing. However he wrote very kindly about you so you must not be too unhappy. Meanwhile I'm afraid you will have to go without a watch. Oh! Winny what a harum scarum fellow you are! You really must give up being so childish. I am sending you £2 with my love. I shall scold you well when we meet.

> Yr loving
> MOTHER

Winston appreciated this letter:

Winston to Lady Randolph

24 April [1894]   Sandhurst

My dearest Mamma,

Thank you so much for your letter — which I have just received. Papa wrote me a long letter about the watch and seems to be very cross. I wrote back at once saying how sorry I was and explaining the whole affair & got a letter by return of post — last night. I think that by his letter Papa is somewhat mollified. I hope so indeed. But how on earth could I help it. I had no waistcoat to put the watch in and so have had to wear it in the pocket of my tunic.

Papa writes, he is sending me a Waterbury — which is rather a come down.

I am very sorry it should have happened — as you can well believe — and sorrier still that Papa should have heard of it. But I feel quite clear in my own mind that I am not to blame except for having brought so good a watch back here — where there is everything in the way of its safety.

However a Waterbury is as the regulations say "more suited to my position as a cadet" and there is not much time to lament, here now.

It is so dear of you to have written me such a kind letter & for sending me the £2. You are the best and sweetest Mamma in all the world. With lots of love & kisses,

I remain, Ever your loving son
WINSTON S. CHURCHILL

But Winston was not quite sure whether in fact his father had been "mollified." On April 30 he writes to his mother: "Papa has not written to me for some time and I am uncertain whether he is still angry with me or not." And on the following day: "I hope he is not incensed about the watch anymore. I wish you would send me a line on the subject. Also I wd be very grateful if you would draw Papa's attention to the date (May 1) as I am not particularly rich owing to the £3 I had to disburse for my watch."

Winston to Lord Randolph

(Blenheim Papers)

30 April [1894]   Sandhurst

My dear Papa,

I got the watch on Saturday morning — for which many thanks. I do hope you are not angry with me anymore about it. On Sunday I stayed with Col Brabazon at Aldershot. He very kindly asked me down and I enjoyed myself very much indeed.

We are going through a course of Musketry which is very interesting and which we all like as it does not begin until half past seven and so we get a little longer in bed. The riding is going on very well and so is work etc.

This morning I had a letter from a man offering to lend me money on note of hand — I took it to Major Ball and he has forwarded it to the Governor — but I am afraid there is no chance of bringing the man to book.

I will write you again very soon — but for the present have nothing more to say.

Hoping that you will not think any more of the watch and with best love

I remain, ever your loving son
WINSTON S. CHURCHILL

Lord Randolph drew the incident to a close in a calmer tone than he had adopted at the beginning:

Lord Randolph to Winston

1 May 1894   50 Grosvenor Square

Dear Winston,

You need not trouble any more about the watch. It is quite clear that the rough work of Sandhurst is not suitable for a watch made by Dent. I daresay you had a pleasant Sunday with Colonel Braba-zon. I am glad to hear the work is going on well, and the riding. I suppose your old volunteer experiences [at Harrow] will make the course of musketry less strange to you. Never attend to money-lenders, put their letters into the waste paper basket. If you would like to come up on the 5th of May I am afraid you won't find me at dinner for I dine at the Royal Academy dinner, but your mother will be here & you might do a play.

Ever your affte father
RANDOLPH S. C.

The affair of the moneylender was treated with great earnestness. The papers were forwarded to the Director of Public Prosecutions with a view to prosecuting the moneylender, one Fred Ellis, for attempting to obtain business from a minor. But after careful enquiries it emerged that the moneylender's letter had not been sent to Winston direct at Sandhurst (where the moneylender must have known he was writing to a minor) but had been forwarded from Blenheim. No action was consequently taken.

Winston had seen Colonel Brabazon the previous month when the latter, "magnificently dressed," had come over from Aldershot to

Camberley to officiate at the Staff College riding examination there. Winston told his father (March 13): "He has asked me to go and stay at Aldershot the first Saturday we are here after Easter."

Colonel Brabazon, a 10th Hussar, had just taken command of the 4th Hussars at Aldershot. An impoverished Irish landlord, his military career had on several occasions suffered for lack of funds. Nevertheless, by his dash and gallantry in the field and by the sheer force of his personality off it, he established himself as a man of redoubtable character in the eyes of the War Office and of Society. Lord and Lady Randolph had known him for many years and it seemed therefore natural that Winston should have turned to him for help in his efforts to get into the cavalry.

Winston to Lady Randolph

EXTRACT

11 January [1894]   Hindlip Hall
                                                    Near Worcester

My dearest Mamma,

I have written to Colonel Brabazon and have stated my various arguments in favour of cavalry regiment. I have asked him to say whether or no they are correct — when he writes to you — but in case he should not state this clearly I will put them down for you.

1. Promotions much quicker in Cavalry than in Infantry (60th Rifles slowest regiment in the army).

2. Obtain your commission (3 or 4 months) in Cav much sooner than in Infantry.

3. 4th Hussars are going to India shortly. If I join before "Augmentation" I should have 6 or 7 subalterns below me in a very short time.

4. Cavalry regiments are always given good stations in India and generally taken great care of by the Government — while Infantry have to take what they can get.

5. If you want to keep a horse you can do it much cheaper in the cavalry than in infantry — government will provide stabling — forage — and labour.

6. Sentimental advantages grouped under heading of
    a. uniform
    b. increased interest of a "life among horses" etc

   c. advantages of riding over walk

   d. advantages of joining a regiment some of whose officers you
      know. i.e. 4th Hussars.

The first 5 of these reasons I wrote to Col Brabazon the last I write
to you.

There you are — now don't ever say I did not give you any reasons
— There are 5 good solid arguments.

On April 26 Brabazon had confirmed in writing his verbal invitation to Winston to spend Saturday to Monday with the 4th Hussars:
"If you can come go and see Captain Julian Byng of the 10th Hussars
who is coming over also. You might come over with him." Winston
duly went with the future hero of Vimy Ridge but news of the visit
travelled fast and on the Sunday Lady Randolph wrote: "A bird
whispered to me that you did not sleep in yr own bed last night.
Write to me all about it. I am not sure if Papa wld approve." Lady
Randolph had divined the ulterior motive behind Winston's visit
which Lord Randolph, from his letter, did not seem to have guessed
at. Winston did not trouble to hide it from her:

Winston to Lady Randolph

EXTRACT

1 May [1894]   Sandhurst

My dearest Mamma,

   I have just got your letter. I should not think that Papa would
object to my having stayed with Col Brab at Aldershot. He distinctly
wrote to me that he did not want me to come up to London much.
I wrote yesterday to him and told him all about it.

   I should like to come up on Saturday as I have not been to London once this term — and want to see Jack & yourself. I altogether
protest against being perpetually immured down here.

   I had great fun at Aldershot — the regiment is awfully smart. — I
think they did not always have a good name — but Col Brab did
not take long in knocking them into shape. I met Capt Bobby
White who asked to be remembered to you.

   How I wish I were going into the 4th instead of those old Rifles.
It would not cost a penny more & the regiment goes to India in 3

years which is just right for me. I hate the Infantry — in which physical weaknesses will render me nearly useless on service & the only thing I am showing an aptitude for athletically — riding — will be no good to me.

Furthermore of all regiments in the Army the Rifles is slowest for promotion. However it is not much good writing down these cogent arguments — but if I pass high at the end of the term I will tackle Papa on the subject. . . .

To his father, however, he did not confide these hopes:

Winston to Lord Randolph

3 May [1894]   Sandhurst

My dear Papa,

I was so delighted to get your letter of yesterday & shall be delighted to come up for Saturday. It was very pleasant staying with Colonel Brabazon at Aldershot. He has made such a smart regiment of the 4th. They used to be considered very slack — but he has worked a wonderful change. It was quite extraordinary how clean and smart the men were. It was the first time I have ever messed with a regiment — and the ceremony interested me very much. In the afternoon we went for a walk to the Mausoleum Chislehurst.

Everything is going very well here and I am getting on steadily in my work. Out of a riding class of 29 there are only about 6 who have not yet been off — but I have so far avoided a fall. Next term I hope to be in the First Ride. However that is looking ahead.

I have nearly finished Hamley [*The Operations of War*]. It is a very solid but interesting work. I am reading a very good book I got from Bain on Artillery which will take some time. This letter consists entirely of "shop" but I know you take an interest and won't mind.

Thanking you once more for writing, & with best love.

Ever your loving son
WINSTON S. CHURCHILL

Although Winston had after all obtained a place in the infantry list, Lord Randolph was determined to leave nothing to chance; he had sought out the Duke of Cambridge to remind him of a former promise to get Winston into his regiment, the 6oth Rifles. The

October meeting at Newmarket provided the ideal opportunity. On 12 October 1893 Lord Randolph reported from the Jockey Club Rooms to both his mother and to Lady Randolph that he had settled the matter and that the Duke had promised to get Winston into the 60th; but Winston, as we have seen, and soon Brabazon himself, had other ideas.

*

Winston's increasing independence showed itself in a determination to choose not only his own career but also his own friends, especially those among his relations. The very size of the Marlborough family and the extensive correspondence among them which the scattered nature of their homes entailed lent itself to the building up of formidable legends about individuals, some based on fact or bitter experience, others on mere hearsay or a desire to make mischief. Duchess Lily who had early befriended Winston came under Lord Randolph's gravest suspicion:

Lord Randolph to Frances, Duchess of Marlborough

EXTRACT

28 October 1893

... Winston has gone to Eton to spend a day & night with Mr Little. He comes back here on tomorrow. He wanted to go & stay with Dss of Lily but I told him he had seen nothing of his mother & ought to devote himself to her. For some reason or other also I do not care about his being with the Duchess Lily. A dinner or lunch *"ça se passe"* but staying in her house is not vy good for him. You never know what state she may be in. . . .

This would seem to imply that Duchess Lily was bibulous; apart from Lord Randolph's passing remark there is no evidence for this. Sir Shane Leslie, who knew her when he was a young man, has told the author that as far as he knew the suggestion is untrue. Lord Randolph had for some years effectively cut himself off from his brother the 8th Duke. The breach over the Aylesford affair was healed for a brief period following the death of their father in 1883; but almost immediately it was reopened when the new Duke decided to sell the great collection of paintings at Blenheim. Apart from a few nights' shelter at Blenheim for Winston and Jack when Duchess Fanny asked them to Blenheim to escape the diphtheria in 1888, Lord Randolph's family was completely estranged from the Duke. So that when he died unexpectedly in November 1892 Winston hardly knew his cousin Sunny, who succeeded as 9th Duke a few days before his twenty-first birthday. When it was time to make arrangements for Christmas the following year, it was hoped that Winston and his brother Jack would spend the holiday with their uncle's family, the Leslies at Glaslough in Ireland, and this was indeed arranged by Lady Randolph. But a more attractive proposition presented itself and Winston gladly availed himself of it. Lady Blandford, "Bertha," the new Duke's mother, now came back to Blenheim and invited him there.

This fitted in well with his plans for he had intended to spend a few days in Worcestershire with Lord and Lady Hindlip, their son Charles Allsopp and their niece, Molly Hacket. "I arrived here last night after rather a cold journey," Winston wrote to his father from Blenheim on Christmas Eve. "Sunny and Lady Blandford are very kind to me and want me to stay here till Tuesday week. If you think fit I shall stay here until I go to Hindlip as you can go straight from here without the necessity of going to London." Lord Randolph commented in a letter to his mother: "I do not mind his going to Blenheim as long as I dont go there myself. They seem to make a fuss with him & of course he knows nothing of the past."

Winston was fascinated by Blenheim:

Winston to Lady Randolph

25 December [1893]   Blenheim

My dear Mamma,

   I am enjoying myself here very much — though there is plenty of divine service. Every one is very kind and civil to me & Lady Blandford has really gone out of her way to make me comfortable. I suggested going on Tuesday but she would not hear of it & told me that she expected me to stay until the following Monday. It would be very convenient if I were to go direct from here to Hindlip as it is only an hour and a quarter — by train.

There is no sort of party & I am quite alone with Sunny. He is very good company and we have sat talking till 1.30 every night since I have been here.

I have also had long talks with Lady Blandford or "Aunt Bertha" as I am getting to call her. She really is most kind. Altogether I am quite content at the prospect of staying a week here & am in no hurry to get back to town.

On my way back from Hindlip I think I shall go — with your permission — and stay with the Dillon's at Ditchley . . . but that can be arranged later.

Hoping you were not bored to death in town — that Papa looked well — and that you had a "Happy Christmas"

I remain Ever your loving son
WINSTON S. CHURCHILL

To his aunt Leonie he wrote on Boxing Day from Blenheim: "Perhaps you are astonished at the paper. Sunny very kindly asked me down here for the Christmas week. He is such an interesting companion and anything but the idiot I was taught to believe him to be." And a few days later he wrote to his mother:

Winston to Lady Randolph

EXTRACT

30 December [1893]   Blenheim

. . . Sunday has been very kind and we have had very lengthy conversations. It is most untrue to say he is stupid. He is very sensible & I think clever — extremely industrious and attentive to business and he seems to have made himself very popular among the tenantry and neighbours. . . . I shall be extremely sorry to leave on Monday and nothing but the thought of the beautiful Polly Hacket consoles me. Lilian & Nora [*his cousins*] are very amusing and rather pretty. Lady B [Blandford] is charming. Altogether I have had a very pleasant week and I am particularly glad to have made Sunny's acquaintance. . . .

P.S. Mind you don't show this letter to anybody.

Winston's friendship with his cousin became a firm and lasting one, and it remained constant, despite family quarrels of the past and political differences, over the next forty years.

*

Riding, it will have been noted, was one of Winston's main interests and undoubtedly he did extremely well, only just failing in the end to be at the head of the riding class. He owed much of his success to the extra lessons which he received during his holidays in Hyde Park from Captain Burt, the riding master of the Life Guards. In his academic examinations he was also proving very successful and the results of his first term in December 1893 placed him among the first twenty of his course. He obtained 1198 out of 1500 marks, his best subjects being Tactics for which he got 278 out of 300 and Military Law (276). Only in Military Topography (199) did he have much leeway to make up. The official remarks under the heading "Conduct" were "Good but unpunctual." In July 1894, his marks fell away somewhat and he scored only 1140. While he had made up a lot of ground in Fortifications, scoring 254 as against 215 in December, he lost a lot on Military Law (218) and on Military Administration (195 instead of 230). The comment on his conduct was this time merely "Unpunctual." Either Winston was not as punctual as he thought he was or his standards declined as his self-confidence grew. Certainly in later life he was notoriously unpunctual, but since from an early age trains, cars and ships — and later aeroplanes — waited for him he was seldom conscious of this social weakness.

Two letters written about this time from Miss Mabel Love, a young musical comedy actress at the Lyric Theatre, survive. There is nothing to show what degree of intimacy existed between the young people:

Miss Mabel Love to Winston

[? July 1894]   169 Buckingham Palace Road
                                                          [London S.W.]

Dear Mr Churchill,

I must apologise for not having returned the photos sooner but I have been very busy lately on account of my rehearsals for the Lyric. I am afraid I don't know anything funny or amusing so have just written my name. I shall look forward to seeing you when you come to town.

Yrs sincerely
MABEL LOVE

Miss Mabel Love to Winston

[? September 1894]   169 Buckingham Palace Road

Dear Mr Churchill,

   I signed and addressed the photos you sent me some time ago, and have only just come across them finding they had been mislaid instead of posted, so am sending a line to apologise for my seeming rudeness.

Yrs v. truly
MABEL LOVE

That Miss Love was widely admired is attested by the enthusiasm with which Winston's acquaintance with her was saluted in a letter from a contemporary Harrow friend, George Wilson: "How did you manage to meet Mabel Love, I rather envy you as pretty females are few and far between down here," in Bannockburn.

In his last term at Sandhurst Winston became involved in a highly enjoyable escapade arising out of a campaign by a Mrs Ormiston Chant and members of the London County Council to separate the bars of the Empire Theatre in Leicester Square from the adjoining promenade where attractive and good-natured ladies of the town used to parade themselves, particularly on a Saturday evening. The whole of the story — and perhaps more than the whole of the story — is preserved with exceptional verve and brilliance in *My Early Life*. This account should be consulted by all readers who are interested to recall the passions that this episode aroused. Writing nearly forty years later Winston was to relate how he went up to London from Sandhurst to be present at the formation of "The Entertainments Protection League" in defence of the old Empire, and how at a seedy London hotel he met the founder and one and only member of the League. The well-constructed speech which was in his pocket no doubt later formed the basis of the letter which he contributed over his initials to the correspondence on the fate of the Empire Theatre which raged in the *Westminster Gazette*. This letter, signed WLSC, was his first publication in a national newspaper:

> The improvement in the standard of public decency is due rather to improved social conditions and to the spread of education than to

the prowling of the prudes. . . . Now, Sir, I submit that the only method of reforming human nature and of obtaining a higher standard of morality is by educating the mind of the individual and improving the social conditions under which he lives. This is a long and gradual process, the result of which is not to be obtained in our generation. It is slow, but it is sure. . . .

In the meantime it is the plain duty of every Government to endeavour, as far as possible, to localise and minimise the physical effects of the moral evil. . . . In England we have too long obeyed the voice of the prude. Well-meaning but misguided people, of which class Mrs Ormiston Chant is a fair specimen, have prevailed upon Government to disclaim a responsibility which it was their bounden duty to accept. . . .

If our impetuous reformers could only be persuaded to wait, and to take a broader and perhaps a more charitable view of social problems, they would better serve the cause they have at heart. But these "old women in a hurry" will not have patience, but are trying to improve things by repressive measures — a dangerous method, usually leading to reaction.

But his most dramatic action in this episode took place on November 3, the Saturday after the partitions had been erected, when he was at the head of a mob of two or three hundred which stormed the barricades and tore them down.

Mounting on the debris and indeed partially emerging from them, [he wrote in *My Early Life*] I addressed the tumultuous crowd. No very accurate report of my words has been preserved. They did not, however, fall unheeded, and I have heard about them several times since. I discarded the constitutional argument entirely and appealed directly to sentiment and even passion, finishing up by saying, "You have seen us tear down these barricades to-night; see that you pull down those who are responsible for them at the coming [municipal] election."

To his brother Jack he wrote disarmingly: "It was I who led the rioters — and made a speech to the crowd. I enclose a cutting from one of the papers so that you may see."

Winston was always a courageous and candid boy, and he made

little secret of his part in these activities. He wrote to his mother, to his aunt Leonie and to Lord Randolph about them. Referring to his letter to the *Westminster Gazette* in the issue of October 18 he wrote to Lady Randolph:

Meanwhile I have been making an essay of journalism. The County Council wish to close the Empire and a most bitter controversy is raging in every paper on the subject. I enclose you the *Westminster Gazette* in which I have a letter — which they were good enough to print. It may perhaps interest Papa. Tomorrow I have got a long letter in the *Daily Telegraph* which I will send you. Of course I only sign them W.L.S.C.

Unfortunately the *Daily Telegraph* had closed its correspondence on the subject by the time Winston's letter was received. To his aunt, Mrs Leslie, Winston wrote:

It is hard to say whether one dislikes the prudes or the weak-minded creatures who listen to them most. Both are to me extremely detestable. In trying to be original they have merely lapsed into the aboriginal. The "new woman" is merely the old Eve in a divided skirt.

And to his father he had written:

Winston to Lord Randolph

EXTRACT

29 October [1894]   [Sandhurst]

. . . The Empire is closed. The last scene was quite pathetic. On Friday night the whole audience remained after the fall of the curtain groaning the County Council and calling for George Edwardes who eventually came forward and made a short speech, when a scene of extraordinary enthusiasm took place — The great audience standing up and cheering themselves hoarse. But Saturday the place was closed and the "prudes" have gained a great victory.

I don't quite know what your opinion on the subject may be — but I am sure you will disapprove of so coercive and futile a measure. Lord Rosebery, by the way was very cautious and would give no opinion. . . .

Lord Randolph by this time was scarcely in a position to pass judgement, though this Winston did not yet know. Three months before Lord Randolph's health had started to deteriorate to an alarming extent; the older members of the family knew that he was suffering from a severe mental disease. His speeches both in the country and in the House had become increasingly embarrassing; he often became confused and lost the thread of his argument; his enemies chattered or left the House; his friends absented themselves discreetly or sat in silence in embarrassed grief. Sir Henry Lucy, *Punch's* Parliamentary correspondent, had described how in April 1894 during a debate in the House Balfour listened to Lord Randolph "bowed down with physical and mental suffering." Lord Rosebery was to write in his sensitive memoir of Lord Randolph: "There was no curtain, no retirement, he died by inches in public."

The doctors prescribed rest but this Lord Randolph would not undertake. He seemed quite oblivious to the deterioration of his powers or the anguish suffered by his friends and family. It was decided that Lady Randolph should take him on a world tour as the likeliest chance of effecting a cure, or at least arresting the progress of the disease. Some members of the family were concerned at the idea of Lady Randolph accompanying him since, as Marjoribanks wrote to Lord Rosebery, she "always grates on his nerves." According to Lord Randolph in a letter to his mother quoted in Winston's Life, the doctors at first verbally agreed to a journey round the world on condition he gave up political life for a year; almost at the last minute the doctors became alarmed at the idea of so prolonged an absence from their care:

Drs Thomas Buzzard & Robson Roose to Lady Randolph

25 June 1894   74 Grosvenor Gardens W.
Private

Dear Lady Randolph Churchill,

As you are aware, it is against our advice that Lord Randolph is starting for the United States, and you have doubtless seen the letter which we sent to his Lordship. Our wish was that previous to his attempting a lengthened journey he should go with a Medical man to some place near at hand by way of experiment as to the effect of change upon him. In these circumstances it appears to us advisable to repeat in writing, what we have already expressed by word of mouth, that we cannot help feeling a good deal of anxiety in regard to the future, and would earnestly counsel your Ladyship to insist upon an immediate return to England in case Lord Randolph should shew any fresh symptom pointing possibly to disturbance of the Mental faculties.

As it is necessary that Dr Keith, as well as your Ladyship, should be thoroughly aware of our views, we are sending him a duplicate of this letter. We have arranged to hear from him once a week by letter sent to Dr Roose for our joint perusal.

> Believe us to be Yours very truly
> THOMAS BUZZARD
> ROBSON ROOSE

Lord and Lady Randolph sailed for the United States on 27 June 1894 in the S.S. *Majestic*. Winston and Jack came up to London to see their parents off. Rosebery, now Prime Minister, was among those who also came to the station. After a short stay at Bar Harbour in Maine Lord and Lady Randolph went by train across Canada, breaking their journey at Banff in the Rocky Mountains. They visited Vancouver and San Francisco, crossed the Pacific to Japan and then after another long sea voyage across the Indian Ocean arrived in Madras five months after they had left England. It had been intended to make a considerable journey through India but the deterioration in Lord Randolph's health was now so rapid, and his condition often so violent, that on the basis of Keith's reports to Buzzard and Roose in London they recommended his immediate return.

While his parents were going round the world Winston wrote them more than thirty letters. To begin with he did not understand the gravity of his father's illness since there was a family conspiracy to keep bad news from Duchess Fanny and the children. But during October Winston began by degrees to learn a great deal more about his father's illness.

Winston to Lady Randolph

EXTRACT

21 October 1894

. . . We are very much disturbed by Dr Keith's last letter which gives a very unsatisfactory report about Papa. I hope however that there is still an improvement and no cause for immediate worry. Poor old Grandmamma is very low. It seems to me to be unnecessary to send her anything but good reports as any bad news causes her a great deal of trouble. If you only knew what importance she attaches to every cheering good word about Papa — I am sure you would persuade Dr Keith to tell only what is pleasant to hear. Your letter was indeed a treat. I think that the photographs are beautiful and shall always keep them as a souvenir of Japan. It is two months since I got back to Sandhurst and I am now almost at the end of my stay there. . . .

Winston however persuaded Roose to tell him the true facts and his subsequent letters to his mother show how stricken he was by his realization of his father's approaching death.

Winston to Lady Randolph

EXTRACTS

2 November [1894]   50 Grosvenor Square

. . . I persuaded Dr Roose to tell exactly how Papa was — as I thought it was only right that I should know exactly how he was progressing. You see I only hear through grandmamma Jerome who does not take a very sanguine view of things — or through the Duchess who is at one extreme one minute and at the other the next. So I asked Dr Roose and he told me everything and showed me the medical reports. I have told no one — and I beg you above all things not to write to Roose on the subject of his having told me as he told it me in confidence. I need not tell you how anxious I am. I had never realised how ill Papa had been and had never until now believed that there was anything serious the matter. I do trust & hope as sincerely as human beings can that the relapse Keith spoke of in his last report was only temporary and that the improvement of the few months has been maintained. Do, my darling mamma when you write let me know *exactly* what you think. . . .

. . . Now about yourself, Darling Mummy I do hope that you are keeping well and that the fatigues of travelling as well as the anxiety you must feel about Papa — are not telling on you. I can't tell you how I long to see you again and how I look forward to your return. Do what you can with Papa to induce him to allow me to come out and join you. . . .

Winston to Lady Randolph

8 November [1894]   Sandhurst

My dearest darling Mamma,

I got yesterday a report of Papa from Yokohama. Dr Roose was good enough to let me see it. It describes his having been ill with numbness in the hand — I have no doubt you remember the occasion. I am very very sorry to hear that so little improvement has been made, and that apparently there is not much chance of improvement. My darling Mummy — you must not be cross with me for having persuaded Roose to keep me informed as I shall never tell anyone and it is only right I should know. Above all things you must not write to him and scold him — as I promised I would not tell anyone but have made an exception in your case.

I hope and trust as sincerely as it is possible there may still be time for some improvement & some really favourable signs. Do please write and tell me all about him — quite unreservedly. You know you told *me* to write to *you* on *every subject* freely.

Well — all this is very sad to us at home — at least to me — for grandmamma does not know what Dr Keith writes. I fear that much worry will tell upon you — and that the continual anxiety added to the fatigues of travelling will deprive you of any interest & pleasure in the strange things you see. If I were you I would always try and look on the bright side of things and endeavour perpetually to derive interest from everything. Above all don't get ill yourself. Things go on very well here — work and amusements — are both attractive. The end of the term and the examinations are approaching and I hope to pass well so as to have a satisfactory report for Papa.

I will write by next mail again.

With best love my darling Mummy,
Ever your loving son
WINSTON

By this time it was inopportune and hopeless for Lady Randolph to "look on the bright side." By the time she received Winston's letter Lord Randolph was much worse and she had received news of a personal character which cannot have made her task of looking after her husband any easier to bear.

Lady Randolph to Mrs Moreton Frewen

(*Copy: Leslie Papers*)

EXTRACT

18 November 1894   Bay of Bengal

. . . You must not be very angry with me for not having written to you. My letters to Leonie are intended for you & Mama too & I only address them to Leonie as she is the one with a permanent address. I assure you I am always thinking of you darling & I wd give much to be with you all now. The sea is rough & is very hot & this ship is full of beetles, ants, rats etc. We are on our way to Madras from Rangoon. We get there the 21 & stay with the Wenlocks [*Lord Wenlock was Governor*]. We stayed a week at Rangoon intending to go up to Mandalay & Behare 150 miles further North but the steamers did not fit in & we heard there was a lot of cholera & so R was willing to give it up. Keith & I did all we cd to prevent his going to Burma as we feared the heat for him but it was useless. He would have gone alone if we had insisted. After leaving Japan we had 3 days in China seeing Hong Kong & Canton, the latter an extraordinary place. We went there by steamer up the "Pearl River" 12 hrs each way & spent the day in Canton. The "Heathen Chinese" were very nasty glaring at us. They hit Walden [*Lord Randolph's servant*] & spat at Dr Keith so we did not tarry but whisked through the streets in palanquins only setting out to go into shops. From Hong Kong we went to Singapore 5 days sea — every place is 5 days by sea. Mr de Bunsen whom you know travelled with me from Japan to Singapore. He was on his way to Siam as *chargé d'affaires*. Such a nice man. We had long talks about you & Leonie. I have met very few people one cd talk to since we left England. I can't tell you how I pine for a little society. It is so hard to get away from one's thoughts when one is always alone. And yet the worst of it is I dread the chance even of seeing people for his sake. He is quite unfit for society & I hate going to the Wenlocks. One never knows what he may do. At Govt House Singapore he was very bad for 2 days and it was dreadful being with strangers. Since then he has become much quieter & sometimes is quite apathetic but Keith thinks it is a bad sign. I am going to try & get the opinion of another doctor at Madras & I want if possible to get him home or at least near home. I am sure it is quite impossible for us to go travelling about in India. It means staying with people all the time & R is too unfit for it. Of course he does not realise there is anything the matter with him as he feels well physically. Dearest Clarinette I cannot go into all the details of his illness but you cannot imagine anything *more* distracting & desperate than to watch it & see him as he is & to think of him as he was. You will not be surprised that I haven't the heart to write to you about the places & things we see. I try to keep a diary for your sakes but when I write to you I cannot get away from my troubles. I know my letters are dull when they might be interesting. I had a telegram from Charles [Kinsky] at Rangoon telling me of his engagement. I *hate* it. I shall return without a friend in the world & too old to make any more now. Well there! enough about myself. I wish I cd have some good news of you & Moreton poor dear. Your life is not all *couleur de rose.* Whose is? It is so easy to tell people to be philosophical (I can't spell any more) how can one be. I wonder where this will find you. In time to wish you a merry Xmas. Give my best love to Mama & to Leonie. How I wish I could see the boys. I hope they wrote to you. . . .

On November 24 Winston went to Dr Roose's and was shown a telegram just received from Madras that stated that Lord Randolph's condition had become very much worse and that it had been decided to cut short the tour and to return to England immediately. Lord and Lady Randolph reached London on December 24. Despite a few misleading symptoms of recovery there was now no hope that he could live and the family awaited his death with miserable resignation. "For a month," Winston wrote in the Life of his father, "at his mother's house, he lingered pitifully, until very early in the morning of 24 January 1895 the numbing fingers of paralysis laid that weary brain to rest." Seventy years to the day Winston himself was to die. On January 28 Lord Randolph was buried in Bladon churchyard, and a memorial service was held for him in Westminster Abbey.

Winston was just twenty at the time of his father's death and must henceforward be regarded as a man and no longer a boy. Despite his lack of means he plainly felt himself responsible for the small family — there was only his mother and Jack. Both his grandfathers, the Duke and Leonard Jerome, had been dead for some time. His grandmother Jerome was to die within a few months; so too was Everest. The old Duchess died four years later. These three Churchills were to be alone in the world. Lady Randolph still had her private income which she quickly dissipated or mortgaged; and their fortunes were to be increasingly dependent on the impecunious gentleman cadet who was shortly to receive the Queen's Commission in the 4th Hussars with pay of £120 per annum. Within the confinements of his slender means and the limitations of the career to which he was committed — the only one for which he had any training — he was his own master. He had a stout heart, an audacious spirit, colossal ambition, a late-maturing but massive brain from which elements of genius cannot be excluded, a sharp sword; and he was soon to fashion himself a valuable and rewarding pen, which was in the next few years, combined with his thirst for adventure, to liberate him from the thraldom of penury and open all doors during the seventy years that lay ahead.

"It is said," Winston was to write nearly forty years later in his Life of Marlborough, "that famous men are usually the product of an unhappy childhood. The stern compression of circumstances, the twinges of adversity, the spur of slights and taunts in early years, are needed to evoke that ruthless fixity of purpose and tenacious mother-wit without which great actions are seldom accomplished." And in 1898 he wrote of the Mahdi: "Solitary trees, if they grow at all, grow strong; and a boy deprived of a father's care often develops, if he escapes the perils of youth, an independence and vigour of thought which may restore in after life the heavy loss of early days."

There was now no one to help him — or stand in his way; for if Lord Randolph had lived, even in better health, he would have been an obstacle to Winston's career and prospects which were soon to burgeon. He was free to leave the nest and soar through many hazards to the empyrean.

7

The Fourth Hussars

In *My Early Life* Churchill, as we now shall call him, relates how Lord Randolph, in one of his last remarks, had said "Have you got your horses?" Earlier, however, while Lord Randolph was still on his voyage round the world, he had told his son to put the idea of joining the cavalry "out of your head altogether, *at any rate during my lifetime.*" And Lord Randolph had warned: "The Army is the finest profession in the world if you work at it and the worst if you loaf at it." Certainly Churchill seems to have worked hard for his final examinations at Sandhurst in which he obtained the following marks:

	Military Administration	Military Law	Tactics	Fortification	Military Topography
Maximum	300	300	300	600	600
WSC	232	227	263	532	471

	Drill	Gymnastics	Riding	Musketry	Marks awarded by professors
Maximum	100	100	200	—	—
WSC	95	85	190	105	446

For once there was no comment as to his unpunctuality and his conduct was described as "good." Having entered 92nd in a list of 102, he passed out 20th in a class of 130. Before his death Lord Randolph had come to accept the idea that his son should go into the cavalry and not into the infantry; into the 4th Hussars and not into the 60th Rifles to which the Duke of Cambridge, the Queen's first cousin and for nearly forty years Commander-in-Chief of the British Army, had nominated him more than five years before.

Churchill wasted little time. Within a week of Lord Randolph's funeral at Bladon he determined to take the necessary action to start his own career. At his behest his mother telegraphed to Colonel Brabazon who promptly replied on 2 February 1895 suggesting that she should at once get in touch with the Duke of Cambridge. Colonel Brabazon told Lady Randolph to write to the Duke that Lord Randolph had often said that if his son were to go into the cavalry he should like him to join under Brabazon.

Colonel J. P. Brabazon to Lady Randolph

EXTRACT

Saturday [? 2 February 1895]   9 West Halkin Street S.W.

. . . You can say there is *now* a vacancy in the 4th Hussars, that you are very anxious he should not be idling about London & that I personally knew the boy, liked him & was very anxious to have him. I should add — which is the case — that Winston passed very much higher than any of the candidates for Cavalry & hope that the Duke will allow him to be appointed to the 4th Hussars, & thus fulfil one of Randolph's last wishes. . . .

Lady Randolph wrote to the Duke of Cambridge who was at the Hotel Prince de Galles at Cannes on the Riviera. He very promptly replied on February 6 that he would write immediately to the Military Secretary at the War Office and that if the transfer from the list for the 60th Rifles to that for the 4th Hussars could be arranged it would be carried out. "The 4th Hussars is a very good Cavalry Regiment, & Colonel Brabazon an excellent Commanding Officer so I think your selection is in that respect a very good one. I am delighted to hear that your son has passed so well out of Sandhurst, a proof that he has made good use of his stay at the College."

Twelve days after the Duke's letter Churchill reported to the 4th Hussars at Aldershot, and on February 20 he received his Commission. It was signed by H. Campbell-Bannerman, then Secretary of State for War, from whom he was less than eleven years later to receive his first Ministerial appointment as Under-Secretary for the Colonies.

Between arriving at Aldershot and receiving his Commission Churchill found time to write to his mother:

WSC to Lady Randolph

19 February [1895]   IV Hussars
                                                Aldershot

My dear Mamma,

This must necessarily be a short letter as I have but little to say and not much time to say it in. Colonel Brabazon did not come down after all — but I managed all right, though it was rather awkward introducing oneself. As my own room is not yet ready Captain de Moleyns [the Adjutant] has lent me his — also his servant — an excellent man. He does not return until Saturday — before which time I shall have got settled in my own "quarters."

Everybody is very civil and amiable and I have no doubt I shall get on all right with them all. My sedentary life of the last three months has caused me to be dreadfully stiff after two hours riding school, but that will wear off soon.

My room will have to be furnished — but I have made arrangements with a local contractor, who for a small charge will furnish it palatially on the hire system.

There appears to be a very large Harrow element in the regiment — all of whom are very agreeable and nice. The work, though hard and severe is not at present uninteresting, and I trust that the novelty & the many compensating attractions of a military existence — will prevent it from becoming so — at any rate for the next four or five years.

With best love, Your ever loving son
WINSTON S. C.

His regular letters to his mother and to his younger brother Jack at Harrow continue to afford a lively and almost complete account of his early months in the 4th Hussars. At first we learn that "the riding school is fearfully severe and I suffer terribly from stiffness — but what with hot baths and *massage* I hope soon to be better. At present I can hardly walk. I have however been moved up in the 2nd Class recruits which is extremely good. These horses are very different to the Sandhurst screws. Rather too broad I think for me

— and I am rather worried about my old strain [hernia]. Sundry queer pains having manifested themselves, which may or may not be the outcome of the rest of the stiffness."

In a letter to his brother he gives an outline of his daily routine.

WSC to Jack

EXTRACT

21 February [1895]   Aldershot

7.30	Called
7.45	Breakfast in bed
	Papers, Letters, etc
8.45	Riding School — 2 hours
10.45	Hot bath and massage
11.30	Carbine exercises — privately with a Sergeant to catch up a higher class
	Noon "Stables." Lasts 1 hour. I have charge of 1 squadron, 30 men and have to see the horses groomed — watered — fed & the men's rooms clean etc
1 o'clock	Lunch is ready. It does not matter being late
2.15	Drill. 1½ hours nominally — but as I can't walk I get off at present after a half an hour — which is mostly spent in drilling the men myself. After which for the present — hot baths — medical rubber — Elliman's and doctor — until Mess at 8 — Bezique — 3d points. Bed.

With his lack-lustre school days behind him and an unpromising future ahead Churchill plainly aspired to mount and excel in his new profession. The time-table he sent to Jack shows how he sought to gain promotion by extra practice in the mastery of the carbine. Within a week of arriving at Aldershot he was moved up into a higher riding class. "And should all go well," he reported to his mother, "I shall be dismissed riding school in three months instead of the normal twelve." At the same time he was allowed out with the Regiment on a route march. "No one has ever been allowed out before until they have been three to four months in the riding school, so I established a precedent." His only complaint was about Drill, "which as usual I loathe and abominate."

In the evenings he played either bezique for 3d points — "which is a shocking descent from the shillings at Deepdene" (Duchess Lily's new home near Dorking) — or whist — "a most uninteresting game and one at which I have but little luck." Rarely, even in later life, was Churchill apt to take an objective view of affairs. A game at which he did not prevail was naturally a bore. He was already developing that egocentricity which was to become such a predominant characteristic, and to which must be attributed alike his blunders and his triumphant successes.

*

He rode, if anything, rather better than the other young officers of his rank. He early indulged in steeplechasing, and, as soon as he could organise credit on his precarious background, in polo as well. His steeplechasing involved him in an accident early in March. "The animal refused and swerved," he told his mother. "I tried to cram him in and he took the wings. Very nearly did he break my leg, but as it is I am only bruised and very stiff." He was in bed for three days.

But a misadventure of a different kind was in store less than a week later. On March 20 Churchill took part in his first point-to-point at the Cavalry Brigade meeting held at Aldershot; the race for which he entered was for the 4th Hussars Subalterns' Challenge Cup (worth £28 to the winner). It was run over two miles five furlongs and Churchill, riding in the *"nom de guerre"* of Mr Spencer, rode Traveller, one of the two horses owned by his fellow subaltern, Albert Savory. He was not riding under his own name probably because he had reassured his mother only a few days earlier in a letter dated March 15 that he would not be riding in races:

> I think — if you will let me say — that you take rather an extreme view of steeplechasing — when you call it at once "idiotic" and "fatal." Everybody here rides one or other of their chargers in the different military Races which are constantly held. Of course for this year I cannot ride, but I hope to do so next year.
>
> In fact I rather think you are expected to do something that way — ride in the Regimental races at least. However I shall see you long before I can ride and you can discuss it with me.

Since Churchill did not yet have a charger of his own he quite genuinely may have believed that he had no prospects of a ride in a race so soon.

"It was very exciting," he confided to his brother Jack when he described the Challenge Cup race, "and there is no doubt about it being dangerous. I had never jumped a regulation fence before and they are pretty big things as you know. Everybody in the Regiment was very pleased at my riding, more especially as I came in third. They thought it very sporting. I thought so too. It has done me a lot of good here and I think I may say I am popular with everybody." There were four other runners and the race was won by Mr A. O. Francis's Surefoot. Surefoot started at about 6–1 against; Savory's other horse, Lady Margaret, which had won a race the previous day, was favourite at 5–4 on and came second.

Nearly a year later on 20 February 1896 the Racing Calendar announced that the stewards of the National Hunt Committee, their attention having been called to certain irregularities in respect of the 4th Hussars Subalterns' Challenge Cup, had declared the race null and void and the horses which had taken part in it were perpetually disqualified from all races under National Hunt rules. The weekly review *Truth,* edited and owned by Lord Randolph's old friend Henry Labouchere, the Radical member for Northampton, quickly fastened on to this announcement and suggested that Surefoot was in fact a "ringer" — another horse substituted for the one whose name appeared on the race card. It was suggested that a number of officers in the 4th Hussars, among them all those who took part in the race, were in this plot and had profited as a result.

At this time Churchill also became involved in a far more dangerous escapade of which the full facts are still not available. It seems that late in February or early in March 1895 it was learnt that a young man called Allan George Cameron Bruce, who had been at Sandhurst with Churchill, was to join the 4th Hussars. It appears that Churchill and a number of his fellow subalterns had formed an unfavourable opinion of this officer and that they tried to dissuade him from joining the Regiment. They gave him dinner at the Nimrod Club in London and told him among other things that the £500 a year which his father was allowing him would be insufficient to maintain the standards to which the 4th Hussars were accustomed. If Churchill did in fact join his brother officers in such an argument he was being somewhat disingenuous. His own allowance, sometimes paid a little late, seems to have been at this time under £300 a year.

Bruce, notwithstanding the opposition, did join the Regiment; unfortunately for him he seems to have got himself into a number of scrapes with non-commissioned officers and other ranks. Giving the official side of the story to Parliament a year or so later, the Under-Secretary of State for War, Mr Brodrick, alleged that quite early in his career Bruce had to be reproved by his Squadron Commander for using violent and abusive language; then at Bisley he swore at a Colour-Sergeant of another cavalry regiment who all the while was respectfully standing to attention; then finally on the night of Boxing Day Bruce was alleged to have forced his way into the Sergeants' Mess and stayed there drinking for up to an hour. All these events it was alleged showed that Bruce had not understood "what was the proper position of an officer towards non-commissioned officers" and he was accordingly asked to resign from the Army.

Bruce and his father vehemently denied the allegations made against the young officer and called in aid Labouchere's *Truth*, a paper which specialized in exposing minor Service scandals, particularly where personalities could be involved. *Truth* readily obliged the Bruces and vehemently took up their cause. In the course of his campaign Labouchere discovered that a year before (while Churchill was still at Sandhurst) an officer named Hodge, who had joined the 4th Hussars, had been rough-handled and horse-troughed by the young officers in the Regiment who disliked his presence; and that as a result Hodge became so unhappy that he resigned his Commission. The two cases excited all the venom and eloquence of Labouchere's pen; and they were debated in the House of Commons on 19 June 1896 when Mr Brodrick promised a departmental enquiry. *Truth* commented:

> The kernel of the whole case is the undisguised conspiracy formed against this subaltern before he joined to have him out of the regiment unless he consented to go voluntarily. . . . Are we to take it that from Lord Wolseley downward the military authorities approve the principle that a youngster, whose allowance is not, in the judgement of the rowdiest set of subalterns, sufficient to enable him to "go the pace" of the regiment, is out of place in the Army, and should be got rid of by any subterfuge that can be trumped up for the purpose? Are we to take it as now an understood thing that in certain cavalry regiments those sections of the Queen's Regulations which impose

on a Commanding Officer the duty of keeping down his officers' expenditure are a dead letter? Is it now the proper thing in such regiments for the Colonel, instead of taking a fatherly interest in every boy committed to his care, to back up the majority of subalterns in any measures they may take for keeping up "the pace of the regiment," and eliminating individuals who do not go the pace? That, as evidenced by recent events, seems to be the state of things prevailing in the 4th Hussars, and approved of by the War Office and the Commander-in-Chief.

Bruce's case, however, was gravely, even fatally, weakened by a libel his father, Mr A. C. Bruce-Pryce, had perpetrated on Churchill in February 1896 after his son had resigned. Writing to Ian Hogg, brother of Douglas Hogg (later 1st Viscount Hailsham), who was taking Bruce's place and who was purchasing some items of his equipment, Bruce-Pryce alleged that his son knew that Churchill had participated at Sandhurst in "acts of gross immorality of the Oscar Wilde type." Churchill issued a writ within four days of Bruce-Pryce's letter, claimed damages of £20,000 and received within a month a complete withdrawal and apology and £500 damages.

Five months later, even after a War Office enquiry, Labouchere remained dissatisfied and venomous:

The subalterns whose horses ran on this occasion were Messrs Barnes, Savory, Francis, Spencer Churchill, and Walker. Of these Messrs Barnes and Savory assisted just previously in the dragging of Mr Hodge through the horse trough. The whole five of them took part in organising the dinner at the Nimrod Club a few weeks later, when Mr Bruce was invited to hear that he was not wanted in their distinguished regiment. Barnes seems to have been prevented from actually attending the dinner, but the invitation was sent to Mr Bruce in his name. Perhaps the finest stroke of irony in the whole business is that these choice spirits actually took upon themselves — apparently on the strength of some schoolboy tittle-tattle retailed by one of their number — to decide that Mr Bruce, whom the majority of them had never seen, was not a gentleman qualified to grace so select an assemblage as the Officers' Mess of the 4th Hussars. At the very time when this precious gang met to inform Mr Bruce the 4th Hussars really could not have him, five of them (including the ringleader) were fresh from the coup which resulted in the defeat of a hot favourite by the last outsider in the betting, and two others had just been treated to what the Commander-in-Chief facetiously calls "drastic" punishment for that extremely gentlemanly and honourable exploit, the horse-troughing of Mr Hodge. And, to crown the whole thing, the War Office, in its final pronouncement on the Bruce case, solemnly takes its cue from these accomplished judges of all the proprieties, and pleads on their behalf that in vetoing Mr Bruce's appointment that they were acting upon "reports" which had reached the regiment concerning that gentleman. Fancy the heroes of the Hodge outrage and the Surefoot coup shuddering over these "reports," and deciding that they really could not do violence to their feelings by associating with such an ineligible comrade! When Lord Wolseley was casting about for pretexts for washing his hands of the 4th Hussars scandals, I really wonder it did not occur to him to suggest that, in intimating to Mr Bruce that he was not quite up to 4th Hussars form, they were really paying him about as pretty a compliment as he need have desired. That, now, would have been something like an unanswerable argument.

Neither the story of the Challenge Cup nor that of Bruce's reception into the Regiment reads very prettily. The full facts are not known: such as are known have been summarized here and are set out in detail in the companion volume of documents which accompanies this book. Churchill was a singularly high-spirited youth and naturally any escapade in which he was involved was bound to attract attention. After a careful study of all the known facts and a prolonged meditation upon them the author can only conclude that although Churchill's conduct may have been injudicious it was in no way dishonourable.

Certainly Churchill considered himself innocent of the charges brought against him by Labouchere; he was most indignant at the article which named all the subalterns involved and interpreted their action in the worst possible light. He later wrote from India:

WSC to Lady Randolph

EXTRACT

12 November [1896]   Bangalore

. . . Mr Labouchere's last article in *Truth* is really too hot for words. I fail to see any other course than a legal action. He distinctly says that five of us — mentioning my name — were implicated in a "coup" to obtain money by malpractice on the Turf. You must not allow this to go unchallenged as it would be fatal to any future in public life for me. Indeed I daresay I should be exposed to attacks even on the grounds of having helped to turn out Bruce. This racing matter is however more serious. You know the facts — so does Colonel Brabazon. The N.H. [National Hunt] Committee furnished the W.O. [War Office] with a letter expressly vindicating us from any charge of dishonesty or of dishonourable behaviour. A copy of this can be seen at Messrs Weatherby's. Consult a good lawyer — not Lewis — he is Labby's lawyer. Let him see the articles in *Truth:* furnish him with the actual facts and follow his advice. Personally I think the letter alluded to above should be published in *The Times.* You might get Lumley to do this. It clears my character from any suggestion of malpractice. I feel very strongly about this my dearest Mamma. Until something is done to contradict what appeared in *Truth* Oct 22 I appear in a very unpleasant light.

Of course what you do must be done from my point of view alone and not with reference to the regiment — who have no ideas beyond soldiering and care nothing for the opinion of those who are not their friends. I leave matters in your hands — but in my absence my dearest Mamma — you must be the guardian of my young reputation. . . .

And a week later he wrote to his mother again:

I hope you will take steps about the racing article in *Truth.* I trust you my dear Mamma to resent any particularly offensive insinuations he may make — in my absence. He is a scoundrel and one of these days I will make him smart for his impudence. His attacks on us do harm. When he turns his attention to Lord Wolseley and Sir Redvers Buller he is impotent. They can afford to ignore his abuse which falls as far short of its mark — as the mud which a street boy might throw at Nelson's Statue in Trafalgar Square. With us it is different. We are but ground game and within easy range of his invectives. Therefore do muzzle him if you can.

No action, however, appears to have been taken against Labouchere.

*

Winston's honourable instincts and his love for Mrs Everest were now to be shown to advantage. Despite his earlier letter to his mother Mrs Everest does not seem to have been treated very well. She kept writing very complaining, endearing letters to Winston and Jack who were obviously her sole interest in the world. She had spent much of the year 1894 with her former employer the Venerable Thompson Phillips, Archdeacon of Barrow-in-Furness; but during the autumn she broke her arm. "I am always to be a cripple," she wrote to Jack in December, "unless I have it seen to."

On January 31 she wrote to Jack about Lord Randolph's memorial service in Westminster Abbey. She told him that Mr Welldon looked at her rather hard and she thought that he recognized her. She was of course too modest to approach him.

Early in 1895 she went to stay with her sister Mrs Emma Richmond and her family in Crouch Hill, Islington. Churchill did not forget his old nurse:

Mrs Everest to WSC

1 April 1895   15 Crouch Hill

                                            London N.

My darling Precious Boy,

I have just recd £2. 10s from Cox & Co Charing Cross on your account. I thank you very much indeed dearest it is awfully kind & thoughtful of you. My dear dear Boy you are one of ten thousand but I am afraid you will find your income not any too much for your expenses dear. It really is too good & kind of you I don't know how to thank you enough. I am afraid Her Ladyship will think me a terrible imposter. I have written to the London & Westminster Bank today to give them my address. I don't know whether they will forward me the usual remittance that your poor dear Papa arranged for me. I had a letter from Jackie this morning he tells me Grandmamma Jerome is very ill indeed in a critical condition. Her Ladyship is at Tunbridge Wells & Mrs Leslie too. They are both with her, poor Mama she has had a lot of troubles lately. Jackie will have dull holidays again I'm afraid. How are you darling I hope you are keeping well. I should so like to know if you are well. Did you get my letter I wrote you last week. I am longing to see you in your uniform. Do let me know when you are in London. I am quite well & my Arm improving slowly. I can put my hand on the top of my head now & I can use my knife & cut bread & butter. The Duchess has let 50 Gr Square & goes away on the 11th. Where are you going to make your home in your holidays? I hope you will take care of yourself my darling. I hear of your exploits at steeple chasing. I do so dread to hear of it. Remember Count Kinsky broke his nose once at that. It is a dangerous pastime but I suppose you are expected to do it. Only don't be too venturesome. Goodbye darling with much love to you.

I remain ever your loving old

Woom

Mrs Jerome died at Tunbridge Wells on the day after Mrs Everest had written this letter. In May Mrs Everest went to stay at Ventnor with her relations the Balaams and reported that she felt better. On June 4 she wrote to Jack that she was still at Ventnor but was "fit for work." She asked when Lady Randolph would get her new house — she obviously wanted to work for her again. Lady Randolph was in Paris at this time. But in July Mrs Everest fell ill again and died within a few days.

WSC to Lady Randolph

3 July [1895]   Aldershot

My dearest Mamma,

I have just got back from London as I telegraphed to you — poor old Everest died early this morning from peritonitis. They only wired to me on Monday evening — to say her condition was critical. That was the first intimation I had of her illness. I started off and got Keith — who was *too* kind. He thought then that she might pull through — but it was problematical. Instead of rallying however, she only sank into a stupor which gave place to death at 2.15 this morning.

Everything that could be done — was done. I engaged a nurse, but she only arrived for the end. It was very sad & her death was shocking to see — but I do not think she suffered much pain.

She was delighted to see me on Monday and I think my coming made her die happy. Her last words were of Jack. I shall never know such a friend again. I went down to Harrow to tell Jack — early this morning — as I did not want to telegraph the news. He was awfully shocked but tried not to show it.

I made the necessary arrangements for the funeral which takes place on Friday. I ordered a wreath for you from Mackay & I thought you would like to send one.

Please send a wire to Welldon to ask him to let Jack come up for the funeral — as he is very anxious to do so.

Well my dearest Mummy I am very tired as I have been knocking about for two nights & have done all my duty here at the same time. I feel very low — and find that I never realised how much poor old Woom was to me. I don't know what I should do without you.

With best love Ever your loving son
WINSTON S. CHURCHILL

WSC to Lady Randolph

EXTRACT

6 July 1895   Aldershot

My dear Mamma,

I went yesterday to poor Everest's funeral & Welldon let Jack come up too. All her relations were there — a good many of whom had travelled from Ventnor overnight — and I was quite surprised to find how many friends she had made in her quiet and simple life. The coffin was covered with wreaths & everything was as it should be. I felt very despondent and sad — the third funeral I have been to within five months! [*The other two were Lord Randolph's and Mrs. Jerome's.*] It is indeed another link with the past gone — & I look back with regret to the old days at Connaught Place when fortune still smiled.

My darling Mamma — I am longing for the day when you will be able to have a little house of your own and when I can really feel that there is such a place as home. At present I regard the regiment entirely as my head-quarters — and if I go up to London for a couple of days — I always look forward to coming back to my friends and ponies here. I am getting on extraordinarily well and when I see how short a time those who don't get on, stay, I feel that it is very fortunate that I do. . . .

Lady Randolph was evidently not present. But the Archdeacon, with a "long memory for faithful service," travelled all the way down from Cumberland to be at the graveside. Winston paid for a head-stone to be erected on Mrs Everest's grave at the City of London Cemetery in Manor Park with the following simple inscription:

Erected in Memory
of
Elizabeth Anne Everest
who died 3rd July 1895
Aged 62
by
Winston Spencer Churchill
Jack Spencer Churchill

For many years afterwards he paid an annual sum to the local florist for the upkeep of the grave.

Churchill was later to write in *My Early Life* a moving account of Mrs Everest's death. A middle-aged politician battling away in the wilderness against the entrenched debilitating forces of MacDonald, Baldwin and Neville Chamberlain might well have been suspected of seeking popular support by evincing a fabricated solicitude for his old nurse. The action he took on Everest's death and the two letters he wrote to his mother at the time show that he was a proud and generous young man ready to accept family responsibilities for which his mother was unsuited and his brother Jack too young.

*

Churchill was often plagued and sometimes tormented by money matters. He wrote in *My Early Life* about his mother that when he was a small boy she seemed to him a fairy princess: a radiant being possessed of limitless riches and power. He had not then discovered that Lord and Lady Randolph had practically run through all the money they had; and quite soon, as we shall see, his own small patrimony was to be summoned in aid of his mother's extravagances.

His early letters on joining the army were much taken up with finding the money for the outfit and the expenses of joining the Regiment. The cost of joining he put conservatively at £653. 11. 0. and that covered only one charger, for Duchess Lily had given him another worth £200. Cox's the Bankers lent him £100 with which to buy polo ponies. Polo ponies did not cost as much then as they do now; but they must have been inadequate animals if more than one was bought for this price. He was never, throughout his army career, and indeed for several years thereafter, to be out of debt. Some of the tailors' bills for the uniforms which were made for him on joining were not paid until more than six years later when for the first time he had cash in hand. Messrs E. Tautz and Sons, Breeches and Trousers Makers, supplied no fewer than seven pairs of pants, overalls, and breeches during Churchill's first eight weeks with the 4th Hussars at a cost of nearly 40 guineas. And he did not wait long to order himself a satin racing jacket and cap in the chocolate and pink that had been his father's colours.

*

We already know how ardently Churchill had from a very young age followed his father's political career. His father's resignation and the understandable obstinacy of Lord Salisbury to recall Lord Randolph into his Government encouraged his interest in politics; his father's tragic death now quickened that interest, as his letters to his mother increasingly reveal.

He writes to his mother on March 2 of the local government elections in London:

WSC to Lady Randolph

EXTRACT

2 March 1895   Metropole
                                                Brighton

. . . The County Council — at least the Progressive Party — have received a dreadful blow — which will probably have much more widespread results than is generally imagined — at least so I think. Though they will still keep a majority — it will not be large enough to warrant a continuance of their arrogant — grasping and intolerant policy. It is also another blow to the Government who have identified themselves with the Progressives entirely. . . .

And again on the same day about the Primrose League Habitation in Paddington named after his father:

. . . Fardell tells me that the R.C. [Randolph Churchill] Habitation is languishing and in a most effete condition. I sincerely hope that you will not withdraw from the office you hold in it — for it is an institution which assists to commemorate Papa's name — as well as helping on work which he began. . . .

And when in the summer of 1895 Lord Salisbury and the Conservatives were returned to power in the General Election he wrote:

WSC to Lady Randolph

EXTRACT

3 August [1895]   Aldershot

. . . The radical papers go on piling up figures to show that "the verdict of the country" is only a question of chance — and never indicates any real feeling — without for one moment reflecting that this argument knocks the backbone out of their agitation against the Peers. A more disappointed & broken down party never was seen.

Meanwhile the Unionists come in with very nearly every able man in both houses in their cabinet — with the House of Commons at their feet — & the Lords at their back — supported by all sections of the nation — unfettered by promises or hampered by pledges. No party has ever had such a chance — it remains to be seen what use they will make of it.

To my mind they are *too* strong — Too brilliant altogether. They are just the sort of Government to split on the question of Protection. Like a huge ship with powerful engines they will require careful steering — because any collision means destruction. . . .

This was precocious prescience in a young man of twenty. Nearly eight years were to pass before Joseph Chamberlain, having already destroyed the Liberal Party over Home Rule, was to destroy the Tory Party on the tariff issue. It may have been a lucky guess on Churchill's part, but it shows that he was already beginning to think things out for himself rather than to accept the cant thought of the hour. This tendency was to grow throughout his life and was to bring him frequently into collision with large organized sections of unthinking and wrong-headed opinion.

When his cousin the Duke of Marlborough, only three years older than himself, moved the Vote of Thanks in reply to the Loyal Address in the House of Lords, Churchill wrote to his mother on 16 August 1895:

I don't care to dwell on the past, but I could not help thinking as I read it that Papa would have liked to see that he inherited at least some of the family talents and was trying quietly and tactfully to use them.

I wonder now whether he will have the self-control to relapse — for a little longer — into silence.

It is a fine game to play — the game of politics — and it is well worth waiting for a good hand before really plunging.

At any rate — four years of healthy and pleasant existence, combined with both responsibility & discipline can do no harm to me — but rather good. The more I see of soldiering the more I like it, but the more I feel convinced that it is not my *métier*. Well, we shall see — my dearest Mamma.

We can already see that before he was twenty-one he was ardent to emulate and vindicate his father and to carve a career for himself. However, circumscribed as he was, he had to wait another four or five years before he could undertake the battle of politics. Meanwhile he was educating himself and preparing himself for that battle in which he already knew he must engage as soon as he could escape from the poverty of his circumstances and the discipline of the Army.

While the summer at Aldershot dragged on, Churchill's agile mind became increasingly restless. To his mother, who was travelling in France and Switzerland, he wrote:

WSC to Lady Randolph

EXTRACT

24 August 1895   Aldershot

... We have just reached the Saturday of a very hard week — on no day of which have I been in the saddle less than 8 to 9 hours and on no day of which have I omitted to play polo. Next week will be the same only more so — so my time is well employed. . . .

I find I am getting into a state of mental stagnation — when even letter writing becomes an effort & when any reading but that of monthly magazines is impossible. This is of course quite in accordance with the spirit of the army. It is indeed the result of mental forces called into being by discipline and routine. It is a state of mind into which all or nearly all who soldier — fall.

From this "slough of Despond" I try to raise myself by reading & rereading Papa's speeches — many of which I almost know by heart — but I really cannot find the energy to read any other serious work.

I think really that when I am quartered in London I shall go and study one or two hours a week with one of James's men — a most capable fellow — either Economics or Modern History. If you know what I mean, I need some one to point out some specific subject to stimulate & to direct my reading in that subject. The desultory reading I have so far indulged in has only resulted in a jumble of disconnected & ill assorted facts. . . .

We do not possess Lady Randolph's answer, but it was evidently not very helpful.

WSC to Lady Randolph

EXTRACT

31 August 1895   Aldershot

My dearest Mamma,

I write this in answer to your long letter of two days ago. I have considered the subject you suggest "Supply of Army horses." I think it is a subject which has much to commend it to the attention of a cavalry officer: but I am bound to say it is not one which would interest me. It is too technical. It is a narrow question leading to a limited result. A subject more calculated to narrow and groove one's mind than to expand it.

Besides if one hears "horse" talked all day long — in his every form & use — it would seem a surfeit to study his supply as one of the *"beaux-arts."* No — my dearest Mamma — I think something more literary and less material would be the sort of mental medicine I need. And there are so many works — which without making one a specialist on the subject with which they deal — leave much valuable information — and many pleasing thoughts — as a result of reading them. You see — all my life — I have had a purely technical education. Harrow, Sandhurst, James's — were all devoted to studies of which the highest aim was to pass some approaching Examinations. As a result my mind has never received that polish which for instance Oxford or Cambridge gives. At these places one studies questions and sciences with a rather higher object than mere practical utility. One receives in fact a liberal education.

Don't please misunderstand me. I don't mean to imply any sneer at utilitarian studies. Only I say that my daily life is so eminently matter of fact that the kind of reading I require is not the kind which the subject you suggested to me would afford. I have now got a capital book — causing much thought — and of great interest. It is a work on political economy by Fawcett. When I have read it — and it is very long, I shall perhaps feel inclined to go still farther afield in an absorbing subject. But this is a book essentially devoted to "first principles" — and one which would leave at least a clear knowledge of the framework of the subject behind — and would be of use even if the subject were not persevered in.

Then I am going to read Gibbon's *Decline and Fall of the Roman Empire* & Lecky's [*History of*] *European morals*. These will be tasks

more agreeable than the mere piling up of statistics. Well — this far
and no farther — my dearest Mamma — will I investigate a question
which I am sure will bore you in its discussion. . . .

Churchill was a newly joined subaltern of the 4th Hussars. His
letters to his mother show a lively interest in public affairs, and his
hot intention to participate in them; they evince a desire for learning,
an ambition in which he was to prevail the following year in India.

8

New York and Cuba

THAT SUMMER THE 4th Hussars were withdrawn from the Cavalry Brigade at Aldershot. They marched to Hounslow to make leisurely preparations for their departure the following year for nine years' service in India. In those peaceful days with scarcely a shot being fired anywhere in the world, officers, if they could afford it, were allowed five months' leave each year, including one uninterrupted spell of ten weeks. Cavalry subalterns were encouraged to spend the winter fox-hunting. Churchill, who had invested perhaps more than all his money in polo ponies, began to look around for some less expensive and more exciting adventure. Such things were hard to come by, particularly in the military sphere. By the beginning of October, however, he had made up his mind and formulated a plan.

WSC to Lady Randolph

4 October [1895]   Hounslow

My dearest Mamma,

I daresay you will find the content of this letter somewhat startling. The fact is that I have decided to go with a great friend of mine, one of the subalterns in the regiment, to America and the W. Indies. I propose to start from here between Oct 28 & November 2 — according as the boats fit. We shall go to New York & after a stay there move in a steamer to the W. Indies — to Havana where all the Government troops are collecting to go up country and suppress the revolt that is still simmering on; after that back by Jamaica and

Hayti to New York & so home. The cost of the Ticket is £37 a head return — which would be less than a couple of months [hunting] at Leighton Buzzard by a long way. I do not think the whole thing should cost £90 — which would be within by a good margin what I can afford to spend in 2 months. A voyage to those delightful islands at the season of the year when their climate is at its best will be very pleasant to me — who has never been on sea more than a few hours at a time. And how much more safe than a cruise among the fences of the Vale of Aylesbury.

I come home the 24th and hope to see you for a couple of days before we sail.

Now I hope you won't mind my going my dear Mamma — as it will do me good to travel a bit and with a delightful companion who is one of the senior subalterns and acting adjutant of the regiment & very steady.

Please send me a line.

Your ever loving son
WINSTON

Lady Randolph to WSC

Friday [11 October 1895]   Guisachan

My dearest Winston,

You know I am always delighted if you can do anything which interests & amuses you — even if it be a sacrifice to me. I was rather looking forward to our being together & seeing something of you. Remember I only have you & Jack to love me. You certainly have not the art of writing & putting things in their best lights but I understand all right — & of course darling it is natural that you shd want to travel & I won't throw cold water on yr little plans — *but* I'm very much afraid it will cost a good deal more than you think. N.Y. [New York] is *fearfully* expensive & you will be bored to death there — all men are. I *must* know more about yr friend. What is his name? Not that I don't believe you are a good judge but still I shd like to be sure of him. Considering that I provide the funds I think instead of saying "I *have* decided to go" it may have been nicer & perhaps wiser — to have begun by consulting me. But I suppose experience of life will in time teach you that tact is a very essential ingredient in all things.

I leave here tomorrow & go to "Minto House Hawick N.B."
[North Britain, i.e. Scotland]. Write to me there & tell me more —
you have ignored my long letter over yr future career. I shall be in
London the end of next week — possibly before if so I will let you
know. Have you been to Deepdene. Goodbye God bless you dear —

Yr loving Mother
J R C

P.S. I have had a talk with the Tweedmouths over yr plans & they
can help you much in the way of letters to the Gov of Jamaica & in
suggesting a tour. They went to the W.I. [West Indies] & to Mexico
— & know it all well. Once one makes a good *"Itineraire de Voyage"*
one can find out the cost. Would you like me as a birthday pres to
pay yr ticket??

After Lord Randolph's death Lady Randolph abandoned the
initials JSC in favour of JRC. Churchill had already brought his
friend and fellow-subaltern, Reggie Barnes, into the plan and had
persuaded him to accompany him. They had both received permission from the Commanding Officer, Colonel Brabazon, to proceed
"to the seat of war" — an insurrection which the Spanish authorities
were trying to put down in Cuba. Even before he had received his
mother's somewhat grudging assent to the project Churchill was
already laying his plans with his customary thoroughness and on his
lifelong basis of "doing business with the people at the top." He had
written to his father's old Fourth Party friend, Sir Henry Drummond
Wolff, who at this time was her Majesty's Ambassador in Madrid.
He received the following reply:

Sir H. Drummond Wolff to WSC

8 October 1895   San Sebastian

My dear Winston,
    After receiving yesterday your letter I saw the Minister for Foreign
Affairs (The Duke of Tetuan) & spoke to him about your wish to go
to Cuba.
    He said he would get you a letter from the Minister of War & give
you one himself to Marshal Martinez Campos who is personally his

great friend but it must depend on the Marshal what he lets you and Mr Barnes do as everything is in his hands. I fear I can not obtain any thing more but should think these letters would be enough.

How is your mother & what is Jack about?

Pray give them my love.

Yours affecte

H. DRUMMOND WOLFF

Pray write at once if these letters reach you as I am leaving this [address] before long.

It seems as if Brabazon became a little worried that there might be trouble with the War Office; Churchill was advised to consult them. He naturally applied directly to the Commander-in-Chief, Lord Wolseley (formerly Sir Garnet Wolseley), who had recently succeeded the Duke of Cambridge at the Horse Guards, the office of the military headquarters of the whole British Army, the political direction being maintained nearby in the War Office.

Lord Wolseley, like Colonel Brabazon, felt somewhat embarrassed. "He said he quite approved," Churchill wrote to his mother on October 19, "but rather hinted that it would have been better to go without asking leave at all." The fact was that the popular press in England was very much on the side of the Cuban insurgents and the military authorities saw that it would be very undesirable if the expedition of the two young subalterns to the Spanish forces were to be interpreted as anything like an official mission. Nonetheless the Commander-in-Chief, thinking perhaps that he might make the best of it, sent Churchill and Barnes to see General E. F. Chapman, the Director of Military Intelligence. General Chapman furnished them with maps and background information. Moreover, Churchill wrote to Lady Randolph on October 21, "we are also requested to collect information and statistics on various points and particularly as to the effect of the new bullet — its penetration and striking power. This," Churchill concluded, "invests our mission with almost an official character & cannot fail to help one in the future."

At the same time Churchill arranged with the *Daily Graphic,* for whom his father had written from South Africa in 1891, that he should send occasional letters from the front. For this, his first journalistic venture, Churchill was to be paid five guineas a letter.

So all was now "Sir Garnet," to use a popular phrase current at the time: it was the equivalent of the naval phrase "ship-shape." "Sir Garnet" arose from the widespread admiration for Sir Garnet Wolseley who was always sent to any part of the Empire which was in trouble.

Barnes and Churchill sailed from Liverpool in the Cunard Royal Mail Steamship *Etruria*. But the delights of a sea voyage which Churchill had so eagerly anticipated do not seem to have been fulfilled by events. "I do not contemplate ever taking a sea voyage for pleasure," he wrote to his mother on November 8, a day short of New York, "and I shall always look upon journeys by sea as necessary evils which have to be undergone in the carrying out of any definite plan." It was not just the weather — "though we had bad moments we were never sea-sick" — or the lack of amenities — "our cabins are not uncomfortable — but the lack of a comfortable place to sit down and of an interesting occupation have made us look forward eagerly to disembarking." It was the fellow passengers that most irked Churchill: "There are no nice people on board to speak of — certainly none to write of. . . . There is to be a concert on board tonight at which all the stupid people among the passengers intend to perform and the stupider ones to applaud. The days have seemed very long & uninteresting. . . ."

All this was changed as soon as the two young Englishmen got to New York. They stayed at the very comfortable apartment of Mr Bourke Cockran at 763 Fifth Avenue. Cockran, who was then forty-one, was a distinguished lawyer prominent in New York Democratic politics. He had been a member of Congress since 1891 and was coming to the end of his second term. He had aroused considerable controversy by opposing Cleveland for the Democratic nomination in 1892 and in the following year he was to campaign for the Republican nominee, McKinley. Years later in *Thoughts and Adventures* Churchill wrote of Cockran: "I must record the strong impression which this remarkable man made upon my untutored mind. I have never seen his like, or in some respects his equal. With his enormous head, gleaming eyes and flexible countenance, he looked uncommonly like the portraits of Charles James Fox. It was not my fortune to hear any of his orations, but his conversation, in point, in pith, in rotundity, in antithesis, and in comprehension, exceeded anything I have ever heard."

"Every body is very civil," wrote Churchill to his mother, "and we have engagements for every meal for the next few days about three deep. It is very pleasant staying here as the rooms are beautifully furnished and fitted with every convenience & also as Mr Cockran is one of the most charming hosts and interesting men I have ever met."

On his first night in New York Cockran gave in Churchill's honour a big dinner party of leading members of the judiciary, amongst them Judge Ingraham trying a sensational case then going on. This was the trial of David F. Hannigan who had shot and killed one Solomon H. Mann. Hannigan's sister Lettie had stated, to a coroner's jury assembled at her deathbed, that Mann had seduced her and procured an abortion, which was the cause of her death. After a trial lasting nearly four weeks Hannigan was acquitted on November 22 on the grounds of insanity. His aged father William, who had given evidence on his behalf earlier in the trial, died just seventeen minutes before the jury returned its verdict. More than a week before the end of the trial Churchill went to the Court:

WSC to Jack

EXTRACT

15 November [1895]   763 Fifth Avenue

. . . I went and sat on the bench by [the Judge's] side. Quite a strange experience and one which would be impossible in England. The Judge discussing the evidence as it was given with me and generally making himself socially agreeable — & all the while a pale miserable man was fighting for his life. This is a very great country my dear Jack. Not pretty or romantic but great and utilitarian. There seems to be no such thing as reverence or tradition. Everything is eminently practical and things are judged from a matter of fact standpoint. Take for instance the Court house. No robes or wigs or uniformed ushers. Nothing but a lot of men in black coats & tweed suits. Judge prisoner jury counsel & warders all indiscriminately mixed. But they manage to hang a man all the same, and that after all is the great thing. . . .

There was no lack of friends and acquaintances eager to show the young men around New York.

WSC to Lady Randolph

EXTRACT

10 November [1895]   763 Fifth Avenue

. . . A Mr Purdey took us round New York last night to Koster and Bial's & supper at the Waldorf. The Entertainment was good and the supper excellent. Today I snatch a quiet hour to pen you a line — but I lunch with Eva at 1 — call on the Hitts at 3 — the Cornelius Vanderbilts at 5 & dine with Kitty [Mott] at 8 — so you see that there is not much chance of the time hanging heavily. They really make rather a fuss over us here and extend the most lavish hospitality. We are members of all the Clubs and one person seems to vie with another in trying to make our time pleasant. . . .

Churchill's mind might with reasonable excuse have been in something of a whirl. "I feel," he wrote to his aunt Leonie on November 12, "that I should like to think over and digest what I have seen for a few weeks before forming an opinion on it." This letter to Mrs Leslie, as do other contemporary letters to his mother and his brother, reveals that he was already acquiring an eye for detail, the power to reflect and the ability to relate it all together as a clear, concise impression:

WSC to Mrs John Leslie

(Leslie Papers)

EXTRACT

12 November 1895   763 Fifth Avenue

. . . So far I think the means of communication in New York have struck me the most. The comfort and convenience of elevated railways — tramways — cable cars & ferries, harmoniously fitted into a perfect system accessible alike to the richest and the poorest — is extraordinary. And when one reflects that such benefits have been secured to the people not by confiscation of the property of the rich or by arbitrary taxation but simply by business enterprise — out of which the promoters themselves have made colossal fortunes, one cannot fail to be impressed with the excellence of the active system.

But New York is full of contradictions and contrasts. I paid my fare across Brooklyn Bridge with a paper dollar. I should think the most disreputable "coin" the world has ever seen [*He was used to golden sovereigns and half-sovereigns*]. I wondered how to reconcile the magnificent system of communication with the abominable currency for a considerable time and at length I have found what may be a solution. The communication of New York is due to private enterprise while the state is responsible for the currency: and hence I come to the conclusion that the first class men of America are in the counting house and the less brilliant ones in the government. . . .

One evening they went over the ironclad cruiser *New York*. "I was much struck by the sailors: their intelligence, their good looks and civility and their generally businesslike appearance. These interested me more than [the] ship itself, for while any nation can build a battleship — it is the monopoly of the Anglo-Saxon race to breed good seamen."

Then they went to the military academy at West Point. "I am sure," he wrote to his brother, "you will be horrified by some of the Regulations of the Military Academy. The cadets enter from 19–22 & stay 4 years. This means that they are most of them 24 years of age. They are not allowed to smoke or have any money in their possession nor are they given any leave except 2 months after the first two years. In fact they have far less liberty than any *private* school boys in our country. I think such a state of things is positively disgraceful and young men of 24 or 25 who would resign their personal liberty to such an extent can never make good citizens or fine soldiers. A child who rebels against that sort of control should be whipped — so should a man who does not rebel."

And there were diversions. "The other night Mr Cockran got the Fire Commissioner to come with us and we alarmed four or five fire stations. This would have interested you very much. On the alarm bell sounding the horses at once rushed into the shafts — the harness fell on to them — the men slid half dressed down a pole from their sleeping room and in 5½ seconds the engine was galloping down the street to the scene of the fire. An interesting feat which seems incredible unless you have seen it."

"Altogether my dear Aunt Leonie," wrote Churchill, "my mind is full of irreconcilable & conflicting facts. The comfort of their cars & the disgraceful currency — the hospitality of American Society and the vulgarity of their Press — present to me a problem of great complexity."

WSC to Jack

EXTRACT

15 November [1895]   763 Fifth Avenue

. . . The essence of American journalism is vulgarity divested of truth. Their best papers write for a class of snotty housemaids and footmen & even the nicest people here have so much vitiated their taste as to appreciate the style.

I think, mind you, that vulgarity is a sign of strength. A great, crude, strong, young people are the Americans — like a boisterous healthy boy among enervated but well bred ladies and gentlemen. Some day Jack when you are older you must come out here and I think you will feel as I feel — and think as I think today.

Picture to yourself the American people as a great lusty youth — who treads on all your sensibilities, perpetrates every possible horror of ill manners — whom neither age nor just tradition inspire with reverence — but who moves about his affairs with a good hearted freshness which may well be the envy of older nations of the earth. Of course there are here charming people who are just as refined and cultured as the best in any country in the world — but I believe my impressions of the nation are broadly speaking correct. . . .

What had originally been planned as a three-day visit to New York, possibly to be reduced to a day and half, was expanded into a full week. Lady Randolph's dictum that all men found New York very dull was certainly belied in her son's case. After travelling by train to Key West in Florida in thirty-six hours (about the same time as it takes today) Churchill and Barnes embarked on board the Steamer *Olivette* and arrived in Havana Harbour on November 20 — ten days before Churchill's twenty-first birthday.

Cuba was discovered by Christopher Columbus in 1492: his tomb, though not his remains, is still in the cathedral in Havana. In 1511 the Spaniards began the conquest of the island which they ruled until

1762 when Havana was captured by the British, who opened the
port to commerce and the slave trade; it was returned to Spain the
next year in exchange for the Floridas. Cuba became, after the
break-up of the Spanish Empire, the richest of Spain's colonial
possessions, but throughout the nineteenth century the island was
to be the scene of insurrection against Spanish rule. In 1868 there
began a native rebellion which was to simmer for ten years. Afterwards the Captain General, Marshal Martinez Campos, pursued a
conciliatory and humane policy (slavery was formally abolished in
1880 and ended in practice in 1886) but the rapid economic decline
of the country which followed a disastrous fall in sugar prices in
1893–4 once more ripened the native population — creoles as well as
negroes — for revolt. Early in 1895 the rebel leaders of the ten
years' war, Maximo Gomez and Jose Marti, returned from exile in
America and gave leadership to a new insurrection in the island.

From Spain Marshal Martinez Campos was recalled to command a
large expeditionary force to Cuba, and he set out on 2 April 1895
at the head of 200 picked officers and 7,000 men accompanied by
General Valdez, director of the Military School at Madrid, whom he
had selected to be his Chief-of-Staff.

Martinez Campos announced at the outset that his plan was to
occupy the principal towns in Cuba and thus confine the insurrection
to isolated areas, whilst at the same time embarking on a new series
of internal reforms. Unfortunately the isolated outbreaks severely
taxed the Marshal's resources: more and more men, money and
matériel were poured into the island from Spain, yet the strength of
the rebels seemed only to increase. The longer drawn-out the war
became the more sympathy and support was gained by the rebels. In
the United States the Government as well as public opinion openly
espoused their cause.

"Tomorrow we start 'for the front,'" Churchill wrote to his
mother on November 20 from the Gran Hotel Inglaterra, Havana,
"or rather to Santa Clara where the Headquarters Staff are. We go
by rail via Matanzas and Cienfuegos. The journey takes twelve hours
as the trains move very slowly on account of the rebels damaging the
line and trying to wreck the locomotives. I believe they also fire at
the train and throw dynamite cartridges — but the vigilance of the

patrols and also the fact that 40 or 50 riflemen go with each train have reduced risks considerably — and the General recommended the route."

Cuba: Area of Operations

Unfortunately, or perhaps fortunately for Churchill, the General's recommendation did not by itself carry any guarantee of safe conduct. Long before he got to "the front" Churchill had some exciting news for his first despatch to the *Daily Graphic:*

> As far as Colon the journey is safe, but thenceforward the country is much disturbed . . . At Santa Domingo a pilot engine and an armoured car are added to the train, as the rebels often indulge in target practice — from a respectful distance. In the car rides the escort, the passengers being permitted the privilege of using the ordinary compartments. When we reached this place the line thence to Santa Clara had just been cut, and the traffic had to go round by Cruces, thus causing a great delay. On arrival there it was announced that the train which preceded ours, and in which was General Valdes, had been thrown off the line a few miles beyond Santa Domingo, and that fifteen of its occupants had been severely injured.

This had been effected by weakening the supports of a small cul-
vert. The general fortunately escaped uninjured, and at once started
up country. Marshal Campos, to whose headquarters we went, received us very kindly, and readily gave us the necessary passes and
letters. Unfortunately, we found that the column of General Valdes
was already twenty miles away, through a country infested by the
enemy, and it would therefore be necessary to go to Cienfuegos,
thence by steamer to Tuna, and from there on to Sancti Spiritu.
Though this route forms two sides of a triangle, it is — Euclid
notwithstanding — shorter than the other, and we shall catch the
column there.

When Barnes and Churchill got to Tuna, however, they found
that the daily train to Sancti Spiritus had already left — they missed
it by half an hour — and shortly afterwards news came that the insurgents had thrown a bomb at the train.

They then exploded some dynamite successfully, and broke down a
small bridge. As soon as the train arrived at the obstruction it was
fired upon, and when its occupants had had enough they returned
to Tuna to wait until the line was repaired. We were in the same
position, and had to spend the day in the local hotel — an establishment more homely than pretentious.

But the next morning they were able to go to Sancti Spiritus —
"a forsaken place, and in a most unhealthy state. Smallpox and
yellow fever are rife." They beat General Valdez and his column by
a short head and on the following day set out with them on a march
to the village of Iguara, blockaded by the insurgents with the object
of protecting a supply convoy.

On November 29 news came that a band of 4000 insurgents under
Maximo Gomez was encamped a few miles to the east of Iguara and
at 5 a.m. on November 30 General Valdez set out from Arroyo
Blanco, in pursuit of the insurgents.

There was a low mist as we moved off in the early morning, and all
of a sudden the rear of the column was involved in firing. In those

days when people got quite close together in order to fight, and used
— partly, at any rate — large-bore rifles to fight with, loud bangs
were heard and smoke puffs or even flashes could be seen. The firing
seemed about a furlong away and sounded very noisy and startling.
As, however, no bullets seemed to come near me, I was easily reassured. I felt like the optimist "who did not mind what happened,
so long as it did not happen to him."

It was Churchill's twenty-first birthday and on that day, he recalls
in *My Early Life,* "for the first time I heard shots fired in anger and
heard bullets strike flesh or whistle through the air."

From that time onwards the column was in contact with the insurgents almost continually for the next three days. On the afternoon
of December 1, he wrote in his account to the *Graphic:*

> . . . the day was hot, and my companion and I persuaded a couple
> of officers on the Staff to come with us and bathe in the river. The
> water was delightful, being warm and clear, and the spot very beau-
> tiful. We were dressing on the bank when, suddenly, we heard a
> shot fired. Another and another followed; then came a volley. The
> bullets whistled over our heads. It was evident that an attack of
> some sort was in progress. A sentry, sitting on a tree about fifty
> yards higher up stream, popped over it, and, kneeling down behind,
> began to fire at the advancing enemy, who were now not 200 yards
> away. We pulled on our clothes anyhow, and one of the officers, in
> a half-dressed state, ran and collected about fifty men who were
> building shelters for the night close by. Of course they had their
> rifles — in this war no soldier ever goes a yard without his weapon —
> and these men doubled up in high delight and gave the rebels a
> volley from their Mausers which checked the enemy's advance. We
> retired along the river as gracefully as might be, and returned to
> the general's quarters.

That night a bullet came through the hut in which Churchill and
Barnes were sleeping and another wounded an orderly just outside.
The following day came the attack by General Valdez in what was
to become known as the battle of La Reforma. "We advanced right

across open ground under a very heavy fire," he wrote to his mother when he got back to his hotel in Havana on December 6.

> The General, a very brave man — in a white and gold uniform on a grey horse — drew a great deal of fire on to us and I heard enough bullets whistle and hum past to satisfy me for some time to come. He rode right up to within 500 yards of the enemy and there we waited till the fire of the Spanish infantry drove them from their position. We had great luck in not losing more than we did — but as a rule the rebels shot very high. We stayed by the General all the time and so were in the most dangerous place in the field. The General recommended us for the Red Cross — a Spanish Decoration given to Officers — and coming in the train yesterday, by chance I found Marshal Campos and his staff, who told me that it would be sent us in due course.

Though he was not subsequently to be allowed to wear the Spanish decoration, the Red Cross was to be a heavy one to bear in the ensuing weeks. The popular and provincial press both in England and in New York made scathing comments when they heard that Churchill had been with the government forces. "Sensible people," wrote the *Newcastle Leader* on December 7, "will wonder what motive could possibly impel a British officer to mix himself up in a dispute with the merits of which he had absolutely nothing to do. Mr Churchill was supposed to have gone to the West Indies for a holiday, he having obtained leave of absence from his regimental duties at the beginning of October for that purpose. Spending a holiday in fighting other people's battles is rather an extraordinary proceeding even for a Churchill." The *Eastern Morning News* on the same day commented: "Difficulties are certain to arise and Lord Wolseley will probably order him to return at once and report himself."

As soon as he returned to Tampa Churchill denied that he had fought against the Cubans. "I have not even fired a revolver. I am a member of General Valdes's staff by courtesy only, and am decorated with the Red Cross only by courtesy." In New York he gave interviews to the press who received his views with a mixture of grudging respect and tolerant amusement. "One conspicuous feature of this war," he told them, "is the fact that so few men are killed.

There can be no question as to the immense amount of ammunition expended on both sides, but the surprising truth remains that ridiculous little execution is done. It has always been said, you know, that it takes 200 bullets to kill a soldier, but as applied to the Cuban war 200,000 shots would be closer to the mark."

Barely a month after Churchill had taken leave of Marshall Martinez Campos the unfortunate Captain General was dismissed. His friend the Duke of Tetuan resigned in sympathy and the Marshal's place was taken by General Weyler, who had acquired a reputation for ruthlessness in ending the insurrection in 1878: the mere threat of his arrival had been sufficient to bring to an end rioting among the students of Barcelona.

Churchill formed clear and decided views about what he had seen in Cuba. But these did not help him to come down on one side or the other. He had a natural sympathy for people trying to shake off an oppressor, a natural distaste for the high-handed and often stupid actions of the colonial administrators. He saw, moreover, that "the demand for independence is national and unanimous." In his very first despatch he had written: "The insurgents gain adherence continually. There is no doubt that they possess the sympathy of the entire population."

On the other hand he was frankly contemptuous of the ill-organized, ineffective, destructive and often cruel manner in which the rebels conducted their campaign. "They neither fight bravely nor do they use their weapons effectively," he later wrote in the *Saturday Review* on 7 March 1896. "They cannot win a single battle or hold a single town. Their army, consisting to a large extent of coloured men, is an undisciplined rabble." What he saw of the rebel forces and of the havoc wreaked by them on the economy and administration of the country did not inspire in Churchill any confidence that the insurgents would provide a better alternative for Cuba than the Spanish colonial power. "The rebel victory offers little good either to the world in general or to Cuba in particular," he wrote on 15 February 1896 in the *Saturday Review*. "Though the Spanish administration is bad a Cuban Government would be worse, equally corrupt, more capricious, and far less stable. Under such a Government revolutions would be periodic, property insecure, equity unknown."

Sending his friend Bourke Cockran a copy of this article Churchill wrote:

WSC to W. Bourke Cockran

(Cockran Papers)

EXTRACT

29 February [1896]   Bachelors' Club W.

. . . I hope the United States will not force Spain to give up Cuba —
unless you are prepared to accept responsibility for the results of
such action. If the States care to take Cuba — though this would be
very hard on Spain — it would be the best and most expedient course
for both the island and the world in general. But I hold it a
monstrous thing if you are going to merely procure the establishment of another South American Republic — which however de-
graded and irresponsible is to be backed in its action by the American people — without their maintaining any sort of control over its
behaviour.

I do hope that you will not be in agreement with those wild,
and I must say, most irresponsible people who talk of Spain as
"beyond the pale" etc etc. Do write and tell me what you do
think. . . .

No doubt Churchill felt the delicacy of the situation of overly
criticizing the Spaniards who were his hosts and who necessarily were
responsible for his food, his shelter and his safety. Moreover he had
been under fire with the Spaniards on his twenty-first birthday.
Roughing it and encountering some danger with people who are your
hosts inevitably breeds a comradeship which makes completely objective reporting impossible. Just over forty years later he sought to
restrain his son from going to the Spanish civil war to report it for
the *Daily Mail.* He pointed out how difficult it would be to write
objectively about a war (quite apart from the difficulties of censor-
ship) when you were on one side of the lines. He further told his son
that he must on no account later go to the other side; in that case he
would be suspected by both sides of being a spy. This latter advice
was heeded. In retrospect — though it was frustrating at the time —
it was a good thing that General Franco's public relations officers

only allowed the author once to come under fire about two miles outside Madrid.

A year later, writing to his mother from India on 7 January 1897, Churchill expresses his second thoughts about the articles he had written on his return from Cuba:

> I reproach myself somewhat for having written a little uncandidly and for having perhaps done injustice to the insurgents. I rather tried to make out, and in some measure succeeded in making out, a case for Spain. It was politic and did not expose me to the charge of being ungrateful to my hosts, but I am not quite clear whether it was right.
>
> > This above all — to thine [own] self be true
> > And it must follow as the night the day
> > Thou canst not then be false to any man.
>
> I am aware that what I wrote did not shake thrones or upheave empires — but the importance of principles do not depend on the importance of what involves them.

It was not, however, just courtesy to his hosts that coloured Churchill's views when he returned to England after his expedition to Cuba. He foresaw that in the event of a rebel victory the predominant share in government that was likely to be demanded by the negro element among the insurgents, led by Antonio Maceo, would create renewed and even more bitter conflict of a racial kind and thus reduce "the richest island in the world," "the pearl of the Antilles," to ruin. This was the reason that led Churchill to view the rebel cause with less enthusiasm than was popular in large sections of the English Press, and among such of his contemporaries as Hubert Howard, who was reporting for *The Times,* but on the rebel side (and who incidentally was one of the war correspondents later to be killed at Omdurman).

This, too, was the reasoning that led him to look askance at the American Government's recognition of the rebel forces in March 1896. But when America actually intervened and went to war with Spain in 1898 there was no doubt where his sympathy lay. Consistent with the views he had expressed more than two years earlier he now saw the opportunity for firm and stable government in an island which was rich in resources but which had been impoverished and debilitated by mis-government and insurrection. "America can give the Cubans peace," he told the *Morning Post* in an interview on 15 July 1898, "and perhaps prosperity will then return. American annexation is what we must all urge, but possibly we shall not have to urge very long."

The myth has grown up that Churchill was in Cuba during the Spanish-American war, and that he had taken the side of the Spaniards against the Americans. Churchill took every possible step to dispel the myth but it kept recurring, notably at the outbreak of war in 1939 when an American Congressman implied that Churchill had actually been an enemy of the United States in the Spanish-American war.

*

On his return from Cuba there was still another nine months before Churchill was due to embark for India. Since they were going off for eight or nine years ample embarkation leave was provided in addition to normal winter leave, which he had used to such advantage. He had received a cheque from the *Daily Graphic* for 25 guineas for the five articles, and expended some of this in a curious way. The *Western Press* of 21 January 1896 reported that he had bought at a sale at Sotheby's a copy of Gay's *Fables* (1727–38) with plates after Gravelot and others. He did not persist in this incipient interest in rare first editions, though from now on he increasingly bought books to further the self-education on which he was determined.

He was longing to express himself: his new-found friendship with Bourke Cockran provided him with an opportunity to do so. Writing to him from Duchess Lily's house, Deepdene, on 12 April 1896, Churchill declared: "The duty of governments is to be first of all practical. I am for makeshifts and expediency. I would like to make the people who live on this world at the same time as I do better fed and happier generally. If incidentally I benefit posterity — so much the better — but I would not sacrifice my own generation to a principle however high or a truth however great." He went on to criticize a speech which Cockran had made, and which he had sent to Churchill, on the debilitating effect of English rule on Ireland and on Irish industry in particular. Churchill wrote:

> Six years of firm, generous, government in Ireland will create a material prosperity which will counteract the efforts which able and brilliant men — like yourself — make to keep the country up to the proper standard of indignation. Not for twenty years could a Home Rule bill pass the English people — so sick and tired are they of the subject — and by that time the necessity for one will have passed away. Home Rule may not be dead but only sleeping — but it will awake like Rip Van Winkle to a world of new ideas. The problems & the burning questions of today will be solved and Home Rule for Ireland as likely as not will be merged in a wider measure of Imperial Federation.

In his reply from New York dated April 27, Cockran begged Churchill to take up a study of sociology and political economy:

> With your remarkable talent for lucid and attractive expression you would be able to make a great use of the information to be acquired by study of these branches. Indeed I firmly believe you would take a commanding position in public life at the first opportunity which arose, and I have always felt that true capacity either makes or finds its opportunity. . . . I was so profoundly impressed with the vigor of your language and the breadth of your views as I read your criticisms of my speech that I conceived a very high opinion of your future career.

Churchill at this time was twenty-one. He must already have been able, on occasions, to indicate the genius that was to flower in the next half-century. Bourke Cockran must certainly have been a man of profound discernment and judgement of character. As far as we know, he was the first man or woman Churchill met on level terms who really saw his point and his potentialities. At this time Churchill had few friends among his contemporaries and almost none among his elders; his correspondence with Cockran was the first that he entered into with a mature man. Cockran in some ways fulfilled a role that Lord Randolph should have filled if he had survived. As we shall see Churchill was to continue this political correspondence throughout his early manhood and what he wrote to Cockran affords many revealing insights into the development of his mind.

The vivid impression which Cockran made on Churchill's young mind informed and pervaded his subsequent thought and oratory. In what history may decide was one of the most important speeches he ever made — at Fulton, Missouri, under the chairmanship of President Truman on 5 March 1946 — he said: "I have often used words which I learned fifty years ago from a great Irish-American orator, a friend of mine, Mr Bourke Cockran. 'There is enough for all. The earth is a generous mother: she will provide in plentiful abundance food for all her children, if they will but cultivate her soil in justice and in peace.' "

There is an agreeable postcript to this Anglo-American friendship. The author is indebted to his cousin, Anita Leslie, daughter of Churchill's first cousin Sir Shane Leslie, for the following letter:

Anita Leslie to RSC

EXTRACT

20 July 1965

. . . It is just a week since I was sitting in the pavilion at Syon with Adlai Stevenson. . . . Learning I was Winston Churchill's cousin he suddenly started to reminisce about his last meeting with him in the early 1950s. He said: "I asked him something I'd always wanted to know — I asked on whom or what he had based his oratorical style. WSC replied 'It was an American statesman who inspired me when I was 19 & taught me how to use every note of the human voice like an organ.' " "You'd never have heard of him" said AS. "He wasn't a great statesman, just an Irish politician with the gift of the gab, but Winston called him a statesman — his name was Bourke Cockran." I couldn't help interrupting with "He married my mother's sister Anne & darling Uncle Bourke left us every penny we have!" AS looked amazed and said "Well he never said there was a family connection, how strange. . . ." Nor was there really, for Bourke married the sister of Marjorie Ide who married Winston's first cousin my father. But who else in England would have known

all about Bourke! Such a character — I adored him — I was twelve
when he died & his great voice & thickset shoulders & granite ugly
deeply hewn face came back to me. How Bourke would have loved
to have known what *a lot* he could give to that young man. That
his own talent for oratory, wasted on tiresome American financial
problems should in the end help a voice that would hold fortunate
Europe through its most terrible hour.

Adlai was surprised at my interjections but went on, "Winston
then to my amazement started to quote long excerpts from Bourke
Cockran's speeches of sixty years before." Of course AS couldn't
check the absolute accuracy but there was Winston pouring out to
him this tremendous impact on his youth — saying, "He was my
model — I learned from him how to hold thousands in thrall" and
quoting with terrific force.

Within 24 hours of telling me all this — which moved him greatly
— Adlai Stevenson was dead.

I have quoted his words verbatim while they are still distinct in
my memory. . . .

*

Meanwhile Churchill took advantage of his family connections and
of the lively interest and good-will which his name aroused — to
make the acquaintance of many of Lord Randolph's friends and asso-
ciates. All doors were open to him. "What's Randolph's boy like?"
people were inclined to ask. Churchill wondered what his father's
friends were like. He had not met many of them in his father's lifetime. He took advantage of the opportunities now presented. His
mother and Duchess Lily and her new husband, Lord William Beresford, were also most helpful. Lord William was the third son of the
4th Marquess of Waterford, and he had won the Victoria Cross in the
Zulu War. He had recently returned to England after sixteen years
as ADC and Military Secretary to four successive Viceroys of India.

On account of his father's reputation and his mother's influence he
was often asked to visit the famous "Natty" Rothschild at Tring.
Lord Randolph had taken him there two years before. "Natty"
Rothschild was a tremendous and unique figure in English society.
It was only in 1858 that the Bill had been carried removing the civil
disabilities of the Jews. The English have long been a stuffy and

insular race; they tend to resent the intrusion of foreigners in their midst. But the aristocracy were always prepared to accept and assimilate into their ranks foreigners of outstanding quality, particularly if they had a lot of money and proved serviceable to the country.

Thus the Huguenots, who came out of France at the time of the revocation of the Edict of Nantes, found a comfortable haven in East Anglia and revived and fortified the wool trade: self-made men were made knights, baronets and peers (Pitt once said "Any man who has £10,000 a year deserves to be a baronet"): Mr Disraeli became the darling of the Tory party: and Nathaniel Rothschild in 1885 at the early age of forty-four became the first Jewish peer. The Grand Council of Venice around the year 1300 closed its doors to all newcomers; hundreds of Venetian merchants in succeeding centuries made far greater fortunes than many of those possessed by the hereditary Council: but none were admitted. It is astounding that the Venetian Republic maintained its independence alike from foreign aggression and from internal revolt for 500 years until it was extinguished by Napoleon Bonaparte in 1797. The British nation was not extinguished because the aristocracy welcomed not only self-made Englishmen but also Jews and foreigners into their society.

The Rothschilds, in all the countries in which they settled, prospered and proved adaptable and good citizens of the countries of their adoption. They successfully transcended all kinds of snobbery and racial distaste in England, France, Germany and Austria. They acclimatized themselves to the new atmosphere in which they were living, and established rapidly their own standards of comfort, luxury, artistic taste and above all of cuisine. The Rothschildren achieved in many people's eyes the status of minor royalty.

WSC to Lady Randolph

26 January 1896 Tring Park
Tring

My dear Mamma,

There is no hunting tomorrow owing to the death of Mr Lambton, a prominent member of the hunt, so I shall be back in time for luncheon. We have a very interesting party here. Mr & Mrs Asquith — Mr Balfour, the Recorder & Mr Underdown who has great Railway interests in Cuba, several ladies — ugly and dull — Hubert Howard & myself. Lord Rothschild is in excellent spirits & very interesting and full of information. Altogether, as you may imagine, I appreciate meeting such clever people and listening to their conversation very much indeed.

I expect that Dr Jameson and his officers will be dealt with as severely as the government know how. I have not heard a word of excuse or sympathy from anyone. Mr Balfour — particularly — seemed to think that they deserved exemplary punishment & though, as he observed, "it is a case for the Jury" it will not be the fault of HM government if they don't get two years apiece.

I suppose they are right & that these men who never considered us — or English interests — should in their turn receive no consideration from us. But all the same I venture to doubt the advisability of severity. South African opinion & South African interests ought not to be altogether disregarded & the whole of the Cape would vigorously protest against — and bitterly resent the infliction of such a punishment.

Mr Chamberlain has made an excellent speech — but one remark rather sticks in my throat. He says that the aspect of the majority of the population of the Transvaal — paying 9/10 of the taxes and having no representation is an anomaly! Rather a mild term this for a man with the history and political principles of Chamberlain. It was for such an "anomaly" that America rebelled from England & a similar "anomaly" was the prime cause of the French Revolution. However — he has to measure his words. We discussed Cuba also — Howard trying to lure Mr Balfour into recognising the insurgents — but he declined to be caught.

What astonished me in all these discussions of South African affairs is the way people disregard Rhodes. It seems to me to be reckoning without your host. You know what Papa thought of him. I will wager he will turn out to be a factor to be counted on.

Well — *à demain.*

With best love, Ever your loving son
WINSTON

Churchill did not confine his quest for new and interesting personalities and friends to Jewish households. During this period he was sometimes invited into Gentile society. A little later he dined with Mrs Adair who was an American lady and a notable London hostess. "Such an interesting party, Mr Chamberlain — Lord Wolseley, Mr Chaplin — Lord James, Sir Francis Jeune and in fact all the powers that be. Chamberlain was very nice to me and I had quite a long talk with him on South Africa.

"Tonight I am dining with Lord James, who has the Duke of Devonshire and a lot of 'notables' so I hope to be quite *'au fait.'* "

Churchill was not wasting his time in London, prior to his departure for India. At these three social functions he had the opportunity of meeting, among others, the former Home Secretary and future Prime Minister (Asquith); the Leader of the House, First Lord of the Treasury and another future Prime Minister (Balfour); the Colonial Secretary (Chamberlain); the Commander-in-Chief of the British Army (Wolseley); the President of the Local Government Board (Chaplin), the Chancellor of the Duchy of Lancaster (James); the President of the Probate Division and Judge Advocate General (Jeune); and the Lord President of the Council (Devonshire).

Churchill took pains to cultivate the important people he met: he was learning from them about the facts of life and how things were done. He was to make the fullest use of the contacts and friendships which he acquired.

*

Churchill enjoyed these social amenities, but as he many years later said, in an entirely different context, he thought they should be used "as a springboard, not as a sofa." He was for action; and half his interest in meeting all these fascinating and important people was to use them as a personal springboard. The time for his departure for India was approaching: the nearer it came, the less he liked the prospect. For a few brief years he had escaped from nine years of servitude at his private and public schools. Was he now to be imprisoned for another nine years, away from England, the centre of political action?

Whilst still in England he had sought by every means to find adventure elsewhere. When the island of Crete entered one of its periodical phases of conflict and disorder Churchill offered his services as Special Correspondent to the *Daily Chronicle*. This offer was politely declined, though it was suggested that if Churchill were to go of his own accord the paper would be happy to receive his reports. "For, say, five letters of about a column and a half each, we should be willing to pay you for such Correspondence at the rate of ten guineas a letter. I may add that if you were able to send us any news of great importance, or to secure any facts or descriptions of sensational interest, we should be very ready to increase these terms considerably."

Then he heard that the Sirdar, General Sir Herbert Kitchener, was organizing another expedition up the Nile. Churchill asked Captain Philip Green, who had married his god-mother, Lady Camden, two and a half years after the death of her first husband, to try to get him out to the Sudan, if possible as a galloper to Kitchener. Green wrote to such varied people as Pandeli Ralli, a former Liberal MP and a notable member of Anglo-Greek society in London, and the Duke of Montrose. Once again, Churchill's offers were declined. Nor was he more successful when he sought to join Sir Frederick Carrington's expedition against the natives in Matabeleland. Indeed, the manner in which Churchill and his friends and relations kept importuning the War Office led Lord Lansdowne, the Secretary of State for War, to give a word of friendly warning to Lady Randolph:

> May I, as a friend, add this? I am not quite sure that in view of the enquiry which has been promised into the charges made recently against some of the officers of the 4th Hussars, it would be wise on Winston's part to leave England at this moment. There are plenty of ill natured people about, and it is just conceivable that an attempt might be made to misrepresent his action.

As the day of embarkation drew nearer, Churchill grew more hot-tempered and impatient.

WSC to Lady Randolph

EXTRACT

4 August 1896   Hounslow

. . . I daresay you have read in the papers that the 9th Lancers are to go to Durban on the 25th inst. If they are to be sent straight to Rhodesia they will have to take two or three extra subaltern officers

— who will be attached from cavalry regiments. I have applied to their colonel to take me should such a contingency arise — and Bill Beresford has wired to him on my behalf. Consequently it is within the bounds of possibility that I may get out after all — and in the best way too — with an English cavalry regt. This we will talk over on Friday — but my dear Mamma you cannot think how I would like to sail in a few days to scenes of adventure and excitement — to places where I could gain experience and derive advantage — rather than to the tedious land of India —where I shall be equally out of the pleasures of peace and the chances of war.

The future is to me utterly unattractive. I look upon going to India with this unfortunate regiment — (which I now feel so attached to that I cannot leave it for another) — as useless and unprofitable exile.

When I speculate upon what might be and consider that I am letting the golden opportunity go by I feel that I am guilty of an indolent folly that I shall regret all my life. A few months in South Africa would earn me the S.A. medal and in all probability the company's Star. Thence hot foot to Egypt — to return with two more decorations in a year or two — and beat my sword into an iron despatch box. Both are within the bounds of possibility and yet here I am out of both. I cannot believe that with all the influential friends you possess and all those who would do something for me for my father's sake — that I could not be allowed to go — were those influences properly exerted.

It is useless to preach the gospel of patience to me. Others as young are making the running now and what chance have I of ever catching up. I put it down here — definitely on paper — that you really ought to leave no stone unturned to help me at such a period. Years may pass before such chances occur again. It is a little thing for you to ask and a smaller thing for those in authority to grant — but it means so much to me.

Three months leave is what I want & you could get it for me. If I can't get this — perhaps I may be able to go with the 9th [Lancers] — but that might only end in police duty in Natal.

You can't realise how furiously intolerable this life is to me when so much is going on a month away from here. . . .

No answer from Lady Randolph survives. All was settled: all was ordained. He sailed from Southampton for India in S.S. *Britannia* with the 4th Hussars on 11 September 1896.

9

India

MANY YOUNG MEN, at the age of twenty-one, with few attachments at home, would have thought it a high adventure to sail for India and to be stationed there for eight or nine years. Churchill had mixed feelings. He was enraptured by any form of adventure — he had had some of a limited character in Cuba; but he doubted if there would be much opportunity in India. In any case he had already determined that his life should be one of politics. But how to escape from the Army? How to pay his debts? How to achieve an income that would permit his entry into the House of Commons? (Members were not paid until 1911, and then only £400 a year.) These were the ugly and at the time unanswerable questions which were in his mind when he sailed for India.

In those days it was difficult for a young gentleman of good but impecunious family to find a way of earning a living. Trade, commerce and the Stock Exchange were still frowned on in many quarters as unfitting for a gentleman; and these institutions did not much solicit the services of young gentlemen, however gifted. If a young man was not clever enough to go to the Bar, or had not enough influence to get himself into a firm of merchant bankers, he had scarcely any other alternative but to go into the Church, the Army or the Navy, all ill-rewarded professions. Though Churchill was now of age he had inherited no estate. He was, after all, the son of a younger son, and his mother, Jennie, was busy dissipating the remains of a considerable fortune which her father Leonard Jerome had settled upon her. He sailed to India with little more prospects than did Clive; but he did not, like Clive, try to kill himself.

Colonel Brabazon did not sail with the regiment to India; he had relinquished command of the 4th Hussars during the summer and handed over to Colonel William Alexander Ramsay. Colonel Ramsay was, in contrast to his predecessor, a quiet unspectacular officer who suffered from the misfortune of never having seen action in nearly thirty years of service. Churchill's especial friends on the long voyage out were his old travelling companion Reggie Barnes, who had been confirmed as Adjutant in May; Hugo Baring, a son of Lord Revelstoke; Ian Hogg, and, among the senior officers, Major Ronald Kincaid-Smith who was the following year to become second-in-command.

During his voyage Churchill wrote to his mother, posting two letters at Port Said and one on arrival in Bombay. In one of the earlier letters he wrote:

WSC to Lady Randolph

EXTRACT

18 September 1896   S.S. *Britannia*
                                  (between Malta and Alexandria)

. . . I play Picquet with Hugo Baring & chess with Kincaid & in the afternoons and evenings our string band plays — adding to the agreeableness of the voyage. Everyone here pretends the weather is very hot — sleeps on deck etc. But I remain comfortably in the deserted cabin which as I have it to myself at nights is perfectly cool. *We* make a very cheery party ourselves — and as there are nearly a hundred officers on board there is no lack of company. . . .

His letter from Bombay shows that picquet was soon displaced as his main diversion by chess "which is cheaper and more amusing than cards — and which Kincaid-Smith and I have played almost unceasingly for eight days." There was a tournament on board and Churchill reached the semi-final. "I have improved greatly since the voyage began," he wrote just before disembarking, "and I think I shall try and get really good while I am in India." His father had been an excellent chess player in his youth and founded the Oxford University Chess Club. Nine years later, in the Life of his father, Churchill gave with much relish the details of Lord Randolph's

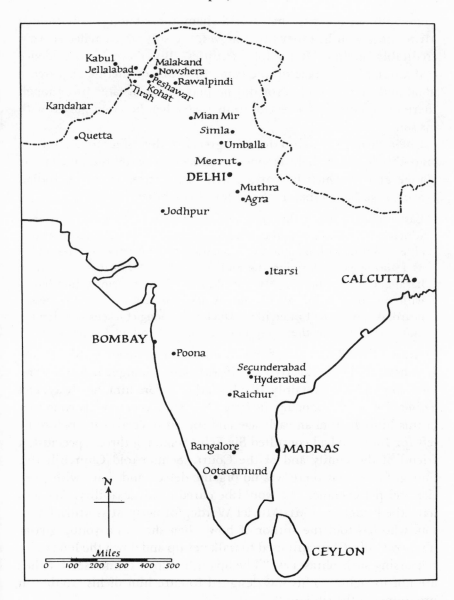

Kabul
Jellalabad
Malakand
Nowshera
Peshawar
Rawalpindi
Kohat
Tirah
Kandahar
Mian Mir
Simla
Quetta
Umballa
Meerut
DELHI
Muthra
Agra
Jodhpur
Itarsi
CALCUTTA
BOMBAY
Poona
Secunderabad
Hyderabad
Raichur
Bangalore
MADRAS
Ootacamund
N
Miles
0   100   200   300   400   500
CEYLON

game with Mr Steinitz, then world champion. Though blindfolded Mr Steinitz won in thirty-three moves, a result which reflected very creditably on Lord Randolph's abilities. But there is no evidence that Churchill did take up the game in India, or that he acquired a notable degree of skill. Nor did he play much in later life, though there was a period of a year or so in 1926 when he often played with his son.

Chess apart, Churchill found agreeable diversion in a kind of "moot" which was held among the officers towards the end of the voyage and in which he participated. In a letter from the Indian Ocean of 30 September 1896, he told his mother:

> Last night we had rather an amusing "Breach of Promise" case in which I was counsel for the defence. To my relief I showed myself able to speak without notes or preparation for twenty minutes and as I succeeded in keeping the audience in constant laughter — my harangue was a success. My impediment did not seem to interfere with my articulation at all and of all who spoke I was the best heard. In the army I came like a Duckling among chickens — I don't know whether I or they were most astonished to find I could swim.

All his life Churchill suffered from an impediment in his speech. It is hard to define exactly what it was; some thought it was a stammer: some a lisp. Certainly, like his father before him, he always had a difficulty in pronouncing the letter "s." He was extremely conscious of this himself from an early age and sought to correct it. Before he left for India he had consulted Sir Felix Semon, a throat specialist, a friend of the family and of the Court. Semon told Churchill (fee four guineas) that there was no organic defect, and that "with practice and perseverance" he would be cured of his disability. We also have the evidence of Mrs Muriel Warde, formerly Miss Muriel Wilson, who has told the author of how when she was a young girl at Tranby Croft, Churchill used to walk her up and down the long drive rehearsing such phrases as, "The Spanish ships I cannot see for they are not in sight." This was designed to cure him of his trouble in pronouncing the sibilant "s."

A few years after his return from India he contemplated marrying Miss Wilson, who was a considerable heiress, as well as being one of the great beauties of her age. She rejected him. Thereafter he decided that he would never marry for money.

Though a lucky man in many ways, Churchill appears to have been unlucky in minor adventures. There had been the pneumonia at Brighton, the misadventures at Harrow, the tumble-down at Branksome Dene, Bournemouth, his fall at steeplechasing at Aldershot. Now, on his arrival at Bombay, he was to experience, through his enthusiasm, a misadventure the effects of which travelled with him for the rest of his life. Eager to go ashore, he tells us in *My Early Life*, he and some of his friends had summoned one of the many tiny boats hovering around the *Britannia* to take them ashore before the rest of the party. After about a quarter of an hour they reached the quays and the Sassoon Dock and "we came alongside of a great stone wall with dripping steps and iron rings for hand-holds. The boat rose and fell four or five feet with the surges. I put out my hand and grasped at a ring; but before I could get my feet on the steps the boat swung away, giving my right shoulder a sharp and peculiar wrench. I scrambled up all right, made a few remarks of a general character, mostly beginning with the earlier letters of the alphabet, hugged my shoulder and soon thought no more about it." He had in fact dislocated his shoulder and for the rest of his life this was to plague him. He had to play polo with the upper part of his arm strapped against his body. Once, he related later, his shoulder very nearly went out through a too expansive gesture in the House of Commons. But he always, as will be seen, liked to attribute his survival two years later of the charge of the Lancers at the Battle of Omdurman to the fact that he was unable to use a sword and instead had to defend himself with the more lethal Mauser pistol.

From Bombay the regiment travelled by train to Bangalore, breaking the journey at Poona. Bangalore was a military cantonment in the Madras Presidency. Despite the rigours of the climate even impecunious subalterns like Churchill seem to have been able to live in considerable comfort and with some degree of elegance:

WSC to Lady Randolph

EXTRACT

14 October [1896]   Bangalore

. . . The climate is very good. The sun even at midday is temperate and the mornings and evenings are fresh and cool. Hugo, Barnes and I are safely installed in a magnificent pink and white stucco palace in the middle of a large and beautiful garden. I will send you a photograph of the bungalow as soon as we are thoroughly settled. For servants we each have a "Butler" whose duties are to wait at table — to manage the household and to supervise the stables: A First Dressing Boy or valet who is assisted by a second DB: and a sais [syce] to every horse or pony. Besides this we share the services of 2 gardeners — 3 Bhistis or water carriers — 4 Dhobies or washermen & 1 watchman. Such is our menage. . . .

Churchill took advantage of his comfortable bungalow and his leisure hours at Bangalore to resume the hobby which he had not pursued since his holidays at Banstead when he was still a Harrow school-boy: collecting butterflies. At Bangalore he found his garden full of Purple Emperors, White Admirals, Swallow Tails and many beautiful and rare species. "I shall be able to make a fine collection with very little trouble and much amusement," he told his brother Jack. He sent to England for his implements, nets, collecting boxes, setting boards, pins and a killing tin. But even before they arrived, he had begun amassing a fine collection — so much so that Hugo Baring and Reggie Barnes, with whom he shared his bungalow, complained that the place was "degenerating into a taxidermist's shop." His rekindled enthusiasm had an unhappy interruption. On 2 December 1896 Churchill wrote to Jack:

My butterfly collection, which included upwards of 65 different sorts, has been destroyed by the malevolence of a rat who crawled into the cabinet and devoured all the specimens. I have however, caught the brute and had him killed by "Winston" the terrier, and have begun again perseveringly.

An entirely new interest was provided by gardening — or more precisely, the growing of roses. The bungalow's previous occupier had left a magnificent collection of standard roses in the garden: "We have now over 50 different kinds of roses," he wrote to his mother on 7 January 1897, "La France, Gloire de Dijon, Marechal Niel and the rest of them — and all the rest we planted on arrival have come up into bright coloured flowers. I take the greatest interest in their growth. In a year or so it will indeed be beautiful." And only a month later he wrote: "The garden is getting on well, though water is badly needed. I have 250 Rose trees & 70 different sorts so that every morning I can cut about 3 great basins full of the most beautiful flowers which nature produces." He became ambitious:

> I am hoping to obtain some orchids from Barnes & if it would not worry you I would like you very much to send a few English seeds — Wallflowers, Stocks, Tulips etc. They are unknown here — but I cannot doubt that in this climate all vegetation must flourish.

At this time he met the first great love of his life, Miss Pamela Plowden. She was seven months older than he and was still alive at his death.

Pamela Plowden's father, Mr Trevor John Chichele Chichele-Plowden, who was in the Indian Civil Service, was at this time Resident at Hyderabad. His first wife, the mother of Pamela, had died four years before, and he had just returned to India with his second wife Beatrice, whom he had married in 1895. Plowden was created KCSI in 1898 and retired in 1900. It appears that Miss Plowden was known to Lady Randolph but when she came on a visit to Bangalore Churchill had to report to his mother (26 October 1896): "Alas — I never met her in England so forbore to call." But the following week, when he went to Secunderabad, just ten miles from Hyderabad, for a polo tournament, Churchill did not let a second opportunity slip. He was smitten with instantaneous love the first time he met Pamela Plowden:

> I was introduced yesterday to Miss Pamela Plowden — who lives here. I must say that she is the most beautiful girl I have ever seen — "Bar none" as the Duchess Lily says. We are going to try and do the City of Hyderabad together — on an elephant. You dare not walk or the natives spit at Europeans — which provokes retaliation leading to riots.

The ride through the city of Hyderabad on an elephant with Miss Plowden was successfully accomplished. "She is," wrote Churchill to his mother, on 12 November 1896, "very beautiful and clever." He dined with the Plowdens at Hyderabad and not unnaturally enjoyed himself. "A civilised dinner with ladies present is delightful in this country after nearly three months of messes and barbarism."

He had little time for the traditional niceties, if such they could be called, of Anglo-Indian society. In his very first letter (4 October 1896) from the mainland he relates how he "saw a lot of horrid Anglo-Indian women at the races. Nasty vulgar creatures all looking as though they thought themselves great beauties. I fear me they are a sorry lot." "Nice people in India are few and far between," he wrote to his mother on 12 November 1896. "They are like oases in the desert. This is an abominable country to live long in. Comfort you get — company you miss. I meet few people worth talking to and there is every tendency to relapse into a purely animal state of existence." He and Hugo Baring went to Calcutta for Christmas. Churchill found the scene there as uninviting as in Bangalore. "Calcutta is full of supremely uninteresting people endeavouring to assume an air of heartiness suitable to the season," he told his mother on 23 December 1896. "This is a very great city and at night with a grey fog and cold wind it almost allows one to imagine that it is London. I shall always be glad to have seen it — for the same reason Papa gave for being glad to have seen Lisbon — namely — 'that it will be unnecessary ever to see it again.' "

Again he had written to Lady Randolph on 18 November 1896:

If I can only get hold of the right people my stay here might be of value. Had I come to India as an MP — however young & foolish, I could have had access to all who know and can convey. As a soldier — my intelligent interests are supposed to stop short at Polo, racing & Orderly Officer. I vegetate — even reading is an effort & I am still in Gibbon.

The newspapers when they arrive are out of date and one gobbles up a week's *Times* in a single morning. The Indian Press is despicable — being chiefly advertisements and hardly a telegram. The articles are written in Pigeon English, by Eurasians or natives — the paper is bad & the printing slovenly.

And he summed up his first eight months at Bangalore:

WSC to Lady Randolph

EXTRACT

14 April [1897] Bangalore

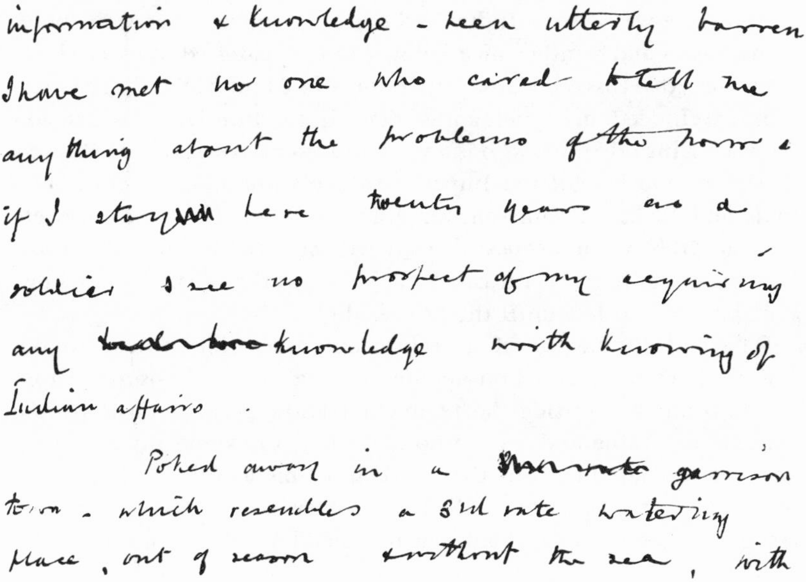
information & knowledge – been utterly barren. I have met no one who cared to tell me anything about the problems of the hour & if I stay here twenty years as a soldier I see no prospect of my acquiring any knowledge worth knowing of Indian affairs.

Poked away in a garrison town – which resembles a 3rd rate watering place, out of season & without the sea, with

. . . The 8 months I have been in this country have as regards Indian information & knowledge been utterly barren. I have met no one who cared to tell me anything about the problems of the hour & if I stay here twenty years as a soldier I see no prospect of my acquiring any knowledge worth knowing of Indian affairs.

Poked away in a garrison town which resembles a 3rd rate watering place, out of season & without the sea, with lots of routine work and a hot and trying sun — without society or good sport — half my friends on leave and the other half ill — my life here would be intolerable were it not for the consolations of literature. The only valuable knowledge I take away from India (soldiering apart) could have been gathered equally well in Cumberland Place. Notwithstanding all this I have not been unhappy, though occasionally very bored, and I contemplate without repugnance returning to my books, my butterflies & my roses. But I must have some holidays & you will be harsher than the Carthaginians if you refuse me them.

I am alone now in the Bungalow Barnes having gone to Ootacamund a hill station for his leave & Hugo [Baring] to Simla to take up his appointment on the Viceroy's staff — so that things are very dull. Only Kincaid & I really are left with a few subalterns who have joined since we came to India & who are for conversational purposes — useless — and a rather nice fellow (Agnew) gazetted to us as Major from the 7th Hussars, whose experiences in Matabeleland are entertaining. Indeed my chief amusement is to stimulate a discussion between Kincaid-Smith who is a wild filibuster & worships the Raiders & Agnew who has all the Imperial soldier's prejudices against colonials and looks on Jameson, Sir John [Willoughby] the whites etc as scoundrels of the deepest dye. It will be terrible when this topic is worn threadbare. With care and judicious treatment it may however be made to last until the 8th of May.

I have lived the life of a recluse out here. The vulgar Anglo-Indians have commented on my not "calling" as is the absurd custom of the country. Outside the regiment I know perhaps three people who are agreeable and I have no ambitions to extend my acquaintance. The consequence is that at such a time as this — when ⅔rds of the regt are on leave or ill, I am somewhat thrown on my own resources. Fortunately these are not slender. But I must take a holiday. . . .

Churchill's letters show that he thought he was in a prison — he had no one to write to except his mother who was occupied with other matters and his brother Jack — more than five years younger than he was — only just leaving Harrow. From the time that he arrived in India he plainly had only two desires: one to read and learn about politics; the other to get out of the Army as soon as he could. Meanwhile, since he had no money he had the idea of going to any little wars that he could find. His industry in this matter was astonishing. First he reminded his mother that he was not at all disheartened by the rebuffs his offers of service had met with before his departure for India. "I suppose," he wrote to her, 18 November 1896, "you have noticed how de Moleyns has got on in S. Africa. The Distinguished Service Order and the command of the New Matabeleland Police have been his reward for a few months of enjoyable

& active life. Compare that with the reward of those who conscientiously perform the routine duties you are always advocating as the road to success."

Once again, he was determined to go to Egypt to join Kitchener's advance up the Nile. *"Please do your best,"* he wrote to his mother the following week. "I should not have forgiven myself if an expedition started next year and I felt it was my own fault I was not there." Even at Christmas time in Calcutta he had written: "I revolve Egypt continuously in my mind. There are many pros and cons but I feel bound to take it if I can get it. Two years in Egypt my dearest Mamma — with a campaign thrown in — would I think qualify me to be allowed to beat my sword into a paper cutter and my sabretache into an election address."

Elections were never very far from his mind as he scanned *The Times.* There was a by-election in November at East Bradford — a constituency in which his father had been much admired and with which Churchill felt he had a strong link. He wrote to his mother on November 4: "Had I been in England I might have contested it and should have won — almost to a certainty. Instead of being an insignificant subaltern I should have had opportunities of learning those things which will be of value to me in the future." When he heard the result and saw that the Conservative had won, he wrote: "What a pity I was not home." Noticing that it was Captain Ronald Greville, formerly of the Life Guards, who won the seat, he added with a touch of bitterness: "I see a soldier got in."

He continued to complain to his mother of the frustration which he felt in India:

WSC to Lady Randolph

EXTRACT

4 November 1896   Trimulgherry
                                                              Deccan

. . . Perhaps it is just as well — that I am condemned to wait — though I will not disguise from you that life out here is stupid dull & uninteresting. That, as a soldier & a young soldier — no one cares to give you information & you meet very few who could even if they would. [Unless] I know more of the influential people who rule the country and unless I get *good letters of introduction* to the *very best* (not socially best) people out here my stay is likely to be utterly valueless. In Cuba I had peculiar facilities of acquiring knowledge. Everyone, no matter of what party or station, was anxious to make me first the recipient & then the exponent of their views. Here no one cares a row of buttons. Probably if I had come out as a vy young member — for three months — I should know more than as a soldier in five years. I shall not stay out here long my dearest Mamma. It is a poor life to lead and even its best pleasures are far below those obtainable in England. I meet none but soldiers and other people equally ignorant of the country and hear nothing talked but "shop" and racing. . . .

The success of others while he was tied down in Bangalore was naturally galling. In Calcutta he met Lord Fincastle who was ADC to the Viceroy and whom he was to encounter several times in the future. "He got three medals out of Egypt and saw hardly any fighting." Later in January he reported: "The adj of the Infantry Regiment here went off to Egypt last night — being appointed to a commission in that service. He had no influence — but of course his age and service stood him in good stead. The general told K-Smith that he had heard I was to go too — but I have so far received no official communication. I want to go to Meerut for the Polo first — but after that — the Pyramids will be a better game."

Sir Herbert Kitchener, writing from the Headquarters of the Frontier Force at Dongola on 30 December 1896 to Lady Randolph, eventually agreed to have her son's name put down on the list for special service with the Egyptian Army, though there were no vacancies at that time in the cavalry. Churchill, who had become very disappointed at the lack of progress he was making in that direction, was delighted. He wrote to his mother on 18 February 1897: "You will see that if I go to Egypt & if things there turn out well, it might be almost worth my while to stick to soldiering. At any rate I am certain of this that unless a good opportunity presents itself of my obtaining a seat in the House of Commons, I *should* continue in the army for two years more. Those two years could not be better spent than on active service. The question is 'where'? Egypt seems the only hope & therefore I beg you to leave no stone unturned in your endeavour to obtain a vacancy for me."

Whether or not this "came off" he was determined not to pass a dull unhealthy summer languishing in Bangalore. Rather than do that he was prepared to spend such small funds as remained to him on taking passage to England for his three months' leave. He had a half-formed idea that he might stop off in Cairo "to pay my respects to the Sirdar" and perhaps be taken on on the spot. Perhaps also he might be able to animate his mother's friends in London to better effect if he were actually there to do it. His mother was against it:

Lady Randolph to WSC

EXTRACT

26 February 1897   35A Gt Cumberland Place

. . . It is absolutely out of the question, not only on account of money, but for the sake of yr reputation. They will say & with some reason that you can't stick to anything. You have only been out 6 months & it is on the cards that you may be called to Egypt. There is plenty for you to do in India. I confess I am quite disheartened about you. You seem to have no real purpose in life & won't realize at the age of 22 that for a man life means work, & hard work if you mean to succeed. Many men at yr age have to work for a living & support their mother. It is useless my saying more — we have been over this ground before — it is not a pleasant one. . . .

"I set great store on going to Egypt if they go on this year," Churchill replied to his mother. "I long for excitement of some sort and the prospect of joining an English expedition attracts me immensely. I do hope you will not relax your efforts."

*

Minor injuries bedevilled his first few months in India. In December he bruised and cut his knee rather badly as a result of a practical joke:

WSC to Lady Randolph

EXTRACT

8 December [1896]   Bangalore

. . . After a somewhat rowdy dinner the other night some one had secretly fastened the reins to the horse's collar — instead of his bit. The result was that off he galloped and spilled Hugo & I and two others at the first corner. Luckily no one was hurt seriously — but I pitched on my knee and cut and bruised it so badly that I shall not be able to play polo for at least a week and possibly a fortnight. Such a nuisance! I write this letter recumbent in a long chair — on my verandah. . . .

Churchill found the cut was slow to heal, a fact that he attributed to the climate, and though he was able to play polo after a few weeks it took more than a month to heal completely. Then in March he fell off his pony playing polo. "I pitched on my shoulder and bruised the muscle so much that I can hardly use my arms. The ground out here is so terribly hard that a fall is no joke." We do not know but it is probable that this was not the dislocated shoulder but the other one.

The following month, however, he had a much more dangerous mishap.

WSC to Lady Randolph

EXTRACT

6 April [1897]   Bangalore

My dearest Mamma,

We live in a world of strange experiences. In Cuba it was my fortune to be under fire, without being wounded. At Bangalore I have been wounded without being under fire. Four days ago I was in charge of the markers in the rifle butts and was sitting on the seat provided, thinking myself perfectly safe — when a bullet struck the iron edge of the Target — flew into splinters & rebounded all over me. One entered my left hand near the thumb and penetrated an inch and a half. Several others stuck in my Khaki coat and many whistled all around. It is to the mercy of God — as some would say — or to the workings of chance or the doctrine of averages — as others prefer, that I was not hit in the eye; — in this case I should have been blinded infallibly. Followed an abominable twenty minutes — probing etc — before the splinter was extracted & since then I have had a bad time every morning when the wound has to be syringed. Knowing, as you do, my keen aversion to physical pain or even discomfort I am sure you will sympathise with me.

I am now indeed a cripple. My left hand is closely bound up and useless. My right arm so stiff I cannot brush my hair & only with difficulty my teeth. However I am healing beautifully and yesterday I managed to play polo with the reins fastened on to my wrist, so that you can see that I am not really very bad. Enough of my ailments, which indeed are insignificant compared with those of some of the others. This climate has not been without its effect on the regiment. We have already invalided two officers & two more — Captain Lafone & one of the younger ones are very dangerously ill — the former with malaria the latter with enteric. While there are only three in the whole regiment who have not been laid up for something since we landed. . . .

In *My Early Life* Churchill described the care and attention the Regiment paid to the art of polo: "It was decided that the regimental polo club should purchase the entire polo stud of twenty-five ponies possessed by the Poona Light Horse; so that these ponies should form the nucleus around which we could gather the means of future victory in the Inter-Regimental Tournament. I can hardly describe the sustained intensity of purpose with which we threw ourselves into this audacious and colossal undertaking. Never in the history of Indian polo had a cavalry regiment from Southern India won the Inter-Regimental cup. We knew it would take two or three years of sacrifice, contrivance and effort. But if all other diversions were put aside, we did not believe that success was beyond our compass. To this task then we settled down with complete absorption."

Every day at five o'clock in the afternoon they played — Churchill in every chukka he could get into, rarely less than eight and more often ten or twelve in an evening.

He had started to play what even in the Army was an expensive game whilst still a cadet at Sandhurst, continuing when he was stationed at Aldershot and Hounslow; and now it was his sole recreation in India, where polo was probably cheaper than anywhere else. From the beginning he seems to have achieved some success:

WSC to Jack

EXTRACT

15 October 1896   Bangalore

. . . The polo here is very bad — and I expect our subaltern's team will easily beat the whole Bangalore garrison. I have only played three times but have made many goals. . . .

At Secunderabad they won the polo tournament and with it a silver cup worth 1,000 rupees (£60). No English regiment had ever won before a first-class tournament within a month of their arrival in India, and the success of the 4th Hussars team caused considerable discussion in the Indian newspapers. Polo attracted the interest of the whole community.

WSC to Lady Randolph

EXTRACT

12 November [1896]   Bangalore

. . . The entire population turns out to watch & betting not infrequently runs into thousands of rupees. Our final match against the Native contingent was witnessed by eight or nine thousand natives who wildly cheered every goal or stroke made by their country men — and were terribly disappointed by the issue. . . .

The centre of the regiment's hopes, and indeed the climax of the year, was the Inter-Regimental Polo Tournament at Meerut one thousand miles to the north. At that time the champions were the great Durham Light Infantry team and Churchill reported that up to the arrival of the 4th Hussars it had been an unheard of thing for a regiment to enter for the Great Tournament in its first year in India — let alone to have a chance of winning. In fact the team never went to Meerut in 1897 for General Sir Mansfield Clarke, the Governor of the Madras Presidency, refused the necessary leave for the polo team to go there. "I think this is most unjust and unfair as there is no precedent for refusing leave for this one tournament which is looked

upon by all out here as the great event of the year." We do not know
the reasons for Sir Mansfield Clarke's decision. Perhaps he simply
thought the 4th Hussars did not stand a chance. Anyway, the winning of the Great Tournament remained the cherished objective and
ambition of Churchill and his friends in the 4th Hussars in India.

Churchill played polo despite his dislocated shoulder, which required the wearing of a leather belt so that his right arm could not
swing too freely. He continued to play until 1927, when, at the age
of fifty-two, he played his last game in Malta with Sir Roger Keyes
who was then Commander-in-Chief Mediterranean. He always described polo to his son as the "emperor of games" and encouraged
him to take it up. Extravagant though his son was he did not feel
that the slender income which was all that Churchill could allow
him would justify such an extravagance.

*

Churchill's first few months in India were clouded by a disagreeable financial fraud into which his mother had stumbled. It appears
that through the introduction of Arthur Cadogan, the second son of
the 4th Earl Cadogan, Lady Randolph's sister Clara (Mrs Moreton
Frewen), Lady Randolph herself and some other friends had been
induced to part with quite considerable sums of money totalling over
£4,000 to one James Henry Irving Cruikshank. Cruikshank purported to be at the head of a syndicate speculating in American
stock. This was what Lady Randolph and her son called "The Spec."
However, from a wire received by Churchill at Port Said on his
journey out to India, it became clear that Lady Randolph and her
friends had in fact been defrauded. It was not just a case of foolish
investment: the money was not invested, it was spent.

WSC to Lady Randolph

EXTRACT

21 September [1896]   Port Said

. . . What an atrocious fraud has been perpetrated on us. I strongly
advise your putting the whole thing in George Lewis' hands. . . .

WSC to Lady Randolph

EXTRACT

30 September 1896   S.S *Britannia*
                                                    In the Indian Ocean

. . . I am very anxious to hear further news of your speculations and the consequent prosecution. It is hard indeed to imagine a more cowardly — mean — and contemptible swindle. The burglar who steals a few pounds worth of plate with an honest gemmy is sent to prison for seven years and it will be simply monstrous if those silken hatted scoundrels are to be left at large to continue their depredations. It is a public duty which you are bound to discharge. . . .

Churchill continued to insist that his mother should prosecute Cruikshank, even though this would not enable her to recover her money. His advice prevailed and a year later on 25 November 1897 Cruikshank pleaded guilty in the Central Criminal Court to obtaining large sums of money by means of fraud and with intent to defraud and to obtaining credit while being an undischarged bankrupt. The Common Serjeant sentenced Cruikshank to four years' penal servitude on each of the two counts, the sentences to be consecutive so that they amounted to eight years' penal servitude. He explained his heavy sentence by saying that "he could not lose sight of the fact that the prisoner was a type of a class — a large, growing, and dangerous class — of men who lived and thrived on the follies of mankind. In that overcrowded metropolis they were surrounded by thousands of the industrious poor struggling, often in vain, to live in decency and in comfort, while men like the prisoner clothed themselves in purple and fine linen and fared sumptuously every day. A Judge, in administering the law, had to remember that, while he punished the prisoner, it was his duty to endeavour to deter men of the same class from following in the same evil footsteps."
Curiously enough Churchill, who alone had been single-minded in his determination to prosecute Cruikshank, was a little shocked by the sentence.

I hope [he wrote to his mother on 2 December 1897], no social considerations increased the Judge's severity. I should have given 3 years

— had I had the decision. At the same time the sentence is only equitable when the contemptible nature of the crime is considered. In the whole matter you have discharged a public duty and can have the satisfaction of knowing that you have deserved well of the great republic of mankind.

*

Duchess Lily had promised Churchill a charger after he had passed the examination into Sandhurst. Now her husband, Lord William Beresford, bought him a racing pony; but the pony had not arrived in India by the time Churchill reached Bombay. The pony, called Lily after the Duchess, caused considerable misgivings to Lady Randolph. "It may be dead for all I know," she wrote to her son from Invermark on 23 September 1896, "but if it is not I want you to promise me to sell it. I had a long talk with the Prince at Tulchan & he begged me to tell you that you ought not to race, only because it is not a good business in India — they are not square & the best of reputations get spoiled over it. *You* don't know but everyone else does that it is next to impossible to race in India & keep clean hands. It appears that Col Brab told the Prince that he wished you hadn't this pony. Sell it & buy polo ponies. I *am sure* that you will regret it if you don't."

Churchill replied:

WSC to Lady Randolph

EXTRACT

14 October [1896]   Bangalore

. . . As to the racing pony "Lily." I have so far heard nothing of it — nor do I know by what steamer or in what condition it will arrive — but at the same time I expect it will be here within a fortnight. I do not at all want to sell it — and I cannot see that it is unwise of me to keep it. Bill Beresford would not be likely to have given it to me if it was certain to involve the unpleasant consequences you anticipate. Everyone out here possesses an animal of one sort or another which they race in the numerous local meetings. Kincaid-Smith among others in the regiment has just bought a pony and

Hoare & two other majors have one each already. Now I cannot believe that all who race — *on this small scale* — must necessarily soil their hands. To condemn a whole enormous class of good fellows — and to judge all by the few exceptions is just the sort of thing Col Brabazon would do. He always loves "glittering generalities" and it is so easy to say, "They are all cheats in India." Such a statement is of course nonsense and I am sure you will not believe it. Still less do I imagine that you will be ready to think that I could not run this mare in a fair and square manner — and must inevitably resort to malpractice or become connected with those who do.

Of course I shall do what you wish in the matter and if you insist upon my getting rid of my pony I will sell her — but I think you will not mind my pointing out how things really stand. In the first place it would be a very great disappointment to me and rob my life out here of one strong interest. In the second — these sort of valuable ponies are not sold every day for £300 when they are untried and unknown and even if I could find a purchaser it would probably mean a big loss — which I cannot afford. Besides this *certain* loss, there is an end to any chance of winning any of the big stakes which would pay my expenses and help me so out here. And thirdly — this pony was given to me by Bill Beresford, not in order that I might convert it into pounds and shillings, but to keep and use. He would be very disappointed as he has taken so much trouble about writing and sending it out etc, and would probably think very little of me for having screwed £125 out of the Duchess on such terms.

Considering all things my dearest Mamma, you must see how difficult my position is. If racing in India was confined — as Col Brab would have you believe — to a few black legs and other disreputable persons — of course I would not hesitate — but when I see *all* those with whom I have to live and many whom I respect owning ponies, I must confess I do not see why you should expect me to deprive myself of a pleasure which they honourably and legitimately enjoy — or why you should distrust my ability to resist the temptation to resort to malpractice.

In your next letter in answer to this write to me on all these points — and let me beg you, my dear Mamma, to bear in mind that it is one thing for you to say "sell" and quite another for me to find any one to buy — except at a ridiculous price. Also do remember that there is no reason why I should not join in the sports of my equals and contemporaries — except on the ground of expense. If you still wish me to get rid of the pony — after you have considered what I have written here — I will do so, but even then I should have to wait my opportunity. I beg you not to ask me to. So much for the subject in this letter. . . .

Lady Randolph repeated that "they all tell me that the racing in India is a very shifty unsatisfactory thing." Churchill retorted blandly: "You should tell His Royal Highness, if he says anything further about racing in India, that I intend to be just as much an example to the Indian turf as he is to the English as far as fair play goes."

The pony arrived at the end of November but even before she was fit for racing Churchill had participated in pony races, wearing his father's old colours of chocolate and pink cap and sleeves. He did not enjoy particular success — he came third three times and when Lily raced at Guindy in March 1897 she ran badly, "as she cannot be acclimatised or trained properly for some time to come."

His lack of success on the Indian turf, however, was no bar to Churchill's election to the Turf Club in London to which he had been proposed by his second cousin, Charles, Marquess of Londonderry. Colonel Brabazon came up specially from Warwickshire to support Churchill's election. His uncle, John Leslie, also came to support him.

＊

Throughout his military career Churchill remained a keen follower of public affairs and an avid reader of the newspapers. At first he confined his comments to military matters; while yet on board ship he deplored the iniquity of officers going to India having to declare articles on which duty must be paid. "Even my regimental saddle is liable to this excise. It seems to me a disgraceful thing to tax public servants going to India by the order of the Government in this extraordinary manner and I cannot see that the Indian Government can be constitutionally right in imposing taxes on Europeans who do not have a vote in such taxes. It is contrary to the fundamental principle of government — no taxation without Representation. But to impose such a tax on a saddle used *only* in military employment is so monstrous an act of injustice that you will find it hard to credit it. I expect I shall find many more instances of this same detestable fruit of bureaucracy."

When Lord Lansdowne advocated an increase in the size of the army Churchill wrote scathingly on 8 December 1896 of his "stupid speech":

WSC to Lady Randolph

EXTRACT

8 December [1896]   Bangalore

. . . I cannot help thinking that he is not as great a man as it is customary to suppose. I hoped no one would be so foolish as to advocate the expenditure of more money on the army. It is a shocking thing that we should be compelled to have a "hundred million budget" every year and you may be sure that the strain of taxation is not without its effect on the prosperity and happiness of the nation. I believe that it is necessary for us to have an unequalled navy: A fleet strong enough to render us superior to a combination of any two powers & with an ample margin for accidents. I would support taxation to almost any extent necessary to attain this end. With such a fleet an army does not become a necessity for defence. For offence an army corps or perhaps two would adequately carry out such enterprises in foreign countries — out of Europe — as might be expedient. The only other duty of the British army is to provide a training ground for our army of occupation here. The increase of the Anglo-Indian forces is a question which I do not consider above. It is one which Lord Lansdowne did not allude to either. It is a matter which rests with the Indian Government. They consider the garrison adequate. Where then is the necessity of an increase to the army? If money is to be spent & taxes imposed — let it at best be employed in making us supreme at sea. Given the unquestioned command of the sea — there is no part of our Empire which our present army could not protect — and without such command there is no part which two such armies could maintain. (India is of course the exception — but that is a matter for the Indian Government). For a man like Lansdowne to voice a petty jealousy & I believe to a great extent an imaginary jealousy — between army and navy — is most improper & unwise. . . .

We shall see how six years later, when he had at last entered the House of Commons, he was to oppose, in a series of highly successful speeches, Mr Brodrick's proposal of three Army Corps. The arguments which he had already propounded to his mother at this time were to mature and fructify.

When it was decided that the Guards were to serve abroad he wrote on 7 January 1897: "Formerly of course 'the Guards' were officered by the nicest fellows in the army & they were a *corps d'elite*. This is now all changed and I would infinitely prefer any Highland regiment or any Rifle Regiment to the Grenadiers, Coldstreams or Scots Guards, either to serve in or with. The army now stands on a democratic basis and 'the Guards' have been sacrificed to the spirit of the age. The name however is not yet wholly divested of its former splendours and 'Eton & the Guards' may still afford solid advantages to the wealthy aspirant for position." And again some weeks later:

WSC to Lady Randolph

EXTRACT

2 March 1897   Bangalore

. . . As to the Guards: I think the War Office have as usual been guilty of meddling & muddling. As usual they have been stupid and tactless. They have proposed a very unpopular change & they have shown no good reason for that change. The Government, also as usual, have had no hesitation in supporting a measure which would seem much better suited to a radical than to a Tory programme. The champions of the Foot Guards in the House of Commons have shown themselves equally tactless. Among the members are a large proportion of soldiers, of whom by far the larger part have served in the Line. Panegyrics on the exceptional efficiency of the Guards Battalions and eulogies on the superior zeal and patriotism of the Guards officers are not the means best calculated to win their votes. I read that Lord A. Compton talked about "levelling down to the line" etc. All this puts everyones back up. I know I should have been irritated myself and should have been inclined to think, that when people have such peculiarly good opinions of themselves, a little quiet solitude on some sea girt rock would do them no harm. However all this does not excuse the government, who will lose many friends by their stupidity.

Two years more will see this government ripe for a fall. A General Election now would probably bring the Radicals in. Certainly if they dropped Home Rule the country would vote for them. The swing of the pendulum has been accelerated by Ld Salisbury's obstinate boorishness, by Balfour's pusilanimous vacillations, by Lansdowne's ridiculous "reforms" & by Curzon's conceit. In two years more they will not command a majority in the country. When that state of things arises any accident might wreck them in the Houses. At least that is how it seems to me — though perhaps I look through bilious-coloured glasses. . . .

Churchill was beginning to express strong views on political matters. Already in November 1896 he had treated his mother to a lengthy and carefully thought out dissertation on the political situation at home. When Lord Rosebery resigned the leadership of the Liberal Party and explained his reasons for doing so in a speech at Edinburgh on October 9, he wrote to his mother:

WSC to Lady Randolph

EXTRACT

4 November [1896]   Trimulgherry
                                                          Deccan

. . . A more statesmanlike & impressive utterance is hard to imagine. He is a great man — and one of these days he will again lead a great party. The only two great men now on the political stage will be drawn irresistibly together. Their political reins already coincide and Ld Rosebery and Joe Chamberlain would be worthy leaders of the Tory Democracy. Such a combination is very distant now — but a fresh deal would bring it into the foreground. Since the question of Home Rule has disappeared from English Politics, the Liberal Unionists have lost their status entirely, and it is only the folly of the Radical party in pretending to cling to the ghost of separation which gives the L.U. an excuse to remain in a Tory government. When the Liberals have the courage to throw over their separatist principles, the L.U. are logically bound to return [to the Liberal Party]. The only thing that will keep them on our side will be the sweets of office. These they will endeavour to take with them and Chamberlain will await a pretext to gather his party up & with them many independent and advanced Tories and so put the Government out. I do not say he will do this deliberately — it may be forced upon him. Suppose the Lowther section of the Tory Party — *the landed interest* (after all the most powerful element on the conservative side) — force Salisbury to raise the question of Protection! The L. Unionists would say (rightly), "We are Unionists but we cannot follow the Union party into the land of Protection — on this question we must differ from you" just as in '86 they said to Mr Gladstone, "We are Liberals — but we cannot agree to Home Rule — on this question we must differ."

The result of so tremendous a juggle would be infallibly — to bring the two popular leaders & finest orators to the front. Divided they would be curbed by the solid remnant of the Conservative party — peers, property, publicans, parsons & turnips. Convergent interests would produce solidarity of action and their similar opinions would interpose no obstacle. Rosebery is only an advanced Tory — Chamberlain a prudent Radical. They would combine, and the fossils & the Fenians — the extremes of either party — would be left in the cold. So much for the Cabinets of the future. This is my final selection — and though it is unwise to prophesy till afterwards — you would do well to "expect the event" which is Gibbon for "await the result. . . ."

In February 1897 Britain, somewhat reluctantly, joined the five Powers in blockading the island of Crete and seeking to prevent Greece from sending reinforcements and supplies to the small Greek expeditionary force "protecting the Christians against the Turks." Lord Salisbury's action was part of his policy of trying to maintain the Concert of Europe, but Churchill wrote to his mother in his most indignant vein:

WSC to Lady Randolph

EXTRACT

25 February 1897   Bangalore

. . . What an atrocious crime the Government have committed in Crete! That Brtish warships should lead the way in protecting the blood bespattered Turkish soldiery from the struggles of their vic-

tims is horrible to contemplate. When Warren Hastings hired out a
British Brigade to a native ruler in order that that ruler might
destroy the Rohillas — he at least obtained in return for his in-
famous action substantial remuneration. But the British Government, in a vain endeavour to obtain the confidence of the Powers,
have not hesitated to commit a crime, equally cruel & more shameless,
in full sight of the world and of history. It is just as well that I am
so young that my opinions do not matter and may be revised and
altered without difficulty if necessary. For in this matter I thoroughly
agree with the Opposition and I cannot help hoping that the Neme-
sis which waits on evil actions may reduce & humble the perpetrators
of such a crime. When I think of all the principles which are bound
up with this Government — the Union — the constitution — Imperialism — even Monarchy itself and when I think of those who have
worked & toiled to make the party what it today is, the spectacle of
great majorities frittered away — of staunch friends alienated — of
splendid opportunities missed — becomes all the more mournful.

Among the leaders of the Tory party are two whom I despise and
detest as politicians above all others — Mr Balfour & George Curzon.
The one — a languid, lazy lackadaisical cynic — the unmonumental
figurehead of the Conservative party; the other the spoiled darling
of politics — blown with conceit — insolent from undeserved success
— the typification of the superior Oxford prig. It is to this pair that
all the criminal muddles of the last 15 months should be ascribed.
Lord Salisbury an able and obstinate man, who joins the brain of a
statesman to the delicate susceptibilities of a mule has been encouraged to blunder tactlessly along till nearly every section of the Union
party & nearly every cabinet in Europe has been irritated or offended.
The result is that abroad we follow the folly that led to that most
idiotic of wars, the Crimea, & keep the ring in which the Turk massacres subjects & at home we see the party to whom so much that is
precious is confided, reduced by the blunders of its leaders to ruin.
So much for politics. It is surprising how easily epithets and indignation rise in the mind, when the sun is hot, has been hot & is daily
getting hotter. Just as religion as it approaches the equator becomes
more full of ceremony and superstition — so language & ideas here
flourish with a florid fertility — which is unknown in more temperate
climes. So you must take 50% off this letter when you read it. . . .

Of course it was not just the sun which led to these ebullitions, of
which Lady Randolph may well have been a sceptical and usually,

as far as is known, an unresponsive audience. Churchill would far
rather have been addressing a crowded House of Commons or mass
meetings from a public platform. These letters are merely another
symptom of his frustration and his mother was the only person to
whom he could blow off steam.

In the matter of Crete, however, she was moved to reply:

Lady Randolph to WSC

EXTRACT

18 March 1897   Brooksby
                                                          Leicester

. . . I hope you have changed yr mind about Crete — subsequent
events must show you that the Concert of Europe were *obliged* to act
as they did altho' they certainly were slow in making up their minds.
I suppose after a bit the Cretans will settle down under a form of
autonomy & afterwards will become annexed to Greece. . . .

WSC to Lady Randolph

EXTRACT

6 April [1897]   Bangalore

. . . I [am] sorry you do not agree with my views on Crete. Certainly I
have seen no reason to alter what I wrote. We are doing a very wicked
thing in firing on the Cretan insurgents & in blockading Greece so that
she cannot succor them. It will take a lot of whitewash to justify
the spectacle of the Seaforth Highlanders fighting by the side of the
Bashi Bazouk. I admit the material arguments are rather on the
other side. That is bound to be the case, I look on this question
from the point of view of right & wrong: Lord Salisbury from that of
profit and loss.

Besides it does not appear to me that we are being dragged by the
nose by the European Powers into this action. Rather does it look as
if we took the lead. We have more ships & more men on the spot and
generally appear to be taking a very leading part. So what? In a
most atrocious crime, where France & Germany have hesitated, we
have rushed in. I am quite sure the people of England do not approve of the use to which their fleets and armies are being put — and
the Government will most certainly have to answer for their conduct.

Lord Salisbury is a strong man & a clever man. He is not running the risk of so much unpopularity for nothing. He does not wish the Russians to get to Constantinople and with this object he is willing to crush the Greeks & Cretans or anyone else whose interests do not coincide with his. The Turkish Empire he is determined to maintain. He does not care a row of buttons for the sufferings of those who are oppressed by that Empire. This is not only wrong but foolish. It is wrong because it is unjustifiable to kill people who are not attacking you — because their continued existence is inconvenient: and because it is an abominable action, which prolongs the servitude under the Turks of the Christian races.

It is foolish because, as surely as night follows day — the Russians are bound to get Constantinople. We could never stop them even if we wished. Nor ought we to wish for anything that could impede the expulsion from Europe of the filthy Oriental.

After all, we do not live in Crimean War days, nor need we repeat the follies of the past. Russia must have Constantinople. It is the birthplace of her religion & the aim of her ambitions. "Were I a Russian as I am an Englishman I would never rest till I saw the Russian eagle floating over St Sophia — never! never! never!" (Pitt on the American Colonies adapted). We shall be mad if we attempt to bar the just aspiration of a mighty people. I would sooner face an avalanche. Seventy millions of people without a warm water port. Is it rational?

But what is Russia doing in Crete? Of all the powers she alone has not the required troops and appears to cooperate most loyally. I do not trust her. Such rectitude would not be human. She cannot be acting in good faith. Every atrocity and every disturbance smooths her path to Constantinople. Is it conceivable she is acting disinterestedly. Never will I believe it.

Our Machiavellian Government had better be careful lest they find themselves even out done in vice. There are no lengths to which I would not go in opposing them were I in the House of Commons. I am a Liberal in all but name. My views excite the pious horror of the Mess. Were it not for Home Rule — to which I will never consent — I would enter Parliament as a Liberal. As it is — Tory Democracy will have to be the standard under which I shall range myself.

1. *Reform at home.* Extension of the Franchise to every male. Universal Education. Equal Establishment of all religions. Wide measures of local self-government. Eight hours. Payment of mem-

bers (on request). A progressive Income Tax. I will vote for them all.

2. Imperialism abroad.

East of Suez Democratic reins are impossible. India must be governed on old principles. The colonies must be federated and a system of Imperial Defense arranged. Also we must combine for Tariff & Commerce.

3. European Politics.

Non Intervention. Keep absolutely unembroiled — Isolated if you like.

4. Defence.

The Colonies must contribute and hence a council must be formed. A mighty navy must keep the seas. The army may be reduced to a training depot for India with one army corps for petty expeditions.

5. To maintain the present constitution of Queens — Lords — Commons — & the Legislative union as at present established.

There! that is the creed of Tory Democracy. Peace & Power abroad — Prosperity & Progress at home — will be the results. . . .

*

When he sailed for India, Churchill embarked on that process of self-education which was to prove so serviceable a substitute for the opportunities which he had neglected or rejected in his formal education. His letters to his mother show that he was already reading, while at Aldershot, Gibbon and Fawcett. There is no information available of what he read on the voyage out on the S.S. *Britannia;* but within a few months of his arrival at Bangalore he was making insatiable demands upon his mother for more books. During his first spell in India (September 1896 — April 1897) his mother sent him at his request 12 volumes of Macaulay (8 of History and 4 of Essays); 27 volumes of the *Annual Register;* and 2 volumes of Adam Smith's *Wealth of Nations.*

With time heavy on his mind (his hands were fully occupied with polo sticks and reins), he eagerly devoured the books that were sent to him. Within eight weeks of receiving the Macaulay, he was able to write to his mother on 17 March 1897: "I have completed Macaulay's History and very nearly finished his Essays." He frequently commented on the authors whom he read: "Macaulay," he wrote to Lady Randolph on 21 January 1897, "is easier reading than Gibbon and in quite a different style. Macaulay crisp and forcible, Gibbon stately and impressive. Both are fascinating and show what a fine language English is since it can be pleasing in styles so different." Two weeks later he wrote: "I have been reading a great deal lately. Fifty pages of Macaulay and twenty-five of Gibbon every day. There are only 100 of the latter's 4,000 odd left now."

In his letters to his mother, he philosophized on his reading. Thuswise, for instance:

WSC to Lady Randolph

EXTRACT

14 January 1897   Bangalore

. . . The eighth volume of Gibbon is still unread as I have been lured from its completion by *The Martyrdom of Man* & a fine translation of the *Republic of Plato*: both of which are fascinating. The former impressed me as being the crystallisation of much that I have for some time reluctantly believed. The writer however does not rise to the level of a philosopher. He is an excellent precis writer & I admired the compactness to which several works I had read were reduced in his pages. He may succeed in proving Christianity false. He completely fails to show that it is wise or expedient to say so. "*Toute verité n'est pas bonne a dire*" — is the criticism I have saddled his book with.

If the human race ever reaches a stage of development — when religion will cease to assist and comfort mankind — Christianity will be put aside as a crutch which is no longer needed, and man will stand erect on the firm legs of reason. But this change will never be accomplished or even accelerated by the success of Winwood Reade. One of these days — perhaps — the cold bright light of science & reason will shine through the cathedral windows & we shall go out into the fields to seek God for ourselves. The great laws of Nature will be understood — our destiny and our past will be clear. We shall then be able to dispense with the religious toys that have agreeably fostered the development of mankind. Till then — anyone who deprives us of our illusions — our pleasant hopeful illusions — is a wicked man & should — (I quote my Plato) — "be refused a chorus. . . ."

I envy Jack — the liberal education of an University. I find my literary tastes growing day by day — and if I only knew Latin & Greek I think I would leave the army and try and take my degree in History, Philosophy & Economics. But I cannot face parsing & Latin prose again. What a strange inversion of fortune — that I should be a soldier & Jack at college. . . .

He was well aware of the influence that Gibbon and his other reading exercised upon his style of writing. "The voyage," he wrote in one letter to his mother, "may be made by literature both profitable and agreeable," and then he crossed these words out, commenting "what a beastly sentence." "I suppress with difficulty," he added, "an impulse to become sententious. Gibbon & Macaulay, however much they may improve one's composition of essays or reports, do not lend themselves to letter writing." To his brother Jack he wrote:

WSC to Jack

EXTRACT

14 February 1897   Bangalore

. . . I am sorry you don't appreciate or approve of my literary style. Gibbon in his autobiography says "The habits of correct writing may produce without labour or design the appearance of art and study." That excuse is good enough for me & I hope you will be graciously pleased to accept it. There are however others. In England, you can in a few hours get an answer to a letter from any part of the country. Hence letter writing becomes short, curt & if I may coin a word "telegrammatic." A hundred years ago letter writing was an art. The Duchess, though not quite a hundred [*she was in fact seventy-four*], writes a letter far better than most people nowadays. In those times pains were taken, to avoid slang, to write good English, to spell well & cultivate style: Letters were few and far between & answers long delayed. You may appreciate the present rapidity of correspondence, but you will hardly claim that modern style is an improvement. Now, out here, I am for all purposes of correspondence in the same state as our great grandfathers were. Only one mail goes each week. Nearly two months elapse before an answer can be obtained. Can you blame me, if, while I suffer the inconveniences of our ancestors, I try to imitate their virtues? But enough of this, I have

been lured into a discussion much longer than I at first anticipated. . . .

To Jack indeed, he often wrote in a different vein:

WSC to Jack

EXTRACT

7 January [1897]   Bangalore

. . . Rudyard Kipling's new book [*The Seven Seas*] is I think very
inferior and not up to the standard of his other works. Few writers
stand the test of success. Rider Haggard — Weyman — Boldrewood
are all losing or have already lost their prowess. What happens is
this. An author toils away & has many failures. Rejected contribu-
tions — books which the publishers won't publish accumulate.
Money does not. One day he writes a book which makes him
famous: *King Solomon's Mines, A Gentleman of France* or *Robbery
Under Arms.* His name now is on every ones lips — his books are
clamoured for by the public. Out come all the old inferior productions from their receptacles, and his financial fortune is made. Few
authors are rich men. Few human beings are insensible to the value
of money. If a book by Weyman is worth a £1000 to him — that
book will be written. Hurried style — exaggerated mannerisms and
plagiarism replace the old careful toil. The author writes no more
for fame but for wealth. Consequently his books become inferior.
All this is very sad but very true — and I am afraid Kipling is
killed. . . .

Actually, far from being "killed," Kipling was still to write *Stalky
& Co, Kim,* the *Just So Stories, Puck of Pook's Hill, Rewards and
Fairies* — among others. *Robbery Under Arms,* however, a stirring
tale which Churchill remembered all his life and which he gave and
recommended to his son, is not much read today.

*

Always eager to find means of self-expression Churchill sought
correspondents other than his mother and his brother. He continued

to correspond with Bourke Cockran; he also found a ready outlet for his ideas in Mr Welldon. As Churchill was leaving for India Welldon had written him a touching letter of advice.

Reverend J. E. C. Welldon to WSC

28 September 1896   Harrow

My dear Churchill,

Thank you very much for your letter. I am very glad to get your letters and will always answer them for I have a strong and even affectionate feeling for you, and that not only because of the relation in which we have stood one to the other as Master and pupil but because your father's death invests your life and Jack's too, with a pathetic interest which is never out of my mind whenever I think of you. But just because I have this feeling I implore you not to let your wild spirits carry you away to any action that may bring dishonour on your school or your name. It is impossible that I should not hear of your follies and impertinences if you are guilty of them and you will recognise that you put a severe strain upon my friendship if you ask me to treat you as a friend when other people speak of you with indignation or contempt.

But enough of this, perhaps too much, and let me now congratulate you upon being sent to India. I would not have you forgo your Indian experience for the world. You will be a witness of the most interesting administrative work that has ever been done among men and you will be witness of it (if I am not mistaken) at a specially interesting moment. Please write and give me your first impressions of India for if second thoughts are said to be wiser than first, though I often doubt if they are, I am sure that first impressions are much truer than second. Tell me most of all what you think of the intellectual and moral capacities displayed by the natives. Speaking of your own life may I urge you to take up some study? There is no reason why you should not learn Latin (so far as it is unknown to you) or even Greek. Hobbes of Malmesbury learnt Greek when he was 70 years old and translated Thucydides. The discipline of study is or may be invaluable to your character.

Above all, my dear Churchill, think more of others than of yourself, be ready to learn from those that are below you and keep your conscience as restful as you can. Jack is very well and has a new room which he likes very much. I feel now as if I must try to be to him both father and brother. Believe me, with the best wishes for your future.

Ever sincerely yours
J. E. C. WELLDON

Gibbon is the greatest of Historians, read him all through.

Mr Welldon's advice may have been sound, but his memory faulty. Thomas Hobbes had learned Greek at the age of six; and though it is true that he was eighty-six when he completed a translation of Homer, he was still under forty when he translated Thucydides. Churchill knew nothing of this: he was distressed by the allusions — as he thought — to his part in the escapades of the 4th Hussars. He forwarded the letter to his mother, and told her:

WSC to Lady Randolph

EXTRACT

12 November [1896]   Bangalore

. . . When next you go down to Harrow — I want you to speak to Welldon about his views on my conduct & to place things before him in their proper light. His letter annoyed me and worried me very much. You must not let him know I forwarded the letter to you — because all correspondence belongs only to the person to whom it is addressed — I ought not really to have passed his letter on. . . .

To his brother he expressed himself more forcibly:

WSC to Jack

EXTRACT

24 November [1896]   Bangalore

. . . As for Welldon's letter: it did not do him credit. If he cared to believe the reports and tales of enemies — his friendship would be valueless. I wrote him back a long and, I think, a powerful vindication. I still entertain the highest opinion of his brains and respect his judgement on nearly every subject — but his ideas have been warped by schoolmastering and contact with clerics: both of which you should avoid. You need not show him this — as I find him a most interesting correspondent. . . .

In fact Churchill's fears about his relations with Welldon were unfounded. His mother wrote:

Lady Randolph to WSC

EXTRACT

11 December [1896]   35A Gt Cumberland Place

. . . I had it out with Welldon about you. He declares he was not thinking of Labouchere's attack & all that business when he wrote to you — but only of your habit (which in this case has cost you a good deal) of putting yrself so much forward. However *no one* pays any attention to anything in *Truth* so you need not worry. Welldon is going to write to you again. . . .

Welldon's letter pacified Churchill, who wrote to his mother:

WSC to Lady Randolph

EXTRACT

16 December 1896   Bangalore

. . . The mail brought a long letter from Welldon in answer to the one I wrote him sometime ago. He writes most affectionately & denies ever having read *Truth's* articles. I am involved in a theological controversy with him on the subject of the Christian Missions — which I deprecate and he defends. His last letter contained a most brilliant and convincing vindication of what I had called "attempts to annoy the heathen" — but I think my rejoinder will be very hard to get round. It is very good of him to carry on this correspondence with me — and I have expressed to him how much I appreciate his kindness. . . .

Two years later Welldon became Bishop of Calcutta and Metropolitan of India. He then became involved in a similar argument with a more formidable controversialist in the person of the Viceroy, Lord Curzon. The policy of the Government was not to interfere with the religious views of the inhabitants of the sub-continent. Curzon prevailed and Welldon returned to England in 1902 to become a Canon of Westminster. Curzon was less successful in his subsequent dispute with the Commander-in-Chief, Lord Kitchener. It was the Viceroy who was returned to England, Kitchener who remained in India.

＊

For all his caustic comments about life in India, for all his desire to leave Bangalore, and, indeed the Army, Churchill took his military duties seriously and appeared to enjoy them.

Mr S. Hallaway, who was his troop sergeant in Bangalore, recalls in Mr David Scott Daniell's *The History of the Fourth Hussars,* published in 1959:

> After a field day Mr Churchill would arrive at stables with rolls of foolscap and lots of lead pencils of all colours, and tackle me on the movements we had done at the exercise. We were nearly always short of stable men, and there were a lot of spare horses to be attended to, so it was quite a hindrance to me. If I was not paying much attention to Mr Churchill's drawings of the manœuvres he would roll the paper up and say, "All right, you are bad-tempered today!" I was not bad-tempered really, but I was a busy man, and I had no time for tactics.

Hallaway also recalls Churchill displaying what was to him unexpected knowledge on the subject of musketry. They were both detailed to attend a course of musketry, and to the sergeant's astonishment Churchill delivered a masterly lecture on the subject and passed out top of the class.

Early in the new year, the regiment went out on two weeks' manœuvres some fifteen miles from Bangalore, living under canvas in "some arid spot . . . under a sun which is getting hotter every day."

WSC to Lady Randolph

28 January [1897]   Kundana Camp
                                                     Madras

My dearest Mamma,

I am afraid I must write you another short letter, this week. We are still under canvas and there is so much to do that when it is all done, but little time and energy remains for letter writing. We have had a week of battles. The camp moves nearly every day and one hot desert is exchanged for a still hotter one. At last the end has been reached. I cannot say I am sorry as the discomforts all the time have been great and the days very long. On the other hand there are contrasting reflections. I have had for the first time in my military experience responsibility & have discharged it, not altogether without success. The regiment has had to adapt itself to the new conditions of a strange country, has had to find out many things which it would have been easy for others to explain; has been exposed to the carping criticism of those Anglo Indian soldiers who look upon soldiering in England as farcical and in spite of all these difficulties its reputation for smartness has been unimpaired. Tomorrow we begin our march back to Bangalore — which we shall reach the day after. Thence, next week, I will write you a longer letter from my own room — in peace and comfort. The heat in this tent is well over 90° — and I have been out for six sunny hours this morning — chasing or being chased by the native cavalry. So my dear Mamma, I know you won't mind my leaving off now.

With best love, Your loving son
WINSTON

When he returned to Bangalore he was acting as Adjutant, having to write "so many memos etc that to touch a pen is an effort." A week later he wrote, quite proudly, to his mother:

WSC to Lady Randolph

EXTRACT

12 February [1897]   Bangalore
                                                     In Camp

. . . We are again in camp doing a "long Reconnaissance" 5 days of discomfort. My face is blistered by the sun so badly that I have had to see a doctor. The inflammation caused by the burns on my chin has inflamed all the glands of my throat & the blister is a horrible sight. I however keep dressings continually on and so manage to go about my business — though in bandaged condition.

I am consoled by the fact that I am doing "Brigade Major" a most important duty and one which in England could never have been obtained under 14 or 15 years service. I am still doing adjutant so that soldiering prospects are very prosperous.

I am becoming my dear Mamma a very "correct" soldier. Full of zeal etc. Even in homoeopathic doses — Responsibility is an exhilarating drink. . . .

He continued to act as Adjutant throughout March and into April when his friend Reggie Barnes returned from leave to resume his duties:

WSC to Lady Randolph

EXTRACT

18 February 1897   Bangalore

... The work is very interesting. It involves a good deal of responsibility. It requires a good deal of tact. I would never have believed
that so much office work was necessary to the maintenance of a regiment and in truth I am disposed to doubt the fact even now. Five
clerks are writing away from morning to night on reports and returns
& memoranda of one kind or another. There is of course a great deal
to do but this kind of work has its compensations. There are many
things to be decided. People older than myself appeal to me about
every sort of subject connected with the regiment. The colonel con-
sults me on nearly all points. Though all is of course on a small
scale, I cannot disguise from myself that it is an excellent training.

Speaking generally — my soldiering prospects are at present very
good. I complete today two years service and am now considered
eligible to sit on courts martial. By an extraordinary run of promotion I have eleven subalterns below me and should I continue to
serve I might easily become a Captain in 3½ more years.

I have also given satisfaction to my superior officers and polo &
other things quite apart I have every reason to believe that I shall
be reported on in the Annual Confidential Report as one of the two
most efficient officers in my rank. ...

*

For some months the financial worries with which Churchill and
his mother had been so beset before his departure for India made no
appearance in their correspondence — with the exception, of course,
of the failure of "The Spec" and the subsequent prosecution.
Churchill explains in *My Early Life* how on arrival in India in those
days, all the cavalry officer had to do was to hand over his uniform and
clothes to the dressing-boy, his ponies to the syce and his money to
the butler, "and you need never trouble any more." True, the extra
allowance paid to cavalry officers in India had increased his Army pay
to about £300 a year; and his allowance from his mother, paid
quarterly, was now £500 a year; but this was never enough:

All the rest, [he recalled in *My Early Life*] had to be borrowed at
usurious rates of interest from the all-too-accommodating native

bankers. Every officer was warned against these gentlemen. I always found them most agreeable; very fat, very urbane, quite honest and mercilessly rapacious. All you had to do was to sign little bits of paper, and produce a polo pony as if by magic. The smiling financier rose to his feet, covered his face with his hands, replaced his slippers, and trotted off contentedly till that day three months. They only charged two per cent a month and made quite a good living out of it. . . .

For the time, then, his financial affairs appeared to be in a tranquil state. The calm was deceptive:

Lady Randolph to WSC

EXTRACT

26 February 1897   35A Gt Cumberland Place

Dearest Winston,
   It is with very unusual feelings that I sit down to write to you my weekly letter. Generally it is a pleasure — but this time is quite the reverse. The enclosed letter will explain why. I went to Cox's this morning & find out that not only you have anticipated the whole of yr quarter's allowance due this month but £45 besides — & now this cheque for £50 — & that *you knew* you had nothing at the bank. The manager told me they had warned you that they would not let you overdraw & the next mail brought this cheque. I *must* say I think it is *too* bad of you — indeed it is hardly honourable knowing as you do that you are dependent on me & that I give you the biggest allowance I *possibly can,* more than I can afford. I am very hard up & this has come at a very inopportune moment & puts me to much inconvenience. I found a £100 for you when you started for India in order that you shld not lose by the speculation we went into & I sent you £50 for yr birthday — all of which I cld ill afford. I understand that you wld get into trouble with yr regiment if this £50 which you got from the banker King (& have probably spent) is not met, therefore I have paid it. But I have told them at Cox's not to apply to me in future as you must manage yr own affairs. I am not responsible. If you cannot live on yr allowance from me & yr pay you will have to leave the 4th Hussars. *I cannot* increase yr allowance. . . .
   . . . I will only repeat that I cannot help you any more & if you have any grit in you & are worth yr salt you will try & live within

yr income & cut down yr expenses in order to do it. You cannot but
feel ashamed of yrself under the present circumstances — I haven't
the heart to write more.

Yr mother

J R C

Churchill tried to make peace with his mother as best he could;
he paid her £30 of the £45 which she had advanced on his behalf,
and promised the rest when "my ship comes home." He blamed it
all on "that stupid Cox" with whom, however, he continued to bank
amicably for the rest of his life. Lady Randolph was obviously
desperately worried:

Lady Randolph to WSC

5 March [1897]   35A Gt Cumberland Place

Dearest Winston,

I was glad to get yr nice letter telling me of yr work as Brigade
Major. What an extraordinary boy you are as regards yr business

affairs. You never say a word about them, & then spring things upon one. If you only told me when you were hard up — & why — perhaps I shld not be so angry. But I don't believe you ever know how you stand with yr account at the Bank. I marvel at their allowing you to overdraw as you do. Neither the Westminster or the National Bank will let me overdraw £5 without telling me at once. Dearest this is the only subject on which we ever fall out. I do wish you wld try & reform — if you only realised how little I have, & how impossible it is for me to get any more. I have raised all I can, & I assure you unless something extraordinary turns up I see ruin staring me in the face.

Out of £2,700 a year £800 of it goes to you 2 boys, £410 for house rent & stables, which leaves me £1,500 for everything — taxes, servants, stables, food, dress, travelling & now I have to pay interest on money borrowed. I really fear for the future. I am telling you all this darling in order that you may see how impossible it is for me to help you — & how you must in future depend on yrself. I make out that you get about £200 pay, which makes yr income for the present £700 a year. Of course it is not much & I can quite understand that you will have to deny yrself many things if you mean to try and live within it. But the fact is, you have got to do more than try. Now when you receive this write me a sensible letter & tell me that I shall be able to count on you.

With best love, Yr loving Mother
J R C

Let me know exactly how you stand.

And when a week later another creditor came presenting a cheque which had apparently been dishonoured, she wrote with the double object of encouraging financial probity and discouraging him from returning to England:

Lady Randolph to WSC

EXTRACT

18 March [1897]   Brooksby
Leicester

. . . I seem only to write disagreeable things, but will you attend to the enclosed & explain it to me. I am sending the man the £11 he asks, but about yr dishonoured cheque I know nothing. My darling boy, you can't think how all this worries me. I have so many money troubles of my own I feel I cannot take on any others. You know how dearly I wld love to help you if I could — & also how much I would like to have you come home — but quite apart [from] the advisability of such a step for such a short time, think of the expense. Every creditor you possess in England will be down upon you, & as far as I can make out you won't have a penny until May & I daresay that is forestalled — of course I can't coerce you & if you have made up yr mind to come, you must, but remember the consequences. I am sure that yr brother officers won't encourage you to come. Yr friend Major Kincaid-Smith wrote me a very kind letter about you — but he deprecated yr coming home. I really think there is a good chance of yr getting to Egypt & in any case you are gaining much military experience in India & showing that you can work & do something. Darling I lay awake last night thinking about you & how much I wanted to help you — if only I had some money I wld do so. I am so proud of you & of all yr great & endearing qualities. I feel sure that if you live you will make a name for yrself but I know to do it you have to be made of stern stuff — & not mind sacrifice & self denial. I feel I am reading you a lecture & you will vote my letters a bore — but you know that I do not mean it in that way. . . .

Churchill replied to his mother:

WSC to Lady Randolph

EXTRACT

6 April [1897]   Bangalore

. . . I am indeed sorry that my cheque was dishonoured. When I left England as I could not pay this man, I gave him a post dated cheque. As the time approached when this cheque should have been presented, being still overdrawn — I wrote and suggested his waiting a little longer. This he does not appear to have done. I wrote also to Cox's telling them to induce the presenter of the cheque to withhold it for a further period. I understand this has been done — though of course White & Co are somewhat annoyed.

All this worries me awfully. Indeed I don't know what will happen in the near future. I must raise a certain sum of money on a Life insurance or some other security & pay off these pressing liabilities lest I obtain a most unenviable reputation. This country is no economy. British cavalry have to pay nearly double for servants, food, forage etc. Of course spending your capital means loss of income — already alas so small, but not to do it is to be almost dishonest in my case. . . .

He had determined, despite his mother's opposition, to return home for leave, though he made it clear that neither his stay in India nor the voyage home would be entirely wasted. "Altogether," he reported on 31 March 1897, shortly before going on leave to England, "since I have been in this country I have read or nearly finished reading (for I read three or four different books at a time to avoid tedium) all Macaulay (12 vols) all Gibbon (begun in England, 4,000 pages) *The Martyrdom of Man* [by Winwood Reade] — *Modern Science and Modern Thought* (Laing) the *Republic of Plato* (Jowett's Translation) Rochefort's *Memoirs* Gibbon's *Life & Memoirs* and one Complete *Annual Register* on English Politics. I have hardly looked at a novel. Will you try and get me the *Memoirs* of the Duc de Saint Simon & also Pascal's *Provincial Letters* — I am very anxious to read both these as Macaulay recommends the one & Gibbon the other."

While on board ship on his way home on leave he planned to read more *Annual Registers*. Six of them he had read and "carefully annotated besides," at Bangalore; they still survive. Most people make use of the *Annual Register,* that admirable institution, of which Edmund Burke was the first editor. Few have read the volumes consecutively in order to gain a comprehensive knowledge of British politics. Churchill was one of the few. Feeling the need for a more detailed knowledge of contemporary English politics and their background, he had written to his mother early in 1897: "Will you send me Hallam's *Constitutional History.* Also do you think you can find out for me — from some able politico or journalist — how and where I can find the detailed Parliamentary history (Debates, Divisions, Parties, cliques and caves) of the last 100 years."

"I hope you have received the books I have sent you," Lady Randolph wrote on 11 March 1897, "& are duly grateful — for I find the *Annual Register* costs 14/– a time — & as you asked for a 100! you will not be surprised if I don't send them all — particularly as I have

them in the library. However I have ordered from 1870 to be sent
2 vols at a time." Churchill was delighted:

WSC to Lady Randolph

EXTRACT

31 March [1897]   Bangalore

. . . The method I pursue with the *Annual Register* is [not] to read
the debate until I have recorded my own opinion on paper of the
subject — having regard only to general principles. After reading
I reconsider and finally write. I hope by a persevering continuance
of this practice to build up a scaffolding of logical and consistent
views which will perhaps tend to the creation of a logical and consistent mind.

Of course the *Annual Register* is valuable only for its facts. A
good knowledge of these would arm me with a sharp sword. Macaulay, Gibbon, Plato etc must train the muscles to wield that sword
to the greatest effect. This is indeed a nice subdivision of the term
"education." The result of one kind of learning is valued by what
you know. Of the other by what you are. The latter is far more
important — but it is useless in the total absence of the former. A
judicious proportion should be observed. How many people forget
this! The education of the school-boy — and of nearly all under-
graduates aims only at stocking the mind with facts. I have no ambition to "stifle my spark of intelligence under the weight of literary
fuel" but I appreciate the power of facts. Hence my toil. . . .

He thus became his own university. He set himself the task, he
examined the topics and in a sense he judged the results. He had
failed to profit by the expensive formal education which his parents
had provided for him: he now prepared to do it for himself. Four of
the *Annual Registers* which his mother sent him, for 1874–5–6–7,
contain carefully thought-out pencil notes, which are still legible
today, pasted in at the appropriate place in the text. He expresses
clear, logical and sometimes unfashionable opinions on a variety of
issues.

Starting in 1874, the year of his birth, he supported in retrospect
a measure introduced in the first few months of Mr Disraeli's second

administration aimed at abolishing lay patronage in the Established Kirk in Scotland and making it over to the congregation: "I am in favour of popular election of religious Ministers — but of course only those interested could vote. The man who does not go to Church has no claim to regulate that Church." This would scarcely have agreed with his father's views on the Established Church — that "lighthouse over a stormy ocean" which "marks the entrance to a port where the millions and the masses of those who are wearied at times with the woes of the world . . . may search for and find that peace which passeth all understanding."

On Gladstone's protest against the new Tory government's decision to reverse a measure introduced by the previous Liberal administration Churchill commented: "I should detest the idea that our laws were unalterable like those of the Medes and Persians." On the Public Worship Regulation Bill to prevent "the advance of ritualism" he wrote: "If a Church is 'established' and receives recognition from the Government . . . it is obvious that the Government should be able to insist on effective control." And on the refusal of Lord Northbrook, Viceroy of India, to prohibit the export of grain from India during the famine of 1873–4: "Lord Northbrook was right in refusing. . . . I should have thought that famine prices would immediately attract the grain without any law being necessary. I am opposed to any interference by Government with private trade."

In the *Annual Register* for 1875 Churchill noted, in a comment on the new coercion laws for Ireland: "The chief, indeed some think the only duty of government, is to afford efficient protection to life and property and in the discharge of that duty they may fairly claim the largest powers. The contention that partial and special legislation is an insult to the Irish people is unfortunately unanswerable. The removal of that insult rests with them." On a bill to establish an intermediate High Court immediately below the House of Lords he wrote: "I like to see modern principles clothed with the picturesque garments of the past. . . . I am inclined to think that the House of Lords is unsuited for the duties of a judicial court, and should prefer a tribunal on the lines suggested. I should very much like to see the functions of a court of appeal extended to criminal cases." The Court of Criminal Appeal was established in 1907.

Churchill supported the Artisans' Dwellings Bill, introduced to give local authorities compulsory powers to carry out slum clearance and improvements. "I affirm the principle that Governments have nothing to give away and hence have no right to be generous: but every class is interested in the extinction of a plague spot." When Mr Henry Fawcett, the Liberal economist whose works Churchill had already read (see p. 251), opposed the measure on the ground that it was "class legislation" — "we do not frame Acts of Parliament to enable noblemen to obtain suitable dwellings" — Churchill commented: "Mr Fawcett's arguments might have claimed the applause of the cavalier parliament or the Oxford Union but such nonsense should not be spoken — still less listened to in the 19th century."

In 1876, during the debate on the purchase of the Suez Canal shares, Mr Robert Lowe, formerly Gladstone's Chancellor of the Exchequer, attributed press support for the deal to self-interest. A "spirited policy," he said, "however expensive it might be to others, was sure to be dear to the newspapers." Churchill noted indignantly: "This is ridiculous. Exciting times cost the newspapers much more in telegrams, correspondents etc than they gained in increased circulation." This was somewhat naive of Churchill at a time when Northcliffe was striding forward to corrupt newspapers. Though Churchill had not perceived it, war and rumours of war were grist to the printing houses of Pulitzer, Hearst and Northcliffe: they were to coin money through these disasters, and Churchill was to be well rewarded for his war correspondence.

On the Royal Titles Bill of 1875, introduced to enable Queen Victoria to become Empress of India, Churchill commented: "I must array myself with those who 'love high sounding titles' since no title that is not high sounding is worth having, and for the present I am not prepared to abolish all titles. There would not be much satisfaction in being styled 'Your Insignificance' or 'Your Squalidity.'"

On the budget introduced in 1876 by Sir Stafford Northcote, which raised Income Tax by a penny to 3d, but which also raised the line of tax exemption from £150 to £200: "I am strongly in favour of exemptions from this tax. Income earned by present work should also be more advantageously dealt with than inherited incomes. Small incomes should not be taxed at all, say under £250 per annum, and only partially if under £500. After that, progressively." Not only was he an early advocate of differentiation between "earned" and "unearned" income, but he also seems to have prognosticated surtax, which was not introduced until 1915 with almost destructive effect, finally reaching 80 per cent of income.

As he read the parliamentary debates for 1876, Churchill came to uphold the right of any parishioner to be buried in the parish churchyard — up to a point. "The law should uphold his claim to 'silent burial' but cannot legislate for the performance of alien rites. These he must do without." But he castigated clergymen who opposed ceremonies of other religions in their churchyards even if no scandal or scene were caused thereby. "It is sad men cannot draw the line for themselves," he reflected.

On the question of women's franchise, to which he early held an objection which was to persist, particularly when his only son was nearly kidnapped by the suffragettes, but which he later embraced since three-quarters of the women voted for him, he wrote:

> On the grounds that it is contrary to natural law and the practice of civilized states — that no necessity is shown — that only the most undesirable class of women are eager for the right — that those women who discharge their duty to the state — viz marrying & giving birth to children — are adequately represented by their husbands — that those who are unmarried can only claim a vote on the ground of property, which claim on democratic principles is inadmissible — that every kind of hysterical fad would gain strength — that religion would become much more intolerant — that priests and parsons would obtain much more power on the ground that it is only the thin end of the wedge — I shall unswervingly oppose this ridiculous movement.
>
> If you give women votes you must ultimately allow women to sit as members of Parliament. True the Civil Servants and Clergymen have votes & don't sit. But they are few & their votes cannot coerce the community. If once you give votes to the vast numbers of women who form the majority of the community, all power passes to their hands.

He favoured compulsory vaccination, and described its opponents as indulging in the least justifiable of mischievous fads. Of the

Deceased Wife's Sister Bill of 1877 he wrote: "There is no natural impediment of consanguinity, and therefore no reason against legalising such marriages." Only six years later, under the influence of Lord Hugh Cecil, he was to take a different view (see Vol. II).

Churchill expressed himself in favour of capital punishment. "Is it a great deterrent?" he asked. "I think so. Perhaps it is because the sentence is irrevocable, because the actual penalty is and must remain unknown." He must have been thinking, in the last sentence, of a possible after-life. Referring to the recent substitution of public executions by private executions he added: "No difficulties should be placed in the way of any (in moderate numbers) who may wish to see the sentence carried out. Justice in every form should not shrink from publicity. The last expiation which she exacts from man should not be hidden from the eyes of his fellow creatures." A few years before he died Churchill told his grandson Winston that he was still in favour of capital punishment in public as he thought that instead of being secretly hanged in a hut the murderer or traitor ought to be allowed to address a crowd as in the case of the first Marquess of Montrose.

On the franchise he wrote: "I would extend the franchise to the whole people not by giving votes to the ignorant and indigent, but by raising those classes to the standard when votes may safely be given." So on elementary education:

Material comforts should precede mental culture. I am inclined to think that we have been precipitate in adopting universal compulsory education. It is however a step in the right direction — and it is impossible to recede now. I am therefore in support of any and every measure which tends to completing a somewhat dangerous experiment. It will obviously be incumbent on the State to provide — *if required* — a meal for children under education. This is unsound economy — but it is a necessary outcome of the violation of the principle previously stated — that "material comfort should precede mental culture."

What sort of education should the individual expect to receive from the state? "Reading and writing, the knowledge of sufficient arithmetic to enable the individual to keep his accounts; the singing

of patriotic songs and a gymnastic course is all that he may expect."
Later, when Churchill was at the Admiralty before the First World
War, he still adhered to the policy of singing patriotic songs and
sought to introduce it into the Royal Navy.

Thus Churchill recorded his thoughts early in 1897 on the issues
of 20 years before. At this time he had seen no action; and his
mother was vexed at his return to England on leave. But from these
comments on the *Annual Register* we can see that his mind was
working, that it was actively engaged in philosophical, economic and
political matters. He had not yet read many books: he was hacking
it all out for himself. No one, not even his mother, suspected the
daemon that was within him, nor foresaw the adventurous and
triumphant days and years that lay ahead. He alone possessed the
secret, the trust and the clue to his destiny.

10

Frontier Wars

CHURCHILL, AS IT HAS already been shown, had dedicated himself to

> Seeking the bubble reputation
> Even in the cannon's mouth.

He was to pursue this course for several years. No other avenue to fame, fortune and Parliament was open to him. Of course, if he had had the money and the opportunity to go into Parliament he would already have left the army; but no glittering legacy hung over his head and he could not at this stage detect any method of paying his debts and acquiring an independent income. He was soon by slow degrees to find a way — the sword and the pen. He early believed that he ought to do business at the top, and he never hesitated to call upon his mother to work on her influential friends, such as the Duke of Cambridge, the Prince of Wales, Sir Edgar Vincent, Lord Salisbury, Sir Evelyn Wood, Lord Kitchener, Lord Cromer and Sir Bindon Blood as the occasion required. People were soon to start attacking him for being "pushy" and even as a "medal-hunter." This sort of talk did not discourage him or deflect him from his purpose. He put up with the flouts and jeers because in his view he was not seeking easy advancement in his profession through influence, but only an opportunity to expose himself to the fire of any enemy of England who happened to be available at the moment. He was tireless and unremitting in his pursuit: what he sought was fame, glory and reputation, and for their sake he was happy to put his life at stake.

So ardent was he in this approach to life that he was even prepared to take part, if only as a witness, in other people's wars. He had already done so in Cuba. Now he wished to go as an observer and report on either side the threatened war between Greece and Turkey over the question of Crete. Before sailing from India he revealed his plans with delightful candour to his mother:

WSC to Lady Randolph
EXTRACT

21 April 1897   Bangalore

My dearest Mamma,

I am afraid you will regard this letter somewhat in the aspect of a bombshell. The Declaration of war by Turkey on Greece has completely changed all my plans. By good fortune I am possessed of the necessary leave and I propose, with your approval, to go to the front as a special correspondent. Now to deal with all possible obstacles & objections. (1) The war may be over before I reach Brindisi, which I expect to do about 20th May. In that case of course I shall come home as originally proposed. (2) The Military authorities. I do not anticipate any difficulty in this matter as my excuse that I did not participate in the fighting in Cuba but merely attended as a spectator was accepted without demur by the War Office; also that I am under the Indian authorities who have given me 3 months leave out of India & will concern themselves no further with me. (3) Which side to go on. This my dearest Mamma must depend on you. Of course all my sympathies are entirely with the Greeks, but on the other hand the Turks are bound to win — are in enormous strength & will be on the offensive the whole time. If I go on this side it will be less glorious but much more safe & as I have no wish to be involved in the confusion of a defeated army my idea is that they would be more suitable. You must decide. If you can get me good letters, to the Turks — to the Turks I will go. If to the Greeks — to the Greeks.

In thinking all this out it has occurred to me that Sir Edgar Vincent could probably do everything for me in Constantinople & could get me attached to some general's staff etc as in Cuba. On the other hand you know the King of Greece and could of course arrange matters in that quarter. These considerations will influence your decision, but I must beg you to remember how important it is to have really good letters and what a difference it makes. One other point in connexion with this question. Please try and find out what prospect there is of British intervention as it would not be expedient for me to be in Turkey if we prohibited her further advance — or in Greece if we blockaded her ports.

(4) Special Correspondent. Of course nearly every paper has one there already, but I have no doubt that you will find one to avail themselves of my services. I would send telegrams and also write signed articles & if necessary crude sketches could be sent. I should expect to be paid £10 or £15 an article — customary rates for telegrams but would bear my own expenses. Lord Rothschild would be the person to arrange this for me as he knows everyone. I should recommend Mackenzie Wallace [of *The Times*] — Borthwick [of the *Morning Post*] or failing everything else the *D. Graphic* who would I am sure be delighted. These arrangements I leave to you and I hope when I arrive at Brindisi I shall find the whole thing cut and dried.

(5) Your personal objections. Of course my dear Mamma — if you don't want me to go I wont — but you must admit I was right over Cuba and that this is a still better chance of gaining experience and of seeing a perhaps never-to-be-repeated spectacle. I know you will not stand in my way in this matter but will facilitate my going just as you did in the case of Cuba. Of course too you will see that all your objections to my coming home and the Prince too — are on my side in this matter.

(6) Money: I shall have about £50 with me when I land at Brindisi and if you can get me good letters I do not think I shall want more than another £50 which you could place to my credit either at Constantinople or Athens according to my destination. This fifty will be repaid out of my letters for which anticipate getting at least £120.

Now to sum up — please write to me at length on all these matters to Poste Restante Brindisi and have a wire waiting for me there in case I may arrive before the letters. Get me the necessary papers and find out the different things I have to ask you to [do]. If you will do this for me you will be a dear — though if you wont you could be nothing else. Of course if there is a prospect of any continuance of the war I could come home for it but I expect it will be short and sharp. Very likely I shall be too late. . . .

His earlier excoriating of the Turks and of the diplomacy of the Great Powers he was prepared to swallow in the cause of action. He sailed from Bombay in the *Ganges* on May 8; but within three days of sailing the Greeks were suing for peace, and long before he reached Brindisi the "war" was over. Disappointed in his expectations of military adventure he travelled back via Naples, where he "did" Pompeii; Rome and Paris, where he paused to see his younger brother Jack; and then home to participate in the "delights of the London season" as a minor and expensive compensation for the lost campaign.

He attended what he later described as a scene from a vanished world, the Duchess of Devonshire's famous fancy dress ball at Devonshire House in Piccadilly — later to be sold for a great sum as a showroom for motor-cars. Lady Randolph went as the Empress Theodora. We do not know how her son was attired except that he was wearing a sword, which came in useful when acting as "second" to his brother Jack, who was challenged to a "duel" in the course of the night's excitements.

Churchill did not allow himself to be completely seduced by the enticements of a London season. He sought, during his three months' leave which he was enforced to spend in England, an opportunity of making his first public speech. His earlier recorded harangue in the Empire Theatre had been anonymous. Now, soon after his arrival in England, he had got in touch with Captain FitzRoy Stewart, a Galloway connection who was Secretary of the Conservative Central Office. He indicated that he would welcome an early opportunity of becoming a candidate. FitzRoy Stewart suggested he might like to make a speech at some Tory function. Churchill wrote in *My Early Life:* "It appeared there were hundreds of indoor meetings and outdoor fêtes, of bazaars and rallies — all of which were clamant for speakers. I surveyed this prospect with the eye of an urchin looking through a pastrycook's window. Finally we selected Bath as the scene of my (official) maiden effort." FitzRoy Stewart wrote to Mr H. D. Skrine, in whose park a rally of the Primrose League was to be held shortly, asking him to allow this "clever young man" to address the meeting. Mr Skrine acquiesced. Monday 26 July 1897 was the date, and Claverton Manor, now the American Museum, near Bath, was the scene of this auspicious event.

After exchanging the customary courtesies Churchill spoke about the Workmen's Compensation Bill which was at that time before Parliament. "When the Radicals brought in their Bill and failed, they called it an Employers' Liability Bill. Observe how much better the Tories do these things. They call this Bill the Workmen's Compensation Bill, and that is a much nicer name. . . . I do not say

that workmen have not been treated well in the past by the kindness
and consideration of their employers, but this measure removes the
question from the shifting sands of charity and places it on the firm
bedrock of law. . . . So far," Churchill told his audience, "the Bill
only applies to dangerous trades." Radicals, and Liberals — "always
liberal with other people's money" — asked why it was not applied
to all trades. "This," said Churchill, "was just like a Radical, just
the slapdash, wholesale, harum-scarum policy of the Radical. It
reminds me of the man who, on being told that ventilation was an
excellent thing, went and smashed every window in his house. That
is not Conservative policy. Conservative policy is essentially a tentative policy, a look-before-you-leap policy, and it is a policy of don't
leap at all if there is a ladder. . . . British workmen have more to
hope for from the rising tide of Tory Democracy than from the
dried-up drain-pipe of Radicalism." He referred to a strike of engineers: "One of the questions which politicians have to face is how to
avoid disputes between Capital and Labour. I hope that ultimately
the labourer may become a shareholder in the profits and may not be
unwilling to share the losses of a bad year because he shared the
profits of a good one." And he concluded with a reference to the
Primrose League:

In 1880 the Tory party was crushed, broken, dispirited. Its great
leader, Lord Beaconsfield, was already touched by the finger of Death.
Its principles were unpopular; its numbers were few; and it appeared
on the verge of extinction. Observe it now. That struggling
remnant of Toryism has swollen into the strongest Government of
modern times. And the great Liberal party which in 1882 was
vigorous, united, supreme, is shrunk to a few discordant factions of
discredited faddists, without numbers, without policy, without concord, without cohesion, around whose necks is bound the millstone
of Home Rule. In all this revolution of public opinion the Primrose League has borne its share. It has kept pegging away, driving
the principles of the Tory party into the heads of the people of this
country, and, though the task has been heavy and the labour long,
they have had in the end a glorious reward. . . .

There was some comment in the evening and the weekly newspapers on this maiden speech, accompanied by speculation as to how

soon Churchill might seek an entry into Parliament. Most of the comments were favourable. *The Lady* wrote on 5 August 1897:

> An auspicious debut on the platform was made the other day by Mr Winston Churchill, elder son of the late Lord Randolph Churchill. He spoke at a large Primrose League meeting, and delighted his audience by the force and mental agility he displayed. Mr Churchill, who is only twenty-three, aspires to a seat in Parliament. He is in the 4th Hussars at present, and is strikingly like his late father in features and colouring.

But lest he should have his head turned there was always a corrective available from some newspaper less favourably disposed towards him:

> He seems to be a young man of some ability [wrote the *Eastern Morning News* of 3 August 1897], anxious to take a part in public affairs. He is, however, in danger of being spoilt by flattery and public notice. . . . Political talent is the least hereditary of any of our tendencies. There are several young members on the Government side of the House whose fate ought to be a warning to Mr Churchill. They began as he is beginning, and their early efforts were attended by a stream of flattery. But now they are in the House they have become political nonentities; they have a name, and that is all.

Having jumped this fence he went to stay at Deepdene with Duchess Lily and her husband Lord William Beresford for Goodwood Races. The ardour with which he broke away at the first opportunity from these gay and colourful events is well recorded in *My Early Life:*

> . . . I was on the lawns of Goodwood in lovely weather and winning my money, when the revolt of the Pathan tribesmen on the Indian frontier began. I read in the newspapers that a Field Force of three brigades had been formed, and that at the head of it stood Sir Bindon Blood. Forthwith I telegraphed reminding him of his promise, and took the train for Brindisi to catch the Indian Mail. . . .

A year before, Churchill had made friends with Sir Bindon Blood at Deepdene and had extracted from him a promise that if ever he commanded another expedition on the Indian frontier he would allow Churchill to accompany him. Before leaving England Churchill wrote to Jack who was still spending his holidays near Paris and who had expected to see his brother before he returned to India. Churchill explained his haste and apologized for the fact that he would not be able to see Jack; and sent from his slender purse "a fiver which I hope will be welcome."

The urgency with which he left is shown in a letter to his mother written from the steamship *Rome* off Aden on August 7 and posted there the following day. He had left behind his polo sticks, he had forgotten to return to old Mr Skrine one of his Primrose League badges, Bain the bookseller had not had time to send him Lord Beaconsfield's and Mr Gladstone's speeches and there were one or two bills which remained unpaid. And when he got to India he remembered that he had intended to take out Peas, his little dog, "and in the hurry and bustle of getting off — of course I forgot him."

In the hope of reputation on a battlefield this impecunious subaltern had sacrificed three weeks of his costly and enjoyable leave and had urgently travelled back to India by the most expensive route. At each port of call, instead of a telegram of welcome from Sir Bindon Blood there was nothing but a forbidding silence. Even when he arrived back with his regiment in the Bangalore cantonment there was no news. It seemed to him that he had hurried back at much expense and with no reward in sight. A few days after his return to Bangalore he wrote to his mother:

WSC to Lady Randolph

EXTRACT

17 August 1897   Bangalore

. . . I have heard nothing more from Sir Bindon Blood. I cannot think he would willingly disappoint me and can only conclude that someone at Headquarters has put a spoke in my wheel. I have still some hopes — but each day they grow less. It is an object lesson of how much my chances of success in the army are worth. I had the most complete assent of my colonel as well as his official recommendation forwarded six months ago. However as all this must be relegated to the past soon — I will not dilate on my disgust. . . .

And a week later:

. . . I am still disgusted at my not being taken. Sir Bindon Blood has never replied to any of my wires since Brindisi or indeed before.

I cannot help thinking that they may have been stopped at the beginning of the Field Telegraph & that he will get them too late. However there is still a chance. The regiment is the next for mobilisation and should an Afghan war break out we may go. The latest reports are alarmist. . . .

As he was writing this despondent letter to his mother there was a letter in the post to him from Upper Swat:

General Sir Bindon Blood to WSC

22 August 1897   Camp Mingaora
                   Upper Swat

My dear Churchill,

 I had to fill my personal staff when I started, and I have not been able to manage a billet for you as yet. I should advise your coming to me as a press correspondent, and when you are here I shall put you on the strength on the 1st opportunity. Fincastle was arranged for in this way, and is now attached to the Guides *vice* an officer killed in action.

 Army Head Qrs make all appointments except personal staff and are very jealous of their patronage. I have hardly managed to get any of my pals on my staff — though I have asked for several. However if you were here I think I could, and certainly would if I could, do a little jobbery on your account.

                  Yours in haste
                  B. BLOOD

To his mother he wrote from the train as it was travelling through India:

WSC to Lady Randolph

EXTRACT

29 August [1897]   In the train near Dhond
                and later near Itarsi

. . . The telegram which I sent you yesterday requires some explanation — though I most sincerely hope you will have done what I asked without awaiting it. Sir Bindon Blood wrote me a letter saying that he had had to make up his staff etc — but that if I could come up as a correspondent (the only excuse possible) he would seize the first opportunity of putting me on the strength of the

Malakand Field Force. I accordingly with much difficulty have obtained a month's leave and starting last night shall in four days
arrive at Nowshera, from whence I hope to join the General. To go
as correspondent, it is necessary to have a special pass and this is in
some cases refused if the paper is not of sufficient importance. I
hope most strongly I shall not arrive at Nowshera to find you have
taken no steps. If I do I shall then have to wire to some Indian
paper with possible failure.

Of course as soon as anyone gets ill or wounded I shall be attached
to the troops and then I must resign, but of this it is not necessary to
speak as yet. The great thing is to get to the front. Lord Fincastle
whom Sir Bindon mentions in his letter, was arranged for in this
way, and if I can get across the frontier all will be well, as when once
attached extension of leave and all else follows. I am taking up
horses and if I am stopped I shall ride from Nowshera up the line
of communications to the Buner Valley where the operations are
now taking place. . . .

. . . Dearest Mamma before this letter reaches you I shall probably
have had several experiences, some of which will contain the element
of danger. I view every possibility with composure. It might not
have been worth my while, who am really no soldier, to risk so
many fair chances on a war which can only help me directly in a
profession I mean to discard. But I have considered everything and
I feel that the fact of having seen service with British troops while
still a young man must give me more weight politically — must add
to my claims to be listened to and may perhaps improve my prospects of gaining popularity with the country. Besides this — I think
I am of an adventurous disposition and shall enjoy myself not so
much *in spite of* as *because* of the risks I run. At any rate I have
decided — and having taken a hand I shall do my best to play a
good game. . . .

WSC to Jack

31 August 1897   In the train near Umballa
                                              N.W. Provinces
My dearest Jack,

Perhaps Mamma will have informed you — (she learnt by my
telegram of Saturday) — of the reason of my journey North. Briefly
it is this: I am going as a War Correspondent — to what paper I do
not yet know — to join the Malakand field force — wh Sir Bindon

Blood is commanding. My hope is based on his promise to place me
on the strength of the expedition at the first opportunity. It is a
chance — perhaps a good chance of seeing active service and securing
a medal. But the future is somewhat vague and uncertain. I have
only a month's leave and if I cannot get regularly attached to the
troops before its expiration — I shall have to come down again.
However I have good hopes.

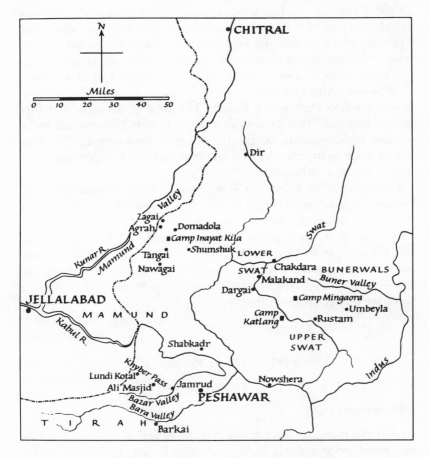

THE NORTH–WEST FRONTIER

Here I am in the development of my scheme at Umballa — a place
in the N.W. of India. Nothing can impress one with the size of this
country so much as to take a journey — as I have done — almost

from North to South. When I went to get my ticket — I asked how far Nowshera — my destination — was. Two thousand and twenty seven miles. Nearly as far that is as across the Atlantic. It is a proud reflection that all this vast expanse of fertile, populous country is ruled and administered by Englishmen. It is all the prouder when we reflect how complete and minute is the ruling — and how few are the rulers.

The frontier is a scene of great trouble and excitement. Practically all the fierce wild warlike tribes of the Afghan stock — the remains [of] the ancient Mohammedan conquest — are in revolt. Some have streamed across the frontier and have been rolled back with terrible losses. Meanwhile the Government has been collecting troops. From every part of India a swift and orderly mobilisation had drawn more than 40,000 additional men to the great military camps of Quetta — Rawal Pindi — Peshawar & Kohat. The time of offensive measures is now at hand. It is impossible for the British Government to be content with repelling an injury — it must be avenged. So we in our turn are to invade Afridis & Orakzais and others who have dared violate the Pax Britannica.

Of this invading force — it is my hope to be an insignificant unit — and if what I wish comes to pass I will write to you at as great length as I can of the events I see. Jack dear — I cannot write more now — as the train is going to move off and if I leave this letter much longer, it will not get to Bombay — wh I am leaving further behind each moment — in time to catch the steamer. Good bye old boy — best love — write to me often and at length and remember you have no better friend than —

Your loving brother
WINSTON S. C.

WSC to Lady Randolph

EXTRACT

5 September [1897]   Malakand Camp

. . . By the time this reaches you everything will be over so that I do not mind writing about it. I have faith in my star — that is that I am intended to do something in the world. If I am mistaken — what does it matter? My life has been a pleasant one and though I should regret to leave it — it would be a regret that perhaps I should never know.

At any rate you will understand that I am bound for many reasons to risk something. Lord Fincastle here will get a Victoria Cross for his courage in a recent action — and though of course I do not aspire to that I am inclined to think that my chance of getting attached would be improved by my behaviour. In any case — I mean to play this game out and if I lose it is obvious that I never could have won any other. The unpleasant contingency is of course a wound which would leave permanent effects and would while leaving me life deprive me of all that make life worth living. But all games have forfeits. Fortunately the odds are good. . . .

*

So far as is known, he had not yet begun his intensive study of Napoleon, whose life was to fascinate him for many years, and of whom he long perpended writing a biography. But like Napoleon he already had a belief in his star. Of course, as he incessantly and spectacularly exposed himself to the fire of the enemy and remained unscathed, this early expression of his belief was progressively fortified. There are records which show that within the next three years, in three different continents, he asserted to three very different people his ardent conviction that he would one day be Prime Minister of England. Once in India to another officer, the second time in South Africa to the son of a station-master, and the third time to his namesake, the distinguished American novelist whom he met when the latter took the chair for him when he was lecturing in Boston in 1900.

In February 1963 the author received a letter from his Suffolk neighbour, Mr Humphrey Bingham, about his father, the Honourable Francis Richard Bingham (later Sir Francis Bingham). When Churchill first went to India, Bingham was a Captain in the Royal Artillery and ADC to the Commander-in-Chief, Madras, Sir Mansfield Clarke, whose daughter he married. "My father," wrote Mr Bingham, "was Master of the Ootacamund Hounds and he was bringing hounds home one day when a young officer in the cavalry regiment rode up to him and, in the course of conversation, said that he had no intention of serving indefinitely in the army and that he proposed eventually to go into Parliament and added that one day he would be Prime Minister." Mr Bingham went on: "I need hardly add that the officer, who was unknown to my father at the time, was smoking a cigar!" They did not meet again until 1917, when Churchill was Minister of Munitions and Bingham was Director-General of Design at the Ministry.

At almost exactly the same time, the author received the following letter from South Africa:

Miss K. M. Clegg to RSC

EXTRACT

[February] 1963   Regent Hotel
                                                   Durban

. . . During the siege of Ladysmith my Grandfather, Mr R. E. Clegg, was the Station Master of Estcourt, at that time the railhead of the British Army, and the station from which the armoured train operated and my Father, George Clegg, was one of the armoured train crew.

At that time Estcourt was crowded with refugees, including my Mother and her family and your Father could not find accommodation, so he was allowed to pitch his tent in my Grandfather's back yard.

Many evenings over the camp fires and in the bar your Father would tell of his adventures as a reporter in India and Egypt. These tales were often so fantastic that my Father and his friends did not believe half of them and would laugh and accuse your Father of telling "tall stories" to impress them.

Then one day your Father said, "Mark my words, I shall be the Prime Minister of England before I'm finished," only to be greeted by more laughter.

The years passed and World War II was upon us, then one morning my Father read in the headlines of the *Natal Mercury* — Winston Churchill — Prime Minister — and suddenly he exclaimed "By jove, he's done it."

Then he told us the story that I have just written. . . .

The author is indebted to the late Mrs John Churchill, daughter-in-law of the American novelist, Winston Churchill, for the third story: When Churchill lectured in Boston on 17 December 1900, shortly after he had been elected to Parliament, but had not yet taken his seat, the American Winston Churchill lunched with him at the Touraine Restaurant. After luncheon the two Winston Churchills walked together and passed over a bridge which spans the Charles River. When they reached the middle of the bridge they paused and looked down the river. The English Winston said to the American Winston, who was three years older than he was: "Why don't you go into politics? I mean to be Prime Minister of England: it would be a great lark if you were President of the United States at the same time." The American Winston did not follow the advice of his namesake, though he was twice elected to be a member of the New Hampshire legislature, in 1903 and 1905; he did, however, live to see the English Winston become Prime Minister.

If these records of Churchill expressing this audacious opinion to three people in three years, in three different continents, are correct, it is legitimate to suppose that he must have expressed it to a score of others. The three people of whom we have record, and no doubt the others, must have thought him a swollen-headed saucy boy who was talking through his already inadequately sized hat.

That he was not utterly alone in his prophecy is shown by a letter which Brother Norwood Coaker of the Community of the Resurrection wrote from Johannesburg to *The Times Literary Supplement* in March 1963:

> My father-in-law, the late Douglas Gilfillan, was a captain in the Imperial Light Horse when the relieving forces entered Ladysmith. I heard him more than once tell the story, and have checked my recollection of it with that of one of his sons.
>
> Captain Gilfillan was one of a group of officers standing conversing round Sir George White in Ladysmith one day soon after the relief. A young officer came up to the group: with a good deal of sang-froid and not much ceremony he made his way through the group until he faced the general, and in a very audible voice at once engaged him in a short conversation, then went off. An older officer said to Sir George, "Who on earth is that?" He answered, "That's Randolph Churchill's son Winston: I don't like the fellow, but he'll be Prime Minister of England one day."

*

Lady Randolph had acted upon her son's urgent request to find a paper for whom he could be a correspondent. She drew a blank with *The Times*. The editor, Mr Buckle, wrote to her regretting that he had already appointed a correspondent (Lord Fincastle) to Sir Bindon Blood's headquarters. She was more fortunate with *The Daily Telegraph,* though she succeeded in obtaining only half the fee which Churchill had expected: "Old Lawson [proprietor of *The Daily Telegraph*] answered a letter I wrote him by telegram saying 'Tell him to post picturesque forcible letters.' I have no doubt if you get a chance of sending any that they will be well paid — of course they must be attractive."

Meanwhile, however, in order to justify his presence at Sir Bindon Blood's headquarters he had acquired accreditation to the *Pioneer,* a paper published in Allahabad which had printed much of Rudyard Kipling's early writing. Churchill's agreement was to cable 300 words a day.

The Daily Telegraph published the first of fifteen "letters" from Churchill on October 6, and Lady Randolph hastened to allay her son's anticipated displeasure:

Lady Randolph to WSC

EXTRACT

7 October 1897   [Edinburgh]

. . . I read yr letters for the *D.T.* to Ld Minto who thought them excellent — but begged me not to sign yr name. He said it was very unusual & might get you into trouble. The 1st one appeared yesterday headed "Indian Frontier — by a young officer." The Editor wired to say they wld give £5 a column — I'm afraid it is not as much as you had hoped — yr first letter was just one column. However I may try & arrange with Lawson for more. I wrote to the Prince & told him to look out for yr letters. Also to lots of people. You will get plenty of kudos (can't spell it) I will see that you do darling boy. I have just bought a *D.T.* of today & see another letter which they seem to have cut in two — if they do that there will be more letters & you will get yr £10. . . .

Churchill was in no way mollified by her action.

WSC to Lady Randolph

EXTRACT

25 October [1897]   [Bangalore]

My dearest Mamma,

I saw in the week's papers that arrived yesterday the first three of my letters to the *D.T.* I will not conceal my disappointment at their not being signed. I had written them with the design, a design which took form as the correspondence advanced, of bringing my personality before the electorate. I had hoped that some political advantage might have accrued. This hope encouraged me to take the very greatest pains with the style and composition and also to avoid alluding to any of my own experiences. I do not think that I have ever written anything better, or to which I would more willingly have signed my name. On such a matter the advice of a soldier was of course worthless. As to getting into trouble with the authorities, I am just as responsible now that they are not signed as if they had been. But in any case I have written nothing that could cause offence. However I left the decision in your hands and you have decided — not for the first time — upon a negative course. I will only add that if I am to avoid doing "unusual" things it is difficult to see what chance I have of being more than an average person. I was proud of the letters and anxious to stake my reputation on them. They are I believe of some literary merit. [*For two of these despatches see the Companion Volume.*]

As I am deprived of all satisfaction on this account, I mean to solace myself financially. I will not accept less than £10 a letter and I shall return any cheque for a less sum. I particularly asked for that amount *"au moins"* and when I think of the circumstances under wh. those letters were written, on the ground in a tent temperature 115° or after a long days action or by a light which it was dangerous to use lest it drew fire — when I was tired and hustled and amid other adverse circumstances — I think they are cheap at the price. The £75 which the *D.T.* propose to give me will hardly pay my ticket for self & horses. The *D. Chronicle* offered me ten pounds a letter to go to Crete and I will not be defrauded in this way. As Dr Johnson says "No man but a blockhead ever wrote except for money."

Will you kindly ask Moreton Frewen if he will go and see the Editor & point out that such a sum is ridiculous and that it is nothing less than a fraud. Correspondents from the theatre of war who pay their own expenses are entitled to special rates for copy. I will not take less than £150 for the series.

As to the printing. I asked that the proofs should be sent to you for correction but I suppose this has not been done as I read in the 2nd letter — the word "frequent" where I wrote "pregnant." This of course makes rubbish. Also at the end of the third letter they have cut out at least ten lines in order to contain the letter within the limit of a column. This spoils the balance of all the concluding sentence. Otherwise the setting up of type is good considering the rough MS wh could not be avoided. I am sorry to write so much about the letters. I had set great store by them and am unhappy that they should have fizzled out in insignificance. Their position in the paper is not good. The *Pall Mall* [*Gazette*] might have appreciated them more.

I was also correspondent for the *Pioneer,* and I will send you my letters and telegrams to that paper in case you care to read them. Perhaps you will have them put in a book, as they might be useful if I wished at any time to concoct another account. I am still thinking seriously of writing *The Story of the Malakand Field Force.* It would of course sell well and might do me good. I know all the people to get information from. The novel [*Savrola*] however interests me so much and is so full of promise that I am undecided & am loath to put it by for a time. I see there has been a vacancy in Lancashire wh might have suited me. But I was better employed. . . .

He did not mind so much about the fee: what he minded was that his mother had exercised the option which he had given her of suppressing his name. Why? On "the advice of a soldier."

Many older people, and perhaps still more his contemporaries, were apt at this period to denounce Churchill as a pushing "medal-hunter." This cannot be denied. In the light of the letters printed above it would be absurd to attempt to do so. He was ardent for distinction. How could he ever hope for advancement without prestige? Much though he honoured and treasured his father's memory, he did not want to trade on it. He already knew that he could write, and his command of the English language was developing rapidly. He sought fame and glory so that he could lay aside his sword, and seize the pen with which he could liberate himself from financial thraldom. He wished to enter Parliament more or less on a level with his better educated and more prosperous contemporaries. As he was gladly willing to venture his life on these foolhardy enterprises, who shall say that his motives were contemptible?

After spending a few days at Sir Bindon Blood's Headquarters, Churchill had been invited by Sir Bindon to attach himself to Brigadier-General P. D. Jeffreys' Brigade, which was to go on a punitive expedition into the Mamund Valley. Here on 16 September 1897, Churchill took part in his first real action as a combatant. In his newspaper despatches and later in his account in *The Story of the Malakand Field Force*, he was suitably modest and even self-effacing as to his role. He revealed his true thoughts to his mother:

WSC to Lady Randolph

[In pencil]

19 September [1897]   Camp Inayat Kila
Private

Dearest Mamma,

The enclosed 3 letters to the *Daily Telegraph* will tell you a good deal of what happened here. Please do whatever you think fit with them. I am tired of writing as these long letters take several hours. But I must give you some account of my personal experiences on the 16th. I started with the Cavalry and saw the first shot fired. After half an hour's skirmishing I rode forward with the 35th Sikhs until firing got so hot that my grey pony was unsafe. I proceeded on foot. When the retirement began I remained till the last and here I was perhaps very near my end. If you read between the lines of my letter you will see that this retirement was an awful rout in which the wounded were left to be cut up horribly by these wild beasts. I was close to both officers when they were hit almost simultaneously and fired my revolver at a man at 30 yards who tried to cut up poor Hughes' body. He dropped but came on again. A subaltern — Bethune by name — and I carried a wounded Sepoy for some distance and might perhaps, had there been any gallery, have received some notice. My pants are still stained with the man's blood. We also remained till the enemy came to within 40 yards firing our revolvers. They actually threw stones at us. It was a horrible business. For there was no help for the man that went down. I felt no excitement and very little fear. All the excitement went out when things became really deadly. Later on I used a rifle which a wounded man had dropped and fired 40 rounds with some effect at close quarters. I cannot be certain, but I think I hit 4 men. At any rate they fell. The regiment was fairly on the run and only stopped at the bottom by want of breath. Then I went about with a friend of mine, a subaltern in the Buffs. But, after this first thing, all else was tame. The skirmishing did not even excite me, though the young officers of this regiment were highly delighted at a few bullets that whistled about or kicked up the dust close by and considered each a tremendous escape. It was a very nice regiment and works well but they have not yet seen what it means to be well punished.

Altogether I was shot at from 7.30 [a.m.] till 8 [p.m.] on this day and now begin to consider myself a veteran. Sir Bindon has made me his orderly officer, so that I shall get a medal and perhaps a couple of clasps.

We fought again yesterday. But this time things were well managed and loss was only 7. [September] 16th was biggest thing in India since Afghan war. There will be more tomorrow, but I think the worst is over. When I think what the Empire might have lost I am relieved.

I hope you can make out this scrawl dearest Mamma — tell Jack details. In my novel I develop the idea that a "politician" very often possesses mere physical courage. Military opinion is of course contrary. But at any rate whatever I do afterwards, no one can say anything against me on this score. I rode on my grey pony all along the skirmish line where everyone else was lying down in cover. Foolish perhaps but I play for high stakes and given an audience there is no act too daring or too noble. Without the gallery things are different.

I will write again soon if all goes well, if not you know my life has been a pleasant one, quality not quantity is after all what we should strive for. Still I should like to come back and wear my medals at some big dinner or some other function.

The novel takes a great deal of shape in my brain. It will I hope be a really good thing. It is certainly original. I am a little lonely here at times as I have never a friend to talk to as when with Sir Bindon or the Regiment. And I do not look ahead more than a day — or further than the hills that surround the valley. I suppose other things have happened in the last week — but I did not realise it. Europe is infinitely remote. — England infinitely small — Bangalore a speck on the map of India — but here everything is life size and flesh colour.

Ever your loving son
WINSTON

Two weeks later Churchill was involved in another engagement:

WSC to Lady Randolph

[In pencil]

EXTRACT

2 October [1897]   Inayat Kila

My dearest Mamma,

Since I last wrote to you — we have had another severe action. Agrah — 30th September — I was under fire for five hours — but did not get into the hottest corners. Our loss was 60 killed and wounded — out of the poor 1200 we can muster. Compare these figures with actions like Firket in Egypt — wh are cracked up as great battles and wh are commemorated by clasps & medals etc etc. Here out of one brigade we have lost in a fortnight 245 killed and wounded and nearly 25 officers. I hope you will talk about this to the Prince and others — as if any fuss is made, they may give a special clasp for Mamund Valley. This has been the hardest fighting on the frontier for forty years. I have been attached as a matter of extreme urgency — to 31st Punjaub Infantry. A change from British cavalry to Native Infantry! Still it means the medal and also that next time I go into action I shall command a hundred men — and possibly I may bring off some *"coup."* Besides I shall have some other motive for taking chances than merely love of adventure.

Today and yesterday I have fever. 103° and an awful head — but I hope to be alright tomorrow. We expect another action on the 5th — Sir Bindon Blood is coming up himself and bringing two more batteries and two fresh Battalions. The danger & difficulty of attacking these active — fierce hill men is extreme. They can get up the hills twice as fast as we can — and shoot wonderfully well with Martini Henry Rifles. It is a war without quarter. They kill and mutilate everyone they catch and we do not hesitate to finish their wounded off. I have seen several things wh have not been very pretty since I have been up here — but as you will believe I have not soiled my hands with any dirty work — though I recognise the necessity of some things. All this however you need not publish. If I get through alright — and I have faith in my luck — I shall try and come home next year for a couple of months. Meanwhile the game amuses me — dangerous though it is — and I shall stay as long as I can. It is a strange life. Here I am lying in a hole — dug two feet deep in the ground — to protect me against the night firing — on a mackintosh with an awful headache — and the tent & my temperature getting hotter every moment as the sun climbs higher and higher. But after all, food and a philosophic temperament are man's only necessities. . . .

All his life Churchill thought that military service was an essential ingredient of a political career. When he came to a powerful station he never cared much — though he sometimes had to condone it — for putting ministers into his government or shadow cabinet who had not exposed themselves to the fire of the enemy in either of the two world wars. In later life, notably the 1945 election, he naïvely supposed that good war records would encourage the electorate to vote for candidates who possessed them. He persuaded those with such records (many of them generally against their better judgement) to stand for Parliament. Those who had gained the Victoria Cross or the DSO were almost invariably unsuccessful. Moreover he encouraged all Tory candidates who had served, like the author, without any particular merit or glory, to wear uniform and any such military tributes they had gained in the war. Mr Julian Amery and the author, standing for the double-barrelled seat at Preston, were among those who disregarded his advice. They were both defeated by a narrow majority, but neither of them ever subsequently felt it had made any difference.

Churchill's hope of medals, though it was to be disappointed, was not altogether without foundation:

General Sir Bindon Blood to Colonel J. P. Brabazon

EXTRACT

4 October 1897   Camp Inayat Kili
                                                    Bajaur

My dear Brabazon,
    Young Winston Churchill will have told you that I have been looking after him and putting him in the way of seeing some real

tough fighting. He is now pro tem an officer of native Infantry — of the 31st P. I. [Punjab Infantry] I have put him in as he was the only spare officer within reach, and he is working away equal to two ordinary subalterns. He has been mentioned in despatches already, and if he gets a chance will have the VC or a DSO — and here such chances have *sometimes gone begging.* . . .

He did not get the VC or the DSO; apart from the campaign medal, he had to make do with a mention in despatches. The citation read: "And finally hé [Brigadier-General Jeffreys] has praised the courage and resolution of Lieutenant W. L. S. Churchill, 4th Hussars, the correspondent of the *Pioneer* newspaper with the force who made himself useful at a critical moment."

His mother forwarded this news to him, and he replied:

WSC to Lady Randolph

EXTRACT

2 December [1897]   Hyderabad

. . . I cannot tell you with what feelings of hope and satisfaction I receive your information that I have been mentioned in despatches by Sir Bindon Blood. If that is the case — and I daresay it may be — I shall feel compensated for any thing. I am more ambitious for a reputation for personal courage than [for] anything else in the world. A young man should worship a young man's ideals. The despatches should be published soon and I shall know for certain. Meanwhile I live in hope. As to deserving such an honour — I feel that I took every chance and displayed myself with ostentation wherever there was danger — but I had no military command and could not expect to receive credit for what should after all be merely the behaviour of a philosopher — who is also a gentleman. . . .

On the same day he wrote to his brother Jack, who by this time was nearly eighteen:

WSC to Jack

EXTRACT

2 December 1897   Hyderabad

. . . I was delighted to hear from Mamma this mail that Sir Bindon Blood had mentioned me in despatches. I had never imagined such a thing possible. I had no military command and only rode about trying to attract attention — when things looked a little dangerous. Perhaps my good grey pony caught the speaker's eye. I hope it is true. Being in many ways a coward — particularly at school — there is no ambition I cherish so keenly as to gain a reputation of personal courage. At any rate we shall see soon as the despatches will be published shortly. In the meantime I shall hope. . . .

Churchill wrote to his mother on December 9: "I do not suppose any honour or dignity which it may be my fortune in life to deserve or receive will give me equal pleasure . . ." And again:

WSC to Lady Randolph

EXTRACT

22 December [1897]   [Bangalore]

. . . I am very gratified to hear that my follies have not been altogether unnoticed. To ride a grey pony along a skirmish line is not a common experience. But I had to play for high stakes and have been lucky to win. I did this three times, on the 18th, 23rd and 30th, but no one officially above me noticed it until the third time when poor Jeffreys — a nice man but a bad general — happened to see the white pony. Hence my good fortune.

Bullets — to a philosopher my dear Mamma — are not worth considering. Besides I am so conceited I do not believe the Gods would create so potent a being as myself for so prosaic an ending. Any way it does not matter. . . .

Later Churchill explained his true motives in a letter to his mother. It was not military glory but to get into politics:

WSC to Lady Randolph

EXTRACT

26 January 1898   [Bangalore]

. . . In politics a man I take it, gets on not so much by what he *does,* as by what he *is.* It is not so much a question of brains as of character & originality. It is for these reasons that I would not allow others to suggest ideas and that I am somewhat impatient of advice as to my beginning in politics. Introduction — connections — powerful friends — a name — good advice well followed — all these things count — but they lead only to a certain point. As it were they may ensure admission to the scales. Ultimately — every man has to be weighed — and if found wanting nothing can procure him the public confidence.

Nor would I desire it under such circumstances. If I am not good enough — others are welcome to take my place. I should never care to bolster up a sham reputation and hold my position by disguising my personality. Of course — as you have known for some time — I believe in myself. If I did not I might perhaps take other views. . . .

On his return to Bangalore with his grey pony after his service with the Malakand Field Force, Churchill laid aside his half-completed novel, *Savrola*. Instead, he started the first of the many books he was destined to write in the intervals of a crowded life. He wrote *The Story of the Malakand Field Force*.

WSC to Lady Randolph

EXTRACT

10 November [1897]   [Bangalore]

. . . I have been incited to it in some way as a means of repairing the non-signature of my letters. It is a great undertaking but if carried out will yield substantial results in every way, financially, politically, and even, though do I care a damn, militarily. At any rate I am fully committed now as I have written to all the colonels and knowledgeable people I met up there for facts etc and I do not doubt I shall receive volumes by return of post. Such is the modesty of the age. Few people are above saying what really happened from their point of view. Of course I shall have to discriminate . . .

After a fortnight of intense activity he received a set-back:

WSC to Lady Randolph

EXTRACT

24 November [1897]   [Bangalore]

. . . I am working very hard at the book and am daily receiving facts and letters from the frontier concerning it. I hear Ld Fincastle is also writing one and has received the pictures I had hoped to obtain. A great nuisance this as the subject is so small that there is not room for two books on it. He has not treated me with much consideration in the matter as he knew I was contemplating writing and might at least have informed me that he wanted to tell the tale.

Had he done so I would have given way as the novel filled & still fills my mind. As it is — I have got so far — and the book promises so well — that I do not mean to give in. It will of course make all the difference which comes out first. I want you therefore to approach the publishers on the subject and write to me. I hope to send the MS home in six weeks at the latest. It need not be sent out later for corrections — as I am having it typewritten. . . .

Churchill worked hard:

WSC to Lady Randolph

EXTRACT

22 December [1897]   [Bangalore]

. . . I hope you will like it. I am pleased with it chiefly because I have discovered a great power of application which I did not think I possessed. For two months I have worked not less than 5 hours a day and had I more time I should like to take another three or four months and produce something of value as well as of interest. I will write you a covering letter with the MS explaining my views on the subject of its publication. But it should be worth a good deal of money. This we cannot afford to throw away. . . .

WSC to Lady Randolph

31 December [1897]   [Bangalore]

My dearest Mamma,

Herewith the book. It has by a great effort been finished a week earlier than I had expected. Maps & a photograph of Sir Bindon Blood for frontispiece, I hope by next mail, but do not delay publication on their account.

I have hurried vy much & it is possible there are still a few slips and errors of writing in the MS. I cannot have the proofs sent out here as that would take too much time. I want you therefore to ask Moreton Frewen if he will undertake the work of revising and correcting them for me. I shall be vy grateful indeed if he will. I enclose some notes as to publication & as to the points I want whoever revises to look out for.

Failing Moreton — Ivor Guest and failing him do find some one well read and clever. I do not see why you should not do it yourself, but proof correcting is a great labour and involves many technicalities and conventional signs. Moreton would be best of all and I am sure he would do it for me.

Now dearest Mamma I don't want anything modified or toned down in any way. I will stand or fall by what I have written. I only want bad sentences polished & any repetitions of phrase or fact weeded out. I have regarded time as the most important element. Do not I beg you lose one single day in taking the MS to some publisher. Fincastle's book may for all I know be ready now.

As to price. I have no idea what the book is worth but don't throw it away. A little money is always worth having. I should recommend Moreton's treating with the publishers, it is so much easier for a man. If the book runs to a second edition, I shall add another three or four chapters on Buner which is now impending. I have wired to Blood to take me again on this new advance. I do not expect to go. Allow nothing to prevent the publication of this book. I have taken great pains — nor do I think the result altogether unworthy.

I have gone to the expense of sending this by letter post in order to save the week of sea journey. So I beg you do not lose time. I don't think I ought to get less than £300 for the first edition with some royalty on each copy — but if the book hits the mark I might get much more.

No more my dear Mamma. Believe me I am weary of the pen. No letter from England at all for me this week. But I look forward to your next. Write and tell me all about the book and wire me result of any bargain you may make. You need only say the price & then the royalty & the probable date of publication. My last words, like the bishop's are "verify my quotations."

Ever your loving son
WINSTON

He repeated this last injunction on 19 January 1898: ". . . I must again repeat — *"Verify my quotations"* particularly the date of Ld Salisbury's Guildhall speech. . . ."

Lady Randolph, on the advice of no less an authority than Mr Arthur Balfour, entrusted the book to A. P. Watt, the literary agent, who found in Longmans a ready publisher.

A. P. Watt to Lady Randolph

20 January 1898　　　　　　　　　　　　　Hastings House

Dear Madam,

As the result of my negotiations with Mr Longman, I have pleasure to inform you that he is willing to publish Mr Churchill's book *The*

Story of the Malakand Field Force on the following terms, which I have no hesitation in advising you are such as you may with entire confidence accept. They are:

1. That Mr Longman will probably publish the book at 6/- at his own risk and expense, and will pay a royalty of 15% on the first three thousand copies of the English edition sold.

2. A royalty of 20% on all copies sold after three thousand.

3. Threepence a copy on the Colonial Library Edition.

4. 10% on the first thousand copies sold in America and 15% on all copies sold beyond one thousand.

5. On the day of publication he will pay in advance the sum of £50 on account of these royalties.

Mr Longman estimates that there will be three maps required, one printed in colours and two in black and white. For these there is no "copy," but he has little doubt that the map engravers can supply it. If, however, Mr Churchill has sent "copy" of the maps, perhaps you will kindly forward it at once to me.

As I have impressed Mr Longman with the necessity there is for having the book produced without any delay, I should be glad if you would be kind enough to telegraph to me tomorrow if the arrangement which I have made meets with your approval, when I shall at once inform Mr Longman and the book can be put in hand.

I telephoned to you before writing this letter but found that you had just left town.

I am, dear Madam, Very truly yours

A. P. WATT

P.S. Please note that my telegraphic address is "Longevity, London."

Churchill entertained great hopes:

WSC to Lady Randolph

EXTRACT

26 January 1898   [Bangalore]

. . . The publication of the book will be certainly the most noteworthy act of my life. Up to date (of course). By its reception — I shall measure the chances of my possible success in the world. Although on a larger subject and with more time I am capable of a purer and more easy style and of more deeply considered views — yet it is a sample of my mental cast. If it goes down then all may be well. . . .

The first edition ran to 2,000 copies at home and another 2,000 abroad. Altogether 8,500 copies were published in the nine months between March 1898 and January 1899.

But even as he was finishing his book, Churchill showed himself keen to hurry off to other scenes of action. He did not think that the risks he had run with the Malakand Field Force had gained him the reputation which he believed he had deserved. Three months after he had returned to dull regimental soldiering at Bangalore the Tirah Campaign, also on the Afghan frontier, was already under way. It had opened inauspiciously. Churchill was still burning for distinction. To seek a new opportunity for reputation he was prepared to sacrifice his leave and spend money which he could not afford in making a four-day train journey from Bangalore to Calcutta, which was then the capital of India. He spent sixty interesting but abortive hours in Calcutta, and then had to return to Bangalore with sadness and frustration in his heart.

Though abortive, his visit to Calcutta was enjoyable. He stayed with the Viceroy, Lord Elgin, under whom he was later to serve as Under-Secretary at the Colonial Office; he dined with the Commander-in-Chief, Sir George White, with whom he was to dine again, under quite different circumstances, at Ladysmith two years later; and he rode a horse which he was lent in the local point-to-point.

WSC to Lady Randolph

EXTRACT

19 January 1898   Raichur

My dearest Mamma,

I am on my way back from Calcutta where I have had a pleasant & I hope, a useful visit. The trains do not connect well and I have to wait here six hours, which may be conveniently employed in writing my mail letters. At Calcutta I stayed at Government House with the Elgins. Hugo Baring who was stopping there mentioned my name and they civilly invited me. From one cause and another I found myself hospitably entertained by everyone — in contrast to last year when I knew nobody. My stay there was very short — but I met a lot of useful people, particularly military people. I dined one night with the C-in-C and generally discoursed with generals.

All were unanimous in advising me to employ every effort to get to

Egypt. My friend Col Ian Hamilton who is the next officer to get a Brigade & will command the force sent to Egypt, should one go from India — has promised to try and take me on his staff. But up to date it does not seem that they will use Indian troops. A great mistake as troops from this country understand warfare in tropical countries and take the field with so much ease and rapidity.

I think I could have obtained a vacancy in the Gwalior Transport Train now serving with the Tirah Expeditionary force — on duty in the Khyber pass — but in the hopes of Egypt I did not press the matter. Indeed there appears to be no prospect of further operations on a big scale. . . .

While Churchill was seeking to earn a reputation for courage on the North-West frontier, he was constantly on the alert with a view to finding a Parliamentary opening.

WSC to Lady Randolph

EXTRACT

17 November [1897]   [Bangalore]

. . . You must keep your eye on the political situation. Although I know & hear nothing out here, it is evident to me that a very marked reaction against the decision of the last general election has taken place. These numerous bye elections might, had I been in England, have given me my chance of getting in. However my experience out here has been of greater value and interest than anything else would be, or perhaps can ever be. Of course should a vacancy occur in Paddington — you must weigh in for me & I will come by the next ship. They would probably elect me even if I could not get back in time. I suppose Ld Salisbury's retirement is now only a matter of months. There might be sweeping changes after that. Chamberlain would not be likely to tolerate Balfour [as] PM unless in the Lords, and would the Londonderry type of Tory allow Chamberlain to dominate even more than at present? Should a split occur, I should remember that a tory democrat is a tory first and a democrat after. The reactionary remnant might always be whipped up. . . .

Lord Salisbury, who had become Prime Minister for the first time as long ago as 1885, had formed his third administration in June 1895; a considerable Unionist victory at the general election had followed. A number of by-elections during the Christmas recess early in 1898 — notably the defeat of Churchill's cousin, Ivor Guest, at Plymouth — suggested that the Government's popularity was declining. Nevertheless, Lord Salisbury was to fight — and win — another general election and did not consider it necessary to retire until July 1902.

On his return to Bangalore Churchill found disquieting news. His mother's financial affairs had got into such a state that she felt obliged to seek a fresh loan amounting altogether to £17,000 with which to pay off a series of minor loans and also to clear some pressing debt. The security for such a loan was to be life insurance policies on both her life and on Winston's. What was now required was that Winston should guarantee at least the premiums on these life insurance policies amounting in all to £700 per annum which would also cover the interest on the loans. Lady Randolph did not trouble to inform her son of these important financial transactions but merely caused the solicitors Lumley & Lumley to send to Churchill the necessary forms for signature.

Churchill loved his mother dearly and wished to help her. But he was not prepared to be stripped of his modest competence in this way. He wrote to her.

WSC to Lady Randolph

EXTRACT

28 January 1898   [Bangalore]

. . . Speaking quite frankly on the subject — there is no doubt that we are both you & I equally thoughtless — spendthrift and extravagant. We both know what is good — and we both like to have it. Arrangements for paying are left to the future. My extravagances are on a smaller scale than yours. I take no credit to myself in this matter as you have kept up the house & have had to maintain a position in London. At the same time we shall vy soon come to the end of our tether — unless a considerable change comes over our fortunes and dispositions. As long as I am dead sure & certain of an ultimate £1000 a year — I do not much care — as I could always make money on the press — and might marry. But at the same time there would be a limit.

I rather wish you had written me a letter on the subject — to explain things to me — as I may be quite wrong in my conceptions of the affair. I hope you will not mind my writing in a candid manner. I sympathise with all your extravagances — even more than you do with mine — it seems just as suicidal to me when you spend £200 on a ball dress as it does to you when I purchase a new polo pony for £100. And yet I feel that you ought to have the dress & I the polo pony. The pinch of the whole matter is we are damned poor. . . .

After he had made these remonstrances, Churchill signed the necessary documents that Lumley & Lumley had sent him. He did so, however, only on the condition that Jack should share the burden of £700 a year if and when he came into his own money.

WSC to Lady Randolph
EXTRACT

30 January 1898   [Bangalore]

. . . I need not say — how painful it is to me to have to write in so formal a strain or to take such precautions. But I am bound to protect myself in the future — as I do not wish to be left — should I survive you — in poverty. In three years from my father's death you have spent a quarter of our entire fortune in the world. I have also been extravagant: but my extravagances are a very small matter beside yours.

I am glad to see that this £14,000 is to include everything. It would be impossible for this transaction to be repeated. Indeed you will see that the 1st. condition I have made — will make me independent and enable me to decide as I will.

If this letter does not please you — you must balance your annoyance against my reluctance to be £700 a year poorer and then I think you will admit that my side of the account is the heavier.

I hope you will write me a special answer to this letter — saying what you think about what I have said & requested. I write in full love and amity and you will do very wrong to be angry at the unpleasant things it is necessary to express. . . .

*

Towards the end of February 1898, Churchill went to Meerut for the Polo Tournament, in which he distinguished himself. The 4th Hussars beat the 5th Dragoon Guards, but lost in the second round to the famous Durham Light Infantry, the only Infantry Regiment ever to win the Regimental Polo Tournament and to do so three years running. But Churchill's restless mind was not on polo: it was still with the nagging campaign that was being waged on the Northern frontier in Tirah. Constantly he was devising means of joining it. At Meerut he was staying with Sir Bindon Blood and it was there that he conceived the idea of going to Peshawar, the railhead for the Tirah expedition, to see if he could not find employment at Headquarters there. As he explains in *My Early Life,* there was a considerable element of risk attached to this enterprise. Though Meerut was 1,400 miles north of Bangalore, it was still 600 miles short of Peshawar. His leave expired three days after the final match of the tournament — the three days it would take the polo team to return to Bangalore. So if he took train to Peshawar, which would take him a day and a half, and found no employment there, he would be two, if not three, days late returning to Bangalore.

Characteristically, Churchill decided to take the risk. He had received some encouragement in a letter from his friend Ian Hamilton who commanded one of the brigades in the Tirah expedition:

WSC to Lady Randolph

EXTRACT

25 February [1898]   c/o Sir B. Blood KCB
                                            Meerut

. . . I have had a long and vy interesting letter from General Hamilton — who has just assumed the command of the 3rd Brigade Tirah Expdy Force and who is a great friend of mine. He describes at length several vy neat & clever operations he has recently conducted which have ended by placing his Brigade nearest to the enemy. As the Gordon Highlanders form part of it — they will acquit themselves well — if hostilities are resumed.

If he can find a higher post for his present orderly officer — (a major & too senior for such employ) he will wire for me. Indeed I have considerable hopes of getting the field again — and in that expectation have brought with me tents, saddlery, uniform, etc. *Nous verrons.* . . .

On 7 March 1898, Churchill was able to report success:

WSC to Lady Randolph

7 March [1898]   Camp Ali Musjid
                                    Khyber Pass

My dearest Mamma,

But for my telegram the address might astonish you. I came on to Peshawar after the Polo Tournament as I told you I proposed to do. I went to see Sir Wm Lockhart in the hopes of being allowed to go and see General Hamilton — but without any expectation of employment. To my astonishment — I have been taken on his (Sir Wm's) staff as Orderly Officer. The appointment has not yet been sanctioned from Army Head Quarters — but I should think it extremely unlikely, in view of Sir William's approaching command [*as Commander-in-Chief, India*], that any obstacle will be raised. If it should be sanctioned I shall wire to you.

The success which has attended my *coup* is in some measure I feel, deserved. But I have received a most remarkable assistance from Captain Haldane — the general's ADC. I have never met this man before and I am at a loss to know why he should have espoused my cause — with so strange an earnestness. Of this I shall learn more later. But in the meanwhile I am greatly interested. He is a very clever, daring, conscientious & ambitious fellow — his influence over the general is extraordinary. Indeed I think he has pulled the wires all through this war and is in great measure responsible for its success or failure. He is extremely unpopular and takes no pains to cultivate friends in the force. My idea is that my reputation — for whatever it may be worth — has interested him. Of course you will destroy this letter and show it to no one. For though I am under a considerable obligation to this officer I cannot say that I approve of a system which places the reins of power in the hands of so young and unknown a man. I fear this is the explanation of much. However, destroy this and repeat to none — or I may be found a fool as well as an ingrate.

Sir Wm is himself a charming man — vy amiable and intelligent. But the situation is full of interest. Now for Heaven's sake say nothing about this.

As to the future — the outlook is I fear pacific. The Tribes will probably submit and if so the General is off home on the 26th inst. Still they will probably find something for me & so I may be up here for some months — until Egypt in fact — on which point concentrate your efforts.

If the tribes don't submit — we resume operations Friday week and shall enter the Bara & Bazar valleys. This will of course mean some fighting. The odds are about 3–1 for peace. Of these matters the papers will inform you. Meanwhile — I will write you some interesting letters.

We move on to Landi Kotal tomorrow — and I shall then have seen the whole of the Khyber pass — a most interesting trip. Then we return to Peshawar — pending developments. Weather vy cold in tents & raining.

Ever your loving son
WINSTON S. CHURCHILL

The key to his success was, as he indicated in his letter and as he generously pointed out in *My Early Life,* "remarkable assistance from Captain Haldane." Aylmer Haldane was at that time serving as a Captain in the Gordon Highlanders. A member of a closely knit and brilliant Scottish family — Richard Burdon Haldane, later to be Secretary of State for War and Lord Chancellor, was a cousin of his — he had soon made his mark as a staff officer in India. Churchill recalls in *My Early Life* how he had been warned that Haldane had immense influence — "in fact, they say throughout the Army, too much." We do not know what it was about the young Churchill that led to Haldane's benevolent attitude towards him. For apart from ambition, they neither of them seemed to have much in common: "He is indiscreet — over-bearing — irritating [in] manner — possessed by a great desire to confer favours — but in some ways a remarkable man — and works like a machine," Churchill wrote to his mother on March 31. Earlier he had said: "Haldane and I get on capitally. He is not as clever as I thought originally — but I think an able fellow. He likes me and in spite of the disparity in age, we talk unreservedly." Haldane was twelve years older: that he got on well with Churchill is proved not only by the fact that he took all steps to ensure the success of Churchill's attachment to Sir William Lockhart's staff, but also by the way in which he unburdened intimate details about his unhappy married life to the young subaltern. Churchill "kept up" with Haldane after he left the Tirah Field Force; as will be seen, they were to meet again in new and more hazardous surroundings not long afterwards.

Churchill soon found that there was no war and not likely to be one: "Of course I do hope for a fight, but I do not delude myself," he wrote to his mother:

WSC to Lady Randolph

EXTRACT

18 March [1898]   Camp Peshawar

. . . Both sides are sick of it. . . . Though I now fear fighting is all over — [this] cannot be a bad business. I shall possibly get an extra clasp on my medal. It counts in my record of service and as an extra campaign. But the chief value lies elsewhere. I now know all the generals who are likely to have commands in the next few years. Sir William Lockhart will always give me an appointment with any Field Force and I have now a great many friends in high places — as far as soldiering is concerned.

I have also now seen nearly the whole frontier, indeed with the exception of the Samana & the Kurram I have been all over it. This under peculiarly interesting circumstances is not without value.

My vanity is also gratified in many small ways. But of these it is unnecessary to write. I am entitled to 3 months leave on full pay in consequence of having been attached to the Field Force — so that you see, as I have already written — that there is only one black cloud on the skyline. . . .

One of the ways in which his vanity was flattered was as follows:

WSC to Lady Randolph

EXTRACT

31 March [1898]   Camp Peshawar

. . . I have been instrumental in stopping a vy great blunder. General Nicholson the Chief of Staff and the next Adjutant-General in India was so stung by an article in the *Fortnightly* that he actually wrote an answer and signed it "Chief of the Staff." I need not say how ill judged this was — or rather would have been. I happened to hear about it from Haldane — and meeting the General I told him my opinion — and that Lord Wolseley and the Prince would both disapprove most strongly. He was vy civil — and has since wired to prevent publication. This of course is a story which should not be repeated. . . .

Churchill went even further and actually wrote a letter for publication to Lord Charles Beresford, Admiral and MP, the flamboyant brother of Lord William Beresford. This was a defence of those serving in India and an attack on those who under cloak of anonymity in newspaper articles and letters to Members of Parliament were attacking the conduct of the campaign. "I have asked him to publish it," Churchill explained to his mother on March 31, "signed by me — and as if by an indiscretion. It is an indirect method which in this case is more suitable. The letter will establish my position with the Indian military authorities on unshakeable foundations. They are extraordinarily sensitive of Press Criticism and welcome the slightest favourable comment." This letter was duly published in *The Times* on 3 May 1898, but *The Broad Arrow,* the organ of the military Establishment in London, purported to read into it a subtle attack on the military authorities and offered the severest strictures on the presumptuous young subaltern.

Undoubtedly Churchill had brought upon himself a good deal of hostility, both in Simla, where the Indian Army mandarins held court, and at the War Office. Even Lord Roberts had refused to help Churchill to get to the front, and Churchill was genuinely shocked and hurt. Churchill had asked his mother to approach Lord Roberts, who was at this time commanding the forces in Ireland, on the grounds of his father's friendship with — and considerable services to — the Field Marshal. Only a few years before Lord Roberts had been pleased to accompany Lord Randolph to Harrow. Now Churchill commented: "I don't understand Lord Roberts' refusal. A good instance of ingratitude in a fortunate and very much overrated man."

Even in the midst of the excitements and new surroundings of Sir William Lockhart's Headquarters at Peshawar, Churchill was able to write that he was thinking of his book, *The Story of the Malakand Field Force*, "more than of anything else." "I have not yet received the proofs or the volume," he wrote to his mother on March 18, "but I am sure it has been managed as well as it could possibly have been." The correction of his proofs had been entrusted to Moreton Frewen, his uncle, who on the strength of a slender work in bimetallism was regarded as the literary member of the family. He had two nicknames: "Mortal Ruin" and "Silver Tongue." On March 21 the proofs arrived at Peshawar.

WSC to Lady Randolph

EXTRACT

22 March [1898]   Peshawar

My dear Mamma,

I add this letter to tell you that the "revised proofs" reached me yesterday and that I spent a very miserable afternoon in reading the gross & fearful blunders which I suppose have got into the finished copies. In the hope of stopping publication I have wired to Longmans, but I fear I am already too late. Still I may catch the Indian edition, in which the absurdities would be most laughed at.

I blame no one — but myself. I might have known that no one could or would take the pains that an author would bestow. The result, however, destroys all the pleasure I had hoped to get from the book and leaves only shame that such an impertinence should be presented to the public — a type of the careless slapdash spirit of the age and an example of what my father would have called my slovenly shiftless habits. . . .

He goes on in this letter and the next, on March 25, to give pages and pages of examples of "emendations made by Moreton which have the effect of making the passage as bald as if written by a Harrow boy." He complained of the "strange stupidity" of words which he had printed for clearer legibility in capitals appearing in capitals in the book — "how any intelligent person could have passed this is a mystery to me"; of mis-spellings — "hideous sights"; of misprints — "absurdities . . . , which, thank God, cannot be attributed to the author"; and of "absolutely haphazard" arrangements.

Altogether there are about 200 misprints, blunders & mistakes, though some of these, perhaps 100 will only be apparent to me. With great courage Moreton has in places altered what I wrote & made it appear nice and plain and simple so that an idiot in an almshouse could make no mistake — but though he has taken these liberties with my text so good a classic has allowed the word "fulcrums" to pass uncorrected. Perhaps I had better state that I meant fulcra (plural) but in the hurry made a mistake.

All this as I said reveals to the world my mind & nature as shallow — ill educated — slovenly etc. All this destroys my pleasure in the book and makes its very sight odious to me. All this will prevent it from ever reaching a second edition — where these mistakes could be corrected.

I have had an evil presentiment. But I risked mistakes for one reason — to get it published before Lord Fincastle's book.

Whereas, I see his is now already out, and mine when the mail left was still being embellished as I have described.

God forbid that I should blame you my dearest mamma. I blame myself — and myself alone for this act of folly & laziness which has made me ridiculous to all whose good opinion I would have hoped for.

I writhed all yesterday afternoon — but today I feel nothing but shame and disappointment. You could not be expected to know many of these things — but as far as Moreton is concerned, I now understand why his life has been a failure in the city and elsewhere.

For my own part unhappy as I feel and in spite of all the ridicule I shall have to face, I still have confidence in myself. My style is good — even in parts classic. The book reads much better than the MS & were [it] what I wanted down on its pages, I should be proud of it. And I have learnt a lesson.

I pray to God that the printers' devil may have altered some of the more glaring misprints. But in any case enough will remain to damn & destroy the merit of the work.

Do not I beg you write and tell me that indiscriminating people have praised it or that charitable editors have puffed it. If you want to imagine my feelings — read Lord Macaulay's essay on Mr Robert Montgomery's poems. I feel as that wretched man did when he first read it. . . .

In view of all this the letter of thanks he wrote to Moreton Frewen was a masterpiece of restraint and deserves to be quoted:

WSC to Moreton Frewen

(Copy: Leslie Papers)

EXTRACT

2 April 1898   Camp Peshawar

My dear Moreton,

Many thanks for your letter of the 7th March. I have read the advance copy of the book and I see that you have taken a great deal of trouble in the matter and have modified a good many of my statements — perhaps judiciously. I am very grateful to you for your kindness in all this matter. It is a very invidious task to come between an author and his proofs — and I felt this fully when I asked you to undertake the business of revision. I agree with you as to the signs of haste and indeed reading the book a second time in print I have found many passages I would gladly alter.

There are two or three unfortunate slips as

> [page] 30 Chitral wall for Chitral road
>
> page 165 The Koh-i-mohr . . . . a splendid peak *in*visible
> alike from Peshawar and Malakand.
>
> page 203 fulcrums for fulcra.

This was in my MS. And when I noticed it I thought of writing but did not as I thought you would see it. I fear Mr Welldon will be very much shocked.

The book has been very well brought out by Longmans and the maps are excellent with only two mistakes noticeable.

If it reaches a second edition I shall make some extensive alterations as you suggest.

Once more thanking you let me pass the subject. . . .

In fact the book was received with enthusiasm everywhere — except for *The Broad Arrow,* which commented sourly on the fact that a young cavalry officer should be permitted to shift the burden of monotonous duty at Bangalore on to other shoulders "in order to obtain preferential treatment at the front. A knight of the sword has no prescriptive right to constitute himself a knight of the pen, in order that he may provide himself with an opportunity of using both indiscriminately. . . ." The weird punctuation was the one criticism that most discerning writers made. The review that Churchill was probably most pleased with was that in the *Athenaeum:*

The operations of the Malakand Field Force have yielded two excellent books [*the other by Lord Fincastle*]. That now before us is a literary phenomenon. Lieut Winston Spencer Churchill, named, if we mistake not, after the father of the first Duke of Marlborough, omits, indeed, the family hyphen from his name, but has evidently much of the genius of his uncle, of his father, and of their best known progenitor. May he become as great a soldier as the last, and a straighter politician! *The Story of the Malakand Field Force* (Longmans) needs only a little correction of each page to make its second edition a military classic. As it stands, it suggests in style a volume by Disraeli revised by a mad printer's reader. Disraeli's books all showed signs of the influence of Bolingbroke and of Burke; Mr Churchill may be only a reader of Burke and of Disraeli, but in many passages these writers speak again, and the application of Burke's style in particular to the affairs of war yields here and there passages worthy of Napier's great history — the model of military literature. Yet one word is printed for another, words are defaced by shameful blunders, and sentence after sentence ruined by the punctuation of an idiot or of a school-boy in the lowest form. . . .

Churchill commented in forwarding this review to his mother:

Here is one of those opinions to which I must bow. The vy great praise bestowed upon my style is more than ever in my most sanguine moments I had hoped for. The condemnation is less severe than that I should have myself pronounced.

The glittering prize of literary appreciation which has hung before my eyes has been snatched away — as soon as it was won.

However I have learnt my lesson. I may live to write something that will take its place in permanent literature — for the faults need not be repeated — and the power of writing will remain.

I am glad I wrote a kind letter to Moreton — the *Athenaeum* has expressed my sentiments with terrible force. . . .

The Prince of Wales wrote. Churchill wrote to his mother (May 10), "he professes himself pleased with the book. I have answered dutifully. The cuttings are vy civil but undeserved. The book as it stands is an eyesore and I scream with disappointment and shame when I contemplate the hideous blunders that deface it. I never had any doubts that the style was good and that the ideas were pleasing.

But such slovenly work is a dreadful disgrace. Literary excellence is what I aim at. However there is plenty of time — barring accidents.
. . ." Had he known that the Prince of Wales was sending a copy of the book to his sister, the Empress Victoria of Germany, his good opinion of himself and of the Prince might well have been even enhanced, for as he said he was "Tory enough" to be flattered by such things.

Mr Welldon also wrote to Churchill, which gave him great pleasure. "If the work reaches a second edition," he told his mother, "you must telegraph to me. I will then ask Welldon to revise the punctuation as I am rather ignorant in this respect & have alas made one bad grammatical mistake in the misuse of the Present Participle. . . ."

One of the first results of the success of *The Story of the Malakand Field Force* was a series of invitations from magazine editors and publishers to write articles or books. He had already sent a short story "Unus Contra Mundum" which he wanted to sell to one of the magazines. He had also sent a long and rather exuberant article on the art of oratory and the philosophical implications of it called The Scaffolding of Rhetoric. Neither of these two articles seem to have been published, though the script of the latter survives. Now the Editor of the *United Services Magazine* asked him to write an article on the Ethics of Frontier Policy, which was published in the magazine in the following August. The publishing house of James Nisbet and Co wrote to ask if he would write a life of the great Duke of Marlborough and whether he would consider writing a life of Lord Randolph. He like the idea of writing the life of Marlborough — as a "memoir." He did not wish to poach on his cousin Sunny's preserves, Churchill told his mother (May 10). "At the same time I think it would produce something that would ring like a trumpet call." To the suggestion that he should write the life of Lord Randolph he replied that he thought the time had not yet come when such a life could be written, "and if ever I attempted it I should make it a labour of years."

Already Churchill was laying down some principles for himself. He realized that he would not be able, in his writings, to express himself as forcibly as he might wish: "The Tirah Campaign has been cruelly mismanaged," he wrote to his mother on March 3. "The malice with which I was myself pursued might well have inspired me to state forcibly what is here said on all sides. But a young man must cultivate early a sense of responsibility in public criticism — if he wants attention paid to his utterances." And to his brother Jack, who was about to accompany his employer, Mr Ernest Cassel, on a business trip to Egypt, he gave this advice: "There is a great deal to be seen in every Eastern town — and first impressions are often original and always valuable. You should try and put them down on paper — not necessarily for publication — but as a practice in good composition. The art of observing is one which can be cultivated — and it is an excellent thing to try and see the odd, queer and unnoticed side of things."

For the *Pioneer* newspaper he was writing five "letters" on the Cuban revolt which was just coming to a head with American intervention, articles based, presumably, on his experiences eighteen months before.

The idea of writing, now that he had achieved this success with his first book, appealed to him immensely:

WSC to Lady Randolph

EXTRACT

25 April 1898   Bangalore

. . . This literary sphere of action may enable me in a few years to largely supplement my income. Indeed I look forward to becoming sooner or later independent. We shall see. I have in my eye a long series of volumes which I am convinced I can write well.

1. A life of Garibaldi.
2. A short & dramatic History of the American Civil War.
3. A volume of short stories called "The Correspondent of the *New York Examiner.*"

(The one I sent you last mail would be included — of the others there are about five, blocked roughly).

I hope, if I live, to produce something that may remain, and if on looking into Garibaldi — of whose wonderful career no good account exists — I find that the materials are congenial — I may perhaps make a classic. *The Story of the M.F.F.* took but 5 weeks to write. But I will take 3 years over the others.

Ian Hamilton, to whom he had entrusted the article for the *United Services Magazine,* gave a word of warning. He wrote from the ship that was to take him from India to England:

Colonel Ian Hamilton to WSC

25 April 1898   SS *Shamron*

My dear Churchill,

Your kind letter and the magazine article. The latter is of great though unequal power. I see what they mean about your punctuation. You have a habit of putting a comma in between the relative and its subject which is unusual. But punctuation is a matter of fancy after all & this does not matter a d——, one way or the other. You have in you the raw material for several successful careers. But altho' art is long, life is short and, whatever your ambition, be sure you lose no time in getting on to the direct and recognised track which leads up to it. The admirable Crichton — many-sided sort of career leads to dispersion of effort, indefiniteness of aim and ultimate disappointment and defeat. Rather select your line of country forthwith and break in and curb all your talents to be merely subsidiary appendages to help you towards your goal. It would be satisfactory to achieve the combination of Marlborough, Napier and Pitt, but in the existing specialized era, such dreams are of the idlest texture. The period has arrived when you will only be losing time and training if you continue to hang between the two or three avenues which radiate from your feet & lead towards fame each in its own way & through its characteristic country. Suppose you attain to Khartum & get promised a brevet the day you are gazetted Captain then what a sad waste if you ultimately drop the soldier, especially as the title of Major would not help you in politics. Briefly then I hold that you should decide now, and either stand for Parliament on the very first occasion or else determine to be a soldier and leave politics alone until you can approach them from the fixed & serene basis of a seat in the House of Lords. I will certainly pay my respects to Lady Randolph if they allow me to stay long enough in town. Your MS I will post to her in London; it will only be 24 hours later than if I posted it on the ship. May we meet again, and soon, when the bugles are blowing and drums are beating and khaki is the colour we wear.

Yours very sincly

IAN HAMILTON

P.S. Have you read my wife's article in *Chapman's Magazine* of some months back: "Till we meet again." It is good of its kind. No I never got the copy of your book but I bought one & read it with much delight not only in the matter but also in the style. Send me one some day *signed*. I have a fad for author's copies. I.H.

P.S. *No* 2. Remember about the special medal *or* supplementary decoration for N.W.F. operation 1897–1898! I am doing all I know. I.H.

*

While he had been travelling long distances to and from Calcutta, fruitlessly as it seemed, to join the Tirah campaign, even while he was enjoying his fugitive delights there and again on his return to Bangalore he was still maturing his long-considered project of somehow or other getting to a much bigger war — the re-conquest of the Sudan. Since 1896 Sir Herbert Kitchener, the Sirdar of the Egyptian Army, had been advancing by short stages up the Nile, building a railway as he went along. His force of Egyptians, with a stiffening of English units, grew more powerful as the railway became longer.

WSC to Lady Randolph

EXTRACT

10 January 1898   Bangalore

. . . Oh how I wish I could work you up over Egypt! I know you could do it with all your influence — and all the people you know. It is a pushing age and we must shove with the best. After Tirah & Egypt — then I think I shall turn from war to peace & politics. If, that is, I get through all right. I think myself I shall, but of course one only has to look at Nature and see how very little store she sets by life. Its sanctity is entirely a human idea. You may think of a beautiful butterfly — 12 million feathers on his wings, 16,000 lenses in his eye — a mouthful for a bird. Let us laugh at Fate. It might please her. . . .

WSC to Jack

EXTRACT

19 January 1898   Raichur

. . . I am concentrating all my efforts on the Egyptian line of attack. I wish Mamma would help. So far I have had to [do] all these things myself. . . .

Lady Randolph to WSC

EXTRACT

13 January 1898   Chatsworth

. . . I wrote to the Sirdar — but I do not expect any result. I'm told you must have 4 years service to be taken. The advance on Khartoum will not be until the Spring — May — & if they fight now it will be at once, before you could get there. Caryl Ramsden who is in the Seaforth Highlanders has gone up with his batt: a great piece of good luck for him — but of course Malta & Crete for a year was not pleasant. . . .

WSC to Lady Randolph

EXTRACT

2 February 1898   [Bangalore]

. . . As to Egypt: I beg you to continue to try from every side. My plans have crystallized since I knew the advance was not till the autumn. I shall take my 3 months leave June 15 to Sept 15 — and go to Egypt — as a Correspondent if they will allow — failing all other capacities — but I hope you will be able to get me attached — at any rate temporarily. I shall go if I am alive — and I think I shall prevail ultimately. . . .

As it happened Lady Randolph already had a plan to spend part of the winter in Egypt. It was thus easy for her to comply with her son's urgent request. Churchill, unaware of his mother's plan, flattered himself that her expedition was undertaken solely in his interests. Naturally he was ecstatic in his thanks:

WSC to Lady Randolph

EXTRACT

16 February 1898   [Bangalore]

. . . Your telegram reached me on Saturday — and I can assure you
I feel vy grateful indeed to you for going to Egypt. It is an action
which — if ever I have a biographer — will certainly be admired by
others. I hope you may be successful. I feel almost certain you will.
Your wit & tact & beauty should overcome all obstacles. . . .

Churchill, however, did not, as he himself would have said in later
years, "weary of well-doing." Only nine days later we find him writing to his mother from Meerut where he had gone to stay with Sir
Bindon Blood for the Regimental Polo Tournament:

WSC to Lady Randolph

EXTRACT

25 February [1898]   Meerut

. . . Meanwhile I hope you are making all things smooth in Egypt.
As I have been attached to a Field Force I am entitled to three
months leave on full pay and shall proceed to Egypt — subject to
the approval of Providence — the last week in June. You should
make certain of my being employed then. This will be an easier
matter than an official attachment to the Egyptian army and is more
likely to be allowed as it involves the Egyptian Govt in no extra
expense. Sir Evelyn Wood has promised Lady Jeune that he will
in that contingency assist me as much as lies in his power. But you
probably know that it all rests with the Sirdar who can do as he
likes. You must leave directions for any letters which I address Poste
Restante, Cairo, — to be forwarded without delay — should they
arrive after you have left for England.

I hope you will enjoy Cairo — I believe at this season it is for
climate and company delightful. . . .

Like Antony and Napoleon before him, Churchill ardently aspired
for action on the Nile.

WSC to Lady Randolph

31 March [1898]   Camp Peshawar

. . . Lady Jeune telegraphed to me yesterday "Soudan all right —
writing" from which I gather she has worked things for me. She is
a clever woman and tho I believe you do not like her she is worth
knowing. She would not have gone to the expense of telegraphing
to this country unless she was sure.

And this brings me to a great project. If I hear by her letter that
I am to be selected as a Special Service Officer — and to be sent out
"on duty" — then there will be no occasion for me to sacrifice my
3 month Privilege leave — and if the regiment can spare me I shall
with your concurrence come home as soon as possible and try and
have a month in England before the Nile.

My heart leaps towards such a prospect — in a way that you very
likely do not realise. . . .

On April 8, Kitchener put 16,000 Dervishes to flight at the Atbara.
Churchill was not slow to hear of this and to see the military signifi-
cance, especially in so far as it concerned his own fortunes:

WSC to Lady Randolph

EXTRACT

13 April [1898]   Bombay

. . . It was evident from the moment that the Dervishes evacuated
Metemmah and Shendy and moved round the Egyptian left flank
with a view to threatening & possibly assailing Sir Herbert Kitchener's communications — that a battle was imminent.

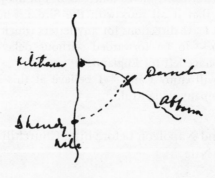

The Dervishes were "formed to a flank" i.e. had their line of retreat in prolongation of their front. For an army to be beaten in such a strategic position is for it to be destroyed. This has happened many times in military history. We all expected a battle therefore — but when it did not come off — Sir B.B. concluded that the Egyptian troops must have been considered worthless and that the Sirdar did not feel strong enough to seize the glorious opportunity presented. He said "in two days more we shall see." The next morning we got the news.

I need not tell you how bitter my own feelings were to think I had not been there. Still my conscience is easy and as I was actually on field service at the time, I cannot complain.

I do not think this will alter the prospects of an autumn campaign, tho it may diminish the resistance to be encountered. The Nile will not rise before it is ready, and I am quite easy in my mind that even July would be time enough. We shall see. If I am too late and all is over I can only conclude that perhaps Fate intervened because Chance would have been malicious had I gone.

Meanwhile relax not a volt of your energy. "The Importunate Widow" and the appropriate scriptural instances occur to me.

I expect to find Lady Jeune's letter awaiting me at Bangalore and will then write to you and tell you what my plans are. I fear England must not be included in them. As soon as I can get my leave I am off to Egypt. The reason is that if Lady Jeune has been able to arrange for my being sent out as a special service officer — it will be desirable for me to be on the spot before the others, so as to ensure my not being left on the line of communications. However, I reason without any facts. Next week will show. . . .

His brother Jack, who was then eighteen years old, wrote him what was obviously a discouraging letter about the prospects; his letter unfortunately does not survive. However Churchill's reply is extant:

WSC to Jack

EXTRACT

9 May [1898]   Government House
                                        Ootacamund

. . . I do not at all agree with you that the Atbara is the end of the Soudan campaign. Much more severe fighting will ensue — especially at Omdurman. I hear they are making great preparations at Woolwich — for high explosive shells & 5 inch rifled guns — to breach the fortress — which does not look as if all were over.

It seems good fighting — short and sharp. But I don't expect it is any more exciting & less dangerous than the frontier. At Atbara — 16,000 men — lost 500 killed & wounded (60 killed). On 16th Sept in Mamund valley 1000 men — lost 150 — (of whom 50 killed) or four times as heavy a proportion. Also the Egyptian fight lasted 28 minutes. I was under fire exactly 13 hours on the 16th. However I look forward with much interest to see both kinds. . . .

Evidently the hoped for reply did not await him at Bangalore. But his determination to reach the impending scene of war as soon as possible remained unabated despite all discouragements:

WSC to Lady Randolph

EXTRACT

22 May 1898 [Bangalore]

. . . Egypt. Please redouble your efforts in this direction. My plans for the future will be much influenced by this. I am determined to go to Egypt and if I cannot get employment or at least sufficient leave, I will not remain in the army. There are other and better things ahead. But the additional campaign will be valuable as an educational experience — agreeable from the point of view of an adventure — and profitable as far as finance goes as I shall write a book about it — easily and without the blunders which disfigure my first attempt. This of course if all goes well. Don't fail to wire me any news of an advance. . . .

II

The River War

NOTHING WAS CERTAIN. Yet Churchill, impecunious as he was, took up his three months' leave and sailed from Bombay on June 18. He arrived in London in early July. At once he animated his mother to pull any strings that had not yet been pulled. By this time many friendly agents were already at work. His mother was doing all she could: Lady Jeune was intriguing with Sir Evelyn Wood, the Adjutant General of the Forces. But none of this seemed to be of avail.

Churchill now recognized that all the best endeavours of his mother with Kitchener and those of Lady Jeune with Sir Evelyn Wood had miscarried. He was beginning to feel that he had wasted his time when, out of the blue, there arrived a potential life-line inspired by memories of the past. Lord Salisbury, then Prime Minister and Foreign Secretary, had chanced to read *The Story of the Malakand Field Force*. Evidently he was not put off by the misprints and poor punctuation which had so distressed the author. He invited him to come and see him. Churchill recounts the story admirably in *My Early Life*:

> The Great Man, Master of the British world, the unchallenged leader of the Conservative Party, a third time Prime Minister and Foreign Secretary at the height of his long career, received me at the appointed hour, and I entered for the first time that spacious room overlooking the Horseguards Parade in which I was afterwards for many years from time to time to see much grave business done in Peace and War.
>
> There was a tremendous air about this wise old Statesman. Lord

Salisbury, for all his resistance to modern ideas, and perhaps in some way because of it, played a greater part in gathering together the growing strength of the British Empire for a time of trial which few could foresee and none could measure, than any other historic figure that can be cited. I remember well the old-world courtesy with which he met me at the door and with a charming gesture of welcome and salute conducted me to a seat on a small sofa in the midst of his vast room.

"I have been keenly interested in your book. I have read it with the greatest pleasure and, if I may say so, with admiration not only for its matter but for its style. The debates in both Houses of Parliament about the Indian frontier policy have been acrimonious, much misunderstanding has confused them. I myself have been able to form a truer picture of the kind of fighting that has been going on in these frontier valleys from your writings than from any other documents which it has been my duty to read."

I thought twenty minutes would be about the limit of my favour, which I had by no means the intention to outrun, and I accordingly made as if to depart after that period had expired. But he kept me for over half an hour, and when he finally conducted me again across the wide expanse of carpet to the door, he dismissed me in the following terms, "I hope you will allow me to say how much you remind me of your father, with whom such important days of my political life were lived. If there is anything at any time that I can do which would be of assistance to you, pray do not fail to let me know. . . ."

Churchill jumped at the opportunity. Where petticoat influence had failed, he would succeed. He wrote to Lord Salisbury:

WSC to Lord Salisbury

(Salisbury Papers)

18 July [1898]   35A Great Cumberland Place

Dear Lord Salisbury,

I am vy anxious to go to Egypt and to proceed to Khartoum with the Expedition. It is not my intention, under any circumstances to stay in the army long. I want to go, first, because the recapture of Khartoum will be a historic event: second, because I can, I anticipate, write a book about it which from a monetary, as well as from other points of view, will be useful to me.

I was assured five months ago, on the authority of the Adjutant General, that I might count on being employed; and hence I have postponed offering myself to a newspaper as correspondent until all the principal ones have already correspondents and there is no vacancy.

From a military point of view there can be no objection to me. I enclose a letter from Sir Evelyn Wood, which will show you that he has tried to do his best on my behalf. From the journalistic point of view: — either Sir William Lockhart or Sir Bindon Blood will testify that what I have hitherto written has been entirely agreeable to the military authorities and for the public advantage. There is no reason why I should not be employed as a soldier, except that there are others with greater claims remaining unemployed. That is undoubted. But there are others, I venture to think, with less claims who are employed.

Sir Evelyn Wood has tried his best — so he assures me — on my behalf. My mother has exerted what influence she can for two years. Even HRH has allowed his name to be used as a recommendation. All have failed.

I therefore venture to ask you to help me in the matter. I am convinced that if you will write a letter to Lord Cromer and say that on personal grounds you wish me to go — the affair will be immediately arranged. Either I should be attached to the Expeditionary Force direct, or allowed to proceed to the front as correspondent of some, perhaps insignificant, paper and after a few casualties be appointed to fill a vacancy — as I was on the N.W. Frontier.

I am loth to afflict you with this matter. Yet the choice lies between doing so, and abandoning a project which I have set my heart on for a long time. I feel that you will not be unwilling to help me, if that can be done without hurt to the public service and I venture to think that no hurt will result, but rather benefit. The affair is after all of extreme insignificance to any but me.

          I beg you will believe me, Yours very sincerely

                  WINSTON S. CHURCHILL

Lord Salisbury asked Lord Cromer, who for so many years had been the political master of Egypt, to write to Kitchener: "But I am afraid I cannot advise you to rely too confidently on the result of his letter," warned the Prime Minister in his reply to Churchill. In the event, the intervention of these distinguished personages was not necessary. Churchill relates in *My Early Life* how Lady Jeune had told Sir Evelyn Wood that she had heard somebody at the dinner table express the opinion that Kitchener was going too far in picking and choosing between particular officers recommended by the War Office.

> The Egyptian Army no doubt was a sphere within which the Sirdar's wishes must be absolute, but the British contingent (of an Infantry Division, a Brigade of Artillery and a British Cavalry regiment, the 21st Lancers) was a part of the Expeditionary Force, the internal composition of which rested exclusively with the War Office. Lady Jeune told me indeed that Sir Evelyn Wood had evinced considerable feeling upon this subject. Then I said, "Have you told him that the Prime Minister has telegraphed personally on my behalf?" She said she had not. "Do so," I said, "and let us see whether he will stand up for his prerogatives."
>
> Two days later I received the following laconic intimation from the War Office:
>
> "You have been attached as a supernumerary Lieutenant to the 21st Lancers for the Soudan Campaign. You are to report at once at the Abbasiya Barracks, Cairo, to the Regimental Headquarters. It is understood that you will proceed at your own expense and that in the event of your being killed or wounded in the impending operations, or for any other reason, no charge of any kind will fall on British Army Funds."

It was the death of a young officer in the 21st Lancers, Lieutenant P. Chapman, that created the vacancy which provided Churchill with his opportunity. Only one thing it seems now stood between Churchill and his goal: the necessary leave from the Indian Army authorities to take part in the Sudan Campaign. Characteristically, he decided not to wait for this leave to be given, but on the contrary to depart at once in case an adverse order might arrive from India. Instead of travelling more speedily by P & O via Brindisi, or more comfortably by Austrian Lloyd via Trieste, Churchill opted for a third route, slower and more uncomfortable than either, one that would place him out of communication with the Indian military authorities as soon as possible. Once he was in Egypt it would be impossible for them to recall him; indeed they would hardly know where he was. Thus he travelled to Marseilles and there caught the Messageries Maritime Paquebot *Sindh* — "a filthy tramp — manned by these detestable French sailors" as he described it to his mother.

*

While he crossed the Mediterranean he must, despite his excitement about the voyage and his anxiety as to whether he would be intercepted by an order to return, have had time to reflect on what was for him an important public speech, only the second of his career. He made this twelve days before he left London at Bradford, his father's old stamping-ground.

WSC to Lady Randolph

15 July [1898]   Bradford

My dearest Mamma,

The meeting was a complete success. The hall was not a vy large one — but it was closely packed. I was listened to with the greatest attention for 55 minutes at the end of which time there were loud & general cries of "Go on." Five or six times they applauded for about two minutes without stopping and at the end of the peroration — which the newspapers cut owing to necessities of printing — many people mounted their chairs and there was really a very great deal of enthusiasm. In reply to a vote of thanks I said that I had already spoken for nearly an hour and that only three minutes remained, whereupon they shouted "Go on for another hour" & "Coom back lad" etc. All of which was vy gratifying.

As to tangible results: — there was a supper afterwards at the Midland Hotel at which about 30 of the most important local men were present and in the numerous speeches that went on till midnight the vy broadest hints were made to me to keep my eye on the Central Division. Mr Wanklyn the Member has it appears given great offence here and is also concerned in some company transaction which they are furious about. R. Greville told me plainly that they were profoundly impressed and delighted by my speech and that the idea of having me back to Bradford in what they called "another capacity" was vy strong.

Personally — I was intensely pleased with the event. The keenness of the audience stirred my blood — and altho I stuck to my notes rigidly I certainly succeeded in rousing & in amusing them. They burst out of the hall & pressed all round the carriage to shake hands and cheered till we had driven quite away.

The conclusions I form are these — with practice I shall obtain great power on a public platform. My impediment is no hindrance. My voice sufficiently powerful, and — this is vital — my ideas & modes of thought are pleasing to men.

It may be perhaps the hand of Fate, which by a strange coincidence closed one line of advance and aspiration in the morning and in the evening pointed out another with an encouraging gesture. At any rate my decision to resign my commission is definite.

> With best love, Your ever loving son
> WINSTON

His speech had provoked praise from some unexpected sources. For instance — Haldane, the Liberal philosopher and future Secretary of State for War, wrote to Lady Randolph:

R. B. Haldane to Lady Randolph

15 July 1898   House of Commons

Dear Lady Randolph,

Contrary to my habit — I asked for a *Morning Post* today — I read the speech at Bradford — I thought it very good — broad in tone — fresh & vigorous — I hope he will soon be in the House, for there is in his voice something of the strong quality of one that is — alas — still — to the loss of all of us, & of you most of all.

> Yours vy sincerely
> R. B. HALDANE

A great sense of destiny, of power and of greatness was already deeply impregnated in Churchill. He was, by this time, markedly egocentric and self-expressive. This alienated many of his contemporaries and to a lesser extent those who were older than he was and who had known his father and were fascinated by the thought that he would prove to be a serviceable successor. Already by this time he had become an object of conversation and controversy. It was facile to say that he was trading on his father's reputation, that he pulled all the strings he could and made use of all the influence which he had inherited. But none could gainsay his courage or the ardour of his ambition. All this, however, did not make him very popular. He was still living in the twilight of a Victorian era in which many of his activities were regarded by older people as "ungentlemanly."

He recognized all this, but with his eyes open decided to run the risks. After all, he had nothing to lose. He was penniless; indeed, in debt. He was a soldier of fortune. He had to make his way, he had to make his name. It was a help being the son of Lord Randolph. Many people, like Lord Salisbury, Sir Michael Hicks-Beach and Sir Henry Drummond Wolff, who had had important transactions with Lord Randolph, were prepared to help him. But their help would have been of no avail without his own primordial thrust. As these pages unfold, it will be seen that though he took the fullest opportunity of connections which he had inherited from his father, it was his own daemon which led him on to fame, prosperity and honour.

*

No message from the Indian authorities intercepted him. When he reached Luxor on August 5, he permitted himself a sigh of relief: "As there has been no cancelling order and a fortnight has already passed, I think I may now conclude with certainty that 'silence has given consent.' "

Churchill continued in the same letter to his mother:

WSC to Lady Randolph

EXTRACT

5 August 1898   Luxor

. . . It is a very strange transformation scene that the last 8 days have worked. When I think of the London streets — dinners, balls etc and then look at the Khaki soldiers — the great lumbering barges full of horses — the muddy river and behind and beyond the palm trees and the sails of the Dahabiahs. And the change in my

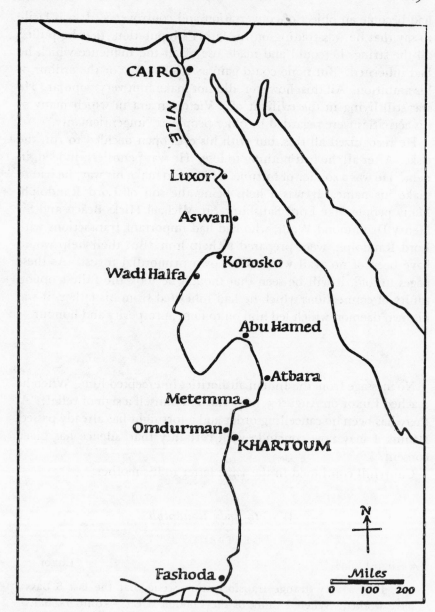

THE ADVANCE UP THE NILE

own mind is even more complete. The ideals & speculations of politics are gone. I no longer contemplate harangues. The anticipations of Parliament — of speeches — of political life generally have faded before more vivid possibilities and prospects and my thoughts are more concerned with swords — lances — pistols & soft-nosed bullets — than with Bills — Acts & bye elections. . . .

Very few personal letters of Churchill's during this campaign survive. He took his military duties seriously and often found it difficult to write his despatches for the *Morning Post,* who had contracted to pay him £15 a column. We must, therefore, for the next few weeks, rely principally upon these despatches and the account he gave of his travels and adventures in *The River War.* This book, which was published in two volumes fifteen months after the recapture of Khartoum, is still regarded by many good judges of literature as one of the best books he ever wrote. It has been reprinted several times. Here are a few extracts which chronicle his journey from the barracks at Abbasiya, where he had reported, until he joined Kitchener's forces a few miles short of Khartoum.

Cairo. On the 2nd of August we paraded in the panoply of modern war — *khaki* uniforms, sun-helmets, "Sam Brown" belts, revolvers, field-glasses, and Stohwasser gaiters — at Abbasiya barracks. The railway runs conveniently by the cavalry lines, and a long train of carriages for the men and of cattle trucks for the horses was waiting. The entraining of troops is always a wearying affair. The soldiers — arrayed in what they call "Christmas Tree order," and dangling from every part of their bodies with water-bottles, haversacks, canteen-straps, cloaks, swords, and carbines clank awkwardly into the carriages. Then the baggage has to be loaded, kit-bags must be stowed, and provision made for food and filtered water. With infantry the business is laborious; but with cavalry the difficulties are more than doubled. Saddlery, forage, and above all horses, have to be packed into the trucks. When I mention that the horses were stallion Arabs, it will easily be realised what a kicking and squealing the stowage of this last item caused. But perseverance overcomes everything, even the vivacity of the little Arab horse, though at times he seems to be actually infected with the fanaticism of the human inhabitants of the land of his birth. At length all

things are accomplished. The band strikes up "Auld Lang Syne."
For a moment the train is linked to the platform by the handshaking
of those who go and of those who stay. Then it slowly moves off,
gaining pace and increasing the distance gradually, until its growing
rattle drowns the cheering and the fitful strains of the band. We are
off. Whither? Southward to Khartoum and perhaps beyond —
perhaps very far beyond for some. . . .

Aswan. I viewed the celebrated ruins of the temple with an hostility so keen that I am provoked to a long digression.

In brief, Churchill traces the difficulties experienced over many
years in finding the money necessary for the building of a dam which
would provide irrigation for large stretches of Egypt, and then goes
on to criticize the fact that when at last sufficient funds were made
available for the construction of a dam, it was found that one obstacle, the temple of Philae, stood in the way of increasing the store
of water from 1,065,000 to 2,550,000 cubic metres, by merely raising
the height of the dam 8 metres.

. . . The profits of the people and Government of Egypt would be
more than doubled. The wealth and happiness of the amiable
peasants of the Delta would grow; their contentment would react
on the prosperity of other countries. All the world would gain
advantage from those extra eight metres of masonry.
    The Temple of Philae intervenes. The raising of the water-level
would submerge it. I will not assail the small but beautiful ruin.
Let us believe that the god to whom it was raised was once worthy
of human reverence, and would willingly accept as a nobler memorial the life-giving lake beneath which his temple would be
buried. If it were not so, then indeed it would be time for a rational
and utilitarian generation to tear the monument of such a monster
to pieces, so that no stone remained upon the other, and thus prevent for ever the sacrifice of 1,485 million cubic metres of water —
the most cruel, most wicked, and most senseless sacrifice ever offered
on the altar of a false religion. But the quarrel of the philosopher is
not with the temple. Behind it stand the archaeologists. Because
a few persons whose functions are far removed from those which may
benefit mankind — profitless chippers of stone, rummagers in the

dust-heaps of the past — have raised an outcry, nominally on account of the tourists, the sacrifice of water — the life-blood of Egypt — is being offered up. The State must struggle and the people starve, in order that professors may exult and tourists find some space on which to scratch their names. . . .

The temple was partially submerged as a result of these operations, and wholly submerged after the dam was enlarged in 1907.

Atbara. Early on the morning of the 16th, while the stars were yet in the sky, the convoy and its escort started. . . . I remained behind, having to hand over surplus stores, and intending to catch up the column in the evening at its first camp, about fifteen miles away. The business I had to do consumed more time than I had anticipated, and it was not until the sun was on the horizon that the little ferry steamer *Tahra* landed me again on the west bank. I made inquiries about the road. "It is perfectly simple," they said. "You just go due south until you see the campfires and then turn towards the river." This I proceeded to do. I had gone about a mile when the sun sank and the world went into darkness. The bushes by the Nile were thick and thorny, and to avoid these I struck into the desert, steering due south by keeping my back to the Pole star. I rode on at a trot for nearly two hours, thinking all the time that it would be a welcome moment when I sat down to dinner, and above all to a drink. Suddenly, to my dismay, the sky began to cloud over, and my guiding-star and the pointers of the Great Bear faded and became invisible. For another hour I endeavoured to pursue my old direction, but the realisation that I was out of my bearings grew stronger every moment. At last the truth could be no longer disguised. I was lost. No dinner, no drink; nothing for the pony; nothing to do but wait for daylight!

One thing seemed clear in the obscurity. It was futile to go on at random and to exhaust the animal on whom alone depended my chance of catching up the troops. So I selected a sandy spot behind a rock and, passing the reins round my waist, endeavoured to sleep. Thirst and the fidgeting of the pony effectually prevented this, and philosophic meditation was my sole and altogether insufficient consolation. Although the sky remained clouded, the night was hot. The view in every direction was concealed by the darkness, but the barrenness of the desert was none the less apparent. The realisation of its utter waste and desolation grew. A hot, restless, weary wind blew continuously with a mournful sound over the miles and miles of sand and rock, as if conscious of its own uselessness: a rainless wind over a sterile soil. In the distance there was a noise like the rattle of a train. It was more wind blowing over more desert. The possibility of Dervishes was too remote to be considered; but as the night wore on, the annoyance at missing a needed dinner and the discomfort of my position were intensified by another sensation — a horrible sensation of powerlessness, just like that which a man feels when his horse bolts and will not be stopped. Supposing morning should reveal nothing but desert, and the trees by the Nile should be hidden by the ground and by the low hills and knolls which rose on all sides! Of course, by riding towards the rising sun, I must strike the Nile sooner or later. But how far was I from it? The idea that the distance might be beyond the powers of my horse jarred unpleasantly. Reason, coming to the rescue, checked such imaginings with the comfortable reflection that twenty miles was the most I could have ridden altogether. Meanwhile the hours passed without hurrying.

At about half-past three in the morning the clouds cleared from one part of the sky and the glorious constellation of Orion came into view. Never did the giant look more splendid. Forthwith I mounted and rode in his direction, for at this season of the year he lies along the Nile before dawn with his head to the north. After two hours' riding the desert scrub rose into higher bushes, and these, becoming more frequent and denser, showed that the Nile was not far off. Meanwhile the sky in the east began to pale, and against it there drew out in silhouette the tracery of the foliage and palm-trees by the river's drink. The thirsty pony pricked up his ears. In the gloom we brushed through the thorny bushes, spurred on by a common desire. Suddenly the undergrowth parted, and at our feet, immense and mysterious in the growing light, gleamed the Nile. I have written much of the great river. Here it thrusts itself on the page. Jumping off my horse, I walked into the flood till it rose above my knees, and began eagerly to drink its waters, as many a thirsty man has done before; while the pony, plunging his nose deep into the stream, gulped and gulped in pleasure and relief, as if he could never swallow enough. Water had been found; it remained to discover the column.

After much riding I reached their camping-ground, only to find it deserted. They had already marched. There was a village near by. Once it had consisted of many houses and had supported a large population. Now only a few miserable people moved about the mud walls. War and famine had destroyed nine-tenths of the inhabitants. I selected one of the remainder, whose *tarboush,* or fez, proclaimed him a man of some self-respect, and perhaps even of some local importance, and applied to him for breakfast and a guide. He spoke nothing but Arabic: I, only one word of that language. Still we conversed fluently. By opening and shutting my mouth and pointing to my stomach, I excited his curiosity, if not his wonder. Then I employed the one and indispensable Arabic word, *Backsheesh!* After that all difficulties melted. From a corner of the mud house in which he lived he produced a clean white cloth full of dates. From another corner some *doura* satisfied the pony. From an inner apartment, which smelt stale and acrid, three women and several children appeared. The women smiled amicably and began to wait on me, handing me the dates one by one in fingers the dark skin of which alone protected them from the reproach of dirt. The children regarded the strangely garbed stranger with large eyes which seemed full of reflection, but without intelligent result. Meanwhile the lord of these splendours had departed with a wooden bowl. Presently he returned, bearing it filled with fresh, sweet, but dirty milk. This completed a repast which, if it would not gratify the palate of the epicure, might yet sustain the stomach of the traveller.

I next proceeded to ask for information as to the column. With the point of my sword I drew on the red mud wall the picture of a Lancer — grotesque, disproportioned, yet, as the event proved, not unrecognisable. The women laughed, the man talked and gesticulated with energy. Even the children became excited. Yes, it was true. Such a one had passed through the village early that morning. He pointed at the sun and then to the eastern horizon. But not one — many. He began to make scratches on the wall to show how many. They had watered their horses in the river — he lapped vigorously from his hand — and had gone on swiftly. He pointed southwards, and made the motion of running. Then he gazed hard at me, and, with an expression of ferocious satisfaction, pronounced the word "Omdurman." He was of the Jaalin, and, looking at the ruins and the desolation around, I could not wonder that he rejoiced that the strong and implacable arm of civilisation was raised to chastise his merciless enemies. I replied to his speech by repeating with considerable solemnity the word *Backsheesh,* and at this, without more ado, he put on his boots and a dirtier blue shirt, picked up his broad-bladed sword, and started. But I will not be wearisome with a further account of my wanderings in the riparian bush, or of the other meals of dates and milk I was forced, and indeed fain, to eat. In the evening I caught up the column at its camp, and washed away the taste and recollection of native food and native life with one of the most popular drinks of the modern world.

Um Teref. We had the day to ourselves, and passed it visiting our friends in the camp or resting either under the invaluable Soudan umbrellas — which, rising here and there like mushroom clusters, marked the officers' quarters — or under the trees, whose leaves gave a good shade and some relief from the glare. Fatigue parties of Egyptian soldiers soon arrived with axes to destroy these natural shelters that the gunboats might have wood, and in spite of protests all were cut down except a single tree, which, partly because it gave shade to the mess and partly because it was too thick, was left standing.

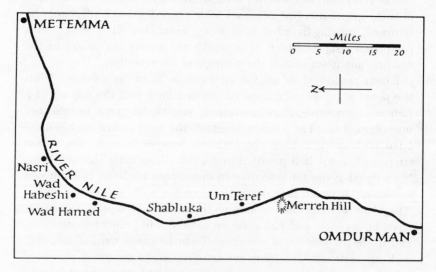

THE APPROACH TO OMDURMAN

One incident I must relate which arose out of this wood-cutting. The army had been accompanied by a large number of black women, presumably the wives of the Soudanese soldiers. These the Sirdar had constantly endeavoured to banish, refusing to make any provision for them and forbidding them to follow the line of march. But they treated his orders with profound disdain, and they were seen daily trudging along after the troops, carrying their goods and chattels on their heads, in spite of the dust, the sun, the danger, and the length of the road. I had often felt sorry for them and their fatigues. Yet I suppose theirs was a labour of love. Four of these beauties were now encamped beneath a tree. A stalwart Egyptian soldier advanced to cut it down according to his orders. Forthwith they summoned him to desist, and on his paying no attention to their imprecations the whole four rose in a bunch and rushed upon him, knocking him down, beating him, and pulling his ears. The soldier, rising with a great effort, succeeded in freeing himself, and incontinently fled, pursued by the taunts of the damsels, who retired again to their tree — *which was not cut down.* . . .

Merreh Hill. Trotting out the next morning — the 31st — as the light strengthened, we soon reached the hill of Merreh, and while the horses were being watered, I climbed to the top to view the scene. The sun had just risen, and the atmosphere was clear. A wonderful spectacle was displayed. The grand army of the Nile marched towards its goal: a long row of great brown masses of infantry and artillery, with a fringe of cavalry dotting the plain for miles in front, with the Camel Corps — chocolate-coloured men on cream-coloured camels — stretching into the desert on the right, and the white gunboats stealing silently up the river on the left, scrutinising the banks with their guns. Far in rear the transport trailed away into the mirage, and far in front the field-glass disclosed the enemy's patrols. Behind the moving army a long thread of wire made an Empire share its quarrel; before it a long account awaited settlement. . . .

For all his preoccupations Churchill did have time to send back some philosophical reflections:

WSC to Lady Randolph

EXTRACT

24 August 1898   Wad Hebeshi
                                                    before Shabluka

. . . Within the next ten days there will be a general action — perhaps a vy severe one. I may be killed. I do not think so. But if I am you must avail yourself of the consolations of philosophy and reflect on the utter insignificance of all human beings. I want to come back and shall hope all will be well. But I can assure you I do not flinch — though I do not accept the Christian or any other form of religious belief. We shall see what will happen; and in that spirit I would leave the subject. Nothing — not even the certain knowledge of approaching destruction would make me turn back now — even if I could with honour.

But I shall come back afterwards the wiser and stronger for my gamble. And then we will think of other and wider spheres of action. I have plenty of faith — in what I do not know — that I shall not be hurt. After all there will be nothing hotter than the 16th Sept of last year, and I am sure that of the next world we may say — If any then better. . . .

He also found time to write a long letter to his friend Captain Aylmer Haldane, the gist of which, after many courtesies and some description of his activities is contained in the following paragraph:

WSC to Captain Aylmer Haldane

(Aylmer Haldane Papers)

EXTRACT

11 August [1898]   near Wadi Halfa

. . . One thing particularly I write about. It is this. In common with the ingenuous Bellew [*a Lieutenant in the 16th Lancers*] I am entitled to a medal and two clasps for my gallantry for the hardships & dangers I encountered with the T.E.F. [Tirah Expeditionary Force]. I am possessed of a keen desire to mount the ribbon on my breast while I face the Dervishes here. It may induce them to pause. But when will it be issued? If you will do me a favour and materially add to my joy as well as to my gratitude please write me a letter to say exactly when I may consider my medal as issued & enclose in the envelope a little slip of ribbon. I ought to come in among the first lot — Staff always take precedence — of mere, common regimental officers. If you write to me and tell me that it is alright I will duly put it on. . . .

When Churchill's squadron of the 21st Lancers joined up with the main army at Shabluka a week before the battle of Omdurman he wrote:

WSC to Lady Randolph

EXTRACT

26 August 1898   N. of Shabluka

. . . F. Rhodes [Colonel Frank Rhodes, Correspondent of *The Times*] vy kind and amiable. He talked to Sirdar about me. Kitchener said he had known I was not going to stay in army — was only making a convenience of it; that he had disapproved of my coming in place of others whose professions were at stake & that E. Wood had acted wrongly & had annoyed him by sending me. But that I was quite right to try my best. Taken in conjunction with his letter to you you can see that whatever his knowledge of war may be his acquaintance with truth is rudimentary. He may be a general — but never a gentleman. Perhaps however I shall meet him. I have however not pressed for an introduction since hearing. If I live he will recognise that it might have been worth while to impress me with his ideas on Egypt & the Sudan. As it is I shall form my own. . . .

This arrogant quip proved to be an omen of better relations between the two men in the distant future. Though Churchill was later in the *Morning Post* and in *The River War* to attack Kitchener for having desecrated the Mahdi's tomb, there was to come a day when Kitchener found himself in a position to make a strikingly magnanimous gesture to Churchill who was by then virtually his equal in government. In May 1915 Asquith's Liberal Government fell, mainly because of Lord Fisher's resignation as First Sea Lord and to a lesser extent because of the shell crisis, and it was obvious that Churchill was going to be compelled to leave the Admiralty. There was an uneasy gap in the formation of a new Coalition Government but Churchill knew at an early stage that he, with Haldane, had been singled out by the Tories as their victims and as their price for joining the new Coalition. In Volume II of *The World Crisis* Churchill was to write:

. . . It was during this interval that I had the honour of receiving a visit of ceremony from Lord Kitchener. I was not at first aware of what it was about. We had differed strongly and on a broad front at the last meeting of the War Council. Moreover, no decision of any importance on naval and military affairs could be taken during the hiatus. We talked about the situation. After some general remarks he asked me whether it was settled that I should leave the Admiralty. I said it was. He asked what I was going to do. I said I had no idea; nothing was settled. He spoke very kindly about our work together. He evidently had no idea how narrowly he had escaped my fate. As he got up to go he turned and said, in the impressive and almost majestic manner which was natural to him, "Well, there is one thing at any rate they cannot take from you. The Fleet was ready." After that he was gone. During the months that we were still to serve together in the new Cabinet I was condemned often to differ from him, to oppose him and to criticize him. But I cannot forget the rugged kindness and warm-hearted courtesy which led him to pay me this visit. . . .

*

Only a few days after writing the letter of August 26 quoted above, on September 1, Churchill was destined by an unusual chance to come face to face with the Sirdar himself. This incident is vividly described in *The River War:*

. . . The great army, however, still advanced majestically, pressing the cavalry back before it; and it was evident that if the Khalifa's movement continued, and in spite of it being nearly one o'clock, there would be a collision between the main forces before the night. I was sent back to describe the state of affairs to the Sirdar.

To make certain of the position of the Expeditionary Force before starting in search of it, I climbed the black hill of Surgham and looked around.

From the summit the scene was extraordinary. The great army of Dervishes was dwarfed by the size of the landscape to mere dark smears and smudges on the brown of the plain. Looking east, another army was now visible — the British and Egyptian army. All six brigades had passed the Kerreri Hills, and now stood drawn up in a crescent, with their backs to the Nile. The transport and the houses of the village of Egeiga filled the enclosed space. Neither force could see the other, though but five miles divided them. I looked alternately at each array. That of the enemy was, without doubt, both longer and deeper. Yet there seemed a superior strength in the stolid battalions, whose lines were so straight that they might have been drawn with a ruler.

The urgency of my message allowed only a momentary view. But the impression produced by the sight of two armies thus approaching each other with hostile intent — for the Arab advance was very rapid — was so tremendous, that I found it necessary, lest my excitement should be apparent, to walk for a quarter of a mile before delivering my account.

The Sirdar, followed by a dozen Staff officers, was riding a few hundred yards from the *zeriba*. He had not yet seen the Dervish army, and was at the moment going to the hill of Surgham to take a general view. Nevertheless, he invited me to describe the situation as seen from the advanced squadrons. This I did, though neither at such length nor perhaps with such facility as in these pages. The swift advance of the enemy brought the moment very near. They were now but four miles away. In an hour, if they continued their movement, the action must begin. All the results of many years of preparation and three years of war must stand upon the issue of the event. If there had been a miscalculation, if the expedition was not strong enough, or if any accident or misfortune such as are common in battles were to occur, then utter ruin would descend upon the enterprise. The Sirdar was very calm. His confidence had been communicated to his Staff. "We want nothing better," they said. "Here is a good field of fire. They may as well come to-day as to-morrow." . . .

After completing his brief verbal report to the Sirdar, Churchill rode back to the *zeriba* where a large body of troops was encamped. They had been told to stand to arms at 2 p.m. It seemed likely at the time that the Dervish army would attack them that afternoon or possibly during the night. Churchill had come in search of a quick luncheon. He met a friend who took him into a Mess tent where he found himself in the company of the Director of Intelligence, Colonel Wingate, Slatin Pasha the famous administrator in the Sudan, Colonel Rhodes *The Times* correspondent, and the Foreign Attachés who were accompanying the Headquarters of the Nile Expedition. In *The River War* he records a conversation he had with Baron von Tiedmann, the German Military Attaché: " 'This is the 1st of September,' he said. 'Our great day, and now your great day; Sedan and Soudan.' I laughed at his ponderous wit; nor have I since been able to decide whether or not it cloaked a rather bitter sarcasm."

It must have been after the 21st Lancers retired behind the *zeriba* with the main body of the army that Churchill enjoyed the "happy experience" he related in *My Early Life*. He was strolling along the bank of the Nile with a brother officer, when they were hailed from one of the gunboats lying twenty or thirty feet from the shore. "How are you off for drinks?" the Naval Lieutenant in command asked. "We have got everything in the world on board here. Can you catch?" and almost immediately a large bottle of champagne was thrown from the gunboat to the shore. "It fell in the waters of the Nile, but happily where a gracious Providence decreed them to be shallow and the bottom soft. I nipped into the water up to my knees, and reaching down seized the precious gift which we bore in triumph back to our Mess." The name of the lieutenant in command of the gunboat was David Beatty, who only eighteen years later, after the Battle of Jutland, succeeded Admiral Jellicoe in the Command of the Grand Fleet.

There was no attack by the Dervish army that afternoon. Many of Kitchener's troops had made long marches and needed rest. All units, including the 21st Lancers, who had been on patrol and reconnaissance all day were withdrawn inside the vast crescent-shaped *zeriba* with its back to the Nile. There were many in the Army who thought that this was a dangerous posture in which to leave this vast expeditionary force during the night. Perhaps the Dervishes would attack under cover of darkness, and vast confusion might be caused. The numerous horses, mules and camels might stampede and the Dervishes, despite the accurate fire of highly trained British troops, might conceivably break into the *zeriba*. Churchill, inexhaustible in his quest for information and knowledge, chose to perambulate the outside of the *zeriba* after dark. It is clear that Kitchener's decisions were much debated in the camp that night. Churchill came to the conclusion that Kitchener had clung to a true decision; but in any case by dawn Kitchener's decision had been vindicated by events. The Dervishes feared the dark, and they did not attack.

Before first light the 21st Lancers were sent out to the high ground which divided the two armies in order to report on the enemy's movements. To quote again from *The River War:*

> Even before it became light several squadrons of British and Egyptian cavalry were pushed swiftly forward to gain contact with the enemy and learn his intentions. The first of these, under Captain [Everard] Baring [*a brother of Hugo*], occupied Surgham Hill, and waited in the gloom until the whereabouts of the Dervishes should be disclosed by the dawn. It was a perilous undertaking, for he might have found them unexpectedly near.
>
> As the sun rose, the 21st Lancers trotted out of the *zeriba* and threw out a spray of officers' patrols. With one of these it was my fortune to be sent to reconnoitre Surgham Hill. We galloped forward, and as we did not know that the Egyptian squadron and its officer had already looked over the ridge, we enjoyed all the excitement without any of the danger, and were also elated by the thought that we were the first to see what lay beyond. As there had been no night attack, I had expected that the Dervish army would have retired to their original position or entered the town. I rejected the idea that they would advance across the open ground to attack the *zeriba* by daylight, as it seemed absurd. Indeed, it appeared more probable that their hearts had failed them in the night, and that they had melted away into the deserts. But these anticipations were immediately dispelled by the scene which was visible from the crest of the ridge.
>
> It was a quarter to six. The light was dim, but growing stronger every minute. There in the plain lay the enemy, their numbers unaltered, their confidence and intentions apparently unshaken. Their front was now nearly five miles long, and composed of great masses of men joined together by thinner lines. Behind and to the flanks were large reserves. From where I stood they looked dark blurs and streaks, relieved and diversified with an odd-looking shimmer of light from the spear-points.
>
> After making the necessary reports I continued to watch the strange and impressive spectacle. As it became broad daylight — that is to say, about ten minutes to six — I suddenly realised that all the masses were in motion and advancing swiftly. Their Emirs galloped about and before their ranks. Scouts and patrols scattered themselves all over the front. Then they began to cheer. They were still a mile away from the hill, and were concealed from the Sirdar's army by the

folds of the ground. The noise of the shouting was heard, albeit faintly, by the troops down by the river. But to us, watching on the hill, a tremendous roar came up in waves of intense sound, like the tumult of the rising wind and sea before a storm. In spite of the confidence which I felt in the weapons of civilisation — for all doubts had dispersed with the darkness — the formidable aspect of this great host of implacable savages, hurrying eagerly to the attack of the *zeriba*, provoked a feeling of loneliness, which was shared, I think, by the rest of the little patrol. Partly to clear the mind of such unnecessary emotions, and also with the design of thereafter writing this account, I moved to a point on the ridge which afforded a view of both armies.

The British and Egyptian force was arranged in line with its back to the river. Its flanks were secured by the gunboats lying moored in the stream. Before it was the rolling sandy plain, looking from the slight elevation of the ridge smooth and flat as a table. To the right rose the rocky hills of the Kerreri position, near which the Egyptian cavalry were drawn up — a dark solid mass of men and horses. On the left the 21st Lancers, with a single squadron thrown out in advance, were halted watching their patrols, who climbed about Surgham Hill, stretched forward beyond it, or perched, as we did, on the ridge.

By a singular piece of historical good fortune the "necessary reports" to which Churchill referred have survived. He took it upon himself in view of the urgency of the matter to address two written reports scribbled in pencil direct to the Sirdar, and a copy to his commanding officer, Colonel Martin. The duplicates do not survive, but the top copy, addressed to the Sirdar, was preserved by his Deputy Assistant Adjutant-General, Captain Sir Henry Rawlinson. Later, during the First World War, Rawlinson and Churchill became close friends. In 1920, Rawlinson, who by then had become a full General and a peer, and was sorting out his papers, wrote to Churchill:

General Lord Rawlinson to WSC

5 January 1920   Government House
                                                 Farnborough Hants
My dear Winston,

In looking through some old Sudan note books today I came across the two enclosed messages which I think you will like to have in remembrance of a warm day's work which neither of us will forget.

Yours sincerely

RAWLINSON

These are the two somewhat crumpled messages which Rawlinson had preserved:

WSC to Sir H. Kitchener

No I   *Date* Sept 2 1898

From   Lieut Churchill

Place   Left Advd Patrol 21st L.

To   Sirdar

Place   near Omdurman

Duplicate to O.C. 21st Lancers

Dervish army, strength unchanged, occupies last nights position with their left well extended. Their patrols have reported the advance and loud cheering is going on. There is no *zeriba*.

Nothing hostile is between a line drawn from Heliograph Hill to Mahdi's tomb, and river. Nothing is within three miles from the camp.

Signature WINSTON S. CHURCHILL

Lieut 4th Hussars

attd 21st Lancers

And half an hour later:

WSC to Sir H. Kitchener

From   Lieut Churchill

To   Sirdar   *Desp* 6 h. 20 m.

About ¼ Dervish army is on their right which they have refused at present. Should this force continue to advance it would come the South side of Heliograph hill.

Most of the Cavalry are with this force.

Duplicate to Col Martin

Signature WINSTON S. CHURCHILL

Lieut 4th Hussars

Churchill wrote lively accounts of the Battle of Omdurman both for the *Morning Post* and later in *The River War*. Of even greater interest are two letters he wrote — the first to his mother two days after the battle on September 4 and another to Ian Hamilton on September 16. These were written while the battle was still vividly in his mind.

WSC to Lady Randolph

4 September 1898   Khartoum
                                              and be damned to it.

My dearest Mamma,

I hope that this letter will not long precede me — certainly not more than a fortnight. You will have been relieved by my telegram which I sent off at once. I was under fire all day and rode through the charge. You know my luck in these things. I was about the only officer whose clothes, saddlery, or horse were uninjured. I fired 10 shots with my pistol — all necessary — and just got to the end of it as we cleared the crush. I never felt the slightest nervousness and felt as cool as I do now. I pulled up and reloaded within 30 yards of their mass and then trotted after my troop who were then about 100 yards away. I am sorry to say I shot 5 men for certain and two doubtful. The pistol was the best thing in the world. The charge was nothing like as alarming as the retirement on the 16th of Sept last year. It passed like a dream and some part I cannot quite recall. The Dervishes showed no fear of cavalry and would not move unless you knocked them over with the horse. They tried to hamstring the horses, to cut the bridles — reins — slashed and stabbed in all directions and fired rifles at a few feet range. Nothing touched me. I destroyed those who molested me and so passed out without any disturbance of body or mind.

Poor Grenfell — with whom I made great friends and with whom and Molyneux I always lived and eat — was killed and this took the pleasure and exultation out of the whole affair, as far as I was concerned. Dick Molyneux too had a bad sword cut and a wonderful escape. Jack Brinton a slash across his shoulder. I heard at midday of Colonel Rhodes being wounded and at night of poor Hubert Howard being killed. He had ridden out our charge unhurt and it was indeed the irony of fate to kill him with a friendly shell. These things — and at the time they were reported as worse — made me anxious and worried during the night and I speculated on the shoddiness of war. You cannot gild it. The raw comes through. The metaphors are mixed but expressive.

I am just off with Lord Tullibardine to ride over the field. It will smell I expect as there are 7,000 bodies lying there. I hope to get some spears etc. I shall write a history of this war. Colonel F.R. is going to edit it and will give me all his photos. He is a brave gallant man. Nothing depresses him. Oh, there is such a lot to tell that it is useless my trying to write it now that the post is going off.

I will send 3 M.P. [*Morning Post*] letters during the next 3 days. And now I shall get back alive in all human probability and will tell you all about it myself.

I have told Molyneux to come & see you. We made great friends. He is a brave and cheery friend. Our losses are worth thinking of. Out of 20 officers and 280 men and horses we lost 5 officers, 70 men and 135 horses killed and wounded in 120 seconds. [*Corrected casualty figures are given in the next letter.*] Pursuit another seven. Meanwhile, arrange me some good meetings in October, Bradford & Birmingham. Sunny will help.

Your loving son
WINSTON

WSC to Colonel Ian Hamilton

(*Ian Hamilton Papers*)

EXTRACT

16 September 1898   In the train
Sudan Military Ry

. . . I had a patrol on 2nd Sept and was I think the first to see the enemy — certainly the first to hear their bullets. Never shall I see such a sight again. At the very least there were 40,000 men — five miles long in lines with great humps and squares at intervals — and I can assure you that when I heard them all shouting their war songs from my coign of vantage on the ridge of Heliograph Hill I and my little patrol felt very lonely. And though I never doubted the issue — I was in great awe.

Then they advanced and I watched them, fascinated and of course scribbling messages perpetually to the Sirdar and O.C. 21st Lancers. Their cavalry patrols which consisted of five or six horsemen each made no attempt to drive me back and I waited until one great brigade of perhaps 2000 men got to within 400 yards. I didn't realize they could shoot and thought they were all spearmen. Then they halted for a quarter of an hour and treated me and my 7 Lancers with complete disdain. Foolishly I dismounted 4 and opened magazine into the brown of them. Thereat they sent out 20 Riflemen and began to make very close practice. Finally I had to gallop and as we did so I did not hear less than 30 bullets. Luckily — (you know how capricious Fortune is) — we never had a man touched. If we had it would have meant others.

I then sent the patrol behind the hill and went up to the top myself. I dismounted but my grey pony was a target and it got too hot for me to stay although the scene was worth looking at. Various frantic people — Adjutant trumpeters etc then arrived and brought me back to my Squadron. But I assumed so very lofty a position — pointing out that no one was even hurt (and they admitted the value of the information) that I was allowed to go off again. I attributed the fact that we had no casualties to my "experience" etc. It was really due to the Almighty's amiability. For candidly the fire was for the time being as hot as anything I have seen — barring only those 10 minutes with the 35th Sikhs — a year ago today.

Then the whole attack developed and they cleared the cavalry into the *zeriba* and we listened for an hour to 20,000 rifles, near 60 guns and 20 maxims without seeing much. Watered and fed etc. A few bullets — all high as good cover down by bank. At 8.30 the attack weakened and we were bustled out of the *zeriba* to left flank. We halted on the old ridge and messed about with carbines for a quarter of an hour. Beyond the ridge thousands of Dervishes could be seen, as I thought fugitives — "meet to be cut up." I made use of the expression "supine apathy" here.

At 8.40 we mounted and rode slowly towards these crowds. I was confident that we should spear them till we could not sit on our horses. But between us and the distant fugitives was a single line of 150 men. We all thought these spearmen. They let us get within 250 yards in silence. We proposed — at least I think this was the idea — to move round their flank and slip a squadron at them and then on to the better things beyond. The ground looked all right and besides we did not intend doing anything from that direction.

We trotted in column of troops across their front from right to left. As we did so the enemy got down on their knees and opened a very sharp fire. There was a loud brisk crackle of musketry. The distance was too short for it to be harmless on so big a target and I realised that there were only two courses open viz: Left wheel into line and gallop off — coming back for wounded — a bad business; & Right wheel into line and charge. I think everybody made his own decision. At any rate while the trumpet was still jerking we were all at the gallop towards them. The fire was too hot to allow of second lines — flank squadrons or anything like that being arranged. The only order given was Right Wheel into Line. Gallop & Charge were understood.

I went through the first 100 yards looking over my left shoulder to see what sort of effect the fire was producing. It seemed small. Then I drew my Mauser pistol — a ripper — and cocked it. Then I looked to my front. Instead of the 150 riflemen who were still blazing I saw a line nearly (in the middle) — 12 deep and a little less than our own front of closely jammed spearmen — all in a *nullah* with steep sloping sides 6 foot deep & 20 foot broad.

After the Frontier I thought — capital — the more the merrier. I must explain my position. I was right troop leader but one. I saw we overlapped. I was afraid we would charge into air. I shouted to Wormald 7th Hussars (an excellent officer) to shoulder and we actually struck the enemy in a crescent formation. Result of our shoulder was this — my troop struck the *nullah* diagonally and their decreasing slope enabled us to gallop through not jump it. Result we struck — faster and more formed than the centre troops.

Opposite me they were about 4 deep. But they all fell knocked A.O.T. [arse over tip] and we passed through without any sort of shock. One man in my troop fell. He was cut to pieces. Five or six horses were wounded by back handers etc. But otherwise unscathed. Then we emerged into a region of scattered men and personal combats. The troop broke up and disappeared. I pulled into a trot and rode up to individuals firing my pistols in their faces and killing several — 3 for certain — 2 doubtful — one very doubtful. Then I looked round and saw the Dervish mass reforming. The charge had passed through knocking over nearly half. They were getting on their legs again and their Emirs were trying to collect them into a lump again. I realised that this mass was about 20 yards away and I looked at them stupidly for what may have been 2 seconds. Then I saw two men get down on their knees and take aim with rifles — and for the first time the danger & peril came home to me. I turned and galloped. The squadron was reforming nearly 150 yards away. As I turned both shots were fired and at that close range I was grievously anxious. But I heard none of their bullets — which went

Heaven knows where. So I pulled into a canter and rejoined my troop — having fired exactly 10 shots & emptied my pistol — but without a hair of my horse or a stitch of my clothing being touched. Very few can say the same.

I am glad to have added the experience of a cavalry charge to my military repertoire. But really though dangerous it was not in the least exciting and it did not look dangerous — at least not to me. You see I was so confident we would open them and hunt them and the realisation of our loss did not come to me until we reformed and I saw the wounded etc. It was I suppose the most dangerous 2 minutes I shall live to see. Out of 310 officers & men we lost — 1 officer and 20 men killed — 4 officers & 45 men wounded and 119 horses of which 56 were bullet wounds. All this in 120 seconds!

I never saw better men than the 21st Lancers. I don't mean to say I admired their discipline or their general training — both I thought inferior. But they were the 6 year British soldier type — and every man was an intelligent human being that knew his own mind. My faith in our race & blood was much strengthened. As soon as we got through I reformed my troop getting about 15 together and I told them they would have to go back and perhaps back again after that. Whereupon my centre guide said in a loud voice, "All right sir — we're ready — as many times as you like."

I asked my second sergeant if he had enjoyed himself. He replied "Well, I don't exactly say I enjoyed it Sir, but I think I'll get more used to it next time." This mind you was at 9.15 a.m. and looking out on the possibilities of the day — I thought he should have lots more.

I was very anxious for the regiment to charge back — because it would have been a very fine performance and men and officers could easily have done it while they were warm. But the dismounted fire was more useful, though I would have liked the charge — *"pour la gloire"* — and to buck up British cavalry. We all got a little cold an hour afterwards and I was quite relieved to see that "heroics" were "off" for the day at least.

I send you a rough sketch, which may interest you. I did not distinguish myself in any way — although as my composure was undisturbed my vanity is of course increased. I informed the attached officers on the way up that there was only one part of the despatch in which they could hope to be mentioned. They asked what part. I replied, "The casualty list." And the words were nearly prophetic because out of 8 we had 1 killed & 2 badly wounded.

I am in great disfavour with the authorities here. Kitchener was furious with Sir E. Wood for sending me out and expressed himself freely. My remarks on the treatment of the wounded — again disgraceful — were repeated to him and generally things have been a little unpleasant. He is a great general but he has yet to be accused of being a great gentleman. It is hard to throw stones at the rising sun and my personal dislike may have warped my judgment, but if I am not blinded, he has been on a certainty from start to finish and has had the devil's luck to help him beside. . . .

12

Return to India

As soon as the battle was over Churchill was keen to return to England and go from there to India to take part in the Inter-Regimental Polo Tournament. He arrived back in England early in October. At this time he received another letter from the Prince of Wales. Some months before the Prince had written: "You have plenty of time before you, and should certainly stick to the Army before adding MP to your name." Churchill's answer does not survive, but the Prince of Wales wrote back:

Prince of Wales to WSC

6 October [1898]   Mar Lodge
                                                        Braemar

My dear Winston,

Many thanks for your letter received today and for having taken in such good part the remarks I made in my previous letter. I fear in matters of discipline in the Army I may be considered old fashioned — & I must say that I think that an officer serving in a campaign should not write letters for the newspapers or express strong opinions of how the operations are carried out.

If the Sirdar as you say viewed your joining his Force with dislike — it is I am sure merely because he knows you write, for which he has the greatest objection I understand, & I cannot help agreeing with him, but I feel sure he could have nothing personal against you.

Your writing a book with an account of the campaign is quite another matter — & I feel sure that you will write it as a history &

not with military criticism which so young an officer as yourself, however clever you may be, should avoid as a matter of discipline. That the military authorities at home do not like officers writing you must be fully aware of as there are certain laid down rules in the Service on the subject — still they wink at it & some encourage it — (who shall be nameless). When I return to Town which will probably be in about 10 days time I hope you will come & see me & tell me all about the recent campaign & about your future plans.

I can well understand that it must be very difficult for you to make up your mind what to do, but I cannot help feeling that Parliamentary & literary life is what would suit you best as the monotony of military life in an Indian station can have no attraction for you — though fortunately some officers do put up with it or else we should have no Army at all!

Believe me, Yours very sincerely
ALBERT EDWARD

I shall be delighted to accept the new edition of *The Malakand Field Force* which you kindly propose sending me.

Churchill went to Marlborough House two weeks later to dine with the Prince of Wales.

Pending his return to India for his final spell and to take part in the Polo Tournament he made full use of the military laxity which at that time permitted a serving officer to make political speeches. He made three, at Rotherhithe, Dover and Southsea. Churchill, like so many other politicians of his day, had an exaggerated idea of the influence of the newspaper press. Though he did not trim his sails to their winds, he always sought to keep on good terms with newspaper proprietors. He was already friends with Oliver Borthwick, the son of Lord Glenesk the proprietor of the *Morning Post,* and he made friends with Alfred Harmsworth, later Lord Northcliffe. "Harmsworth is very civil and will report the speech at Dover well," Churchill wrote to his mother on October 21. In the same letter he reported that at dinner the day before, given by Ernest Cassel, he sat next to Moberly Bell, the Manager of *The Times.* "We get on capitally," Churchill reported with some pride.

After his speech at Dover, he wrote to his mother:

WSC to Lady Randolph

27 October [1898]   35A Great Cumberland Place

Dearest Mamma,

I daresay you will have gathered from the papers that the Dover speech was successful. I think Wyndham was impressed. I had one moment when I lost my train of thought — but I remained silent until I found it again — and I don't think it mattered.

Perhaps I shall speak at Portsmouth on Monday night. I am vy tired and will write no more.

Ever your loving son
WINSTON S. CHURCHILL

At a dinner of the Southsea Conservative Association on October 31, Churchill concluded a long speech with the following peroration:

To keep the Empire you must have the Imperial spark. Where is the glory of an armed sluggard living on the terror he has excited in the past? That is the debauched Imperialism of Ancient Rome. Where is the glory of the starving peasant arrayed in purple and in cloth of gold? That is the Imperialism of modern Russia. That is the Imperialism which some people in England appear to admire, but that is not the Imperialism of the Tory Democracy.

To keep our Empire we must have a free people, an educated and well fed people. That is why we are in favour of social reform. That is why we long for Old Age Pensions and the like. The Radicals — I do not mean Radical Imperialists like Lord Rosebery — for Radical Imperialist is, if you tell the truth, only Tory Democrat spelled another way — the Radicals (I mean those of Mr Morley's school) would have no Empire at all. We would have one and make all share the glory. *"Imperium et Libertas"* is the motto of the Primrose League, and it may also be the motto of Progressive Toryism. You have two duties to perform — the support of the Empire abroad and the support of liberty at home. It is by the interplay and the counter action of these two forces that our development is now to be guided. We want young men who do not mind danger, and we want older and perhaps wiser men who do not fear responsibility. The difficulties and emergencies with which the Empire is confronted will give us these men in plentiful abundance — and they in their turn will help to preserve that very Empire that calls them forth.

So the great game goes on, and, gentlemen, it is for you to say that it shall go on — that it shall not be interrupted until we are come through all the peril and trial, and rule in majesty and tranquillity by merit as well as by strength over the fairest and happiest regions of the world in which we live.

Churchill became involved at an early stage with some of the controversies that surrounded the conduct of the Omdurman campaign. On October 19, the Editor of *Concord,* a pacifist magazine, had written to the *Westminster Gazette* deploring the massacres of Dervishes at Omdurman both during and after the battle, as "deliberately planned and executed in cold blood." He cited in support of his contention, among others, "Lieutenant Churchill's account of how the enemy was 'destroyed, not conquered by machinery,' and of the terrible scenes on the battlefield afterwards." Churchill in his spirited reply, declined to enter into a discussion of "the legitimacy of the practice of killing the wounded." "The ethics of human destruction," he wrote in his letter to the Editor of the *Westminster Gazette* on October 24, "must necessarily be somewhat obscure. Neither rhetoric nor hysteria will help us to determine them." Churchill confined his argument with the Editor of *Concord* to the allegation that the Dervish loss was caused by the unnecessary bloodthirstiness of the British and Egyptian forces.

Had "The Editor of *Concord"* been present in the *zeriba* on the morning of September 2, and had he seen 40,000 savages advancing with hostile intent, he would not have protested against the soldiers opening fire. He would as a reasonable man have perceived that if the spearmen came to close quarters with the troops, a far greater slaughter would take place than actually occurred — a slaughter in which he himself might have been unfortunately included. Once fire was opened the loss of the Dervishes was mechanical. There was a hail of bullets. The Dervish advance continued, and, in the interests of the Peace Preservation Society, it was necessary that the hail of bullets should also continue. The courage of the enemy was their destruction. When they had had enough they withdrew.

"The Editor of *Concord"* preaches principles with which few will not sympathise. But he should be logical; judging by his literary vehemence, he appears to be a most pugnacious peace maker: a man who disapproves so entirely of physical force that he would employ physical force to prevent it. He should also be just. It will be open to him, if he is dissatisfied with the war on the Nile, to attack the Ministry responsible for that war. They will probably be able to justify their action to the satisfaction of the majority of the electorate. But I submit, that it is unfair as well as irrational to attribute cruelty and bloodthirstiness to soldiers who, placed in a position where they have to defend their lives, use the weapons with which they are armed with skill, judgement, and effect.

Though at this time Churchill sought to soft-pedal the issue, subsequent disclosures forced him to be more outspoken. For instance, he wrote to his mother after he had gone back to India — (26 January 1899): "I shall merely say that the victory at Omdurman was disgraced by the inhuman slaughter of the wounded and that Kitchener was responsible for this."

Before he left for India he wrote to his steady love, Miss Pamela Plowden, with whom he plainly had had words and controversy:

WSC to Miss Pamela Plowden

(Lytton Papers)

28 November [1898]   35A Great Cumberland Place

My dear Miss Pamela,

I am going to India on Friday: I want to come and see you before then. It was vy good of you to write me so long a letter. I venture to copy a few lines out of Genl Gordon's Journals at Khartoum which I am now compelled to read for the purposes of *The River War.* They rather bear out my view of these things.

"We may be quite certain that Jones cares more for where he is going to dine, or what he has got for dinner, than he does for what Smith has done, so we need not fret ourselves for what the world says."

I said or tried to say something to this effect. It is true. Having thus asserted the general principle — I will admit that you are quite right and that I make unnecessary enemies. The question is — Is it worth it? I confess I think so in many cases. It is an extravagance that is all. Besides Public and Private life are distinct provinces of action. Many a wise Chancellor of the Exchequer has been a spend-thrift himself. For all that I will try and take your advice. In any case believe that I am grateful for it. I remain persuaded rather than convinced.

The book is getting on magnificently and I am quite satisfied with what is thus far completed. Gordon was an extraordinary character. General, fanatic & wit. A vy rare combination. I met a young lady the other day who is I think — I judge only from the standpoint of reason — nearly as clever & wise as you. I certainly had much the worst of it in an argument on a purely philosophical subject. Hence I rank her one above Plato. I wonder if I arouse your curiosity. I hope so for then you may ask me to come to see you. Were I wise I would not allay it — by telling you that she is less beautiful.

One thing I take exception to in your letter. Why do you say I am incapable of affection? Perish the thought. I love one above all

thought. I love one above all others. And I shall be constant. I am no fickle gallant capriciously following the journey of the

others. And I shall be constant. I am no fickle gallant capriciously following the fancy of the hour. My love is deep and strong. Nothing will ever change it. I might it is true divide it. But the greater part would remain true — will remain true till death. Who is this that I love. Listen — as the French say — over the page I will tell you

Yours vy sincerely

Winston S. Churchill

Churchill was obviously in love with this beautiful girl whom he had met in India two years before. But such were his ambition and his slender means that he was not yet prepared to commit himself. This letter was cool, distant and provocative. He was obviously far from settled in his mind as to his course of action. After all, he was only on the eve of his twenty-fourth birthday; he had no money, nor had Miss Plowden, and he was still thinking ferociously about his future.

From Brindisi he wrote to his brother Jack: "Mind you try and make Cassel take you to Egypt. You can't push too much in all things." He had earlier written to his mother, "This is a pushing age, we must push with the best." He was clearly still of the same opinion.

Churchill was determined not to allow the same mistake to occur in *The River War* as had occurred over *The Malakand Field Force*. This time he did not depend upon Moreton Frewen. Before he left for India he had embarked on some enquiries. He wrote to officers who had taken part in the campaigns on the Nile. One of the surviving letters seeking this information is addressed to Major E. J. M. Stuart-Wortley, who commanded the irregulars on the East Bank in the Omdurman campaign. "The fuller it is and the more descriptive you can make it, the better," Churchill wrote, asking for an account of his doings. "I should like also very much to learn your views on war and policy in the Soudan and any comparisons you draw between the campaign of 1885 and the recent one." Churchill went on: "I would like to learn something of the characteristics of Inalin and Dervishes. Did not Wood behave with great gallantry on one occasion?"

On his way to India he wrote to his mother:

WSC to Lady Randolph

11 December [1898]   S.S. *Shannon*
                                                         off Aden

My dearest Mamma,

I daresay you will expect a letter — though in truth there is nothing to tell. We have had a vy rough passage down the Red Sea — of all places — and I have not enjoyed myself excessively. I have however made good progress with the book. Three vy long chapters are now almost entirely completed. The chapter describing the fall of Khartoum Gordon's death etc is I think quite the most lofty passage I have ever written. The only thing which has pleased me apart from the pleasure of writing is that there are two copies of *The Malakand Field Force* on board which are very regularly read.

Please send without delay the *Annual Registers* of 1884, 1885 & 1886. I want them.

Ever your loving son
WINSTON

And from Bangalore, only ten days later, he wrote to his mother:

I work all day & every day at the book and have done about a third. You must forgive my short letter on that account. Time is so precious and there is so much to do. I have done nearly a third. I beg you not to retaliate by writing short answers. My hand gets so cramped. I am writing every word twice & some parts three times. It ought to be good since it is the best I can do. . . .

In a letter written to Lady Randolph on New Year's Day 1899:

I have not received any fresh information re book on Nile since reaching this country, I expect I shall have to finish it in England. It is now half done and it is I think better than *The M.F.F.* . . . Talk to F. Rhodes and make him send me lots of material. . . . I must go on with my book now; I am very industrious. But the climate is enervating. . . .

In his next letter he goes on:

Meanwhile I work continually at the book and progress slowly but still I think what is written is really good. Let me quote you one sentence — it is about the Mahdi who was left while still quite young an orphan. "Solitary trees, if they grow at all, grow strong: and a boy deprived of a father's care often develops, if he escape the perils of youth, an independence and a vigour of thought which may restore in after life the heavy loss of early days."

This reflection must have been prompted by his own experience.

*

In all probability he would not have returned to India at all except for the lure of the polo:

WSC to Lady Randolph

EXTRACT

11 January 1899   Bangalore

. . . I am going next week to Madras to play polo and shall stay at
Government House. The week after that Jodhpore where we all stay
practising for the Tournament with Sir Pertab Singh. Then Meerut
for the Inter-Regimental Tournament, where I stay with Sir B. B.
& after that Umballa for the Championship — a very pleasant six
weeks. Then home and the more serious pleasures of life. . . .

. . . I am playing polo quite well now. Never again shall I be able
to do so. Everything will have to go to the war chest. . . .

His next letter to his brother shows how the splendid plan nearly
miscarried:

WSC to Jack

EXTRACT

9 February 1899   [Jodhpore]

. . . I am staying with Sir Pertab Singh for a week before the Inter-
Regimental Tournament. All the rest of our team are here and
everything smiled until last night — when I fell down stairs &
sprained both my ankles and dislocated my right shoulder. I am
going to struggle on to the polo ground this afternoon — but I fear
I shall not be able to play in the Tournament as my arm is weak and
stiff & may come out again at any moment. It is one of the most
unfortunate things that I have ever had happen to me and is a bitter
disappointment. I had been playing well and my loss is a considerable blow to our chances of winning. I try to be philosophic but it is
very hard. Of course it is better to have bad luck in the minor
pleasures of life than in one's bigger undertakings. But I am very
low & unhappy about it. Nor is it any consolation that next year
I shall have forgotten all about it. . . .

In a similar letter to his mother written on the same day he adds
the reflection: "I trust the misfortune will propitiate the gods —
offended perhaps at my success & luck elsewhere."

The 4th Hussars had taken the standard precaution of having with them a fifth man and Churchill advised them to play this reserve and to leave him out of the team. But after due deliberation the other members of the team, Major Reginald Hoare, Albert Savory and Churchill's old friend and companion in arms, Reginald Barnes, decided in the end that it was worth playing Churchill even if he was unable to hit the ball very much. "In those days," Churchill recalled in *My Early Life*, "the off-side rule existed, and the No 1 was engaged in a ceaseless duel with the opposing back who, turning and twisting his pony, always endeavoured to put his opponent off-side. If the No 1 was able to occupy the back, ride him out of the game and hamper him at every turn, then he could serve his side far better than by overmuch hitting of the ball. We knew that Captain Hargress Lloyd, afterwards an international player against the United States, was the back and most formidable member of the 4th Dragoon Guards, the strongest team we should have to meet."

Churchill played with his right upper arm strapped tightly to his side so that his shoulder would not come out again but giving him only a restricted arc in which to swing his stick. Notwithstanding this, success attended the 4th Hussars — and Churchill — in the first two rounds.

WSC to Lady Randolph

EXTRACT

23 February 1899   Meerut

. . . The Polo Tournament is going on vy well. We beat the 5th Dragoon Guards in the first round by 16 goals to 2 — an amazing score. Yesterday we beat the 9th Lancers by 2 goals to 1 after a vy exciting match. You will perhaps remember their beating us at Hurlingham in 1896. I then bet them £100 to 90 that we could beat them before I left the regiment. It is satisfactory to have achieved this small object. Tomorrow we play in the Final match with the 4th Dragoon Guards. I do not expect to win. Still it is a vy open game. My shoulder and arms are still vy weak and I have to play all tied up which weakens us a good deal. . . .

The final, played on February 24, "before a large assembly in perfect weather," was as exciting as had been anticipated. The

Dragoons took the lead in the first chukka. Churchill in his thrilling account in *My Early Life* states that the Dragoons scored two goals in the first chukka but the contemporary account in the *Pioneer Mail* reported that their second goal did not come until the sixth chukka. It was in the fourth chukka that Hoare hit the Hussars' first goal. Two more goals for the Hussars followed in the next two minutes. "Suddenly," wrote Churchill in *My Early Life,* "in the midst of a confused scrimmage close by the enemy goal, I saw the ball spin towards me. It was on my near side. I was able to lift the stick over and bending forward gave it a feeble forward tap. Through the goalposts it rolled. . . . Presently I had another chance. Again the ball came to me close to the hostile goal. This time it was travelling fast, and I had no more to do in one fleeting second than to stretch out my stick and send it rolling between the posts."

Churchill in his account in *My Early Life* suggests that by this time the score was 3–2 in favour of the 4th Hussars and that shortly afterwards the Dragoons scored again to level the scores. There is some discrepancy between this and the account in the *Pioneer Mail* of March 3 in which it is stated that the Hussars scored three goals in the fourth chukka, one by Hoare and two by Savory. This account then goes on to relate how the Dragoons scored their second goal in the sixth chukka and how Churchill scored the Hussars' fourth goal in same chukka. This final goal Churchill describes: "Once again fortune came to me, and I gave a little feeble hit at the ball among the ponies' hoofs, and for the third time saw it pass through the goal. This brought the 7th chukka to an end." According to the *Pioneer Mail* it was in the seventh chukka that the Dragoons scored again to make the score four goals to three to the Hussars. Both Churchill and the *Pioneer Mail* are agreed that the final result depended on the last chukka because the Dragoons had scored one subsidiary more than the Hussars so that if the Dragoons scored one more goal to make the score four goals each they would be declared the winners. However, the Dragoons did not score again and the 4th Hussars had won the Inter-Regimental Tournament of 1899.

There could be no doubt, notwithstanding the report to the contrary in the *Pioneer Mail,* that Churchill believed that he had scored three of the four goals. He wrote to his mother from Calcutta on

March 3: "You will be glad to hear that we won the Inter-Regimental Polo Tournament — a very great triumph for it is perhaps the biggest sporting event in India. I hit three goals out of four in the winning match so that my journey to India was not futile as far as the regiment was concerned." A leading polo authority, Brigadier Jack Gannon, who reported polo for *The Field* for nearly twenty years has told the author: "The number of times a long shot reaches the goal mouth and then is finally popped through by a player covered from sight by others is fairly frequent, and without checking you don't know who did touch it through." It is more likely that the correspondent of the *Pioneer Mail* mistook the identity of the actual scorer of the Hussars' second and third goals than that Churchill should so soon after the match have assumed the role of hero when he could easily have been exposed as a braggart.

Churchill's interest in polo in India did not end with his brilliant performance at Meerut. A day or two later he attended a meeting of the Indian Polo Association where a measure was put forward to limit the height of polo ponies. Major John Sherston, at this time Assistant Adjutant-General, Bengal, and a well-known polo umpire in India, proposed this measure; Churchill was opposed to it. The following extract from the *Pioneer Mail* gives some idea of the controversy:

WSC: This system will subject polo ponies to the same rigorous preparations that the poor racing ponies are suffering from at present, and the wretched polo ponies will have to be walked about with sacks on their backs and be drugged like the racing ponies. Far from increasing the evil we should try to reduce it.

SHERSTON: The Calcutta Turf Club is at present taking steps to prevent these practices.

WSC: What guarantee have we of this? Besides in some cases the polo clubs are far from the railway.

SHERSTON: There will be two official measurers paid to go to all such places.

WSC: Will two official measurers be sufficient to go all over India? However much you pay a man he cannot possibly be in two places at once. (*Laughter*).

*

Before Churchill had left London in December 1898 on his last journey to India, Lady Randolph conceived the idea of starting a literary magazine. Churchill showed much enthusiasm for the project and he hoped that it would do his mother and her reputation a great deal of good.

WSC to Lady Randolph

EXTRACT

1 January 1899   [Bangalore]

. . . You will have an occupation and an interest in life which will make up for all the silly social amusements you will cease to shine in as time goes on and which will give you in the latter part of your life as fine a position in the world of taste & thought as formerly, & now in that of elegance & beauty. It is wise & philosophic. It may also be profitable. If you could make a £1000 a year out of it, I think that would be a little lift in the dark clouds. . . .

He was helpful in making the initial advances to publishers and copious in his advice as to the style and format and the title of the new venture. He even saw a remunerative occupation in it for himself.

. . . I agree that it is better to have a skilled & trained journalist as sub editor. I should have liked to have undertaken that part myself and my mania for exact printing etc might have fitted me, but on the whole I think that at any rate in its initial stages it is better to have an experienced man. Do not make any arrangement for more than one year — as the opportunity of my earning two hundred pounds a year — would make a very sensible addition to the advantages we derive from the venture. Of course I will help you in any way that I can and I do not doubt the affair can be made a success. . . .

The title of the magazine caused him a good deal of mental perturbation. Churchill agreed to consult Dr Welldon — he had, towards the end of the previous year, arrived in Calcutta as the new Bishop of Calcutta and Metropolitan of India — on this momentous literary decision. Churchill liked none of the new titles such as

"International Quarterly," or the "Arena" which had been put forward: "There must be some good sounding word or expression that would express either 'The beginning of a new cycle with new ideas & almost boundless possibilities' or 'A feast for a literary epicure.' " The title which he liked least was "The Anglo-Saxon." "It means nothing & has not the slightest relation to the ideas and purpose of the magazine," he told his mother on February 16. "Most unsuitable," he told his mother again a week later, "it might do for a vy popular periodical meant to appeal to great masses on either side of the Atlantic. It is very inappropriate to a Magazine de Luxe, meant only for the cultivated few and with a distinct suspicion [of] cosmopolitanism about it." By the time he got to Calcutta, he found his mother pressing on with her ideas of "The Anglo-Saxon" to which she now added a motto. Churchill was horrified:

WSC to Lady Randolph

EXTRACT

2 March 1899   Calcutta

... I must now turn to the Magazine. I am vy glad that you will not publish until June. I repeat all I wrote a fortnight ago about there being no hurry. But I think you have quite lost the original idea of a magazine de luxe. Your title "The Anglo-Saxon" with its motto "Blood is thicker than water" only needs the Union Jack & the Star Spangled Banner crossed on the cover to be suited to one of Harms-worth's cheap Imperialist productions. I don't say that these have

not done good and paid but they are produced for thousands of vulgar people at a popular price. People don't pay a guinea for such stuff. And besides there is a falling market as regards Imperialism now.

As for the motto "Blood is thicker than water" I thought that that had long ago been relegated to the pothouse Music Hall.

In the crowded literary market there was I believe just room for an expensive magazine published luxuriously and typical of a certain *dilettante* excellence — a magazine that might be read equally by the educated people of Paris of Petersburg of London or New York. Literary, artistic scholarly always — but blood and thunder never. But your apparent conception of a hearty production frothing with patriotism and a popular idea of the Anglo-American alliance — that wild impossibility — will find no room among the literary ventures of the day. You may say that this is not your idea. It is certainly what the title suggests. I confess I shivered when I read your letter.

There is another point. If you publish at a guinea you must give people a guinea's worth. I don't think it would be possible or fair to make more profit than 2/6 a number after everything was paid, otherwise your magazine would be supported only by charity, would run for a couple of numbers and then perish. It must hold its own by its own intrinsic value & excellence. Not by the favour of friends good enough to subscribe "Its only a fiver, my dear."

To make this thing a success you must have at least a dozen good writers who will undertake to put it on its legs & keep it going. It must have a strong backing, literary talent, interested — I do not say interested pecuniarily — in the success of the enterprise. If you start without this sort of support — money or no money you will come to a full stop.

Of course as a title "Cosmopolis" would have done excellently. But it is taken already. Literature is essentially cosmopolitan. Patriotism and art mix as little as oil and water. I don't want to be discouraging but I foresee so many difficulties and I am afraid that there is only one narrow road which will lead to success. I am dining with the Bishop tonight and will have a long talk with him about the subject. When I saw him for a moment yesterday, he seemed vy doubtful as to whether such a thing could be made to pay. But he was ironical at the idea of "The Anglo Saxon." I did not dare mention that "Blood was thicker than water." Let me suggest as an alternative motto "Let 'em all come."

I am afraid you won't like my criticisms: but I am as anxious as you are that the enterprise should be successful. I shall be home within three weeks of your receiving this and we can then discuss the whole project from every point of view. I am sure that it is possible to make a success of the scheme. Of course it would have been more interesting at half a crown monthly. Poor Rudyard Kipling is I fear at the point of death. It is a terrible loss to the English speaking world. [*He was dangerously ill with pneumonia in New York, but recovered and lived until 1936.*]

Ever your loving son
WINSTON

P.S. I think "The Imperial Magazine," is less open to objection than the "Anglo Saxon." There is a sort of idea of excellence about it — an Imperial pint is bigger than an ordinary pint.

My article on Rhetoric is not good enough for the Magazine. It would do for the Nineteenth Century — but it is too much to expect it to make its own reputation as well as that of the paper.

But Anglo-Saxon it was, and Churchill agreed to stop carping at a title which he never came to like. *The Anglo-Saxon Review* was first published in June 1899 and continued for ten numbers until September 1901.

*

Curzon had succeeded Lord Elgin as Viceroy on 6 January 1899, and not long afterwards, on his way back from the Inter-Regimental Polo Tournament, Churchill stayed for a week with the Viceroy in Calcutta. All his previous hostility evaporated under the impact of the Curzon charm:

WSC to Lady Randolph

EXTRACT

2 March 1899   Calcutta

... Everything is vy pleasant and I have found him very delightful to talk to. His manners are wonderful. All the aggressiveness wh irritated me at home is gone. They have both won everybody's heart. But I fear he works too hard — nearly eleven hours every single day

— so his secretary tells me. And you would be shocked to see how Lady C is changed. I was vy pained to see her. She has had a sharp attack of fever and will not I think stand the climate which will spoil the whole thing. She sends all sorts of messages to you and speaks with great affection for you. . . .

In a letter to his mother written on March 9, he confesses: "Really I misunderstood his manner entirely," and to his grandmother he wrote (March 26): "I spent a pleasant week at Calcutta & had several long and delightful talks with Lord Curzon. I understand the success he has obtained. He is a remarkable man — and to my surprise I found he had a great charm of manner. I had not expected this from reading his speeches. I think his Viceroyalty will be a signal success. They are both already vy popular."

Churchill obviously made a good impression during his stay in Calcutta. Lady Curzon wrote to Lady Randolph on 14 March 1899: "People in India have an immense opinion of Winston & his book. You hear his praises so often I know Jennie — but you can never hear them too often can you! Lockhart & Sir Wm Nicholson, and Bindon Blood as you know and Welldon all swear by him & make no limitations as to how far he will go."

*

Before he had left England, Churchill had once again taken in hand his novel which had languished for more than a year, its composition having been interrupted by three military campaigns and two books about them. He had sent the typescript to his grandmother, asking her to comment, particularly on the character of the heroine Lucile. The old Duchess replied:

Frances, Duchess of Marlborough to WSC

29 November [1898]   Castlemead
                                                       Windsor

You have set me a difficult task in the question you ask me to answer! There is so much that is clever and graphic in your Novel and you describe very well, the fighting and horrors of the Barricades. At the same time there is a want of interest in the plot and I quite agree with you that Lucile is a weak and uninteresting personality. It is clear you have not yet attained a knowledge of Women — and it is evident you have (I am thankful to see) no experience of Love! Now as to the policy of publishing the Book I can see no objection to it. It cannot injure your reputation in a literary Point of View for the faults are those of youth and inexperience and not Want of Ability, 250£ is not to be despised and to my mind you have earned it.

It is a pity you wrote those letters to the *Morn Post* for I fear it has laid you open to the Charge of breaking your word. But it cannot be helped now — Had you asked me I should have said — Certainly not. In this case howr there is really no objection and the Book whatever its imperfections does you credit in point of talent. As to the future I wish you would return to your Regiment and give up Parliament till the Dissolution! I have *all* along advised this. I am quite sure your dear Father would have urged it.

I will return the 2 Packets by tonight's Post. I scribble this by early Post and on the spur of the Moment. I am rather tired which must account for Blots and errors. Have you got Lord Glenesk [Proprietor of the *Morning Post*] or Mr Dicey [a former editor of the *Observer*] or others of your Father's Literary Friends to read your novel. Lord James also is a good judge. To my mind there is so much merit and originality in the composition that one regrets some of its inequalities. And now goodbye dear Winston. I thank you for your affectionate expressions and sincerely return them.

Affectly

G<small>D</small> M<small>OTHER</small>

The outline of the heroine Lucile was sketched for him by his aunt Leonie. But it seems he did not have time or opportunity to improve, as he had hoped, the character of Lucile, for almost immediately *Macmillan's Magazine* offered £100 for the serial rights which Churchill gladly accepted. "It is a great compliment it's being serialised" he wrote to his mother on 1 January 1899, "very good and only the successful novels are serialised."

*

A letter from Churchill to Aylmer Haldane written on the train between Bombay and Bangalore reveals that even though Churchill had avowedly only returned to India in order to play in the Polo Tournament, the least prospect of military adventure caused him to send cables to his friends on the frontier. The letter also reveals that his longing for medals remained undiminished.

WSC to Captain Aylmer Haldane

(*Aylmer Haldane Papers*)

18 December [1898]   in the train near Wadi

My dear Haldane,

You must forgive my horrid writing which the address will explain and I think excuse. Of course the frontier war has not come off. I never thought it would as the work was so thoroughly done last year. I have written to Sir William [Lockhart] to thank him for his telegram for which I also thank you. I am concerned to think that the reply cost more than I had prepaid. I therefore enclose a cheque on King, King & Co which I beg you will fill up and thus discharge the lesser part of my obligation.

There is another matter about which I want to ask you. I am leaving the army in April. I have come back merely for the Polo Tournaments. I naturally want to wear my medals while I have a uniform to wear them on. They have already sent me the Egyptian one. I cannot think why the Frontier one has not arrived. Young Life Guardsmen on Sir B. Blood's staff in Buner have already got theirs. Do try and get mine for me as soon as possible. Otherwise it will never be worn. I come in either as attd to 31st P.I. in Malakand Field Force or on Sir William's staff. The latter would of course be the best place to figure in. Will you try and get the medal sent me — there is only the general clasp — so that there should be no great difficulty.

I have had a beastly passage out: vy rough and only one nice person on board. However I am glad to get back to my regiment. The book is about 1/3 finished and I hope to have it completed by April 1 — an auspicious date. I hear General Rundle pronounced my description of the battle in the *M. Post* to be "correct." He did not agree with the criticisms.

I can quite understand your all being vy disgusted at the fuss they make over Lord Kitchener. But then [the] British public are always extremists. Write to me to Bangalore and do what you can about the medal.

Yours very sincerely
WINSTON S. CHURCHILL

A few weeks after arriving back in India, Churchill's plans for completing *The River War* received a serious set-back. Major Watson, "on whom I counted for a great deal of important information," who had been aide-de-camp to Kitchener during the campaign, had been forbidden by the Sirdar to supply him with any information. But if anything, this seemed to make Churchill all the more determined. "This will cause delay but it shall not prevent me from writing the account," he told his mother on January 26. It was one more black mark against Kitchener. "I am duly appreciative of the civility," he remarked drily.

What the set-back meant was that he would have to spend some days in Cairo on his way home from India; and indeed this proved a very worth-while visit — so much so that he extended his stay in Cairo by a week. Churchill finally left India in the middle of March. When he arrived in Cairo at the end of the month, he had completed — or thought he had completed — eighteen of the twenty-three chapters and expected to finish the book in a month. "The book will now take a somewhat longer time," he wrote to his mother on March 30. "I have found a great many things which are of great interest and which rather alter the narrative as I have told it."

At first he had found little to say in favour of Kitchener: "The book grows rather in bitterness about K," he had written to his mother on 29 December 1898; "I feel that in spite of my intention it will be evident no friend has written it. I expect they had just about had enough of him when he went back to his Soudan. A vulgar common man — without much of the non-brutal elements in his composition." But after a few days in Cairo he wrote on March 30:

WSC to Lady Randolph

EXTRACT

30 March [1899]   Savoy Hotel
                                                              Cairo

. . . A great many of my more acrid criticisms of the Sirdar I shall tone down or cut out. I have quite got over any feeling of resentment and I do not wish to profit by the reaction which has set in against him. Major Watson by a lucky chance is in Cairo so that whatever information he was not allowed to give me by writing, I may procure from him by word of mouth. I lunched yesterday with Lord Cromer and he afterwards did me the honour of talking to me about the Soudan, its past and its future with reference to my book for more than two hours and a half.

What I then learned makes it necessary to considerably modify the earlier chapter dealing with the Gordon episode. I feel that it will be impossible for me to sacrifice all the fine phrases and pleasing paragraphs I have written about Gordon, but Cromer was very bitter about him and begged me not to pander to the popular belief on the subject. Of course there is no doubt that Gordon as a political figure was absolutely hopeless. He was so erratic, capricious, utterly unreliable, his mood changed so often, his temper was abominable, he was frequently drunk, and yet with all he had a tremendous sense of honour and great abilities, and a still greater obstinacy. Pray do not mention this otherwise than as coming from me because my conversation was naturally private. . . .

Lord Cromer, indeed, turned out to be of great help to Churchill in putting *The River War* into historical perspective.

WSC to Lady Randolph

EXTRACT

3 April 1899   Savoy Hotel
                                                                   Cairo

. . . I have been very much flattered by the great kindness and attention which Lord Cromer has shown me here. He has given me letters of introduction to everybody who is of importance in Cairo and has taken great trouble to explain all sorts of matters connected with Egyptian politics to me. I have had three long talks with him of more than an hour and a half each and he certainly has impressed me as a wonderful man. He presented me to the Khedive the other morning. I was much amused by observing the relations between the British Agent and the *de jure* Ruler of Egypt. The Khedive's attitude reminded me of a school-boy who is brought to see another school-boy in the presence of the head-master. But he seemed to me to be an amiable young man who tries to take an intelligent interest in the affairs of his kingdom, which, since they have passed entirely beyond his control, is, to say the least of it, very praiseworthy. . . .

*

Churchill's ambition, of which much has already been written, was never hidden from his friends and acquaintances, nor did he delude himself about it. In one of his rare political comments from India, Churchill told his mother:

WSC to Lady Randolph

EXTRACT

11 January 1899   [Bangalore]

. . . Joe C. [Chamberlain] is losing ground a good deal. I feel it instinctively. I know I am right. I have got instinct in these things. Inherited probably. This life is vy pleasant and I pass the time quickly and worthily — but I have no right to dally in the pleasant valleys of amusement. What an awful thing it will be if I don't come off. It will break my heart for I have nothing else but ambition to cling to. . . .

From Suez, while at sea, Churchill penned a letter to his grandmother, Duchess Fanny, formally acquainting her with his decision to leave the Army. He had of course informed his mother earlier.

WSC to Frances, Duchess of Marlborough

EXTRACT

26 March [1899]   Suez

. . . My reason in writing now that I shall so soon be home and after waiting so long is to tell you — what you may have guessed from the address of this letter — that I am about to leave the army, and have already forwarded my papers to the Horse Guards. I fear that you will not commend my decision, but I have thought a great deal about it and although it is possible I may live to regret it, I don't think I shall ever regard it as unreasonable. On one point I am clear — the time had come when it was necessary to choose definitely. Had the army been a source of income to me instead of a channel of expenditure — I might have felt compelled to stick to it. But I can live cheaper & earn more as a writer, special correspondent or journalist: and this work is moreover more congenial and more likely to assist me in pursuing the larger ends of life. It has nevertheless been a great wrench and I was vy sorry to leave all my friends & put on my uniform & medals for the last time. . . .

Churchill's decision to send in his papers and resign his commission was courageous, even audacious. He was trained for no other profession save the Army. Here it would be a long time before he could gain advancement and earn a competence. How would he ever be able to pay off his debts and acquire an income sufficient to sustain a parliamentary career? He had high hopes of some financial return from *The River War*; but this was still uncompleted and there is no record that he had received any advance for it. Doubtless he had already aspired to write his father's Life, but the decision was not in his hands. He had not yet approached his father's literary trustees; when he did they were somewhat sceptical of his fitness for the task.

Nonetheless he returned to England full of hope and projects. He was always ready to run risks on the field of battle, in politics, and in his own personal finances. Fortune does not always favour the brave: Churchill in later life had his ups and downs. But fortune was with him in his youth and again in what for most men would have been regarded as old age.

13

Boer War

ON HIS ARRIVAL in London from Cairo at the end of April Churchill decided to get on with the battle of life as quickly as possible; he could not afford overmuch time for dalliance.

WSC to Lady Randolph

EXTRACT

3 May 1899   35A Great Cumberland Place

. . . I have replied to Birmingham diplomatically, expressing my desire to accept, yet hesitating about my ability. I dined last night at the Rothschilds — a delightful dinner — Mr Balfour, Mr Asquith, Lord Acton, self, Evelina [Lord Rothschild's daughter] & Lord and Lady R. [Rothschild]. AJB was markedly civil to me — I thought — agreed with and paid great attention to everything I said. I talked well and not too much — in my opinion.

The Accrington people are arriving and I must go. . . . Miss P. [Plowden] has been vy much impressed with the Proofs of the first two chapters of *The River War*. . . .

Already he was being waited on by deputations of notables from Conservative Constituency Associations who sought to persuade him to stand as their candidate at the election, which was expected to take place within the next eighteen months.

Churchill had, it seems, consulted a fashionable palmist, Mrs Robinson, who had claimed to see favourable omens in his hand. Certainly his entry into active politics could scarcely have been more unexpected. He tells in *My Early Life* how he had been sounded out by Mr Robert Ascroft, one of the two members for Oldham, which was in those days a two-member constituency, to become his "running mate" at the next election, as the other Unionist member, Mr James Oswald, was ailing. In the event it was Mr Ascroft who died suddenly on 19 June 1899. It was thought expedient to ask Mr Oswald to resign at the same time. Mindful of their late member's wishes the Oldham Conservative Association immediately turned to Churchill. He reported on his first meeting straightaway to Miss Pamela Plowden:

WSC to Miss Pamela Plowden

(Lytton Papers)

20 June 1899   35A Great Cumberland Place

Pamela,

I have just returned from Oldham tonight. The whole thing is in my hands as far as the Tory Party there go. I fight the seat & am trying to find second candidate. If Ivor Guest were in England I could ensure his being accepted. I got on famously with the committee. I've vy nearly arranged a compromise by which I should have been the Tory Member. Now there must be a fight with very uncertain chances. I begin my meetings tonight.

Yours ever

WINSTON

Leading members of the local Tory and Liberal parties had hoped to arrive at some accommodation whereby they would return, unopposed, one Tory and one Liberal member; but these ideas were quickly thrown aside by the enthusiastic rank-and-file supporters of both sides. So Churchill's fellow Conservative candidate was Mr James Mawdsley, the General Secretary of the Lancashire branch of the Amalgamated Association of Cotton Spinners. The late Mr Ascroft had, it was believed, owed his success to the fact that he had been for some years the trusted solicitor to this Trade Union and it was considered to be a shrewd move towards securing the Labour vote to invite Mr Mawdsley to stand. Thus the Scion and the Socialist, as they were dubbed, fought the seat together. They issued separate election addresses. Churchill naturally stressed the fact that he was a Tory democrat. "I regard the improvement of the condition of the British people as the main end of modern government." As a Unionist, he also had a sharp word to say against Home Rule: "All true Unionists must, therefore, be prepared to greet the reappearance of that odious measure with the most strenuous opposition." Churchill in his election address emphasized measures against what he described as "the lawlessness in the Church." There were measures before Parliament at this time to deal with ritualism and extreme High Church practices in the forms of worship being carried on by some of the clergy of the Church of England. He went on: "The ecclesiastical machinery devised to deal with such persons has been found defective. I am of the opinion, if this be true, that it must be speedily repaired or replaced . . . But I believe that there must exist means of enforcing discipline in the National Church as well as in other public institutions, and if the authority of the bishops is not exerted or obeyed, stronger measures will be necessary."

No doubt these words were intended for the approval of the chapel folk who comprised a large proportion of the electorate of Oldham. Churchill had good reason for seeking to propitiate them. For some time Lord Salisbury's Government had had on its hands the Clerical Tithes Bill, a measure intended to benefit the clergy of the Church of England and the Church Schools. This Bill was quickly nicknamed by the Radicals the Clerical Doles Bill and it at once aroused the opposition of Nonconformists everywhere and of Methodists in Lancashire in particular. From the outset, Churchill and his supporters realized that this Bill would greatly diminish his prospects of success. "This Clerical Tithes Bill Balfour has foolishly introduced," Churchill wrote to his cousin, the Duke of Marlborough on June 29, "is simply playing the deuce with the Lancashire electors." Churchill, it will be remembered, had never shown himself deeply committed on religious matters and the niceties of ecclesiastical partisanship often escaped him.

As he was to relate in *My Early Life*: "As I was ignorant of the needs which had inspired it and detached from the passions which it aroused, the temptation to discard it was very great. I yielded to the temptation." Just three days before polling he announced in reply to a question at his meeting at the Primitive Methodist School, Washbrook, that if he had represented Oldham when the House of Commons divided on the Clerical Tithes Bill the previous week he would, out of consideration for the views of his constituents, have voted against the Bill. His announcement was greeted with loud cheers; but later Churchill was to admit that it had been a frightful mistake. "It is not the slightest use defending Governments or parties unless you defend the very worst thing about which they are attacked."

Opposing Churchill and Mawdsley were two outstanding candidates: Mr Alfred Emmott and Mr Walter Runciman. Emmott's family had been mill-owners for several generations and Runciman came from a shipping family. As Churchill wryly remarked: "My poor Trade Unionist friend and I would have had very great difficulty in finding £500 between us, yet we were accused of representing the vested interest of society, while our opponents, who were certainly good for a quarter of a million, claimed to champion in generous fashion the causes of the poor and needy." Three of the candidates were to reach Cabinet rank: Churchill and Runciman in 1908; Emmott in 1914. Mr Mawdsley died in 1902.

Churchill kept up a steady stream of correspondence with his mother and with Pamela Plowden, trying to persuade both to come to Oldham to help him in the campaign. Quite early on his left tonsil had become inflamed which made public speaking difficult, but Dr Robson Roose — as ever a friend of the family — promised to send down a special spray. "The throat is the only thing that worries me," he wrote cheerfully to Lady Randolph on 26 June 1899, "but it would be no more extraordinary to win the Oldham election with a sore throat, than it was to win the Polo Tournament with a dislocated shoulder."

Pamela Plowden refused to come: "I quite understand your not coming," he wrote to her on June 28, "it would perhaps have been a mistake — but I shall be sorry nevertheless." And as the campaign drew to an end, he told his mother: "Mrs Runciman goes everywhere with her husband and it is thought that this is of value to him. How much more! — but you will complete the sentence for yourself."

Churchill was confident that as public speakers and as men "in all that makes for popularity — in all that ensures attention" —

Mawdsley and he were "far superior to the Radical candidates." But he had little illusion about the outcome. "My private impression," he wrote to the Duke of Marlborough on 29 June 1899, "is that we shall be beaten in spite of Mawdsley, and in spite of everything I can do, and we shall be beaten simply because the Government have brought forward this stupid Bill which can do them no possible good." In another letter to Pamela Plowden, he sums up the campaign and his feelings:

WSC to Miss Pamela Plowden

(Lytton Papers)

EXTRACT

2 July 1899   Oldham

Pamela,

A vy busy week has closed. I now make speeches involuntarily. Yesterday I delivered no fewer than eight. But the good air up here has given me three times the health and strength I enjoyed in London.

Well we are nearing the end now. I don't think anyone has the vaguest idea how it will turn out. There is no doubt that I personally — have made a vy good impression. Mawdsley is a good fellow but who can tell how the Trades Unions will vote? There are so many cross currents in this fight that the regular party tides are disturbed. Whiteley's resignation and venomous speech has done a great deal of harm. I will make him regret this treachery one of these days. . . .

George Whiteley, Conservative MP for Stockport, had resigned from the Conservative Party and crossed the floor on the passing of the Clerical Tithes Bill on June 29, declaring it to be "A bare-faced and cynical revival of the dole system, by which the clergy were to profit." Churchill did not foresee that he was quite soon to cross the floor himself and was to be subjected to similar taunts. He continued to Miss Plowden:

. . . But whatever the result may be it has been a strange experience and I shall never forget the succession of great halls packed with excited people until there was not room for one single person more — speech after speech, meeting after meeting — three even four in one night — intermittent flashes of Heat & Light & enthusiasm — with cold air and the rattle of a carriage in between: a great experience. And I improve every time — I have hardly repeated myself at all. And at each meeting I am conscious of growing powers and facilities of speech, and it is in this that I shall find my consolation should the result be, as is probable, unfortunate. But I still wear your charm — so who can tell. Write to me Pamela — I have had you in my mind more perhaps this week than ever. I am glad to think that when all is finished we shall meet at Blenheim on the 15th another quiet Sunday. The London papers are fulsome and if there is a severe reverse here they will have made me seem vy ridiculous. But after all — the battle in the end must be to the strong.

Yours ever
WINSTON S. CHURCHILL

The result was declared late in the evening of July 6 and was as follows:

Emmott (Radical)	12,976
Runciman (Radical)	12,770
Churchill (Conservative) . . .	11,477
Mawdsley (Conservative) . . .	11,449

The majority of Emmott over Churchill, 1,499. The figures at the previous election were:

Ascroft (Conservative) . . .	13,085
Oswald (Conservative) . . .	12,465
Lee (Radical)	12,249
Hibbert (Radical)	12,092

Mr Ascroft's personal popularity had clearly been exceptional; bearing this in mind, the total swing of about two per cent to the Radicals was not disgraceful, and Churchill could afford to take a calm view of the result.

The Tory *Manchester Courier* of July 7 reported that Churchill "looked upon the process of counting with amusement. A smile lighted up his features, and the result of the election did not disturb him. He might have been defeated, but he was conscious that in this fight he had not been disgraced."

From Balfour, indeed, he received a kind letter of encouragement: "Never mind," he concluded, "it will all come right; and this small reverse will have no permanent ill effect upon your political fortunes." Balfour, thinking of Churchill's switch on the Clerical Tithes Bill, had however remarked in London at this time: "I thought he was a young man of promise, but it appears he is a young man of promises." Churchill was not yet twenty-five when he lost the election.

*

At the time of the Jameson Raid at the end of 1895 Churchill was only twenty-one. We have seen the excited interest with which the young subaltern followed the fortunes of the raiders and how he was conscious of the profound effect of this raid on English relations with the Boers in South Africa. There is extant in his papers a long memorandum entitled "Our Account with the Boers" probably written by him towards the end of 1896 or early in 1897 and, as far as can be traced, not published anywhere. This gives a comprehensive account of the problems as seen at that time by a fair-minded patriotic Englishman. He wrote: "Imperial aid must redress the wrongs of the Outlanders; Imperial troops must curb the insolence of the Boers. There must be no half measures. The forces employed must be strong enough to bear down all opposition from the Transvaal and the Free State; and at the same time to overawe all sympathisers in Cape Colony. There will not be wanting those who will call such a policy unscrupulous. If it be unscrupulous for the people of Great Britain to defend their most vital interests, to extend their protection to their fellow countrymen in distress and to maintain the integrity of their empire, 'unscrupulous' is a word we shall have to face." And he concluded: "Sooner or later, in a righteous cause or a picked quarrel, with the approval of Europe, or in the teeth of Germany, for the sake of our Empire, for the sake of our honour, for the sake of the race, we must fight the Boers." So by the summer of 1899 he was well aware of the clash which was impending in South Africa.

In 1877, England had abortively annexed the Transvaal, not only for political, military and economic reasons but also in the hope that her action would promote a Federation of the different territories in South Africa. The scheme misfired and in 1881 the Boers reasserted their independence after defeating the English at Majuba Hill. This incident apart, however, the English did not, on the whole, interfere with the Boers who had trekked to the interior of South Africa until the discovery of gold on the Witwatersrand in 1886. The Transvaal rapidly became the most industrialized and wealthy land on the African continent. It became a profitable market not only for overseas suppliers but also for farmers and traders of the Cape, and the Transvaal Republic was able to strengthen its armed forces and demonstrate its hostility towards Britain in a variety of ways.

Fortune seekers from all parts of the world flocked to the Rand and it soon became clear to the Boers that these men had little respect for the Boer way of life. As their numbers grew, the Republican authorities progressively made it more difficult for the Uitlanders, as they were called, to acquire the vote and to settle. "If I grant the franchise," said their President, Paul Kruger, "I may as well pull the Republican flag down."

Britain, on the other hand, championed the cause of the Uitlanders, partly because most of them were British and they had genuine grievances, but also because she hoped this would strengthen her influence in the Transvaal. After the Jameson Raid, the Transvaal Republic increased its purchase of arms and rallied opinion in the Cape and other parts of South Africa to its cause. The Orange Free State, for example, formed a military alliance with the Transvaal and leaders like Smuts gave up their British nationality and settled in what was called the South African Republic.

Early in 1899, the Uitlanders on the Rand petitioned the Queen. Whereas previously their cause had been pleaded by the great capitalists and investors in the Rand, now it was the ordinary working man and settler that took matters into their own hands. Sir Alfred Milner, the High Commissioner in Cape Colony, backed their protest: "The spectacle," he wrote in a famous despatch, "of thousands of British subjects permanently in a position of helots, constantly chafing under undoubted grievances and calling vainly to Her Majesty's Government for redress does steadily undermine the influence and reputation of Great Britain and the respect for the British Government within the Queen's dominions." Milner was ordered by the Government at home to negotiate with the Boers on behalf of the Uitlanders and at Bloemfontein Milner met Kruger from May 31 to June 5.

It was the popular view at that time that the Colonial Secretary, Mr Joseph Chamberlain, was impatient and thirsting for a "showdown." The documents of the period seem to show on the other hand that it was Milner who was thirsting for aggressive action. The Bloemfontein negotiations broke down and thereafter, despite various other offers by the British Government to the Boers, the two sides edged ever nearer towards war. A final offer to accept the enfranchisement of the Uitlanders on the Boers' original terms was made by Chamberlain on September 8. This was conciliatory enough to win the support of the Cape Dutch and of Boer sympathizers in England; but it was rejected by the Boer Republics within a few days.

Churchill was by now convinced that there would be war, and so was a large body of opinion in England. On September 18 Alfred Harmsworth, proprietor of the *Daily Mail,* telegraphed to Churchill asking him to act as his paper's war correspondent. Churchill immediately telegraphed to his friend Oliver Borthwick of the *Morning Post,* telling him of Harmsworth's invitation. Churchill suggested to Borthwick that he should go to South Africa for the *Morning Post,* after all his earliest backer, in return for expenses, copyright of his work and £1,000 for four months' shore to shore (£250 per month) and £200 a month thereafter. Within hours Churchill's offer was accepted and he told his mother (September 18): "I am at their disposal." This was probably the most lucrative contract into which any newspaper war correspondent had entered up to this time; and it served to elevate the scale of journalists' salaries in general.

Before he left London Churchill wrote to the Colonial Secretary, Mr Chamberlain, and went to see him. He was anxious to obtain letters of introduction to important people in South Africa. Chamberlain at first wrote back in a guarded fashion, but when, early in October, war was seen to be inevitable, he showed himself to be rather more enthusiastic:

Joseph Chamberlain to WSC

4 October 1899   Birmingham

My dear Winston,

    I have your telegram & I will write to Milner tonight asking his good offices for the son of my old friend. I am sure he will do all in his power. I shall be in London on Monday but I gather that you leave before then. If so good luck & best wishes!

Yours very truly

J. CHAMBERLAIN

Unlike the War Office, which, Churchill wrote to his mother on October 2, "is working very crankily," he was making his preparations for departure with brisk efficiency. These were the very early days of the film; but Churchill already seems to have been seized of the potential of this medium, and he gladly agreed to go half shares with a Mr Murray Guthrie in a scheme to record the South African war on a biograph machine. Guthrie was a distant connection by his marriage to the sister-in-law of Churchill's aunt Leonie Leslie, and was the newly elected Member of Parliament for Bow and Bromley (where he had defeated George Lansbury). He was to be responsible for the business and technical aspects of the scheme, while Churchill promised, with the help of an "expert" who was to go out with the machine, to "obtain some very strange pictures." But then came the news that the American Biograph Company was already literally in the field, and no more was heard of Churchill's project.

*

Churchill never believed that war should be needlessly uncomfortable: he made his dispositions accordingly. There is preserved a list of the stores with which he equipped himself before sailing to South Africa.

Account

Bought of W. Callaghan & Co Opticians

EXTRACT

6 October 1899   23A New Bond Street W.

£   s.   d.

Repairing & adjusting "Ross" Telescope
new sling to case   14   6

Repairing Voigtländer Field Glass, refitting top mountings etc	18	6
A saddle back fitted to pigskin case	17	6
A Bronzed Needle Compass fitted in of do 1	5	0

[3   15   6]

Account

to Randolph Payne & Sons, Importer of Wines, Spirits and Liqueurs

EXTRACT

6 October 1899   61 St James's Street S.W.

[per dozen]

6 Bottles 1889 Vin d'Ay Sec	110/–	2	15	0
18 bottles St Emilion	24/–	1	16	0
6 bottles light Port	42/–	1	1	0
6 bottles French Vermouth	36/–		18	0
18 bottles Scotch Whiskey (10 years old)	48/–	3	12	0
6 bottles Very Old Eau de Vie landed 1866	160/–	4	0	0
12 Rose's Cordial Lime Juice	15/–		15	0
6 × 1 dozen cases for same packing, marking etc			10	0
Cartage Dock charges & Insurance			13	0
Sent by S.S. *Dunottar Castle* to South Africa		16	0	0

By this time, of course, Churchill was a civilian and he had no military status. This, he could foresee, might be irksome if opportunity were to present itself for further military glory. He had moreover been at one time promised a place on the staff of General Sir Redvers Buller who was going out to take command of the British forces in South Africa. So that he might be in a position to take advantage of such opportunities if he wished, he wrote before his departure to obtain a commission in the Royal Bucks Yeomanry, accompanying his formal application with a personal appeal to the Honorary Colonel — Lord Chesham. This application, however, was never in fact forwarded, for when he got on board ship he discovered that it might be easier to obtain a Yeomanry commission from the Adjutant of the 9th Yeomanry Brigade which was under the command of his father's old friend Lord Gerard, of the Lancashire Hussars, who was accompanying Sir Redvers Buller as ADC.

Although both Britain and the South African Republic had drafted ultimatums it was the Boer ultimatum calling for the withdrawal of British troops that in fact proved decisive; it was despatched on October 9 and expired on October 11. The first shots were fired at Kraaipan on October 12. Churchill sailed from Southampton in the *Dunottar Castle* two days later on October 14. On the same ship were Buller and his staff, and many war correspondents. In his first despatch to the *Morning Post* he wrote:

26 October 1899   RMS *Dunottar Castle*
                                                           at sea

. . . What an odious affair is a modern sea journey! In ancient times there were greater discomforts and perils; but they were recognised. A man took ship prepared for the worst. Nowadays he expects the best as a matter of course, and is therefore, disappointed. Besides how slowly we travel! . . .

He was very fond in later life of quoting Dr Johnson's famous phrase: "Being in a ship is being in a jail, with the chance of being drowned." To be kept prisoner, as it were, in a boat, cut off from all news of the outside world, while a war was actually going on thousands of miles away, was a frustration Churchill found difficult to endure. Earlier he had written:

WSC to Lady Randolph

17 October [1899]   Madeira
                                              en route to South Africa

My dearest Mamma,

We have had a nasty rough passage & I have been grievously sick. The roll of the vessel still very pronounced prevents my writing much, and besides there is nothing to say. Sir R. Buller is vy amiable and I do not doubt that he is well disposed towards me. There are a good many people on board — military or journalistic — whom

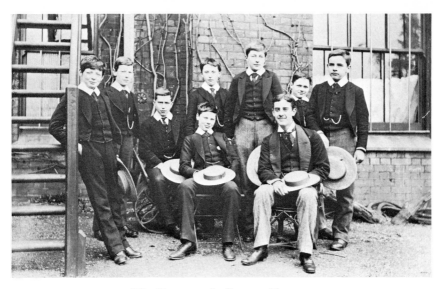

MR DAVIDSON'S SMALL HOUSE

Harrow, 1888–9. Winston is at the left

H. O. D. DAVIDSON

First Housemaster

ROBERT SOMERVELL

English Master

REVEREND J. E. C. WELLDON
Headmaster of Harrow, 1885–98
From a portrait by Hon. John Collier

BERNARD MINSSEN
French Master

LOUIS MORIARTY
Army Class Master

REVEREND F. C. SEARLE
Under-Housemaster, Headmaster's House

"Your Deputy-Mother"
Laura Caroline, Lady Wilton

Lady Randolph
and Admirers
Count Kinsky (left),
Lord Dudley (right)

SANDHURST: PARADE AFTER THE HALF-MILE DONKEY RACE, MAY 1894
Churchill as Pierrot, back row left

DUCHESS LILY   COLONEL BRABAZON

MURIEL WILSON AS VASHTI
In Abercrombie's *Emblems of Love*

MOLLY HACKET

MABEL LOVE
In *Little Christopher Columbus*
at the Lyric

LORD RANDOLPH,
1893

IN THE FAR EAST ON THEIR WORLD TOUR
Lord and Lady Randolph and Dr Keith

HEAD OF THE FAMILY
Churchill with Lady Randolph after the death of his father

SIR BINDON BLOOD

IAN HAMILTON
In camp, Kohat,
February 1898

BUNGALOW AT BANGALORE
Churchill, extreme left

THE REGIMENTAL POLO TEAM, 1898–9
From left: Savory, Barres, Churchill, Hoare

ATTACHED TO 21ST LANCERS: IN CAIRO, 1898

NEAR OMDURMAN
2 SEPTEMBER 1898

The two messages sent by Churchill
to the Sirdar before the battle

THE ARMOURED TRAIN: THE DAY AFTER THE ACTION

CAPTAIN AYLMER HALDANE
AND
LIEUTENANT LE MESURIER

On arrival at Lorenço
Marques after their escape

PAMELA PLOWDEN,
1892

WINSTON CHURCHILL,
1900

Two drawings by
Lady Granby (later
Duchess of Rutland)

"WINSTON"

Vanity Fair Cartoon by Spy, 10 July 1900

"He is a clever fellow who has the courage of his opinions . . . He can write and he can fight . . . he has hankered after Politics since he was a small boy, and it is probable that his every effort, military or literary, has been made with political bent . . . He is something of a sportsman; who prides himself on being practical rather than a dandy; he is ambitious; he means to get on, and he loves his country. But he can hardly be the slave of any Party . . ."

MEMBER FOR OLDHAM

I know and all are vy civil — but I cannot say that I am greatly
interested in any of them.

I wonder what news we shall find at Madeira! Evidently the
General expects that nothing of importance will happen until he gets
there. But I rather think events will have taken the bit between their
teeth.

I won't write more — but please fire off a weekly letter and stimulate everyone else to write too. I hope that the second number [of
the *Anglo-Saxon Review*] will be a success.

Ever your loving son
WINSTON

But at Madeira they found nothing; "nothing, though satisfactory,
is very hard to understand," he wrote in his *Morning Post* despatch
of October 26. "Why did they declare war if they had nothing up
their sleeves? Why do they waste time now?" For two weeks there
was no news. Churchill, like the rest of the company on board ship,
gave himself up to wild surmise:

WSC to Lady Randolph

EXTRACT

25 October [1899]   RMS *Dunottar Castle*
                                           en route

My dearest Mamma,

We are having a cool & prosperous voyage, and although the ship is
crowded and ill-found, I cannot say I hate it as much as I expected to.
I am vy excited to know what will have happened when we land.
Fourteen days is a long time in war, especially at the beginning.
I expect George [Cornwallis-West *whom she was soon to marry*] will
be in S.A. within a fortnight of my getting there and I will go and
see him. The main campaign — as I learn on the best possible
authority — for who can foresee such things — will begin about the
25th December and we should be at Pretoria, *via* Fourteen Streams
and Bloemfontein by the end of February. I may therefore be home
in March: George I expect will see the Derby. But it is perhaps early
to make such speculations. . . .

Then on October 29 they sighted a homeward bound steamer, the
Australasian, which displayed a black board on which was painted

in white "Boers defeated; Three battles; Penn Symons killed."
Churchill had known Symons in India but it was not his death that
cast a gloom over the passengers of the *Dunottar Castle*. It was the
news of the three battles and the Boer defeat: the three battles in
which they had not participated. It seemed likely, they argued, that
it would be all over before they got to Cape Town.

*

While Churchill was at sea his book *The River War* was in the
press. It was to be published in two volumes a week after his arrival
in Cape Town. It was generally very well received and was much
praised by the literary and military critics of the day. The courage
and fearlessness with which he made his criticisms of Lord Kitchener
were commented on as much as his presumption and "cocksureness"
in making them. Some critics singled out the first volume as being
particularly impressive; others enjoyed the verve with which he described, in "forcible and picturesque" language, the exciting incidents which he had himself witnessed in the second volume. Nearly
all the critics united in acclaiming *The River War* as the standard
history of the campaign. Only the *Saturday Review,* the weekly to
which Churchill himself had three years before contributed on
Cuban affairs, carried a notice that was almost wholly hostile: "Only
this astonishing young man," it wrote on 18 November 1899, "could
have written these two ponderous and pretentious volumes. . . . The
annoying feature in the book is the irrepressible egoism of its author.
. . . The airs of infallibility he assumes are irritating. . . . He is
perpetually finding fault is this 'terrible cornet of horse.' " Perhaps
the most balanced review is that which appeared in the *Daily Mail* of
November 7:

> Mr Winston Spencer Churchill is an astonishing young man, and
> his *River War* (Longmans) is an astonishing triumph. It is well-
> written, it is impartial, it is conclusive, and we do not think that any
> other living man could have produced it. Of course, it has its faults.
> It is far too long, for instance.
> To devote nearly a thousand pages to what will appear a century
> hence a mere episode in modern history is like setting a wheel to

break a butterfly, especially as the whole story might have been packed into 500 pages, and nothing lost.

Moreover the book is not one, but two. The first part is the serious narrative of the past, a summing up (so to say) of British endeavour and British failure. And this part is written in the severe style of Gibbon. The simple fact is put as a general statement; antitheses are suggested where none are possible; and Mr Churchill, having the *Decline and Fall* up his sleeve, forgets that only a great occasion justifies the music of the organ.

But the latter part of the book is the work of a war correspondent. Mr Churchill describes the scenes of which he was a witness, and he describes them with admirable movement and energy. And all the while he keeps his head perfectly straight. No excitement disturbs his balance, and, though the book in style and dash is the book of a young man who has read Gibbon, in judgement it is the work of mature intelligence. Take, for instance, the account of Gordon's mission to Khartoum. Nothing can exceed Mr Churchill's admiration of the hero, nor his anger at the hero's desertion. Yet never does he plead his cause extravagantly. He is always rather a judge than an advocate.

Judicial, also, is his account of Omdurman and of the fateful charge. Nor even in his treatment of Fashoda is he betrayed into excess. Indeed, he understates rather than overstates his case. For instance, there is no doubt that the invasion of Marchand was part of a triple plot, in which Abyssinia and the Marquis de Mores were to be engaged. So much has been freely confessed by the leaders of the Nationalist party, who, always indiscreet, were compelled after Fashoda to brag of the beautiful plan that had miscarried. Indeed, the French at Fashoda were only trying, as they have tried many times in their history, to fight a friendly Power under an alien flag; and we think that Mr Churchill might have asserted with courage the truth at which he does no more than hint.

But the *River War* is an excellent book — excellent in spite of the faults which we have named; in spite, also, of the *obiter dicta* which interrupt its pages.

The initial print of 2,000 copies was soon sold out at 36/– and two further impressions, making another 1,000 copies in all, were published within six months. But it was to be many weeks after the reviews had appeared that Churchill had the satisfaction of reading them; for within ten days of the book's publication, he was a prisoner of war. His capture and escape may well have promoted the sales of this comparatively expensive work.

*

On October 31, the *Dunottar Castle* arrived in Cape Town and her passengers were left in little doubt that there would still be plenty

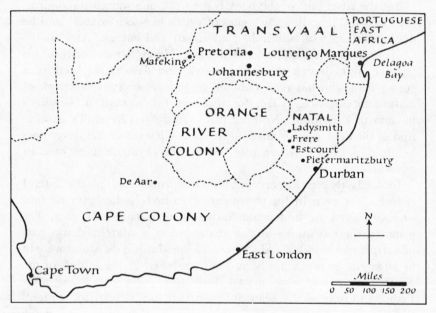

SOUTH AFRICA, 1899

for them to do. While Sir Redvers Buller and his staff decided to continue their comfortable and leisurely progress in the *Dunottar Castle* to Durban, Churchill and two of his fellow correspondents, Captain Campbell of the Laffans News Agency and J. B. Atkins of the *Manchester Guardian,* had discovered that by taking a train from Cape Town to East London (by way of De Aar), and thence by steamer to Durban, they would arrive three or four days earlier than the General and his staff.

Churchill, though understandably anxious to arrive at the scene of battle ahead of the Commander-in-Chief, found time to avail him-

self of the letter of introduction which Joseph Chamberlain had sent
to the Governor of Cape Colony, Sir Alfred Milner.

WSC to Lady Randolph

EXTRACT

3 November [1899]   In the train near East London

. . . We have greatly underestimated the military strength and
spirit of the Boers. I vy much doubt whether one army Corps will be
enough to overcome their resistance — at any rate a fierce and bloody
struggle is before us in which at least ten or twelve thousand lives
will be sacrificed and from which the Boers are absolutely certain
that they will emerge victorious. Naturally I do not share that last
opinion — but it is as well to bear it in mind. Sir Alfred Milner
told me that the whole of Cape Colony was "trembling on the verge
of Rebellion" [*a phrase used in his despatch to the* Morning Post
of November 1] and this will further complicate the issue. I will
write to you from Ladysmith. We have had good luck so far, this
being the last train to get through from De Aar, and we have gained
four days on all the other correspondents. I shall believe I am to be
preserved for future things. . . .

Churchill's account of his short cut to the front is confirmed and
supplemented by a recollection of Atkins which is recorded in
Winston Churchill and Harrow by E. D. W. Chaplin:

. . . By the time we reached Cape Town we had tied our fortunes
together at least for the Natal campaign. We would go to the sound
of the guns near Ladysmith as quickly as possible. That meant leaving the ship at once and going by train and another ship to Durban.
At East London we joined a tiny coasting vessel and had a gruelling
passage, both of us being very seasick. . . .

It must have been a very rough passage. "You were not concerned
in the simple calculation whether or not you were a good sailor,"
wrote Atkins in his contemporary account: "it was rather a question
whether you had a good enough head to sit on the shoulder of a
spinning peg-top without reeling from giddiness."

In Durban harbour, near their own coaster's moorings, lay the
hospital ship *Sumatra*. There Churchill found a number of old
friends among the wounded, one of them Reggie Barnes, his compan-

ion in Cuba and fellow polo-player in India. Barnes, who had been
shot through the groin in the attack on Elandslaagte, told him of the
courageous and successful manner in which the Boers were fighting
the war.

It was evident that Buller would not be arriving in Durban for
three days and that, after assembling his stores, there would be a
considerable delay before the new General Headquarters moved to
the front. Churchill and Atkins naturally anticipated these cumber-
some activities. At Durban Churchill heard that Ian Hamilton, now
a General, had arrived in Ladysmith on the last train before the
Boers had advanced and cut the railway line near Chieveley. He
decided to go to the front as quickly as he could by rail.

Again Atkins takes up the story:

> Then by train to Maritzburg, where we hired a special train for
> Ladysmith. Many miles short of Ladysmith, however, we came to a
> stop — the line was cut; the Boers were across it; Ladysmith was in-
> vested. Perhaps it was as well that we failed.
>
> We pitched our tents in the railway yard at Estcourt. We had
> found a good cook and we had some good wine. We entertained
> friends every evening, to our pleasure and professional advantage
> and, we believed, to their satisfaction.
>
> One memorable evening we entertained the officer commanding at
> Estcourt. While we were dining the clang of field guns being loaded
> into trucks went on unceasingly; for the officer, as he told us, had
> decided that the position at Estcourt could hardly be held and that a
> retirement to better ground nearer Maritzburg was necessary. As
> dinner proceeded Winston, with an assurance which I partly envied
> and partly deprecated, argued that Joubert was probably too cau-
> tious to advance yet; that he was no doubt delighted with the security
> of the Tugela River; that it would be a pity to point the way to
> Maritzburg, and so on. Shortly after our guest had left us the clang-
> ing in the trucks, which had ceased, began again. The trucks were
> being unloaded. Winston gleamed "*I* did that!" he said; but added
> gracefully, "*We* did that!" Whether he did it or not we shall never
> know. The officer may have acted on fresh information. At least
> Winston's effort was singular for persuasive reasoning.

Churchill's old friend from frontier days in India, Aylmer Haldane, was at Estcourt. Many years later in his memoirs he recalled:

As I came out of the office [in Estcourt] feeling rather lugubrious I noticed Churchill, who, as well as some other correspondents, was hanging about to pick up such crumbs of information for his news-paper as might be available. I told him what I had been ordered to do and, aware that he had been out in the train and knew some-thing of the country through which it was wont to travel, suggested that he might care to accompany me next day. Although he was not at all keen he consented to do so, and arranged to be at the station in time for the start.

Churchill's own account of the journey of the armoured train, first transmitted to the *Morning Post* from Durban and published on 1 January 1900, has remained unchallenged and substantially un-altered over the years. It is reprinted in its entirety in *My Early Life*. Of more interest, in a way, is the official account which was written by Haldane in prison at Pretoria, but which was not despatched until well after Churchill had completed his escape.

Captain Aylmer Haldane to Chief of Staff, Natal Field Force

(Royal Archives)

3 January 1900   Pretoria

Sir,
    I have the honour to forward the following report concerning the capture of an armoured train which left Estcourt under my com-mand on the 15th November 1899.

    1. On the night of the 14th November, I received verbal instruc-tions from Colonel Long, R.A., commanding at Estcourt, to take a 9-pr muzzle-loading Naval gun and detachment, HMS *Tartar,* one company 2nd Bn Dublin Fusiliers, and one company Durban Light Infantry, and with the armoured train reconnoitre in the direction of Colenso, proceeding with caution and keeping out of range of the enemy's guns. The train, which was made up and manned as follows:
        Ordinary truck — gun and detachment,
        Armoured truck — ¾ company, 2nd Bn Dublin Fusiliers,
        Engine,
        Tender,
    2 armoured trucks —$\left\{\begin{array}{l}\text{1 company, 2nd Bn Dublin Fusiliers,}\\\text{1 company, Durban Light Infantry,}\end{array}\right.$
        Breakdown gang truck,

left Escourt at 5.10 a.m. and on arrival at Frere Station at 6.20 a.m. I reported that no enemy had been seen. Here I met a party of eight men of the Natal Mounted Police, from whom I learnt that their patrols were in advance reconnoitring towards Chieveley, whither I proceeded after a halt of 15 minutes. On reaching there at 7.10 a.m., I received the following message by telephone from Estcourt, "Remain at Frere in observation, watching your safe retreat. Remember that Chieveley station was last night occupied by the enemy. Nothing occurred here yet. Do not place reliance on any reports from local residents as they may be untrustworthy," and in acknowledging it stated that a party of about 50 Boers and three wagons was visible moving south on the west side of the railway.

3. I at once retired towards Frere, and on rounding the spur of a hill which commanded the line the enemy opened on us at 600 yards with artillery, one shell striking the leading truck. The driver put on full steam and we ran down the gradient at a high speed, and almost immediately on reaching the level three-quarters of a mile from Frere, the breakdown gang truck and two armoured trucks, which preceded the engine were derailed, one of the latter standing partly across the track. The enemy, lying in ambush, had allowed the train to pass towards Chieveley, and had then placed a stone on the line, which the guard, probably owing to the shell fire, had neither seen or reported.

4. Mr Winston Churchill, special correspondent of the *Morning Post* who was with me in the truck next the gun-truck offered me his services, and knowing how thoroughly I could rely on him, I gladly accepted them, and undertook to keep down the enemy's fire while he endeavoured to clear the line. Our gun came into action at 900 yards, but after four rounds, was struck by a shell and knocked over. I recalled the gun detachment into the armoured truck, whence a continuous fire was kept up on the enemy's guns, considerably disconcerting their aim, as I was afterwards informed, killing two and wounding four men.

The Boers maintained a hot fire with rifles, 3–15 pr Creusot guns and a Maxim shell fire, but as the shells struck the engine and truck obliquely the armour-plating was only occasionally penetrated. For an hour efforts to clear the line were unsuccessful, as the trucks were heavy and jammed together, and the break-down gang could not be found, but Mr Churchill with indomitable perseverance continued his difficult task, and about 8.30 a.m. the engine forced its way past the obstructing truck, which, however, again fell forward some inches across the line.

Shortly before this the couplings which fastened the armoured and gun trucks to the engine had been broken by a shell, and when the engine cleared the wreckage they were left behind. Perhaps it was possible to again remove the wreckage and re-couple the trucks to the engine, but as the cab of the latter was now crammed with wounded, who would have been scalded had a shell struck the boiler, as the pipe of the reserve water-tank was torn open and the water rushing out, as the front of the engine was in flames, and because I apprehended lest the enemy, seeing the engine free, should again tamper with the line, I resolved to allow the engine to retreat out of range towards Frere, and withdrawing the men from the trucks, made a run for some houses, 800 yards distant, where I had some hope of making a further resistance. As the enemy had not relaxed his artillery and musketry fire, and there was absolutely no cover, the men became considerably scattered along the line, and in a formation ill adapted to offer resistance. To my disgust, and in direct disobedience of my orders, I saw two men 200 yards in front of me holding up white handkerchiefs. I shouted and ran towards them, but at this moment the Boers, who, unperceived by us, had left the hill on our right rear, and, seeing the signal, had stopped firing, galloped among the retreating soldiers, who remained uncertain what to do, and called upon them to surrender. Under these circumstances, at 8.50 a.m., I, 2nd Lieutenant T. Frankland, 2nd Bn Royal Dublin Fusiliers, and 50 men, were captured; the remainder, on whom the Boers continued to fire, making good their retreat across the railway bridge to Frere Station, whence I understand they and the engine reached the British lines at Estcourt in safety.

5. I venture here with some diffidence, owing to the unfortunate termination of the reconnaissance, to record my acknowledgements of the services of the following:

2nd Lieutenant T. C. Frankland, 2nd Bn Royal Dublin Fusiliers, a gallant young Officer who carried out my orders with coolness.

A.B. Seaman E. Read, HMS *Tartar,* No 6300 Lance-Corporal W. Connell, Privates Phoenix and Kavanagh, 2nd Bn Royal Dublin Fusiliers, who, notwithstanding that they were repeatedly knocked down by the concussion of the shells striking the armoured truck, continued steadily to fire until ordered to cease. Captain Wylie and the men of the Durban Light Infantry, who ably assisted in covering the working party engaged in clearing the line, and who were much exposed to the enemy's fire. I regret I am unable to give exact details of any deserving special mention, but I beg to suggest that Captain Wylie be called upon for a report.

Mr Winston S. Churchill, whose valuable services have already been detailed in the text of this report, and whom, owing to the urgency of the circumstances, I formally placed on duty.

I would point out that while engaged on the work of saving the engine, for which he was mainly responsible, he was frequently exposed to the full fire of the enemy. I cannot speak too highly of his gallant conduct.

The driver of the engine, who, though wounded, remained at his post.

The telegraphist attached to the train, who showed a fine example of cheerfulness and indifference to danger.

Lastly, under this heading, I desire to mention the bearing of all the troops under my command, which, under the trying circumstances of this small affair, was admirable.

6. I understand that the Boers buried four of the killed, and that they have 13 wounded in hospital. Of the 52 taken prisoner, seven, including Mr Churchill, are slightly wounded.

7. I should like to be accorded an opportunity of making a report in detail of the many defects of the armoured train, and the dangers and disabilities under which it lies in an unsupported reconnaissance; but the popular opinion of this flimsy military machine may best be shown by the fact that in camp it was known as "Wilson's death-trap."

8. I attach rough sketch of the scene of action.

I have the honour to be, Sir, Your obedient Servant
AYLMER HALDANE
Captain, 2nd Bn Gordon Highlanders

Natal Witness, *17 November 1899*

EXTRACT

Thursday 9.40 a.m.   Estcourt

. . . Capt Wylie, who is doing well, describes Mr Winston Churchill's conduct in the most enthusiastic terms as that of as brave a man as could be found. It was on Mr Churchill's initiative that Capt Wylie and a number of his men worked to get the trucks blocking the line out of the way.

After that task had been accomplished, amid a hail of missiles, and the engine and tender were able to move forward, Mr Churchill again directed the engine-driver to steam back to the rear trucks, which were still on the line, with the object of hooking them on and so saving most of the men. Unfortunately, he found the leading truck had been injured, probably by shells, as it could not be coupled on, and Mr Churchill then directed the driver to proceed slowly while he got as many wounded as possible on the tender.

It was while he was co-operating with Mr Churchill in this work that Capt Wylie was shot through the hip. Before collapsing Capt Wylie succeeded in getting his head behind a large boulder, and there he lay on his face, helpless. While in that position a shell struck the boulder and smashed it to pieces, without further injury to the wounded officer.

When the engine came past again, he was placed on the tender.

Previous to being shot down Capt Wylie had seen that all his men were on the move in retreat.

Mr Churchill accompanied the wounded to Frere Station, and then returned to the scene of the fight to attend to the wounded left on the field. All firing had then ceased, so that Mr Churchill, like those missing, must be a prisoner.

All is quiet so far this morning. . . .

Leo Amery of *The Times,* J. B. Atkins of the *Manchester Guardian,* G. W. Steevens of the *Daily Mail,* and Bennett Burleigh of the *Daily Telegraph* all agreed that Churchill had behaved with great gallantry at the armoured train disaster. The more Radical newspapers were inclined to suspect that this was a mutual admiration society among war correspondents but this impression was quickly dispelled by similar tributes from the Natal railway authorities.

Inspector Campbell of the Natal Government Railways sent the following letter to the General Manager of the Railways on behalf of the railway employees who escaped with the armoured train; it was published in the *Natal Witness* on November 17:

The railway men who accompanied the armoured train this morning ask me to convey to you their admiration of the coolness

and pluck displayed by Mr Winston Churchill, the war correspondent who accompanied the train, and to whose efforts, backed up by
those of the driver, Wagner, is due the fact that the armoured train
and tender were brought successfully out, after being hampered by
the derailed trucks in front, and that it became possible to bring
the wounded in here. The whole of our men are loud in their
praises of Mr Churchill, who, I regret to say, has been taken prisoner. I respectfully ask you to convey their admiration to a brave
man.

Many of the reports suggested that Churchill would be recommended for the Victoria Cross. But perhaps the most touching
account was published in the *Morning Post* on December 12; it
consisted of a letter written by Lord Randolph's, and now Churchill's, servant Walden to Lady Randolph:

Thomas Walden to Lady Randolph

17 November 1899   Horseshoe Hotel
                                                        Maritzburg
                                                          Natal

My Lady,
    I am sorry to say Mr Churchill is a prisoner, but I am almost cer-
tain he is not wounded. I came down to Maritzburg yesterday to
bring all his kit until Mr Winston gets free. I am going back to
Estcourt this afternoon. I have joined the Imperial Light Horse
on Colonel Long's advice, although I asked him first if I could join
as I wanted to be near Mr Winston as soon as he is free. So Colonel
Long said he would arrange for me to leave the regiment as soon as
Mr C. wanted me. I came down in the armoured train with the
driver, who is wounded in the head with a shell. He told me all
about Mr Winston. He says there is not a braver gentleman in the
Army. The driver was one of the first wounded, and he said to
Mr Winston: "I am finished." So Mr Winston said to him: "Buck
up a bit, I will stick to you," and he threw off his revolver and
field-glasses and helped the driver pick 20 wounded up and put
them on the tender of the engine. Every officer in Estcourt thinks
Mr C. and the engine-driver will get the V.C. It took them two
hours to clear the road. They had to knock the iron trucks off
the road by running into them with the engine. The shells had

knocked them all to pieces. How the engine escaped being blown
up I don't know; it was a total wreck. The engine, with Mr C. on
it, got back to Frere station safe, and then Mr C. would get off and
go back to look after Captain Haldane. Mr C. left his field glasses
and revolver on the engine, and the driver says he had lost his hat.
It was a frightful morning too. It had been raining for about
twenty-four hours, and it rained in torrents all day, so he must have
been very wet; he had a good mackintosh on though. The driver
says he was as cool as anything and worked like a nigger, and how
he escaped he doesn't know, as about fifty shells hit the engine.
Everyone in Maritzburg is talking about Mr Churchill. I am pleased
to say he was in the best of health when I last saw him, as I believe
he is now.

I remain, your obedient servant
T. WALDEN

It is interesting to compare these reports with that sent by General
Joubert, who was in command of the Boer forces, to Francis W. Reitz,
the former President of the Orange Free State and now State Secretary of the Transvaal.

General P. J. Joubert to F. W. Reitz

(South African Government Archives)

(TRANSLATION)

15 November 1899   Headquarters Ladysmith

In our plans of operation the decision was, and is, to hold Ladysmith by having our guards in the area and with our Commandos
operating past Estcourt. The day before yesterday I arrived at
Colenso. Yesterday was the day set for reconnoitring the position.
We discerned English guards. They were also moving out towards
the patrol under the command of Commandant David Joubert.
However, this did not lead to a clash of arms, although a train
rushed down upon three of our burghers. They fired upon the
train which turned back. Nonetheless it was clear that we must
take the position. Therefore commandos of Ermelo, Middelburg
and a portion of Krugersdorp immediately proceeded to take the
place while the other burghers only left at 3 o'clock this morning.
When I arrived at the position, the train was coming into view.

Fortunately one of our Commandos had marched round. When the train noticed us and rushed on, the Commando had already thrown boulders on to the line. The train was derailed, but the site was unsuitable for our cannons and even worse for the burghers; for it was an armoured train consisting of three armoured coaches. As soon as the train was derailed, they fired on us with an Armstrong and a Maxim. On our side, five were slightly wounded and a few more seriously. Eventually the engine was freed and it departed with half of the train.

We consequently captured only five trucks of which three were armoured. On the side of the enemy, two were killed, ten wounded and 56 captured, among whom was Winston Spencer Churchill, a reporter of the *Morning Post,* who is at present being sent to Pretoria. It is now raining heavily. All the burghers and prisoners are wet. I have not yet succeeded in getting the officers together. Nor have I yet seen the Free State Commando that was to have accompanied us. We are expecting a much stronger attack. I have been away from Ladysmith these three days and hear strong rumours of Kaffir Commandos. Yesterday I gave L. de Jager orders to commandeer the Natal burghers and to check the kaffirs.

A number of unofficial versions of Churchill's part in the Armoured Train action survive. The following deserves special attention.

Lizzie B. Walls to Lady Randolph

18 December 1899   The Glen
                                              Lewisham Road S.E.
Dear Madam,

I am taking the liberty of sending you an extract from a letter I received this aft from my brother, who is a Private in the Durban Light Infantry (volunteers). He was in the Armoured train disaster at Estcourt & amongst other things in a most interesting letter says:

"Thanks to young Churchill (a son of Lord Randolph's) who was with us as correspondent for some paper, we managed to get the engine clear after about an hour. Churchill is a splendid fellow. He walked about in it all as coolly as if nothing was going on, & called for volunteers to give him a hand to get the truck out of the road.

"His presence and way of going on were as much good as 50 men would have been. After the engine got clear he came about ½ mile on it and then coolly got off & walked back to help the others. He is now a prisoner in Pretoria. I got shot through the left foot shortly after the start so couldn't do much more than lie still & shout, & just as the engine was getting clear, I got shot through the throat, so I had my share of it."

Trusting you will excuse the liberty I have taken,

I remain, Yrs very faithfully

LIZZIE B. WALLS

Numerous accounts are extant of the exact circumstances in which Churchill was captured. His own in *My Early Life,* though not exact in all details, deserves to be cited first.

I had not retraced my steps 200 yards when, instead of Haldane and his company, two figures in plain clothes appeared upon the line. "Platelayers!" I said to myself, and then with a surge of realization, "Boers!" My mind retains its impression of these tall figures, full of energy, clad in dark, flapping clothes, with slouch, storm-driven hats, poising on their levelled rifles hardly a hundred yards away. I turned again and ran back towards the engine, the two Boers firing as I ran between the metals. Their bullets, sucking to right and left, seemed to miss only by inches. We were in a small cutting with banks about six feet high on either side. I flung myself against the bank of the cutting. It gave no cover. Another glance at the two figures; one was now kneeling to aim. Movement seemed the only chance. Again I darted forward: again two soft kisses sucked in the air; but nothing struck me. This could not endure. I must get out of the cutting — that damnable corridor! I jigged to the left, and scrambled up the bank. The earth sprang up beside me. I got through the wire fence unhurt. Outside the cutting was a tiny depression. I crouched in this, struggling to get my breath again.

Fifty yards away was a small platelayers' cabin of masonry; there was cover there. About 200 yards away was the rocky gorge of the Blue Krantz River; there was plenty of cover there. I determined to make a dash for the river. I rose to my feet. Suddenly on the other side of the railway, separated from me by the rails and two uncut wire fences, I saw a horseman galloping furiously, a tall, dark figure, holding his rifle in his right hand. He pulled up his horse almost in its own length and shaking the rifle at me shouted a loud command. We were forty yards apart. That morning I had taken with me, Correspondent-status notwithstanding, my Mauser pistol. I thought I could kill this man, and after the treatment I had received I earnestly desired to do so. I put my hand to my belt, the pistol was not there. When engaged in clearing the line, getting in and out of the engine, etc, I had taken it off. It came safely home on the engine. I have it now! But at this moment I was quite unarmed. Meanwhile, I suppose in about the time this takes to tell, the Boer horseman, still seated on his horse, had covered me with his rifle. The animal stood stock still, so did he, and so did I. I looked towards the river, I looked towards the platelayers' hut. The Boer continued to look along his sights. I thought there was absolutely no chance of escape, if he fired he would surely hit me, so I held up my hands and surrendered myself a prisoner of war.

"When one is alone and unarmed," said the great Napoleon, in words which flowed into my mind in the poignant minutes that followed, "a surrender may be pardoned." Still he might have missed; and the Blue Krantz ravine was very near and the two wire fences were still uncut. However, the deed was done. Thereupon my captor lowered his rifle and beckoned to me to come across to him. I obeyed.

. . . Such is the episode of the armoured train and the story of my capture on November 15, 1899.

It was not until three years later, when the Boer Generals visited England to ask for some loan or assistance on behalf of their devastated country, that I was introduced at a private luncheon to their leader, General Botha. We talked of the war and I briefly told the story of my capture. Botha listened in silence; then he said, "Don't you recognise me? I was that man. It was I who took you prisoner. I, myself," and his bright eyes twinkled with pleasure. Botha in white shirt and frock coat looked very different in all save size and darkness of complexion from the wild war-time figure I had seen that rough day in Natal. But about the extraordinary fact there can be no doubt. He had entered upon the invasion of Natal as a burgher; his own disapproval of the war had excluded him from any high command at its outset. This was his first action. But as a simple private burgher serving in the ranks he had galloped ahead and in front of the whole Boer forces in the ardour of pursuit. Thus we met.

History depends wherever it can on first-hand accounts. But it should be one of the strictest precepts of the historian to subject everything that comes before him to a cold and sceptical scrutiny. This applies with special force to moments of action, passion and excitement. The man who is hotly engaged in action has all his faculties fully absorbed in the current emergency. Unless he has special aptitudes or is a trained reporter it is unlikely that he will see things in their true perspective or even perceive what were the salient or dominating events of the action. In retrospect, of course, many events may be reassessed and assigned in different proportion, many illusory fears dismissed, many fugitive hopes relegated to a proper limbo. But when there are a number of witnesses, all of them equally unprejudiced, all of them equally truthful, it may still be that some facts will be etched more sharply in one man's memory than in another's.

Memory often plays us quirks. Churchill once told the author a story of Sir Walter Raleigh during his imprisonment in the Tower of London. Sir Walter was passing his time writing his immense *History of the World*. One morning he looked out of his window which faced on a courtyard and saw a man come through an archway. Another man emerged from a doorway. Words were exchanged, an altercation ensued, blows were struck and one man fell dead. The Governor of the Tower ordered an inquiry: six independent witnesses, none of whose interests was remotely engaged, were summoned, as well as Sir Walter. Their accounts differed in almost every particular. Despairing of human credibility Sir Walter abandoned his History. Perhaps he was bored with it anyway.

These reflections are not put forward with the object of inducing a similar mood of defeatism in other historians, but solely as a corrective to gullibility. The chronicler must assemble all the evidence he can, deploy it, weigh it judiciously, consider its plausibility and then tell his tale with his utmost candour.

The cloud of testimony, and it is indeed a cloud which shrouds this particular episode, makes it very hard for the historian to determine who was the actual physical captor. The author has received accounts, some of them conflicting, from many sources. L. C. B. Howard of the Transvaal thinks that it was Botha; Dr Keuzenkamp, now living in North Carolina and who was in the action as a boy of seventeen, thinks that it was not. Dr Ploeger of Pretoria suggests that it was Field-Cornet Oosthuizen, who was killed later in the war. A telegram from one of the local commanders, Captain Theron, dated 28 November 1899 (see page 467) points unequivocally to Oosthuizen as the captor. However, among a number of other suggestions, Mr Lyonel Capstickdale of Johannesburg sent the author in a letter dated 8 June 1965 a recent cutting of a paragraph in the Johannesburg *Star,* which denies that Botha had anything to do with it, and which states emphatically that Adolph de la Rey and Francois Changuion, serving in Oosthuizen's commando, actually effected the capture.

A close study of all the accounts has been made by the author and one of his assistants, Mr Martin Mauthner, who was resident in South Africa for many years. In the Johannesburg *Sunday Times* in June 1963, Mauthner, with the author's approval, summed up the central issue thus:

> . . . Does this then mean that Botha had no part in the capture? Not necessarily. In fact, the evidence suggests that Botha was in the neighbourhood at the time, and probably in overall command of that particular area. It is quite possible that, although he himself did not capture Sir Winston, he had the young prisoner brought before him for questioning. . . .

This conclusion is fortified by Mr A. M. Davey, of the University of South Africa, who has done extensive research into this question. In a letter to the author on 5 December 1962 he states:

> . . . It is known that Louis Botha's command of English was poor; he probably failed to make his meaning clear to Sir Winston. My guess is that Botha intended to indicate that he was in overall command of the area in which the armoured train affair took place. . . .

The probability that it was not Botha who captured Churchill is fortified by the fact that it is not mentioned in the Boer documents.

When Churchill was captured neither he nor Botha were famous men. In the next few years both had an interest to be respectively the captive and the captor. Of course, many other South African burghers in the neighbourhood of Frere found it agreeable in their old age when Churchill had become famous to approximate themselves as closely as possible to his capture.

Despite the numerous doubts which have been shown to surround this topic Churchill himself to the end of his days remained obdurate in his conviction that it was Botha who was his captor. It often happens that when one has in good faith told a story a great many times it becomes increasingly vivid each time it is told. In July 1960 the author wrote to his father drawing his attention to an article by Mr H. P. H. Behrens in the Johannesburg *Star* of 30 April 1960 in which it was stated that it was certainly not Botha but probably was Field-Cornet Oosthuizen who had captured him. Churchill replied: "The writer is mistaken and I was captured by Botha *personally* as stated in my book," the word "personally" being inserted in his own handwriting in what was otherwise a typed letter. Nor is the report true that Jaap Botha (no relation) who died at 83 in March 1966 was one of the captors.

*

Haldane, who was eventually to rise to the rank of full General, has left in his *A Soldier's Saga* a first-hand account of Churchill's demeanour immediately after his capture.

> . . . At this time we were all feeling, not unnaturally, very disconsolate, but Churchill must have been cheered by the thought, which he communicated to me, that what had taken place, though it had caused the temporary loss of his post as war correspondent, would help considerably in opening the door for him to enter the House of Commons. As we trudged along wearily over the damp veldt he remarked to me that in allotting him what I might call the "star turn" I had effaced myself, while his work of clearing the line had brought him into prominence and in full view of the Durban Light Infantry and the railway personnel, and that those of them who had escaped on the engine would not fail to make the most of what they had seen when they got back to Estcourt. He added that

so far as I was concerned he would at first opportunity publish the facts in his newspaper, to which, while thanking him, I replied that being satisfied that I had done my duty and acted in what I considered the wisest way in the circumstances, no explanation as to what had occurred was necessary. . . .

After his escape from Pretoria Churchill rejoined the army and he gave some account of his capture to his friend Atkins of the *Manchester Guardian,* who in his book *The Relief of Ladysmith* published by Methuen in 1900 wrote the following:

He explained how the party in the armoured train came to surrender. "Now mind — no surrender!" Haldane had said as the party left the train to fall back on some cottages. How often I had heard Haldane and Churchill crying out upon the number of prisoners taken in this campaign! But two Tommies waved handkerchiefs without authority, and in a moment the Boers were sweeping round them — it was out of question to fire when the signal had been accepted — "rounding us up," as Churchill said, "like cattle! The greatest indignity of my life!"

When the prisoners had been rounded up they were marched off to the nearest railway station. For an eye-witness account of what happened we are indebted to Dr Keuzenkamp, who wrote in his letter to the author dated 19 March 1963:

. . . It began to rain very hard so we rode to a small railroad station called Modderspruit (Mud Spring). More in order to get the prisoners out of the rain we placed the uniformed prisoners in the Baggage room and Mr Churchill in the ticket office. As I observed the ticket office with its copper bars under which tickets were sold I felt it answered to the appearance of a jail. General Botha told me to watch the door which I did. I could hear the prisoner walking up and down the office.

When a train arrived from the direction of Dundee or Newcastle Mr Churchill was released from the ticket office and placed in the passenger compartment of the train. Passing from the ticket office to the train he spoke to me but being unable to speak English at that time all I could do was to shake my head. . . .

News of Churchill's capture was cabled speedily all around the world; and though Lady Randolph was in Yorkshire, she was soon informed. The first news reached her from Moreton Frewen: later his communications were to prove more tardy than those from other sources. He telegraphed that there was "Unpleasant news capture hundred men from armoured train Ladysmith." The first full account came from the Editor of the *Morning Post* who telegraphed Lady Randolph at her London address; this was forwarded to her in Yorkshire by Jack. The telegram, dated November 16, stated: "I regret to inform you that Mr Winston Churchill has been captured by the Boers: he fought gallantly after an armoured train in which he was travelling had been trapped."

Jack, the next day, again passed on the news:

Jack to Lady Randolph

TELEGRAM

17 November 1899   Edgware Road
Time received 8.55 a.m.

Oliver Borthwick has telegraphed Winston undoubtedly taken prisoner in armoured train Estcourt. He is not wounded and was taken while trying to save wounded. Telegram says his bravery splendid. Dont be frightened. I will be here when you come home.

JACK

*

After a march of two days the captives had reached the small railway station of Modderspruit. From there the journey by rail to Pretoria took the best part of 24 hours. On arrival at the Boer capital the officers were taken to the State Model School while the other ranks were imprisoned in a cantonment on a race course. The State Model School was indeed a model. Opened less than three years before, it had just begun its educational functions when they were cut short by being commandeered by the military authorities as a prison. It still remains a fine solid building, worthy of the sturdy Boers, and after the war it served for many years as a school and stands as a historical monument. A plaque commemorating Churchill's incarceration was put up in 1963.

WSC to Lady Randolph

18 November 1899 Pretoria

Dearest Mamma,

A line to explain that I was captured in the armoured train at Frere on the 15th, with some 50 officers and soldiers and some other noncombatants and platelayers and such like. As I was quite unarmed and in possession of my full credentials as a Press correspondent, I do not imagine they will keep me. They have always treated Press correspondents well and after Majuba Hill the *Morning Post* correspondent was released after a few days detention. You need not be anxious in any way but I trust you will do all in your power to procure my release. After all this is a new experience — as was the heavy shell fire.

Your loving son
WINSTON S. CHURCHILL

PS Cox's should be instructed to cash any cheques I may draw. Their cheques are the ones cashed here easiest. WSC

WSC to Miss Pamela Plowden

(Lytton Papers)

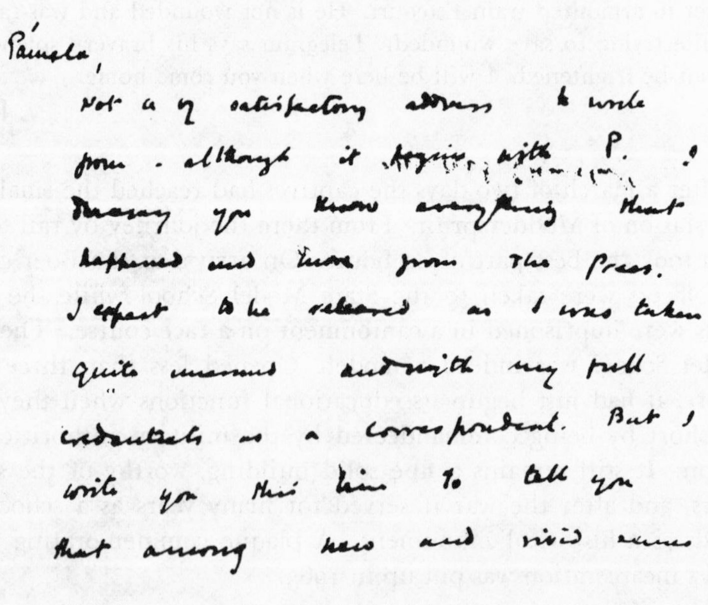
Pamela,
Not a vy satisfactory address to write from – although it begins with P. !
I daresay you know everything that happened and more from the Press.
I expect to be released as I was taken quite unarmed and with my full credentials as a correspondent. But I write you this line to tell you that among new and vivid scenes

18 November [1899]   Pretoria

Pamela,
Not a vy satisfactory address to write from — although it begins
with P. I daresay you know everything that happened and more from
the Press. I expect to be released as I was taken quite unarmed and
with my full credentials as a correspondent. But I write you this
line to tell you that among new and vivid scenes I think often of you.

Yours always
WINSTON S. CHURCHILL

The letter to Lady Randolph reached London on New Year's Day
1900. Churchill had escaped more than a fortnight before. The
reader will observe the care with which Churchill had to write in
these and subsequent letters partly in order to camouflage the somewhat un-civilian role he had played in the action and partly in order
to convey through the censors to the Boer authorities a plausible
argument for his release.

On the same day that Churchill wrote these letters he also began
an artful correspondence with the Boer authorities in the person of
L. de Souza, the Transvaal Republic's Secretary of State for War.
This quite possibly might have secured his release, but it was also
calculated to conceal the plans already being formed for an escape
that would have been far more spectacular than a prosaic release.

WSC to L. de Souza
(*SA Govt Archives*)

18 November 1899   Pretoria

Sir,
1. I was acting as special correspondent of the *Morning Post* newspaper with the detachment of British troops captured by the forces
of the South African Republic on the 15th instant at Frere, Natal,
and conveyed here with the other prisoners.
2. I have the honour to request that I may be set at liberty and permitted to return to the British lines by such *route* as may be considered expedient, and in support of this request I would respectfully
draw the attention of the Secretary of State to the following facts:

   a. I presented my credentials as special correspondent immediately
      after the British force surrendered and desired that they might

be forwarded to the proper authority. This was promised accordingly.

b. I was unarmed.

c. My identity has been clearly established.

3. I desire to state that on my journey from the scene of action to this town I have been treated with much consideration and kindness by the various officers and other burghers of the Republic with whom I have been brought into contact.

I am Sir, Your obedient servant
WINSTON SPENCER CHURCHILL
Special correspondent, *The Morning Post,* London

General P. J. Joubert to F. W. Reitz

(*SA Govt Archives*)

TELEGRAM

(*Translation*)

19 November 1899   Ladysmith

I understand that the son of Lord Churchill maintains that he is only a newspaper reporter and therefore wants the privilege of being released. From a newspaper it appears entirely otherwise and it is for this reason that I urge you that he must be guarded and watched as dangerous for our war; otherwise he can still do us a lot of harm. In one word, he must not be released during the war. It is through his active part that *one section* of the armoured train got away.

[*Note on telegram:*]

The Government will act accordingly. Thereafter the Commandant-General's Office will be instructed to act accordingly. F.W.R. [Reitz] 22.XI.99.

Churchill continued to bombard the Boer authorities, both verbally and in writing, with requests for his release.

WSC to L. de Souza

(*SA Govt Archives*)

26 November 1899   [Pretoria]

Sir,

In further support of my application for release on the grounds that I am a non-combatant and a Press correspondent forwarded to you on the 18th instant, I have the honour to urge the following facts.

1. I have consistently adhered to my character as a press representative, taking no part in the defence of the armoured train and being quite unarmed. Although in any case the *onus probandi* that I have departed from the non-combatant attitude would rest with the Government of the South African Republic, I append hereto a certificate from the officer who commanded the train. I have learned that it is alleged that I took an active part in the said defence. This I deny, although being for an hour and a half exposed in the open to the artillery of the Transvaal force, I naturally did all I could to escape from so perilous a situation and to save my life. Indeed in this aspect my conduct was precisely that of the civilian platelayers & railway servants, who have since been released by your Government.

2. My case while under detention as a prisoner of war has doubtless attracted a great deal of attention abroad and my release would be welcomed as a graceful act of correct international behaviour by the world's press.

3. The kindness and consideration with which I have been treated by the burghers in the field and by various members of the Executive in Pretoria has left a pleasant impression in my mind and if I am released from my mistaken imprisonment, I am at least as likely as anyone else to chronicle the events of the war with truth and fairness.

4. My further detention as a prisoner will most certainly be attributed in Europe and America to the fact that being well known I am regarded as a kind of hostage; and this will excite criticism and even ridicule.

5. I am willing — though I desire to continue my journalistic work — to give any *parole* the Transvaal Government may require *viz* either to continue to observe noncombatant character or to withdraw altogether from South Africa during the war.

6. The *Morning Post* newspaper will pay all expenses the Government of the South African Republic has been or may be put to on my account.

7. I have the honour to request that in the common courtesy of war I may be favoured with an answer to this and my previous application explaining the attitude which the Transvaal authorities propose to adopt respecting me, and the reasons for it.

I am Sir, Your obedient servant
WINSTON SPENCER CHURCHILL
Sp correspondent, *The Morning Post*

Appended Certificate

19 November 1899   Pretoria

I certify on my honour that Mr Winston Churchill, Correspondent of the *Morning Post* accompanied the armoured train on the 15 November as a non-combatant, unarmed and took no part in the defence of the train.

A. HALDANE Captain, Gordon Highlanders

Churchill was continuing to be crafty with the Boer authorities. The Boers were very sensitive to world opinion, on which they much relied. In the testimonial to the good treatment he had received from his captors the Boers had a guarantee that he could not after release complain of ill-usage.

There was a rumour at this time that the Boers might be prepared to exchange prisoners. Churchill was not prepared to forgo this opportunity despite his "non-combatant" status. He wrote on November 30 to Colonel F. W. Stopford, Assistant Adjutant-General at the War Office: "Unless I am regarded for the purpose of exchange as a military officer, I am likely to fall between two stools. Pray do your best for me." Colonel Stopford did not receive the letter until December 28 when he was able to write back: "I am very glad to know that you do not require my help, wh I wd gladly have given." Fifteen years later Churchill was to encounter Stopford again as one of Kitchener's dug-outs commanding a Corps at Suvla Bay. In his *World Crisis* Churchill was impelled to write of the lack of energy with which the successful and unopposed landing at Suvla Bay was to be exploited, thereby stultifying the entire operation.

As to releasing Churchill the local Boer commanders remained adamant.

Captain D. Theron to F. W. Reitz

(SA Govt Archives)

(Translation)

28 November 1899   Colenso

I should like to state that in the *Natal Witness* & *Natal Mercury* of the 17th of this month full reports appeared of the active and prominent part taken by the newspaper reporter Winston Churchill in the battle with the armoured train at Frere Station. Churchill called

for volunteers and led them at a time when the officers were in confusion. According to *Volkstem* and *Standard & Digger News,* he now
claims that he took no part in the battle. That is all lies. He also
refused to stand still until Field-Cornet Oosthuizen warned him to
surrender. He surrendered only when he aimed his gun at him. In
my view Churchill is one of the most dangerous prisoners in our
hands. The Natal papers are making a big hero out of him.

General P. J. Joubert to F. W. Reitz

(SA Govt Archives)

(Translation)

28 November 1899   [Colenso]

I see a rumour in the newspapers that the son of Lord Churchill,
Lieutenant Churchill, reporter of the *Morning Post,* is to be released
by the Government. I object most strongly against this. If this person
is released then any prisoner of war whatever may as well be released for he played a very active part at the armoured train and led
the soldiers in the attempt to let the train escape. He was thus made
a prisoner of war while seriously hampering our operation. He must
therefore be treated like other prisoners of war, and, if necessary, be
even more strictly guarded.

The politicians agreed with the soldiers. Reitz replied: "Your
telegram re Lieutenant Churchill. The Government does not intend
to release Mr Churchill."

On November 30, his twenty-fifth birthday, Churchill wrote two
long letters, one to the Prince of Wales, the other to Bourke Cockran.
Conscious of the censor who was going to read them, Churchill
reiterated in both letters that he regarded his detention as unjustifiable. But while the letter to the Prince gave details of the armoured train action and drew attention to the gallantry of the engine
driver, Churchill permitted himself some reflections of a more general
nature in the letter to Cockran: "I think more experience of war
would make me religious. The powerlessness of the atom is terribly
brought home to me, and from the highest human court of appeals
we feel a great desire to apply to a yet higher authority. Philosophy
cannot convince the bullet." And as a postscript: "I am 25 today —
it is terrible to think how little time remains!"

When the decision of the authorities not to release him was conveyed to Churchill at the beginning of December he realized that he would have to avail himself of other means to secure his release from captivity. Nevertheless, partly no doubt to distract the attention of the authorities from his clandestine preparations, he made one more attempt to obtain his release.

WSC to L. de Souza

(SA Govt Archives)

8 December 1899   Pretoria

Sir,

1. I understand that the question of my release rests ultimately with the commandant general, and I therefore request that my previous application may be forwarded to him so that he may have an opportunity of learning my side of the case.

2. I would point out that I did not fight against the Boer forces, but only assisted in clearing the line from the *debris*. This is precisely what the civilian platelayers and railway staff did. They have since been released.

3. I have now been kept a close prisoner for 24 days.

4. If I am released I will give any *parole* that may be required not to serve against the Republican forces or to give any information affecting the military situation.

I am, Sir, Your obedient servant
WINSTON S. CHURCHILL
Sp correspondent, *The Morning Post*

Joubert remained sceptical; but he seems to have grown weary of the business, and was not prepared to press his objections to Churchill's release any further.

General P. J. Joubert to F. W. Reitz

(SA Govt Archives)

(Translation)

12 December 1899   Volksrust

Referring to the request by Lt Churchill which was forwarded to me, I desire to state that he is entirely unknown to me; and I would not in the least have noticed him if the British newspapers had not mentioned him as being Lt Churchill, with an account of all the highly appreciated services rendered by him in the British Army for years and on different occasions.

These culminated in the attacks on the armoured train, when, owing to his actions, the engine or a section of the train escaped being captured. It is even mentioned in an exaggerated way that but for his presence on the train, not a single Englishman or soldier would have escaped. After the train was forced to a standstill the officers and men would definitely have fallen into enemy hands had he not directed proceedings in such a clever and thorough way, whilst walking alongside the engine, that the train together with its load escaped capture.

All this became known throughout the world, and I suppose the British Empire, through the newspapers. All this however is denied by Mr Churchill, and I have to accept his word in preference to all the journalists and reporters. If I accept his word, then my objections to his release cease. Seeing that a parole was promised him and that he suggested leaving Africa to return to Europe where he would report and speak only the truth of his experiences — and if the Government accepts this and he does so — then I have no further objections to his being set free, without our accepting somebody else in exchange.

P. J. JOUBERT, Commandant
PS Will he tell the truth? He will also be a chip off the old block.

But, by the time this telegram reached the authorities in Pretoria, its content had become irrelevant to the situation.

14

Escape

WHILE THIS PROTRACTED and seemingly abortive correspondence was passing between Churchill and the Boer authorities, plans for escape had from the earliest been afoot in the State Model School. "We thought of nothing else but freedom, and from morn till night we racked our brains to discover a way to escape." The original plan which is described in *My Early Life* in vivid detail was one of breath-taking audacity. It involved nothing less than the 60 British officers seizing control of the State Model School by a *coup de main* in the middle of the night; thereafter liberating 2,000 British other ranks who were in a prisoner-of-war cage a mile and a half away on the race-course; and then, with their aid, seizing control of Pretoria, the Boer capital, together with President Kruger and his Government. This exciting plan had to be abandoned since it was over-ruled by the senior British officers in the State Model School. Though there is no documentary evidence, the plan was so original and it is de-scribed by Churchill with such loving and indeed mouth-watering expectation that the reader may incline to believe that he was its "true and onlie begetter."

While the more grandiose plan was being studied and soon aban-doned, Haldane and "Lieutenant" A. Brockie had been maturing their own plans for a joint escape. Brockie, who was in fact a Regi-mental Sergeant Major in the Imperial Light Horse, but who, on his capture near Ladysmith, had succeeded in passing himself off as a Lieutenant of the Natal Carabineers with the object of being placed in the officers' prisoner-of-war camp, was a Johannesburg man who spoke Afrikaans and a native language also. For this reason he was considered by Haldane essential to his plan of escape. Churchill now sought to attach himself to this enterprise. Haldane was at first reluctant; he considered that Churchill, already a conspicuous and marked man in the State Model School, would have his absence from the camp noticed sooner than others. Eventually Haldane agreed to let Churchill come, but he did not make him privy to every detail of the plan. Brockie had also objected to an addition to the party. Churchill succeeded in persuading Haldane, partly by pointing out that he could after all have got away at the time of attack on the armoured train; and partly because Churchill did not scruple to use the argument that Haldane had expressed himself as very grateful to him for his conduct on that occasion. Brockie was compelled to acquiesce.

The plan that Haldane and Brockie had formulated was to climb out of a circular-shaped latrine in the back yard of the School. The spot was chosen because the electric light did not shine upon it. A sentry normally stood close by, but if he happened to move a few paces away, which he usually did during the dinner hour in order to converse with another sentry patrolling another side of the yard, an attempt to climb over the fencing could be made unobserved.

On December 11 the trio made what proved an unsuccessful attempt. Just before 7 p.m. Haldane and Churchill strolled over to the latrine which abutted on the perimeter of the camp, ahead of Brockie; but after a few minutes' inspection it was plain that there was nothing doing. A sentry was on duty just in front of them. He refused to move. They returned to their quarters.

The following night at the same hour Haldane and Churchill once again went to the latrine. Many accounts, some of them contradictory, have appeared about the exact details of Churchill's escape; in his own contemporary accounts he was compelled to give reports that were necessarily obfuscating in order to protect his comrades in the prison and those who were to help him outside. Churchill's most considered account was not to be put down until 1912 when it became necessary for him to bring an action for libel against *Blackwood's Magazine,* which, having libelled him already in 1900, had incontinently libelled him again. Churchill at that time put on paper his careful recollections of the events. This 1912 memorandum, which has never been published (and the portion in square brackets was not even included in the final version), reads in part:

before the moon rose, Haldane and I both got into the
roundhouse and waited for a chance of climbing over; but
after much hesitation we thought it too dangerous; and
came back to the veranda. Brockie then came up and
asked us why we had not got over. Haldane explained
the difficulty of the sentry's position, and Brockie
said; "You're afraid". Haldane replied: "You can go
and see for yourself". Brockie then went across the
yard, got into the roundhouse, and remained there some
time. Then I said: "I will go back again". I went
across the yard, and at the entrance to the roundhouse
I met Brockie coming out, but we dare not speak to each

. . . Haldane and I both got into the roundhouse and waited for a chance of climbing over, but after much hesitation we could not make up our minds to it, we thought it too dangerous; and came back to the veranda again. Brockie then came up and asked us why we had not got over. Haldane explained the difficulty of the sentry's position, and Brockie said: "You're afraid." Haldane replied: "You can go and see for yourself." Brockie then went across the yard, got into the roundhouse, and remained there some time. Then I said to Haldane: "I will go back again." I went across the yard, and at an entrance to the roundhouse I met Brockie coming out, but we dared not speak to each other in the presence of the sentry, and though he muttered something as he went by, I did not hear what it was. [I had come to the conclusion that we should waste the whole night in hesitations unless the matter were clinched once and for all; and as the sentry turned to light his pipe, I jumped on to the ledge of the wall and in a few seconds had dropped into the garden safely on the other side. Here I crouched down and waited for the others to come.

I expected them to come every minute. My position in the garden was a very anxious one because I had only a few small and leafless bushes to hide behind, and people kept passing to and fro, and the lights of the house were burning. Altogether I waited more than an hour and a half in the garden for the others to join me. Twice a man from the house walked along a path within 7 or 8 yards of me.]

Meanwhile Brockie had rejoined Haldane, had agreed with him that the sentry's position made the attempt too dangerous, and both of them went in to the dining room where the evening meal had already begun. They had not abandoned the attempt for the night, and meant to have another try after dinner.

After I had waited about a quarter of an hour, I managed to attract the attention, by tapping gently, of an officer whose name I forget, who had come to the roundhouse for a private purpose, and told him to tell Haldane that I had succeeded in getting over, and that he must come and make the attempt to join me as soon as he could. Both he and Brockie then came back, and I suppose about half an hour after I had got over, Haldane attempted to climb the wall. Whether he made some slight noise, or just through bad luck, the sentry turned round at the moment and he was seen as his shoulders were about level with the top of the wall by the sentry. The sentry immediately challenged him, levelled his rifle at him, and ordered him to come back, which of course he was forced to do. It was very lucky for him that the sentry was a humane man who gave him a chance to come back instead of firing at once, which at that very close range would probably have been fatal. The sentry seems not to have believed that a serious attempt to escape was in progress, and took no further notice of Haldane once he had come down and gone back to the main building, though he thenceforward changed his position and stood so as to make it quite impossible for anyone to go over the wall without being seen.

Meanwhile, I was waiting in the greatest anxiety in the garden on the other side, and of course knew nothing of all this. At length I heard someone in the roundhouse trying to communicate with me by tapping, and going close to the wall I had a conversation with Haldane who had come to tell me that he had made his attempt and had been stopped by the sentry; that the position of the sentry now made it quite impossible for him or Brockie to follow that night. This was of course a tremendous blow to me and seemed to make my position absolutely hopeless. I could not climb back in because the wall was higher on the outside than on the in, and there was no ledge to help me. Had I attempted to come back, I should have made a tremendous noise and been instantly detected. If I had walked round to the front of the building and given myself up to the sentry, an instant enquiry would have been made and our loophole of escape would have been effectually closed in the future. On the other hand, to go on alone seemed quite hopeless; Brockie with his knowledge of Kaffir and Dutch had been our only chance of buying food without being detected. How was I alone, without any local knowledge, without even a compass or a map, or any fixed plan what to do except to walk by night and hide by day, to cover 300 miles of wild and hostile country to the frontier? So hopeless did this appear that I would gladly have climbed back again had this been possible. Haldane and I discussed the situation in whispers through the chinks in the corrugated iron fence; he quite agreed with me that it was impossible to come back, and that I must go on alone. It was a great disappointment to him to be left behind, but he bade me good-bye and wished me good luck.

I am sure he thought my chances of getting clear away were practically nil, and I took the same view myself. If I had not believed that I was certain to be recaptured, I should never have run the risks which were necessary to success; but I felt that I would have a run for my money and see how far I could get.

I immediately made up my mind not to attempt to walk through the country by night and hide by day, as we had intended to do had we been three together and with Brockie. I did not feel equal to the physical strain, and I was sure I should be starved out if I tried it. One of the few things we knew was that there was a train to Delagoa Bay each night: we had several times discussed the possibilities of getting into this train, but had rejected it on account of the danger, and chosen instead the alternative of walking. I felt, however, that the train was my only chance, though a desperate one.

I had waited in the garden now for one hour and a half, and got up without any attempt at concealment and walked straight out at the gate into the road. Passing another sentry who stood in the roadway at a distance of 2 or 3 yards, in full moonlight and electric light. . . .

The incidents of the next few hours are amply chronicled in *London to Ladysmith,* in the *Strand Magazine* of December 1923 and January 1924, and in *My Early Life.* How he, choosing the middle of the road, walked through the streets of Pretoria humming a tune (not whistling, for this was a habit he always deprecated); how he stumbled unconvinced upon the railway to Delagoa Bay in Portuguese East Africa. How he calculated that his best chance of boarding a train would be 200 yards from the station, when the train would not have gathered much steam, on an uphill gradient, when it would be slowing down, and on an outward curve, when he would be hidden from the view of both the engine driver and the guard. How, when a train came along, he clambered on to its couplings and then on to a truck full of empty coal bags, and how he thought it prudent to descend from the train before first light; how he quenched his thirst at a stream; how a few hours later, sheltering from the sun, he had as his sole companion a hungry looking vulture; and how, when night fell, lost on the veld, and with few resources, he marched resolutely towards the only light he saw.

Thus far in his escape Churchill has been the sole witness: the tale is simple and it needs no unravelling. From now on there are almost as many accounts as there are of his capture with the armoured train. Fortunately these accounts do not markedly differ; but they were set down at many different periods and each narrator was struck by different aspects of the adventure. There is Churchill's full account, first given in the *Strand Magazine* and later in *My Early Life;* there is Captain Haldane's in *How We Escaped from Pretoria* (1901) which is based on first-hand knowledge. There are then the accounts of two of Churchill's rescuers — John Howard, in a letter to the Johannesburg *Star* which he forwarded to Churchill in 1907 and in an interview with the same newspaper in 1923; and Charles A. Burnham, also in a letter to Churchill written in 1908 and in an interview with the *Star* in 1923. And finally, there is the additional information supplied by Howard's son, Mr L. C. B. Howard, to the author in 1963. Some of these accounts have never been published before: the story that follows draws on all of them.

The house which Churchill approached belonged to John Howard, manager of the Transvaal and Delagoa Bay Collieries at Witbank. It was situated near the railway at Balmoral, seventy-five miles to the east of Pretoria and nearly two hundred miles to the west of the frontier with Portuguese East Africa at Komati Poort. Howard had spent the evening playing cards with some neighbours, who had left him about 1 a.m. It was a warm night and he was lying on his bed still awake, when, about 1.30 a.m., he was roused by a knock at his bedroom door which opened on to the verandah. John Howard recalled in 1923:

> . . . I seized my revolver, and then opened the door. I saw before me a man below medium height, and dripping water from the waist. His hair was red, his eyes blue, and his face inclined to be freckled. He said: "Are you an Englishman?" and I in turn asked him what he wanted and who he was. He replied: "I am Dr Bentick. I have fallen off the train and lost my way."
>
> Personally I believed he was a Boer spy, and keeping him covered with my revolver I ordered him into the dining room. He seemed very much knocked about and agitated, and he was no sooner in the dining room than he sank into a chair that was at the head of the table. I stood at the other end, revolver still in hand. I told him it was an insult to my intelligence to say that he had fallen off his train and lost his way on a bright moonlight night. After a little wordy sparring I said to him, "You shan't leave this room without my permission. I advise you to play the open game." You will understand that, believing him to be a Boer spy, I had to be very careful of what I said. His expression at intervals changed, giving place to one of doubt, and eventually determination, when he explained, "I am Winston Churchill."

Churchill then made a clean breast of the matter. According to Churchill, Howard locked the door, came over and shook his hand and exclaimed: "Thank God you have come here! It is the only house for twenty miles where you would not have been handed over, but we are all British here, and we will see you through."

It seems strange that Howard did not instantly guess the identity of his visitor. Churchill's escape had become known at 9.30 a.m. the previous morning and within a few hours an official of the Transvaal Government had called at the mine and given a description of the escaped prisoner-of-war. Howard, in common with a number of other British subjects in the neighbourhood, had assumed Transvaal citizenship a few years before the war; but because they were of British descent and also because their presence was vital to the running of the mine, they were not called up for service with the Boer army when the war broke out. Now, although as a Transvaal citizen

Howard was running a grave risk in harbouring Churchill, he at once started to make plans for the next stage of the escape. He decided to call in a number of his friends and enlist their advice and help. Accordingly, before sunrise, he had assembled John Adams, the secretary of the mine; Dan Dewsnap, the engineer, formerly an Oldham man; and two Scots miners, Joe McKenna, the mine captain, and Joe McHenry. Dr Gillespie, the mine doctor, was also brought into their deliberations.

No detailed plan could be concerted that night, but it was decided that Churchill should be secreted at the bottom of a mine, in a stable that had recently been constructed for the pit ponies. Churchill entered the pithead cage with Howard and Dewsnap:

> Down we shot into the bowels of the earth. At the bottom of the mine were the two Scottish miners with lanterns and a big bundle which afterwards proved to be a mattress and blankets. We walked for some time through the pitchy labyrinth, with frequent turns, twists, and alterations of level, and finally stopped in a sort of chamber where the air was cool and fresh. Here my guide set down his bundle, and Mr Howard handed me a couple of candles, a bottle of whisky, and a box of cigars.
>
> "There's no difficulty about these," he said. "I keep them under lock and key. Now we must plan how to feed you tomorrow."
>
> "Don't you move from here whatever happens," was the parting injunction. "There will be Kaffirs about the mine after daylight, but we shall be on the look-out that none of them wanders this way. None of them has seen anything so far."

Howard's reference to there being no difficulty about the whisky and cigars because they had been under lock and key plainly implied that the servants would not notice their disappearance: on the other hand he was apprehensive that the servants might notice the disappearance of food.

*

Nearly thirty-six hours had now elapsed since Churchill's escape and nearly twenty-four since the authorities had discovered his absence. Haldane recalls how Churchill's departure was discovered:

We made up a dummy which, placed in his bed, had such a natural appearance that early on the morning of the 13th it was invited to accept a cup of coffee by a soldier servant. No reply being vouchsafed, the beverage was placed on a chair. But our attempts to defer the evil hour of discovery were speedily frustrated; for a barber of the town, who, watched by a policeman, plied his trade on certain days in the school, came by appointment at 8 a.m. and failing to find his client, roused suspicion in the mind of his escort. These suspicions were confirmed to Dr Gunning [*the civilian administrator of the camp*], who came himself to see what was the matter. I had endeavoured to get rid of the barber by telling him that he was not required that morning, but, unfortunately, he was an inquisitive, persistent fellow, who was unwilling to depart before earning his expected fee. Dr Gunning came and made inquiries about Churchill's whereabouts but obtained no information.

At 9.30 a.m. when the commandant returned a roll was called, and each prisoner's absence carefully noted. The fact of there being an absentee became apparent.

Churchill had left behind him a letter of a saucy character which the authorities were to read after his flight had become known. The envelope, addressed to the Under-Secretary for War, was marked "p.p.c." — *pour prendre congé*.

WSC to L. de Souza

(Copy: Mrs O. E. de Souza Papers)

11 December 1899   State School Prison
                                                                  Pretoria

Dear Mr de Souza,

I do not concede that your Government was justified in holding me, a press correspondent and a non-combatant, a prisoner and I have consequently resolved to escape. The arrangements I have succeeded in making [in] conjunction with my friends outside are such to give me every confidence.

But I wish, in leaving you thus hastily and unceremoniously, to once more place on record my appreciation of the kindness which has been shown to me and the other prisoners by you, the Commandant and by Dr Gunning, and my admiration of the chivalrous and humane character of the Republican forces.

My views on the general question of the war remain unchanged, but I shall always retain a feeling of high respect for the several classes of burghers I have met and, on reaching the British lines, I will set forth a truthful and impartial account of my experiences in Pretoria.

In conclusion, I desire to express my obligations to you and to hope that when this most grievous and unhappy war shall have come to an end, a state of affairs may be created which shall preserve at once the national pride of the Boers and the security of the British and put a final stop to the rivalry and enmity of both races. Regretting the circumstances have not permitted me to bid you a personal farewell, believe me

Yours vy sincerely
WINSTON S. CHURCHILL

The Commandant of the camp also had to write to Mr. de Souza:

R. W. L. Opperman to L. de Souza

(SA Government Archives)

(Translation)

13 December 1899   Guard Office
                                                State Model School
                                                Pretoria

I have the honour to inform you that one of the prisoners of war escaped during the night (W. S. Churchill, correspondent of the *Morning Post*). During the past 4 or 5 days his behaviour was most unusual. He hardly spoke to any of the other prisoners and dreamily wandered alone around the building.

In my view the only way he could have escaped was by bribing one or more of the guards, because the guards were so placed that it would have been impossible for him to escape without their knowledge.

I have the honour to be
Your Excellency's obedient servant
R. W. L. OPPERMAN

After Churchill's escape a formal enquiry was held by the Boers into its circumstances. No evidence emerged then or since that bribes were offered or taken. The records are preserved in the State and Leyds archives. It appears that these guards were somewhat slack in the execution of their duties. One of them, Guard Bodenstein, told the Court of Enquiry that Churchill often slept on the verandah — it being near Christmas time and very warm. Another, Corporal Scheepers, recalled that Churchill would walk around the compound until three or four o'clock in the morning. There was no roll-call. The guards, though they were described as members of the South African Republic Police, were in fact either too old or too young or too unfit for military service. The Commandant, Opperman, had only been at the State Model School for a month. But the most important fact that emerged from the enquiry was that instead of ten men being on duty as was normal and as was expected, there were for some reason only eight men posted around the State Model School at the time that Churchill escaped, thus leaving unguarded what was to be his bolt-hole.

The letter that Churchill had left for Mr de Souza was deliberately misleading. The references to friends outside immediately made the Boer authorities assume that he had accomplices in Pretoria. The warrant for searching houses in Pretoria which was issued by the Magistrate, P. Maritz Botha, shortly after the escape states that "There is reason to believe that W. Churchill, a prisoner of war who escaped from the building of the Model School, is hidden in a certain house in this town inhabited by certain parties, to be pointed out by Detective Donovan." Detective Donovan must have pointed out a great number of houses that day and in the ensuing night. Mrs Catherine Holmes, who was six years old at the time, recalls in a letter to the author written in 1963: "I can remember clearly waking up in the middle of the night & being very frightened as I could hear my parents talking to a cousin of ours & they seemed to be very excited. Our family of 7 lived in houses next to each other — my grandmother & five uncles & aunts, & our home. As there was a 7 o'clock curfew nobody could be out late & my cousin had crept through the windows of the houses to warn us all that the Boer soldiers were coming to search the houses for Sir Winston. As there had been a lot of looting for food, we had to hide any surplus food so that the soldiers would not confiscate it. This memory is as clear to me as the night it happened."

Some English people living in Pretoria were ordered out of the Transvaal altogether on the pretext that they were suspected of having aided Churchill in his escape. Soon descriptions of Churchill were circulated throughout the country; almost as soon false reports about him having been seen and even recaptured came in to the authorities.

The first description of Churchill stated that he was "about 5 ft 8" or 9", blonde with light thin small moustache, walks with slight stoop, cannot speak any Dutch, during long conversations he occasionally makes a rattling noise [*voggeld* in original] in his throat." It was not until December 18 that the first photographs of Churchill were issued to the police, and a reward of £25 was set on his head, dead or alive.

General Joubert's reaction on hearing of Churchill's escape was to telegraph to the State Secretary in Pretoria on December 15: "With reference to Churchill's escape I [wonder] whether it would not be a good thing to make public the correspondence about the release of Churchill to show the world what a scoundrel he is."

The news of the escape was soon flashed around the world. Oliver Borthwick wrote to Lady Randolph on December 14: "Just received the following from Reuter, 'Churchill escaped.' The country being free from Boers & knowing his practical turn of mind I have no doubt that he knows what he is about and will turn up with an extra chapter of his book finished in a few days time at some English encampment. So do not be uneasy." The news appeared in the morning papers in London on December 15. The bald announcement — a Reuter telegram from Lourenço Marques — was accompanied by speculation in all the newspapers as to what would happen to Churchill if he were recaptured. With stories of his gallant behaviour at the armoured train incident still fresh in their minds, it was considered unlikely that the Boer authorities would treat him leniently. The *Daily Telegraph* commented: "If Mr Churchill is caught the Boers won't let him have the privileges of a prisoner-of-war again. He cannot be shot unless he uses arms to resist capture, but he may be subjected to confinement rigorous enough to control the innate daring and resourcefulness of which he inherits his full share."

His friends must have held their breath fearing recapture on the open veld; but there were not lacking those who, while one of their own fellow countrymen was still on the run, did not scruple to attack him and to encourage the Boers to take reprisals against his fellow prisoners. Thus, the *Daily Nation* (of Dublin) of December 16:

> Mr Winston Churchill's escape is not regarded in military circles as either a brilliant or an honourable exploit. He was captured as a combatant, and, of course, placed under the same parole as the officers taken prisoner. He has, however, chosen to disregard an honourable undertaking, and it would not be surprising if the Pretoria authorities adopted more strenuous measures to prevent such conduct.

General Joubert's wish to have the character of Churchill maligned was thus gratified sooner than he could ever have expected. There has of course always been a noisy pacifist or nationalist element in Britain who are ready to traduce the conduct of their fellow countrymen who are helping to fight their country's battles. Naturally, being silly billies they know nothing of the traditions of the British Army nor in their passionate hatred of their own country do they mind what lies they tell. British officers and troops are not allowed to give their parole — it is indeed laid down that it is their plain duty to escape. It is true — though this was not the point of the *Daily Nation* — that Churchill did not hold a commission and was a civilian war correspondent; he could have given his parole: indeed, he offered it if he were to be released. But since his suggestions were rebuffed, all bets were off. Churchill was not to know that at the very time he was escaping the authorities were considering in a more favourable light the possibility of his release.

During subsequent years Churchill was compelled to bring various legal actions and to issue various statements in denial of the allegation that he "broke his parole." It is a classic example of how the truth can never catch up with lies, particularly when they have been published in the gutter press. Even on the occasion of Churchill's ninetieth birthday the lie was repeated by his wartime colleague, Lord Morrison of Lambeth, in what was supposed to be a television "tribute." In this broadcast Morrison lightly said in answer to a question put to him by Mr Eamonn Andrews: "I think I remember his name in the Boer War where he was taken prisoner and then was put on parole and he broke his parole." Lord Morrison was induced to apologise, and it is only fair to him to recall that he had been a conscientious objector in the first World War and was not deeply imbued with British military traditions.

But in fact few newspapers at the time gave Churchill much chance of success and within two days stories were being published in all the morning and evening papers in London of his reported recapture at Waterval-Boven (complete with picture of the railway station where the capture was effected) or alternatively at Komati Poort.

This seems a convenient moment to dispose of one of the other lies that was to pursue Churchill throughout his career, namely that he had incontinently abandoned his two comrades in escape, Haldane and Brockie, and had dishonourably made off on his own. The account already given shows the absurdity of this; and Haldane, in his contemporary account, made no such suggestion. Nor did his correspondence with Churchill in the next few years indicate that he felt any grievance; indeed, he went out of his way to help Churchill to refute some of the lies with which he was beset.

Haldane, Brockie and Lieutenant Frederick Neil Le Mesurier of the Dublin Fusiliers were themselves to escape three months later in a singularly imaginative fashion. Churchill took the first opportunity of giving an account of this escape, publishing extracts, in *Ian Hamilton's March,* from the diary of Lieutenant Frankland, who had been in the same room as Churchill and the other escapers. Shortly after Churchill's own escape Haldane had devised a plan for making a tunnel from under his room in the State Model School across the road. A trap-door under their floor revealed below a series of compartments about 24 feet by 4 feet and in one of these they began to dig; but after they had made a shaft of about 6 feet they struck water and try as they might to bail it out the shaft was always flooded in the morning and they had to abandon this particular enterprise. Towards the end of February, however, the officers learned that they were to be moved from the State Model School in two days to a new prison in Pretoria. Haldane, Brockie and Le Mesurier decided that they would "go to earth now." They opened the trap-door and disappeared into the compartment below, waiting for the prison to be empty of prisoners and guards when they would merely walk out.

This they did on the night of February 26–27. Unfortunately, it soon became apparent that the prison was not to be vacated as soon as they had hoped. Haldane and his two companions, however, refused to give up, and gradually, with the aid of prisoners in an adjoining room, began tunnelling sideways through two cross walls each 2 feet thick until they dug their way into a large end room whose outer wall lay opposite the yard of a house then used as part of the prison. For nineteen days the three men remained underground, being fed all the time by Frankland and one or two brother officers who were let into the secret. Finally on March 16 the State Model School was evacuated and Haldane, Brockie and Le Mesurier were able to make good their escape and reached Lourenço Marques two weeks later, having followed much the same route as Churchill and having indeed been harboured by Mr Howard and his friends at the Witbank colliery.

A further quotation from Churchill's 1912 memorandum is necessary at this point.

My conscience is absolutely clear on the whole episode; I acted with perfect comradeship and honour the whole way through. I would not consent to escape on the 15th November on the engine while he [Haldane] and others were left behind. I gave up a certain means of escape, with honour and credit, from a scene of disaster, in order to return and fight it out with those who were left behind. I was a party to all the discussions about plans for escape from the very first day of our captivity, and the only reason why I did not decide to go with them until about a week before the time, was that I expected to be released by the Transvaal Government as a civilian. After our attempt on the 11th, we were all fully resolved that we must at all costs get over on the night of the 12th. There was no more agreement, or bargain, or stipulation, as to who should go first, or how we should go, than there is among a dozen people in the hunting field who are waiting to take their turn at an awkward gap. When I had got over, I waited for an hour and a half at imminent risk of recapture, for the others to come, and the fact that they were not able to come seemed to me and seemed to them to deprive me of all reasonable chance of escape.

In these circumstances, it is monstrous that any misunderstanding, however honest, for which I am not in the slightest degree responsible, should be allowed to serve as a basis for the abominable charges and slanders of which I have been repeatedly the object. I have no doubt that every word of the above statement will be corroborated by Captain Frankland of the Dublin Fusiliers who is now at the Staff College. He was taken prisoner with us in the armoured train, and knows the whole circumstances in every detail; and he it was who afterwards rendered a supreme service to Haldane and Brockie by feeding them when they were concealed underground, thus giving up for their benefit his own chance of escape.

Churchill had hoped that Haldane would testify in his action for libel against *Blackwood's Magazine* which was heard before Mr Justice Darling and a special jury on 20 May 1912. Haldane, although he indicated that he would certainly not testify against Churchill, seemed reluctant to testify for him, particularly when it became apparent that the case would be uncontested and that Blackwood's were to apologise. Up till then Haldane, for various reasons, although he did not see very much of Churchill, appeared to be on very good terms with him and had made no complaints about his conduct. But in the year 1924, in his Diary which he re-wrote and amplified in 1935, he set down his account of the affair which shows that he had become embittered and that his grievances had rankled with him. The Diaries of Sir Aylmer Haldane (as he had become in 1918) are preserved in the National Library of Scotland. As they have never been published it seems desirable to make considerable extracts from them so that all may be assured that everything that it has been possible to discover is placed before the reader. The relevant portion of the Diaries, which are published by permission of the late Sir Aylmer Haldane's Trustees, will be found in the Companion Volume. Here let it suffice that Haldane claimed that Brockie could not have allowed Churchill to go it alone: that it had always been inherent in the scheme that it was a three-man and not a one-man job: that Churchill twisted the story to his own advantage and was not entirely truthful in what he subsequently wrote: and that Brockie, Frankland and Le Mesurier would have corroborated Haldane's view of the matter had they been alive.

No one can be sure what would have been Frankland's views at the time Haldane wrote in 1924, for he was killed fighting as a Major on the Gallipoli Peninsula during the First World War. He plainly harboured no resentment against Churchill as late as 1908, for on the occasion of Churchill's marriage he sent him Maxwell's two-volume *Life of Wellington,* handsomely bound in full red morocco with the Churchill arms emblazoned on both of them in gold, and the family motto *Fiel pero desdichado* (Faithful but unfortunate) underneath. A note inserted read: "From J. H. C. Frankland in Memory of November 15th 1899." November 15 was the date of their capture after the armoured train disaster. Haldane's resentment also does not seem to have gone very deep. When his *A Soldier's Saga* was published in 1948 (by Blackwood's) he sent a copy to Churchill with the inscription: "With the profound admiration of an old Ally."

*

It was dark in the mine. When Churchill awoke he felt for his candle but could not find it. He went back to sleep. It was not until the evening that an advancing lantern heralded Howard's return with a chicken and some books; he expressed surprise that Churchill had not lighted his candle. Churchill explained that he could not find it. Howard said: "You cannot have put it under your mattress." He then explained that the rats must have got it.

Howard reported that the Boers were making a widespread search for him, and that he must lie quiet for the moment. Churchill was to spend another two nights and days in the mine, and Howard's greatest anxiety was how to feed him without arousing the suspicion of his Dutch and native servants. The chicken had, it seems, come from Dr Gillespie, who lived some distance away. But soon two young ladies who helped run a boarding house nearby, Ada London and Ellen David, were brought into the plot and it was they who henceforth supplied Churchill with food. On the evening of the third day Churchill was brought up from the mine. His new friends were concerned for his health, and insisted on his taking a walk in the dark. Dr Gillespie was also summoned: he suggested that Churchill should be found accommodation above ground. So it was decided that he should be hidden in the spare room of the office — a sort of storeroom.

The plan to take train to Delagoa Bay was now being concerted.

Mr Charles Burnham, who had also been drawn into the plot, was the local storekeeper, as well as an agent for shipping wool; he had a consignment of bales that was to be put on a train for Lourenço Marques. It was decided to load it on the train leaving Witbank at 11 p.m. on December 19. The idea was that a *cache* should be created among the bales where Churchill could lie in comfort and secrecy.

Churchill was duly smuggled aboard, together with a revolver, two roast chickens, some slices of cold meat, a loaf of bread, a melon and three bottles of cold tea. Fifteen months later eight gold watches, suitably inscribed, were on the way to the Witbank Colliery as a token of Churchill's gratitude to those who had helped him during these six days.

At the last moment Mr Burnham decided, and it was well that he

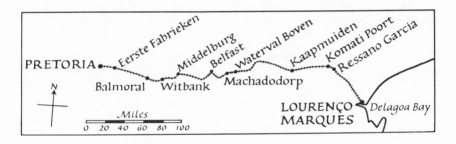

THE RAILWAY TO FREEDOM

did, to accompany the train himself. Later Burnham was to write to Churchill an account of their journey, of which he naturally had seen a great deal more than Churchill:

Charles A. Burnham to WSC

EXTRACT

8 March 1908   Transvaal & Delagoa Bay Collieries
                                              P.O. Witbank

. . . My first obstacle to overcome was at Middleburg where they wanted to shunt your truck into a side track and there leave it until next day, a few drinks and a tip to the shunter soon put him in a good frame of mind, and on we went after a short delay.

The next at Waterval-Onder, when the guard told me that your truck would have to remain there as the next train leaving was not a freight train, I did not argue this point with him but dispensed a bottle of Whisky between the Shunter and the guard taking the next train on; when the time came to leave he told me it was all right he had fixed the trucks on to the passenger train.

When we arrived at Kaap Muiden Station the platform was crowded with armed Boers and on looking out of my compartment I noticed an old Boer leaning against the very truck you were in; it struck me at once that I must get him away at all costs. I at once walked up to him and asked if he could direct me to the Buffet which happened to be just opposite. He looked at me in surprise, and then pointed at it saying, "Why, there is the place." I simply said "Oh yes, will you not join me in a cup of coffee?" Although I had never seen him before in my life, he came at once.

All went smoothly and luck had not deserted us at Komati Poort the border Station where the whole train was searched. I happened to be acquainted with the Chief Detective there, by name, Morris; after a short talk with him he gave orders to his subordinates that nothing belonging to me was to be touched and that the wool was to continue on its journey without interruption; at Ressano Garcia the first station in Portuguese territory, I was disappointed at having to leave you behind, as the Station Master there was the only one on the whole journey who was proof against a bribe. I offered him up to £20 to allow the trucks to continue with the passenger train. All I could get from him was a promise that the trucks would be forwarded on within half an hour; on hearing I wished to wait and continue my journey with you on the goods train but this being against their regulations he would not allow, there was nothing else for me to do but to go on with the passenger train and await your arrival at Lourenço Marques. . . .

Churchill had memorized the names of all the stations, and when he saw through slits of the truck that he had reached Ressàno Garcia, which he knew to be the first station in Portuguese East Africa, he surfaced from the privacy of his bales and "sang and shouted and crowed at the top of my voice." Indeed, he recalls that he was "so carried away by thankfulness and delight that I fired my revolver two or three times in the air as a *feu de joie*. None of these follies led to any evil results."

In the goods yard of Lourenço Marques he was met by the admirable Mr Burnham who, while waiting there, had been arrested by a Portuguese official for "loitering with intent." He had however been quickly released, and now he guided Churchill discreetly to the office of the British Consul. By this time it was late in the afternoon. At the Consulate he was turned away by a secretary, who not unnaturally did not recognise him; he became so angry and made so much noise that the Consul looked out of the window and came down and asked who he was. Thereafter he was warmly welcomed. "A hot bath, clean clothes, an excellent dinner, means of telegraphing, all I could want," he wrote later. "I devoured the file of newspapers which was placed before me. Great events had taken place since I had climbed the walls of the State Model School. The Black Week of the Boer War had descended on the British Army. General Gatacre at Stormberg, Lord Methuen at Magersfontein, and Sir Redvers Buller at Colenso, had all suffered staggering defeats, and casualties on a scale unknown to England since the Crimean War. All this made me eager to rejoin the army, and the Consul himself was no less anxious to get me out of Lourenço Marques which was full of Boers and Boer sympathisers." The steamer *Induna* was sailing that night for Durban. These Boer sympathizers might have sought to kidnap Churchill from the neutral territory of Portuguese East Africa. Anticipating this possibility a group of Churchill's fellow countrymen, "fully armed," spontaneously gathered in the Consulate garden to escort him to the quay and see him safely on board. As it proved, there was no trouble and the *Induna* sailed with Churchill aboard.

On the afternoon of the day after next, December 23, the *Induna* docked at Durban. Churchill arrived to find that he had become world famous overnight. The Black Week of which he had read in Lourenço Marques only served as a sombre backcloth which set off his personal achievement in the most vivid colours. He might well have exclaimed, as Lord Byron did after the publication of *Childe Harold*: "I awoke one morning and found myself famous."

The headlines of the world's press screamed the news: telegrams poured upon him: he was hailed in Durban as a popular hero. The most welcome telegram probably only reached him much later. It was from Miss Plowden to his mother, and read: "Thank God — Pamela."

*

Elated by his ovation from the Durban crowd, one of the most loyal communities of the British Empire, and having made a stirring address from the steps of the Town Hall, Churchill took train the same afternoon to Pietermaritzburg where he stayed the night as the guest of the Governor of Natal, Sir Walter Hely-Hutchinson, and from where on the following morning he set out for the Headquarters of Sir Redvers Buller at Chieveley. "He really is a fine fellow," Buller wrote to Lady Londonderry, "and I must say I admire him greatly. I wish he was leading regular troops instead of writing for a rotten paper."

He spent that night, Christmas Eve, in the platelayers' hut a few hundred yards from the place where he had been captured thirty-six days before.

15

Ladysmith to London

IN AN EXUBERANTLY patriotic mood, doubtless animated by the triumph of his escape, Churchill cabled a dispatch to the *Morning Post* in the course of which he wrote: "More irregular corps are wanted. Are the gentlemen of England all fox-hunting? Why not an English Light Horse? For the sake of our manhood, our devoted colonists, and our dead soldiers, we must persevere with the war." This was not well received in all sections of London society. Churchill himself recalls in *London to Ladysmith* that he received a cable from a London acquaintance saying:

Best friends here hope you won't go making further ass of yourself —
McNEILL

No one seemed to know who McNeill was: it was surmised that he must have been very rich, or he would hardly have spent £3 bandying pleasantries by cable with a complete stranger.

From Chieveley Churchill went up to the forward groups of Buller's army who were preparing to attack the Boer positions around the Tugela River near Colenso. From there he wrote to his mother, on 6 January 1900, that Buller had given him a Lieutenancy in the South African Light Horse without requiring him to abandon his status as a war correspondent. This was most remarkable: it was largely because of his activities as an officer-correspondent in the Omdurman campaign that a rule had been established that the two jobs could not be doubled. Churchill was the first and as far as is known the only individual for whom it was relaxed. This, he added in his artless way, "may have been done to qualify me for some reward they might care to give me." This expectation was to be disappointed; he had already acquired too many enemies.

In his letter he went on to compliment his mother on her "enterprise & energy in coming out to manage the *Maine*." This was a hospital ship which had been provided as a gesture of Anglo-American solidarity by a group of well-wishers in England and New England who raised more than £40,000 in two months. It bore the name of the United States battleship *Maine* which was blown up in Havana Harbour in February 1898, which deed served as a pretext for the Spanish-American war, as a result of which Spain was stripped of her possessions in the Caribbean and the Philippines. "Remember the *Maine*" had become the watchword of the United States during that brief but decisive war.

Churchill went on in the same letter:

> I have another piece of [news] that will surprise you. Jack sailed from England on the 5th and I have obtained him a lieutenancy in the S.A. Light Horse too. I feel the responsibility heavily but I knew he would be longing to come and I think everyone should do something for the country in these times of trouble & crisis. I particularly stipulated that Cassel should agree, and I hope you will not mind.

Jack, who had sailed a few days later than his mother, was by good fortune able to join Lady Randolph and the *Maine* in Cape Town; they sailed together to Durban.

Churchill was to remain in South Africa for another six months. He was to be present at a number of skirmishes around the Tugela River, at the battle of Spion Kop, at Hussar Hill and Potgieter's Ferry. He was to be among the first to enter Ladysmith and, later, Pretoria. He was to accompany General Sir Ian Hamilton's campaign through the Orange Free State and the Transvaal, bicycle through Boer-infested Johannesburg, and finally distinguish himself on reconnaissance at the battle of Diamond Hill. All these incidents have been described in detail in Churchill's contemporary despatches to the *Morning Post,* in *London to Ladysmith* and *Ian Hamilton's March,* and in *My Early Life.* These despatches are fortified in a number of letters which survive to his mother, to his brother, to Miss

Pamela Plowden and to the Colonial Secretary, Mr Joseph Chamberlain.

Churchill ends the letter of January 6 to his mother: "I think a great deal of Pamela; she loves me vy dearly." Four days later, when he had already been in action with Buller's troops in one of the many skirmishes around the Tugela River, he wrote to Miss Plowden:

WSC to Miss Pamela Plowden

(Lytton Papers)

EXTRACT

10 January 1900   Chieveley
Natal

. . . Alas dearest we are again in retreat. Buller started out full of determination to do or die but his courage soon ebbed and we stood still and watched while one poor wretched brigade was pounded and hammered and we were not allowed to help them. I cannot begin to criticise — for I should never stop. If there were any one to take Buller's place I would cut and slash — but there is no well known General who is as big a man as he is and *faute de mieux* we must back him for all he is worth — which at this moment is very little. You will see that my telegrams do not waver or flinch. Nor must anyone in public attack the best men the state can find. I know one great general — but the War Office will not consider him — Sir Bindon Blood — so what is the use of crabbing the man at the wheel.

And the horrible part of it all is that Ladysmith will probably fall and all our brave friends be led off to captivity and shame. Thank God we are going to have one more try — if they will only let us attack instead of pulling us back — we will make a most desperate effort. I pray to God that I may have no thoughts for myself when the time comes — but for you my darling always. Nothing that can happen in Natal can prevent our victory; so be brave and confident and do not let the incidents of war obscure the general trend of events. The Republics are wearing thin. I will write again soon.
Ever your loving and devoted
WINSTON

Even when he recounted the story of the abortive battle of Spion Kop he made every excuse for Buller's indecisiveness in his despatches to the *Morning Post.* In a letter to Miss Plowden, written from Durban on January 28, he gave some hint of the dangers he had encountered: "The scenes on Spion Kop were among the strangest and most terrible I have ever witnessed." And again: "I had five very dangerous days — continually under shell and rifle fire and once the feather on my hat was cut through by a bullet. But in the end I came serenely through."

Miss Plowden had urged him, in her letters, to come home. He understood her anxiety — "though I know you are too wise to be timid." But he dismissed the idea. "For good or ill I am committed and I am content. I do not know whether I shall see the end or not, but I am quite certain that I will not leave Africa till the matter is settled. I should forfeit my self-respect for ever if I tried to shield myself like that behind an easily obtained reputation for courage. No possible advantage politically could compensate — besides believe me none would result . . . but I have a good belief that I am to be of some use and therefore to be spared."

His faith in his star was one of his recurrent themes. No doubt it was encouraged by communications such as the one he received in March from Captain Percy Scott, the Commander of the cruiser *Terrible,* who had landed and transported four 7-inch naval guns for the defence of Ladysmith:

> I am very proud to have met you, because without any luck you have made a wonderful career. Though I did not shake hands with you before I left PMB [Pietermaritzburg] I feel certain that I shall some-day shake hands with you as Prime Minister of England, you possess the two necessary qualifications genius and plod.

Churchill had gone to Durban at the end of January to meet his mother and his brother Jack who were arriving from Cape Town in the *Maine.* "Oh why did you not come out as secretary?" he wrote to Miss Plowden. "Why did you not come out in the *Maine* so that I should be going to meet you now. Perhaps you are wise." Churchill expressed anxiety about his brother. He had taken the responsibility for bringing him out, hoping that at least the relief of Ladysmith would have been effected before he arrived. "But now we have the bloodiest fight of the war immediately before us — a supreme effort to break through the Boer lines."

Churchill's anxiety proved justified sooner than he could have feared. On February 12, in his first action — a minor skirmish during a reconnaissance at Hussar Hill above the Tugela — Jack was shot in the calf by a Boer bullet.

WSC to Lady Randolph

EXTRACT

13 February 1900   Chieveley Camp
                                      Natal

My dearest Mamma,

It is coincidence that one of the first patients on board the *Maine* should be your own son. Jack, who brings this letter, will tell you about the skirmish and the other action he took part in. He behaved very well and pluckily and the Adjutant, the Colonel and his squadron leader speak highly of his conduct. There was for ten minutes quite a hot fire. And we had about ten men hit. Jack's wound is slight though not officially classed as such. The doctors tell me that he will take a month to recover and I advise you not to allow him to go back before he is quite well. He is unhappy at being taken off the board so early in the game and of course it is a great nuisance, but you may be glad with me that he is out of harm's way for a month. There will be a great battle in a few days and his presence — though I would not lift a finger to prevent him — adds much to my anxiety when there is fighting. . . .

J. B. Atkins, Churchill's fellow war correspondent, commented on Jack's wound: "It seemed as though he had paid his brother's debts." Churchill himself wrote, in a letter to Miss Plowden, on February 21: "Here is an instance of Fortune's caprice. There was a very hot fire — bullets hitting the ground or whizzing by in dozens. Jack — whose luck was fresh — was lying down. I was walking about without any cover — I who have tempted fortune so often. Jack was hit. I am glad he is out of harm's way *honourably* for a month."

Slowly, despite the blundering and indecisiveness of the higher command, and at considerable cost in lives, the approaches to Ladysmith were cleared of Boers. "We have advanced," wrote Churchill to Miss Plowden on February 25, "crossed the Tugela and are struggling towards Ladysmith. Very fierce and bloody fighting all day and night. Progress very slow and the danger to the whole army is great . . . I was very nearly killed two hours ago by a shrapnel. But though I was in the full burst God preserved me. Eight men were wounded by it. I wonder whether we shall get through and whether I shall live to see the end." A few days before he had again written: "I am safe — preserved by my strange luck, or the favour of Heaven — which you will — perhaps because I am to be of use."

Churchill entered Ladysmith with the first relief column, on the evening of February 28. With him he had brought a box of food which Miss Plowden had sent to him for her brother-in-law, Major Edgar Lafone. Unfortunately Major Lafone was not well enough to enjoy these delicacies and Churchill had to report that he was impelled to eat them himself. That night he dined with the defender of Ladysmith, Sir George White. Next to him sat Ian Hamilton, and next but one General Hunter. "Never before have I sat in such brave company nor stood so close to a great event."

With the relief of Ladysmith the war in Natal receded north into the fastness of the Drakensberg mountain range. Churchill remained in Ladysmith for some weeks, attending to personal and political matters. Even before the crossing of the Tugela, while he was hotly engaged in the fighting around Spion Kop, he had received a telegram from the Southport Divisional Conservative Association, inviting him to be adopted as Conservative Candidate at the next election. Churchill had wired back from Spearman's Farm: "Impossible decide here." But though he was pressed by the Southport Tories, Churchill decided that his first loyalties, for the moment at any rate, lay with Oldham. He was not unmindful, perhaps, of Mr Dan Dewsnap's words just before he was secreted in the mine at Witbank, when that citizen of Oldham pressed his hand and whispered: "They'll all vote for you next time."

There were also business matters to attend to. Now that he had been taken prisoner and had escaped he considered that the value of his next book, which was *London to Ladysmith*, was far greater than could have been expected when he had originally made a contract with his publishers. "Make sure that I get two thousand pounds on account of the royalties," he told his mother. Then there were offers to write magazine articles and an offer from a lecture agent in

America, Mr Pond, to go on a lecture tour. He even had an idea, which he entrusted to Miss Plowden, of writing a play about the South African war — to be produced by Herbert Beerbohm Tree at Her Majesty's Theatre in the autumn. "It will be perfectly true to life in every respect and the scenic effects should be of such a novel and startling character that the audience will imagine themselves under fire." But Lady Randolph, who had been told of this project by Miss Plowden, discouraged it: "*Honestly* it would not do. People won't stand any war play — you forget how it wld harrow their feelings & it wd be thought bad taste."

*

During his stay in Ladysmith, Churchill was able to read the reviews of his novel *Savrola,* which had been published in New York on February 3 and in London ten days later. Though it was the third of his books to be published, it was, as we have seen, the first which he had begun; its completion, however, had been delayed by *The Malakand Field Force* and *The River War.* The book bore many signs of immaturity; few of the critics pretended there was much originality, though at least one claimed that it had "literary merit of a high order" and quite a few drew a parallel with Disraeli. One of the most detailed and interesting reviews appeared in *The Star*:

> This is Mr Winston Churchill's first novel. It was written in 1897, when the author was three years younger than he is now. It will not add to the reputation he gained by *The River War,* compared with which it is in many respects crude and immature; but it is, nevertheless, a brilliant, witty, and exciting political tale. Mr Churchill follows the Disraelian tradition. He is ambitious; he is a perfect poseur; and he is an adept in the arts of notoriety. He has turned war correspondence into a gigantic advertisement of his modest personality. The novel is a sideshow which, as Dizzy knew, is an excellent means of keeping up public interest. *Savrola* (Longmans) is by way of being a political satire, but it is inchoate, random, and vague in its import. Mr Churchill had not found himself when he wrote it. Laurania, the republic in which the lively events of the story take place, is as nebulous as Ruritania. Indeed, it is more so. It is on the shores of the Mediterranean but whether it is in Europe or

Africa we can hardly make out. It has African colonies and it has
a dispute with Great Britain. It has a fleet, and an army withal,
and a spirited foreign policy. But its nationality is dubious, the
names of its public men being French, Italian, Spanish, and what
not. A revolution is brewing, however, against the Government,
which had refused to give the franchise to the citizens. The story
relates the overthrow of the Government by the rebels. Savrola is a
Disraelian young man, cynical, cultured, philosophic, who leads the
people against the military dictator, Antonio Molara. Molara uses
his beautiful wife as a decoy and a Delilah. But Lucile and Savrola
fall in love with each other, and there are complications.

There is no realisation of the various personages. They are the
stock puppets of brisk romance. We are told that Savrola and Lucile
fall in love, but we are not shown the transitional processes. Tried
by the test of the vitality of the characters, the novel is a failure. But
it is a fairly good specimen of the romantic quick-firing gun. It is
rapid and thrilling, and crammed with fighting.

It would be unfair to give away the plot, but the fighting scenes
are full of movement and the suspense that makes you breathe hard
in your armchair. Tiro's desperate climb along the telephone wires
is, I fancy, a really new spasm. But perhaps the best thing in the
book is Savrola's calm walk across a fire-swept open space, though his
bout with Molara is very full of tingling peril.

> Savrola looked at the pistol barrel, a black spot encircled by a
> ring of bright steel; all the rest of the picture was a blank. He
> could just see the rifling of the barrel; the lands showed faintly.
> That was a wonderful invention — to make a bullet spin as it
> travelled. He imagined it churning his brain with hideous energy.
> He tried to think, to . . .

The writing is unequal. There are vivid flashes, of course, as:

> Civilisation . . . a state of society where moral force begins to
> escape from the tyranny of physical forces.

> Evolution does not say "always" but "ultimately."

When Civilisation degenerates:

> Our morals will be gone, but our Maxims will remain.

Life is a riddle:

> "We shall learn the answer when we die."

> "If I thought that," said Savrola, "I should kill myself tonight out
> of irresistible curiosity."

Of death:
> When the notes of life ring false, men should correct them by referring to the tuning-fork of death.

Of a stupid general:
> A good staff would run him all right, sir; he is very placid and easily led.

Of art and honor:
> Art is to beauty what honor is to honesty, an unnatural allotropic form. Art and honor belong to gentlemen; beauty and honesty are good enough for men.

Here the desire for smartness involves a fallacy. *Does* art belong to "gentlemen?"

There is a tinge of sarcasm in the description of the Government Press. The "Hour" ("the organ of orthodox mediocrity") suggests *The Times,* "The Courtier" ("the respectable morning journal of the upper classes"), the *Morning Post,* the "Diurnal Gusher" ("a paper with enormous circulation," "fruity sentiment," and "morbid imagination"), the *Daily Mail.* The picture of the orator preparing his speech is neat:
> "Instinctively he alliterated." . . . That was a point: could not tautology help it?

But the signs of precocious immaturity are plentiful, e.g. the description of Savrola's library. Mr Churchill selects this sentence from Macaulay — a volume of his essays lay open on the writing table, and "that sublime passage whereby the genius of one man has immortalised the genius of another was marked in pencil":
> And history, while for the warning of vehement, high, and daring natures he notes his many errors, will yet deliberately pronounce that among the eminent men whose bones lie near his, scarcely one has left a more stainless and none a more splendid name.

"Sublime?" Hardly. It is obvious, indeed, that Macaulay has been Mr Churchill's model. His influence is bad, leading to false antitheses and forced emphasis as:
> The rest of the table was occupied by papers on files. The floor, in spite of the ample waste-paper-basket, was littered with scraps. It was the writing-table of a public man.

The floor? Again:
> Her tall figure was instinct with grace, and the almost classic dress she wore enhanced her beauty *and harmonised with her surroundings.*

And here is a split infinitive:
Nor did he care to longer hide from himself the reason.

Yes, Mr Churchill has travelled far in the three years since he wrote *Savrola*.

Most of the reviewers agreed that the "depiction of action" was vivid — "brilliant in the extreme," wrote the local Tory paper, the *Manchester Courier*; but most were also agreed that the delineation of the characters left much to be desired. They complained of the "lack of flesh and bloodness" in the characters, in that of Lucile in particular. As for the love scenes, the *Echo* summed up:

> . . . The novelist, indeed, depends on plenty of fighting and blood-shed to eke out a plot that is singularly slight and not too well elaborated. Add to this that his love scenes are shirked as far as possible, that his heroine, unlike his men, is little more than a lay figure and that his dialogue makes too desperate efforts after intellectuality (and therefore dullness) and you will see that Mr Winston Churchill scarcely possesses at present all the qualifications of a successful romancer. Still as a talented young author's first attempt in an unfamiliar vein, *Savrola* merits being regarded as a novel of undoubted interest and no little promise. . . .

Perhaps there would have been no continuing interest in *Savrola* if Churchill had not subsequently made such a name for himself in the world. But Mr Bryan Magee, writing in *Encounter* in October 1965, observed that *Savrola*

> . . . could quite probably have survived regardless of its authorship. In the library of my old school there is a thumb-blackened copy of the original edition to show that it has done so already for sixty-five years. But today its main interest is extrinsic. Boys may still read it purely for the story, but it is hard for any adult to pick it up who does not now have a greater interest in the author than in the book. However, it is comparatively neglected by adult readers, and this is a pity. It was not written for children, after all, and besides being a good adventure story it throws a fascinating light on its author's early ideas and beliefs which only adults will appreciate. Every writer, whatever his subject, reveals more about himself in

his writing than he intends or even realises. However skilfully he may try to project a certain image of himself he can no more entirely determine the impression his readers form of him than he can jump on his own shadow. The young Churchill was no exception. He was not trying to make the reader think he was a fine fellow — except in one or two respects his book is free from self-consciousness — but he reveals in his novel a great deal about his attitudes to politics, oratory, ambition, power, death, war, army life, religion, philosophy, and relations between the sexes. But the overriding fascination is in his portrayal of the central figure, Savrola.

Any number of things about Savrola, from the books he has read to his way of preparing a speech, are exactly like Winston Churchill. He is the only character with whom the author identifies so completely that no criticism of him is uttered or even implied. He constantly expresses opinions which in the book as a whole the author reveals as his own. Normally it is rash to identify an author with one of his characters, but every reader of this book I have come across gets the impression that here the identification of author with hero is complete — Savrola has the same talents and qualities of character as Churchill has, thinks what Churchill thinks, and one has the irresistible feeling that as a fictional hero he does the things Churchill would like to do. . . .

Later in the same article Magee commented:

. . . The book can be said to contain innumerable vignettes of the author's later self, especially as war leader. "In that scene of confusion and indecision he looked magnificent. His very presence imparted a feeling of confidence to his followers." We see him reading all the newspapers every morning in bed before he gets up. We see him scribbling pungent comments on the official papers submitted to him. In the crucial moment of the fighting, when everything lies in the balance, he calmly takes a nap. The author even sees that his hero's supreme gift is not for original political thought, of which he produces little or none, but for personifying and articulating mass-thoughts and mass-emotions. "Do you think I am what I am, because I have changed all those minds, or because I best express their views? Am I their master or their slave? Believe me, I have no illusions."

*

At this time Churchill received a long and encouraging letter from the Colonial Secretary, Joseph Chamberlain.

Joseph Chamberlain to WSC

2 March 1900   40 Princes' Gardens S.W.

My dear Churchill,

I received your letter of many weeks ago & have kept it ever since on my table. I had no heart to write again as long as the military situation was so unsatisfactory. Now I am full of congratulations — firstly on your good work & clever escape from the Boers; secondly upon the admirable & graphic letters which you have since been sending home; and thirdly & chiefly, on the success which has at last attended our arms.

I read your *River War* with great pleasure, but your next history of an Expedition will be of even greater interest & value.

The lessons of this war are already most important. It has shown that there is no falling off in the bravery & endurance of the rank & file, but our generalship is, I fear, open to some of the criticism which has been so plentifully poured upon it by our foreign critics.

It has also been proved that our extended Empire renders us liable to a strain on our military resources for which we are insufficiently prepared. The whole system must be reviewed after the war, and I hope that one result will be that our War Office will give more attention to the splendid material that we have in our Militia & Volunteers, and will not treat them as they hitherto have done as toy soldiers in peace time & useless in war.

On the whole the Boers seem to have behaved well, to have treated our prisoners & wounded with kindness & to have shown a tenacity & courage beyond all praise.

It has been my conviction all along that they are much less numerous than our people have supposed, but their instinct of self-protection which enables them always to obtain good cover, & their mobility, have assisted them to maintain a successful defence against superior forces.

There has been, even in the worst time of depression, no flinching on the part of the public. On the contrary with each reverse the determination to bring the matter to a final & satisfactory issue has been strengthened. I think this feeling will continue to the end & the Government will have a vast majority at their back in insisting on terms which will for ever prevent a recurrence of this trouble & will place beyond a doubt the supremacy of the British flag in South Africa.

I hope you keep well & wish you continued success & distinction.

I was sorry to see that your brother has been wounded, but I hope, like yourself not seriously.

Believe me, yours very truly
J. CHAMBERLAIN

Churchill replied:

WSC to Joseph Chamberlain

(J. Chamberlain Papers)

7 April 1900   In the train near De Aar

Dear Mr Chamberlain,

It was a great pleasure to me to receive and read your letter and I think it vy kind of you to write when you are so busy and I daresay so anxious.

You will understand how keen were our feelings of joy and triumph to succeed at last in relieving Ladysmith and in bringing food to all our starving friends. I expect indeed that your satisfaction at home was even greater than ours, for it is more painful to read of disasters at a distance when one cannot do anything to restore them and cannot accurately measure their extent than it is to sustain them on the spot. At home people's eyes are fixed on the loss and misfortune and the fact that the army still remains strong and determined is vy often overlooked or forgotten.

I hope, now that it is over, the nation will not complain of the Ladysmith "entanglement" for it makes a fine page in English history and besides it is becoming vy clear that the Boers threw away around Ladysmith their best chance of success. Fancy if they had flung their main strength upon the Cape Colony at the very beginning and stood strictly on the defensive at Laing's Nek. The Natal army which was practically the only strong force in S. Africa would have been unable to get at them and meanwhile every Dutchman from the Orange River to the sea would have risen in rebellion. The Boer doctrine that Natal rightly belongs to them has ruined them, or at least has led them into a most serious error.

I have left Natal, I think for good, and am now on my way to join Lord Roberts at Bloemfontein. The situation has in the last fortnight changed considerably for the worse. The Field Marshal did not surround and destroy Olivier's southern commando because, first, his own cavalry were exhausted and secondly, he did not want to break them up behind him, but rather to allow all his enemies to collect in front. The result has been most unfortunate and the

campaign consequently prolonged. I earnestly hope that the resolve
of the country will not weaken, but I fear that they will regard a
new series of misfortunes, such as may vy easily come to us, as an
anticlimax. However we all have entire confidence in Lord Roberts.
If he cannot carry this war to a prosperous issue, no one else in the
British Empire will be likely to succeed. I hear he has had occasion
to put Lord Kitchener in his place several times and there is no
doubt out here as to who commands the army or whose brain directs
its movements.

I cannot of course come home until the end of the war or at least
until the Transvaal is in our hands: but I shall hope to find a seat
before the dissolution, as I should like to record a vote on many
points which will arise both out of the settlement of S. Africa and
the disturbance of Pall Mall [*the reorganisation of the War Office*].
I have tried to form my own opinion on the state of affairs and
society here without accepting the usual formulas, and in consequence I have many doubts. But I do see three things quite clearly.
The Republics must go: we should not treat with their civil government or negotiate with either President except in his military
capacity: and it will not be possible to effect a satisfactory settlement by means of a [Afrikaner] Bond Ministry.

Touching this last matter, when we have been freely terminating
men's lives, I cannot see why we should hesitate to temporarily
abrogate a constitution.

With all good wishes and my best congratulations on the success
with which you have dealt with your many bitter enemies,

I remain Yours sincerely

WINSTON S. CHURCHILL

*

Churchill had meanwhile become involved in a controversy concerning the treatment that had been meted out to those Boers in
Natal and elsewhere who had rebelled but who were now once again
under British jurisdiction. In a letter to the *Natal Witness,* published on 29 March 1900, he wrote:

. . . I urge generous counsels upon the people of Natal. . . . Many
eyes are' upon you now, all admiring, some reluctantly admiring.
Let not these watching multitudes be surprised and disappointed.
Do not act or speak so that it may be said, "It is true, the Natal
colonists have fought well; but they were drunk with racial animosity. They were brave in battle; but they are spiteful in victory."

Peace and happiness can only come to South Africa through the fusion and concord of the Dutch and British races, who must forever live side by side under the supremacy of Britain. . . .

"I earnestly hope, expect and urge," he wrote in a *Morning Post* despatch at the same time, "that a generous and forgiving policy will be followed." Churchill's appeal met with loud-voiced condemnation. Both the *Morning Post* and the *Natal Witness* wrote editorials in disagreement. In England the Conservative press and some speakers jeered at Churchill; in Natal he became the object of letters of angry abuse and sorrowful criticism. "We can only be true to ourselves by punishing those who have proved untrue," wrote one citizen of Ladysmith. "I am rooted to this country by having four children born in it. You are not. I have to live in this country side by side with the rebels when the British Army leaves it, you will probably be the other side of the world. These are two very important differences."

Jack, who had left hospital and rejoined his Regiment at Ladysmith, wrote to Lady Randolph, who had sailed home in the *Maine* in the middle of March, accompanying a boatload of wounded:

Jack to Lady Randolph

EXTRACT

3 April 1900   Ladysmith

. . . Winston is being severely criticised about his Peaceful telegrams — and everyone here in Natal is going against his views. They say that even if you are going to treat these Boers well after their surrender, this is not the time to say so. For knowing that they will lose nothing and may gain a lot, they may go on fighting. . . .

Sir Walter Hely-Hutchinson, the enlightened Governor of Natal with whom Churchill had made friends, wrote: "Leniency may be the best course. We must be careful, however, not to alienate loyal feeling in South Africa. . . ."

*

Eager to see more fighting, Churchill applied to join the army which Field Marshal Lord Roberts, newly arrived from England, was preparing for a push through the Orange Free State into the heart of the Boer territory, the Transvaal. Churchill believed he had some claim on his goodwill; moreover he was entitled, in common with all war correspondents, to go to the front. Now, for the second time — just as when three years before Churchill had tried to get up to the frontier in India — the Field Marshal proved niggardly with his favours. For a long time after Churchill had applied to be attached as war correspondent he heard nothing. Then, gradually, it became known to him that Lord Roberts did not wish to have him. Two reasons were advanced. First, that Churchill's presence would annoy Roberts's Chief of Staff, none other than Lord Kitchener, who bitterly resented criticism made by Churchill in *The River War*, which had been published the previous November. Secondly, Lord Roberts was displeased with Churchill on account of a criticism he had ventured in one of his despatches of a sermon preached by an army chaplain on the eve of the battle of Vaal Krantz, just after the bloody battle of Spion Kop:

I attended a church parade this morning. What a chance this was for a man of great soul who feared God! On every side were drawn up deep masses of soldiery, rank behind rank — perhaps, in all, five thousand. In the hollow square stood the General, the man on whom everything depended. All around were men who within the week had been face to face with Death, and were going to face him again in a few hours. Life seemed very precarious, in spite of the sunlit landscape. What was it all for? What was the good of human effort? How should it befall a man who died in a quarrel he did not understand? All the anxious questionings of weak spirits. It was one of those occasions when a fine preacher might have given comfort and strength where both were sorely needed, and have printed on many minds a permanent impression. The bridegroom Opportunity had come. But the Church had her lamp untrimmed. A chaplain with a raucous voice discoursed on the details of "The siege and surrender of Jericho." The soldiers froze into apathy, and after a while the formal perfunctory service reached its welcome conclusion.

As I marched home an officer said to me: "Why is it, when the Church spends so much on missionary work among heathens, she does not take the trouble to send good men to preach in time of war? The medical profession is represented by some of its greatest exponents. Why are men's wounded souls left to the care of a village practitioner?" Nor could I answer; but I remembered the venerable figure and noble character of Father Brindle in the River War, and wondered whether Rome was again seizing the opportunity which Canterbury disdained — the opportunity of telling the glad tidings to soldiers about to die. . . .

Lord Roberts felt that the Army chaplains had been unjustly treated, and the very fact that learned divines from cathedral closes all over England had instantly volunteered their services in South Africa only seemed to make the matter worse.

Churchill, however, had two friends at court: General Ian Hamilton and General Nicholson, both intimate confidants of Lord Roberts. Their pleas on Churchill's behalf prevailed, and eventually the Field Marshal's private secretary, Colonel Neville Chamberlain — not the same Neville Chamberlain who went to Munich and later conducted Britain into the Second World War: he never served in the armed forces — wrote:

Colonel Neville Chamberlain to WSC

11 April 1900   Bloemfontein

My dear Churchill,
    Lord Roberts desires me to say that he is willing to permit you to accompany this force as a correspondent—*for your father's sake.*

Yours sincerely
NEVILLE CHAMBERLAIN

"You will form your own opinion," wrote Churchill to his mother, "as to the justice of making me accept as a favour what was already mine as a right."

Roberts continued to ignore Churchill until, nearly six weeks later, the young war correspondent undertook a daring bicycle ride through Boer-held Johannesburg in order to bring to Roberts an important message from Hamilton, and also the first news that Johannesburg was being evacuated by the enemy. Only then did Roberts relent. Churchill had however already softened the ground by relieving the Commander-in-Chief of one of a superfluity of dukes which encumbered his staff. The Radical press had made mock of the fact that Roberts had on his staff the Dukes of Norfolk, Marlborough and Westminster. Churchill took Marlborough off with him on the march with Ian Hamilton.

Churchill first attached himself to the Brigade of Imperial Yeomanry commanded by his old friend and Commanding Officer, Brabazon. It was during the few days he spent with him that he had one of his narrowest escapes in the war — "Indeed," he wrote to his mother afterwards, "I do not think I have ever been so near destruction." He had gone on an impetuous sortie with Captain Angus McNeill and Montmorency's Scouts, racing a contingent of Boers to an important kopje near Dewetsdorp. They had just dismounted at a wire fence about a hundred yards from the summit and were cutting the wire, thinking they were the first to arrive, when from behind some rocks on the summit itself appeared the heads of a dozen Boers — "Grim, hairy, terrible." Young McNeill shouted:

WITH BULLER AND HAMILTON

"Too late, back to the other kopje!" But as Churchill tried to remount, his horse, terrified by the firing, plunged wildly. Churchill lost his stirrup; he tried to jump into the saddle, but the saddle only slipped beneath the animal, which broke away and bolted.

Barely a hundred yards from the enemy, with the rest of the Scouts two hundred yards away by now and no cover for a mile around, Churchill's position seemed hopeless. But as he ran to dodge the bullets, a scout came riding across his front. Churchill describes the incident in his despatch to the *Morning Post*: "A tall man with skull and crossbones badge, and on a pale horse. Death in Revelation but life to me!" Churchill shouted to the scout: "Give me a stirrup." To his surprise he stopped at once and told him to get up behind him. Churchill ran to him, mounted, and away they rode, out of range of the Boer bullets, but not before the scout's horse had been hit. "Oh my poor horse," moaned the trooper. "Never mind," said Churchill, "you've saved my life." "Ah," rejoined the scout, "but it's the horse I'm thinking about."

It was Trooper Clement Roberts who had come to Churchill's rescue. Churchill immediately paid tribute to him in his *Morning Post* despatch. "All the officers were agreed that the man who pulled up in such a situation to help another was worthy of some honourable distinction. Indeed, I have heard that Trooper Roberts — note the name, which seems familiar in this connection — was to have his name considered for the Victoria Cross. As to this I will not pronounce, for I feel some diffidence in writing impartially on a man who certainly saved me from a great danger." But six years later, when Roberts had settled in Cape Colony, he had still received no reward. He wrote to Churchill, who by that time had become Under-Secretary of State for the Colonies, and who sent him £10. What Roberts wanted, however, was not money. Mr R. J. N. Orpen, a local dignitary, who had espoused Roberts's cause, explained to Churchill's cousin Dudley Marjoribanks, who was in the High Commissioner's office at Johannesburg:

R. J. N. Orpen to Captain Dudley Marjoribanks

EXTRACT

4 October 1906   Barkly East
                                                      Cape Colony

. . . what he has so long looked forward to receiving is the much prized Victoria Cross — which he was given to understand he was fully entitled to receive at the time of the battle of Dewetsdorp, but not that he thought at the moment of receiving anything for the humane act he was thankful to be able to perform with some difficulty in rescuing a fellow creature from danger, Mr Roberts wishes also to state that the occurrence was witnessed by many people — officers and men — including General Rundle and General Chermside who were present. Mr Roberts would be very thankful if Mr Churchill, the High Commissioner — and yourself — would put him in the way to get the *Victoria Cross — which is in itself a recommendation through life, and would help his family. . . .*

Churchill had the case reopened, and in 1907 Roberts was awarded the Distinguished Conduct Medal.

Churchill had also recommended the driver, Wagner, and the fireman, Stewart, of the armoured train for some reward. This he was unable to arrange until 1910 when he was Home Secretary and had some patronage at his disposal. He then caused Wagner and his companion Stewart to receive the Albert Medal.

C. Wagner to WSC

6 August 1910   Durban

Sir,

I have the honour to inform you that I have received the Albert Medal for the part I took in the Armoured Train when you were present — as I have no doubt that you have been largely Instrumental in securing this Honour for myself and Mr Stewart — I desire to convey to you my thanks for the trouble and Interest you have taken in us which I can assure you I will always remember. I am still as I was on that memorable occasion a Driver on the N.G.R. [Natal Government Railways] now S.A.R. [South African Railways] and it seems to me as promotion is so slow on the System that I am likely to remain in the same position for the rest of my days. Again thanking you.

I have the honour to be Sir, Your obedient Servant
C. WAGNER

*

At the beginning of May, Churchill, together with his cousin the Duke of Marlborough, had joined General Ian Hamilton's column, which was to make its way through the Orange Free State into the Transvaal on one flank or another of Roberts's army. For this expedition Churchill had equipped himself and Marlborough with a wagon and a team of four horses. There was a false bottom to the wagon in which were installed "the best tinned provisions and alcoholic stimulants which London could supply."

Ian Hamilton's column consisted of:

11,000 men
4,600 horses
8,000 mules
36 field guns
23 machine guns
6 pom-poms

There were only eight small actions in the course of the march, and the four hundred mile advance was accomplished in 45 days including ten days of halts *en route*. Simultaneously Lord Roberts was advancing along an approximately similar axis with the main army of some nine divisions. In all, in order to capture Pretoria, a force of more than 200,000 men was brought into action. The Boers, recognizing that they were being overwhelmed by superior numbers, prudently withdrew their forces to the east.

Pretoria was reached on June 5. Churchill and Marlborough galloped ahead of the main force of Hamilton's column. Churchill's first concern was for the prisoners. He knew that the State Model School had been evacuated, but he quickly found his way to the new prison. There the British prisoners, who had during the night before narrowly prevented the Commandant from moving them away, were waiting anxiously. Lieutenant Frankland records:

> Presently at about half past eight, two figures in khaki came round the corner, crossed the little brook and galloped towards us. Were they Boers come to order our removal? — the advance scouts, perhaps, of a commando to enforce the order! — or were they our friends at last? Yes, thank God! One of the horsemen raised his hat and cheered. There was a wild rush across the enclosure, hoarse discordant yells, and the prisoners tore like madmen to welcome the first of their deliverers.

Who should I see on reaching the gate but Churchill, who, with his cousin, the Duke of Marlborough, had galloped on in front of the army to bring us the good tidings.

Another record of Churchill's arrival is preserved by Mrs Norah C. Brown, of Halifax, Yorkshire, whose father Augustus Melville Goodacre, a Reservist Engineer, wrote in his diary, now in her possession:

. . . suddenly Winston Churchill came galloping over the hill and tore down the Boer flag, and hoisted ours amidst cheers and our people some of which had been in for 6 months or more were free and at once the Boer guards were put inside and our prisoners guard over *them!* It was roarable and splendid. . . .

Thus less than six months after his escape Churchill was back in Pretoria.

While the Army had been marching towards Pretoria, Mafeking was relieved by two flying columns under the command of Colonel Bryan Mahon and Colonel H. C. O. Plumer (the former became a General and C-in-C, Ireland; the latter a Field Marshal and C-in-C, Rhine Army) after a siege lasting 217 days. The London crowds went mad and the word "maffiking" has passed into the language. When, three weeks later, the Boer capital of Pretoria was captured, it seemed to most people that the war was over.

WSC to Lady Randolph

EXTRACT

9 June 1900   Pretoria — Again

. . . Now that Pretoria is taken I propose to come home, although as the line is at present cut by the Boers, and I may possibly go with General Hamilton to Heidelberg, there may be some delay in starting. We shall, I think, fight an action tomorrow, which should have the effect of clearing the country east and north east of Pretoria, and should I come through all right I will seriously turn my face towards home . . .

. . . I need not say how anxious I am to come back to England. Politics, Pamela, finances and books all need my attention. . . .

The action of which he had warned his mother took place two days later and took the name of Diamond Hill. Though the Boer War was to drag on for another two years this was the last engagement in which Churchill was to take part; and he displayed his usual spirit. In 1944 Sir Ian Hamilton wrote in his book *Listening for the Drums*:

... Winston gave the embattled hosts at Diamond Hill an exhibition of conspicuous gallantry (the phrase often used in recommendations for the V.C.) for which he has never received full credit. Here is the story: — My Column, including Broadwood's cavalry and a lot of guns, lay opposite and below a grassy mound, bare of rocks or trees, not unlike our own South Downs where they meet the sea. The crestline was held by the Boer left. The key to the battlefield lay on the summit but nobody knew it until Winston, who had been attached to my column by the High Command, somehow managed to give me the slip and climb this mountain, most of it being dead ground to the Boers lining the crestline as they had to keep their heads down owing to our heavy gunfire. He climbed this mountain as our scouts were trained to climb on the Indian frontier and ensconced himself in a niche not much more than a pistol shot directly below the Boer commandos — no mean feat of arms in broad daylight and one showing a fine trust in the accuracy of our own guns. Had even half a dozen of the Burghers run twenty yards over the brow they could have knocked him off his perch with a volley of stones. Thus it was that from his lofty perch Winston had the nerve to signal me, if I remember right, with his handkerchief on a stick, that if I could only manage to gallop up at the head of my mounted Infantry we ought to be able to rush this summit. . . .

The capture of Diamond Hill meant the winning of the battle, ending as it did with a general retirement by the Boers; also it meant that it was the turning point of the war. The capture of Pretoria had not been the true turning point but rather this battle of Diamond Hill which proved that, humanly speaking, Pretoria would not be retaken. Persistent efforts were made by me to get some mention made or notice taken of Winston's initiative and daring and of how he had grasped the whole layout of the battlefield; but he had two big dislikes against him, — those of Bobs and K. And he had only been a Press Correspondent — they declared — so nothing happened. As it was under me at Guddakalai [*on the Indian frontier*] that he had enjoyed a brief but very strenuous course of study in the art of using ground to best advantage, either for attack or defence, this made me furious with impotent rage and I would like the numbers of pen men who are making good copy out of Winston every day to bear this fact more constantly in mind: that he had his full share of bad luck as well as of good before he reached his present high perch on the political Diamond Hill, where now everyone shouts "Bravo!" each time he opens his mouth.

A month later, on July 4, Churchill, who had paused in Cape Town to have some interesting talks with the British High Commissioner, Sir Alfred Milner, and also a day's fox-hunting with the Duke of Westminster and Milner, sailed for home in the same ship which had brought him out, the *Dunottar Castle*. In eight months he had managed to make a name for himself both at home and abroad. He had established that reputation for courage to which he so ardently aspired: he had made friends as well as enemies in high places: he had confirmed that he could earn his living with his pen: he had learned to think for himself and — that most blessed of all gifts of the statesman — to form independent views: he had matured and developed and now felt fully qualified to mount a more important stage.

16

Oldham and America

CHURCHILL LANDED from the *Dunottar Castle* at Southampton on 20 July 1900. On the voyage home he had occupied himself with completing his forthcoming book, *Ian Hamilton's March,* which largely consisted of his despatches to the *Morning Post.* His previous book, *London to Ladysmith via Pretoria,* had been published five days before the relief of Mafeking; he was to sell 14,000 copies of this in England, the Colonies and America. *Ian Hamilton's March,* also published by Longmans, was not to come out until October. It sold 8,000 copies.

His mother was not at Southampton to greet him. She was on the point of marrying Captain George Cornwallis-West. He was sixteen days older than Churchill and twenty years younger than Lady Randolph and was the most handsome man of his time. Though his sister was soon to marry the Duke of Westminster, he was, after paying Lady Randolph's debts, to be very hard up. Lady Randolph's new marriage was improvident and unsuitable. It lasted on and off for thirteen years until Cornwallis-West left Lady Randolph to marry Mrs Patrick Campbell, the famous and beautiful actress, so glorified by George Bernard Shaw. Mrs Campbell's description of the married state is worthy to be put upon the record: "The deep deep bliss of the double bed after the hurly-burly of the *chaise longue.*"

A General Election was in the air. With Mr Dewsnap's words at the mine still echoing in his ears, Churchill had no Parliamentary thoughts save of Oldham, where he had been defeated at the by-election a year before by 12,770 to 11,477: Churchill had been in a minority of 1,293 votes to the Liberals. On his return to Oldham he received what he described in a letter to his brother as "an extraordinary reception." "Over 10,000 people turned out in the streets with flags and drums beating and shouted themselves hoarse for two hours, and although it was 12 o'clock before I left the Conservative Club, the streets were still crowded with people. I don't think the two Radical members are at all pleased with the idea of my standing against them." Churchill was readopted as the Conservative candidate; and as his running mate they selected Mr C. B. Crisp, a London stockbroker, in place of Mr Mawdsley, the Conservative workingman candidate.

Churchill at once made the necessary preliminary arrangements for the coming election. It had always been thought that the election would take place in October and it was not until September that Parliament was dissolved and that the date of the election was definitely established. George Wyndham, Under-Secretary of State for War, and soon to be Chief Secretary for Ireland, took Churchill to the House of Commons. "I was treated with great civility by many people," he wrote to his brother on July 31. "All sorts of members from Mr Chamberlain downwards came up and generally gave me a very friendly reception. I have greatly improved my position in England by the events of the last year."

Wyndham told Churchill that the War Office had received the official despatch on the armoured train incident (which is quoted on page 447). "I was very favourably spoken of," Churchill wrote to his brother, "but I do not expect I shall get anything out of it, not at any rate the one thing that I want. I have, however, had a very good puff." Wyndham asked Churchill to stay with him in Northumberland, as earlier Lord Rosebery had asked him to stay at The Durdans, Epsom. From both of them he imbibed a good deal of the current political atmosphere.

Churchill quickly found that he was to be in great demand as a speaker, and that he would have to limit his engagements to helping personal friends. He was determined not to make any mistake over Oldham this time. He wrote to his mother on August 12 from Earl Grey's seat:

WSC to Lady Randolph

EXTRACT

12 August 1900   Howick
                                                        Lesbury
                                                        Northumberland

. . . I have had an enormous number of invitations to speak for
people about the country but have had, steadily, to refuse them,
with the exception of Plymouth [*for his cousin Ivor Guest*] on the
17th of this month and Staly Bridge [*for George Wyndham*] on the
28th of September.

I must concentrate all my efforts upon Oldham. I am going to
have a thorough campaign from the 20th to the 23rd of this month,
speaking at 2 or 3 meetings every night upon the African question,
and trotting through Cotton Mills and Iron works by day. . . .

Marlborough, with whom he spent some days at Blenheim, accompanied Churchill on this speaking tour during August. He was also
to give him £400 towards his election expenses and £100 per annum
towards the expenses of registration in his constituency. At the
beginning of September the two of them, together with Ivor Guest,
went to Paris for a few days. They went to see the International
Exhibition on which Churchill had some strictures to make in a
letter to his aunt Leonie:

WSC to Mrs John Leslie

(*Stour Papers*)

EXTRACT

8 September 1900   105 Mount Street

. . . the buildings are fine, the scale is colossal, but the arrangements
do not seem to me to be inspired with any cleverness in catering for
the public taste. Large areas of the Exhibition only resemble parts
of Whiteley's shop; side shows of all kinds are equal to what you
see at a village fair in England; the arrangement of no less than
three people, the ticket seller, the ticket puncher & the ticket collector
at the doorway, shows there is bad business instinct about the whole
concern and I do not wonder that, apart from their manners, the
French have not made a financial success of the enterprise. . . .

It was on this occasion that Marlborough snubbed the Grand Duke
Michael of Russia:

Lady Stanley to Lord Stanley

(Derby Papers)

EXTRACT

9 September 1900   Witherslack

. . . It will amuse you to hear of the D. of Marlborough who is in
Paris with Winston Churchill and accepted to dine one night with
the G.D. Michael. Just before the day came the D. of Marlborough
wrote "my dear Grand Duke, Winston Churchill has made other
arrangements for me so I am sorry I cannot dine with you." Poor
Miche was terribly upset as much by the way he was addressed as by
the scant courtesy of the excuse! . . .

But perhaps the most notable service that Marlborough rendered
to Churchill at this time was to provide him, at least temporarily,
with a home. Lady Randolph had said that she wanted to let 35A
Great Cumberland Place and that after an extended honeymoon she
proposed to live at Salisbury Hall near St Albans. As a result, Churchill had to find new accommodation for himself. Marlborough
generously handed over to him the unexpired two years of a lease
he held on a flat at 105 Mount Street — "fine rooms," he wrote to his
aunt Leonie, "and . . . much more comfortable than I was at Cumberland Place. But of course I no longer live for nothing." He had
written to his aunt to enlist her help in furnishing his new home.
"You cannot imagine how that kind of material arrangement irritates
me," he wrote. "So long as my table is clear and there is plenty of
paper I do not worry about the rest."

Parliament was formally dissolved on September 17 and Churchill
began his election campaign in Oldham two days later. "I prepare
myself for defeat," he wrote to Lord Rosebery. "But yet I cannot
quite exclude the hope of victory." After the first full day of cam-
paigning, Churchill was writing to Lady Randolph: "The excitement
is already great and I have no doubt that before the end of the campaign the town will be in a state of frenzy." He begged his mother
to come down to Oldham to help; as in the campaign of the previous
year he found that feminine assistance was demanded by local cus-

tom. On the very next day, September 21, he again appealed to his mother, who was in Scotland:

WSC to Lady Randolph

EXTRACT

21 September 1900   Crompton Hall

My dear Mamma,

I write again to impress upon you how very useful your presence will be down here providing you really felt equal to coming down and doing some work. Mr Crisp the other candidate has brought his wife down and she is indefatigable, going about trying to secure voters and generally keeping the thing going. I know how many calls there are on your time and from a point of view of pleasure I cannot recommend you to exchange the tranquil air of Scotland for the smoky tumult here, but I think it will be worth your while to see the close of the contest. We shall poll on the 3rd or 4th of next month certainly before the 5th, and in the last three or four days your help and intervention would be useful. They have spoken to me several times have the committee as to whether you would be likely to come down. I need not say that it would be very pleasing to me to see a little more of you in that way. . . .

The campaign was short — shorter even than Churchill had anticipated, for polling day in Oldham was to be October 1. Mr Emmott, the senior Radical member and local mill-owner, was again the most formidable of the other candidates. Mr Runciman, the other Radical member, was a Liberal Imperialist — that is, he belonged to that faction in the Liberal party led by Rosebery, Asquith, Grey and Haldane, that supported the prosecution of the South African war. Churchill had some talk with Runciman before the campaign, and also some correspondence.

Walter Runciman to WSC

EXTRACT

8 August 1900   11 Windsor Terrace
                                                 Newcastle-upon-Tyne

. . . Such are the possibilities of double seats that the success of either of us need not necessarily mean the discomfiture of the other. It would be odd to find that we were to become colleagues!

I fear that is a remote chance and one of us will have to go down.

It is a satisfaction to know that we don't enter in this contest in any ungenerous spirit. . . .

Mr Crisp, Churchill told his mother, was improving every day, "and I think he will finish up by being a very strong candidate, and he certainly means business."

Churchill was by no means convinced that the enthusiasm that was displayed on his triumphant return from the war two months before would be translated into votes:

WSC to Lady Randolph

EXTRACT

21 September 1900   Crompton Hall

. . . I do not feel any great confidence in the result for although there is a great deal of enthusiasm everywhere and although things are better than last time I fear that in this constituency the organisation is still far from perfect as they will insist on managing it themselves, not allowing an expert or paid agent to do the work properly, the consequence is that you get an inefficient organisation. However I am not altogether without hope. . . .

Churchill wrote to Mr Balfour asking him to fulfil a vague promise to come over from Manchester and speak for him, but he did not come. At some inconvenience however — his return journey by railway took more than four hours in the middle of the night — Chamberlain came up from Birmingham to speak on behalf of the son of his old adversary and friend. This khaki election has been described as Chamberlain's election, just as the war had come to be regarded as Chamberlain's war. The Colonial Secretary's appearance on his platform at Oldham, which was probably of more use than Balfour's could have been, must have left a deep impression upon Churchill, for he cherished the memory thirty years later when he came to write *My Early Life*.

. . . There was more enthusiasm over him at this moment than after the Great War for Mr Lloyd George and Sir Douglas Haig combined.

There was at the same time a tremendous opposition; but antagonism had not wholly excluded admiration from their breasts. We drove to our great meeting together in an open carriage. Our friends had filled the theatre; our opponents thronged its approaches. At the door of the theatre our carriage was jammed tight for some minutes in an immense hostile crowd, all groaning and booing at the tops of their voices, and grinning with the excitement of seeing a famous fellow-citizen whom it was their right and duty to oppose. I watched my honoured guest with close attention. He loved the roar of the multitude, and with my father could always say, "I have never feared the English democracy." The blood mantled in his cheek, and his eye as it caught mine twinkled with pure enjoyment. I must explain that in those days we had a real political democracy led by a hierarchy of statesmen, and not a fluid mass distracted by newspapers. There was a structure in which statesmen, electors and the press all played their part. Inside the meeting we were all surprised at Mr Chamberlain's restraint. His soft purring voice and reasoned incisive sentences, for most of which he had a careful note, made a remarkable impression. He spoke for over an hour; but what pleased the audience most was that, having made a mistake in some fact or figure to the prejudice of his opponents, he went back and corrected it, observing that he must not be unfair. All this was before the liquefaction of the British political system had set in. . . .

Churchill was to need all the support he could find. For when the votes came to be counted it was found that the Liberals had retained their over-all majority in Oldham. Only because some 400 electors had split the straight party vote in order to make him one of their choices did Churchill prevail by a small margin. The figures were as follows:

Emmott	12,947
Churchill	12,931
Runciman	12,709
Crisp	12,522

Thus Churchill was returned in Runciman's place by 222 votes. The result was announced shortly before midnight and the morning papers of October 2 all carried the announcement; *The Times*, however, contrived to say that Churchill had been defeated, though it made amends the following day with an apology and a leading article that welcomed his arrival in Parliament.

In those days, when polling in the various constituencies was spread over three weeks, the early results could have a considerable influence on the rest of the country, where polling had not yet taken place. A clear gain by the Conservatives from the Liberals at Oldham naturally put the former in good heart, and a telegram of congratulations from Lord Salisbury was received by Churchill that same night. On the following day Arthur Balfour, who had found it impossible to assist in Oldham, asked Churchill to abandon any idea of returning to London and instead begged him to go to Manchester to speak on his behalf. When he arrived at the hall, Churchill recalled, "the whole meeting rose and shouted at my entry. With his great air the Leader of the House of Commons presented me to the audience. After this I never addressed any but the greatest meetings." For the next three weeks he was the star speaker in tours of marginal constituencies organized for him by the party managers. First, he spent two days at Chamberlain's home, Highbury, Birmingham, being carried from one Midlands meeting to another by special train. Then he travelled widely afield, to wherever the party managers thought he would be most helpful in swaying votes. "Quite a few victories followed in my wake," he recalled. It seemed to him like a triumphal progress.

The Conservatives won a decisive victory, gaining an overall majority of 134. This, it is true, was 18 less than Lord Salisbury's majority in 1895: but that majority had been whittled away by by-elections to the extent of 12 seats (24 on a division), which was now partly made good at the General Election. Many were the letters of congratulation that poured in on the new MP. One of the most delightful came from the gardener at Banstead, the house near Newmarket which Lord Randolph had taken and where Churchill had spent some of his holidays as a schoolboy. It was a far cry from those days:

T. Ranner to WSC

10 October 1900   Banstead Manor

Dear Sir,

I Tommy Ranner, Gardener of Banstead Manor, do heartily congratulate you as being MP of Oldham.

I have many and many a time thought of what you last said to me when leaving the old Manor House and during the past 9 months have talked a lot about you. I said when you was taken prisoner by the Boer's that they would have a D——d hard job to keep you if you was anything like you was when I knew you. And I had an extra glass when you escaped. I am taking a great liberty in writing too you but I know that you will like to know that little old Tommy is still alive and glad to hear of your success.

I remain Dear Sir, Yours Sincerely

TOMMY RANNER

*

Even while he was still in South Africa, Churchill had been attracted by offers to give lectures on the war and on his experiences. First, there had come the offer from Major J. B. Pond, an American agent. In March Churchill had written to his mother asking her to find out about Pond and to make arrangements. "I would not go to the United States unless guaranteed *at least* a thousand pounds a month for three months and I should expect a great deal more. Five thousand pounds is not too much for making oneself so cheap. I beg of you to take the best advice on these matters. I have so much need of money and we cannot afford to throw away a single shilling." The following month came offers to lecture in England. Churchill did not relish the idea: "But you must remember how much money means to me and how much I need it for political expense and other purposes," he wrote to his mother, "and if I can make three thousand pounds by giving a score of lectures in the big towns throughout England on the purely military aspect of the war, it is very hard for me to refuse, but I should like you to ask Mr Balfour and Mr Chamberlain what they may think of such a course and whether it would likely to weaken my political position if I appeared as a paid lecturer on public platforms in this connection."

The reply they gave must have been reassuring, for soon after his return to England, Churchill had set about assiduously collecting eminent men to preside at his lectures in the various cities. Lord Wolseley, still Commander-in-Chief, for the inaugural lecture at St James's Hall in London; Lord Rosebery at Edinburgh; Mr Chamberlain at Birmingham — a local notable to suit every town. Churchill went back to his old school, Harrow, for a practice run for these lectures — "The War as I saw it" — on October 26. He only made £27 there but it was worth-while for another reason: "The lecture requires much condensation," he discovered. "I only got a quarter through my notes in an hour and a half." Evidently he had paced himself more evenly by the time he gave his first public lecture at the St James's Hall on October 30. "It says not a little for his qualities as a lecturer," reported *The Times,* "that for an hour and a half he was able to hold fast the attention of everyone in that very spacious auditorium."

Between October 30 and his twenty-sixth birthday, November 30, Mr Christie's lecture agency (the author lectured under the same auspices more than thirty years later) had arranged twenty-nine lectures throughout the kingdom. His biggest share of the takings was at Liverpool on November 22 where he made £273 14s. 9d. (as against £265 6s. 2d. for a capacity crowd at the St James's Hall), and the next biggest audience appears to have been at Cheltenham on November 30 where Churchill made £220. In all in that month of lecturing in England Churchill's share of the proceeds was £3,782 15s. 5d.

By contrast, the American lecture tour was to prove more exhausting and less rewarding. He arrived in New York on board the *Lucania* on December 8. In Washington, where he was the guest of Senator Chauncey Depew, he met President McKinley; from New York, where he was the guest of his old friend Bourke Cockran, he went to Albany to dine with Governor Theodore Roosevelt — recently elected Vice-Président and soon to become President of the United States following the assassination of McKinley in September 1901. In the United States, as in Britain, Churchill had distinguished men to take the chair for him at his meetings — Mark Twain in New York, Winston Churchill, the American novelist, in Boston. In his introductory speech Mark Twain said:

> I think that England sinned when she got herself into a war in South Africa which she could have avoided, just as we have sinned in getting into a similar war in the Philippines. Mr. Churchill by his

To be good is noble; to teach others how to be good is nobler, & no trouble.

Truly Yours

Mark Twain

Jan. 27, 1901.

father is an Englishman, by his mother he is an American, no doubt a blend that makes the perfect man. England and America; we are kin. And now that we are also kin in sin, there is nothing more to be desired. The harmony is perfect — like Mr Churchill himself, whom I now have the honour to present to you.

Churchill took advantage of his meeting with Mark Twain to get him to sign all of the *Writings of Mark Twain,* the edition was limited to 1,000. All twenty-five — save Volume 12 — survive to this day. But financially the tour was disappointing:

WSC to Lady Randolph

EXTRACT

21 December 1900   Hotel Touraine
                                         Boston

. . . I encountered a great deal of difficulty in starting my tour properly. First of all the interest is not what Maj Pond made out and secondly there is a strong pro-Boer feeling, which has been fomented against me by the leaders of the Dutch, particularly in New York. However, all is now in train, but the profits are small compared to England and so far the result to me as follows:

Philadelphia	£120	
New York	£150	
Newhaven	£ 40	
Washington	£ 50	
Baltimore	£ 35	average about
Boston	£ 66	£50 per lecture
New Bedford	£ 40	
Springfield	£ 30	
Hartford	£ 10	
Fall River	£ 40	

His dissatisfaction was voiced even more emphatically in a letter to his mother written at the turn of the century:

WSC to Lady Randolph

EXTRACT

1 January 1901   Toronto

. . . I was vy glad yesterday to get another letter from you. The lecture tour is by no means the success I had expected, although here in Canada there is a great deal more interest than in the States. Pond's terms are vy grasping compared to Christie's and he has been vy foolish in selling for fixed sums to local agents some of the best towns. For instance he sold Toronto for 500 dollars (£100) and the takings at the door amounted to near £450, out of which on his arrangement I got only £70. Naturally I protested against this sort of thing and we had a most unpleasant squabble. He is a vulgar Yankee impressario and poured a lot of very mendacious statements into the ears of the reporters and the whole business has been discussed in whole columns of all the papers. Peace has, however, been patched up on my terms, and I propose to go through with the tour. I had magnificent audiences in Montreal, Ottawa, & Toronto and had great success with them, but did not benefit financially as I should have done, for the reason explained. Had I been able to forsee all this I would not have come but would have gone on with my tour in

England which was more pleasant & far more profitable. However I shall remain till Feb 2 (when I sail) — making £50 a night clear and perhaps a little more. . . .

Churchill had spent Christmas in Ottawa as the guest of Lord and Lady Minto at Government House. By good fortune or good management, Miss Plowden was there. Shortly before he had returned from South Africa Lady Randolph had written to him from England: "Pamela is devoted to you and if yr love has grown as hers — I have no doubt it is only a question of time for you 2 to marry." Yet by October it was common talk in London society that Churchill had "put off" with Miss Plowden. "Pamela was there," Churchill wrote to his mother from Ottawa, "very pretty and apparently quite happy. We had no painful discussions, but there is no doubt in my mind that she is the only woman I could ever live happily with." Lord Minto reported to Lady Randolph of Winston's visit: "I think he ran no risks here — everything seemed to me to be very tolerably platonic — but I am becoming so humdrum that it is difficult for me to imagine that anyone ever had any other feelings than those of Plato."

Altogether Churchill cleared some £1,600 from his American tour. He wrote to his mother in the same letter:

WSC to Lady Randolph

EXTRACT

1 January 1901   Toronto

. . . I am vy proud of the fact that there is not one person in a million who at my age could have earned £10,000 without any capital in less than two years. But sometimes it is vy unpleasant work. For instance last week, I arrived to lecture in an American town & found Pond had not arranged any public lecture but that I was hired out for £40 to perform at an evening party in a private house — like a conjuror. Several times I have harangued in local theatres to almost empty benches. I have been horribly vulgarised by the odious advertisements Pond and Myrmidons think it necessary to circulate — and only my cynical vein has helped me to go on. . . .

Churchill was on his last lectures in Winnipeg when the news arrived of the death of Queen Victoria:

WSC to Lady Randolph

EXTRACT

22 January 1901   [Winnipeg]

. . . So the Queen is dead. The news reached us at Winnipeg and this city far away among the snows — fourteen hundred miles from any British town of importance began to hang its head and hoist half-masted flags. A great and solemn event: but I am curious to know about the King. Will it entirely revolutionise his way of life? Will he sell his horses and scatter his Jews or will Reuben Sassoon be enshrined among the crown jewels and other regalia? Will he become desperately serious? Will he continue to be friendly to you? Will the Keppel be appointed 1st Lady of the Bedchamber? Write to tell me all about this to Queenstown. (SS *Etruria* leaving New York on the 2nd prox).

I contemplated sending a letter of condolence and congratulations mixed, but I am uncertain how to address it and also whether such procedure would be etiquette. You must tell me. I am most interested and feel rather vulgar about the matter. I should like to know an Emperor and a King. Edward the VIIth — gadzooks what a long way that seems to take one back! I am glad he has got his innings at last, and am most interested to watch how he plays it. . . .

The Queen's funeral took place on February 2. A day of mourning was proclaimed throughout the Empire. On that day, Churchill sailed from New York on the SS *Etruria* for England. He had entered a new century and a new reign.

Genealogical Tables

Table I

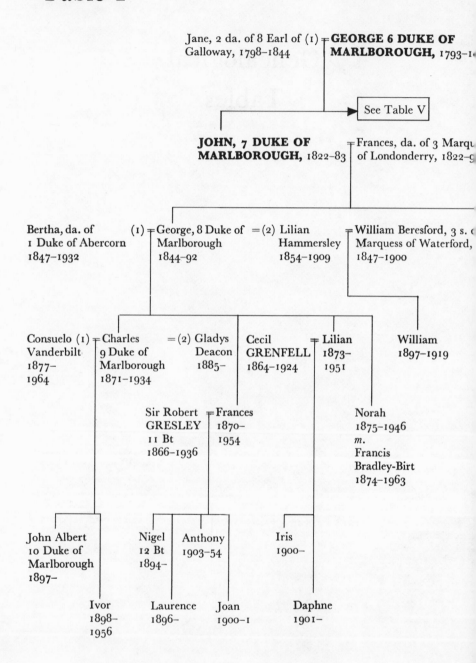

Jane, 2 da. of 8 Earl of (1) ╤ **GEORGE 6 DUKE OF**
Galloway, 1798–1844   **MARLBOROUGH,** 1793–1⸱

See Table V

JOHN, 7 DUKE OF   ╤ Frances, da. of 3 Marqu
MARLBOROUGH, 1822–83   of Londonderry, 1822–⸱

Bertha, da. of   (1) ╤ George, 8 Duke of   = (2) Lilian   ╤ William Beresford, 3 s. ⸱
1 Duke of Abercorn   Marlborough   Hammersley   Marquess of Waterford,
1847–1932   1844–92   1854–1909   1847–1900

Consuelo (1) ╤ Charles   = (2) Gladys   Cecil   ╤ Lilian   William
Vanderbilt   9 Duke of   Deacon   GRENFELL   1873–   1897–1919
1877–   Marlborough   1885–   1864–1924   1951
1964   1871–1934

Sir Robert ╤ Frances   Norah
GRESLEY   1870–   1875–1946
11 Bt   1954   *m.*
1866–1936   Francis
                       Bradley-Birt
                       1874–1963

John Albert   Nigel   Anthony   Iris
10 Duke of   12 Bt   1903–54   1900–
Marlborough   1894–
1897–

Ivor   Laurence   Joan   Daphne
1898–   1896–   1900–1   1901–
1956

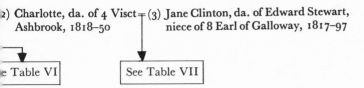

2) Charlotte, da. of 4 Visct ╤ (3) Jane Clinton, da. of Edward Stewart,
    Ashbrook, 1818–50   niece of 8 Earl of Galloway, 1817–97

e Table VI   See Table VII

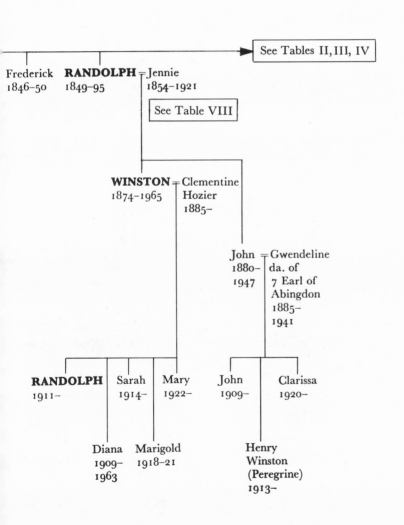

See Tables II, III, IV

Frederick   **RANDOLPH** ╤ Jennie
1846–50   1849–95   1854–1921

See Table VIII

WINSTON ╤ Clementine
1874–1965   Hozier
           1885–

John ╤ Gwendeline
1880–   da. of
1947   7 Earl of
      Abingdon
      1885–
      1941

RANDOLPH   Sarah   Mary   John   Clarissa
1911–   1914–   1922–   1909–   1920–

Diana   Marigold   Henry
1909–   1918–21   Winston
1963   (Peregrine)
                   1913–

Table II

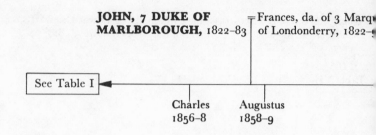

JOHN, 7 DUKE OF MARLBOROUGH, 1822–83 = Frances, da. of 3 Marq of Londonderry, 1822–

See Table I

Charles 1856–8 Augustus 1858–9

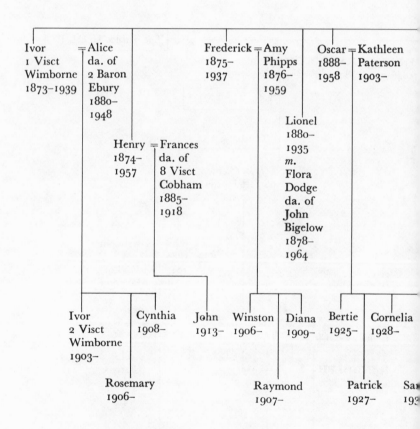

Ivor 1 Visct Wimborne 1873–1939 = Alice da. of 2 Baron Ebury 1880–1948

Frederick 1875–1937 = Amy Phipps 1876–1959

Oscar 1888–1958 = Kathleen Paterson 1903–

Henry 1874–1957 = Frances da. of 8 Visct Cobham 1885–1918

Lionel 1880–1935 m. Flora Dodge da. of John Bigelow 1878–1964

Ivor 2 Visct Wimborne 1903–

Cynthia 1908–

John 1913–

Winston 1906–

Diana 1909–

Bertie 1925–

Cornelia 1928–

Rosemary 1906–

Raymond 1907–

Patrick 1927–

Sa 19

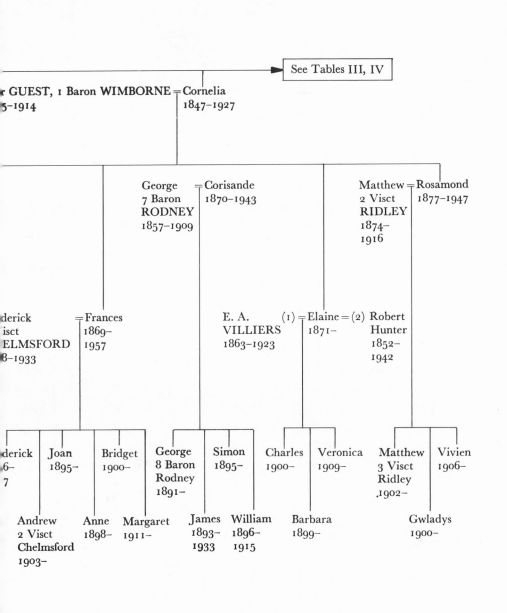

See Tables III, IV

GUEST, 1 Baron WIMBORNE = Cornelia
5–1914   1847–1927

George = Corisande   Matthew = Rosamond
7 Baron 1870–1943   2 Visct   1877–1947
RODNEY   RIDLEY
1857–1909   1874–
                            1916

derick = Frances   E. A.   (1) = Elaine = (2) Robert
isct   1869–   VILLIERS   1871–   Hunter
ELMSFORD 1957   1863–1923   1852–
8–1933   1942

derick Joan   Bridget   George   Simon   Charles Veronica   Matthew   Vivien
6–   1895– 1900–   8 Baron   1895–   1900–   1909–   3 Visct   1906–
7   Rodney   Ridley
                         1891–   .1902–

    Andrew   Anne   Margaret   James   William   Barbara   Gwladys
    2 Visct 1898– 1911–   1893–   1896–   1899–   1900–
    Chelmsford   1933   1915
    1903–

Table III

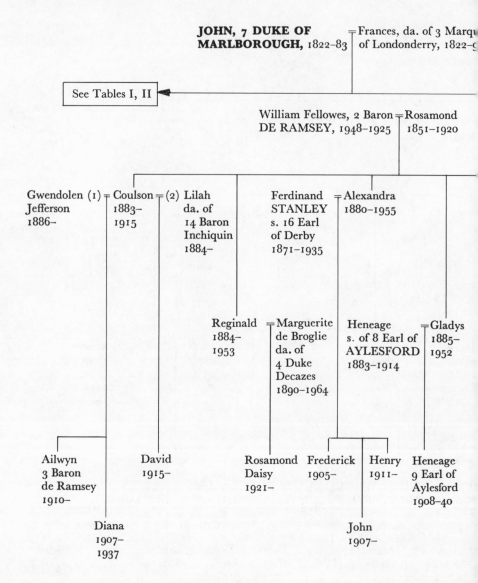

JOHN, 7 DUKE OF
MARLBOROUGH, 1822–83 ╤ Frances, da. of 3 Marqu
of Londonderry, 1822–9

See Tables I, II

William Fellowes, 2 Baron ╤ Rosamond
DE RAMSEY, 1948–1925 1851–1920

Gwendolen (1) ╤ Coulson ╤ (2) Lilah
Jefferson   1883–   da. of
1886–   1915   14 Baron
                              Inchiquin
                              1884–

Ferdinand ╤ Alexandra
STANLEY   1880–1955
s. 16 Earl
of Derby
1871–1935

Reginald ╤ Marguerite
1884–   de Broglie
1953   da. of
           4 Duke
           Decazes
           1890–1964

Heneage   ╤ Gladys
s. of 8 Earl of 1885–
AYLESFORD   1952
1883–1914

Ailwyn
3 Baron
de Ramsey
1910–

David
1915–

Rosamond Frederick Henry   Heneage
Daisy   1905–   1911–   9 Earl of
1921–   Aylesford
                             1908–40

Diana
1907–
1937

John
1907–

See Table IV

Edward, 2 Baron TWEEDMOUTH ⊤ Fanny
1849–1909   1853–1904

ne   (1) ⊤ Hermione ⊤ (2) Baron   Dudley   ⊤ Muriel
•RDON-   1886–   Rudolf   3 Baron   da. of
NNOX   Cederstrom   Tweedmouth   2 Earl
f 7   1871–1947   1874–1935   Midleton
ke of   1881–
hmond
5–1949

                              James, 5   ⊤ Sybil
                              Marquess of   1888–
                              ORMONDE   1948
                              1890–1949

Reginald   Brita   James   Moyra
1910–   1924–   1916–   1902–
                            1940

                            Moyra   Joan
                            1920–   1906–
                            1959

Table IV

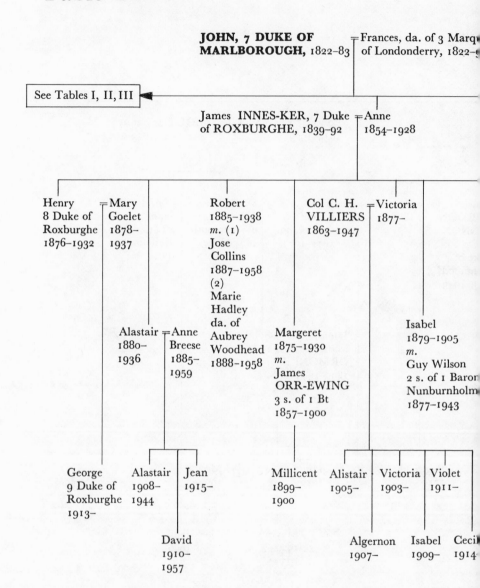

JOHN, 7 DUKE OF MARLBOROUGH, 1822–83 ⊤ Frances, da. of 3 Marq⧧ of Londonderry, 1822–⧧

See Tables I, II, III ◄

James INNES-KER, 7 Duke of ROXBURGHE, 1839–92 ⊤ Anne 1854–1928

Henry 8 Duke of Roxburghe 1876–1932 ⊤ Mary Goelet 1878–1937

Robert 1885–1938 m. (1) Jose Collins 1887–1958 (2) Marie Hadley da. of Aubrey Woodhead 1888–1958

Col C. H. VILLIERS 1863–1947 ⊤ Victoria 1877–

Alastair 1880–1936 ⊤ Anne Breese 1885–1959

Margeret 1875–1930 m. James ORR-EWING 3 s. of 1 Bt 1857–1900

Isabel 1879–1905 m. Guy Wilson 2 s. of 1 Baron Nunburnholm⧧ 1877–1943

George 9 Duke of Roxburghe 1913–

Alastair 1908–1944

Jean 1915–

Millicent 1899–1900

Alistair 1905–

Victoria 1903–

Violet 1911–

David 1910–1957

Algernon 1907–

Isabel 1909–

Cecil 1914⧧

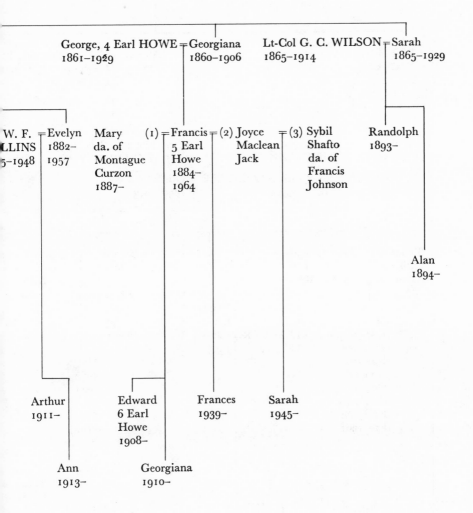

George, 4 Earl HOWE = Georgiana   Lt-Col G. C. WILSON = Sarah
1861–1929   1860–1906   1865–1914   1865–1929

W. F. = Evelyn   Mary   (1) = Francis = (2) Joyce   = (3) Sybil   Randolph
LLINS   1882–   da. of   5 Earl   Maclean   Shafto   1893–
5–1948   1957   Montague   Howe   Jack   da. of
              Curzon   1884–   Francis
              1887–   1964   Johnson

Alan
1894–

Arthur   Edward   Frances   Sarah
1911–   6 Earl   1939–   1945–
            Howe
            1908–

Ann   Georgiana
1913–   1910–

Table V

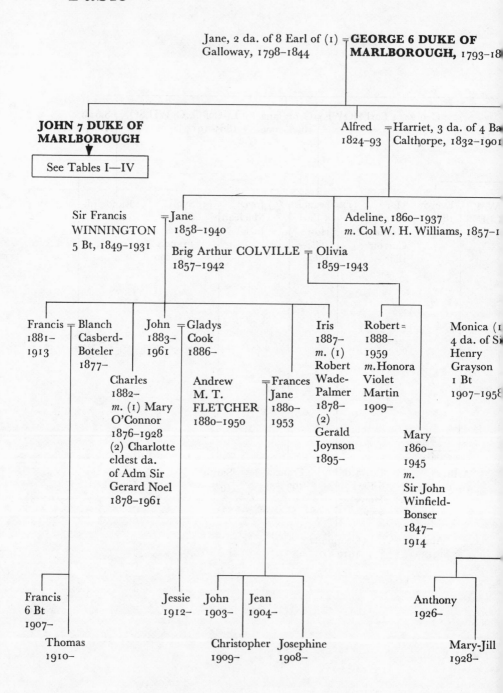

Jane, 2 da. of 8 Earl of (1) = **GEORGE 6 DUKE OF**
Galloway, 1798–1844   **MARLBOROUGH,** 1793–18

JOHN 7 DUKE OF
MARLBOROUGH

See Tables I—IV

Alfred = Harriet, 3 da. of 4 Ba
1824–93   Calthorpe, 1832–1901

Sir Francis = Jane
WINNINGTON   1858–1940
5 Bt, 1849–1931

Brig Arthur COLVILLE = Olivia
1857–1942   1859–1943

Adeline, 1860–1937
m. Col W. H. Williams, 1857–1

Francis = Blanch
1881–   Casberd-
1913   Boteler
     1877–

Charles
1882–
m. (1) Mary
O'Connor
1876–1928
(2) Charlotte
eldest da.
of Adm Sir
Gerard Noel
1878–1961

John = Gladys
1883–   Cook
1961   1886–

Andrew   = Frances
M. T.   Jane
FLETCHER   1880–
1880–1950   1953

Iris
1887–
m. (1)
Robert
Wade-
Palmer
1878–
(2)
Gerald
Joynson
1895–

Robert =
1888–
1959
m. Honora
Violet
Martin
1909–

Mary
1860–
1945
m.
Sir John
Winfield-
Bonser
1847–
1914

Monica (1
4 da. of S
Henry
Grayson
1 Bt
1907–1958

Francis
6 Bt
1907–

Thomas
1910–

Jessie
1912–

John
1903–

Jean
1904–

Christopher Josephine
1909–   1908–

Anthony
1926–

Mary-Jill
1928–

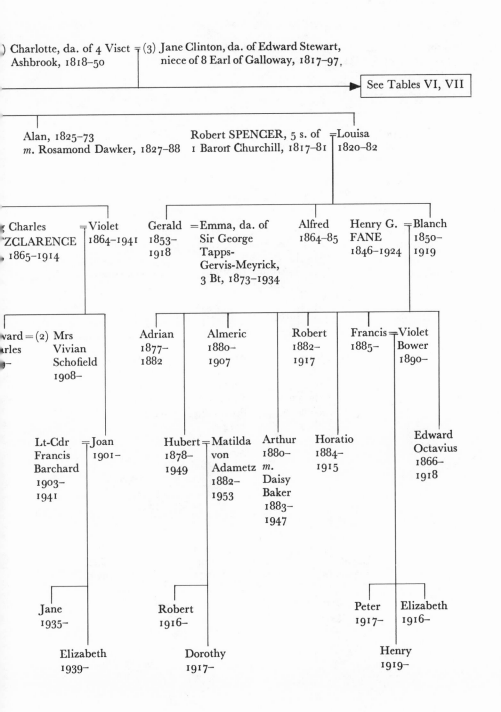

) Charlotte, da. of 4 Visct ⊤(3) Jane Clinton, da. of Edward Stewart,
Ashbrook, 1818–50   niece of 8 Earl of Galloway, 1817–97.

See Tables VI, VII

Alan, 1825–73   Robert SPENCER, 5 s. of ⊤Louisa
m. Rosamond Dawker, 1827–88   1 Baron Churchill, 1817–81 1820–82

; Charles   ⊤Violet   Gerald   =Emma, da. of   Alfred   Henry G. ⊤Blanch
ʼZCLARENCE   1864–1941   1853–   Sir George   1864–85   FANE   1850–
, 1865–1914   1918   Tapps-   1846–1924 1919
                                    Gervis-Meyrick,
                                    3 Bt, 1873–1934

vard =(2) Mrs   Adrian   Almeric   Robert   Francis =Violet
ırles   Vivian   1877–   1880–   1882–   1885–   Bower
ı–   Schofield 1882   1907   1917   1890–
           1908–

Lt-Cdr   =Joan   Hubert=Matilda   Arthur   Horatio   Edward
Francis   1901–   1878– von   1880–   1884–   Octavius
Barchard   1949   Adametz   m.   1915   1866–
1903–   1882–   Daisy   1918
1941   1953   Baker
                                      1883–
                                      1947

Jane   Robert   Peter   Elizabeth
1935–   1916–   1917–   1916–

Elizabeth   Dorothy   Henry
1939–   1917–   1919–

Table VI

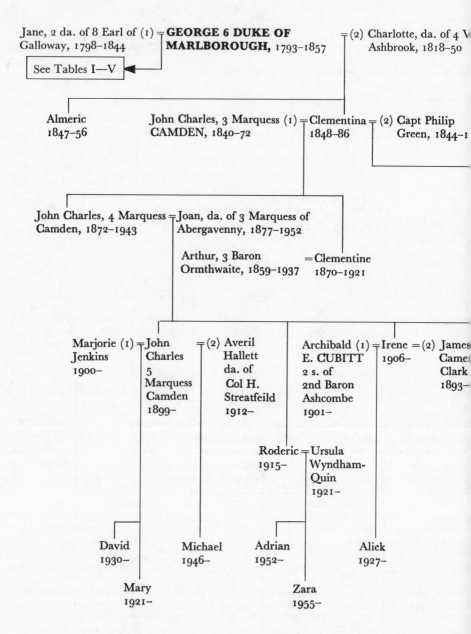

Jane, 2 da. of 8 Earl of (1) ⚭ **GEORGE 6 DUKE OF**   ⚭ (2) Charlotte, da. of 4 V
Galloway, 1798–1844   **MARLBOROUGH,** 1793–1857   Ashbrook, 1818–50

See Tables I—V

Almeric   John Charles, 3 Marquess (1) ⚭ Clementina ⚭ (2) Capt Philip
1847–56   CAMDEN, 1840–72   1848–86   Green, 1844–1

John Charles, 4 Marquess ⚭ Joan, da. of 3 Marquess of
Camden, 1872–1943   Abergavenny, 1877–1952

Arthur, 3 Baron   = Clementine
Ormthwaite, 1859–1937   1870–1921

Marjorie (1) ⚭ John   ⚭ (2) Averil   Archibald (1) ⚭ Irene = (2) James
Jenkins   Charles   Hallett   E. CUBITT   1906–   Came
1900–   5   da. of   2 s. of   Clark
   Marquess   Col H.   2nd Baron   1893–
   Camden   Streatfeild   Ashcombe
   1899–   1912–   1901–

Roderic ⚭ Ursula
1915–   Wyndham-
   Quin
   1921–

David   Michael   Adrian   Alick
1930–   1946–   1952–   1927–

Mary   Zara
1921–   1955–

) Jane Clinton, da. of Edward Stewart,
 niece of 8 Earl of Galloway, 1817–97

→ | See Table VII |

:lyn, 1881–   , *m.* (1) Col Paul LEVKOVIC, 1874–
                    (2) Luke Hansard, *d.* 1927

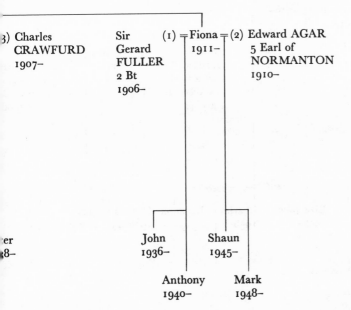

3) Charles   Sir   (1) ⲧFionaⲧ(2) Edward AGAR
   CRAWFURD   Gerard   1911–   5 Earl of
   1907–   FULLER   NORMANTON
                    2 Bt   1910–
                    1906–

:er   John   Shaun
8–   1936–   1945–

                         Anthony   Mark
                         1940–   1948–

Table VII

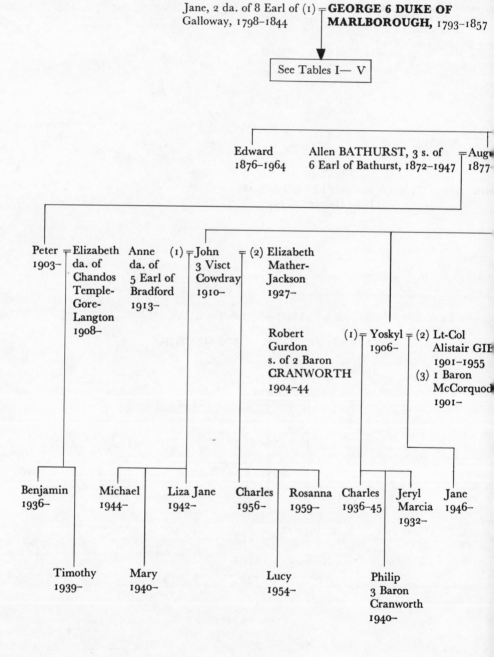

Jane, 2 da. of 8 Earl of (1) ⚭ **GEORGE 6 DUKE OF**
Galloway, 1798–1844   **MARLBOROUGH,** 1793–1857

See Tables I— V

Edward   Allen BATHURST, 3 s. of   ⚭Aug
1876–1964   6 Earl of Bathurst, 1872–1947   1877

Peter ⚭Elizabeth   Anne   (1) ⚭John   ⚭ (2) Elizabeth
1903–   da. of   da. of   3 Visct   Mather-
     Chandos   5 Earl of   Cowdray   Jackson
     Temple-   Bradford   1910–   1927–
     Gore-   1913–
     Langton
     1908–

Robert   (1) ⚭ Yoskyl ⚭ (2) Lt-Col
Gurdon   1906–   Alistair GIB
s. of 2 Baron   1901–1955
CRANWORTH   (3) 1 Baron
1904–44   McCorquod
                   1901–

Benjamin   Michael   Liza Jane   Charles   Rosanna   Charles   Jeryl   Jane
1936–   1944–   1942–   1956–   1959–   1936–45   Marcia   1946–
                                                                    1932–

Timothy   Mary   Lucy   Philip
1939–   1940–   1954–   3 Baron
                                             Cranworth
                                             1940–

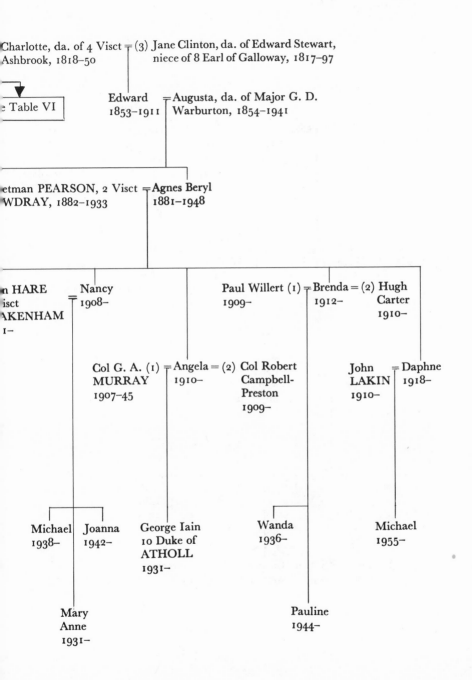

Charlotte, da. of 4 Visct = (3) Jane Clinton, da. of Edward Stewart,
Ashbrook, 1818–50   niece of 8 Earl of Galloway, 1817–97

e Table VI

Edward   = Augusta, da. of Major G. D.
1853–1911 | Warburton, 1854–1941

etman PEARSON, 2 Visct = Agnes Beryl
WDRAY, 1882–1933   1881–1948

n HARE   Nancy   Paul Willert (1) = Brenda = (2) Hugh
isct   = 1908–   1909–   1912–   Carter
KENHAM   1910–
1–

Col G. A. (1) = Angela = (2) Col Robert   John   = Daphne
MURRAY   1910–   Campbell-   LAKIN   1918–
1907–45   Preston   1910–
1909–

Michael   Joanna   George Iain   Wanda   Michael
1938–   1942–   10 Duke of   1936–   1955–
ATHOLL
1931–

Mary   Pauline
Anne   1944–
1931–

Table VIII

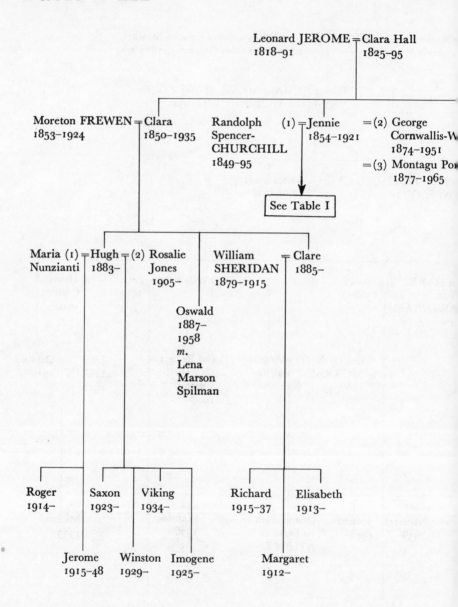

Leonard JEROME = Clara Hall
1818–91   1825–95

Moreton FREWEN = Clara
1853–1924   1850–1935

Randolph   (1) = Jennie   = (2) George
Spencer-   1854–1921   Cornwallis-W
CHURCHILL   1874–1951
1849–95   = (3) Montagu Po
                                     1877–1965

See Table I

Maria (1) = Hugh = (2) Rosalie   William   = Clare
Nunzianti   1883–   Jones   SHERIDAN   1885–
                      1905–   1879–1915

Oswald
1887–
1958
m.
Lena
Marson
Spilman

Roger   Saxon   Viking   Richard   Elisabeth
1914–   1923–   1934–   1915–37   1913–

        Jerome   Winston Imogene   Margaret
        1915–48   1929–   1925–   1912–

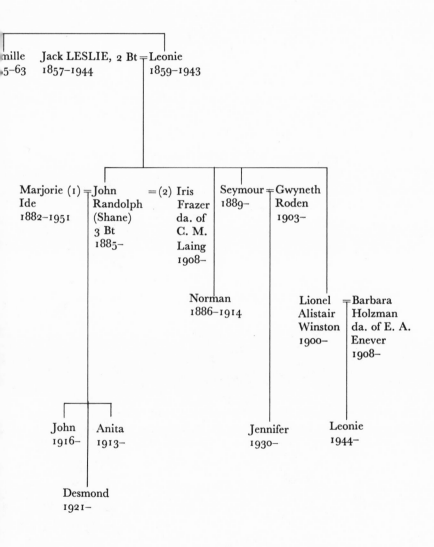

mille   Jack LESLIE, 2 Bt ╤ Leonie
5–63   1857–1944   1859–1943

Marjorie (1) ╤ John   = (2) Iris   Seymour ╤ Gwyneth
Ide   Randolph   Frazer   1889–   Roden
1882–1951   (Shane)   da. of   1903–
               3 Bt   C. M.
               1885–   Laing
                                   1908–

                             Norman   Lionel   ╤ Barbara
                             1886–1914   Alistair   Holzman
                                                      Winston   da. of E. A.
                                                      1900–   Enever
                                                                   1908–

John   Anita   Jennifer   Leonie
1916–   1913–   1930–   1944–

Desmond
1921–

Index

Index

COMPILED BY G. NORMAN KNIGHT, M.A.

CHAIRMAN OF THE SOCIETY OF INDEXERS

The name of Winston Churchill occurs on almost every page of the text. To avoid unnecessary overloading the entry under this name has not been made a table of contents of the entire volume but has been confined to those headings which cannot be readily found under other entries.

Throughout the index his name has been abbreviated to WSC and that of his son, the author, to RSC.

CAPITALS for a surname denote that it is the subject of a short biography between page xxvii and page xxxviii.

Page reference numbers in **bold type** indicate that more than a few lines are devoted to the subject. Reference numbers in *italics* indicate illustrations or their captions, or maps. *qv* stands for *quod vide* (which see).

bis after a reference number denotes that the item is quite separately mentioned twice on the same page of the text, and *ter* three times. *q.* stands for "quoted." *passim* denotes that the references are scattered.

Subheadings have been arranged mainly in chronological order.

The method of alphabetical arrangement is word-by-word.

Northcote, Sir Stafford—*continued*
St James's Place (1880), 39; his Diary quoted on Prince of Wales's attitude to Lord Randolph, 39–40; his position as Leader of the House is undermined by Lord Randolph's intervention over Bradlaugh (1882), 42–3; Conservative party leadership is divided between Salisbury and him (1884), 56; Lord Randolph refuses to join government under his leadership (1885), 65; goes to House of Lords as Earl of Iddesleigh (1885), 65; his budget of 1876, WSC on (1897), 324
Nowshera (N.W. Frontier), WSC at, on way to Malakand F.F., 336, 338

Oaks, the, won by Lord Randolph's "L'Abbesse" (1889), 130
Oldham:
WSC's first Parliamentary candidature for (1899), 430–5; three out of the four candidates later reach Cabinet rank, 432; loses by-election, 434; tumultuous ovation to WSC on return from Boer War (1900), 516; WSC's General Election candidature (1900), 515–7, 518–23; Joseph Chamberlain speaks on WSC's platform, 520–1; for this two-member seat Emmott (Lib) and WSC (Cons) are returned, 521; WSC takes Runciman's place by 222 votes, 521
Oldham Conservative Association, 430
Olivette, SS, WSC and Barnes go to Cuba in, 261
Olivier, Commandant, why Roberts did not destroy his commando (1900), 503
Omdurman, Battle of (Sept, 1898), xxxiii, 269, 394–405
Map of the approaches to Omdurman, *390;* prediction of, by WSC (May, 1898), 375–6; WSC reports his reconnaissance result verbally to Kitchener, 394–5; WSC reports his patrol findings to C.O. and Kitchener, 397–399; WSC takes part in 21st Lancers'

Omdurman, Battle of—*continued*
charge, 283, 400–1, 402–4; WSC "shot 5 men for certain and two doubtful," 400; WSC attributed his survival to his having to use pistol instead of sword, 283, 400; casualty list, 401, 404; the massacre is attacked by Editor of *Concord,* citing WSC, 409; WSC's reply, 409–10; slaughter of wounded attacked by WSC (1899), 410; a reviewer calls WSC's account of the charge in his *River War* "judicial," 443; results of WSC's officer-correspondent role, 491
Oosthuizen, Field-Cornet:
was he WSC's captor (1899)?, 458, 459, 467; killed later in the Boer War, 458
Ootacamund Hounds, the, Madras, 339
Opperman, R. W. L. (Prisoner of War Camp Commandant):
WSC mentions his kindness in his "p.p.c." letter (1899), 478–9; corresponds with de Souza about the escape, 479
Orange Free State, the, 435
forms a military alliance with Transvaal Republic (1899), 436; is "wearing thin"—WSC (1900), 493; it "must go" —WSC (1900), 504; Ian Hamilton's march through, 492, 510–11
Orpen, R. J. N. (of Cape Colony), writes about Tpr Roberts's award for gallantry (1906), 509–10
Oswald, James Francis, QC (1838–1908):
one of two Conservative MPs for Oldham (1895–9), 430, 434; is induced to resign on death of his "running mate" (1899), 430
Otho de Leon (Churchill ancestor), 6
Ottawa:
WSC's lecture at (1900), 526; WSC and Pamela Plowden spend Christmas (1900) with Lord and Lady Minto at Government House, 527
Our Account with the Boers' (paper by WSC, 1896 or 1897), 435